"The Word"
MADE ▾ FRESH

A down to Earth version of The Old Testament

"Let there be "light" ... Andy Edington

by Andy Edington

EAKIN PRESS ★ Austin, Texas

VOL. I
The Old Testament
Second Printing

Copyright © 1988
By Andy Edington

Published in the United States of America
By Eakin Press, P.O. Box 23069, Austin, Texas 78735

VOL. I   ISBN 0-89015-681-6
VOL. II   ISBN 0-89015-682-4
2 VOL. SET   ISBN 0-89015-683-2

Dedication

This book is dedicated to the great cloud of witnesses who have surrounded my life, including my family; my wife Marguerite, daughter, Rita, son, David, plus my parents, brothers, a sister, grandchildren, nephews, nieces, those here and those who have gone before, a host of friends, including preachers and teachers — they are all in the book.

All of these influences, plus the energy to do the work, have been undergirded and made both strong and binding by a Word, a Name, and a Sign.

CONTENTS

FOREWORD

It is so easy for us to forget that the people of Biblical times were human beings. Their humanity was as real as ours. The events which grasped their lives generated the same doubts and affirmations, fears and hopes, joys and sadnesses which claim us.

In The 'Word' Made Fresh, Andrew Edington seeks to reveal our identification with their humanity, the beautiful humanity with which the One, true and living God has been pleased to deal through the ages. These pages do not give us a word by word translation, but rather selected scriptural accounts using today's images as vehicles for the timeless truth.

Volume 1 of The 'Word' Made Fresh moves through the history of Israel. Further volumes will introduce us anew to the prophets and the New Testament.

In his twenty-one year investment in the lives of young people while President of Schreiner Junior College and High School, one of Dr. Edington's central purposes was the development of interest in the Holy Scriptures on the part of students. His concern continues to be the awakening of interest in the "words" which communicate the Word of God, and which may lead to commitment to Him who is the living Word of Life.

Sam M. Junkin, President
Schreiner Junior College

AUTHOR'S COMMENT

The Word Made Fresh is being republished in two volumes, covering all sixty-six books of the Bible, and re-published with a slightly altered format.

This publication is made possible because of the interest and vision of MeJ and John O'Neal, who have felt that *The Word Made Fresh* is a vehicle for developing an interest in the Bible among those whose exposure to the Bible has been either quite limited or non-existent, as well as being a treatment of the Biblical word that might stimulate new thought areas for those people who are already conversant with the Bible.

It is my hope that every time a 12-year-old or a disadvantaged person, or anyone else receives a new and helpful insight into the word of God through *The Word Made Fresh* that the Lord will add a new blessing into the lives of MeJ and John O'Neal.

Andrew Edington

In the beginning God created everything from nothing, for there was no earth or heaven and darkness was total and only the spirit of God moved.

And God said, "Let there be light", and there was light. God checked it and found it to be good. God designated the presence of light as "day" and the presence of darkness as "night". This was the first phase of creation.

Next God said let there be a firmament dividing all the various waters in their varied forms. God divided the waters underneath from those that were above and he called the upper part Heaven. This was the second phase.

Then God ordered the waters under the heavens to be gathered together and dry land appeared. This dry land was called 'Earth' and the waters which were gathered together were called 'Seas'. God said, "Let the grass now grow, and the plants, and the fruit trees, each after it's kind," and God checked all this and saw that it was good, and this was the third phase of creation.

God then decided there should be specific lights in the heavens, working orderly, to control the seasons and the times. The two principal lights God made were one greater for the day and a lesser one for the night. God also made the stars and set them in the firmament. After all this was done God checked it and found it to be a good system. This was the fourth phase of creation.

Then God's planned creation began developing in living creatures of the sea, even such as whales, and also the winged fowl of the air and God encouraged their productivity and he saw the way it was working and thought it was good. This was the fifth phase of creation.

God then saw to it that the earth began to bring forth living creatures, each of its own kind and he made the cattle, and the creeping things, each different. God saw that this was good and so He decided to make man; to make him different from all the other creatures, to model man after the image of God, and to empower man to look out for all other living things, to have dominion over the fowl of the air and the fish of the sea, and over all the creeping things. God made man male and female, and he blessed them, and he instructed them to multiply. God also told them to exercise proper care of the earth, to replenish and conserve.

God told man that all things were given to him for his benefit and to properly use God's creation. God observed all that He had done and He considered it a good plan.

Now the seventh phase of God's creation was for rest and growth. God blessed the seventh phase particularly. God watched the clouds form, and rain come, and plants grow and the earth and all His creation becoming active. It was during this phase that God breathed into man a living soul, and man's difference became permanently established.

The first area to develop as a garden was called Eden. There were four rivers having their source here and God watched as man developed this area and lived in it.

God ordered man, however, not to eat of the tree of knowledge, for knowledge of life would bring into man's experience knowledge of death. God let man name all of the plants and animals and God provided woman for man. God called the helpmate woman for she was made from man and was of the same flesh. It is proper, therefore, that a man cleave to a woman and that they become one for this is the beginning of family, the basic unit of God's plan for man.

Chap.
3

Sometime after this, Curiosity, the name of the first serpent, began working on a woman named Eve. The serpent said that God was running a bluff, and that all knowledge would mean would be equality with God. The fruit of the tree looked good and the reasoning seemed adequate; so Eve disobeyed God and then induced Adam rather easily to join her in disobedience. The knowledge which the two acquired for all mankind was knowledge of their nakedness, knowledge of the existence of good and evil, and knowledge of death.

And God said to the woman, "What is this that you have done?"

She replied, "Curiosity got the best of me."

And God said to the serpent Curiosity, "From henceforth you are to be cursed and despised over all cattle and all beasts, and you shall crawl on your belly in the dust the remainder of your existence. I will also create enmity between you and woman, and you shall bite at the legs of her and her offspring, and they shall strike at your head."

To the woman God said, "Your punishment shall be labor in childbirth and you shall be subject to man."

God spoke to Adam and said, "Because you joined Eve in this folly, you will have to work. You will plant, and fight weeds, and you shall live and prosper by the sweat of your brow."

God, however, still caring for His special creation, provided skins for clothes for Adam and Eve.

God then noted that man would have to be expelled from the presence of the place of God; and this place known as Eden was closed to man. Enclosed in God's place is the tree of eternal life and this was no longer available simply for man's easy taking.

Chap.
4

It was not long after this that Eve became pregnant and her first son was named Cain. Later there came another son and his name was Abel. In due time Cain was assigned the job of looking out for sheep and Abel was the farmer. Each brought appropriate offerings to God, but Cain had a poor attitude. The Lord was therefore pleased with Abel's gift and not with Cain's. This disturbed Cain and he vented his anger on Abel, and killed him. God punished Cain by relating a vagabond and lost feeling to sin, and Cain groaned under the penalty. God also placed a mark on Cain that would encourage others to let him live and prolong him in his misery.

Cain departed from the area with his wife and started a new life. Down through the years there were many descendants of Cain, and there began to develop through the years skills in music, and art, and the working of metals. Eve had still another son, Seth, and he was a fine boy and he began another line and gradually man began to work at the job of subduing the earth, and about this time man became sensitive to his need for God.

Chap.
5

Now there were multiple descendants of Adam and finally there came one named Enoch. Enoch was the first great seeker of God, and Enoch walked with God. In his later years, one day Enoch walked off with God and did not return.

Chap.
6

Many generations later, as time had passed and man was expanding in numbers and in wickedness, there was born a man named Noah, and he worshipped God. It was now that the Lord began to restrict the longevity of man. God said that He would not always be at odds with man, but since man was of flesh his time should be limited.

There were big men on the earth in these days and they chased the girls, taking many wives. Wickedness increased and God wondered if He had been wise in turning man loose on the earth. Now Noah was a good man, and God rejoiced in him. The earth was full of violence and evil and God revealed to Noah that He planned to clean up the place.

God told Noah to build an ark, large enough to hold all of Noah's family and representatives from all the animals. Noah gathered stores of food as instructed, and he built an ark, and he ignored all the smart remarks made by local yokels.

Chap.
7

God gave Noah seven days to load the ark after it was finished and then He caused the rains to descend for forty days and forty nights and the earth was flooded. As the waters increased the ark was lifted and the ark floated, to the great joy of Noah. All living substance that was not in the ark was destroyed, all men, and cattle, and the creeping things.

Chap.
8

God did not forget Noah, but He sent a wind to begin to blow upon the waters and the rain was stopped. There was no way for

Noah to tell if the waters were receding and so he sent forth a raven who never returned. After waiting a long time, Noah sent forth a dove and the dove returned weary from flying. After another period of waiting, Noah sent the dove a second time, and this time the dove returned with a green twig, an olive leaf. Finally mountain tops became visible in the distance.

At long last the Ark rested on dry ground and God spoke to Noah and told him it was time to lower the gangway and start life going again on the earth.

Noah was the first down the ramp and onto the dry ground, and he immediately built an altar and thanked God. This pleased God mightily and God smelled a sweet savor, and so God said in His heart that He would not again curse the ground because of man and again smite every living thing at once. God further promised not to tamper with the seasons, but that without interruption there would be seedtime and harvest, cold and heat, summer and winter, day and night, without ceasing.

Chap.
9

God blessed Noah and He renewed His instructions to man through Noah to be fruitful and multiply, to keep the earth in good shape, to practice conservation, and to avoid the shedding of the blood of his fellowman.

God made a covenant with Noah and with mankind that He would not again destroy as He had with the flood and that the sign of the covenant would be the rainbow, and the rainbow would be a reminder to God of His agreement.

Now Noah had three sons and he named them Tom[1], Dick[2], and Harry[3] and they scattered and through them came into being all the races of the world.

Noah was at a loss for something to do and so he planted a vineyard. After this he gathered the grapes, made wine, and got drunk. Harry saw the old man naked and drunk and left in disgust, but the two older boys took pity on Noah and covered him with a garment. When Noah learned of this, he chewed out his younger son and praised the other two, telling the younger that he would never amount to anything but that the older boys would prosper.

And at the proper time Noah died.

Chap
10

Noah's sons had children, and their children had children, and so went the development and spread of mankind. Among one of the generations there developed a young man named Nimrod and he was the first of the great hunters.

Chap.
11

As man progressed, he also began to develop arrogance and one group decided that they were now smart enough to look God in the eye. All men spoke one language and as the making of bricks was

[1]Shem   [2]Ham   [3]Japheth

devised, the men began to build a tower which was to reach to Heaven.

The Lord brought this project to a screeching halt by confounding their language; so that the confusion prevented communication. Then God called the name of this place Babel. The men ceased then in their efforts and scattered themselves abroad, as the Lord had planned for them to do.

Time went by, and many, many generations came into being, and man spread himself across the face of the earth.

There was born eventually a man named Joe[1] and he had a son named Abe[2]. Now God inspired Joe to take his family to the land of Canaan and establish there a new nation, but Joe stopped on the way at a place called Palm Springs[3], and he liked it there and there he stayed.

Chap. 12

In time God spoke unto Abe and challenged him saying, "Get yourself out of this country, get away from your kinfolks and from the protection of your father, and I will show you a new land and give you a chance to found a great nation. I will give every reasonable help, and if you take advantage of the opportunity, yours shall become a great name, and the families of the earth shall be blessed because of you."

Abe took Sara, his wife, and a nephew named Lot along with a few herdsmen and departed on the great trip of his life. The group journeyed to the land of Caanan, and the Lord assured Abe that this was the promised land. In recognition of this occasion Abe built an altar and thanked God.

In due time a famine arose in the land because of the drought, and so Abe gathered his possessions and headed for Egypt.

Abe had inquired a bit about Egypt and its customs and so he spoke to Sara, his wife, as they neared the land of Egypt and said, "Sara, you are a very beautiful girl. The Egyptions will notice this and they will decide to kill me in order to possess you; so I want you to pose as my sister, then I can bargain with them for you."

Sure enough, the Egyption girl watchers noticed Sara, and word was passed to the palace crowd and then to Pharoah, and Sara was taken into the girls' dormitory of Pharoah's palace in exchange for numerous sheep, oxen, men servants, maid servants, camels, and similar booty.

The Lord began to create problems in Pharoah's house because Sara was actually Abe's wife.

Pharoah soon learned that Sara was Abe's wife, and that this was the source of his difficulties and so he sent for Abe and told him to take Sara, take his possessions, and get out of Egypt. Abe left, of course, and he was now a pretty rich man.

[1]Terah   [2]Abram   [3]Haran

Abe and Lot returned to the homesite in Canaan, and both men were wealthy from their trip to Egypt. In fact, both became so affluent that there was not room enough in one area for the two of them. Soon strife arose between the herdsmen of Lot and those of Abe.

Abe one day suggested to Lot that in the interest of peace that they separate. Abe said that he would move with his possessions in the opposite direction from Lot and that Lot should choose first.

Lot agreed and immediately began to figure on the best direction. It did not take him long to decide to go east to the fertile plains of Jordan, toward the cities of Sodom and Gomar[1]; so Abe dwelled in Canaan and Lot in the city of Sodom. Now the men of Sodom were wicked and sinful and Lot lived in the midst of them.

Then the Lord told Abe to travel the length and breadth of the land and to become acquainted with it, for the Lord planned that Abe and his offspring should rule it. Abe did as he was told, and at some places, such as St. Louis[2], he built an altar to God.

And it came to pass that the various kings began to do battle with one another, and there was strife and rebellion in the land. The kings of Sodom and Gomar banded together and in an encounter on the plains they were defeated, and they lost their possessions and also many of their people were taken captive, including Lot.

A messenger came and reported this to Abe and he decided to rescue Lot. Abe assembled a group of about 318 roughriders and he went in pursuit of the victorious kings. By using the strategy of dividing his men and attacking at night, Abe rescued Lot and recovered the people and the lost possessions. Needless to say, Abe was given a triumphant and hearty reception when he returned the people to Sodom. The king of Sodom offered to give Abe all the booty, but Abe said, "Let me keep some of the people and you can have the goods." Abe said that he served the one true God, and that he would not take so much as a shoe lace that did not belong to him. Among other things, Abe said he did not want the king of Sodom to be able to say that he had made Abe rich.

Abe did allow the three platoon leaders who were with him to take their share of the booty, but for himself Abe kept nothing.

Sometime after this Abe sensed the presence of God in a vision and God reminded Abe of His support and the promise of reward.

"How can this promise be fulfilled if I remain childless?" asked Abe. The nearest thing to an heir, Abe pointed out, was some kid who happened to be born in Abe's house.

Again the word of the Lord came to Abe saying that the child in the house would not be the heir, but the promise was renewed of an offspring of his own flesh and blood. Abe believed this, and was

[1]Gomorrah   [2]Mamre

comforted. God promised Abe that as he viewed the heavens and saw the many stars so ultimately would be the number of his descendants.

Abe thought often of these things and asked God for a sign of encouragement. As a result, Abe initiated a little ceremony, with burnt offerings, and after the long and intense ceremony, a deep sleep fell upon Abe and a nightmare of darkness.

While in his sleep the Lord came to Abe saying that his descendants would have difficulties and would spend 400 years as captives, but that God would punish the captors. Abe, however, was assured that he would die in peace, and that ultimately the land of Canaan would belong to the seed of Abe.

Chap.
16

Sara still was not pregnant and she was worried about the descendant problem. Sara had a house maid that was a nice girl named Lilly[1] and Sara reasoned that if Abe would marry her and have two wives in one tent that this would double the chances of offspring. The arrangement was agreeable to Abe and as a result Lilly became pregnant.

The new arrangement did not work smoothly, however, as Lilly elevated herself to number one wife and Sara began to fret. When Sara complained to Abe he told Sara that Lilly was her problem and to do with her as she pleased. Sara immediately began to make life so miserable for Lilly that Lilly headed for the hills.

Now when Lilly found herself weary and in poor circumstances in the wilderness by an oasis, she prayed and an angel of the Lord appeared to her and advised her to return and submit herself to Sara's rule and that as a result God would see to it that her child would be born, that the child would be a boy, and that she should name him Mike[2]. The angel promised that God would make Mike the father of a great race of wild and vigorous people.

Lilly was grateful to God and she named the place of her prayer Holy Water[3]. Lilly returned as instructed and had her son and she named him Mike.

Chap.
17

Time rolled along and still there was no sign of pregnancy with Sara and Abe was beginning to think that maybe he and Sara were too old to have a child; so God renewed his covenant with Abe. Because of Abe's great faithfulness, God changed his name to Abraham, and again God renewed His promise to eventually give unto the seed of Abraham the land of Canaan.

As a sign of recognition of this covenant, Abraham agreed to see that every male child would be circumcised and that this would be a physical symbol of a spiritual agreement.

God said that since to Sara there was to come God's extra blessing that a superlative was to be added also to her name, and she

[1]Hagar   [2]Ishmael   [3]Beerlahairoi

would be called Sarah.

God said that Sarah would be pregnant soon and that the son was to be Isaac. God reminded Abraham again that God was a keeper of the promises and that both Mike and Isaac would become established heads of future great races. Then God ceased talking to Abraham.

Abraham immediately began the process of circumcising all the males attached to his household or under his command.

One day Abraham was sitting in front of his tent in meditation in the presence of God, and he saw three men approaching. Abraham rightly assumed that these three had been sent by God and he welcomed them profusely, offering coffee, water, bread, and instant cookies.

Abraham then went and selected a fine calf and had one of the servants prepare it and before long there was a wonderful steak dinner with all the trimmings prepared for the visitors.

One of the men said, "Where is Sarah, your wife?"

"She's in the tent," replied Abraham.

"I will return unto thee, in accordance with Sarah's time of life, and see that Sarah has a son."

Now Sarah overheard this and she laughed in derision.

Abraham said to the men, "But Sarah has passed the menopause."

The Lord said then to Abraham that Sarah should not have laughed for nothing is impossible with God. The representatives of God again affirmed that Sarah would have a son.

Sarah then denied that she had laughed but she knew she was wrong, and she was afraid.

God spoke through one of the visitors and said, "Because the howling of Sodom and Gomar is great and their sin even greater, we are going to check on them and if it is as it appears, we will destroy the cities."

As soon as the visitors departed, Abraham appeared before God and prayed saying, "Will you destroy the righteous with the wicked? If there are 50 good people in the city, will you save it?"

"Yes," replied God, "if there are 50 good people in Sodom I'll save it."

"Perhaps there are only 45. Would you save the city for 45?"

"Yes," replied God. "I'll save it for 45."

"What about 40?" said Abraham.

"I'll save it for 40," replied God.

"How do you feel about 30?" asked Abraham.

"I'll save it for 30," said God.

"Ten less would be 20," asserted Abraham.

"I'll save it for 20," said God.

"This is the last time I'll speak, but God, will you save it for 10?"

"Yes," said God, and at that God ceased communicating with Abraham.

Shortly after this two men, representatives of God, came to Sodom and Lot invited them to spend the night at his house. They finally accepted his invitation and that evening enjoyed a fine dinner at Lot's home.

Some of the wild and unruly men of Sodom, however, learned that there were strangers at Lot's house and they came to make sport of them and harass them. Lot pleaded with the people, but to no avail. In fact, Lot said that he had two daughters that he would release to the pleasure of the crowd, but that the two men were his guests and shouldn't be violated.

This was not well received and the unruly mob began to threaten Lot so that the two guests finally pulled Lot into the house for his own safety. The representatives or angels of God then detonated a tear bomb on the front porch and men "wearied themselves trying to find the door."

The angels then turned to Lot and said, "Get your family together. The Lord has sent us to destroy Sodom and we want to get you and your family to a safe place first."

Now Lot had a couple of married daughters, but Lot's sons-in-law laughed at his warning and would not leave; so he took his wife and two daughters and left the city.

One of the angels told them to flee to the mountains and that they were not to look back on the city. Lot bucked at this injunction, however, as he claimed he was no rancher or mountain man and that he needed to live in the city. Lot said that a little city would do, but that it had to be a city.

The angels agreed and headed Lot to Zoar. Brimstone and fire then rained down upon Sodom and Gomar, and Lot's wife couldn't resist looking back on the disaster and she was burned to where only salt was left.

Abraham saw the smoke rise from the destruction of Sodom and Gomar and trusted that God had delivered Lot as promised.

Lot, however, became unhappy in Zoar as the people were not friendly to him, a refugee from hated Sodom; so finally Lot left Zoar with his two daughters and began to dwell in a lonely mountain region.

The oldest of Lot's daughters decided that the two girls would be left forever in the mountains and would never have any children; so she proposed a plan whereby they would get their father drunk and then lie with him when he was too stoned to know what was happening. The eldest daughter was the first to pull the trick and then she talked the youngest into doing the same thing. As a result both girls became pregnant by their father, without his knowledge, for he was apparently real drunk on both occasions.[1]

The Lord provided, however, that the sons of Lot's daughters would be the source from which came the people of Mississippi[2] and the Moscow Muggers[3].

Again Abraham decided to journey to the south and to visit in the land of Winston,[4] king of Filter[5]. As he had done once in Egypt, Abraham explained that Sarah was his sister. Because of this, Winston asked Sarah to be one of his wives and she was placed in the girls' dormitory.

God revealed to Winston, however, the fraud, and Winston was afraid, for he believed it to be a great wrong to take another man's wife. As a result, Winston gave Abraham a big fee to take his wife back and Winston explained that he had not had an occasion to go to bed with Sarah; so there was no harm done.

When Winston complained to Abraham about the deceit, however, Abraham said that actually Sarah was his half-sister anyway, and so his lie was not as bad as Winston thought. Abraham also said that he had mentioned the sister deal for fear of the ungodly attitude of Winston's people.

For the second time in his life, Abraham returned to his homeland with significant riches. Winston could not resist criticising Sarah and he told her that she didn't need to wear a veil any more with a husband that did such a deceiving job for her.[6]

Because of the generous fee, Abraham asked God to bless Winston and to let pregnancy again abound in his household, and God relieved the tension in the palace and children were again in process.

God fulfilled also his promise to Sarah, and she conceived and gave birth to a son, who was named Isaac. Sarah and Abraham were both middle aged and they were elated over the baby. Sarah said that the Lord had finally made her happy and she wanted everyone to be joyful. Abraham gave a big barbecue in celebration.

Now Lilly's son began to tease Sarah about her baby and so Sarah asked Abraham to send Lilly and Mike away. Abraham did not want to do this, as he was fond of both of them.

God told Abraham not to worry, however, as it would be good for Lilly to leave and take Mike to another area and begin another nation. When Lilly left, Abraham gave her provisions.

Lilly was never much of an outdoor person and soon she was lost in the wilderness and the water was all gone as well as the food. Lilly put the child Mike in the shade and then she went apart as she

[1] I personally never cared for Lot, anyway
[2] Moab
[3] Ammon
[4] Abimelech
[5] Gerar
[6] "You don't need a veil" is no longer an insult

said she could not stand to see him die.

The little boy then prayed to God for help and God heard him so that when Lilly opened her eyes she found water and gave it to the boy. As a result, the two lived and the boy became very proficient with the bow and arrow and when he was old enough, Lilly selected a wife for him among the Egyptians.

Winston and Abraham met some time later and Winston urged that the two of them agree to arbitrate any difficulties that might arise and discuss things together so there would be no war.

A chance to practice this came pretty soon as some of Winston's men captured one of Abraham's wells. Winston assured Abraham that he had known nothing of it and so the error was corrected and Abraham offered public sacrifice so all would know that things were well between Abraham and Winston. Abraham gave Winston seven ewe lambs so that Winston would remember that the well was dug and owned by Abraham. Abraham used this occasion to praise God, and to establish a place of worship.

Chap. 22

A few years later when Isaac was still a small boy, God spoke to Abraham and told him to take his only son Isaac, whom he dearly loved, and to go to a holy mountain and to sacrifice him. Abraham obeyed, and he took Isaac, two servents, and wood for the altar of sacrifice. En route to the mountain Isaac said to his father, "We have the wood, but where is the sacrifice?"

Abraham replied, "The Lord will provide."

Upon arriving near the site, Abraham left the servants behind and took only the wood and Isaac up the mountain. Once there Abraham built an altar and then tied Isaac to the altar. As Abraham raised very slowly the sacrificial knife, the voice of the Lord came to him saying that he should stop and look behind him. When Abraham turned around there was a ram caught in the bushes and God told Abraham to sacrifice the ram instead of Isaac.

God told Abraham that because of his extreme willingness to obey God to such a degree that God would see that ultimately all the nations on the earth would be blessed through the descendants of Abraham.

Upon returning home, Abraham was told of the various additions to the family through his brother Nat[1], who had now totalled 8 children by one of his wives, a girl named Mildred.[2]

Chap. 23

Sarah died on a trip and Abraham wanted to bury her on the spot so he could see that it was properly done. Abraham found a cave in a field and he sought to purchase this from the owner, a young man called Ronnie.[3] The purchase was agreed upon and Abraham bought the field and the cave, and Abraham mourned for Sarah, his true wife.

[1]Nahor
[2]Milcah
[3]Ephon the Hittite

As Abraham became very old he worried about getting a wife for Isaac and he called his trusted ranch foreman and made him promise to find a wife for Isaac in the next county and not to let him marry a local girl who might simply be after his money.

Abraham told the foreman to go seeking a wife in the area of Palm Springs[1], but not to take Isaac on the trip.

The foreman said, "How do I select a wife?"

Abraham replied, "I will ask God to have an angel help. If the chosen girl won't return with you, you are released from this vow."

The foreman took ten camels and many provisions, plus jewelry and gifts and went into the next county, stopping at a prominent water well. At this point the foreman prayed saying, "O Lord, help me. Send the right girl today so that I will make a wise choice. As a test, I will ask each girl that comes for water for a drink, and if she says she will give me to drink from the pitcher and then offers to water the camels, I will know that this is God's choice."

Sure enough, a beautiful girl, Becky,[2] a granddaughter of Mildred, came to the well and responded favorably to the foreman and she also offered to water the camels.

The foreman thanked Becky and gave her beautiful rings as well as some hard cash and gold earrings. Then the foreman asked for her name and if it was possible for him to spend the night and meet the family. Becky invited the foreman to the house. The foreman thanked God for his help.

Of course, Becky ran home and told everybody what had happened and she impressed her brother Laban very much with the jewelry and the money. Laban then ran to meet the foreman and offered him the full hospitality of his house.

After washing his feet, the foreman came to dinner, but said that he could not eat until he had explained his errand.

"First, let me admit that the Lord has made my boss, Abraham, very rich and very powerful. Now Abraham has an only son who will inherit everything and I've come to secure a wife for the son," said the foreman.

The foreman then went on to explain how he had prayed and he had selected Becky.

Becky's father was dead and the eldest brother, Laban, ruled the ranch, and so he spoke, "This is apparently a matter of God's doing. You may take Becky and let her become your master's son's wife."

At this point the foreman thanked God again, and then broke out the jewelry, money, and gifts for the family. A feast ensued and an all night celebration took place.

The next day the foreman was ready to take Becky back, but the brother and sister asked to keep Becky a few days so she wouldn't have to pack in a hurry.

[1]Haran   [2]Rebecca

The foreman urged them and they decided to let Becky decide for herself.

Becky said, "Saddle up, I'm ready."

The home folks waved good-bye to Becky, saying such encouraging things as "Be the mother of thousands!"

As Becky, her two servants, and the foreman neared the ranch headquarters back home, Isaac was sitting on a rock meditating and he arose to meet the group approaching.

"Who is that?" asked Becky.

"That's Isaac," said the foreman.

Whereupon Becky coyly covered her features with her veil.

Shortly thereafter, however, the young couple were married and Isaac who had been grieving over his mother's death was comforted in Becky, and he fell in love with her.

Chap. 25

Abraham soon made a gift to Isaac of all his major possessions, but he gave many gifts and what he considered a fair amount to the sons of his other wives as well as to his illegitimate children and asked them all to leave the area so that Isaac might begin his own operations as head of his own family.

Shortly after this Abraham died, and he was buried in the cave with Sarah his wife.

Mike[1], Abraham's son by Lilly[2], died after a fruitful life and after properly establishing a new nation.

Isaac prayed to God that Becky would become pregnant and she wondered during her pregnancy about all the discomfort. God told her, in response to her prayer, that she would be the mother of two nations, and they would often struggle, with the younger being stronger than the elder.

Becky in time gave birth to twins and the first, a hairy boy, was named Esau and the second was named Jacob.

The boys grew and Esau became a cunning hunter and Jacob was a mother's boy, and stayed close to the house. Now Isaac was particularly fond of Esau because he enjoyed the venison he brought him, but Becky was partial to Jacob.

One day Esau came in famished and pooped out from deer hunting.

"How about some food?" he asked.

"I'll sell you some," said Jacob.

"If I don't eat I'll die; so what's the price?" asked Esau.

"Your right to the ranch," said Jacob.

Whereupon Esau sold his rights to the ranch for a square meal. Esau obviously placed very little value on inheriting the ranch.

Chap. 26

A periodic drought came to the land and Isaac did as his father had done and went south in the land of Winston[3], king of Filter[4].

[1]Ishmael   [3]Abimelech
[2]Hagar   [4]Gerar

Isaac also remembered about his father's fear of being killed because of having a beautiful wife and so he told the people that Becky was his sister, for she, as Sarah had been, was beautiful.

Isaac prospered in the land and his possessions grew. One day, however, Winston was looking out the window and he saw Isaac loving Becky; so he sent for him. Winston told Isaac that he knew that Becky must be his wife and he lectured Isaac, saying that some of the   Fascists could have gone to bed with Becky and defiled themselves; so he asked Isaac to leave the country.

Winston told Isaac that he could not order him out as Isaac had more men than Winston had, but Issac agreed to leave in the interests of harmony and peace. Isaac had, however, become rich in the process.

Isaac took his people to a portion of the country where his father had dug wells, but the wells had been plugged by the Fascists.

The servants of Isaac went to work and dug again one of the wells of Abraham in a valley, and herdsmen from Filter came and claimed the well. Isaac then dug another of the wells, and then another, surrendering each when claimed by   Fascist herdsmen. Winston had observed the continued prosperity of Isaac and thought that God was providing continuous water for Isaac; so he journeyed to Isaac and made a covenant of peace with him.

After this Isaac dug another well and no one contested it. Isaac was pleased with this, but he and Becky were both displeased to learn that the eldest son Esau had married two Hippie[1] girls.

Chap. 27

In time Isaac became old and almost blind and one day he sent for Esau and asked him to go kill a deer and bring him some fresh venison for he loved deer meat very much. Becky heard this and she told Jacob to kill two kid goats and bring them and she would cook them like venison and let Jacob present them to Isaac and receive Isaac's blessing.

"But, Mother," said Jacob, "Daddy will know it is me by feeling my smooth hands, for Esau is hairy."

"Don't be so stupid. Just do as I say," replied Becky.

So Becky fixed the meat and made it savory, and then she dressed Jacob in Esau's clothes and put on his hands the gloves she had made from the young goats' hides. Jacob then took the meat to his father.

"Hello, Father," said Jacob.

"Which one are you, son?" asked Isaac.

"I am Esau. I have done as you asked. Bless me and enjoy the meat."

"How did you get the deer so quickly?" asked Isaac.

"The Lord, thy God, helped me," said Jacob.

[1]Hittite

"Come near," said Isaac, "that I may feel thee, and know you are Esau."

Jacob came near and Isaac felt his hands and said, "The voice is the voice of Jacob, but the hands are the hands of Esau."

Again Isaac said, "Art thou Esau?"

Again Jacob replied, "I am."

So Isaac bestowed his blessing on Jacob and thereby his possessions. Isaac smelled the garments of Esau which Jacob wore and he said, "These are of the field which God has blessed and may the Lord give thee the dew of heaven, the abundance of the earth, and plenty of corn and wine, and let everyone that despises you be despised and everyone that blesses you, let him be blessed."

Shortly after this Esau returned with the venison and brought it to Jacob, saying "I am Esau, thy son, and I seek thy blessing."

Isaac trembled with anger and told Esau that Jacob had used subtility to secure the blessing, but there was only one blessing that he could give and it was given.

Esau wept in his anguish and vowed that after his father's death he would kill Jacob.

The words of Esau about killing Jacob were reported to Becky and so she sent for Jacob and said, "Esau plans to kill you. Flee to Palm Springs and visit my brother Laban until Esau has had time to cool it. I will send for you when all is well." Becky then came to Isaac and said that she was afraid Jacob would marry locally and that was a sickening thought.

Chap. 28

As a result, Isaac sent for Jacob and ordered him not to marry locally but to find a girl from his mother's country, and he then dismissed Jacob with his blessing.

When Esau learned that Isaac had blessed Jacob again and had sent him to Palm Springs to find a wife because the girls of Canaan did not please him, then he took additonal wives of Mike's descendants for himself, in hopes of pleasing Isaac.

As Jacob proceeded toward Palm Springs he tarried to rest on the way and used a stone for a pillow. While he was asleep he dreamed that he saw a ladder reach from the earth to heaven and the angels of God going up and down the ladder. In his dream he heard the voice of God from the top of the ladder saying that for Abraham's sake he would bless Jacob and his offspring. Jacob awoke and was afraid for he reasoned that surely the Lord was in this place. As a result, Jacob took the stone he had used as a pillow, poured oil on it, and made it an altar, vowing that if God would bring him home safely that he would worship God and believe in him completely. In his enthusiasm, Jacob also promised to tithe.

Chap. 29

As Jacob traveled east he found a well and there were three flocks there being watered. Jacob asked the herdsmen if they knew a rancher named Laban and they said they did.

"Is he alive and well?" asked Jacob.

"Yes," replied one of the herdsmen, "In fact, there comes one of his daughters, Rachel, bringing the sheep to water now."

As Rachel approached, Jacob rolled away the stone which closed the well, told Rachel that they were kissing kin, and kissed her. Rachel ran to tell her father about the new cousin she had found and Laban came forth to meet Jacob.

Jacob stayed on the ranch working for Laban for about a month, and Laban said one day that he thought he should start paying Jacob.

Now Laban had two daughters, the eldest was Leah, a plain but wholesome girl, and Rachel, who was very beautiful.

Jacob fell in love with Rachel and he told Laban that he would work for seven years and his wages would be the hand of Rachel in marriage. The seven years seemed but as a few days to Jacob because of his love for Rachel.

At the end of the seven years, Laban ordered a marriage feast and Jacob was married to the heavily veiled girl that Laban brought to the church. The next morning, when the sun made bright the honeymoon tent, Jacob had his suspicion confirmed that he had married the wrong girl, for it was obviously Leah at his side.

Jacob at once complained bitterly to Laban about the trick played on him.

Laban explained that it was an old family custom that the eldest daughter had to be wed first.

"Next week," said Laban, "we will have another wedding and you can marry Rachel and work another seven years."

Jacob married Rachel the next week, and he loved Rachel more than Leah.

Because Jacob showed favoritism to Rachel, the Lord blessed Leah with children and caused Rachel to be barren. Leah had four straight sons, Reuben, Butch[1], Max[2], and Judah, and each time she had a son she expected to impress Jacob.

Rachel envied Leah and complained to Jacob about not having children. Jacob said, "It is God's doing. Don't blame me."

Rachel then asked Jacob to have intercourse with her maid Babe[3] so that Rachel could count a child to her tent's credit. As a result Babe produced two sons, then Leah became jealous and threw her handmaid into the contest. When Leah's handmaid Zelda became pregnant, she was so large that Leah said she looked as if she was going to give birth to an army and she named the large son that was born Troop[4].

During all of this Jacob had quit going to bed with Leah. One day, however, Rachel asked Leah for some material and Leah said

[1]Simeon   [2]Levi   [3]Bilhah
[4]Hebrew word is Gad

she would sell it for one night again with Jacob. When Jacob came in that evening, Leah told Jacob that he was purchased for her tent that evening and so he lay with Leah and from this she had her fifth son by Jacob. Leah then had a sixth son by Jacob and a daughter that she named Dinah[1].

The Lord now remembered Rachel and she finally had a son who was named Joseph.

Jacob decided that it was time to return to his homeland and he also asked permission from Laban to leave, but Laban said, " You can deal with me for a raise in pay, but you can't leave." The ranch had been prospering and Jacob had been doing most of the work.

Jacob pointed out to Laban how everything had increased under Jacob's supervision, and he agreed to remain and to care for all the ranch and cattle, but he said, "I will go through the ranch and select all the spotted cattle for myself and leave all the blemish-free for you. From now on, Laban, all the speckled are mine and all the solids are yours."

Jacob then moved his tents about ten miles away on another part of the ranch, but he continued to feed and water all the stock of the ranch.

Now Jacob devised a way of doctoring the feed of the cattle so that all of the offspring began to be produced with specks, and in a very few years, practically all of the cattle everywhere were flecked. Jacob omitted this treatment only in the case of weak or sick cattle. Jacob flourished and became rich while Laban sat on the porch and rocked, not knowing that his cattle were gradually all being marked for Jacob.

Chap. 31

Some of the sons of Laban, however, began to wise up a bit and Jacob decided that he had better make his move. The Lord favored Jacob's plan to move back to Canaan.

Jacob called Leah and Rachel to him and told them how Laban had always cheated on his wages and that God had been on the side of Jacob and had caused the speckled rams to leap upon the pure cattle and that God was helping Jacob. At least Jacob said that's what he dreamed.

Rachel and Leah said Laban had never given them anything and they were ready to take all they could get and leave; so Jacob rose up and departed with his wives, and sons, and all his goods. While Laban was away shearing sheep, Rachel had slipped into the house and taken the jewelry.

Three days later, Laban was told of the departure of Jacob; so he pursued him and in seven days he caught up and God warned Laban in a dream to be careful of what he said to Jacob.

When Laban came to talk with Jacob, he accused him of

[1]She had 10 brothers; so nobody was in the kitchen but Dinah

stealing away with his daughters and grandchildren. Laban even suggested that he might have given Jacob a farewell party.

Laban went on to say that except for the warning of God he might get physical with Jacob for stealing all his goods.

Jacob insisted that nothing had been stolen and told Laban he could search, for Jacob did not know that Rachel had stolen the jewelry.

Laban immediatley went into Jacob's tent, then to Leah's tent, and then to Rachel's. Rachel had taken the jewelry and was sitting on it when Laban entered. Laban searched the tent and did not find the jewelry. Rachel told Laban not to be displeased that she did not rise when her father entered but that she was in her menstrual period.

When Laban failed to find anything he could claim, Jacob became angry and yelled, "What's eating you? What do you think I've done? Why do you pursue and harass me? I worked hard for 20 years and this is all the thanks I get. I've been out in the cold, looked out for your ranch, and you've cheated me ten times on my wages. In fact, if it weren't for God I'd be broke.[1] Furthermore, the daughters are mine, the sons are mine, the cattle are mine. Now put up or shut up, though I'll offer an agreement for the sake of the children."

So a place was marked with stones and Laban said let this place be a witness between us and "the Lord watch between me and thee when we are absent one from the other." And Laban added that neither would ever cross the pile of stones seeking to harm the other.

Jacob then offered a sacrifice and early in the morning Laban arose, kissed his daughters and grandchildren good-bye, and returned home.

Jacob proceeded toward Canaan and the angels of the Lord met him, and Jacob named the place God's Country[2].

Jacob dispatched messengers to Esau to tell him of his return and inquire into the state of affairs. The messengers returned and said that Esau was coming to meet Jacob with 400 men and the news terrified Jacob; so he instructed his followers to divide into two groups and he told them that when Esau attacked one group, the other was to flee to safety.

At this point Jacob prayed saying that he was completely unworthy of God's mercies, but that he was afraid of Esau and that he needed to be delivered. Jacob also mentioned that Esau would probably kill mothers and their children.

Jacob then assembled an abundance of gifts for Esau, separated widely one group of gift bearers from the other and Jacob told the first of the servants to tell Esau that all the possessions were Jacob's and that they were gifts for Esau. He commanded the same for the second, third, and all the gift bearers. Jacob also told the servants to tell Esau that Jacob was coming last, and Jacob hoped that by the time Esau got to Jacob the gifts would have soothed him.

[1]I doubt if anyone present believed this.   [2]Mahanaim

After the gift bearers had crossed the boundary stream and it was night. Jacob sent his two wives, the two handmaidens, and his eleven sons[1] and they forded the brook. Jacob remained on the safe side.

During the night a man appeared and he wrestled with Jacob. Jacob would not release the man, although the man threw Jacob's hip out of joint. Jacob was certain that the man was an angel of God and Jacob promised to release him in exchange for a blessing. The man blessed Jacob and told him that henceforth his name would be Israel for he had overcome his difficulties and he had shown strength in dealing with man and God.

From this time forth the children of Israel no longer ate meat from the hollow of thighs in remembrance of this occasion.

Chap. 33

The next morning Esau arrived with 400 men. Jacob sent the handmaidens with their children first, then Leah and her children, then Rachel and Joseph last. [2] Jacob then went forward himself, bowing seven times en route and when he came near Esau embraced him and welcomed him with forgiving love.

"Who are all these people?" asked Esau.

"My family," replied Jacob.

"What was all that convoy I met?"

"They were my servants with gifts for you," replied Jacob, "as I wanted to please you."

"Keep your stuff, brother, I have plenty."

Jacob, however, insisted, saying that God had prospered him and that he was making the gifts as a blessing and so Esau accepted the presents.

"Let's go," said Esau.

"My people are not in shape, Esau, and the feet of my stock are tender; so let us go slowly and we will see you later at the ranch."

"All right," said Esau, "but at least let me leave a few servants to help you as I am interested in being helpful to you."

Jacob proceeded to Kansas City[3] and there built a house and stockyards. Jacob also began to buy land in the surrounding area.

Chap. 34

Dinah, the daughter of Jacob, went roaming around looking at the new land and one of the native sons saw her. He grabbed her and lay with her, and ended her virginity. The young man, whose name was Sandy[4], actually fell in love with Dinah and began to speak sweetly to her. Sandy then asked his father to make a deal with Jacob so that Sandy could marry Dinah.

In the meantime, Jacob had heard that Dinah had been raped, but he took no action, waiting until all his sons were home. Soon Harvard[5], the father of Sandy, came to Jacob and said that Sandy

[1] Dinah no doubt also, but girls were rarely counted in this era   [2] Obvious partiality   [3] Succoth   [4] Shechem   [5] Hamor

wanted to marry Dinah and that he thought it would be good to have some of the new people to intermarry with the natives.

Harvard was very gracious and expressed a willingness to pay any reasonable dowry and to encourage friendliness in the land.

The sons of Jacob were very angry so they decided to deceive the Harvard people. The spokesman for the group told Harvard that their sister would not marry into an uncircumcised family, but that if every male would consent to be circumcised that the marriage would be approved.

As a result, Sandy and Harvard returned to their neighborhood and persuaded all the men to consent to being circumcised, telling them of the benefits of accommodating the tourists. Consequently, every male was circumcised.

On the third day following this, when the wounds of circumcision were the very sorest, Butch[1] and Max[2], the blood brothers of Dinah, took their swords and attacked the helpless men, killing Harvard and Sandy, taking Dinah forcibly home, while the other brothers made spoil of the neighborhood, taking all the sheep, oxen, jewelry, wives and children, and vandalizing the whole community.

Chap.
35

Jacob rebuked his sons claiming that they had ruined his reputation and that the other inhabitants would rise up against them. All the sons said was that they weren't going to let anybody take advantage of their sister.[3]

Jacob then declared a household reform and told all his family to put on clean clothes, to destroy all false gods and images, and Jacob collected all the jewelry representative of pagan concepts and then he led the whole crowd on the journey to Bethel.

God appeared to Jacob and renewed his blessing and told Jacob that because of his recent faith and trust, that God was changing his name to Israel, and that he would receive the promise given to Abraham and Isaac; so Jacob built a small memorial church on the spot.

As they journeyed from this place Rachel came into labor and died giving birth to a son named Benjamin.

Israel, formerly named Jacob, continued to have some family problems. It was noted, for instance, that his eldest son Reuben had been trifling with Israel's mistress.

At last Jacob (Israel) journeyed to see his father Isaac who was very old. Not long after this Isaac died and Esau and Jacob attended the funeral.

[1] Simeon   [2] Levi

[3] How much advantage is questionable

Esau, in the meantime, had prospered so greatly that he felt the land was too small for all that he and Jacob both owned, so Esau gethered all his people and all his possessions and departed from Canaan.

Joseph remained in Canaan and helped his older brothers feeding the cattle, but he also reported critically on them to his father. Now Jacob loved Joseph more than his other sons and they all knew it; so they hated Joseph.

Joseph did not help matters by telling his older brothers that he dreamed that all the family were binding sheaves in the field and that Joseph's sheaf stood upright while all the others bowed to him.

"Does this mean that you will rule over us?" asked the superstitious brothers.

Joseph poured it on with another dream that showed the sun, and the moon, and eleven stars bowing to him and they hated Joseph all the more.

Not many months later Jacob sent Joseph to find his brothers and get a report on where they were and how well they were doing with the cattle.

Joseph, who had received a spectacular sport coat of many colors from his father, set forth on the trip. The brothers, who were by now jealous of Joseph and the coat, saw him in the distance and they plotted to kill him.

Reuben, however, argued against killing Joseph and suggested that he be thrown into a nearby pit. Reuben secretly planned to save Joseph from the pit.

Consequently, when Joseph arrived his brothers took his coat and then threw him in a deep, dry pit.

Later, while they were eating, a group of slavetraders came along and one of the brothers suggested that they sell Joseph and split the money. This sounded like a good idea. Unknown to the brothers, however, some gypsies found Joseph, took him from the pit, sold him to the slave traders, and the slave traders took Joseph to Egypt.

Reuben discovered the empty pit and was extremely upset. The other brothers, however, decided to take the coat of Joseph, dip it in goat's blood, and tell their father that Joseph was killed by a lion.

On returning home, this was the story they told and Jacob believed it, and Jacob went into deep and sorrowful mourning for his favorite son. No one could comfort him and Jacob said he would grieve all his life for his dead son.

The slave traders sold Joseph to a man named Pat[1], a big shot friend of Pharoah, ruler of Egypt.

[1]Potiphar

One day Judah, a grown son of Jacob, went to visit his friend Tommy[1] in the next county and during the visit he fell for a girl named Sheila[2]. The marriage to Sheila resulted in Sheila having three sons by Judah, the eldest being named Al[3]. When Al became of age Judah arranged for him to marry a girl named Dolly[4]. Al, however, was a bad boy and the Lord deprived him of his life before he could become a father.

Judah was worried about the widow Dolly having no children so he instructed the second son, Olaf[5], to have intercourse with Dolly and produce a son. Olaf did not want to have a son through his brother's wife and so he spilled his sperm on the ground when he was in the tent with Dolly. The Lord then caused Olaf to lose his life.

Then Judah told his daughter-in-law Dolly to return to her father's house until the third son Sam[6] was old enough to marry.

Shortly after this Sheila died and Judah sought comfort in travel, visiting again his friend Tommy. Dolly learned of this and she was unhappy that Judah had not provided marriage and a son for her, as Sam was grown and no arrangement had been made with Dolly.

Dolly was a desirable woman and so she shed her widow's garb and dressed herself fetchingly, covering her face with a veil, and she placed herself in a prominent place knowing that Judah, her father-in-law, would see her. Judah saw Dolly and thought that she was a whore; so he propositioned her.

"What will you pay?" asked Dolly.

"A kid from the flock," replied Judah, "and I will leave you a pledge until the kid arrives."

"I'll take your ring, a bracelet, and your staff," said Dolly.

Judah gave it to her and then he lay with her, not knowing it was Dolly. After this episode Dolly returned to her father's house and put her widow's clothes on again.

Judah later asked his friend Tommy to take a kid to the harlot and retrieve his ring, bracelet and staff. Tommy sent word to Judah that no one knew of a harlot answering Judah's description in the little town of Camelot[7] where this incident occurred.

About three months later word came to Judah that his daughter-in-law Dolly was pregnant, and that the child would be illegitimate.

"Bring her here and we'll burn her to death," said Judah.

Dolly appeared before Judah.

"Hello, Dolly," said Judah, "you have played the part of a harlot."

[1] Hirah
[2] Shuah
[3] Er

[4] Tamar
[5] Onan
[6] Shelah

[7] Timnath

"Yes," said Dolly, "and the man left me a pledge," and so saying she showed Judah the ring, bracelet and staff.

"You have been more right than I have been," confessed Judah, "for I failed to remember my promise about Sam. You are forgiven." Judah had no further dealings with Dolly, who later had twins.

Chap.
39

In the meantime, Joseph, who was sold in Egypt to Pat, was progressing nicely. Joseph was a good boy and smart and the Lord blessed the work that he did for Pat so that Joseph had finally been promoted to General Manager and handled all of Pat's affairs.

Trouble started, however, when Pat's wife asked Joseph to go to bed with her.

Joseph said, "I just can't do it. Your husband has trusted me with all his affairs, and it would be not only a sin against God, but a dirty trick to play on Pat. I'm real sorry, but I can't go to bed with you."

The wife disregarded this negative reply and began to speak daily to Joseph, suggesting that they at least do a little necking, but Joseph continued to refuse.

One day the wife caught Joseph alone in the house and grabbed him by the shirt saying, "Love me!"

Joseph ran, but in leaving a part of his shirt was left torn in the lady's hand. This really tore it for the wife and she called to the servants and made a little speech saying, "Pat brought this Hebrew Joseph in to mock us and rule our lives. He actually tried to attack me and so I yelled, and in running away he tore his shirt and here is the piece of it."

When Pat returned he heard his wife's story and had Joseph thrown into prison. The Lord, however, was with Joseph even in prison and soon Joseph became a trusty and was really running the prison.

Chap.
40

Sometime later Pharaoh's butler and baker were sent to prison and came under Joseph's jurisdiction.

One morning the butler and the baker appeared especially sad and they explained to Joseph that each had dreamed the night before and neither one could interpret their dream.

Joseph asked them to relate their dreams. The butler said that he dreamed he saw a vine and there were three branches and the buds came forth and grapes grew and he gathered them, squeezed them into a cup and gave them to Pharoah.

Joseph said that this simply meant that in three days the butler would be restored in favor and get his old job back with Pharaoh.

"Now when this occurs," Joseph said, "remember me, and ask Pharaoh to get me out of this dungeon."

The chief baker said that he had dreamed of three white baskets on his head and that the birds began eating the goodies out of the top basket.

Joseph said this dream meant that in three days Pharaoh would cut off his head and hang his body out to be pecked by the birds.

Three days later Pharaoh had a birthday and to celebrate he restored the butler to his former position and he had the baker hanged.

Unfortunately, the butler forgot all about Joseph.

Chap.
41

Two years later Pharaoh dreamed that seven fat cows came out of the river and began grazing and along came seven skinny cows and they ate the fat ones. Pharaoh also dreamed that seven good, full grained ears of corn were consumed by seven poor ears. Pharaoh was glad to wake up and realize it was a dream, but he wanted an interpretation.

Pharaoh sent for the educators, the astrologists, and the consultants, but none could interpret the dream.

The chief butler spoke up, however, saying, "A couple of years ago when I was in prison along with the baker, we had dreams and a trusty there named Joseph interpreted our dreams and did so correctly."

Joseph, after shaving and dressing properly, appeared before Pharaoh, as requested.

Pharaoh told Joseph of his problem and Joseph said that God alone could interpret dreams, but that God sometimes worked through Joseph. Pharaoh then repeated the dreams to Joseph.

Joseph said, "God has decided to show Pharaoh what God is planning to do. The seven good cows and the seven good ears represent seven years of plenty and the seven skinny cows and poor ears are seven years of famine. This is the cycle that is forthcoming, for there shall be seven years of gracious plenty in Egypt and then seven years of grievous famine and hardship."

"Ugh," said Pharaoh.

"My suggestion," said Joseph, "is for you to appoint one man to take charge. Select a wise person who knows what this is all about, and let him gradually corner the grain market in Egypt, and store grain in the good years to provide for the lean years. When the lean years come, Pharaoh's warehouses will have all the grain that is available. It will be a financial bonanza."

"How can I find anyone who is better qualified than you? God has shown you these things and so I hereby make you General Manager of Egypt."

Whereupon Pharaoh put a special ring on Joseph's finger, bought him some fancy clothes, and arranged for him to ride in the second chariot during Mardi Gras parades. Pharaoh publicly declared Joseph the chief ruler saying, "Let no man lift a hand or a foot without permission from Joseph."

Pharaoh then said that Joseph's new name was to be Bing[1] and Pharaoh also gave him a wife, Arlene[2], a high class local favorite.

Joseph was a young man at this time and with great energy and enthusiasm he went forth and during the seven good years he accumulated corn as sand of the sea until it was too much to be numbered.

Joseph had two sons during this period, the eldest, who made him forget how tired he was, he called Zip[3], and the second son he named Carl[4], who reminded him of God's blessings.

The seven years of plenty ended and throughout the whole Middle East there came a time of great need, and there was food only in Egypt, in the warehouses under Joseph's control. Soon the people began to cry unto Pharaoh and he sent them to Joseph, and Joseph sold the grain to the Egyptians and to the people from the far countries who came to buy.

Chap. 42

Meanwhile, back at the ranch in Canaan, Jacob said to his sons, "Why do you sit around staring at each other? There is corn in Egypt, and we've got to have corn; so go down and buy some, else we die."

The ten older brothers set out for Egypt, leaving the youngest, Ben, at home, for he was still a bit young for such a hazardous trip.

The brothers arrived in Egypt and as was the case with all foreign buyers, they had to present themselves before Joseph to make a plea for corn. Now Joseph recognized his brothers, but he was careful to see that he was disguised enough so that they would not know him.

Joseph spoke harshly to them saying, "From where did you birds come?"

"We are from the land of Canaan and we come to buy food."

"You are spies. You have come to see how bare our land is."

"No, sir. We are one man's sons, we are sincere people, and we are not spies."

"You look like spies to me."

"We are twelve all told. The youngest we left at home and one brother is no longer alive."

"You are spies! In fact, I'll test you. You stay in Egypt until the youngest comes here. I will let one go back to Canaan for the youngest and I'll keep the others here in jail until the two return."

Whereupon he put them all in custody for three days. At the end of this period, Joseph told them that since he was a God-fearing man, he would give them a chance to live and told them to leave one brother bound in prison, take the corn that was needed, and then return later with the youngest.

[1]Zaphenathphaneah   [3]Manassahs,
[2]Asenath   [4]Ephraim

Joseph was speaking to them through an interpreter and they did not know that he knew their language, but Joseph understood perfectly the conversation they had following his final pronouncement.

"We are guilty concerning our lost brother," said one, "therefore this trouble has come upon us."

Reuben said, "I told you meatheads not to sin against the child and you would not listen."

The brothers agreed to the arrangement and they left Butch[1] bound. Joseph then ordered their sacks to be filled with corn and secretly he had their money placed back in the sacks, also provisions. The sacks were placed on the donkeys and they departed. The first night on the road one of the brothers opened one of the sacks to feed his donkey and saw the money in the mouth of the sack.

"My money is restored," he told his brothers.

This scared all of them and they said that it must be part of God's punishment.

Upon arriving at home, they told the whole story to Jacob.

Jacob immediately complained, "You are gradually getting rid of all my children. Joseph is long gone, Butch is lost in prison, and you want to take Ben away. You're doing all these things to spite me."

"I'll be responsible for Ben. Let me have him and I'll bring him back. If I fail you can kill my two sons, your grandsons," said Reuben.

"You're nuts. Ben shall not go to Egypt. Joseph's dead and Ben is the only son of Rachel left, and it would be too much if anything happened to him."

Chap.
43

Famine, however, grew worse in the land and the corn from Egypt was gone.

Jacob said, "All right, boys, go again to Egypt."

Judah spoke, "The man made it clear. No Ben, no corn. We will

go if Ben goes."

"Why did you big mouth goofs tell the man that there was another son in the first place?" asked Jacob.

"He asked us," they replied. "How were we to know that he'd want to see the youngest one?"

"Send the lad with me," said Judah, "so that we can all live. If I don't bring Ben back I'll take the full blame."

"All right," said Jacob, "if you must go, take plenty of gifts, take exotic aftershave lotion, some honey, salted pecans, and take double the money, both the money you brought back and the new amount needed. Maybe the money left in the sacks was an oversight.

[1]Simeon

Take your brother Ben, and God Almighty give you mercy before the ruler of Egypt that he may release Butch and let you bring Ben home. If I lose my children I lose everything."

The brothers came again and appeared before Joseph and this time Ben was with them. When Joseph saw Ben he told his aides to invite the brothers to lunch. The brothers were terrified to learn that they were invited to the ruler's house, and they feared that they would be attacked and made slaves.

The minute the brothers hit the door of Joseph's house they began explaining about the money to the business manager.

"Peace be with you, and fear not," said the business manager, "your God and the God of your father hath put the money in the sacks." Then he presented Butch to them.

The business manager saw that the brothers had a chance to wash and prepare for lunch.

When Joseph arrived the brothers gave him the presents and bowed themselves to the earth.

"Is your father well?" asked Joseph.

"Yes," they said.

Joseph then looked upon Ben and asked if this was the youngest son and they told him that it was. Joseph blessed him then. In fact, Joseph was so happy to see Ben and the other brothers that he had to leave to get hold of himself before the time for eating.

There were separate tables for lunch for Joseph, a Hebrew, could not eat with the Egyptians present, the Egyptians could not eat with the foreigners from Canaan, and the foreigners did not know that Joseph was a Hebrew.

Joseph, however, sent the food from his own table to the brothers' table but he put the choice cuts on Ben's plate. They all ate, drank, and were merry.

Chap.
44

After the meal, Joseph privately told the business manager to fill the sacks again with corn, to again replace the money, and this time to conceal a silver cup in Ben's sack. Needless to say, the business manager did it.

The next morning the brothers departed for Canaan.

Joseph instructed his business manager to let them get a couple of miles out of town and then they were to be stopped and searched by the customs people. The customs people were to say such things as "Why do you repay a kind host in such a manner?"

This was done and the brothers replied, "Why do you accuse us? We would not do anything wrong. Did we not bring the money back that was left in our sacks before? If there is anything stolen, search us and the culprit will surely die, and we will voluntarily be slaves."

The customs officers said, "That is not necessary. I will merely take as my slave anyone who is trying to steal or smuggle."

So beginning at the eldest, each was searched and the silver cup was found in Ben's sack.

The brothers tore their clothes and gnashed their teeth, and returned together to face the ruler again. Upon arriving, they fell on their faces again before Joseph.

"What deed have you done? Do you think I'm so stupid as to let you get away with this theft?"

Judah spoke then, "What can we say? How can we clear ourselves? We are even now your slaves, all of us."

"Sorry about that," said Joseph, "but I must keep the guilty on as my slave and the rest of you can return to the ranch."

Judah stepped forth then and said, "Don't get mad, but please listen. We know you are as powerful as Pharaoh, but listen. Do you remember asking if we had a father or a brother? Well, we said we had a father, an old man now, and a younger brother, a son of his old age, a little one, and his blood brother is dead, and only the little one is left of the mother, and the father loves him dearly. Then you said, 'Bring him down.' We said the old man would die if anything happened to the boy. Now father reminded us that his great love, Rachel, had only two sons, and one was torn to pieces, and if he loses this last one, he will perish. As a result, I declared myself surety for Ben. Let me therefore be your slave instead of Ben, for I cannot return to my father without Ben for I could not stand to see him suffer so much."

Chap. 45

After this speech, Joseph could not contain himself and he ordered everyone from the room except the brothers and then he declared himself unto them. In fact, Joseph carried on so everyone in the house could hear him.

The brothers couldn't believe it. It was too startling to comprehend.

Joseph then approached to them and said, "I am Joseph, your brother, whom you sold into Egypt. Do not be grieved or angry with yourselves that you treated me as you did, for God did send me before you to preserve life. For two years now there has been famine and there are five more years to come. God has really sent me before you to preserve a posterity for you in the earth, and to save your lives by a great deliverance; so really, it was not you, but God who did this thing, for God has made me as a father to Pharaoh, and a ruler throughout all Egypt.

"Make haste. Go to my father and say to him, 'Thus saith thy son Joseph. God hath made me ruler of Egypt, come to see me, and make haste.

I will give you land in Texas[1], where there is room for all of you, and your children, and your flocks, and all you have, and I will

---

[1]Goshen

feed you during the remaining years of famine. Look, you can see now that I am Joseph, and so can Ben. Don't forget to tell father of all my glory in Egypt, and hurry, and bring my father to me."

Joseph then embraced his brother Ben and then all the brothers got into the act.

The word of this soon leaked out and Pharaoh heard of the coming of Joseph's father and he was glad. Pharaoh ordered wagons to be acquired and given to the brothers to help with the move and Pharaoh said that what they didn't bring, Pharaoh would supply. So the brothers departed, with many gifts and many provisions.

Finally they arrived in Canaan and told Jacob that Joseph was alive and governor over the whole land of Egypt, and then Jacob fainted. As soon as he could listen they told Jacob all the things that Joseph said, and they showed him the wagons, and Jacob began to recover.

Jacob then said, "It is enough. Joseph my son is alive. I will go and see him before I die."

Chap. 46

As soon as everyone was packed Jacob and all his sons, and grandsons, the wives, the servants, and with all the possessions, they departed in one group. At a place where they stopped, the Lord spoke to Jacob and said, "I am God. Be not afraid to go to Egypt. I will be with thee. I will make of you a great nation and will in time deliver your descendants from Egypt. You will also see Joseph."

Judah went ahead to confer with Joseph and to locate Texas. Joseph then went in a chariot to meet his father and embrace him.

Joseph told his father and his brethren that although they had been raising sheep and goats that they were to tell Pharaoh and all the Egyptians that they were cattlemen and not to mention being shepherds, as a shepherd was an abomination in Egypt.

Chap. 47

Upon arriving in the presence of Pharaoh, however, the five selected brothers were asked by Pharaoh, "What is your occupation?"

"We are shepherds," they replied. "We have no pasture in our land and we would like to dwell in Texas, which we understand is not widely settled and there is much space there."

"Fine with me," said Pharaoh, "and if any of you have any experience in the cattle business I will be glad to employ you to help on my ranch."

Joseph brought Jacob to meet Pharaoh and Jacob blessed Pharaoh.

"How old are you?" asked Pharaoh.

"Older than seems possible, yet younger and more evil than my fathers," said Jacob, and then he departed.

Joseph saw to it that his father and his brethren were all nourished and well settled in Texas.

Joseph began gathering together all the money that was owed for all the corn that had been sold and he brought the money to Pharoah for safekeeping.

Now as the famine increased the people came to Joseph for corn, but they had no money. Joseph said that he would accept cattle in place of money so the people brought their cattle in exchange for food for a year.

The next year the people came for food and Joseph said that in exchange for food he would take land and the people then transferred all their deeds to Joseph for a year's supply of food.

Finally, Joseph told the people that they would now work the fields, all of which were now owned by the government, and they would be given food for their labor. And so it was made a law that the people would work and 20% of all that they made was given to Pharaoh. The only land exempt was church property.

Jacob was getting old to the point of thinking of death and he sent for Joseph and made him promise to bury him back home. Joseph promised.

Chap. 48

Word came to Joseph some months later that his father was dying; so Joseph took his two sons Zip and Carl and went to his father's bedside. At the approach of Joseph, the old man revived a bit and began to talk. Jacob said that he would like to bless the two sons of Joseph and they drew near, Jacob placed his right hand on the head of Carl, the younger, and the left on Zip.

Jacob prayed, saying, "God, before whom my father and grandfather walked, God who fed me all the days of my life, and the spirit which redeemed me from evil, bless these boys, let my name be their name, and let them grow into a multitude in the midst of the earth."

When Joseph saw that the right hand of Jacob was on Carl's head he told his father that the hands should be changed, but Jacob said he knew what he was doing, for great as the older boy would be, the younger would be greater.

"Joseph, I die," said Israel[1], "and I am leaving you an extra portion of my property, being some land I took away from a Frenchman[2]."

Then Jacob called the whole family together and pronounced a prophecy on each tribe.

"Reuben, your tribe represents power and strength, but it is not stable, and shall not excel, because of that incident with my mistress."

"Butch[3] and Max[4] are cruel. They are cursed for their violence

---

[1]Same as Jacob
[2]An Amorite

[3]Simeon
[4]Levi

and their wrath. I will divide them and scatter them."

"Judah shall be praised. The rule shall not depart from Judah and his tribe shall be neat and well kept."

"Jack Tar[1] shall be the seafaring ones, and in charge of the ports."

"Jeeves[2] is a worker and he shall be the servant tribe."

"Dan shall be a judge, and full of tricks."

"Troop[3] shall have trouble with troops, but will finally be victorious."

"Duncan Hines[4] shall be the eater and and furnish the gourmet cooks."

"Hubert[5] is a great talker with a mouth full of goodly words."

"Joseph is a fruitful bough growing by a well. The archers shoot at him and worry him, but he is made strong by the mighty God of Jacob. The blessings of my father shall be on the head of Joseph."

"Ben shall be like a wolf prowling in the morning and then counting his money at night."

Then Jacob blessed them all and charged them to see that he was buried in the same cemetery with Sarah, Abraham, Isaac, Becky and Leah.

Jacob, who sat for the blessing period, then climbed into bed and died immediately.

Chap.
50

Joseph mourned the passing of his father. Having had his father embalmed, he then at the end of the mourning period went to Pharaoh for a visa to leave the country to go and bury his father as requested.

There went with Joseph a great company of chariots and horsemen and the sons of Jacob buried him as he asked.

The brothers of Joseph then began to worry that Joseph might seek some revenge on them since their father was no longer alive to be a peacemaker, and so they went to Joseph and asked for forgiveness for their cruel behavior to him when he was a boy.

"Be not afraid," said Joseph, "I am not God. Granted that you planned evil against me, but God meant it for good, to bring to pass, as illustrated now, to save many people. Fear not, for I will continue to nourish you and your little ones." Thus he comforted them and spoke kindly to them.

Joseph lived to see his grandchildren grow and then as his own death approached he said unto his people, "I am going to die. God will visit you though and finally bring you out of this land, as he promsied Abraham, Isaac, and Jacob."

Joseph died and was embalmed and buried in a tomb in Egypt.

[1]Zebulon   [3]Gad
[2]Issachar   [4]Asher
                    [5]Naphtali

EXODUS

The twelve sons of Jacob prospered and multiplied and their descendants became strong and plentiful in the land. Many years later, long after Joseph was dead, a new Pharaoh came into power who had never heard of Joseph or all that he had done for Egypt.

The new Pharaoh, however, was increasingly alarmed over the growing power of the Hebrews and he reasoned that if an enemy attacked the land the Hebrews might join them and Egypt would be doomed. As a result, he began to take various steps to prevent this.

One thing he ordered was work. Pharaoh made the Egyptian overseers or taskmasters compell the Hebrews to make brick and do the laboring and servant chores of the land.

In view of the population explosion problem among the Hebrews, Pharaoh ordered all the midwives to kill any male Hebrew as soon as he was delivered. Because of the fear of God and the madness of this order, the midwives refused to obey. When challenged by Pharaoh, they denied their disobedience, telling Pharaoh that Hebrew women were more lively than Egyptian women and that the sons were being born before the midwives arrived. Pharaoh said, "A likely story."

God blessed the midwives for their attitude.

Pharaoh finally ordered the death of every male Hebrew child.

There was born one day to a Hebrew family a boy and the couple managed to hide the baby for over three months. Then the mother fixed a small boat out of reeds and during the day the teen-age sister would baby sit while the infant floated in the boat, hidden in the marsh grass.

One day some young ladies came down to the creek to frolic and swim. One of them was Pharaoh's daughter and she saw the baby and immediately went soft-hearted and said, "This is a Hebrew baby, but I want to keep it."

At this point the quick-thinking baby sitter arrived and said, "Do you want me to go and employ a nurse for you to use for the baby?"

"You bet I do," said Pharaoh's daughter.

Whereupon the sister went and brought the baby's mother.

"Take the baby and nurse it and I'll pay you wages," said Pharaoh's daughter.

The child grew, and the mother brought the baby, now named Moses[1], to Pharaoh's daughter regularly and Moses lived and grew up in a palace.

When Moses became grown he moved about the city observing all the work being done, and one day he saw an Egyptian striking a Hebrew slave. Moses carefully looked in every direction and decided

[1]Means one drawn from the water

32

that he was not observed, so he attacked and killed the Egyptian.

The next day Moses saw two Hebrews fighting and he attempted to be a peace maker, but he was rebuked by one of the Hebrews who mentioned that he knew Moses had killed a man and probably considered himself above the law.

Word of this shortly reached Pharaoh and he put out an APB on Moses, who had already fled to the wilderness in the land of Midian.

Moses visited an oasis as this was the place to see about getting a job. One of the county commissioners in this area who was also a prominent rancher had seven daughters but no sons; so the daughters brought the flocks to the oasis for water. Here the herdsmen from the other ranches made them wait until last to water. Moses, who was a trained Egyptian warrior, told them this was not fair, and began to beat the herdsmen with his war stick. In a few minutes the herdsmen decided Moses was right, and they let the seven girls water their stock first.

Upon returning home early for the first time, their father, Mr. Cartwright[1], wondered how they got to water early.

The girls said, "An Egyptian, Hoss Moses, delivered us and also drew the water."

"Where is this fellow?" asked the old man. "Invite him to dinner."

Hoss Moses found a happy home on the range. Soon he was given his choice of daughters to marry and he chose Zsa Zsa[2] and Moses began a period of great joy and contentment. He had it made.

In the meantime, however, back in Egypt, Pharaoh had died, and the bondage of the Hebrew people was increased and they began to cry mightily to the Lord for deliverance. God heard their moans and groans and He was not unmindful of His promise to Abraham and Isaac, and He looked upon the children of Israel and decided to help them.

Chap.
3

One day when Moses had the duty on a faraway part of the ranch, an angel of the Lord appeared in the middle of a bush which though it burned, it did not seem to be consumed.

Moses said to himself, "I think I'll ease over and see more closely this strange sight."

As Moses approached, God called to him saying, "Moses."

"Here I am," said Moses.

"Put off your shoes, this is a holy place, and holy ground, for I am here," said the Lord. "I am the God of your father, and the God of Abraham, Isaac, and Jacob."

Moses was afraid and hid his face.

"I have seen the affliction of my people," the Lord continued, "at the hands of the Egyptians and I know their sorrows, and so I am

[1]Reuel (Jethro)   [2]Zipporah

here to initiate their deliverance, for I want them to leave Egypt and go to a good land, flowing with milk and honey, a place now inhabited by Canaanites, Hippies[1], Indians[2], Anglo-Saxons[3], Canadians[4], and Germans.[5] I have heard the prayers of my people of Israel and I am depending on you to return to Egypt and to lead in their liberation."

"Who am I, Lord?" asked Moses. "I am a nobody to Pharaoh."

"I will be with you," said God, "and I promise that after the deliverance of the people you will return here and serve God at this very place."

"When I come to the children of Israel and tell them that the God of their fathers has sent me, they shall surely say 'what is His name?'"

"Tell them that I Am That I Am," said God. "Tell them I am the God of Abraham, Isaac, and Jacob. Tell them to gather their leaders together and tell them of my promise, and they shall finally listen to you. It will not be easy, Moses, for the king of Egypt will work against you, but in the long run the Israelites will follow you, and they will receive gifts from the Egyptians to help them with their journey."

Chap.
4

"But, God, these people won't believe me," insisted Moses.

"All right, Moses. Take the rod that is in your hand and throw it on the ground."

Upon doing this, Moses saw the rod turn into a serpent and he jumped at least 12 feet.

"Now pick it up, Moses," said God. When Moses grasped the tail of the snake it turned again into a rod.

"Feel better, now?" asked God. "Then put your hand in your shirt."

Moses put his hand in his shirt and when he withdrew it, he was a leper.

"Now put it back in your shirt." Moses placed his trembling hand in his shirt and when he withdrew it he was whole again.

"Believe me, Moses," said God, "I will work as many signs as are necessary to get my people free from Egypt."

"All this sounds fine, O Lord," replied Moses, "but I am not a public speaker. When I get up before a crowd my tongue sticks to the roof of my mouth."

"Who do you think made you? Who made the dumb or the deaf or the seeing or the blind? Have I not made them all, and they are mine. Now get up and go and let me worry about your mouth."

"But, God, why not send someone who is already prepared?"

[1]Hittites   [2]Amorites   [3]Perizzites
[4]Hivites   [5]Jebusites

And God became miffed with Moses and said reluctantly, "All right. I will have Aaron meet you and Aaron is a great speaker, though he can do nothing else. You can put words in Aaron's mouth after I have placed them in yours. Now take the rod which I have blessed and for the last time 'get gone!'"

Moses returned to the ranch house and told his father-in-law of his encounter with the Lord and the father-in-law blessed him and sent Moses away in peace.

The Lord then comforted Moses by telling him that his picture was no longer in the Post Office in Egypt and that the group who had sworn to kill him were all dead.

Moses then put his wife[1] and sons on a donkey and departed for Egypt. En route Moses had a fight at a motel which apparently Moses interpreted as objection from God that the eldest son was not circumcised. As a consequence, Zsa Zsa[2] took a sharp stone and circumcised the son, which was a bloody operation, and then she threw the foreskin at Moses[3], calling him a bloody brawler.

After this incident, the mother and boy returned to the ranch.[4]

As promised by God, Aaron met Moses in the wilderness and there Moses told Aaron all the words of the Lord and told him of all the signs which were at Moses' disposal.

Upon arriving in Egypt Moses and Aaron gathered together all the leaders of the children of Israel and Aaron spoke to them, telling them all the words of the Lord, and the people bowed their heads and worshipped God.

Shortly thereafter Moses and Aaron visited Pharaoh and told him that God had a message for Pharaoh and it was "let my people go".

"Who is the Lord that I should obey him? I don't know him and I won't let Israel go," replied Pharaoh.

"We believe in God and He has met with us and ordered us to take the people into the wilderness for a feast. How about letting them off for three days, just a long weekend?"

"You're trying to get the people out of work. Nuts to you both!"

As a result of this confrontation, Pharaoh ordered the workload to be increased on the Hebrews, including requiring them to secure their own straw for the bricks. All this was done and the punishment was severe.

The local leaders of the Hebrew people then came to Pharaoh and asked, "What brought all this trouble on us?"

"You are idle," said Pharaoh, "and want to spend time in the wilderness at a feast. Your workload will stay as I ordered."

---

[1] Some scholars question her enthusiam for the trip
[2] Zipporah   [3] Some scholars were right
[4] Indications are that wife and sons all returned.

After leaving the palace the leaders encountered Moses and Aaron and denounced them saying, "The Lord should judge you all and punish you all for what you have caused to happen to us. You made us stink in the nose of Pharaoh and also his rulers, and they have gotten tough with us."

Moses then went to the Lord and moaned, "Why, O Lord, did you get me into this mess? What's more, ever since I've come here there has been nothing but trouble and no deliverance, not even a tiny bit."

Chap.
6

"Calm down, now, Moses. Wait and see what I will do in my own time. I assure you that Pharaoh will gladly release the Hebrews when I am finished with him. You forget, Moses, that I am the Lord. I am the God of Abraham, Isaac, and of Jacob. I am Jehovah. My promises will always be kept. I have heard the groans of my people and will give them Canaan, it will be so, for I am the Keeper of the Promises. I will redeem my people, and I will take them to me for a people, and I shall be their God."

Moses repeated these assertions to the people, but they would not listen.

God then spoke to Moses again and said, "Go see Pharaoh again."

"But, God," said Moses, "if the Hebrews won't listen to me, how do you expect Pharaoh to listen?"

"Remember who you are. You, Moses and Aaron, are descendants of my people down through years. Act like it!"

"I still don't think Pharaoh will listen," replied Moses.

Chap.
7

"Now, Moses," said God, "I have caused Pharaoh to think highly of you. Aaron can say the words. Pharaoh will not be easy, but I will use his hardness of heart to demonstrate my power, so that finally even the Egyptians shall know that I am the Lord."

Moses and Aaron then did as God ordered and appeared before Pharaoh, who immediately asked that they show him a miracle of God. As God had instructed him, Aaron then threw his cane on the ground and it turned into a snake.

Pharaoh, however, called for some of his own magicians and they did the same thing, but the snake of Aaron ate up the other snakes. This just made Pharaoh mad.[1]

The Lord then told Moses the next day to go stand by the water pool where Pharaoh came to drink and take the rod and when Pharaoh came to say "The Lord God of the Hebrews says 'Let my people go!'"

Then the Lord instructed Moses to have Aaron stroke the waters with his cane, and as a result all the waters turned red and were polluted, and the fish died, and the river stank, but Pharaoh just

[1]Pharoah may have asked them to stay over a day and do the trick before Rotary

got madder. The Egyptians had to dig for fresh water as the pollution
lasted a week.

The Lord then told Moses to go to Pharaoh and say again that
he was to let the people go, and threaten him this time with frogs.
Moses then told Aaron to stretch forth his cane and frogs began to
arise from the rivers and the pools and the swamps so that there was
a frog jubilee. The magicians claimed to be doing this same thing but
Pharaoh got his fill of frogs and sent for Moses and told him that he
would let the people go.

"Hurrah for me," said Moses. "I'll get the frog withdrawal going
tomorrow." And the Lord heard the prayer of Moses and the frogs
died out of houses, and the villages, and the streets.

When the frogs were gone, however, Pharaoh relented and
cancelled the release of the people.

God then spoke to Moses and said, "Hit them with lice." Aaron,
on the order of Moses, then struck the dust with his cane and lice
began to get over everything everywhere.

Pharaoh's magicians could not handle this one, and they told
Pharaoh that the lice touch had to come from God. Pharaoh was not
impressed, as he still did not believe in God.

The Lord then waited a few days and spoke to Moses and said
that it was now time to use flies on Pharaoh and the Egyptians, but
that the land of Texas, where the Hebrews dwelled, would be spared.
So the Lord released swarms of flies, and they covered the land, and
the people, and the beasts.

Pharaoh then sent for Moses and said, "All right, tell your
people to have their picnic, but have it here."

"No," said Moses, "it must be three days in the wilderness."

"All right, but don't go far," said Pharaoh, swatting flies as he
spoke.

Moses then asked the Lord to remove the flies and He did so,
but Pharaoh hardened his heart again and would not let them go.

The Lord then told Moses to go to Pharaoh and tell him that
the hand of the Lord would be upon the cattle if Pharaoh did not let
the people go, and there would be a terrible murain among all the
livestock.

So the Lord struck the cattle and all over Egypt they began to
die. The cattle of Israel had been separated and they did not get the
disease.

Pharaoh just got madder and madder.

The Lord then told Moses and Aaron to prepare ashes and to
cast them in the air in sight of Pharaoh and there would be boils and
infections in the land. The magicians who were summoned could not
stand still for the boils that were upon them, but Pharaoh would not
turn from his resolve to hold the people.

After the Lord had seen again how bull-headed Pharaoh was, He told Moses that he would now smite the people with a tremendous hail, the worst that Egypt had ever seen. God said He wanted to teach the Egyptians that there was none mighty like unto Him.

On the next day, as the Lord had commanded, Moses stretched forth his cane and the Lord sent forth thunder and hail, and lightning ran along the ground, and hail rained down on the land of Egypt. The hail broke down trees and destroyed all of the standing crops.

Pharaoh this time sent for Moses and Aaron and said, "I quit. You win. I have sinned. The Lord is righteous and I and my people are wicked. Ask God to cut the thunder and the hail and I'll let your people go."

"As soon as I leave the city, I will spread forth my hands to God and the thunder and the hail will cease, but I doubt if you and your servants are really converted. I'm of the opinion that you're just scared."

Now when quiet had come and Pharaoh saw that only the flax and barley had been destroyed for the wheat and rye had not grown up, he sinned all over again, renounced his promise, and again hardened his intention to keep the Hebrews in subjugation.

Chap.
10

The Lord then told Moses that all of these things had been done to teach a great lesson, not so much to Pharaoh as to God's people, that down through the ages they might pass the word from father to son of the power of God and of His mighty acts.

This time, God told Moses, "Hit them with the locusts."

The servants of Pharaoh then implored Pharaoh saying, "How long will we have to put up with Moses and these plagues? Let the dog-gone people go!"

Pharaoh then sent for Moses and Aaron again and said, "You can go. I want to know, though, who will go with you and what you will take."

Moses said, "We will go with our young and our old, with our flocks, and our herds, for we must hold a feast for the Lord."

"No deal," said Pharaoh. "I will let the men go, but kids aren't needed for worship and you can leave the women and children behind. The interview is over!"

Moses stretched forth his hand as God had commanded and the locusts with an east wind began to swarm into Egypt and eat up every herb, and the locusts covered the land so that it was darkened, and anything that the hail had left the locusts ate.

Pharaoh summoned Moses in haste, confessed his sin, and begged for relief. The Lord then sent a strong west wind which drove the locusts away and again the heart of Pharaoh was hardened.

The Lord then told Moses to stretch forth his hand to heaven and he would bring a great darkness to the land of Egypt for three days and no one could see another person for the darkness, and everyone stayed at home during the big blackout.

Pharaoh then told Moses that the people could go, including the women and children, but that they could not take any livestock or any possessions with them.

Moses said, "No deal. You must give us sacrifices to take for burnt offerings and all our cattle go with us."

Pharaoh would not agree and called off the release again, saying to Moses, "Get out. I never want to see your face again. If you ever return I will see that you are executed."

"That suits me fine, Bub," said Moses, "because that means I'll never see your face again either."

Chap.
11

After this the Lord spoke to Moses and told him that one more terrible plague would be used against Pharaoh and that the last one would work.

First, Moses was to prepare all the Hebrew people for a sudden departure. Moses instructed the people to borrow everything they could from the Egyptians. By this time the name of Moses was important and the Egyptians were generous in their gifts and loans to the Hebrew people. There was much talk in the land, and Moses departed from Pharaoh in anger and Pharaoh's heart and head were hardened.

Chap.
12

"What I plan to do," said God, "is so important that from now on this shall be known as the first month of the year. For I will pass through the land of Egypt in the night and will smite the first born in every family, unless there be the blood of the lamb marked on the door, such houses I shall pass over. Let the Hebrew people carefully and liturgically mark their doors for this night, and if there be a family too poor to have a lamb, let them use the blood of a neighbor's lamb. Let it be remembered that this shall be a memorial day and feast day for my people forever."

"Years from now," continued God, "when your children shall ask why you observe this occasion, you tell them that it is the sacrifice of the Lord's passover."

And the children of Israel did as commanded. And it happened as the Lord said, for the angel of death passed through the land of Egypt and the eldest son in each place from Pharaoh's palace to the dungeons was taken by death, and also the eldest of the livestock. There was a great cry and sadness in Egypt, for there was no house in which there was not one dead.

The Lord told Moses and Aaron to get the show on the road, and they aroused the people, and the Egyptians urged them to leave, and they gave gifts and loaned articles, until the children of Israel had almost cleaned the Egyptians out of their possessions.

Now there were some 600,000 men plus women, children, livestock, vehicles that departed, after serving in bondage in Egypt for four hundred and thirty years.

The Lord spoke strongly to Moses regarding the keeping of the feast of the Passover, insisting that it be taught from generation to generation, for it should be a sign and a memorial for God said, "With a strong hand hath the Lord brought thee out of Egypt. Therefore keep the ordinance of the passover in its season from year to year."

On leaving Egypt Moses, as inspired by God, did not take the people the short route through the land of the Fascists, lest they encounter a warlike people and return to Egypt, but he led them through the way of the Red Sea.

Moses took the bones of Joseph with him for it was recorded by Joseph that eventually God would deliver, and that Joseph wanted his bones to make the trip.

Now the Lord led the children of Israel, using a cloud by day and a pillar of fire by night, and at no time did He take these away from the people.

The Lord planned that the Hebrew people should pitch camp by the sea, taking the long way so that Pharaoh would think the people lost in the wilderness. All this was done in order that the Lord could work His wondrous way on Pharaoh, and that he and all the Egyptians would know that there is only the one true God.

And so it happened that the Egyptians began to relent over the release of all their cheap labor and they encouraged Pharaoh to pursue the Hebrews, which he did with 600 chariots of high speed and all the mighty men of the army of Egypt.

When the children of Israel, camped by the Red Sea, saw the dust in the distance and the sun shining on the armor of the Egyptian army, they were terrified.

The first committee to immediately descend on Moses said sarcastically, "Were there no cemeteries in Egypt, was it for this that we were brought into the desert to die?"

The second committee appeared then and said, "Moses, we told you and we told you to leave us alone in Egypt. Now look what has happened. It would have been better for us to serve the Egyptians than to die in the wilderness."

Moses said, "Sit tight and don't be afraid, and you shall undoubtedly see the salvation of the Lord. You won't have to deal with the Egyptians any more after today for the Lord will fight for you."

Then Moses went and cried unto the Lord.

"Why cry unto me, Moses?" asked God. "Speak to the children of Israel and tell them to go forward!"

And God instructed Moses to hold his cane over the waters of the Red Sea as the people marched forward.

The angel of the Lord then removed himself from the front of the people to their rear and the pillar of fire moved behind them and the cloud came between the camp of the Egyptians and the Hebrews and it prevented the people from seeing each other and they were afraid saying, "The Lord fights for the Hebrews, let us flee."

As God had commanded, Moses stretched forth his hand over the sea and the wind began to subside in the night, and in the morning the tidal wave came down upon the main part of the Egyptian army that was in the sea, and the waters covered the chariots and the horsemen and they perished.

And Israel saw the great work which the Lord had done, and they feared and worshipped God, and believed God and his servant Moses.

Chap.
15

The children of Israel celebrated, and the folk song and ballad writers became very active and they put to music the "Red Sea Story". The songs all told of the greatness of God, the terrible destruction which fell upon the Egyptians, and everyone seemed to get into the act.

Miriam, sister of Aaron, led the women in a big dance scene, playing timbrels and singing the Ballad of the Red Sea, and there was feasting and rejoicing, and the praising of God.

After a few days the celebrating ceased and Moses began to lead the people through the wilderness. The Hebrews were no longer afraid, for they predicted that the people of Canaan would be afraid after they were told of the great victory over the Egyptians and so they followed Moses confidently.

The first major camping spot was selected for its trees and water. The water, however, was bitter and the people immediately began complaining. Naturally they appointed a committee to call on Moses and to gripe for the whole crew.

"Now we're in a terrible fix, Moses," the committee stated, "for the water is too bitter to drink."

Moses asked God for help and the Lord made it known to Moses that all that was needed was leaves from a sassafras tree. As soon as the leaves were put in the water, the water became sweet and the people quit griping for a few days.

Moses said to the people, "If you will obey God, and do that which pleases Him, you will have no health problems such as the sinful and wicked Egyptians have."

Chap.
16

Two and a half months later the food ran out and the supplies of flour, sugar, and staples from Egypt were all gone. The people immediately began to complain. Typical of the moans was the expression "Would to God that we had died natural deaths in Egypt rather than starving to death in this weird wilderness."

The Lord, the keeper of the promises, told Moses that he would provide food, but that the people would have to obey the rules of conservation.

Each morning following the heavy dew there would be small white pieces of ambrosia, which the Hebrews called manna, and each evening there would be quail, weary of flying, that could be caught on the ground.

The rules were simple. All the manna was to be gathered each day and on the sixth day of each week, a double portion of manna and quail were to be gathered in order that the seventh day be a day of rest.

Some of the people immediately goofed. First, there were some who would get tired and leave some manna on the ground, and it spoiled and smelled. Then there were some who went out to gather food on the sabbath day. The Lord was displeased with this.

The manna tasted like biscuit and honey and the people lived primarily on this for forty years.

Chap.
17

The next hardship that brought forth major complaints was lack of water. Again they howled to Moses and Moses prayed to God saying, "What can I do with these griping people? They are ready to stone me because of the water problem."

And the Lord told Moses to go and assemble the people with their leaders and smite the rock Niagara,[1] and that he would cause water to fall out of it for the people to drink. Moses did as God suggested and water came and Moses snapped a bit at the people saying, "Is God with us or not? Where is your faith?"

Not long after this the Capone[2] gang came to harass the Israelites and Moses ordered Joshua, a strong young warrior, to gather up a few vigilantes and fight them. During the struggle the Hebrews did well as long as Moses kept his hands raised in encouragement; so they put stones under his elbows to keep his arms high, and Joshua prevailed. And the Lord said that this occurrence was to be remembered and that He would always hold this against the Capone gang, and that He would fight them and their kind from generation to generation.

Chap.
18

Now back at the ranch in Midian, word came to Mr. Cartwright, Moses' father-in-law, about the great deliverance from Egypt and the trip that Moses was conducting for the children of Israel; so Mr. Cartwright decided to visit Moses when the pilgrimage approached his area, and to take Moses' wife and two sons to see Moses. The wife had returned home mad after Moses had gotten in a fight at the motel on the way to Egypt.

Moses welcomed his father-in-law and his family and had a big dinner in their honor. The next day Mr. Cartwright was amazed to see that Moses arose early and took the seat of judgment and spent all day and late into the evening judging the people, answering their questions, and settling disputes.

[1]Horeb   [2]Amalek

Mr. Cartwright spoke to Moses and said, "This has got to be the stupid way to live. You will not only wear yourself out, but you'll wear the people out and only trouble will result."

"Somebody has to make the rulings and explain right and wrong to the people," replied Moses.

"Yes," said Mr. Cartwright, "but what makes you think you are the only one that can do it? What will the people do when you have a stroke in the next few months?"

"What do you suggest that I do?" asked Moses.

"It will take a little organization," said Mr. Cartwright, "but you should choose the best possible men and make them the supreme court to rule over the many thousands, then set up a system of lower courts, down to a judge for as few as ten families or one row of tents. Let the lesser judge deal with small matters, and the next highest judge with more important matters, and so on until only the major matters of import come to your attention."

"Sounds like a great idea," said Moses, "I will try it."

As a result a system was inaugurated of courts and appeals. Mr. Cartwright had made a wise suggestion and Moses had been smart enough to accept the advice.

Mr. Cartwright then returned to the ranch.

Chap. 19

With a system of courts the need arose for specific laws and God spoke to Moses and said, "Tell the people again that I am God. Remind them of what I did to the Egyptians and assure them that if they will keep my commandments I will treasure them as a nation, and they shall be to me as if they were a nation of ministers and priests."

The Lord then further expressed the need for the people to be prepared for His revelation of law; so Moses instructed them to take three days of preparation, to bathe, clean their possessions, scrub their tents and lockers, and not to even have intercourse with their wives for this period in order that they might be ready in mind and body to be aware of the presence of God.

On the morning of the third day there came forth great thunder and lightning, the whole mountain of Sinai was engulfed in a dark cloud, and smoke came forth from the mountains. Moses climbed the mountain into the cloud and God told him to make certain that none of the others, save Aaron, should touch the mountain.

Moses said, "I had already thought of that, and put barriers up and blocked the trails so that no one would get too close to the mountain."

"All right," said God, "return to the people and I will speak from the mountain."

And God spoke and said, "I am the Lord thy God. I am the one that brought you all out of the house of bondage that you all had in Egypt."

"In the first place, be sure and know that I am the only one true God, and I must be considered unquestionably number one in all things.

"You are not, therefore, to make graven images in the likeness of any object or person to which you will bow down, or for whom you commit your whole being. I will not accept secondary service, for I do not hesitate to punish, even though it may affect one generation after another for several generations, and yet I am merciful in great plenty to the thousands who love me and attest thereby in their lives.

"Do not try to use my name for your own purposes. You cannot claim to speak or act in God's name unless I authorize you to do so.

"Observe Sunday. It is a different day. It is a day set aside in recognition of creation and the creator. You are not to pursue the regular work of the week. You are to acknowledge on this day that God is Lord, and this seventh day is to be for His glory, and for refreshment, and you are to influence your family and associates in this connection.

"Recognize and adhere to the basic scheme of man's development which is the concept of the family unit. Respect the family unit as this is the only way for a full and meaningful life.

"You do not personally have the right to decide whether another person shall live or die.

"Adultery is forbidden for it works against the basic family plan.

"To steal is a violation of the law of God.

"You do not have the right to give a wrong impression about your neighbor or repeat things about anyone that is not absolutely true.

"You also are not to desire the things or conditions that are not yours. You are not to desire your neighbor's house to the dissatisfaction of your own, or your neighbor's wife, or his golf clubs, nor his ranch, nor anything that he has that might appear preferable to what you have."

The people heard the mighty thundering, and saw the lightning, and the billows of smoke coming from the mountain, and they backed away and were afraid. The people told Moses that in the future let Moses speak to them anytime, but do not let God speak straight for it is too terrifying.

Moses said, "Don't get so fretful. God is just teaching you a good lesson; so that you do not sin."

God said to Moses, "Now tell the people that I do not want them to make any more images of silver and gold as objects of worship. If you wish to recognize God and worship Him, just build a small altar of stones, and do not even bother to cut or break the stones as the simplicity appeals to me."

Then through Moses there were established many detailed laws and rulings as a system of jurisprudence in order that the people might know how to relate themselves to their neighbors, and a person could thereby know what to expect of the law.

If a man hurt a woman who was with child and caused a miscarriage, the beating was to be left in the hands of the husband, but the judges would determine the fine.[1]

And God spoke again to Moses and said, "Come up near to me, bring Aaron and the elders and let them worship at a distance."

Moses told the people of the laws and of God's promises if they would obey and the people promised to obey. And Moses wrote all the words of the Lord and built an altar to God of twelve stones, representing the twelve tribes of Israel.

Then went Moses and Aaron and the elders up to the mountain, but only Moses went up on the mountain. A cloud covered the mountain for six days and on the seventh day God called to Moses out of the cloud. The sight of the glory of God appeared as a devouring flame bursting out of the top of the mountain and Moses disappeared into the cloud on the mountain and remained there in meditation for forty days and forty nights.

God spoke to Moses and said, "Tell the people to bring gifts of gold and valuables, as much as each will willingly give, and let the money be used to build the ark of the covenant, and this shall be a symbol of God's house, and here we shall regularly commune, one with another. There is also to be built a church[2] to house the ark.[3]"

The Lord then told Moses to take Aaron and his sons and set them apart as priests and ministers, to array them in special robes, and to train them in a proper liturgy of worship.

Moses was also instructed in special rites of ordination for Aaron and his sons and the special garment was designed saying 'Holiness to the Lord.'

"When all of this is done," said the Lord, "then in the tabernacle I will meet with the people, and I will sanctify the church with my glory and bless the altar and I will dwell with the children of Israel and will be their God and they will know that I am the Lord their God, that brought them forth out of the land of Egypt. I am the Lord!"

[1]A sample of the law   [2]Tabernacle
[3]Complete description Exodus 25, 26, 27

Chap.
30

Further instructions were then given in the area of craftsmanship.[1]

Chap.
31

Now the Lord had provided in the diversity of creation that there should be men with special talents and God called to Moses attention the fact that there were such among the people and that these talented persons were the ones to be named in charge of the construction of the ark and the tabernacle.

Chap.
32

The people, however, began to get restless after Moses failed to return from the mountain in a few days and many rumors began to circulate about his going AWOL or dying or the like.

After a while the people came to Aaron and said they despaired of Moses returning and that they needed a new god and a new leader; so Aaron agreed to help with a false god, and acting as their new leader he assisted in the construction of a golden calf.

God beheld all this and He spoke to Moses on the mountain saying "You had better get back to camp. The people have corrupted themselves. I perceive that they are a stiff-necked outfit and have already forgotten me. I will completely destroy them and start a whole new nation from you."

"Please don't do that, God," urged Moses. "In the first place, the Egyptians would be pleased. Also remember your promise to Abraham, Isaac, and Jacob. Let me have a chance at them again."

The Lord agreed to this, and so Moses came down from the mountain with the two tablets of law in his hands and there he was met by a fine young man named Joshua.

"The noise the people are making," said Joshua, "sounds like the noise of war."

"No," said Moses, "it doesn't sound like people shouting for mastery, nor do I hear sounds of people being struck, but it sounds to me more like a bunch of drunks singing."

When Moses came to the camp he saw the people dancing and singing, full of wine, naked, and going wild around the golden calf.

Moses roared and he threw the stone tablets at the people and he threw the golden calf in the fire and he ground it to pieces and made the people drink it in their water.

Moses turned to Aaron and stormed, "What did the people do to you to force you to do this thing?"

"Nothing," replied Aaron, "they just asked me to do it and brought me the money. It was one of those 'boys will be boys' deals."

Then Moses stood forth before the people and cried, "Who is on the Lord's side? Everyone that is faithful come stand by my side."

[1]Exodus 30

Many men then came to stand by Moses, and Moses spoke to them, and told them to take swords to go through all the camp and to kill everyone that did not repent. Then Moses said that he might be able to go to God and seek His blessing again. So the men went forth and as a result something in the neighborhood of 3,000 men were killed before order was restored.

Then Moses came into the presence of God and spoke saying, "Lord, these people have sinned greatly. Forgive them. I am willing to sacrifice my own life for their sake."

"Thank you, Moses, but that is not necessary. I'll tend to the punishment. Start your trip again and I will let my angel again guide you, but I'm going to make the trip a tough one and I'm going to exercise reasonable punishment on the people."

Chap.
33

And the Lord told Moses to get the people together and to depart, but God also said that although He would be with Moses and the people when they arrived in Canaan, He would not be with them on the remainder of the trip, for they must suffer for their disobedience.

The news of this disturbed the people but there was nothing they could do about it. In fact, God instructed Moses to place the tabernacle well outside the camp and that at this location God would deal with his servant Moses, in whom God had great delight.

When Moses left the camp and entered the tabernacle in the distance, the people saw the cloud of God descend on the tabernacle, and they worshipped. The young man Joshua was present at the tabernacle with Moses, and God spoke to Moses as a friend speaks to a friend.

"You have told me, God," said Moses, "to bring this people to a new land. I want to know who is going to help me."

"My presence will go with you, Moses, and I will give you rest," said the Lord.

"All right, but agree to cancel the trip if you withdraw your presence, for it is your presence that makes us a people different from other people."

"I will agree to your request, Moses, for you have found favor in my sight and I even know you by name."

"Show me a sample of your presence, Lord," said Moses.

"All right," God said. "I will cause my goodness to pass near you, and I will pronounce my name. You cannot see me, for no one can behold God and live, but I will let you get in the crevice of a rock wall and I'll pass by and you can feel my presence and behold my departure, but my hand will cover you as I pass."

Chap.
34

"I'm ready," said Moses.

"First, however, you must hew me two tablets of stone in order that I might write on them the ten commandments exactly as they were on the tablets you broke when angry with the people. Do this by morning."

And Moses hewed the stone tablets and rose early in the morning and climbed Mount Sinai and the Lord descended in a cloud and stood there with Moses and proclaimed His presence and spoke saying, "The Lord God is merciful and gracious, long suffering, and abundant in goodness, showing mercy to thousands, forgiving iniquity and sin for those who repent, but visiting the unrepentant iniquity of the fathers unto the children for four generations."

Moses bowed his head and worshipped. Then Moses prayed saying, "Lord, I pray for your presence. Stay with us. I know the people are stiffnecked and sinful, but pardon us, and let us be thy people."

God spoke then saying, "I will make an agreement that I will do some marvels in sight of the people such as have never been done. I will drive out the Hippies, the gypsies, and the Russians from before you, but do not dare try to make side deals with any of them. Destroy their altars, break their images, and you people are to worship no other God, for I am a jealous God."

"Be very careful," God continued, "that you do not join with other inhabitants in strange worship, nor should you intermarry with them, and don't forget to tithe. The first fruits are mine. Observe the proper feast days and make certain that all the kids go to church at least three times a year. This is my covenant with my people."

When Moses came down from the mountain after visiting with God and carrying the ten commandments on the stone tablets, the face of Moses shone. The people were terrified and so Moses covered his face with a veil while he revealed the commandments of God and told the people of the covenant.

Chap.
35

Moses appeared again before the people and called for a thank offering. Moses urged that all the people who were moved in their hearts by the goodness of God to bring gifts of all kinds in order that the tabernacle, and the ark of the covenant, could all be properly completed.

The people did this and trained craftsmen were assembled and all were put under the care of Mr. Disney,[1] whom God himself had blessed with great talents. And Mr. Disney assembled other talented people and trained them, and then they set forth to do the building and the making of the garments.

Chap.
36

The people were moved by this great activity and continued to make gifts until Moses announced that enough was already on hand and no further gifts were needed.[2]

[1]Bezaleel   [2]They over-subscribed the budget

Chap.
37, 38, 39

The building and the equipment, the garments and symbols were all set forth with great skill and in great detail[1] and all was approved by Moses and Moses saw that it had all been done in accordance with the will of God, and so Moses blessed all of those who had helped in any way.

Chap.
40

God told Moses that now the tabernacle could be placed within the camp. It came about that all these things were completed after two years and Moses set up the bulletin board as the very last thing, and the tabernacle was finished. Then a cloud covered the area of the congregation and the glory of the Lord filled the tabernacle. From thenceforth the cloud of the Lord was in the sight of all during the day and the fire shown at night, and the people journeyed only when the cloud moved or the fire advanced.

[1]Read Exodus 37, 38 for details

LEVITICUS

Note: The book of Leviticus is a compilation of laws, liturgical procedures and admonitions. The following paraphrases are samples from the book and are selected passages.

Chapters 1-7 deals with the manner, nature and method of burnt offerings for peace as well as trespass offerings.

Chapters 8-10 set forth instructions for the garments of Aaron and his sons as priests as well as such admonitions as the prohibition of the use of wine or strong drink by the priest or minister before conducting the service in the tabernacle or church.

Chapter 11 made distinctions between the various animals to be eaten or sacrificed.

Chapters 12-15 expressed views on health habits and preventive medicine in specific areas of post-pregnant conditions, blood problems, leprosy, and purification or cleanliness cautions for travel in the wilderness.

Chapter 16 described procedures for priests in connection with tabernacle service and Chapter 17 emphasized the error of the eating of blood.

Chap.
18

At a later time God spoke to Moses and told him to remind the people that they were under the one true God and they must obey His admonitions. God stated the sins of the Egyptians had been their undoing and that the Canaanites were guilty of the same sins. The children of Israel must observe God's orders, or they too would encounter difficulty.

One of the prominent errors of the Egyptians was the matter of indecent exposure. God, speaking through Moses, reminded the people that careless nakedness and the intentional exposure of a person was prohibited. Man was not to participate in any act of a homosexual character, nor was he to attempt intercourse with animals. Women also were told this was forbidden. Respect for relatives and neighbors meant that a person did not have the right of free love and the exercising of such constituted wickedness.

Chap.
19

The Lord explained to Moses various other matters dealing with the behavior and attitudes of the people.

God said to Moses, "You are to be holy for I the Lord am holy."

This meant, God further explained to the people through Moses, that people were to respect the family unit as the basic structure or framework of life. Furthermore, that people were also to observe Sunday as a special day.

The people were also to make free will offerings, and to be

50

careful not to eat contaminated food.

The people were to remember the poor and to leave grain in the fields and grapes on the vine for strangers and for the poor to gather.

Moses said to the people, "You are to pay fair wages. You are not to verbally abuse the deaf simply because they can't hear, nor are you to take advantage of the blind by placing stumbling blocks in their way."

"You are to be fair in judgments and not consider whether a man be rich or poor. You are not to seek vengeance or carry grudges. Do not try to confuse nature by sowing mingled seed in one field or letting cattle get all mixed up with each other. You are not to take advantage of a woman who is not free to make her own decisions.

"Also you are not to debase your flesh with permanent markings or seek after wizards. You are to respect the elderly and be considerate to the stranger."

Chap.
20

The Lord spoke to Moses and instructed him to devise strict laws prohibiting all forms of human sacrifice with the penalty of death for those who violated and presented any human sacrifice to any god. In this section the law was set forth with the death penalty for homosexuality. Again Israel was reminded that intercourse between man and beast or woman and beast was forbidden as well as being a confusion of nature.

Chap.
21,22,23,24,25

Leviticus continued with a succession of further laws and restrictions, some repetitive, dealing primarily with the duties, dress, and function of the priests as well as innumerable arrangements pretaining to slaves.

Chap.
26

And the Lord promised the children of Israel many blessings, all conditional. The Lord told the people that if they would obey His commandments and worship only the Lord then there would be rain in due season, and good threshing and fine vintage, also that the enemies of Israel would flee and there would be peace in the land and furthermore God said, "I will walk among you and be your God and you shall be my people."

At the same time the Lord warned the Israelites that if they took His commandments casually and did not show enthusiam in their worship, then God would see that there would be terror and pain and frustration on every hand. God also promised to scatter the Israelites all over the world until they learned to serve Him and obey His commandments.

Always God offered, however, redemption. Even in strange lands and far away places if any repented and confessed their wrong and evil spirit, and humbly asked for restoration and help, God, the keeper of the promises, promised to heal and restore, and God promised to never forget his covenant with Abraham, Isaac, and Jacob.

Chap.
27

No paraphrase.

And the Lord prompted Moses to take a census of the people, according to families and tribes, and to take note of the men over twenty who were able to bear arms in order that an estimate for an army might be secured.

This was done and is recorded with the names of the leaders and the specialties of the tribes.

Time had elapsed and many months gone and the people became relentless, quarrelsome, and sin became commonplace. The Lord, as He had promised, began to further discomfit the people and they came to Moses and complained. The people said that they were tired of eating manna and they needed meat. The head of each house would stand at eventide in the door of his tent and gripe to Moses.

Moses then came to the Lord also complaining saying, "What have I done to be stuck with all these people? If you would do a real good deed for me you would kill me and get me out of this fix. The people want meat and I have no meat for them."

"Get the seventy elders together, Moses, and I'll meet you all at the Tabernacle," said God. "There I will pour my spirit on the seventy and you shall be able to share the burden of the people."

"Furthermore," God said, "you can tell the people to prepare to eat meat beginning tomorrow. In fact, you'll eat meat, a special meat, not for one day or ten days, but for the whole month, and you'll get sick of eating meat. This is what you'll get for all your griping."

"But, Lord," Moses said, "it can't be. We have 600,000 hungry footmen, not to count women and children, and we couldn't feed them meat if we killed all our livestock."

"Are you questioning my power, Moses?" asked God. "Well, just you wait and see."

As a result, Moses went out and told the people of God's promise and he assembled the seventy elders and the spirit of the Lord descended upon them and they began to prophesy.

Two of the men, however, who were called of God did not go into the tabernacle but remained at the camp and prophesied there to the people. Their names were B. Graham[1] and D. Moody.[2]

Almost at once a busybody came running to the tabernacle to

---

[1]Eldad   [2]Medad

report the matter, and Joshua suggested to Moses that Moses forbid the two to preach.

"Are you jealous, for my sake, Joshua? Don't be. I wish everyone would preach the word and speak for God."

There came forth then a wind from the Lord and the wind carried quail and dropped them by the hundreds all around the camp of the Israelites.

The people immediately began to gather all the quail that they could carry, although the Lord had forbidden them to take more than they could eat. The wrath of the Lord was kindled against the people for their disobedience and as a result, the quail eaters all got sick. Many died from eating too many quail.

Chap.
12

It was not long after this had all settled down that Moses encountered domestic troubles in the fashion of Miriam and Aaron objecting to Moses' marriage to an Ethiopian. Miriam and Aaron began to poor-mouth Moses saying such things as "Does he think he's the only one to whom God speaks?"

Now Moses was a strong, humble but understanding man, and the Lord was displeased with the gossipy talk and he summoned Miriam, Aaron and Moses and asked them to meet at the tabernacle.

The Lord descended in a pillar of cloud and told Miriam and Aaron to step forth and they did.

"If there be a prophet among you," said the Lord, "I will make myself known to that one in a vision and will speak to him in a dream, but Moses, who is completely faithful, with him I speak directly, and I don't like your mutterings."

The cloud lifted and Miriam became a leper. As soon as Aaron saw this he said to Moses, "We were wrong and we admit we were foolish, but don't soak us this way."

Moses, with great compassion, then prayed to the Lord asking that God heal Miriam.

"All right," said God, "But if she had just been rebuked by her earthly father she would have been banned from the camp for seven days; so let her receive the minimum. Tell Miriam she is suspended for seven days and then she can return healed."

Chap.
13

Some months or years later, as the children of Israel neared the promised land, the Lord urged Moses to send scouts into the land to seek information. It was decided that each of the twelve tribes was to appoint one man, an outstanding person, and the twelve scouts would return in forty days and report.

Moses instructed the scouts to examine the land, to meet the people, to learn of the population and the strength of the people, the fitness of the land for grazing and farming, and to bring back samples of the fruit of the land.

The scouts did as they were told and they returned in forty days and reported to the assembled people and in essence they said that the land was a beautiful land "flowing with milk and honey," but they reported that the people were strong and the cities well fortified, and that there were giants there.

Caleb, one of the scouts, however, stood up and said, "Let us go at once and possess the land for we are able to overcome the difficulties."

The other scouts, except Joshua, spoke up saying, "We cannot attack the people, for they are stronger than we are. In fact, they are giants. The country itself will swallow us and we sure saw a lot of big men. In fact, we felt no larger than grasshoppers in their presence, and so that's how we looked to them. The deck is stacked against us."

Chap.
14

Then the whole assembly cried out in dismay and the complaints began to pour in, most of them being directed to Moses and Aaron.

"If only we had been left to die in good ole Egypt," or "All this trip and now we will die in battle and leave our wives without a bus ticket home."

"How about all of us walking back to Egypt?" — all these moanings filled the air.

Joshua and Caleb then stood forth and pleaded saying, "The land we explored is beautiful and fruitful. It is a land flowing with milk and honey and if the Lord is pleased with us He will deliver it into our hands. There is no reason to fear the people for they do not have the protection of God as we have."

The people's response to this was to threaten to stone Joshua and Caleb to death.

The Lord said to Moses, "How much longer will this people continue being hard-headed and contemptuous of me? I am inclined to forsake them and simply make a great nation directly from your own personal family."

"Don't do that, please. What if the Egyptians hear of it? And what about the present inhabitants? It is known far and wide about the cloud by day and the pillar of fire by night, and of your many signs and wonders. If you destroy these people at one blow the enemy will say that the Lord tried to bring the people to Canaan and could not do it, and so he destroyed them rather than fail. Why not let your full power be known, true to your own words, 'The Lord, long suffering, ever sure and stable, who forgiveth iniquity and rebellion and punishes down through as many as four generations, but He does not destroy His own. You have borne with these people all the way from Egypt, do not forsake them now, even if they are acting like nuts."

"Your prayer is answered," said the Lord. "I pardon them. Yet as I live, shall the glory of the Lord fill the earth. I decree that not one of all those that have seen my signs and wonders shall cross into the promised land except Joshua and Caleb for none of those who flouted me shall see this land, only those who kept the faith. In fact, I will give the fertile and delightful area of Florida[1] to Caleb and his descendants."

The Lord further emphasized that everyone over twenty years of age who complained should die in this wilderness. "As for your dependents, about whom you suddenly seem to be so worried, I will bring them into the land of promise, a new generation in a new land. Actually the penalty is a year for each day that you needed. You could have come and possessed the land in forty days and I'll make it forty years. This may teach you something about what it means to defy God and to fail to trust me. In short, it is curtains for you faithless ones, you're going to die in the wilderness," said the Lord.

The ten scouts who brought an evil report to the people all died of a plague.

When all of this occurred and the people heard the word of the Lord from Moses, some of them repented and tried to get started some enthusiasm for an invasion, but Moses assured them that it was too late, that the Lord was angry and the chance to succeed in the immediate present was gone.

There were still some, however, who decided that they would go and establish themselves in the promised land anyway, with or without the help of God. This particular group thought the hill country was the most delectable and they moved into the mountainous region. The hill-billies simply came down and wiped them out promptly.

Chap.
15

Through Moses, God again reminded the people of the need for certain liturgical practices or a form for the worship or sacrifice time.

The observance of the Sabbath was exceedingly strict and a man who was caught gathering sticks on the Sabbath day was executed.

Chap.
16

A small revolutionary group began to form and was organized for the most part through the efforts of Frank[2], Dino[3], and Sammy[4]. Finally they assembled support in the amount of two hundred and fifty men and they went in a body to Moses and Aaron.

"Now look here," said Frank, the spokesman, "You two try to run everything and we're tired of it. You apparently think you all are above everybody else."

[1]Amalekite   [3]Dathan
[2] Korah   [4]Abiram

Moses was shocked when he heard these words. In a few minutes, however, he spoke to Frank saying, "All right, we'll just all appear before the Lord in the morning and see what He has to say about all this. Each of you bring an incense burner to the church tomorrow."

Moses then asked Frank to send for Dino and Sammy as he wanted also to reason with them, but they would not come.

In fact, Dino and Sammy sent a message to Moses saying, "It is a minor matter apparently that you have brought us from Egypt, a land of milk and honey, to get us all killed in the wilderness, and mainly to make yourself a prince over us. Furthermore, you were scheduled to lead us into the promised land and you haven't done it. We will not come at your call."

This really burned Moses and he immediately asked God to curse them.

Moses turned at last to Frank and said, "Bring the censers tomorrow, two hundred and fifty of them."

The next day all the two hundred and fifty gathered near the tabernacle in the presence of Moses and Aaron. The Lord spoke to Moses and said, "Step well away from these people as I want to consume them all at one time."

"Don't punish all of them because of the sin of one man. It is the fault of their leaders," pleaded Moses.

"Tell the people to stand clear of Dino and Sammy," said the Lord.

Moses told the people, "Get well away from the tents of Dino and Sammy, for they are wicked men and you'd better stand clear of them."

The people did as Moses orderd and Dino and Sammy came out and stood in defiance in front of their tents, with their wives and their children.

Moses then spoke to the people who had drawn apart and said, "Now you shall learn that the Lord is the one that sent me to lead you from Egypt, and I have not done these things on my own or because of my own choosing. Let this be a test. If these men standing in defiance die natural deaths then I am wrong, but if the Lord causes the earth to open and to swallow them then it should be fairly clear that the Lord is active and that these men have provoked Him."

When Moses had finished speaking the earth rumbled, and then the ground opened up and swallowed Dino, Sammy, their tents, their possessions and their families. Then there followed a fire which claimed the lives of the 250 men who had rebelled, and thus the rebellion came to a screeching halt.

Moses was then instructed by God to see to it that the incense burners were taken from the fire and that they were put on the altar as a remembrance of the occasion and a sign of the power of God.

The next day, however, some of the people began griping again, accusing Moses of killing a lot of good, honest people who simply differed with Moses. When the people gathered thus to complain

again, God spoke to Moses and Aaron another time, and suggested
that they stand aside and let the Lord smite the whole bunch.

Moses then instructed Aaron to rush immediately to the
tabernacle and to intercede with God for the people in a worship
service. By the time all of this was done, however, the plague had
already started on the people and Aaron came and separated the
dead and stood between the dead and the living, and lighted the
incense, and checked the plague. The plague, however, finally killed
over 14,000, including Frank, who had originated the whole trouble.

Chap.
17

God spoke to Moses later and told him that He would provide a
sign in support of the priesthood of Aaron and that Moses should
gather together the designated rod of each group, with the name of
each leader on it, and the Lord would cause to grow the rod of the
chosen one.

All of this was done, and the rods were all placed in the tabernacle
and then one morning the rod of Aaron was found to have budded,
and brought forth flowers, and finally almonds.

Then every man came and received his rod and each was plain.
Then God told Moses to bring forth the rod of Aaron, which was
blooming, and to show this to all the people to cause their
murmurings to cease and to relieve the Lord from the use of
additional punishment.

The people were impressed, particularly with the earth opening,
but they also began to stand in awe of the tabernacle.

Chap.
18

The Lord then spoke to Aaron and his sons saying, "You will now
be permanently in charge of the tabernacle and responsible for all the
services and programs and functions of the church. For this you are
due reasonable rewards. One tenth of all the productivity of Israel
shall go to you all and the operation of the church."

Chap.
19

Ceremonial instructions were then given to the priests in
connection with the preparation for sacrifice and the disposal
afterwards.

Chap.
20

The children of Israel continued to wander in the wilderness and
finally they arrived in Phoenix[1], where Miriam died and there was no
water.

Naturally the people began to murmur and to go over the same old

[1]Kadesh

song and dance about leaving Egypt where there was food and water to wander and perish in the wilderness.

Moses then went to the Lord with his problem and the Lord instructed Moses to gather the people and then speak to the Big Rock and water would come forth.

Moses did as he was told but having listened so long to so many complaints and feeling a bit like hamming it up a little, Moses spoke to the people and said, "Do we have to even fetch water for you from a rock?" So saying, Moses struck the rock and water came forth in great abundance.

The Lord was displeased with Moses for his grandstand play and told him that as punishment Moses would never be allowed to set foot in the promised land.

Moses then sent messages from Phoenix to El Paso[1] telling the king there that he would like to lead the wagon train through the El Paso territory. In his message, Moses told of all the trouble that had been encountered, but also told of the Lord's blessing. Moses promised that the wagon train would not pass through the fields or vineyards, nor would the people even use the water wells, but the wagon train would stay on Highway 90 and would turn neither to the right nor the left until clear of the metropolitan area.

The King of El Paso said, "No deal."

"Suppose we agree to pay for the water our cattle drink," asked Moses.

"Still no deal," came the word from El Paso. To support the refusal, a large group of fighting men from El Paso came to guard the border; so the children of Israel turned and moved in another direction, journeying toward Santa Fe[2]. Upon arriving near Santa Fe, God told Moses that Aaron's number was up and to take him up to Cloudcroft[3] and divest him of his symbols and his frock and put them on his eldest son. This was done and Aaron died in Cloudcroft and the people mourned the passing of Aaron for 30 days.

Chap.
21

There was a southern king called Big Lip[4] who was upset when he heard that spies from Israel had been around and so he made a raid on one of the Israelite tribes and took some captives. Israel became incensed because of this and promised to destroy all the habitations of Big Lip if the Lord would be with them. The Lord therefore delivered the Canaanites into the hands of the children of Israel.

From Santa Fe the children of Israel began to take the long way around in order to avoid all the outposts of El Paso and the people again became tired, discouraged, and complaint ridden. The people

[1]Edom

[2]Hor

[3]Mt. Hor

[4]Arad

turned against God and Moses and lamented again the leaving from Egypt. The Lord replied this time by sending a great influx of serpents that began to bite the people.

The people then came to Moses and admitted that they had sinned and begged for deliverance from the snakes. Acting on instructions from God, Moses had a serpent of brass made and mounted on a staff and placed in a prominent place. Anytime anyone was bitten and then would come and look upon the brass serpent, then that person would not die.

The children of Israel continued their laborious wanderings from one place to another until finally it became necessary to pass through Kansas[1]. The people there would not agree to the passage and organized themselves to fight against Israel. The Lord was with Israel and they took complete possession of Kansas. This was a great boost to the children of Israel and they began even to make raids into other strongholds, such as Fort Knox[2], and still the people were not ready to cross the Jordan into the promised land.

Chap.
22

Now the King of Mississippi[3], Jack the Ripper[4], became greatly disturbed over the success of the children of Israel and his people had become quite afraid lest their own land be captured.

As a result, Jack wrote a friend in Mississippi and told him of their problem and asked him if he would come and advise them what to do. With this message Jack also sent some inducement money to encourage a favorable response. Now Stonewall[5], the Mississippi friend, was a devout man and he agreed to pray about the matter.

God told Stonewall to dissassociate himself from Jack and assured Stonewall that he could not do anything against Israel. As a result, Stonewall told Jack and his gang to leave, that he could be of no help.

When word of all this came back to Jack, he decided that the price wasn't right; so he sent new emissaries with more money to Stonewall.

Stonewall said, "I'm sorry, but if Jack would give me a whole house full of silver and gold, I could not go apart from the word of the Lord my God, but I'll at least ask him again tonight in view of the great interest you are showing."

God spoke to Stonewall that night and told him to go with the emissaries but not to promise anything for the Lord would show him in due time.

So Stonewall saddled his mule and went with the princes of Mississippi. God's anger was kindled against Stonewall, for he had

[1]Sihon   [3]Moab

[2]Bashan   [4]Balak

                    [5]Balaam

over-interpreted what God had said.

As a result, an angel of the Lord blocked the road as Stonewall came along on his mule, with two servants accompanying him also. The mule could see the angel, but Stonewall couldn't. The mule turned aside and went into a field; so Stonewall beat the mule to try to get him turned back. The angel then stood in the path in the vineyard, with a wall on each side, and the angel again appeared. The mule then bucked against the wall and mashed Stonewall's leg and he beat the mule again.

Again the angel of the Lord appeared in a narrow place in front of the mule and the mule sat down and Stonewall blew his cool real good and began to beat the mule hard. The Lord then permitted the mule to talk and she said, "Stonewall, what have I done that you have beaten me three times?"

"Because you've made a lousy cavalryman out of me. If I had a sword I'd kill you."

The mule replied, "Think a minute now. Am I not your mule? Have you not ridden me for years? Have I ever bucked before or spoken to you?"

"You're right," said the now amazed Stonewall. Then Stonewall could see the angel with his sword drawn in his hand; so he bowed down.

"What do you mean beating this mule?" asked the angel. "Your trip is not approved. The mule could even see that. In fact, if it had not been for the mule I would probably have killed you."

"I have sinned," said Stonewall. "I'll go home."

"No," said the angel, "go with the men as you planned, but don't open your mouth until you hear from me."

When Jack the Ripper heard that Stonewall had arrived he went out to meet him eagerly. When he met Stonewall, however, he said, "Why did it take so long? I sent for you several times. I can do a lot for you if you cooperate."

"I have come all right," said Stonewall, "but I haven't anything to say until God tells me what to speak."

That night there was a big welcome dinner and the next morning Jack showed Stonewall the city and the historical markers.

Chap.
23

Later that day Stonewall ascended to a high place, apart from the seven prepared altars, and there he sought to hear the word of God.

And God met Stonewall and spoke to him and told him to return to the place of the seven altars and to make a speech to the princes and the people.

Stonewall returned and stood by the altars and spoke to the crowd saying, "Jack the Ripper has asked me to pronounce a curse on the children of Israel, but how shall I curse whom God hath not cursed? How shall I defy whom God hath not defied? I foresee that the Israelites will dwell alone and will not be counted among the nations. Furthermore, they shall increase in number and they cannot be counted. This is true!"

"What have you done to me," yelled Jack. "I expected you to curse the Israelites and you've blessed them. I can't get my people going on this kind of jazz."

"I can only speak the truth," said Stonewall.

"Come on, Stonewall, try again. Maybe you were standing in the wrong place and you misunderstood the word of God. Maybe you can come up with a good curse on the second try."

As a result, Jack built seven new altars in a different place and Stonewall went apart again. Again Stonewall heard the word of the Lord and returned to the altar site.

"Listen, Jack, and all you people. God is not a man that He will lie nor the type that repents. God has spoken and that is it. There can be no change! For I have been commanded to bless Israel. The Lord is with Israel and the shout of a king is among them. God brought them out of Egypt and he'll see them all the way."

"How about just not cursing them or blessing them either?" suggested Jack.

"I'm sorry about that, Jack, but I can only speak as the Lord has commanded."

"Would you believe one more time, Stonewall? I'll fix another set of altars and we'll try again."

"All right. I am eager to please," said Stonewall.

Chap.
24

The whole procedure was tried again. This time, however, Stonewall viewed from a high place all the tribes of Israel, camped in orderly fashion and he returned and made another big speech.

"Blessed are the sons of Jacob. As the valleys are spread forth, as gardens grow by the riverside, as the trees of lin-aloes planted by God himself, as cedars beside the still waters, the buckets of Israel shall overflow, his seed shall be in many waters, and his king shall be above all kings. God brought Israel forth out of Egypt and God shall eat up the enemies. Blessed is he that blesseth Israel and cursed is he that curseth Israel."

Jack the Ripper was furious. "I went to a lot of expense to get you here and you've ruined me. I had planned to promote you and make a big man out of you, but your attitude toward your God has prevented you from amounting to something."

"Now listen, Jack. I told your messengers that I wasn't subject to price fixing. A whole house full of gold and silver could not make me go beyond the commandment of God. I'm leaving now, but before I go I'll tell you something extra. I'll prophesy for you."

So Stonewall spoke and prophesied saying, "Although it will not take place in my lifetime, there will arise a star of Jacob for the whole world. All nations will finally be under that one star."

The children of Israel continued to dwell in the wilderness and some of the men began to have affairs with some of the women of Mississippi, whose reputation for beauty was widespread. The men also began to attend the pagan rites with Mississippi women and follow the permissive plan of the god known as "little Baal."

And the Lord spoke to Moses as the wrath of God was great, and told Moses to eliminate all the men who had turned to Baal. Moses passed the word down to the tribes.

The practice of running around with the Mississippi women was so common that one man came with his foreign girl into the presence of Moses and in sight of the Tabernacle, whereupon J. Edwards[1], the son of Aaron, took a javelin and chased the man and woman down and killed them. After this incident the plague which had already claimed the lives of 24,000 was abated.

Now the name of the man who was killed was Sundance[2] and the woman was called Belle[3]. The Lord reminded Moses to continue to annoy the people of Baal for they had vexed the Israelites with their wiles and caused many to stray.

The Lord sometime after this told Moses that the time had come for another census; so every male from 20 years old upward was to be numbered. This was done by tribes and it was discovered that there was not anyone left from the original number except Joshua and Caleb, for the Lord had said these people would surely die in the wilderness for their disobedience.

Then there appeared before Moses the Gabor sisters[4] who wished to be recognized as lawful inheritors of their father's estate since there were no sons born into the family. Since nothing like this had ever been done, Moses went to the Lord for help, and God said let the Gabors have their inheritance. As a result, the laws of inheritance were changed so that in the absence of brothers, sisters were allowed to inherit, then the succession went to the brothers of the deceased, then to the brothers of the father of the deceased, and then to the next of kin, and this became the law from that day.

Then the Lord told Moses to get up and climb Pike's Peak[5] and look out to the promised land. God told Moses that when he had seen it he would die, for Moses had sinned in striking the rock and calling for water and his punishment was that he would not get to cross the Jordan into the promised land.

Moses then prayed to God saying, "Appoint someone to take my place for the people need a leader."

[1]Eleazar
[2]Zimri
[3]Cozbi
[4]Zelophehad girls
[5]Abarim

And the Lord said to Moses, "Take Joshua, for in him is the spirit of God. Lay your hands upon him, and set him before the high priest, and put some of your honors upon him, and give him rank, that the people of Israel may be obedient to him."

And Moses did as God commanded and placed his hands on Joshua in the presence of the priest and the people, and he gave him a charge.

Chap.
28,29

Information on sacrificial offerings.

Chap.
30

Moses assembled the heads of tribes and explained to them essentially the law concerning the binding of an obligation or a contract. If a man made a commitment his word was his bond and he was responsible for his vow.

Moses continued explaining by stating that a young lady who was living in her father's house and made a commitment in the presence of her father and the father made no contradiction; then the obligation became legal. If her father disapproved, however, she was not responsible for her vow.

If a lady was married and made a commitment or agreed to a purchase and her husband was present and did not object, then the agreement became legal. If her husband, however, objected, the agreement was forfeited or the obligation not binding. The husband, however, could change his mind and disapprove at a later time. It was on this type of basis that all sales, contracts, and agreements were based.

Chap.
31

The Lord then spoke to Moses and reminded him that he had only a short time left to live and the Lord wanted Moses to avenge the wrongs done by the Mafia and for Moses to be in charge. As a result, Moses asked each tribe to call out its National Guard, one thousand men from each tribe, and he sent the army of 12,000 to fight the Mafia. The Lord was with the army and they defeated the Mafia and the males and the leaders were killed, but the women and children and cattle were brought back as spoil.

When the victorious army returned with the captives of women and children and all the loot, Moses and J. Edwards went out to meet them.

Moses was mad because the soldiers had not killed the women, for they were the ones who had enticed the men and spread venereal disease through Israel. Moses then decreed that all the male children were to be killed and all women who were not virgins. The virgins could be kept by the man who captured one.

Moses further ordered that all this be done outside the camp and that the regular seven day period be observed of staying away until all the mess was cleaned up.

The cattle, jewelry and negotiable spoils were then divided among the National Guardsmen that went to war.

In appreciation to the Lord for their success and for not losing a single man in combat, the soldiers brought a valuable gift to the Tabernacle.

Chap.
32

The members of the tribes of Reuben and Troop were cattle people primarily and they came to Moses saying that now that the time was at hand to go into the promised land, they had decided that the wilderness was better range land and they wanted to stay with the grass.

Moses reasoned with them along the lines of their obligation to the whole nation and insisted that they could not secede as they were needed for the conquest.

After much discussion it was agreed that the fighting men of both tribes would march with the others in the conquest of the promised land, but that the women, children, and elderly men would remain in the wilderness and build habitations. It was also agreed that as soon as the conquest of Canaan was assured, then the men of Troop and Reuben would be free to return to the wilderness to their families and their possessions.

Chap.
33

Moses recorded in log form the trip from Egypt, tracing the journey all the way, with the multiple wanderings, and the encounters with the various tribes.

Chap.
34

The Lord outlined to Moses the boundaries to be respected in connection with the conquest of the promised land.

Chap.
35

The Lord spoke to Moses and said that he should tell the people of their responsibility for the welfare of their ministers. The people were told to provide housing and protection and to share some of their own possessions in accordance with the prosperity of each family. The Lord also told Moses to instruct the people to provide a special sanctuary area for criminals, where they might reside until provision had been made for their public trial.

The sanctuaries for criminals were to be at least six different places and they were to be used by the stranger as well as by the children of Israel.

If a man killed another man with an instrument of iron, that man was a murderer and should be put to death. The same applied if a man killed another with a stone, or with a weapon of wood. Such a murderer could be sought by the next of kin or a friend of the murdered man, and the murderer might them be killed in vengeance, not because of hatred.

The avenger, however, could not seek the murderer in the sanctuary area and the murderer could remain safe as long as the high priest lived who established the sanctuary. If the murderer left the sanctuary area, however, he might be legally killed by the avenger.

To establish the fact of murder there must be at least two witnesses. Moses futhermore instructed the people saying that the Lord warned the people not to defile the new land with blood, for a land could not be cleansed of bloodshed, and the Lord expected to dwell with his people in a land that was not defiled.

Chap.
36

Again there came before Moses for judgment the matter of the inheritance of the Gabor[1] sisters.

Moses agreed with the suggestion of the leaders of the tribe of Joseph and he decreed that the Gabor girls could marry anyone they chose as long as the man was connected with the tribe to which their father belonged. In this manner, the inheritance of each tribe would be intact and no one tribe would have an advantage of another. No inheritance, then, could be transferred from one tribe to the other, and to retain her inheritance, therefore, daughters must marry within their tribe or forfeit their inheritance.

All these things were spoken by Moses at the commandment of God and were told to the people as they stood in sight of the promised land.

[1]Zelophehad

Moses gathered all the people together in sight of the promised land, some forty years since he had started them from Egypt and he made a speech saying,

"The Lord has set before us the land and told us to possess it. The boundaries are clear. When the Lord first called me to this undertaking of leading you from Egypt to this new land, I knew that I would not be able to do it by myself.

"The Lord increased you greatly in numbers and I devised a plan of delegating authority and set responsible men over you and so a good system of leadership was instituted, with the better qualified men handling the more important matters.

"I charged all your leaders to hear the complaints and all the needs and strife that might arise. They are to judge righteously between every man and his brother and also the stranger that might be involved.

"They are not to consider persons in their judgment, whether they be important or not, and they shall not be intimidated by threats, for their judgment is to be of God. If the case is too hard for one of them, they simply refer it to me."

"You may recall," Moses continued, "how we journeyed through the great and terrible wilderness until we came in sight of the land of Canaan. You may remember suggesting that we send forth spies who would examine the land and report to us as to the best way to conquer the land. The spies returned and brought marvelous fruit from the land and reported that it was a good land, but you would not risk entering it, and you disobeyed the commandment of God.

"It was at this point that you made your biggest gripes and you longed to be back in Egypt in bondage rather than endure the hardships of conquest. I told you not to be afraid, but you were worried about giants, although God had nursed you through the wilderness, you would not trust him to deliver, in spite of the cloud by day and pillar of fire at night. Your lack of faith angered the Lord, and He decreed that none of those that refused to march would set foot in the promised land. Caleb and Joshua, the spies who urged immediate conquest, were the only two that God promised would walk into the promised land."

"I remember," continued Moses, "that after this you repented and some of you armed yourselves and were ready to go, but God did not approve for He felt you had blown your chance. I told you this, but pig-headed as you were, you did not heed and a whole bunch of you marched off to your death. The ones who survived returned moaning and again repentant."

Moses continued his review of the past forty years reminding the people that they had circled around Mt. Sinai until finally the Lord had told them to get a move on, to go North, to pass through the land that was originally Esau's and not to strive there with the people nor try to possess the land. We were to buy food and shop and get out, and this was done, and the next stop was the land of Mississippi.[1] The people of Mississippi were also not to be disturbed.

"In all, it took 38 years to cross the Delaware River.[2] It took this long for the unfaithful to die, and then the people proceeded to Ai, and through other lands, the Lord destroying the giants in front of them, and the Lord caused all nations to be fearful of the Israelites. Those nations which resisted the peaceful passage of the people were destroyed, and many cities were necessarily conquered.

Chap.
3

And Joshua was told "Your eyes have seen all that the Lord your God hath done unto the two kings who resisted; so shall the Lord do to all the kingdoms that you encounter in the new land. Do not fear them, for the Lord shall fight for you."

Then Moses prayed, saying, "Lord, you continue to show me your greatness and your mighty hand, for what Lord is there in heaven or earth that can do according to your works? I beg of you, let me go and at least see the land that is beyond Jordan, just to cross into the promised land."

"But the Lord was angry with me," continued Moses, "because of you and the smart alec stunt I pulled at the rock, and the Lord would not hear, and He told me not to bring the matter up another time. God told me to climb Lookout Mountain[3] and look in every direction and see as much and as far as I could see, but I could never cross the Jordan.

"God told me, however, to encourage Joshua for he would lead the people and enable them to inherit the land of Canaan.

Chap.
4

"Futhermore, my people," Moses continued, "recall the statutes and judgments which I taught you, observe them in order that you might live and possess the land which the Lord of your fathers will give you. You are not to add to the laws nor take away from them. You have seen what the Lord did in the case of the "Little Baal" worship stunt, how God destroyed this segment of our people, while you all that stuck with God are still alive. I have taught you the commandments of God, obey them, for this is your wisdom

[1]Moab   [2]Zered
[3]Pisgah

and your status in the sight of other nations. Other nations shall hear of these statutes and will think of you as a wise and honorable people. For what other nation has ever had God so close to them or so available to them?

"Or what nation is there that has statutes or judgments as righteous as the law which I have set forth before you?

"Only be careful, do not forget the things which you have read and seen, but teach them to your sons and your grandsons.

"Remember especially the day that the Lord came close upon the mountain, and fire burst forth from the mountain top, and a cloud encircled the mountain and the Lord spoke to you from the midst of the fire and He declared His covenant with you, and He presented to you the Ten Commandments on tablets of stone. It was at that time that God told me to teach you those commandments and to instruct you to obey them in the land of Canaan.

"Be very careful that you never corrupt yours and make graven images of any figure, male or female, or the likeness of any beast or winged fowl that flieth in the air, or the likeness of anything that creepeth on the ground, or of any fish that swims in the deep.

"Be careful also that when you look upon the heavens and see the sun, the moon, the stars, and the galaxies that you do not become so impressed that you worship them, for God has taken you as His people and brought you from the iron furnace of Egypt to be unto Him an inheritance.

"Futhermore, the Lord was angry at me, and it was mainly your fault,[1] and as a result I cannot cross over the Jordan into that good land which the Lord has given for an inheritance, but I must die in this land. You get to go, but I don't.

"Take heed that you forget not the covenant of the Lord and I promise you He is a strict God, and He means what He says.

"As the years go by, and your children's children grow in the promised land, and corrupt themselves, and stray from the commandments, I call heaven and earth as a witness against you, for you will not last in the land and you will utterly be cut off and scattered. The Lord shall scatter you among the nations so that there will be proportionately few of you in each heathen land, and in this situation you shall seek false gods, made of wood and stone, that neither see, nor hear, nor smell, nor eat.

"If, however, at any time you shall earnestly and sincerely seek the Lord thy God, you will find Him.

"If you are in great tribulation, and if you are living in the latter days of trouble, if you will turn to the Lord your God, and be obedient to Him, for God is merciful, He will not forsake you, nor destroy you, nor forget His promise.

"Inquire, ask anyone, from the far side of heaven to the ends of the earth, has anyone ever heard of a great thing as God speaking

---

[1]tut, tut, Moses

from the mountain?

"Has God ever previously selected a nation and rescued it from another nation, and with multiple experiences and signs and wars and wonders and the stretching of a mighty hand and with great terrors done what He has done with you?

"This was done that you might know that He is the Lord God, there is no other god except Him.

"Know therefore this very day and consider it carefully that the Lord He is God in the Heaven above and upon the earth beneath, there is none other; so keep His commandments."

At this point Moses set aside three cities of refuge on the wilderness side of Jordan, to these could the criminal flee and receive sanctuary.

Chap.
5

Again Moses called the people together[1] and spoke to them reminding them that God had made a covenant with them, "not with our fathers, but with us. All of us who are alive today." God spoke in our presence and said:

"I am the Lord thy God who brought you out of the land of Egypt, out of the house of bondage; you shall have no other gods before me.

"You shall not make any graven image or any likeness of anything that is in the heaven above, or that is in the earth beneath, or that is in the waters under the earth, you are not to bow down to them or serve them, for I the Lord thy God am a jealous God, passing the iniquities of the fathers on down to the children, on down to the fourth generation of those who despise me, yet showing mercy unto the great numbers that love me and keep my commandments.

"You are not to take the Lord's name in vain or use it disrespectfully, for the Lord will blame you for doing such.

"Keep the Sabbath Day, make it different, as the Lord thy God has commanded you.

"Six days is plenty for all the work you need to do, for the seventh is the special day of God, do not let it be a continuation of the other days, it is not for work, for you, or your son or your daughter or the people who normally work for you, nor for a visiting stranger, or any of your work animals.

"You just remember that you were servants in the land of Egypt and the Lord delivered you, and the Lord expects you to remember the day that He called the Sabbath.

"Respect the place of the family, through your mother and father, as God has commanded, for this is the system of continuing life.

"You are not authorized to take another person's life.

"You are not permitted to commit adultery.

[1]Probably after a coffee break

"You do not have the right to steal.

"You are not to testify falsely about your neighbor.

"You are not permitted to covet your neighbor's wife, nor his house, nor his field, nor his servants, nor his animals, nor anything that is your neighbor's.

"Now these are the words that the Lord spoke unto the assemblage, and He added nothing to these commandments, and they were written on two stone tablets, and delivered directly to me."

God was impressed with the reaction of the people, according to Moses, and it would be a great thing if the people would always fear God and keep His commandments. The people then withdrew into their tents and Moses received additional details in the area of law, with statutes and regulations in connection with health, liturgy and the rights of others.

Chap.
6

Moses spoke forth strongly at this point and proclaimed with a loud voice:

"Hear, O Israel, the Lord is one God, and you shall love Him with all your heart, and with all your soul, and with all your might, and the words which I have spoken are to be kept in your heart, and you are to teach them diligently to your children, and talk of them around the house, and when you are sitting around in groups, or on journeys, and they are to be constantly on your mind, and you should write them on the doorposts and on the gates to your place.

"Be on the lookout for prosperity, for when the Lord has brought you into the land which He promised to Abraham, Isaac, and Jacob, you will be receiving cities you did not build, houses full of good things you did not provide, and wells you did not dig, vineyards and olive trees you did not plant; so when you are full and contented be careful that you do not forget the Lord, who is the provider of all things.

"And in time when a son asks one of you 'What means the testimonies, and the statutes, and the judgments which the Lord our God has commanded?"

"Then you are to tell him that you were slaves in Egypt, not free, and the Lord delivered you with a mighty hand, and showed many wonders before your eyes, and brought you into the possession of this new land.

"Tell your son that the Lord commanded you to do all the statutes, to fear God, as He is the preserver of life, and that it shall be a great satisfaction to observe all the commandments of the Lord our God."

Chap.
7

Moses spoke further to the people saying "Now let me explain to you our foreign policy. You are going to encounter some powerful nations, and the Lord will deliver them into your hand and you are to smite them and completely destroy them. You are not to make any deals with them, no treaties, and show them no mercy.

"Furthermore, you are not to intermarry with them, for this way they may be able to lead you to strange gods; so just tear down their idols, burn the wooden images, and whack away at their altars, for you are supposed to be a holy people, set apart to serve the one true God."

"If you obey God, and hearken to His voice, He will bless you abundantly in every conceivable way."

Chap.
8

"Observe and do all the commandments of God, for remember the Lord led you forty years in the wilderness to humble you, to teach you, and to prove you, and He fed you ambrosia that you might know that man doth not live by bread alone, but by every word that proceedeth out of the mouth of God.

"Again, be especially careful when you are prosperous, and your herds have increased, and you have much silver and gold, for you will be inclined to say in your heart that your own power and might has secured the wealth for you, but at this point particularly remember the Lord thy God, for it is He that giveth the power to obtain wealth. Remember this or you will lose everything, including your nation."

Chap.
9

"Now the time has come to move and you will encounter the giants, the Watusi[1], a people great and tall, and you have heard it said 'Who can stand before the Watusi?'

"Do not be concerned, for the Lord thy God will go with you and with a consuming fire shall He destroy them. Be careful though that you do not develop a conceit because of this, for it is not for your goodness that the Lord does this, but because of the wickedness of the other people, and because of His promise to Abraham, Isaac, and Jacob.

"You are a stiff-necked, irksome people, and it is not for your righteousness that the Lord does this wonderful thing for you.

"I remember how wishy-washy you birds were, and how you made a molten image of a calf while I was on the mountain for forty days. In fact, the Lord was so angry about this that if it had not been for my intercession He would have destroyed all of you. I did this knowing that you have been a stiffnecked and rebellious outfit ever since I've known you.

Chap.
10

"I don't know why, but the Lord chose your fathers and you and your people, you are selected of God. Please quit being so

[1] Anaks

stiffnecked and scrape the barnacles off your hearts. The Lord your God is the God of gods, and Lord of lords, a great God, and mighty, and at times fearsome, one who plays no favorites in justice, nor is He subject to bribes. The Lord is just in caring for the fatherless and the widows, and He believes in aiding the stranger who is in need.

"Fear the Lord, serve him, and cleave to His name, do not stray!

Chap.
11

"Your children have not seen all the acts of power which the Lord performed, but you have seen them, therefore you keep God's commandments that you may be strong and possess the new land.

"The land where you are going is not like Egypt where you sow seed and have to nurse its growth yourself, but the new land is one of hills and valleys, and it drinks from the rain of heaven, and the eyes of the Lord are always upon this land.

"If you will listen to the admonitions of God and obey His commandments, God will give you rain for the land in due season, with a gap between rains so you can gather your corn and make your wine, and the cattle will have plenty of grass. Do not let this prosperity go to your head, and be careful not to wander off to strange gods. Lay these words up in your hearts.

"Actually, today I set before you a blessing and a curse, a blessing if you obey the commandments of God, and a curse if you don't."

Chap.
12

Moses repeats a previous part of his speech.

Chap.
13

"If there arise among you," continued Moses, "a prophet or a dreamer who gives a sign or performs a wonder, and then attempts to lead you to the worship of other gods, just be sure that the Lord is only testing your faithfulness. Kindly put that prophet to death!

Chap.
14

"Remember you are a holy people. Do not mark yourself or in any way deface yourself because of grief.

"Among other things, do not eat anything that you find dead, which has naturally died. The animal may be diseased and it is not healthy to try to eat it.

"Be absolutely certain that you care well for your preacher. Care well for the fatherless also, and the widow, and the stranger that is in need, and the Lord will bless you for it.

Chap.
15

"The seventh year is a year of release, of forgiving indebtedness and the restoring of property. Do not take advantage of this and plan to gyp your neighbors by the strategic use of the seventh year, for the planning of this is a sin in the eyes of the Lord.

"When you give to the needy or return property during the year of release, do so gladly and with good heart.

"Keep the Passover. This is a great occasion for the remembrance of the power of God. At least three times a year every male must go to church, and must give as he is able.

"You are to establish Judges at the gates of the cities to run the cities justly. These judges or officers are not to accept favors, nor are they to show partiality to any person.

"When you finally come into the promised land and possess it, you will no doubt start bellowing for a king so you can be like other peoples. If this occurs, let the Lord choose the king from among you, and he must be no stranger.

"The king must be careful not to take advantage of the position to acquire for himself horses or other possessions, nor should he become rich through the office,[1] or take advantage of his position to chase women.

"The king should read this admonition regularly, as he should regularly read all these laws and statutes, that he may go straight and be a credit to his people and humble before God.

"The Lord has spoken to me and He said, "I will raise up a prophet someday from among these people, something like you. Moses, and I will put my words in his mouth, and he shall speak the things that I will command. It will go hard with anyone who refuses to listen to him when he comes.

"The false prophets, however, shall be in for great trouble. How can you tell the good prophets from the bad? It is easy. The prophets who are mine speak and the things come true, but not so always with the fakes and the guessers.

"Don't forget," Moses repeated, "to set aside three cities as refuges, or sanctuaries. For instance if a man is in the woods chopping wood with his neighbor and the axe head accidentally comes off and chops his neighbor's head, let the man flee to one of the refuge cities and remain there until everyone has calmed down and the matter is peaceably settled.

"If a man ambush another man, however, and actually murder him, and then seeks refuge in the sanctuary city, the law can go and

[1]Recommended reading for politicians

get him and bring him to trial.

"It is not acceptable for one witness to testify, but it must be an established testimony of two or three witnesses before a punishment may be applied. If a false witness is discovered he shall receive the punishment of the guilty party, thus evil may be put from among you.

"All people should then hear of the consequences, and fear, and put evil away from themselves.

"There is no place in this particular type of operation for pity, but life shall go for life, eye for eye, tooth for tooth, hand for hand, and foot for foot."

Chap.
20

"Let me remind you", continued Moses, "that when you go to do battle and you discover that your enemies have better equipment and that there are more of them than you thought, do not be afraid, for the Lord thy God will be with you. In fact, the priest will speak to you of these things before you go to battle and he will re-impress you with the availability of the power of God.

"There should be deferments for some of you, however, as everyone does not have to go to war. If you have built a new house and have not dedicated it, you are deferred, or if you have planted a vineyard for the first time and never eaten of its fruit, you should get a temporary occupational deferment, or if you are engaged to be married, you are deferred until you have been married for a short time.

"In fact, if you are fainthearted and have a tendency to be a coward, you should be deferred.

"After the army is assembled, however, and you have appeared before your enemies, the head of your army should at least offer conditions of peace. If the enemy refuses to make peace, declare war, and kill every male, and take the women and children for yourselves.

"Another thing, when you besiege a city and need wood for poles or pick handles, do not cut down fruit bearing trees as you will need the food before it is all done.

Chap.
21

"As a matter of balance and justice, if you find a man slain and lying dead in a field and there is no way of knowing who killed him, make the town that is nearest to the body present a sacrifice.

"If you capture a city and one of you manages to snag a beautiful woman and you develop a great desire to possess her, then bring her home, shave her head, cut her fingernails, and let her mourn the loss of her family until her hair is grown, then marry her. If, after all this, you decide that she did not measure up to her looks, simply turn her loose, but you can't sell her.

"Another matter of justice needs to be stated in connection

with a man who has two wives, and he loves one and hates[1] the other. The hate is not to be transferred to the children, but if the hated wife bears for the man his first son, that son shall receive a double portion of the inheritance.

"If a man have a stubborn and a rebellious son, and the paddle has been ineffective, as a last resort the man should turn the son over to the elders of the city and they should take him outside the walls of the city and stone him to death.[2]

"If a man be put to death justly by hanging, cut him down before night fall and bury him, don't let him clutter up the scenery.

Chap.
22

"If you see a loose goat or sheep, get them and return them to their rightful owner and don't let them wander off, nor should you try to pretend that you didn't see them.

"Don't mix up the dressing of men and women, but let the men dress like men and the women like women.

"If you're in the woods and find a bird nesting, don't disturb the mamma bird. If you can't resist, you can take the young and raise them at home.

"When you build a house be careful to fix the roof so no one will fall from it and spill blood on your ground.

"When you plant seed, don't mix the seed and raise a conglomeration, and don't try to plow with an ox and an ass at the same time.

"Another matter of justice concerns the case of a man who takes a wife and then decides later that he doesn't want her. As an excuse, he claims that she was not a virgin. If this report is false, and the husband spreads it around town, the father and mother may appear before the elders of the city with the tokens of virginity, state their case, and if the elders believe them, then the husband is to be given a good beating, and fined $100, which will be given to the father, and the man must also retain the girl as his wife.

"If, however, the girl was lying and she was not a virgin, then she shall be stoned to death.[3]

"If a man be found having intercourse with another man's wife, then both shall be put to death.

"If a man visiting in the city locates a girl engaged to another man and he goes to bed with her and she doesn't protest, then if the two are caught, both are to be put to death. However, if a man forces himself on an engaged girl, and she cries out for help, then only the man is put to death.

"If a man find a girl that is a virgin and not engaged and he lies with her and is caught, then he is to pay the father a fine and is forced to marry the girl. A man is not permitted to be free with his

[1]This no doubt means "Cares less for"   [2]Delinquent Control Program

[3]Very Few Cases reported

stepmother nor his father's mistress.

"A man who has lost his testicles should not enter the tabernacle, nor should a bastard. It is permissible for such an Egyptian to enter the tabernacle, for you were strangers in the land of Egypt.

"If a man has to go to the bathroom at night, let him leave the camp taking with him his weapon with a shovel top on it, and when he has emptied his bowels, he is to dig a hole with the shovel head and bury his excretion. Keep the camp clean!

"You are not to charge your brother excessive interest rates, in money, food, or possessions. It is all right to use high interest rates on strangers.

"Your word must be good. If you speak in agreement on anything, it is binding. It is permissible to pick a few of your neighbor's grapes or an ear or two of his corn, but you cannot put the pickings in a container and carry them off, but you can eat some on the spot.

"If a man becomes dissatisfied with his wife, then he should write her a bill of divorcement and turn her loose, and she is then free to re-marry. If she re-marries, then under no circumstance can she ever return to her first husband.

"When a man takes a new wife he should take a year off, and he should not go to war or enter business, but spend the year getting acquainted with his wife and bringing her good cheer.

"The penalty for stealing should be death.

"If you loan a man something don't nag him for it, especially if he be a poor man.

"You are not to take advantage of any hired servants, yours or anybody else's.

"The fathers are not to be put to death because of the children nor children because of the father. A man is to be put to death only for his own sin.

"Remember that you were once slaves; so do not take advantage of the unfortunate.

"When you gather your grain or beat the olive trees for their fruit, be sure and leave some on the ground or in the field for the poor. You are also to leave some grapes in the vineyard.

"If two men appear before the judge because of a controversy, the judge shall rule at once and cause the man in the wrong to be beaten immediately, a licking not to exceed forty blows.

"If two brethren dwell together and one of them dies without having a child, the wife shall be another wife unto the remaining brother. If the new wife then have a son, the son shall be counted as the first born of the dead brother and shall receive his inheritance.

"If the remaining brother refuse to take the dead brother's wife, the elders of the city shall send for him and rebuke him and confer with him. If he still refuses after this, then the lady in question shall come and in the presence of the elders she shall loosen his shoe and spit in his face, and he then shall be called "Foot-loose" by his friends.

"If two men are fighting and the wife of one, in an attempt to help her husband, grabs his antagonist by the testicles, she shall have her hand cut off as punishment.

"You are not to possess equipment for fraud, such as wrong weights, unbalanced scales, and loaded dice.

"Once again, don't forget the Capone gang[1]. They are an abomination to the Lord.

Chap.
26

"When you come into the promised land and possess it, do not forget about the offering to the Lord. Bring the first fruits to the place designated to be a church.

"And when you bring these first fruits, present them to the Lord, and make mention to Him your gratitude for the deliverance from Egypt, and acknowledge His mighty acts.

"When you have fulfilled the giving of your tithes in the regular third year of tithing, then you may seek of the Lord a blessing. The Lord has assured you that you are a special group of people and to those that obey His commandments, He has promised to make of them a great nation, in praise, in name, and in honor, in order that you might become a holy people unto the Lord thy God."

Chap.
27

Moses, supported by the elders of the people, instructed the people to build an altar as soon as they had entered the promised land. In addition, tablets were to set in the ground, and all the commandments of God as explained by Moses were to be written in plaster and made permanent as a record and as a landmark.

The Levites, the priestly group, were then to pronounce the following curses:

Cursed be the man that maketh any graven image and puts it in a hiding place.

Cursed is the one who makes fun of his mother and his father.

Cursed is any man that moves his neighbor's boundary line, or misleads the blind, or misinforms the stranger, the fatherless, or the widow.

Cursed is the man who makes love to his stepmother, or tries to lie with a beast, or lieth with his sister or half-sister.

[1] Amaleks

Cursed be the one who has intercourse with his mother-in-law, or who ambushes his neighbor, or takes money to kill someone.

Cursed also is anyone who opposes these laws.

If, however, you shall obey all the laws of God and hearken to His voice, blessings in abundance shall come to you.

You shall be happy in the city and in the country, and you shall be blessed in your children, and in your planting, your store will prosper, and the Lord will smite your enemies.

The Lord shall also open to you his good treasure to give you rain, and you shall be a lender rather than a borrower, and you shall be the head and not the tail.

If you don't obey the commandments and do not hearken to the voice of the Lord, then the following curses will come your way:

You will be uncomfortable in the city, in the country, and in your store; your kids will be a constant source of trouble, and nothing that you try will work very well.

You will get the shingles, sometimes fever, and the Lord will withhold rain. Your enemies will overcome you and leave you to the buzzards. You are also apt to get hemorrhoids and the itch, some of you will go mad or blind. You will court a girl and another man will take her to bed, you'll build a house and never live in it, and plant fields and vineyards and never harvest the grain or pick the grapes. Your ox will drop dead in front of you and you will lose your ass.[1] Your sheep will be stolen and you won't recover them. Your sons and daughters shall be captured and you will be powerless to prevent it.

A strange nation shall devour your land and oppress you. You will have trouble with arthritis and your knees will hurt, and the king who you have selected will be defeated by another nation and you will be scattered. You will become a byword and people will make sport of your name.

All the good things promised will be reversed and you will get the little end of every stick. All because you fail to serve God and worship Him.

The Lord will bring a nation from afar off, one that operates like an eagle, a nation whose language you do not know. It will be a fierce nation, and it shall be merciless to old and young. This nation shall lay siege to your cities and you shall become depraved because of hunger. All these things will happen unless you obey the laws of this book and stand in awe of the glorious name, the Lord thy God.

If you are disobedient, you shall become few in number, you shall perish from sickness, and the Lord will scatter the remaining few throughout the nations of the world, and you will have no ease or real home among the nations.

[1]donkey or beast of burden

You will be so miserable that each morning you will say, "Would that it were already evening." Often you will be put up for sale and there will be no buyers.

Chap.
29

Moses called forth then even more vehemently. "You know of all the mighty acts of God, the signs, the wonders, the miracles, yet you seem unimpressed. I have led you forty years in the wilderness. You are well prepared, yet you stand this day before the Lord, you, your wives, your little ones, the hewers of wood and the drawers of water, and you are to enter into a covenant with the Lord thy God on this day.

"Do not for one minute think that you can deceive God. Lip service will not be sufficient. You cannot say one thing and do another.

"There are some unknown things, and they belong to God, but His revelation belongs to us and to our children, if we obey his law.

Chap.
30

After you have gone through the periods of blessing and cursing, and you remember all the things that I have told you, and you decide to return to the Lord and obey Him, then the Lord will deliver you from captivity, and have compassion on you, and bring you from all the nations whereto you have been scattered, even if there are some on the moon, God will fetch them, and bring you again to your native land, the land promised to you. The Lord will bless you in this.

"This commandment and this pronouncement which I make to you today is clear. It is not on Mars so that you might wonder about it, nor is it beyond the sun, but the word is clear and at hand and you can hear it.

"I have placed before you today life and good or death and evil.

"I commend you today to love God, to walk in His ways, to keep His commandments and His statutes and His judgments, and the Lord thy God will bless thee. If you turn away, however, and do not heed so that you wander off and worship strange gods, then I denounce you this day for you shall surely perish. I call heaven and earth as a witness this day, for I have set before you life and death, blessing and cursing. Therefore choose life, for the children's sake; decide that you will love the Lord thy God and that you will obey his voice, for He is your life and the controller of your days, and then you may dwell in the land that the Lord promised to Abraham, Isaac, and Jacob.

Chap.
31

Moses continued, saying, "I am an old man. I am no longer nimble and barely mobile, also the Lord has told me that I can't cross the Jordan, but the Lord will go with you, and he will not fail you."

Moses then summoned Joshua and spoke to him saying, "Be strong and of good courage for you must go with these people into the land promised by God, and you will help them take the land, and God will be with you, He will not fail you nor forsake you; so fear not, and never be discouraged."

And all this was written and handed to the priests for safekeeping.

The Lord then spoke to Moses and reminded him that the time was short and told him to appear with Joshua in the tabernacle to receive the Lord's blessing. Then Moses and Joshua presented themselves, and the Lord appeared before them in a cloud that hovered above the door of the tabernacle.

The Lord spoke to Moses and said, "Your time has come. You will pass away and the people will in time forget and wander into strange religions. They will forsake me and break my covenant, then I shall be angry with them, and I will leave them to their miseries. Write this now in a song, to be recorded, as a witness against them. This song shall testify against them when they have found a home in the land flowing with milk and honey, and when they have forgotten me." Moses that day wrote the song.

Moses then gave Joshua, the son of Nun, a charge and instructed him to lead the children of Israel.

When all of this was written in a book, Moses had the writing placed in the ark of the covenant, that it might be there as a witness.

"I know you," repeated Moses, "You are a stiff-necked and rebellious people and when I'm dead you are going to forsake God. You even did it with me around; so I know you'll do it after I've gone." Thus Moses spoke to all of them and told them again of the punishment of God in the latter days for those who disobey.

Chap.
32

Moses decided to speak again, pleading, and saying, "Listen everyone, everywhere, my teachings are coming down as the rain, my speech like the still dew. It is as soft water to the grass, because I proclaim the glory of God, to God I ascribe greatness. He is the Rock, His works are perfect, all His ways are full of understanding, a God of truth, just and right, while the people are a perverse and crooked generation.

"O you foolish people, is God not the father that saved you? Didn't he make you and put you here?

"Remember the olden days. Ask your fathers, ask the elders. From the very beginning you have been the Lord's portion of the people.

"Jacob is a good illustration. God found him in the desert, in a howling wasteland. God kept him and instructed him. As an eagle wing sweeps the nest, and flutters over its young, and spreads its wings so the young may ride on the broad wings; so the Lord did with Jacob, and there was no following of strange gods for Jacob.

"Jacob rode on the high places and was abundantly blessed, but some of you are just fat slobs, who have forsaken God.

"What a shame that you act as a nation without common sense. It would be wonderful if you were wise and understood. How could it be that two could chase ten thousand, except the Lord were handling the matter? The rock of our enemies is not like our Rock, their grapes, even, are grapes of gall.

The Lord shall judge His people. The Lord shall ask of the people, "Where are your gods now that you are in all this trouble? Why don't you get them to help you?"

"You should know that there is only one God. He kills and He makes alive. He will avenge himself of the enemies and He will have mercy on those who love Him and keep His commandments."

Moses spoke all these things also to the people, and it was a new day.

That day God told Moses to climb Mt. Nebo and look over the land of Canaan which would be given to the children of Israel. God told Moses that the climb would kill him and he would then be gathered to God's home among his people.

"You can see the land, Moses," God said, "but you can't enter it."

Moses then blessed the people before he departed. Moses blessed each of the tribes in turn and he added, "May the shoes of all of you be of brass and iron, and may you retain your strength as long as you live. There is only one God, who ruleth the heaven, and he is your refuge, and underneath are the everlasting arms. God shall thrust forth your enemies, and Israel shall be at peace. Happy you should be, O Israel, a people delivered by God, who is as a shield for all of you."

Chap.
34

Then Moses ascended Mt. Nebo to the top of Lookout Mountain,[1] in sight of Jericho. The Lord said to him, "Moses, there she is. As far as you can see. This is the land that I promised to Abraham, Isaac, and Jacob."

Then Moses died and was buried in land where he had ranched, but no one knows the place. Moses was still in possession of all his faculties when he died, and his eye was clear. The children of Israel mourned for Moses the full thirty days.

Then Joshua took Moses' place, for Moses had laid his hands on Joshua and blessed him, and taught him wisdom, and the people listened to Joshua.

There never was a prophet like Moses, one to whom God spoke mouth to mouth, and knew face to face. Through Moses the Lord performed tremendous signs and wonders and did mighty things through his servant Moses.

[1]Pisgah

JOSHUA

After the death of Moses the Lord spoke to his assistant minister, Joshua, and told him to get up and go, to cross the Jordan and to conquer the land promised by the Lord through Moses, and the Lord reminded Joshua that no enemy would be strong enough to prevent his success. The Lord said "As I was with Moses so shall I be with you. I will not fail you nor forsake you. You be strong and of good courage and observe the law as I explained it to Moses. The book of the law of God should never depart from you, speak from it, let it be your guide, and there will be no problem."

"Have at it, Josh, but tough and strong, for I am with you all the way!"

Joshua then had the word passed among the people that they had 3 days to pack.[1] To the tribes that had voted to remain in the wilderness, Joshua reminded them that all the able-bodied men were to remain in the Army until the promised land was secured, and then they could return to their chosen homes and cities. The men agreed to do as Joshua ordered, for they said they would adhere to Joshua as well as they had to Moses[2], and would execute anybody who rebelled.

Chap.
2

Joshua then selected two men to go to Jericho and spy for him and bring back a report. The spies entered Jericho and lodged in the only desegregated boarding house available, which was run by a lady named Sophie[3].

Word was passed to the Mayor of Jericho about the strangers, however, and he sent word to Sophie to bring the men to him for questioning as he suspected that they were spies.

Sophie, however, didn't care much for City Hall and so she hid the men and sent word to the Mayor that the men had been there and left and failed to leave a forwarding address. Sophie did report, however, that she had seen two similar looking men slipping out of the gate of the city only a few minutes before dark and she thought that the Mayor and the Vigilante Committee could catch them by heading north. This was a great opportunity for action so the whole posse went north in mad pursuit of two men.

Sophie, who had hidden the spies under some straw on the roof top, came to the two spies and said "I know you men are from the camp of those under the Lord God and I know that this collection of yellow-bellies here in Jericho are absolutely terrified. Everyone has heard of the Red Sea incident, and what happened to the Mafia, and

[1]Some housewives no doubt mentioned that it couldn't be done in 3 days.
[2]which fell short of 100%

[3]Rahab mentioned as harlot, but this also could simply mean an early Lib movement girl.

83

the Capone Gang, and the hearts of the people in this area are just plain melted. We know that the Lord your God is the real God, both in the heaven and on earth. Now promise me, under oath to your God, that in exchange for the kindness that I have shown you that you will return the favor and that when your army comes to capture Jericho that you will not destroy this my father's home, nor will you kill my father, my mother, my brothers, or my sisters."

"It's a deal, Sophie", said both the men together, and they shook on it.[1]

Sophie then let them over the wall by use of a rope and she said to them "Go south to the mountains so you won't run into the vigilantes that I sent north and hide for about 3 days, for that's about as long as a posse lasts in this county."

The men were highly appreciative and they suggested that in order that no mistake be made, Sophie tie a red ribbon in the window of her house and promised to deliver her people, but warned them not to go out the front door into the street when the fight started as they would very likely get clobbered, but that they should all escape down a rope from the same window even as the spies were escaping."

Everything then being arranged they left and Sophie tied a red ribbon to the window. Just as Sophie thought, on the third day the posse returned worn out and most of them went and got boozed up for their trouble.

The spies hid during this three day period as Sophie had suggested and then they returned to Joshua and reported.

"The Lord has already delivered those people into our hands," reported the top ranking of the two spies, "for the people there are already scared to death."

Chap.
3

Joshua got up early in the morning and ordered the people to assemble near the edge of the Jordan and here began the three days of preparation for the crossing[2] and the appointed leaders went all through the camps passing the word that when the ark of the covenant crossed over the Jordan, then to break camp and get going.

"Do not get too close to the ark of the covenant for the ark is to be your guide and you can watch. Furthermore, prepare yourselves for the trip, no wild parties or the like, but thought and prayer, for the Lord will begin the very first day working wonders through you," said the leaders.

Joshua then told the priests to pick up the ark of the covenant and begin the trip.

The Lord then spoke to Joshua and said "This day I will begin to increase your importance with your people that they may be

---

[1]or kissed her, depending on Sophie   [2]No doubt with a few more complaints

certain that I am with you as I was with Moses."

The Lord went on to say to Joshua that he should tell the bearers of the ark to stand still when they entered the Jordan. When this was done Joshua addressed the people again and said "Now you will know why you should enter the promised land without fear and you can be sure of your victories for the ark of the covenant of the Lord of all the earth shall proceed you."

Joshua then had each tribe select a man to be present as a witness, for he said the Lord will cause the waters that fill the Jordan to cease when the bearers of the ark enter the waters, and the tribes of Israel would cross the Jordan on dry ground. The sources of the waters of the Jordan dried up and the river bed was dry until the tribes of Israel had crossed the Jordan, and it was witnessed and the glory of God was there.

Chap.
4

Then the Lord made a suggestion to Joshua that he require one man from each of the tribes of Israel to lift a stone from the Jordan and to place the twelve stones together in a pile on the bank of the Jordan river close to where the crossing occurred. This would serve as an historical marker and when the children down through the years would ask their fathers for the meaning of these stones then the fathers could tell them of how the flow from the sources of the Jordan was stopped in order that the ark of the covenant might pass over the Jordan and that these stones would serve as a memorial for this occasion.

The representatives of the tribes each did as he was commanded and Joshua saw to it that the stones were properly placed and they are there today.

After this was done, and all the people had crossed the Jordan, and the ark of the covenant was safely secured across the Jordan, then Joshua prepared an army of 40,000 select men who were to march onto the plains of Jericho and besiege the city. At this very time, the Lord magnified Joshua in the eyes of all the people so that they respected him as they had respected Moses.

When the priests carrying the ark of the covenant had come forth from the trickling waters and secured the ark on dry land, then the Lord released the waters again from the sources of the Jordan and the river returned to its natural flow.

Joshua then made a brief speech[1] to the children of Israel and spoke to them saying "As the Lord your God did to the Red Sea as you entered the wilderness so did he to the Jordan River as you left the wilderness in order that all the people of the earth might know the power of the Lord, and that He is mighty, and that you must stand in awe of the Lord thy God forever."

---

[1]He was never as long-winded as Moses

When news of the drying up deal of the Jordan had spread through the various towns and cities in Canaan[1], then all of these people became faint hearted and feared greatly these same people who some few years earlier had seemed to be as grasshoppers in their eyes.

During the wilderness wanderings and the constant mobility of the whole nation, none of the children born in the wilderness had been circumcised. As a result, Joshua ordered every male to be circumcised and this was a painful and time consuming operation, and Joshua ordered the people to remain in camp until everyone had healed and some of the gripping had died down.

The children of Israel then observed the feast of the passover and on the next day there was no manna, nor did the children of Israel ever have to eat manna again, for they began to eat of the fruit of the land of Canaan.

Now Joshua decided to go and have a look himself at the city of Jericho to plan his attack and as he came in full view he was confronted by a man with a sword in his hand, as if he were ready to do battle. Joshua spoke to the man and asked if he was for Israel or against Israel.

"I am the captain of the host of the Lord" said the man, and Joshua bowed his head to the ground, and asked what he should do.

"Loose your shoes and take them off your feet, for you are on holy ground," replied the man. Joshua did as he was told.

The city of Jericho had been put under martial law and there was no coming and going through the gates of the city and commerce was at a standstill.

The Lord said then to Joshua "See, the people of Jericho, even the warriors already know that they've had it. They are terrified. Use some psychological warfare on them and get all your men of valor and march around the city for six days, parading, and taunting them. Let the priests with the ark of the covenant lead the parade, and let them sound forth their trumpets, and let it be a joyful, triumphant type of march, then on the seventh day march around the city seven times and at the end of the seventh time around the city on the seventh day let the priests give a mighty blast with rams' horns and then instruct the people to shout with a great triumphant shout, and storm the walls of Jericho, for the walls will be flattened before them."

Everything was carried out exactly as the Lord said, and Joshua only reminded the people of Israel to preserve the house of Sophie and the family of hers that were there, and also to bring all the loot

---

[1]no doubt with added touches.

to the synagogue.

Joshua explained that this was the Lord's victory and that all silver, brass, gold, and precious things were to be brought to the Lord's house.

So when the people shouted at the final blast of the rams' horns, the mighty warriors of Israel, 40,000 strong charged the walls, and they were flattened before them and they took the city, and destroyed everything in the city, men and women, cattle and cats, and Joshua sent the two spies to protect Sophie and her household and they delivered her safely with her family.

Finally the warriors set fire to the city and burned it to the ground, but gold and silver and valuables were brought to the treasury of the church. Joshua then turned upon the smoking city and pronounced a curse on any man that should attempt to rebuild it.[1]

And the Lord was with Joshua and his fame was spread throughout the land.

Chap.
7

As might be expected, there was one fellow named Fingers Lasky[2] who took some of the silver and jewelry from Jericho and hid it in his tent. No one knew of this, but the Lord, and the Lord was angry because of this.

The next city to be captured was the city of Abilene[3] and Joshua sent a few of his officers to survey the city and report back on the prospects.

The committee returned and told Joshua that Abilene was a small place with only a few warriors around and that it was not necessary to worry with sending the whole army against the city but that 2 or 3 thousand men could handle the capture easily.

As a result, Joshua sent 3 thousand men to attack Abilene and the warriors of Abilene poured forth and began to beat the stew out of the portion of the army that Joshua had dispensed. By the time about 36 men had fallen under the Abilene blows the remainder panicked in fear and became track men, and ran wildly to the safety of the camp.

Joshua was horrified, and immediately fell on his face before the ark of the covenant and prayed to the Lord saying "Why did you let me bring this pack of yellow bellies over the Jordan? I wish we had never crossed the Jordan. I cannot stand to see my army unwilling to stand up and fight. What is more, everyone in the country will hear of this, and they shall no longer fear us and will even lose respect for thy great and holy name."

---

[1]The archeologist are still not exactly positive about the exact place, though I was shown what might have been when I visited the Holy Land.

[2]Achan   [3]Ai

Then the Lord spoke to Joshua and said, "Get up and get with it. Quit your own moaning and groaning. The failure is due to sin, for you have among you one who has stolen from the treasury of the church and has hidden it. Naturally, the children of Israel cannot stand up and fight unless the spirit of the Lord is with them, and I have withheld it because of this sin. Find the offender and punish him."

Immediately Joshua ordered a tent and locker search, tribe by tribe, and the searchers were given a tip that Fingers Lasky had the loot from Jericho, which belonged to the synagogue.

Joshua sent for Fingers and said to him, "Confess."

"I have sinned against God," said Fingers. Then Fingers began to give a big explanation about his need for money, his sick children, his chariot needing repairs, and the high cost of living. Fingers then told Joshua that all the money, jewelry, and garments were hidden in his tent.

Joshua sent men to check his story and they returned with the loot. Then Joshua called an assemblage of representatives from all the tribes and had Fingers and his sons, and all his possessions, and the loot all placed on public view and Joshua said, "Why did you all do this to us? Now the Lord will trouble you for the trouble you have caused."

Then Joshua ordered the people from all the tribes to stone the Lasky family to death and to pile a heap of stones upon the bodies and to make the stones a historical marker and to let the place be known as "Death Valley Days."[1]

Chap.
8

The Lord then encouraged Joshua to again do battle against Abilene, for now that the sin against God was punished, the Lord would be with the army of Israel.

It also occurred to Joshua that Abilene might have been poorly judged by his scouts and he was not going to take the second attempt lightly.

As a result Joshua selected 30,000 of his best men and instructed them to hide themselves during the night behind the walls of Abilene on the opposite side of the city. Joshua explained to them that the remaining group under his command would approach the city from the front and entice the warriors of Abilene out as had been done before. Joshua then said that after a brief encounter this section of the army would again flee and the soldiers then of Abilene sensing a great victory would pour forth from the city to capture the entire fleeing army. When this occurred Joshua told the leaders of the 30,000 crack troops to go into the open gates of the city and to capture it and burn it to the ground, doing to it as was done to Jericho.

[1] The valley of Achor

The plan worked even better than Joshua thought it would, for when the people of Abilene saw Joshua retreating with his army they ran out of the city, every able-bodied man left and there was no one to defend the city when the main army suddenly came from behind the city and entered the open gates. All this was done by pre-arranged signal from Joshua.

When the army of Abilene looked back and saw that the city was lost they were demoralized, and the small portion of the army left with Joshua turned again upon the enemy and smote them right and left. The Mayor of Abilene was taken alive.

There were killed that day about 12,000, some of them women who didn't want to be left out of the action.

The Mayor of Abilene was given special attention as a warning to other mayors and he was hanged by the neck from a tree and his body placed at the entrance to Abilene. Another historical marker was placed there.

Following this victory Joshua built an altar to the Lord, and the stones were placed in proper array, and the commandments of Moses were inscribed on the stones, and the priests and the rulers of the tribes, and the people worshipped God. During the service, Joshua read to the people all the words of the law, the blessings and the cursings, and there was not a word recorded in the law which Joshua did not read.[1]

The word of this second victory created great alarm among all the other mayors and governors of the various places in Canaan and they decided to have a summit meeting and combine their strength to war against Israel. Chap. 9

There was one place called Brooklyn[2], which decided that there might be a slicker way of doing things than war against a highly successful army. As a result they selected a few of their men skilled at deception and dressed them in garments from a faraway place, put old, worn-out saddles on their donkeys, antique wine bottles[3], put worn-out shoes on them, and equipped them with mouldy bread and provisions. These bedraggled looking Brooklyn dodgers came into the camp of Israel saying they had come from a faraway land and would like to arrange an agreement of peace.

The chief of the C.I.A. of Israel immediately said, "How do we know that you are from a far country. You might be from close at hand and next on our list of places to capture?"

Joshua then spoke and said to them, "Who are you? Tell us from where you came?"

The ambassadors then said, "We come from a far away country of which you have never heard. We consider ourselves your servants, for we have heard of the name of the Lord thy God, the fame of

[1]The service definitely lasted well beyond 12 o'clock   [2]Gideon
[3]Sorry, ladies, but we don't know where they are now.

Him, and what happened to the Egyptians, and all that He did to your enemies on either side of the Jordan. When the rulers of our country heard all these things, they gave us beasts of burden and provisions to seek peace with you."

The ambassadors made a point of showing their old bottles and worn saddles, and mouldy provisions.[1]

Joshua then made peace with them, and agreed to spare their lives and the lives of the people they represented.

About three days later one of the C.I.A. boys decided the ambassadors were phony[2] and reported the matter to Joshua. An immediate investigation revealed that the ambassadors had only come from 12 miles away and represented the next group on Joshua's kill and burn schedule.

Joshua and the rulers of Israel, however, had sworn to a treaty of peace, and even though it was because of deceit, Joshua and the rulers would not violate their word. .

In spite of the murmuring of the people and the political pressure, Joshua ordered that the Brooklyn people were to be spared.

Joshua said, "We will let them live, but since they came to us declaring that they were our servants; so shall they be. They shall then be our servants, and they shall be hewers of wood and drawers of water."

Joshua called the ambassadors into conference and asked them why they had tried to deceive him.

"The answer is simple, General Joshua," replied the ambassadors, "for we know that the Lord had promised the land to Moses and we know that you are a "kill 'em all" type of general, and we were afraid for our lives. We are now in your hands and we must submit, but at least we will all live."

Joshua immediately began to assign them to the cutting of wood and drawing of water, and even made them build for Israel a church.

Chap.
10

Now Alex[3], who was mayor of Jerusalem, heard about all these happenings and he was particularly concerned about the treaty with Brooklyn for there were mighty men there and it was a great ctiy. As a result Alex called a meeting of nearby mayors, Sarge from Baltimore[4], Ollie, from Pittsburg[5] Lindsee from Albany[6], and George from Montgomery[7], and entreated them to all join forces and attack Brooklyn. Alex felt that the whole crowd could easily defeat Brooklyn with a portion of its people off working for the children of Israel and not permitted anyway to retain an army.

[1]This would have never fooled Nero Wolfe   [2]Too Late
[3]Adonizedec   [4]Hoham of Hebron   [5]Piram of Jarmuth
[6]Japhia of Lachish   [7]Debir of Eglon

As a result, the mayors all got their armies together and went and encamped around Brooklyn.

Some of the men from Brooklyn then slipped out at night and went two days journey to the camp of Joshua and told him what was happening. The men pleaded with Joshua for instant help.

As a result Joshua immediately gathered all his mighty men of war. The Lord encouraged Joshua in this and told him not to fear the combination of mayors and the cities as the Lord would help deliver them into his hands.

Joshua, always a careful strategist, moved his army silently in the night and suddenly came down upon the gathering of the men surrounding Brooklyn and slew them with a great slaughter. Shortly after the assembled armies began to flee the Lord sent a tremendous hailstorm that struck the warriors down as they fled, and more were killed by the hailstones and the landslides than were killed by the men of Israel.

Then Joshua[1] called upon the Lord to let the sun stand still so his army could keep killing the enemy a few more hours, and the Lord held up the sun for forty minutes[2]. This had never been done before nor would it ever happen again.

The five mayors of the cities involved had not counted on having any trouble, but as soon as the battle started the five of them hid in a cave. A private, bucking for corporal, had spotted them, however, and relayed the information to Joshua. Joshua ordered that the cave be closed with stones until the battle was over and then he would treat mayors as part of the victory celebration.

In a couple of days the remnants of the defeated armies had sought refuge in one of the sanctuary cities and the children of Israel all returned to base after a great victory.

Joshua then ordered the opening of the cave and brought the mayors out before the assemblage of a large crowd.

Joshua then ordered five of the top ranking men of his army to each put a foot on the neck of a mayor. Joshua then said to the heads of his army, "Never be afraid, for the Lord will do to all our enemies as you are doing to the mayors."

As soon as this message had soaked in, Joshua said, "Kill them, and hang their bodies on a tree until dark, then throw the bodies in the cave where they hid, and close the cave." This is exactly what was done.[3]

Then Joshua set forth with his army and began to knock off systematically a number of smaller places, such as Ripley[4], Savannah[5], and Jersey City[6]. Then a rather brash mayor of Chicago[7], named Monthly[8], came with his crowd to fight Joshua and

---

[1]He didn't think much of enemies
[2]There is some evidence that the earth's rotation slowed or stopped at one time.
[3]This may have dampened some election enthusiam in Jerusalem that year
[4]Makkedah [5]Libnah [6]Lachish
[7]Gezer [8]Horam

the children of Israel and Joshua cleaned out his whole army.

Joshua felt that his army had impetus and he immediately moved quickly to knock off Lexington[1], Rochester[2], and even Muleshoe, Texas[3].

Joshua continued his policy of killing everyone that opposed him as he apparently did not have facilities for a POW camp.

Joshua continued to smite and conquer each village and hamlet until he had subdued the whole surrounding area, and then he returned to base camp.

Chap.
11

Word of all this began to spread everywhere and mayors from everywhere became alarmed and finally organized what might be called a grand alliance and brought another army to do battle with the children of Israel, and Joshua brought his highly organized troops against them and the Lord delivered these also to Joshua and there was great slaughter. Joshua then went forth and destroyed by burning all the cities represented against him, but those towns and cities that had not joined the alliance Joshua left standing. The warriors of Israel were now allowed to keep the things captured for themselves and this was a morale booster.

Joshua conquered all the land and the hills of the south country and in every direction, and war took a long time and Joshua was relentless in his conquest as he had been commanded to do by Moses.

Brooklyn was the only place that made peace with Joshua and it alone was spared.

Finally all the kings and mayors were dead and all the cities conquered and Joshua took the whole land according to all that the Lord had said to Moses and he gave all the land as an inheritance to Israel and divided it among the tribes, and the land rested from war.

Chap.
12

A list of the cities, towns, mayors, and kings which were recorded as conquered.

Chap.
13

Now Joshua was getting old and there were still left many areas that were originally promised by the Lord to the children of Israel. The Lord suggested to Joshua that he assign remote areas to the different tribes and to let each tribe as it developed its own army to move and possess new territory until all the land of Canaan was possessed by the children of Israel. This was done, and the property decisions were decided by casting dice and the children of Israel went forth into the land by tribes and increased their possessions and overcame all that opposed them.

The tribe of Levi was not given an inheritance, for these were

[1]Eglon   [2]Hebron   [3]Debir

the priests of God, and it was the responsibility of all tribes to see
that the priests of God were provided for properly in every way.

During all these many decisions and discussions of land there
came to Joshua his old companion who had joined him in the
favorable scouting report to Moses, good, faithful Caleb.

"Joshua, in spite of my years, I am still strong and a sturdy
fighter, I feel no loss of strength from the time I was young, and you
remember I am sure that Moses promised me all the great land and
streams, and mountains in Colorado[1]. No doubt, Joshua, you
remember how everyone was afraid of this area, but if you will deed
me this area and if the Lord be with us, I will take the territory." It
was done.

A description of the cities and areas assigned and conquered by
the tribe of Judah.

The dice were continued to roll in selection of land for the
various tribes, which are named in these chapters.

The Lord then spoke to Joshua and reminded him to set aside
the cities of refuge so that a slayer who was simply guilty of
manslaughter, or self defense might have a safe place to dwell until
things cooled down and justice could be done. "The wanted man is
to have refuge until the judge who would have tried his case is dead,
and then he may return to his house a free man," said the law.

Then Joshua ordered each tribe to assign a portion of their
possessions to the tribe of Levi, who were priests of the Lord.

Then Joshua called to him the leaders of the tribes of Reuben
and Troop and praised them for staying with their agreement to fight
with Joshua until all the land was conquered and told them that they
now could take their possessions and their booty and return to their
families and their cities that they had left on the other side of the
Jordan.

Joshua then reminded them saying, "Take diligent heed to hold
to the commandments of God, to love the Lord your God and to
serve Him with all your heart and all your soul." Then Joshua blessed
them and sent them away.

[1]Land of the Anakims

When the tribes reached the Jordan River and were prepared to cross it, they built there a huge historical marker. Word of this returned to the other tribes and they rose in great indignation, saying one historical marker is enough and we put one there first and now they have built a bigger one and it is sacrilegious.

As a result of this the tribes gathered together a mighty army and went near to the spot of the placing of the big, new historical marker and accused the tribes responsible of turning against God.

A spokesman from the tribe of Reuben said to the leaders of the other tribes, "You are wrong in what you say, this marker is an altar to God. For the previous one is one that you can show to your children and say to them 'see this is the sign of our obedience to God', but what can we say to our children? Our children will not believe we obeyed God, and so this marker is placed here so that we can tell our children that we did as the Lord commanded, we fought with you all at our sides as we agreed, and this marker shows that we crossed and returned, it is to teach our children to obey God."

The speech pleased the leaders of the tribes very much and they shook hands and had a big party instead of a fight.

Chap.
23

There followed then a long period of rest in Israel from all their enemies and Joshua became old and near the time of death. As a result Joshua called for a convention of all the leaders, elders, judges, and officers of all the tribes of Israel and he made a speech to them saying "I have had it. My days are numbered. You have seen all that the Lord has done to your enemies, for it is the Lord your God who has fought for you.

I have divided unto each of your tribes an inheritance of land according to the casting of lots and the Lord will see that you are able to complete the possession of all that has been assigned to you.

Keep your courage. Observe all things that are written in the book of Moses, do not waiver to one side or the other. Be exceedingly careful in the mingling with people of other nations that you do not even mention the names of their strange gods or participate in any of their observances, but cleave unto the Lord your God.

No man has been able to stand before you because of the strength of the Lord and for this reason one man of you is better than a thousand of the enemies of God.

Take heed therefore that you love the Lord. If you begin to get careless, and go astray with some of the women of these nations, or marry them, the Lord will not support you, and these minglings will be snares and traps for you and you will eventually lose this land.

I am about to go the way of all that dwell on the earth and I testify that not one thing has failed within the promises of the Lord, the great keeper of the promises. Even so as all good things have come to you because of your obedience so shall all things turn against you if you transgress the covenant of the Lord your God. If you serve other gods and bow yourselves to them and let other matters become more important to you than the Lord your God, then shall the anger of the Lord be stirred against you and you will lose this land."

Chap.
24

Following lunch, Joshua called the convention to order again and he said, "I have a message from the Lord God of Israel. The Lord has reminded me to tell you that your ancestors go all the way back to the father of Abraham, and God took Abraham into the land of Canaan and gave him Isaac, and Jacob and Esau as grandsons, and gave them lands. God sent Moses and Aaron to deliver the children of Israel after they had been enslaved in Egypt, and God brought your fathers out of Egypt, and destroyed the army of Pharaoh at the Red Sea, and brought your fathers through the wilderness, and brought you across the Jordan and delivered into your hands the men of Jericho and Abilene, and Chicago, and Ripley, and Savannah, and many others. The Lord, has given you a land for which you did not labor, and cities which you did not build, but in which you now live, and vineyards and olive orchards from which you do now eat."

"Now, therefore," continued Joshua, "stand in awe of God, serve him in sincerity and truth, put away from you any thought of the strange gods that some of your ancestors served in Egypt and other places, and serve the Lord.

But, of course, you can choose, you can choose this day whom you will serve, whether you serve strange gods of some of your ancestors, or the gods of the gypsies, but as for me and my house, we will serve the Lord."

The people answered and said, "We will not forsake the Lord, for we know that it was the Lord our God that delivered us, that saved our fathers from the bondage in Egypt, and who has preserved us unto this day. We will serve the Lord, for He is our God."

"Do you really mean this?" asked Joshua. "For the Lord is a jealous God and he does not take these things lightly."

The people again shouted, "We will serve the Lord."

Joshua then said to them, "You are witnesses yourselves that you have chosen the Lord, to serve him."

"We are witnesses", cried the people.

As a result, Joshua had minutes of the meeting recorded, and wrote all these words in the book of the law of the Lord, and marked the place of the testimony with a historical marker under an oak tree, and Joshua reminded the people that the marker was a reminder of their covenant, and then he dismissed the convention.

Not many days later Joshua died and they buried him near Mount Vernon [1].

[1] Timnathserah

After the death of Joshua the children of Israel prayed to the Lord for guidance, for there was no leader to unite all the tribes. The Lord instructed the tribes to each pursue and conquer the enemies within their own areas, the portions which had been assigned to them by lot.

Judah was the first tribe to make its move and the leaders of this tribe asked the tribe of Simeon to join them on a reciprocal agreement, that Judah would then join Simeon in helping with their territory. The plan worked and both tribes completed the conquest of their territories.

Caleb was having some trouble in his area with the Scarlotti[1] gang and he offered as a reward his beautiful daughter Raquel[2] to any man who would lead a successful raid against this mob. The sheriff of Cade County[3] decided to try it, and he succeeded.

Raquel flashed a bit of her charm on her father, and suggested that since the sheriff was poor but honest that it would help matters considerably if Caleb would give her a couple of sections of land that had running water. Caleb consented and all worked well in this matter[4].

Not all of the tribes, however, carried out the injunctions of the Lord. The tribe of Benjamin allowed the Rotarians[5] to remain in Jerusalem, and they are there to this day.

Some of the other tribes, for one reason or another, did not bother to pursue their enemies and they allowed them to remain in their land. The general feeling was that Israel had become so strong that there was no point in further pursuit of frightened people. The enemies of Israel simply interpreted this as weakness, and began to think in terms of rebuilding their own strength.

A man full of the Spirit of the Lord, speaking for the Lord, came to the children of Israel after they had enjoyed many years of prosperity. Joshua was long since dead, and the elders and rulers that Joshua had trained were dead, and new generations had grown up, and they were enjoying themselves too fully to be concerned with the word of the Lord.

The man from God then spoke to them and reminded them of

---

[1]Kirjathsepher   [2]Achsah   [3]Othniel
[4]Particularly for the Sheriff   [5]Jebusites

the covenant of old and warned them about their iniquities, for they were making free with women and worshipping Baal, and following the strange gods of selfishness and greed.

The anger of the Lord was stirred against them and the enemies of Israel began to entrap them and create multiple difficulties for them.

The Lord, however, remained the great Keeper of the Promises and so he began to raise up righteous men, judges in Israel, that were representatives of God's help and his love, and these judges began to deliver the people.

The trouble was that when one of the great judges died, the people would gradually return to evil ways and their enemies would again oppress them. Somewhat in disgust the Lord then decided to let Israel fend for itself for awhile, and He did not drive out their enemies or discomfort them as He had in times past.

Chap.
3

The children of Israel began to degenerate rapidly and they began to intermarry with the enemies of God and they began to violate all the commandments of God, and they became a decadent and deteriorating nation.

As always, there were those few who faithfully worshipped God and began a reform movement and they prayed earnestly to God to help deliver them from their enemies. As a result, the Lord let his spirit enter into the heart of the sheriff of Cade County and he went to war in the name of the Lord, and led the people of Israel to great victories, and delivered them from their enemies, and restored the worship of God. As a result, there was forty years of peace and prosperity in Israel.

Then the sheriff of Cade County died. It wasn't long before sin began again to take its toll and the people wandered from sanctuary habits, and worshipped strange gods, and pursued selfish enterprises. As a result, God stirred up the evil king of New Orleans[1] who gathered together some support from neighboring cities and towns and they swept down upon Israel and conquered their strongholds and subdued the people.

The Israelites had been under this satellite arrangement for 18 years when one of their number, Mac the Knife[2], decided that he would try to do something about the problem. First, he made for himself a special dagger with two edges, and a long thin blade, and he concealed it carefully by sticking it to his thigh with scotch tape.

Now the king of New Orleans was an exceedingly fat man and

[1]Eglon   [2]Ehud

enjoyed flattery and recognition. Mac the Knife was admitted into his presence on the basis of bringing the king a very fine present, and the bearers of the beautiful gift[1] made the presentation and then excused themselves. Mac the Knife told the king that he also had a bit of secret information[2] and asked the king to dismiss his guards so that he might whisper his secret without fear of anyone hearing. The king then ordered the guard to leave him and he remained alone on the summer patio with Mac.

"Great king, I have a message from God for you," said Mac the Knife, whereupon he took his left hand and drew the dagger from his right side and thrust it all the way into the king's stomach, so much so that the fat of the king came over the handle of the dagger and hid it.

Mac the Knife then left the enclosed patio, closed the doors and locked them. When the servants of the king came a few minutes later and found the doors locked they assumed the king was taking his afternoon snooze and did not wish to be disturbed.

Finally, some two hours later, the servants became alarmed and broke down the doors and found the king dead. In the meantime Mac the Knife was long gone.

A couple of days later, Mac sounded the trumpet on a faraway hill to assemble the remaining faithful people of God, and he told them the king was dead and that New Orleans was in great turmoil and that they could win a victory if they attacked immediately. The people responded and descended on New Orleans and its surrounding area with great force and subdued it, killing some ten thousand people in the process. Following this there was sixty years of peace.[3]

Chap. 4

The memory and influence of Mac faded and the children of Israel again did evil in the sight of the Lord and returned to their old tricks of strange gods and foreign women, greed and neglect of the obligations to the church.

There was a strong leader among the people of the hill country named Jesse James[4] and he had accumulated a collection of chariots of iron and the people of Israel stood in great fear of him and were strictly under his thumb.

The children of Israel then began to cry again in their prayers to God and to promise to reform, and the Lord raised up for them a female leader named Carrie[5], which was a big switch in policy[6].

---

[1]possibly a hand carved couch
[3]Wouldn't it be nice if our nation under God-fearing leaders would commit ourselves to Him?

[2]intimated it was a stock tip
[4]Sisera   [5]Deborah
[6]You've come a long way babies

Carrie sent word to the so-called leader of the army of Israel, a man named General Maybe [1] and told him to bring his army of 10,000 men and she would sic them on Jesse James and that the Lord would deliver Jesse with all his iron trains into the hands of Maybe.

General Maybe then sent a note to Carrie saying that he would do this if she would go with him and hold his hand [2]. Carrie said she would at least walk along with him, but that because of his sissy tendency the honor of killing Jesse James would be given to a woman [3].

Carrie set a trap or some inducement of loot down near the Pecos River [4] bottom and Jesse James and his iron chariots fell for the bait. When the iron chariots were in the river bottom Carrie sent General Maybe and his army down from the hill and they thoroughly defeated the James gang.

Jesse fled and sought refuge in the nearest friendly area he could find. As Jesse was running a lady named Mae East [5] called to him and invited him to come and hide in her tent, as her husband was not at home.

Jesse was pooped out from running and laid down in the tent and Mae covered him with a blanket. Jesse was also thirsty and asked for water, but she gave him milk as she said milk would help him more.

Jesse then said, "Mae, honey, please stand in the door of the tent and if any man comes and asks if there is a man hiding in your tent tell him there isn't."

"Okay, Babie", said Mae. However, as soon as Jesse was fast asleep, Mae slipped quietly up beside him and took a huge hammer and a railroad spike and nailed Jesse's head to the ground.

When General Maybe came puffing along a little while later and asked if anyone had seen Jesse James, Mae stepped forth and said, "Sure. I like to deal with winners only; so I have Jesse nailed to the ground in my tent [6]".

Chap.
5

Following this mighty victory, Carrie called for a celebration and she made up a ballad to sing for the people and she sang a mighty song to them, she composed it herself, and it was long, but she sang and they listened [7].

---

[1] Barak
[3] This meant no medal, which hurts a general very much

[2] Not much of a general
[4] Kishon [5] Jael [6] Mae got the medal
[7] This will help prepare us for a woman president

"Praise the Lord", she sang, "His truth is marching on, the people responded to His call, praise the Lord, all of you. The Lord is wonderful indeed, for the Lord shakes the earth, and He causes rain, and great landslides, and then there was the great depression, the villages were empty, travelers walked only on the byways for fear of Jesse James, and then I came along, a great Mother of Israel. I came at a time when there was no army and no enthusiasm, but I bestirred the men, and no longer do the drawers of water at the wells have to worry about the gunslingers of the James gang. How can I help but sing? Didn't I gather together the leaders of Israel and didn't we do a great job?

What a beautiful sight to see the James gang floating facedown in the Pecos River. Curses be on all those of Israel who did not get in the action.

Blessed above all women is the great Mae East. Jesse James asked for water and she gave him milk, she even slipped him some bread with butter on it, and then when he went to sleep she nailed him to the floor. Like wow! she just put her left hand to the nail and the right hand to the hammer, and that ended him. Talk about dead, he was as dead as they come.

Meanwhile back at the gang's ranch in the hills, the mother of Jesse kept wondering why he had not returned.

'What is holding him up?' moaned Jesse's mother. 'What's wrong with his train?'

What happened? The James gang is gone, it is defeated. It is as nailed down as Jesse.

So let all the enemies of the Lord perish, but let those that love the Lord be as the sun when it goes forth on its mighty journey."

The song ended, and Israel had peace for forty years.

Chap.
6

Then comes again the same old story, selfishness, greed, and the strange gods of material things being worshipped instead of God. As always, this meant trouble, this time in the form of the Dalton gang, who dwelt in Midland.

It took the Dalton gang seven years to take over the children of Israel, but they finally subdued them and made of them an impoverished satellite nation.

Then the people cried again to the Lord. Then the Lord sent a prophet unto the people to speak to them and to remind them that God had delivered them from Egypt, and cleaned out the land of Canaan for them, but that the people had disobeyed God and followed after the gods of Wall Street[1].

[1] Amorites

The people repented and prayed again for deliverance.

An angel of the Lord appeared unto a man named Gideon and said to him, "You are a man of great courage."

"Who, me?" asked Gideon in surprise.

"Yes," said the angel, "and the Lord wants you to lead the children of Israel against the Dalton Gang."

"Well, if the Lord is so much for us, why are we in this mess in the first place?" [1]

"Gideon," said the Lord, "All you need to know is that I am with you."

"But, Lord," argued Gideon, "how in the devil can I save Israel? I am a nobody. In fact, my whole family is a poor family, and I am the poorest one in the crowd."

"I will be with you", replied the Lord.

"This is a new thing for me, Lord, and just so I won't think I'm imagining things, show me evidence of your support."

"All right," replied the angel of the Lord. "Bring an uncooked TV dinner and place it on the rock before me."

Gideon did this, and the angel of the Lord stretched forth his staff and fire came out and cooked the TV dinner as if by laser beam.

Gideon was astounded and began to think that because he had seen an angel of the Lord he would be cooked also, but the angel told him to calm down. Gideon then gathered together a few stones and built there an altar to God and worshipped.

That night, Gideon being inspired by God [2] went to town in the middle of the night and took two of his father's oxen and used the oxen to pull down the statue of Baal and the trees around it, right in front of the Dalton Gang's headquarters [3]. Gideon had ten men helping him cut down the trees.

Two bums sitting in front of the country store saw it all and told the Daltons who had done the mischief.

The head of the Dalton Gang was a pretty bright man [4] and he reasoned that there had been no loss of money and no one had touched any of his gang. In fact, he said, "Gideon attacked Baal. If Baal is a real god, let him get up and do something about it. What's the point in worshipping a god who can be defeated by ten men and two oxen." [5]

Gideon then began to send messages out among the tribes announcing the possibility of a revolution, and the unfriendly gangs who supported the Daltons began to gather together and plot,

[1] Some questions just don't get answered
[3] The Daltons being at the saloon at this time of night.
[5] So they went back to the saloon
[2] And probably a little bit impressed with himself
[4] Had finished Jr. College

including a big bunch from Odessa[1].

Gideon began to get a little nervous about this time, as it occurred to him that tearing down a statue and attacking a mighty army were two different things.

As a result, Gideon prayed to the Lord saying, "I will put a rug in front of my door tonight, and if in the morning the rug is wet with dew but the ground all around is dry, I will know you are still with me and I'll get with the army deal."

In the morning Gideon arose and was able to wring a bowl of water from the rug, but the ground around was dry, and Gideon was excited.

That night, however, Gideon prayed again and said, "Lord, don't get mad at me, but I had a science teacher that told me about fleece rugs drawing the moisture out of the air and just so there will be no misunderstanding between us, tonight let the rug remain dry and the ground around it wet.'

And the patient God of all did as Gideon requested, and in the morning the ground was wet, but the fleece was dry.

Chap.
7

The whole personality of Gideon now changed. No longer did he feel himself the poorest of a poor family, but he was General Gideon, leader of the army of the Lord. The first thing General Gideon did was to draft everybody, with no deferments, and ordered them to assemble at Lamesa[2].

The Lord then spoke to Gideon and said that he had too big an army to manage and most of them weren't much help in trying to slug it out with the Daltons anyway.

As a result, General Gideon assembled the army and announced that anybody that wanted to quit and felt that he had a good excuse, or who was afraid, any such could go home. As a result 22,000 left and Colonel Gideon had an army of 10,000.

The Lord spoke to Gideon again and said that there were still too many, that there was a lack of real enthusiasm on the part of many, and that only dedicated, committed men were needed when the power of God was available.

So God inspired Gideon to wisely test his army at the next water hole. Those men who were so dedicated and determined for victory that they walked through the water, lapping the water with their tongues as they passed through were to be kept, while the lukewarm who sprawled out on the ground yelling "coffee break, coffee break" were to be sent home.

[1]Amalekites   [2]Harod

On the other side of the water hole Captain Gideon and his 300 men departed to encounter the Dalton gang and their allies. The Lord told Gideon that with the 300 the Lord would see to the defeat of their enemies.

Gideon arrived with his 300 men and viewed the vast army of the assembled gangs in the valley.

The Lord suggested to Gideon that he go down in the night, with a private going in front in case of booby traps, and that he listen near the tents to hear what the Dalton boys had to say and maybe learn their strategy.

That night as he listened to the Daltons talking he learned they were afraid, for they had heard of the power of the Lord God of Israel, and one of them had dreamed of the crushing of their tents from the landslides that the Lord sometimes used.

Gideon returned and reported to the small group that the whole army was terrified and so he planned the first Halloween. Gideon divided the men into companies of one hundred each and placed them on the hill tops on the 3 sides of the army camped in the valley. Each man was to make an earthern jar, and equip himself with a bamboo trumpet and a torch of fat pine.

Every man had his instructions, and in the middle of the night, when the camp fires were burning low and the bewitching hour was come, Gideon sounded an eerie note on his bamboo trumpet, and then all the others all around did the same, and then they broke their earthern jars and threw them down the hillsides as if the mountains were crumbling, and then they set fire to their torches and came running down from all 3 of the surrounding hills, shouting, "The sword of Gideon and of the Lord has fallen upon you."

The Dalton gang and their allies went to pieces, and in their tremendous eagerness in the darkness to get out of the valley the gangsters began to kill each other in their panic, and they killed more among themselves than were killed by the 300 men of Gideon.

The next day as the terrified gangsters fled helter-skelter, the self-deferred draftees began to come out of the neighboring villages and they joined in the chase and in the slaughter. The Dalton boys themselves, the two leaders, had their heads removed and brought to Gideon's trophy room. Again Israel had called upon the Lord, and deliverance had come.

Chap.
8

The people of Lubbock[1] then became a little jealous of Gideon and his success and they complained to him saying, "Why didn't you

[1]Ephraim

tell us that you were going to make a move against the Dalton gang and the ruffians from Odessa and we would have helped you and been included in the glory?"

Gideon had apparently become a very wise man for he replied to them, "What I have done is nothing compared to what you have been doing in your area. While I was working on the Dalton gang and their allies you did a marvelous job of irrigating and planting, and there is more glory due to you than to me." This made the people of Lubbock satisfied[1].

When Gideon called his original 300 men together he found them hungry, thirsty, and worn out from chasing bandits. As a result he asked the mayor of San Angelo[2] if he would see that his men were fed and given proper rest and treatment.

The mayor said, "Nuts to you. We don't feed stray armies."

Gideon replied, "All right, Mac, we will move along for we have to consolidate our victory and move further north, but on the way back as we come marching through with our whole army we are going to stomp your little city into the dust, and just to add to your worries we will bring thorns and briers and scratch you to bits personally."

The next town was Sterling City[3] from which Gideon received the same reply when asking for food and shelter. Gideon then said to the leaders of Sterling City, "When I come back through with my army you can say goodbye to that big new water tank you have built, for we will pull it to the ground."

After Gideon had consolidated his army and finished the complete defeat of all the Dalton gang and all their allies he returned as he had promised and he tore down the water tower of Sterling City and when he came to San Angelo he sought out the City Council Members and one or two from the school board who had all been designated as the ones responsible for the unwillingness to feed his 300 men, and he captured these persons and took them out on the edge of the city and used briers and cactus thorns to scratch them until they had thoroughly agreed that they had learned a good lesson.

After all these things had happened the people of Israel came to Gideon and asked him to be their ruler and upon his death for his son to be their ruler.

Gideon replied, "I will not rule over you, neither will my son, but the Lord God of Israel will rule over you. However, I will represent him. First, however, I want every man to bring some gold to be put

---

[1]Recommended reading for congress   [2]Succoth
[3]Penuel

in the treasury of the church." It was done. This became a great source of trouble for Gideon as he made no attempt to have this money used, and though his intention was good as an act of worship, the temple funds became a great temptation for thieves.

Gideon had many wives and many children from them, and also a few children from some ladies that he did not quite get around to marrying, but he ruled Israel with justice and there was peace in the land for about forty years, and then Gideon died.

Chap.
9

Again the children of Israel did evil in the sight of the Lord and they were without a great leader for among the many sons of Gideon none had arisen in a godly fashion to lead the people.

Finally one of the sons of Gideon[1], a man named Kaiser[2], called a family reunion and made a little speech to all the other male kinsmen and reminded them that it was impossible for all of them to rule Israel and that he knew it was a tough and dangerous job, but if none of them wanted to do it, he would do it himself.[3]

The family decided that maybe this was best and Kaiser passed his hat among the crowd and collected enough money to get his program going.

After everyone had returned to his own home, Kaiser employed a small band of hoods[4], and contracted with them to go and kill all his uncles and the remaining grandsons of Gideon so that there would be no problem as to which of Gideon's descendents would rule[5]. The hoods killed all on the list except Aesop[6].

Kaiser was then officially made king and began to rule over a large portion of the children of Israel.

Aesop came out of hiding and gathered a big crowd and told them a fable saying, "The trees were doing nicely but they felt that there should be one of them to establish rules and be their king, so they went first to the olive tree and the olive tree said, 'I am sorry, but I don't care to leave my fatness, which honors both me and God.'

Then the trees went to the fig tree and the fig tree said, 'Should I forsake my sweetness and good fruit just for a little recognition?'

The trees then went to the grapevine and said, 'come reign over us', but the vine said, 'why should I leave my wine, which cheereth God and man, just to get promoted and cheered a bit?''

Finally then the trees went to the bramble bush and said, 'what

---

[1]Probably a grandson   [2]Abimelech
[3]He also was the only one who came to the reunion with a sword
[4]Hit men   [5]Also another family reunion would not be necessary.
[6]Jotham

about you reigning over us?'

The bramble replied, 'I will, but if you allow me to reign over you, put your trust in me and agree to live in my shadow, I warn you, that if you turn against me and try to destroy me with fire all the trees will burn along with me.'

"Just think about this," continued Aseop, "for you have put the Bramble Kaiser as your king and he has already choked his own family to death except for me. I tell you now, that when the fire starts, you'll all burn along with ole Bramble Kaiser."[1]

After making this speech, Aesop fled to the hills and stayed hidden in faraway caves.[2]

Needless to say, the people began to fret under the reign of the evil Kaiser and various plots began to develop to overthrow his rule.

The first leader of a rebellion was a man named Big Mouth Lee[3] and he gathered a half-pint sized army and moved into the city of Rochester.

Big Mouth made several speeches saying primarily, "Would to God the people would elect me king instead of ole Bramble Kaiser." Now the mayor of Rochester wasn't real sure how all this would work and he decided to play it safe and sent word to Kaiser about Big Mouth and suggested that he bring his army and then fight Lee's outfit on the plains in front of the Rochester gates.

The mayor of Rochester on the appointed morning[4] stood in front of the gate of the city with Big Mouth Lee when the army of Kaiser began coming down the mountain sides.

"What are those people doing coming down the mountain?" asked Big Mouth.

"I think those are shadows," said the mayor.

"Here come a company of soldiers down the valley. They ain't no shadows," said Big Mouth.

"Where is your mouth now, Lee?" asked the mayor, "didn't I hear you say 'who is ole Bramble Kaiser that we should serve him?' Aren't these the soldiers you despise? You wanted to fight you said, so now is your big chance."

Bramble Kaiser and his well organized army defeated Big Mouth and killed many people in the process.

Bramble Kaiser then decided that the Mayor of Rochester[5] was not to be trusted and he attacked the city and leveled it to the ground. Some of the leaders of the people who had been opposed to the Kaiser anyway hid in a tower and Bramble learned of this; so he went and cut down a tree and told his followers to do the same and

[1]The basic problem in our own politics   [2]Probably writing fables
[3]Gaal   [4]Kaiser had sent him a time schedule
[5]Zebul

then he placed the logs at the foot of the tower and had a big bonfire featuring toasted mayor and councilmen.

Kaiser heard of another place that was rebellious called Houston[1] and he stormed the walls of this city and the people fled to a high tower in the middle of the city. Bramble decided that this would be a good place to have another bonfire. As he was standing at the foot of the tower thinking about this matter, Belle Starr[2] took a large stone and dropped it four stories down for a direct hit on Kaiser's head. It knocked him down and he was flat on his back looking bug-eyed at the laughing girl and so he turned to his trusty armour-bearer and said, "Take your sword and kill me. I couldn't stand to be killed by a woman."[3]

The armour-bearer obeyed immediately.[4] The army then disbanded and everybody went home. The wickedness of Bramble Kaiser had brought his own violent end.

Chap.
10

There then came into the leadership position of Israel a man named Cool Cal[5] and he ruled Israel under God and in peace, and he practically said nothing, and there was peace during the twenty-three years of his reign. Then came Woodrow[6] and he was a good man and judged Israel well for twenty-two years, and then he died.

Following this time, the children of Israel did evil again in the sight of the Lord, and began chasing foreign women and worshipping Baal, and putting the Lord further and further from their thoughts. The anger of the Lord was again aroused and he caused them to fall into the hands of their enemies, who oppressed the Israelites mightily for eighteen years.

Finally, the children of Israel cried again unto the Lord and admitted their sins.

The Lord spoke to them and said, "Did I not deliver you from the Egyptians, the James gang, the Dalton boys, and countless others, yet you always turned back to strange gods, such as Baal. Why don't you pray to them? See if the strange gods will deliver you."

"We deserved that, O Lord," cried the Israelites, "we have sinned and we repent. Please help us." After this prayer they put away the strange gods and served the Lord. The Lord was impressed and he grieved for the afflictions of his people.

The Moscow Muggers[7] gathered together and decided to take advantage of Israel and they camped with their army near Israel. The

[1]Thebez
[3]The disgrace would kill him
[5]Tola
[2]Actually we don't have the girl's name
[4]Kaiser was known as a poor tipper
[6]Jair
[7]Ammonites

children of Israel then said, "Who will lead us against the Moscow Muggers? Anybody who will lead us we will make a judge of Israelites in this area."

There was born in Baldwin[1] county in Israel a man named Big Jake[2], who was a mighty man of valour, strong and courageous, but he also happened to be an illegitimate child. As a result, the brothers and sisters all began to shun him and he was deprived of his portion of the inheritance from his father and the county officials and local gendarmes had him driven out of the county.

It came to pass in time that the Moscow Muggers became active again and began to harass and threaten to take over Baldwin County. The county leaders finally swallowed their pride and went to find Big Jake and asked him to come back and help them.

Big Jake said, "What goes on? Didn't you hate me, and expel me from the county, why come to me now?"

"We've changed our minds. We want you to be our leader for the Moscow Muggers are about to take us to the cleaners."

"All right, but it must be understood that if I come and the Lord delivers the muggers into my hand, then I shall be the new chairman of the county."

"With God as our witness, we agree."

Big Jake then returned and organized for himself a tough outfit and then he presented his cause to the Lord God of Israel at the holy place of Mt. Wesley.[3]

Big Jake then sent messengers to the muggers asking them why they were trying to make war against him. The muggers wrote back saying that they were merely trying to take again the land that was originally theirs[4]. All you have to do is restore our land and we will be happy and peaceful.

Big Jake then wrote back a long letter explaining about the whole trip from Egypt and how Moses had asked the people of Baldwin County to let his people pass through and he would not harm them or take their land, but the county commissioners would not allow this and Israel had to take the long way around Baldwin. Big Jake also said that Moses at the time had said that one day they would pay for this and their refusal of peace at the beginning meant that one of these days Israel would come and capture the land. This was done and God ordered it. The land is ours by order of the Lord, and so what claim can you possibly make? Why didn't you do like good neighbor Sam[5] and let Israel alone and live in peace with the people? Instead of that you chose war and lost, and I strongly suggest that

---

[1]Gilead   [2]Jephthah   [3]Mizpeh
[4]Makes you think about the Indians   [5]Balak

you don't try war again."

But Marx[1] would not listen to this reasoning and made preparation for war against Baldwin County and Big Jake.

Big Jake then prayed to the Lord and made a promise to God saying that if the Lord would grant him a great victory over the muggers that when Big Jake returned in peace to his home town that he would sacrifice whatsoever living thing he first met in sight of his home.[2]

So Big Jake and his band engaged in battle with the muggers and the Lord delivered them into his hands and they chased the muggers as far as Pensacola, Brewton, Atmore, and Greenville, and about 16 more places.

Then Big Jake returned, and to his horror and amazement his daughter came running to meet him, singing and dancing and welcoming him home as a hero, and she was his only child.

When Big Jake saw her he came to pieces, and began to tear his clothes and to moan and lament. Big Jake said, "I have opened my mouth unto the Lord and I cannot relent."

"Father", said the daughter, "If you have made a promise to God about me, you must put God first and fulfill the promise."

Big Jake explained to her what he had promised God and she said, "All right. I will be sacrificed willingly, but first let me go and have a couple of months in the hills to pray and prepare myself, and let me take a couple of my young girl friends with me so that we may lament my fate together."

Big Jake agreed. At the end of the two months she returned and Big Jake sacrificed her to the Lord, according to his vow to the Lord.[3]

Chap.
12

There was a big tribe of people many miles south of Big Jake in his county who heard of his victory over the muggers and they became very angry for not being included, for they could have been in on the plunder, and the money confiscated, and the women captured.

As a result, they brought their forces near to the camp of Big Jake and filed their complaint.

"Your memories are too short," said Big Jake. "In the first place, you never raised a hand when I was thrown out of my own family. What is more, I sent word that we could use more help against the muggers but you thought we'd get a licking; so go jump in the lake."

---

[1]Chief of the muggers   [2]Naturally he figured on one of his cows
[3]This is one of the tough parts to explain. Big Jake was no doubt miserable the rest of his life. What about the mother?

After a few more exchanges like this the armies engaged in battle. The army of Big Jake was victorious and they captured the crossing places along the Jordan. Since there were no uniforms for identification, Big Jake's men guarding the crossing places had difficulty identifying fleeing members of the army until one of the smart boys gave them a good plan. At each crossing place, the representatives of Big Jake would say to every man that came to cross, "What number follows thirteen?"

Those who said "fourteen" were allowed to cross but those who said "foteen" were killed, for their accent betrayed their home county.

Big Jake then judged Israel for six years in peace before he died. Following him were a number of judges of no particular consequence, but they were men of faith and they kept the people mindful of their responsibility to the Lord and his commandments.

Chap.
13

The children of Israel could never make it apparently for more than about 50 or 60 years on the right path, for again they began to do evil in the sight of the Lord, and succumb to greed and worship false gods. As a result the Lord delivered them into the hands of the Fascists[1] and the Fascists controlled them and kept them in submission for forty years.

Again the prayers of some of the faithful touched the heart of God and he sent an angel to appear before a woman named Jean who had no children and was married to a man named Dempsey[2].

The angel said to Jean, "I know you are barren and without child, but you shall soon be pregnant. Take good care of yourself, do not drink any wine or strong drink and be very careful about eating. Your child shall be a boy, and you are not to cut his hair, for this is to be a sign and symbol of the power which God is going to bestow on your son, for he shall deliver Israel."

That night Jean told Dempsey about the man from God and what he had said; so Dempsey then prayed to God and asked the Lord to send the man back to talk to him, as he wanted some instructions about rearing the child.

The angel of the Lord again appeared to Jean, and she ran and got Dempsey and said to him, "Here's that man again."

Dempsey came and spoke to the man and said, "Are you the fellow that talked to my wife?"

"I am," replied the man.

"How about some instructions," said Dempsey.

---

[1]Philistines   [2]Manoah

"There are no further instructions. Just let Jean observe the things I told her."

"Fine. Now will you stay for dinner. We will kill a goat and I'll barbeque some delicious cabrito."

"No, even if I stayed I wouldn't eat. Any offering you make must be to the Lord."

Now Dempsey was not at all of the opinion that this man was an angel; so he said to him, "We really haven't officially met. My name is Dempsey, what is your name?"

"Sorry about that, but my name is a secret."

Dempsey then took the goat and offered a sacrifice to the Lord and as this was taking place the words and expressions of the angel were impressive on Dempsey and Jean. Then as the flame from the fire ascended toward the heavens the angel of the Lord entered the flames and ascended out of sight. Dempsey and Jean then fell on their knees and worshipped and the man did not appear again, and they both knew that he was an angel of the Lord.

Dempsey was really shook up, and said to Jean, "We will surely die, for we have seen God."

"I don't think so, Demps", said Jean, "for I think if the Lord was going to kill us he would not have accepted our worship service. The funeral always comes after you die, not before."

Shortly Jean became pregnant and in the normal time had a son and they named him Samson, and the child grew, and the Lord blessed him, and the spirit of the Lord made him a restless one.

Chap.
14

Young, powerful, restless Samson wandered about the country, and he saw a beautiful girl in Atlantic City[1]. When he returned home he told his father and mother that he had seen the most beautiful girl in the world and he wanted his folks to go and get her for him.[2]

"There are some real sweet girls here near home, daughters of some of our friends, why don't you let us talk to them? This girl you want is a Fascist," complained the mother and father.

Samson said, "Get the Fascist girl for me."

Now the mother and father did not know that this affair was the working of the Lord, for the Lord was seeking a way to get carefree Samson turned against the Fascist.

After some more huffing and puffing on both sides, the father, mother, and Samson all started to Atlantic City to make arrangements for Samson to marry.

Samson moved a great deal faster than his parents and he was a

[1]Timnath   [2]Parents made the proposals in those days

couple of miles ahead of them when he encountered a young lion in the path. The spirit of the Lord came upon him, and he was also pretty full of himself, and he killed the young lion with his bare hands. He did not tell his parents of this, but went ahead and found the girl and had a big time with her.

Arrangements were made, and some weeks later Samson returned for the formal wedding services, which would be under the Fascist system. Enroute this time to Atlantic City Samson saw the carcass of the lion he had killed and the bees had made a hive and there was honey in the carcass; so Samson took some of it and ate and then gave some to his parents to eat, who were going with him to the wedding.

The father and mother of Samson visited with the girl and her people and discussed the wedding plans while Samson went to the bachelor dinner. Since none of Samson's friends had come with him, about thirty friends of the bride came to the feast.

Samson stood up at the feast and said, "I am a betting man. I'll bet you 30 to 1 that I can propose a riddle you can't solve, and I'll give you seven days to get the answer. If you solve the riddle I'll give you each a new suit of clothes and a shirt, and if you can't, each of you must give me one."

"It's a deal. Tell us the riddle," said the companions.

"Out of the eater came forth meat, and out of the strong came forth sweetness."

The Fascists were completely baffled and finally it came down to the seventh day, six days after the wedding and they went to Samson's wife and said, "Entice your husband. Find out the answer to the riddle and tell us, or we will burn you and your father's house to the ground. We can't stand to pay off the bet."

So Samson's wife was on the spot, and she came to Samson and began crying and saying, "You don't love me anymore. You have put a riddle to my friends and you have not told me anything about it."

Samson said, "I haven't told it to my father and mother either and I love them, what's so important about a riddle?"

Samson's wife continued weeping and begging. At last Samson told her just to shut her up, and she told her friends and they came to Samson with the answer, "What is sweeter than honey or stronger than a lion."

Samson said, "You got your information from my wife."

Samson was extremely furious and the spirit of the Lord then descended upon him and accentuated his strength, and he went forth on the board walk at Atlantic City and everytime he came to a fascist he knocked him down and choked him to death, then he took off his

suit and his shirt, and he continued until he had slain thirty men and
had the pay-off for his bet. Then he took the clothes to the friends
of his wife and he left Atlantic City in a rage and returned to his own
home.
    The father of Samson's wife was frantic[1] and he gave
Samson's wife to the best man at the wedding, claiming desertion by
Samson as the equivalent of divorce.[2]

    Sure enough, about nine months later the Atlantic City Belle
had a baby and Samson heard about it and decided to visit his wife.
When Samson knocked on the door, however, the old man wouldn't
let him enter and said, "When you left here so mad I didn't think
you would ever come back, I gave my daughter to one of the local
lads. However, the younger sister is still single and she's a beaut and
I'll be glad to let you marry her."
    Samson left again mad, saying to himself that now the trick
he planned to play on the Fascists would be justified. After this
Samson began to set snares for fox and after some months he had
finally caught 300 of them and kept the foxes all penned up and well
fed.
    At harvest time, when all the standing grain of the Fascists
was ripe and dry and almost ready for gathering, Samson took the
foxes in pairs, tied their tails together with firebrands and set the
torches on fire, turning the foxes, 150 pair of them, loose in all the
grain fields around the country, with each pair furiously dragging a
burning torch. As a result, all the corn, and vineyards, and olive
orchards of the Fascists were completely destroyed.
    It did not take Nero Wolfe to find out who was responsible
and the Fascists then blamed one of their own, the father-in-law of
Samson, for causing all the trouble by giving away Samson's wife.
For vengeance then, they came and burned the father and the
Atlantic City Belle and their house. Samson heard of this and came
to town and killed every Fascist he could find for a couple of weeks,
and then departed feeling that he had evened things us a bit.
    The Fascist then became greatly worried about return visits
from Samson, as no three or four men were a match for him and his
tremendous strength.
    As a result, the Fascists organized a big posse and went to the
area where the tribe of Judah lived.
    "Why do you come with a posse into our area?" asked the
men of Judah.
    "We have come to get Samson, but if you don't turn Samson
over to us we'll turn on you."
    The men of Judah then voted to turn Samson over to the

[1]Odds are he figured she might turn up pregnant
[2]Legal with the Philistines

Fascist.

The men of Judah went to Samson's hideout on Old Smokey[1] and told him of their problem.

"I have only evened things up with the Fascists. They did a few things to me and I did a few things to them," said Samson.

"We are sorry, Samson, but we must bind your hands and turn you over to the Fascists."

"All right," replied Samson, "but promise me that if a fight starts you won't be on the Fascist side. Also don't bind my hands too tightly."

"Agreed. We will bind you and deliver you, but we will not harm you," said the men of Judah.

As a result, Samson came down from Old Smokey and came near to the Fascist posse. At this time the spirit of the Lord came upon Samson and cords binding his wrists seemed only as threads, and he broke them easily, and seeing a hockey stick lying near the roadside he seized it and began killing Fascists as fast as he could get to them. Samson kept his weapon and he continued for several months killing Fascists everytime he could catch one, until he had killed one thousand, which was his goal.

After this he threw away his weapon and went to a beach resort for a little rest praying to God and saying, "You have done a great thing for me and given me a great victory, but I'm tired and thirsty and I have no energy left."

God then caused a healing water to spout forth from the weapon which lay where he had dropped it and he drank from this, and rested and was revived.

For the next twenty years he ruled and judged Israel without any trouble from the Fascists.

Chap. 16

The Fascists were always trying to get Samson but they knew they would have to catch him alone in their territory. Samson's weakness for women gave the opportunity as he had a lady friend in Reno[2] and the Fascists decided to lock the gates of the city while Samson was courting and then catch him in the morning. Some of the girls heard of this and slipped word to Samson; so instead of staying all night, he left his girl at midnight and tore down the gates of the city as well as the posts holding the gates and carried the debris to the top of the nearest hill.

Samson next began to court a lady named Delilah. Delilah was no green kid and Samson was in hog heaven with this affair.

The Fascists, however, came to Delilah and offered her some choice diamonds to do a little sabotage work for them and learn of the source of Samson's strength. In a few minutes she got them to add $5,000 in cash.

[1]Etam   [2]Gaza

As a result, Delilah asked Samson about his strength, and if there was anyway that he could be captured[1].

Samson said, "Come to think of it, if I were bound by green grapevines that had never dried, I'd be as weak as anybody else."

Delilah naturally passed the information along and was given seven green vines. At the first opportunity[2], Delilah let Samson go soundly to sleep and then she tied him with the green vines. Arrangements had been made for men to be in hiding in the house at the time, and Delilah came and awakened Samson saying, "The Fascists are here, wake up."

At this juncture the Fascist came running out of the closet, and Samson broke the green vines as if they were light string and laid out a Fascist or two before they could escape.

Delilah then began to tease Samson and to put on the pout act for his not telling her the truth about his strength.

"Well, I had to have a little fun, but if I'm bound with new rope, I can't do a thing."

The same song, second verse; Delilah bound him when he was asleep, men were hiding in the closests, and when she said, "The Fascists are here", Samson broke the new ropes and banged on a few Fascists.[3]

Delilah was really hot about this, as she was getting in trouble with the Fascists and she didn't like Samson having fun at her expense; so she pleaded with him again.

This time Samson told her to tie his long hair to the beam supporting the house and he would be helpless.

This time the Fascist decided to wait outside and not show up unless the trick worked. Needless to say, Delilah gave Samson the usual treatment of food, wine, and love, and then when he was asleep she tied his hair to the pin beam at the corner of the house. Again she cried, "Samson, the Fascists are here." Samson jumped up and pulled the pin and the beam out and went looking for Fascists, but found only tracks this time.

Delilah did not give up a minute as she really wanted the bonus money. In fact, she kept nagging Samson for the truth, and daily worked on him until he couldn't stand it any longer.[4]

Finally, Samson broke down and told Delilah that his strength came from God, and that the symbol of his strength was his long hair, for it had never been cut as a sign of his faithfulness.

Delilah realized that this was the real thing and she sent word to the Fascist rulers and told them they could come safely.[5] After

---

[1]Delilah could purr

[2]Indications are that Samson may have actually been living with Delilah at this time.

[3]Fascist volunteers were beginning to have to be appointed.

[4]It never occurred to him to give up Delilah

[5]And to bring the money

Delilah had given Samson the full treatment and he had fallen asleep she let his head rest against her knees and then signaled to the barber to come in and cut off Samson's hair.

Delilah herself then began to push on Samson to test his strength and she realized that his power was gone; so she called for the Fascist and they entered the house when she said, "Samson, the Fascist are here."

Samson thought that he would go out as before and knock a few heads around sideways, for he did not realize that the Lord had departed from him. The Fascists seized Samson, bound him, and then burned out both his eyes, and took him to the outskirts of Reno and tied him to a grist mill in place of a donkey and he began to grind grain all day in the grist mill.

During this time, however, the hair began to grow again on Samson's head, and he became thoughtfully repentant.

Meantime, the Fascists decided to have a giant Fiesta to celebrate their victory and to dedicate the celebration to Dracula[1], who was their favorite god at the time. The Fascists all rejoiced saying that their god had delivered Samson into their hands and they began to build a large covering supported by two huge central pillars, and under this cover they were to stage the big celebration, with drinking, dancing and merry making.

After about 3 years the building was finished and during this time Samson had been regaining his strength and had sought forgiveness from God.

The day of the celebration the people insisted that Samson be brought to the Sport's Center in order that they might mock him.

Samson was led into the center by a young lad and Samson said to him, "Lead me to the center of the arena in order that I might hold on to the pillars in the middle on which the whole structure is built."

Now the place was full of men and women and the leaders of the Fascists were there, and there were three thousand men and women on the roof[2].

Then Samson called upon the Lord saying, "Remember, O God, I pray you to strengthen me this one more time. I know I'll die, but give me strength to avenge myself and defy the Fascists and their false god."

Then Samson took hold of the two middle pillars, one with his right arm and one with his left, and he cried, "Lord, let me die with the Fascists," and he pulled with all his strength and the house began to shake and it came tumbling down upon all the people so that in his death Samson killed more people even than he had during his lifetime.

Samson's family came and found his body and gave him a christian burial.

[1]Dagon   [2]This helped

Chap.
17

There was a man who grew up in Israel named Mickey Creep[1] and his mother had $1,500.00 hidden, and it turned up missing. The mother did a great deal of cursing about this, and was very suspicious that Mickey might be responsible.

One day Mickey came to his mother and said, "Mama, I took the $1500.00. I've decided that I shouldn't have done it and I'm returning it to you."

"You're a fine boy, Mickey," said his mother. "Actually, I had saved the money to use some of it for some idols to put around the house, and the rest was in appreciation for you as a son; so I'm giving you the $1500 back." Mickey would not take the money, however.

His mother then took $300 and went to a sculpturer who made her a graven image for her house, which became the house of Mickey shortly, as the mother passed away.

Mickey then began to collect idols so that his house was a house of graven images, and in those days there was no leader in Israel, but every man did his thing just as he thought was proper in his own way.[2]

It so happened that a young seminary student was wandering around the country and he stopped by the house of Mickey to see all the idols.

"Where are you from?" asked Mickey.

"Austin Seminary[3]," replied the young man, "and I'm just looking for a pastorate or the like."

"Well, just stay here," said Mickey, "you can be a father and a priest to me[4] and I'll give you room, board, and $4,000 a year."

"You just secured a father and a priest," said the preacher.

The arrangement worked well, and the preacher made a favorable impression on Mickey and Mickey decided things would go well with him, and that the Lord would bless him for having a priest in his home.

Chap.
18

There was no king or judge in Israel at this time and the tribe of Dan decided to expand a bit and they dispatched five brave men to go on a scouting expedition and to meet together after their wanderings at the house of Mickey Creep on top of Nob Hill[5].

When the five arrived finally at Mickey's house they recognized the priest and began to question him about what he was doing and why he was living here in Mickey's house.

"Mickey offered me a job and I'm here as his father and pastor," said Phil[6] the priest.

"Father Phil, tell us if the Lord is with us on our endeavor

[1]Micah   [2]It just won't work   [3]Bethlehem—Judah
[4]I think Mickey needed both   [5]Ephraim   [6]I never did learn his name

and if we are doing the right thing."

"The Lord is with you and you will succeed," said Father Phil.

The five men noticed the people in the surrounding area, how careless and free they seemed to be, without any law and order, and they returned to their tribe and reported saying, "Let us get up and move against the people of Lazyburg[1] for the land is good and we can take over the place without difficulty."

As a result, they gathered a vigilante type outfit of 600 men and started on the march to Lazyburg. On the trip, they came fairly close to Nob Hill and Mickey's house. While chatting at a coffee break one of the five original spies said, "Do you fellows know that in a house near here there are great treasures. Mickey Creep has been assembling all kinds of valuables, including antique jewelry, not to mention a few graven images. Don't you think we ought to do something about this?"

As a result, they marched the 600 men by Mickey's house and they spoke to Father Phil and then the five scouts went into the house and began to remove all the treasures.

"What are you doing?" asked Phil[2].

"Now Father, just calm down. Mickey isn't home and all you need to do is cover your mouth with your hand[3] and join us as our priest. Isn't it a big promotion to move from a church with only one in the congregation to one that has 600?"

This suited Father Phil fine and he even helped to carry the graven images and some of the loot.

After they had departed some of the neighbors of Mickey Creep got together and came with Mickey to regain his possessions. When they caught up with the 600 men of Dan, the men of Dan turned to Mickey and said, "What's the matter with you, you look pale and angry?"

"You have taken my gods, stolen my treasure, and gone off with my preacher, what more can I say? You ask me what is wrong, you must be nuts."

"Now calm down," said one of the leaders of Dan, "for if you and your friends get noisy some of these 600 men might just start a big killing."

When Mickey realized that they were too heavily outnumbered he returned in sorrow to his house.

The 600 men of Dan proceeded to Lazyburg and smote it with the edge of their swords and burned out a great portion of it, capturing most of the people. Then they established themselves there, and renamed the town Dan.

They set up here the graven images that had been stolen from Mickey.

---

[1]Laish   [2]Fairly silly question   [3]high class way of saying "shutup"

There was still no king or judge in Israel, but there was a circuit riding minister who had a woman with him who was his common-law wife, and her name was Lullabelle[1].

Lullabelle became a bit weary of the tent meetings and she ran away and went back to her father. The minister went after her in a few days to talk her into joining him again.

When Sig[2] arrived at his so-called father-in-law's house he was welcomed by the father of his girl. In fact, they enjoyed each other so eating and drinking and telling jokes that the father of Lullabelle kept Sig around for over a week, but finally he left, and Lullabelle went with him.[3]

After a long journey they came near the city of Saigon[4] and the servant said, "Let us go into Saigon and spend the night."

"Not a chance," said Sig, "for it is no place for a stranger and it is not a city of Israel. We will go to Tel Aviv[5], for it is a city of Israel."

As a result, the servant, the donkeys, Sig, and Lullabelle entered Tel Aviv, but no one would give them lodging for the night.

Finally, an old man came and saw them sitting on the curb and he said, "What's the trouble, Mac?"

"We can find no lodging," said Sig, "even though this is a city of Israel."

"Come stay at my place. I'll be glad to have you," said the kindly old man.

After they were settled in the old man's house, however, some of the local hoodlums who had been drinking came knocking on the door. They called out to the old man saying, "We know you have some strangers in there. Send the man out as we want to chase him up and down the street and have a little sport as we don't want strangers around here."

"I will not do it." said the old man. "This man is under my care by law. I know you are a wild bunch though and if it will keep the peace, I'll let you have my daughter and this visitor's traveling girl friend and you can frolick with them."

The men claimed there were plenty women they could chase.

Sig, however, figured they hadn't seen anybody as desirable as Lullabelle; so he pushed her out the door, reluctantly, but to save his life and the old man's. As a result the men began to abuse Lullabelle, and they took turns, continuing all through the night.

At dawn, when Sig opened the front door, Lullabelle was lying on the threshold, dead from mistreatment. Sig carried her into the old man's house. Then Sig took a knife and cut Lullabelle into twelve pieces and sent one piece to each of the twelve tribes of

---

[1]Tribe of Bethlehem-Judah   [2]A Levite, I'm not certain about the Sig
[3]no indication of enthusiam reported   [4]Jebus   [5]Gibeah

Israel[1]. It was generally agreed that this was the biggest news story of the year. The message with each body piece said "Think about this happening in Israel."

This incident caused a great furor and the representatives and many others from all the tribes from Maine[2] to California[3] gathered together and held a great convention with 400,000 men carrying swords present[4].

Then Sig stood before the whole crowd and told the grisly story and said, "All Israel is disgraced by this. What shall we do?"

The people shouted with great fury and they took a pledge saying that no one would go home until the matter was settled and the wrong avenged.

It was decided to take ten men out of every hundred, using the lottery system, with a thousand selected to provide food for the trip, and all the people of Israel were united for this cause.

As a result, a message was sent to the tribe of Benjamin saying, "Send us the men who were guilty of this crime that we may put them to death and take such evil out of Israel."

The tribe of Benjamin refused to do this, and so they gathered themselves together to do battle with the other tribes. The other tribes had agreed to take vengeance one tribe at a time and the Lord[5] chose Judah to go first.

Now the tribe of Benjamin and all the people from Tel Aviv made a big army, but the tribe of Benjamin had trained 700 left-handed experts with stone slingers[6] and when the armies engaged there was a mighty battle, but the victory went to the tribe of Benjamin.

The children of Israel gathered themselves again and prayed to the Lord, asking if they should go against their brother tribe of Benjamin and the Lord said, "Go."

The second day of battle was another victory for the tribe of Benjamin and that evening the armies of Israel again appeared before the Lord and wept and fasted and prayed earnestly, again asking if they should try another time.

This time the Lord said, "Go up against Benjamin, and I will deliver them into your hands. This time the command of the army of Israel was given to Patton[7]. Patton first placed soldiers in ambush during the night close to the city of Tel Aviv and when in the morning the army of Benjamin came forth to do battle they were overconfident. As Patton had instructed, the first line was to begin fleeing in various directions and as Patton figured the Benjamin outfit scattered in their chase.

[1]This may be where obscene mail started.   [2]Dan   [3]Beersheba
[4]Sounds worse than used car salesman convention
[5]Possibly through the lottery   [6]This was like using a secret weapon
[7]Phinehas

Then when the army of Benjamin was scattered in every direction chasing the fastest runners of Israel, the organized army of Patton arose from close to the city and the Lord was with Israel and while this was happening the original ambush group moved into Tel Aviv and set it afire. When those left fighting for the tribe of Benjamin looked back and saw the burning city they knew they were doomed and defeated.

What men were left of the tribe of Benjamin fled into Mexico[1] and about 600 men made it safely across the border.

Meanwhile, the army of Israel under Patton, since it was already doing well, destroyed a few more cities and made a few more conquests before going home, and for kicks they set fire to all the cities they passed on the way home[2].

Chap.
21

Now at the big convention in Israel another pledge which the people made was that they wouldn't let one of their daughers marry a member of the tribe of Benjamin.

After everybody had cooled down and had been home, some of the people began to lament that on the present basis there would never be 12 tribes of Israel again and this meant changing the flag and other things. The people presented the matter before the Lord and they worshipped God and began to bemoan the loss of the tribe of Benjamin, all because of Lullabelle.

Since everyone had sworn not to let a daughter marry a Benjamite, one of the men of Israel came up with a bright idea. The man's name was Ford[3], and he spoke saying, "I have a better idea than lamenting. There is a town about forty miles from here that has a lot of fine women in it and I suggest that we send 10,000 of our best troops under Patton and let them go and capture 400 young girls and bring them safely to us. Then we can take these girls to the 600 men of Benjamin hiding in Mexico[4] and the tribe of Benjamin can be started again and this will help heal the bad feelings among us."

This motion was seconded and passed unanimously and was done.

Word was sent to the 600 men and the time was set at one of the regular feast days and the plan was to turn the 400 girls loose to dance in the vineyards and the men of Benjamin could come and any girl a man caught he could marry.

Everything worked according to plan and the people all returned to their homes. There was still no king or judge in Israel, and the people operated on a basis of doing whatever seemed right to each man in his own way.

---

[1]Rimmon   [2]Their mothers said "boys will be boys"
[3]Not sure about this name   [4]600 girls would have been an even better idea

RUTH

Years rolled by under various judges and then there came a great famine in the land. There was a sheepherder named Sim[1] and his wife Nan[2] who had two sons, Charles[3] and Walter[4], and they took what sheep they had left and went to Mississippi[5] where they had been told that there was land and grass.

It wasn't long before the boys fell in love with a couple of the Dixie Belles, named Pamela and Ruth.

Not long after this Sim died and then a couple of years later the two sons were killed in an accident[6], which left Nan with two daughters-in-law and no property rights.

Word had also come that the famine was over back home and so the three ladies started to travel back to Judah.

Nan then turned to the two girls and said, "I think it would be better if each of you returned to your mother's house and I will give you my blessing. You were good wives to my sons and you've been good to me, but there is no reason for you to leave your home state. I hope you will find new husbands and a happy home and I hope the Lord will bless you both."

At this point all three began to cry.

"We will see you safely to your own country," said both of the girls.

"It just isn't sensible. I have no more sons for you to marry. I'm too old to find another husband and if I did and became pregnant next week with twins it would be twenty years before you could marry them. It grieves me, for I love you both as if you were my own flesh and blood, but I cannot have you waste your life on an old lady."

This brought on another short period of shedding tears.

Pamela then kissed her mother-in-law, thanked her, and headed home, but Ruth stayed with Nan.

"You'd better go to your own people and your own way of life," said Nan.

"Please don't ask me to leave," said Ruth, "for wherever you go I want to go, where you live I want to live, your people I want to have as my people, and your God as my God. Where you die, there I want to die, and I want to be buried in the same cemetery with you, and I pledge before God that nothing but death shall ever separate us."

Nan realized the sincerity of the statement and she argued no further, so the two of them headed for Bethlehem.

When they arrived in Bethlehem some of the old friends gathered around and said, "Are you really Nan, Sim's wife that left here so many years ago?"

[1]Elimelech   [2]Naomi   [3]Mahlon
[4]Chilion   [5]Moab   [6]chariot drag?

"Yes," said Nan, "but don't call me Nan anymore, call me "Bitterweed",[1] for the Lord has been rough on me. I left here with a full family, husband and two sons, and I return broke and tired and old, with my family dead in Mississippi."

It was harvest time in Bethlehem when Nan and Ruth arrived.

Now Sim, Nan's dead husband, had a cousin whose son had become very wealthy and owned many fields. His name was Bobo.[2]

Ruth said to Nan, "Let me go to the fields and begin to pick the corn and grain that the rich are required to leave for those who will work for it."

"Good idea," said Nan.

So Ruth went and stayed well behind the harvesters as she was required. She picked grain and by chance she chose to work in fields that belonged to Bobo.

Bobo came out from Bethlehem one day to check the work and he said to the harvesters working for him, "Howdy, and may the Lord bless you."

"Same to you, boss," they replied.

Bobo then spied Ruth bending over picking grain and he said to one of his servants, "Whose the doll on welfare?"

The head reaper said, "She is a Mississippi girl[3] and she asked properly for permission to pick the left overs. She came from Mississippi with her mother-in-law, Nan, after her husband was killed."

Bobo then went to Ruth and said, "Do not go to any other fields. Stay in my fields to do your picking. Stay also with the other girls that are reaping here."

Then Bobo turned to the foreman and said, "See to it that none of the young harvesters make any passes at that cute Ruth."

Then Bobo turned to Ruth and said, "When you are thirsty, drink from the barrels that are for my workers."

Ruth then did a little bow with a wiggle and said, "Why are you so kind to poor little ole me?"[4]

Bobo said, "The word has reached me about how hard you work and how good you have been to your mother-in-law. I also am told you have accepted the God of Israel and I hope that the Lord will reward you properly."

"I am anxious to please you for your kindness and for the great comfort that you and your words have brought me. You have been friendly to me even though I am not one of the regular girls, and I am deeply grateful."

Bobo then said, "Not only are you to drink from my barrels, but come to the chuck wagon and eat with my paid workers."

---

[1]Mara   [2]Boaz   [3]Even in those days some Mississippi girls were real beauties.   [4]Life is just like that for pretty girls.

Ruth did this and left for home that evening feeling fine.

The next day or so Bobo had a few more looks at Ruth, who was a real knockout, and he told the regular harvesters to let her gather grain anywhere and not just to pick up the left overs. In fact, Bobo told them to deliberately throw some grain her way and make it easy for her.

At the end of the day, Ruth had a record supply of grain to take home. Nan was tremendously impressed.

"Where did you scrounge for grain today?" saked Nan. "May the Lord bless any man that leaves that much for the poor."

"Well, Nan," said Ruth, "I worked in a field belonging to Bobo, a fine looking man."

"Hot ziggity-dog," squealed Nan, "The Lord has started giving us some breaks. The man is a kinsman and we just might get something going here."

"Well, Nan, he did tell the young men not to chase me around the field and he told me to stay with his regular girls who worked and not to mix with the men or go to other fields."

So Ruth continued working in the fields of Bobo until the harvest time was ended.

Chap.
3

Nan then said to Ruth, "It is time for me to do a little coaching as I want the best for you and I know the ways of dealing with men in this country, the customs, and the rights of the kinsmen."

"I'm all ears," said Ruth.

"Well, tonight is the big celebration of the harvest ending, when they have the eating, drinking, and dancing. First, we are going to give you a tip-to-toe bath, the right kind of perfume, and your snazziest dress, then off to the party."

As soon as Ruth was ready to go Nan said to her, "Now you stay in the background and don't let Bobo see you until he has fininshed eating and had a fair amount of wine. Then you watch when he goes in the big barn to lie down and snooze. Then you go and lie down beside him, take off his shoes, and lie up close to him. When he begins to wake up he'll know what to do."

"I'll do just like you say," replied Ruth.

Off to the party went Ruth and all worked according to plan. After ole Bobo had eaten and had a good bit of wine and was very merry with wine, he went into a corner of a corn bin and laid down among the shucks. Ruth came in and slipped off his shoes and lay close to him.

Bobo awoke about midnight and began to stir and was flabbergasted to find a woman with him.

"Who are you?" asked Bobo, a bit shakily.

"I am Ruth, one of your working girls. I'm the one from Mississippi and since we're sorta cousins you can spread the blanket over the two of us."

Bobo said, "Hurrah for you. You are a remarkable girl. I'm glad you didn't go off with one of the young harvesters tonight. Don't be afraid either of this circumstance, for everybody knows what a virtuous girl you are. Now it is true that I am remotely kin to you, but it so happens that there is a second cousin alive and I think I'm your third cousin; so according to our law the second cousin has first choice."

"We don't play that way in Mississippi," said Ruth.

"I know." said Bobo, "but I must first offer you to Clutch Midas, and if he will not marry you as next of kin, then I will. In the meantime, though, honey, just stay here with me until just before daylight and leave in the dark so no one will know that a woman has been with me all night."

"Just as you say, couz," replied Ruth.

As requested Ruth slipped out of the barn before it was light enough for anyone to see. She also took with her a sack of feed which Bobo gave her as a keepsake.

When Ruth came home Nan could hardly wait to hear all the details. When she saw the sack of grain she said, "You've got him for sure. I bet he will not rest until he has seen the next of kin and figured a way to keep you, but at least you'll get a husband one way or the other."

Chap.
4

The next day Bobo went early down to the courthouse square near the gate of the city and sat until he saw Clutch Midas. Bobo called to him and asked him for a conference, and he requested ten men to listen as witnesses; so there would be no misunderstanding.

"Clutch," said Bobo, "our cousin Sim left years ago and is dead and his widow has returned and claimed the small piece of ground that was Sim's. As you know, it must be offered to the next of kin, which is you, or then to me, before it can be offered publicly."

"Well, I'll buy the land," said Clutch.

"Of course, in fairness to you Clutch, I think I ought to tell you that when you buy the land you also get Nan, the widow. Furthermore, you get a girl she brought from Mississippi, and you'll have to support both of them for the rest of their lives."

"Yow!" cried Clutch. "Of all the things I don't need is a couple of more expensive women. You redeem it, Bobo. You aren't even married and it wouldn't hurt you to support a couple of women."

It was the custom in Israel at that time, that when a contract was made, the party of the first part took off his shoe and gave it to the party of the second part.[1] Clutch gave Bobo his left shoe.

Bobo then turned to the witnesses and said, "You are my witnesses. I have now accepted the responsibility of all that belonged to Sim, Charles and Walter. Furthermore, I have purchased Ruth

[1]Same as "OK it's a deal, let's shake."

for my wife."

"We are witnesses," said all the crowd standing around the gate.

"Good luck, Bobo," said one of the witnesses, "and I hope the Lord makes this Mississippi girl as good as Rachel and Leah, the two who really produced the tribes of Israel."

After this Ruth and Bobo were married and she gave him a son in the proper time.

The friends of Nan congratulated her on becoming a grandmother and told her how this would put new life in her. Nan was elated and she constantly looked out for the baby and kept him when Ruth and Bobo went on trips.

The Lord blessed this marriage and the devotion of Ruth and through her son came the lineage that brought forth King David and it was through this same descendancy that there was born Christ, the Lord.

I SAMUEL

There was a certain man from Birmingham whose name was Toby[1] and he had two legal wives, one was named Hannah and the other was named Penny.[2] Penny produced several sons and daughters[3] but Hannah had no children. Toby, however, particularly loved Hannah; so when he distributed the monthly allowances he gave freely to Hannah, though normally this would not have occurred in most families.

Penny, however, began to put the lip on Hannah and teased her about being childless, calling taunts to her and saying such things as "had any children today?"

This kept up year after year and finally Hannah could hardly eat because of her inferior feeling and the idea that she was good for nothing.

"What is the matter, Hannah?" asked Toby. "It is ridiculous to worry about not having kids. I treat you better than if you had ten sons. Lay off the moaning and groaning."

Actually, this made Hannah all the more anxious to have a son for her husband's sake; so she began to eat and drink again, and then she went to the temple and prayed earnestly to the Lord for help.

Father Eli, a grand old priest of the church, saw her enter the temple and observed her lips moving as if she was mumbling. Actually Hannah was making an arrangement with the Lord, agreeing that if the Lord would bless her with a son she would turn him into the church at an early age and let him grow up as a priest for the Lord.

Father Eli stopped Hannah as she left the temple, for he had observed her mumbling and her tears, and he said, "Hannah, you've got to quit hitting the bottle. How long have you been going too strong on the wine?"

"You are mistaken, Father Eli, I have touched neither wine or strong drink, but I have poured my problems out to the Lord. I have been speaking out of my sorrow, and not from drinking."

Then Father Eli said, "Peace to you. May the Lord God of Israel hear your prayers and grant your request."

"Thank you, Father," said Hannah, and she returned home refreshed and she began to eat and drink normally, and she was no longer a sour puss.

This change in attitude and brightness re-awakened Toby's interest and he again began to have intercourse with Hannah and she became pregnant, and in due time delivered a son and she called him Samuel.

When the time came for one of the regular occasions of going to

---

[1]Elkanah   [2]Peninnah   [3]A real status symbol

church[1] Hannah would not go and said to Toby, "I will stay and nurse the baby, for I will not go to church until he is old enough to be given to the Lord, and to live in church."

"All right," said Toby, "do what you think is right in the eyes of the Lord."

When Samuel was old enough to walk and talk and go to the potty by himself, Hannah took what she had been saving from her allowance and when the time came to go to church she took Samuel and her offering.

When Hannah presented Samuel to Father Eli she said, "Do you remember me? I am the woman who stood in the temple here a few years ago praying, and it was for this child that I prayed. The Lord has answered my prayer, therefore, I am doing as I promised and I bring him now to the temple, to turn him over to the Lord, for he is to grow up as a man of God."[2]

Chap. 2

Hannah then prayed a prayer of thanksgiving saying, "My heart rejoices. I have been blessed because I trusted in the Lord. There is none holy as the Lord, neither is there any rock or support like our God. Don't ever let me speak arrogantly again, for the Lord is a God of knowledge and of actions. The Lord knocks people down and raises them up, he helps the poor and the beggars, the very pillars of the earth are the Lord's and he has built the whole world.

No man will prevail by his own strength, for the Lord will light the path of the righteous and make dark the way of the wicked.

The opponents of God don't have a chance. The Lord shall rule the whole earth, and in his time he will thunder down upon the wicked."

So Hannah left Samuel at the church with Father Eli, and Samuel began to work around the church, helping with the sweeping, and looking out for Father Eli.

Father Eli had two sons of his own, both grown young men, and they began taking advantage of the people who brought offerings to the church, and they were actually stealing a portion of the offerings. This was a great sin, and the Lord was displeased.

Samuel, however, behaved himself and he grew and he learned as a child of God. Every time Samuel's mother came to church[3], she brought Samuel a new coat.

Father Eli also had a special kind word to say to Toby and Hannah and thanked them always for Samuel. After this Hannah had 3 sons and two daughters.

Now Father Eli began to become old and he was disturbed about what was happening with his grown sons, how they were

[1]Three times a year was all you went to church-how about that?
[2]Hannah may be No.1 in the kingdom
[3]Never more than 3 times a year, usually at the yearly feast.

taking from the offering, and how they were making love to various women in the congregation and said to them, "Why do you do these things? The word is that you are living in sin with some of our church women and taking advantage of teen-age girls. Now when you break one of man's laws you simply have to deal with man, but when you break God's law you must deal with God."

The young men paid no attention to their father.

Samuel, all the while, continued to grow in favor both with God and with the people with whom he came in contact.

There came then a man sent from God to Father Eli who said to him, "The Lord is displeased with your house. You have been faithful and a good priest, but your sons are hellions. God is still the Lord, it is the same Lord that delivered the people from Egypt, and this same Lord is a living Lord, and he will not have his offerings stolen and his house abused. As punishment, therefore, you are the end of the line as far as your family name is concerned. Your two sons, Snatch[1] and Wolf[2] shall both be killed at once, and I will raise up a new priesthood and the illegitimate grandsons of this house will have to come and beg bread in the welfare line at the church, and get the needy baskets at Thanksgiving."

Chap.
3

This was an ungodly time in Israel, and the word of the Lord was rarely studied and observed, but Samuel worshipped God. Now Eli was getting old, and his eyes were dim, and Samuel slept nearby to the old man on a cot so that he could be sure that the lamp of the Lord in the temple did not go out, as well as be an aid to Eli.

One night Samuel heard a voice saying, "Samuel."

"I am right here," answered Samuel, thinking that Eli had called, and he went to Eli's side.

"You called me, what do you want?" asked Samuel.

"I didn't call you, boy, go back to bed," said Eli.

"Samuel," came the voice again a little later.

Samuel again went to Eli and said, "Here I am. What do you want?"

"I didn't call you son. Just go on back to bed."[3]

Again, for the third time, came the voice, which was the voice of God, "Samuel, Samuel."

For the third time Samuel went to Eli and insisted that he had heard him call.

Father Eli then finally understood that it was the call of God to the boy, and so he said to him gently, "Go lie down, my boy, and if you hear the call again, do not come to me but say, 'speak, Lord, for thy servant heareth.'"

Samuel returned to his cot and laid down and again the Lord

[1]Hophni   [2]Phinehas
[3]Samuel was about 12 years old and probably took
a dim view of this situation.

called as He had before, "Samuel, Samuel."

Then Samuel said, "Speak, Lord, for thy servant is listening."

Then the Lord spoke to Samuel and said, "I will do a great thing in Israel and it will put a tingle in the ears of the people, and scare the willie-nillie out of some of them. I will destroy the family of Eli for I know of their many sins and will bring them to a violent end."

Samuel lay and pondered on these things and then opened the doors of the temple in the morning, but he did not want to tell Eli of his vision.

"Samuel," called out Eli.

"I'm coming, Father," answered Samuel.

"What is the thing about which the Lord talked with you last night. Do not hide it from me, for I am a man of God, and the words of God should not be hidden from me."

Then Samuel told Eli all that the Lord had said and he did not hold back anything.

"It is truly the word and way of God." said Eli, "Let God do what seems best to Him."

Now Samuel grew into manhood and the Lord was with him, and Samuel wasted no time in idle talk.

The word gradually began to spread everywhere, from Maine to California[1] that Samuel was being recognized as a prophet of the Lord and the Lord appeared again to Samuel in the inspiration of his words.

Chap.
4

The Fascists[2] had again organized themselves and then set themselves up and moved against Israel and its army. Israel could not stand before the Fascist army and was defeated, losing 4,000 men.

When the leaders of Israel gathered together they wondered why they had lost, and why God had forsaken them. One of the elders suggested that it would be a good idea to get the ark of the covenant, and this would be a rallying banner for them.

The people went to Montreat[3] for the ark of the covenant and when it entered the camp there was great rejoicing and the army morale was raised.

Now the Fascists heard all the shouting and the celebrating and they could not understand how you could celebrate a defeat. As a result they sent spies who returned and said that the ark of the covenant of the Lord had arrived in camp.

The Fascists then were terrified and they said, "Our goose is cooked, for God has come into their camp. What can we do? Who can deliver us from the God that destroyed the army of Pharaoh?"

"We don't have any choice. We've got to fight," said one of the

[1]Dan to Beersheba   [2]Philistines   [3]Shiloh

Fascist leaders. "When the going gets tough, the tough get going[1]. If we lose we'll be servants to the Hebrews. Tomorrow we fight like mad."

On the next day the Fascists again engaged in battle with Israel and beat them, and the slaughter was great, and the Israelites fled every one in his own direction, and the Fascists captured the ark of the covenant.

There was a man from the tribe of Benjamin who was one of the better track men and ran all the way to Montreat and told Father Eli that the children of Israel were defeated, that 30,000 had been killed or scared away, that Father Eli's sons, Snatch and Wolf, had both been killed and that the ark of the covenant had been captured.

Upon hearing this news Father Eli had a heart attack and died[2].

About this time Penny was in labor and she heard that her lover[3] had been killed and she died giving birth to a son; so the neighbors named the son Vanish[4] because glory was gone from Israel and the ark of the Lord had been stolen.

Chap.
5

The Fascists then took the ark of the covenant and set it in the place where they kept their idol, for they worshipped a god they called Iron Mike.[5] The next day the statute of Iron Mike had fallen to the ground and been broken in pieces; so the people said, "What will we do with the ark of the covenant, for it is more powerful than Iron Mike?"

Now this occurred in San Antonio[6], and the people began to develop virus trouble, diarrhea was everywhere, and most of the people began to suffer with hemorrhoids and when the men realized all this they decided that it was because of the power of God in the ark of the covenant.

As a result, they appointed a study committee of leaders to deliberate on the matter, and they decided to carry the ark of the covenant to Austin[7], and the hand of the Lord began to disturb these people and they began to have hemorrhoids and rawness in their secret parts.

As a result they sent the ark of the covenant to Waco[8] but the people of Waco protested and said that they didn't want the ark of the covenant in their city as they had enough trouble as it was. The men of Waco said, "Send the ark of the covenant back to Israel, and let them have sore tails, but we are sick of this, and dying with our disorders."

---

[1] A statement not originated by Darrell Royal
[2] Probably a coronary occlusion of the myocardial infractory type.
[3] She apparently was a mistress of Snatch or Butch

[4] Ichabod
[5] Dagon
[6] Ashdod
[7] Gath
[8] Ekron

All this took about seven months, going from one place to another, and the Fascists then went to the fortune tellers and the soothsayers and said, "What shall we do?"

This group suggested returning the ark of the covenant to Israel, but added that it should be conveyed with gifts, some of them being images representing the diseases. "Don't change your mind or get hardhearted about it, but remember what the record says about what happened to Pharaoh and his army when he changed his mind," one said.

"We suggest," said the spokesman, "that you make a new cart for the ark of the covenant, and get the best milk cows to pull it, and put the jewels and images in a box by the side of the ark, and then turn the cows loose and see what happens. If the cows go to Israel we will know it was the Lord plaguing us, but if they don't but stay around here, we will figure that the miseries just came to us by chance."

This was done. It also happened that the Israelites were reaping their wheat at this time and the cows came toward their fields and the people lifted up their eyes and were overjoyed to see the return of the ark.

Now the cart came into the farm of Old McDonald[1], in Scotland[2], and the priests there and the people looked into the ark of the covenant and handled the jewels in the box attached, and the Lord smote them with diseases and a great plague, until they cried to people of England[3] to come and get the ark, for they knew they were not permitted to touch the ark or look into it, and they were sick and afraid.

So the men of England came and took the ark and brought it to Westminister Abbey and it stayed here as a symbol of the people's return to God, and there were years of peace again for the people, though still under the Fascists.

Then Samuel spoke to the people and said, "If you will return to the worship of God with all your heart, and give up your selfish ways and the strange gods you put before the Lord, then the Lord will deliver you from the Fascists and you will no longer be a satellite nation."

The children of Israel listened to Samuel and they put away their phony antics and returned to the Lord.

Then Samuel said, "Gather all the representatives of all the people at Mt. Wesley[4] and I will pray for you to the Lord."

The representatives gathered and they confessed their sins and repented and they worshipped God and brought gifts to the church.

[1]Joshua   [2]Bethshemesh   [3]Kiriathjearim   [4]Mizpeh

The Fascists heard about this gathering and they assembled an army and decided to come to Mt. Wesley and break up the meeting, and the people of Israel were afraid.

Samuel stood before the Lord, he worshipped and he prayed, and he also instructed the men to arm themselves for battle. As the confident Fascists approached the Lord caused a great storm to descend, with howling winds, and driving hail, and the storm terrified the Fascists and scattered them, and the army of Israel pursued them and won a great victory.

Then Samuel placed a historical marker at Mt. Wesley as a memorial to this event. The Fascists were subdued by this battle and the hand of the Lord was against them, and many of the cities were restored to Israel. During this time Samuel acted as a judge and a prophet and a circuit rider going from place to place in Israel.

Chap.
8

As Samuel became older he appointed his sons as judges[1], and the name of one was Hoppa[2] and the other was Grafter[3] and they took bribes, and were money seekers, and were warped in their judgments.

As a result a committee of citizens called on Samuel and told him that his sons were ruining the country and that they thought what they really needed was a king.

Samuel did not like what they had to say, particularly the part asking for a king. Samuel, however, was a man of God, and he prayed about the matter and sought council with God.

The Lord said to Samuel, "Let them have a king. It might teach them a lesson on taxation, at least. These people are not protesting your rule or rejecting you, they are rejecting me. In spite of the multitude of times that I have delivered these people, they still waiver and falter in their duty and devotion. Tell the people, however, what a king is like and the way a king rules and then appoint them a king."

Samuel then said to the people, "I have prayed about this and the Lord has consented to let me appoint a king. First, however, let me remind you what a king will do. He will draft most of your sons and make foot soldiers and chariot drivers out of them, some even will have to run beside the chariots, and some he will put in his fields. Furthermore, he will take the daughters that are pretty and he will put them to work around the palace as cooks, pastry makers, and cocktail waitresses, he will also select some of your best land and declare it government property for parks, and he will take everything you earn, taking at least 10%[4] and then when all these things befall you and you begin to worry about your freedom, you will cry and gripe to the Lord, and the Lord will not hear you."

[1]I've always been dubious about nepotism   [2]Joel
[3]Abiah   [4]Not so bad. Presidents run higher.

The people were not impressed. Some of them said, "Everybody else has a king, why can't we have one?" [1]

Some said, "We want a king. We want somebody who will take the responsibility, and fight our battles for us."

Samuel then repeated all this junk to the Lord. Then God again said to Samuel, "Go get them a king, and maybe they'll learn."

Chap.
9

Now there was a man of the tribe of Benjamin who had properly fed his son vitamins, aside from being a big man himself, and the son grew to be 6 inches taller than the fellows around him, and he was strong, and a good man, and his name was Saul.

Saul's father came one day and reported losing a bunch of donkeys and he sent Saul and one of his servants out to find them. Saul went to Nob Hill[2], and Brownwood[3], and as far as Clovis, New Mexico[4] and he couldn't find them. Saul then said to his servant, "We had better go home. Daddy will begin to worry more about our being lost than the donkeys."

"The fellows at the tavern told me that there was a very wise man staying not far from here and that he might be able to help."

"It's O.K. by me, " said Saul, "but I'm broke. What can we give him for his advice?"

"It just so happens," said the servant, "that I picked up 10 bucks at the dice game last night, and we can give him that."

"That's fine" said Saul, "let's go to the city and find the man."

As they approached the city they encountered some young girls drawing water and they inquired of them if the prophet was still in the city. The girls told Saul that if he went in a hurry he could find the prophet as he was conducting special services and it would be easy to find him today.

Now the Lord had moved Samuel the day before to believe that on the next day he would encounter a young man who would make a good king. God had instructed Samuel to anoint him and had promised that he would help in the troubles with the Fascists who were getting active again.

When Samuel saw Saul approaching the city he knew this was the man of whom God spoke, also the biggest he'd ever seen.

Saul approached Samuel who stood at the gate of the city and said, "Where is the prophet's house, as I would like to see him?"

"I am the so-called fortune teller that you seek. We will eat together today and tomorrow I will tell you all you need to know and send you on your way."

"Incidentally," said Samuel, "the donkeys that were lost are found. Your house is blessed."

"I am a member of the smallest tribe and my family is unimportant even in our tribe, why are you so gracious to me?"

[1]Very familiar   [2]Ephraim   [3]Shalim   [4]Zuph

Samuel then took Saul to dinner and had thirty guests, all key men in the city. It was a special meal, and Samuel said it was particularly in honor of Saul, and Saul ate one whole shoulder of beef to show his appreciation.

Samuel and Saul continued in friendly conversation the next day, and then as time for leaving came Samuel told Saul to send his servant on ahead as he wished to remain in private with Saul and to pass on to him the word of the Lord.

Chap.
10

Then Samuel took ceremonial oil and put it on Saul's head and said, "In the name of the Lord, I annoint you to be the head man over all the Lord's people. As a sign that I know what I'm doing, when you leave here you will find two men by the cemetery near Adamsville[1] and they will say to you that the donkeys have returned home and that your father is now worrying about you. From Adamsville you will go on to Glen Rose[2] and there you will meet three men who will give you a couple of loaves of bread for food, and from there you shall go to a place where there is a revival being held, and the spirit of the Lord will descend upon you at that place and you will become converted and be a new man. When these things occur you will then know that God is with you. Then in a week or so I'll come to you and tell you what to do next."

Everything occurred exactly as Samuel had said, and Saul had a new attitude develop within him, and Saul himself prophesied and spoke forth for God and the people wondered saying, "Is this not the son of that fellow who is the big blacksmith? Has he suddenly become a prophet?" The people talked much about this man Saul and the new circumstances surrounding him.

Upon arriving near his home Saul met his Uncle Ned who said, "Where in the devil have you and your servant been all this time?"

"Well, we went after donkeys," said Saul, "but we couldn't find them. Then we ran into a fellow named Samuel."

"What did Samuel say to you?" asked Uncle Ned.

"He said that the donkeys were found," replied Saul, but he did not tell him the rest of the story.

Samuel then called the people together again at Montreat and said, "In God's name, I remind you that I brought you from Egypt and I have delivered you often, yet in my place you want a king, now therefore present yourselves in the Lord's meeting place here, representatives from all the tribes and I will show you your king."

When all the tribes were gathered, Samuel said, "Where is Saul?"

When they looked for him, they couldn't find him, for he was embarrassed and had hid himself. It wasn't long, however, before they found him, and when he came where the people were it was

---

[1]Zelzah   [2]Tabor

seen that he was a head taller than anyone there.

Then Samuel said, "This is the man the Lord has chosen. Have you ever seen a finer looking fellow?"

And the people shouted, "God save the King."

Samuel then recorded the meeting, and made the selection of the king official.

Saul went home and with him went a bunch of men who were moved of God to join him. The anti-godly element were not pleased and booed him, but Saul held his peace.

Chap.
11

Then a man named Fisty, head of the old Bass Gang,[1] encamped with his raiding party type of army outside of Louisville[2] and threatened the city. Fisty sent a messenger into the city to say that unless every fighting man in the city would let his men blind each one of them in the right eye, Fisty and his raiders would capture the city and kill every man, woman and child.

The city council asked for seven days to think the matter through and appoint committees. Immediately, however, they sent a messenger in secret to Saul and told him of the situation and begged for help, and all the people that heard of this were horrified.

Now when Saul heard of this terrible threat the spirit of the Lord came upon him and he took a yoke of oxen and killed them, and sent a piece of oxen to all the villages, and down all the coast of Israel with the message that any man who failed to report immediately for duty in Saul's army would have his own oxen fixed as the sample indicated.

The fear of the Lord then fell upon the people[3] and then all came to the summons of Saul and he assembled thereby a tremendous army and Saul sent word to Louisville that help would arrive by noon the next day.

So the men of Louisville sent word to Fisty that the next afternoon they would start sending their men out to get their right eyes removed.

Saul divided his gigantic army into three sections and before noon the next day they poured down on the Bass Gang and defeated them easily and scattered the remnants so that no two of the gang left together.

Then the people shouted in gratitude to Saul and they said, "Where are those crummy characters that voted against Saul for king, let's find each one and hang him."[4]

Saul, however, said, "There shall be no man put to death for my sake, for this victory is the Lord's doing."

Samuel then called for a convocation, declared an official assemblage, directed a worship service to the Lord, and crowned Saul

---

[1]Nahash the Ammonite
[2]Jabesh-gilead

[3]Also the fear of losing oxen
[4]Vietnam type of election

With all the great crowd present and the representatives from all the tribes assembled Samuel decided to make a declaration and he spoke to the entire nation saying, "I am getting old and my days are numbered. I want you to stand here as witnesses for me before God and before the new king. Have I ever stolen an ox? Have I ever defrauded anyone? Have I ever taken a bribe or given false information? If I have ever done such to anyone let him step forward and I will repay him."

The people said, "You have never done any of those things."

"You then," said Samuel, "and the new king are my witnesses to God."

"Let me remind, though," continued Samuel, "that it is the Lord who is the deliverer. It is the Lord God of Israel who instructed Moses and Aaron, who punished Israel when the people strayed from the worship of the true God, and then the people repented and the Lord raised up leaders to save the people in God's name. Yet you very people here insisted on an earthly king, when the Lord was willing to be your king.

Now you have a king. The Lord has agreed to the arrangement. Be careful though, for you must serve God and obey his voice and adhere to his commandments, you and your king both or the hand of the Lord will turn against you as surely as he did against any of the previous generations that deserted him."

Samuel let this soak in a bit and then he said, "As a sign that the Lord means business and that he deals in the affairs of man as a living God, I will now call upon God to declare his power in your presence and bring a mighty storm, which will reveal the displeasure of God at your decisions and warn you of his power."

The Lord then sent a mighty storm with roaring thunder and the people were terrified. The people then cried to Samuel and said, "Pray for us, for we know now we have sinned."

Samuel said, "Take it easy. Calm down. You have sinned, yet if you will surrender your lives to God and serve him the Lord will not forsake you. You must turn aside, however, from your greedy pursuit of profit. As for me, I will continue to pray for you and I will continue to teach you the difference between right and wrong as long as I live; so stand in awe of the Lord, serve him with all your heart, be grateful for his goodness to you and all is well, but if you continue to do wickedly you've had it!"

After Saul had been king for about three years he decided that it was time to give some of the army a workout and to become a bit active so he selected three thousand men, took two thousand under his command and one thousand under the command of his son,

Jonathan. The idea was to march against the Fascists who were beginning to stir up a little border trouble again.

Jonathan took his thousand men and attacked a small fort held by the Fascists and won a great victory. Saul had this news spread all over Israel; so that the people felt proud of their victorious nation. Then the Fascists became alarmed over this and gathered an army of 30,000 or more and came in force to the outskirts of Yorktown[1] where the people of Israel could see their numbers. Meanwhile Saul was at Province[2], waiting for Samuel and a little advice.

Samuel did not appear in seven days; so Saul began to worship God on his own, then Samuel came.

Saul said, "I was afraid to wait for you to conduct the services, for fear that the Fascists would get here before you did and God would not be on our side."

"You messed things up, Saul," said Samuel. "You should have not started this in the first place with that silly raid on Fort Sumter."[3]

"In fact", Samuel continued, "the Lord will no doubt want to replace you before long." After saying this Samuel went away mad.

Now Saul had with him about 600 men, for most of the Hebrews had sought hiding places in caves, and on the hills, and many had crossed the Jordan.

Another problem among the Hebrews was that for years the Fascists had been doing all the weapon making and there was no blacksmith in Israel to forge swords. The Fascists had control then of most of the weapons and they divided themselves into three large companies and planned to make raids on cities and subdue the Hebrews and take away captives and spoils. The situation looked very bad.

Chap.
14

Now Jonathan decided that he could take what men he could find and slip up on another unwary fort of the Fascists and have another victory, and raise the morale of the dispirited Hebrews. Since he doubted if his father the king would approve, he went without permission. Jonathan decided to cross the river and attack a garrison that he knew would not be expecting any trouble.

Saul in the meantime was sitting under a tree with about 600 men, all that he had left, and they were bemoaning their fate and pondering the situation.

Jonathan proceeded with his plan and came to the narrow pass between the hills that led down to the garrison. At this point Jonathan said to his gun-bearer, "We will present ourselves suddenly in front of the garrison. It is possible that the Lord will work for us, for numbers make no difference to the Lord, and he can give us victory with a few men as easily as with many."

[1]Michmash [2]Gilgal [3]Geba

Jonathan then said, "We will first suddenly appear in front of the garrison and show ourselves. If they seeing us say to us 'stay where you are. Do not come a step nearer,' then we will get the heck out of there, but if they say 'come on into the garrison' we will know the Lord is going to deliver us and this will be the sign that we are to be victorious."

When Jonathan and his men appeared before the Fascists they said, "Look at the Hebrews, for they have crawled out of their caves for a look at the world."

Then the leader of the Fascists called out and said, "Come on into our garrison and we will show you a thing or two."

Jonathan then yelled "charge" and he and his gun bearer between them killed about twenty men who could not run well because of the plowed ground in front of the garrison. Then the Lord shook the earth with an earthquake, and the Fascists pushed the panic button and the sky was darkened and the Fascists began to kill each other by mistake and there was great bedlam and great slaughter.

Meanwhile, back at the ranch, Saul said, "Let's call the roll and see who we have left." After roll call it was learned that Jonathan and a few others were missing.

Saul then took his 600 men and went to the place of the noise and saw the panic and set himself and his men on the Fascists.

It also happened that a lot of the Hebrews had joined the Fascists a few weeks before, figuring that there was no chance to win and if you can't lick 'em join 'em. These people now, sensing the victory of Saul and his men, also turned against the Fascists, and one of history's most mixed up battles of all time took place.

To add to this another little human touch, the Hebrews who were still hiding in caves and in some of the ladies' restrooms all began to come forth and suddenly join in pursuing the hapless and terrified Fascists. The Lord had again delivered Israel.

There was no celebration, however, as Saul posted a notice saying that no one was to eat anything at all for a whole day, but to continue pursuing the Fascists without even a coffee break.[1] The people didn't like this order.

As a bunch of the men were chasing the Fascists through the woods they passed a place where honey was dripping from a honeycomb. None of the men touched it because of Saul's order, but Jonathan had been so busy all day with his sword that he had not heard the order or seen the bulletin board. Jonathan then took the end of the club he carried in his left hand and dipped it in the honey and ate some and felt better.

One of the soldiers then came to him and said, "That is a no-no. King Saul has pronounced a curse on eating today."

"Well, the king made a big blunder. I already feel stronger and

[1]They did not know about protest marches.

ready to kill more Fascists while you men are fainting and hungry. We could all do better on a full stomach."

The people, however, continued their pursuing of the Fascists without food, as they feared to disobey the king. Finally, however, the people became so hungry they began to kill sheep and oxen and eat the meat raw, for they were perishing of hunger and there was no barbecue pit handy.

Saul was informed of this and took a stone and marked the place so he would remember to make a judgment on their error. Then Saul said, "Let everybody bring meat here and we will cook it and we will eat heartily and properly." Then Saul erected an altar on the spot, as an acknowledgment of the goodness of the Lord.

Saul then thought that it might be a good idea to attack another wing of the Fascist army during the night and so he went with the priest to ask the Lord about this, but there was no reply.

Saul then decided that there had been some instances of sin or disobedience, else the Lord would have replied.

Then Saul spoke to the people and said, "Who has sinned? Let him confess, and even if it be my beloved son Jonathan, the sinner must die."

There was no comment. Saul then said, "We will let God decide where the sin lies. Jonathan and I will be on one side and the people on the other. I will toss a coin, heads you people have sinned, tails, Jonathan or I have sinned." Saul tossed the coin and it came up tails.

Saul then said, "It is between me and my son; so I will toss again, heads I am the sinner, tails, it is Jonathan." The coin came up tails.

Saul then said, "Jonathan, what is it that you have done?"

"All I did was eat a little honey," said Jonathan, "as I didn't know about that silly rule you passed."

"I cannot go back on my word," said Saul, "you must be executed."

The people then put up a big howl. Their spokesman said, "Are you going to execute the man responsible for saving Israel? You must have blown your mind. We the people all agree that he is innocent of wrong and not one hair on his head will you disturb, for he has worked with the Lord our God today and brought us deliverance. Don't you dare touch him."

"All right", said Saul, "since you put it that way."

Saul continued to be king in Israel and was constantly leading selected and trained men against various gangs that would harass the borders of Israel.

The Fascists were still the main enemies who caused most of the trouble. Saul had acquired a family somehow in the middle of all the little wars and raids and he had two sons and two daughters, the youngest, a girl named Greta[1] was truly stunning.

[1]Michal

When Saul would see any strong looking, healthy appearing young man he immediately drafted him into his army for all the time that Saul lived there was war of some sort with the Fascists.

Samuel then came to Saul and said, "Now you remember that I am the one the Lord sent to make you king so I want you to listen to me for I have a word for you from God. The Lord still remembers the Capone gang[1] and all the trouble they caused. This type of gang reorganizes and acts violently and for evil and the Lord is ready to crack down on them again. You are to do it."

"In fact," continued Samuel, "the Lord wants you to go to their area headquarters and destroy, the Lord wants all their possessions destroyed, you are to kill the women, children, donkeys, sheep and cattle."

As a result Saul gathered together over 200,000 armed men and approached Oklahoma City[2] and pitched his camp outside the city limits. Then Saul sent word into Chicago for all the good people and the worshippers of the true God to leave the city as he was going to tear it down and destroy it. Saul also suggested that the Shriners[3] leave the city as they had always been kind to the Israelites.

As soon as those who wished had withdrawn, Saul marched on Chicago with his tremendous army, and destroyed the people with the sword, but the mayor[4] he saved alive. Saul and the people also kept for themselves the best of the cattle and sheep, and they pocketed the jewelry, as well as many of the sporting goods of Abercrombie and Fitch.

Then the word of the Lord came to Samuel imdicating that the Lord was unhappy with the king situation again for Saul had not carried out the instructions that Samuel had relayed to the king.

Samuel was grieved over the matter and prayed earnestly about it. In the morning Samuel arose early and went to call on Saul, but the palace people gave him the runaround, saying Saul had gone to golf at Carmel and that he was going down to Province[5] to fish.

Samuel took out after him and when he found him Saul immediately said to Samuel, "Blessings on thee. I have performed as you told me to do."

Now Samuel was no stoop by a long shot and he said, "Why is it that I hear the cattle mooing in the stockyards of Chicago?"

"The people spared them," said Saul, "to offer as a sacrifice to God and to bring to the church."

"A likely story," said Samuel.

"Now you listen to me, Saul, for the Lord has spoken to me," continued Samuel.

"Speak your piece, Samuel," said the king.

[1]The Amaleks   [2]City of Amalek   [3]Kenites
          [4]Agag   [5]Gilgal

"Do you remember that when you were a nobody even in your own sight, the Lord anointed you instant king of Israel? Now that same God told you to destroy Chicago and all that was in it and you didn't do it."

"Now, Samuel," said Saul, "I obeyed God. I have the mayor in jail. I destroyed the city, but the people are the ones who kept the spoil and they say its for the church."

"Now, Saul, do you think the Lord has as great a delight in burnt offering as in obedience? To obey is better than to sacrifice. You can't buy off the Lord with the Sunday morning offering. For rebellion is a sin, and stubborness is iniquity. Because you, therefore, have rejected the word of God, God is going to reject you as king."

Then Saul said to Samuel, "You are right. I have sinned. I have disobeyed the command of God for fear of the protest marchers among the people. Pardon my sin. Let me again worship with you before God."

Samuel said, "I will not return to you. You rejected the word of God and God rejects you."

As Samuel turned to leave, Saul reached out to hold him by his cloak and the cloak tore and Samuel said, "This is a sign that the Lord is going to take away your kingdom and give it to another fellow, who is better than you are. Remember, God makes no mistakes, so he will not repent in your case."

"I have sinned, Samuel. I truly repent. At least let me worship God with you and stand with me before the altar in the presence of the people."

Samuel agreed and together in the presence of the people they worshipped God.

Then Samuel said, "Bring to me the mayor of Chicago."

The mayor came and approached Samuel very humbly saying, "Surely we've had enough bitterness, let us bury the hatchet and be friends."

"Your gang activities and your meanness and your contracts on people's lives have made many mothers childless, and so shall your mother be," said Samuel. Samuel then picked up a machete knife and cut the mayor into several districts.

Then Samuel went to Richmond[1] to be near the seminary there and Saul returned to Mount Vernon[2], and Samuel came no more to visit Saul. Nevertheless, Samuel grieved over this as he was greatly fond of Saul. The Lord, who never likes for his servants to be unhappy, regretted that Saul had ever been made king, as God knew all along how this would work into trouble for Israel and for Samuel.

Chap.
16

Then the Lord spoke to Samuel and said, "How long will you mourn for Saul? You need to do something beside sitting around and

[1]Ramah   [2]Gibeah

grieving about your playmate. Take the anointing oil and go to Bethlehem and visit Jesse, for I will let you select a new king and a new interest from among the sons of Jesse."

"How can I go, Lord?" said Samuel, "for if my good friend Saul hears of this, it will be called treason and I'll be killed."

"Come, come, Samuel, you know I am with you. Take your liturgical equipment for a service and appear before Jesse and then I'll tell you what to do, and I will reveal to you the one to be anointed."

Samuel did as the Lord said. When Samuel came into the city the town council members were troubled, for Samuel had a reputation for being tough on mayors and the like.

"Do you come peaceably?" they asked.

"Yes, I come peaceably. I come to conduct a service. All of you prepare yourselves to attend and I want to be sure that Jesse and his sons are present."

When the occasion came about, Samuel began to interview the sons of Jesse. The first one was Cary[1] and Samuel thought surely this handsome and talented man was the one, but the Lord said, "Not Cary."

Then the Lord said to Samuel, "Do not judge by his looks, or his weight, or his heighth, for the Lord looks to the inside of a man, to his heart, while man judges by outward appearances."

Then came Henry[2], and the Lord said, "Next". Then came Glenn[3], John, George and on until all seven sons had been interviewed, and all rejected as the new king.

Samuel said to Jesse, "Is that the works?"

"Yes," said Jesse, "except for a teen-ager that I left looking out for the sheep."

"Send for him," said Samuel.

When he came Samuel observed that he was sunburned and handsome and intelligent looking, even for a teen-ager.

The Lord moved within Samuel and Samuel said, "This is the one."

The boy's name was David and he was anointed that day and the spirit of the Lord began to grow within him from that hour.

Samuel went back to Richmond, and Jesse and his sons and the town council all went back to their normal life.[4]

Now the spirit of the Lord left Saul the king and he was depressed and no one could cheer him.

One of the servants suggested that what Saul needed was a little soul music that would make him feel better.

Saul said, "I'll try anything. Bring me a man who can play well and who will lift my spirits."

---

[1]Eliab   [2]Abinadad   [3]Shammah
[4]They probably thought Samuel was senile and a bit off his rocker.

One of the servants said, "There is a young man in Bethlehem who plays a guitar and sings folk songs. He is a handsome lad and the people gather every Saturday night to hear him play."

"Go get him," said Saul.

As a result messengers were sent to Jesse and he was told to let them bring his son David to the king as a folk singer. David came and appeared before Saul and Saul was pleased with him and put him on the payroll at once.

Saul sent a message to Jesse saying that David pleased him and he was keeping him at Mount Vernon.

When Saul became depressed David took his guitar and sang soul music to him and brightened his spirits.

Chap.
17

The Fascists began to activate themselves again for they were always seeking to overcome people and take in new territory. As a result they gathered their army together on Beverly Hill[1] and Israel gathered their army together on an opposite hill, with a valley between the two armies.

There appeared one morning in the valley a Fascist named Goliath, who was truly a giant, about 6 foot 5 weighing around 280, and he was the biggest, strongest man anyone had ever seen in that day. Goliath also had arrayed himself with a big football helmet, shoulder pads, and complete armor, plus carrying a mighty sword. To top it all, he carried a spear that most men could not even lift.

Goliath then shouted a proposal to the army of Israel saying, "Why should we have a big battle and get a lot of people killed, not to mention all the expense, when we could settle the whole matter with two men? You send out your best fighting man and I will fight him. If your man wins, all the Fascists will be your servants and we'll be the satellite nation. I defy you this day and challenge any man. I can lick anybody in the place."

When Saul and all the Israelites heard these words and saw the giant, they were terrified.

Now some of David's brothers were in the army of Israel, but David was back at the ranch tending to the sheep.

Goliath came forth with his same thundering little speech every morning for forty days, and it was wearing on the nerves of the men of Israel as well as Saul.[2]

Jesse, David's father, talked to David at supper one night and said, "Tomorrow I want you to go to the Beverly Hills area and find out what is going on, how your brothers are doing, and what gives with the war. Your mother will send some chocolate chip cookies and some homemade bread."

David arose early in the morning and went to the Beverly Hills area and saw that the armies were preparing for battle. When David

[1]Shochoh   [2]Particularly on Saul who was the biggest man Israel had

had reached the camp and delivered the box from home, he saw the giant Goliath come forth and he heard him issue the challenge as usual. David also observed that all the men around the camp were afraid.

David then said, "What reward has the king offered to the man who will defeat this big slob that defies Israel?"

"The king will bestow on him great riches, shall give him the king's best looking daughter for a wife, and make the man's family tax exempt."

David's oldest brother didn't like David's asking questions and embarrassing the soldiers and he said, "Why don't you go home and tend to the sheep? You're just down here to see the battle and make fun of us."

"What is eating all of you?" said David. "Is there not here a worthy cause?"

Now this conversation was passed along the grapevine to Saul and so he sent for David.

David then spoke to Saul and said, "You can tell the army boys not to be so up tight. I will go and fight the big Fascist."

"You don't have a chance," said Saul, "for you are young and inexperienced, and Goliath is a veteran and twice your size."

Then David said, "Well, when I was keeping my father's sheep there came a lion and a bear and each one raided our flock; so I went after them and killed them, both the lion and the bear. As far as I am concerned, this big gorilla is just like one of them."

"On top of that," said David, "I am confident that the Lord who delivered me from the paw of the lion and the paw of the bear, will certainly deliver me from the heathen with the big mouth."

Saul then ordered that his own personal armor be brought and put upon David. The outfit was so big and heavy that David couldn't move or even see out of it; so he took off the armor.

David decided to go with his own familiar weapons; so he took his shepherd's staff and his sling, and went then to the brook and selected five smooth stones and he went forth to meet the big Fascist.

The Fascist and his shield carrier stepped forth to meet David. When Goliath saw David he scoffed and became enraged saying, "It is an insult. Am I a puppy dog that you send a young boy to fetch?" Then Goliath began to curse something awful.[1]

"If you will step a little nearer, boy," said Goliath, "I will cut you in pieces and feed you to the birds."

David then said calmly, "You come to me with a spear, and a sword, and a shield, but I come to you in the name of the Lord God of hosts, and this day the Lord will deliver you into my hands, and I will remove your head and leave it on the ground for the jackals in order that all men may know that there is a God in Israel.

[1]Most of you can fill in your own words

Furthermore, this whole assemblage shall know that the Lord saves not with the sword and the spear, for the decisions of battles are the Lord's, and he will deliver you today into our hands."

At this point, Goliath began to advance on David; so David took a stone and put it in his sling and began to twirl it around his head and when Goliath was in easy range David snapped the sling free and sent the stone with deadly accuracy right between the eyes of the Fascist and the stone sunk into his forehead and it knocked him out cold.

Since Goliath had an extremely hard head, he was only cool cocked; so David took Goliath's sword and cut off his head while he was out cold, and this ended the engagement.

When the Fascists saw this, they were terrified and ran and the men of Israel came to life and chased them to secure servants or kill those who would not surrender.

David took the head of Goliath to a taxidermist in Jerusalem and then kept Goliath's armour as another souvenir.

When Saul saw David go against the giant he asked his aide saying, "Whose boy is that?"

"I really don't know," said Bouncer.[1]

As a result, when David returned Saul asked him saying, "Who is your father?"

"He is Jesse, a loyal supporter of yours from Bethlehem."

Chap.
18

Now Jonathan had been around while all of this was going on and he became devoted to David, and David enjoyed Jonathan and the two became great and inseparable friends.

Jonathan and David exchanged gifts and made a pact of friendship with each other, and became blood brothers.[2]

David stayed with Saul and behaved wisely. Saul made him a captain in the army and David became very popular with the people as well as with the soldiers.

After the big victory over the Fascists, it was decided to have a big parade in celebration. The women came out in great numbers for the parade[3] and they sang, and danced, and rattled a lot of various noisemakers. The women had also come up with a folk song that they began to sing loudly, the main words of which were, "Saul has slain his thousands, but David has slain tens of thousands."[4]

Now this song went over like a lead balloon with Saul and he began to fret about David. Saul reasoned that David had everything but the kingdom as it was.

As a result, Saul got into one of his depressive spells and so David came with his guitar and played soft music to comfort him.

Apparently David played the wrong song, for Saul picked up a javelin and threw at David twice. David decided he wasn't wanted at

[1]Abner   [2]Indian style   [3]The men were all in the parade
[4]Women still go for the younger men. Too bad, but true.

the time, but Saul was afraid of David for the Lord was with David and was not with Saul.

Saul then promoted David to Colonel and sent him to operate in a different area, and David continued to behave wisely and the Lord was with him.

The people loved David, for he was around them a great deal, and he dealt wisely and fairly with the people.

Saul then said to David, "My oldest daughter[1] I will give you as a wife if you will go forth again and fight the Fascists for me and the Lord."

Now Saul's reasoning was that David was so brave that he would get himself killed.

David said to Saul, however, "Who am I to be the son-in-law of the king. I come from an insignificant family."[2]

In the meantime, an aide to Saul known as Sly Knox,[3] talked Saul into letting him marry Phyllis.[4]

In the meantime, Greta,[5] had fallen for David and the word of this pleased Saul, because he knew his youngest daughter was cute, but also a trouble maker, and Saul had a devious plan to boot.

As a result, Saul sent word to David that he would be honored to have him as his son-in-law, that Saul now was fond of David.

When the servants brought this word David again said, "I am a poor man and I have no dowry or gift to bring such a prize as the king's daughter."

The servants of Saul reported this and Saul sent them back to David saying that the king did not need a dowry of money, but so David would feel that he was bringing something, let him go and bring back an inch of skin off the private parts of 100 Fascists[6]. This pleased David greatly, as he was young and a bit on the warrior side of things.

As a result, David assembled a part of the men under his command and then went out looking for Fascists. Since the operation could be performed more easily on a dead Fascist than a live one, David and his men killed 200 Fascists and brought a double measure of skin to Saul.

Saul realized for sure then that the Lord was with David and that Greta truly loved David, and Saul became all the more afraid of David and his influence.

The Fascists instituted a revenge raid because of what had happened to the 200 of their number and David took his men and handled this situation wisely and merely added to his great prestige.

Chap.
19

Saul became increasingly disturbed about the growing popularity

---

[1]Not the good looking one   [2]David had seen the eldest daughter
[3]Adriel   [4]Merab, the eldest daughter   [5]Michal
[6]Tricky, tricky-Saul thought this would get David killed for sure.

of David and so he spoke to Jonathan and all the soldiers around the palace telling them that David had to be killed.

Jonathan did not go for this and he secretly told David that there was a contract out on him and the hit men were going to look for him the next day and Jonathan suggested that David make himself hard to find.

Jonathan also told David that he would try to change his father's mind.

Jonathan spoke to his father the king and said, "Why pick on David? He's never done anything to you but good things. Didn't David put his life on the line against the Fascists, and through David the Lord delivered Israel. Why should you sin and have an innocent man killed?"

Saul listened to this reasonable approach from Jonathan and cancelled the contract to kill David. Jonathan then brought David into Saul's presence and they were friendly as in earlier times.

The Fascists shortly started a war again and Saul sent David to handle the situation and David had great success and returned home again as a conqueror.

Naturally, Saul turned sour again, and so when David started playing the guitar for Saul, Saul picked up a javelin and threw it at him[1]; so David ducked and left the area.

Saul then sent a few of his killers to watch David's house and to kill him when he came out the next morning. Greta, David's wife, who kept her ear to the ground all the time, told David of this, and suggested that he slip out during the night; so she tied some sheets together and let David out the second story window in the night and he escaped.

Greta then fixed a dummy in the bed and when the messengers from Saul came in the morning and asked for David she said that he was sick in bed.

When the messengers reported this, Saul said that they should go and bring him bed and all and then Saul himself could kill David.

When the messengers came and got the bed they soon realized that there was only a dummy in the bed.

Saul then brought Greta to task and asked her why she helped David escape when David was an enemy of her father.

Greta said, "I had to help him as he threatened to kill me if I didn't." This got Greta off the hook, though it didn't help David.

Word came later to Saul that David had been seen around Mo-Ranch[2] and so he sent a squad of killers to find him there and kill him. When the killers arrived Samuel was conducting a revival meeting and the killers attended looking for David, but became converted and joined the church. Saul sent three different groups on this errand and all of them were converted.

Finally Saul decided to go himself and when he got as far as Black

---

[1]And it wasn't even an electric guitar   [2]Ramah

Mountain[1] he asked saying, "Where are David and Samuel?"

The filling station attendant said, "They are at the Assembly Inn in Mo-Ranch."[2]

As Saul approached the spirit of the Lord again fell upon him and he began to testify as a witness for God. This amazed the people and they wondered if Saul was turning into a prophet.

Chap.
20

Saul's conversion was pretty temporary, however, and only furnished time for David to get away. David went to Jonathan and said, "What gives with all this jazz of killing me? What have I done?"

"I don't know," said Jonathan, "but the old man always consults me on everything, great or small, and I don't think he is trying to kill you."

"You're wrong there, buddy," said David. "I think your father knows of our close friendship and he has not told you what he is doing as he doesn't want to upset you. I'm not kidding, for I'm real close to getting killed."

"Tell me what to do," said Jonathan, "and I'll help anyway I can."

"Well," said David, "tomorrow is the new moon and that's my regular time to play for Saul at dinner. Let me hide in the field outside the palace for 3 days and let's see if Saul misses me playing. If Saul asks for me, tell him I had to go home to Bethlehem to put a rose on my mother's grave. If he accepts this excuse and gives his blessing that's fine, but if he gets furious then I'll know he is still after me. If I am in the wrong, Jon, and have done something worthy of death, then you kill me, but don't turn me in to the king."

"Don't you worry. I'll tell you exactly how things are."

"How will I be able to get the information?" asked David.

Jonathan said, "Let's go out near where you will be hiding and mark a place. After I have sounded out my father and determined his mood then I will send word to you to come to the palace or to flee, as the case may be."

The two young men then made another arrangement between them, obligating themselves to always look out for each other and for each other's family, with the Lord as a witness to the agreement.

Jonathan then told David, "I will send word on the third day by signal. I will come to the field as if to practice with my bow and arrow. I will shoot three arrows and in the direction of the rock we marked, and if I yell to the boy retrieving that the arrows are on this side, then come with me to the palace, but if I say the arrows are away from you, flee, and the Lord always be a witness and a common cause between you and me."

David hid in the field when the new moon came and Saul sat down to dinner. David's accustomed place was empty, but there was no

[1]Sechu   [2]Naioth in Ramah

mention made of it.

On the second day, however, Saul said to Jonathan, "Where is the son of Jesse, for he wasn't here yesterday and is not here today?"

Jonathan said, "David asked permission of me to go to Bethlehem to put a rose on his mother's grave."

Saul then blew his top at Jonathan, and bellowed, "You son of a mean and rebellious woman, don't I know that you are a close friend of David? I tell you this, as long as David lives, you shall not be settled and you will not inherit the kingdom. Now go and find him and bring him here to me, for I want to execute him."

Jonathan then said, "What has he done to deserve death?"

Then Saul tossed a javelin at Jonathan,[1] which left him under the impression that all was not well at home.

Jonathan was greatly disturbed over his father's actions and words and he grieved greatly over the matter.

The next day Jonathan went out to the field with his boy retriever as if to practice with the bow and arrow.

As the lad started out in the field Jonathan shot 3 arrows well beyond him and called to him saying, "The arrows are well beyond you. Hurry, get them, and run back here." The boy did as he was told.

Jonathan then gave his bow and arrows to the boy and said, "Take them back to the house."

As soon as the boy was gone, David came out of hiding and he and Jonathan had a reunion, with tears.[2] Then the two shook hands and wished each other well. Jonathan returned to the city while David fled to the hills.

Chap.
21

David was without food and he had no weapons with him; so he went to the church in Jerusalem and asked the minister for some bread. The minister knew something was wrong and he could not understand why this prominent man was by himself, and without food, and was asking for supplies.

The priest said that it so happened at that moment that there was no bread available for travelers and that all that was on hand was the communion bread. David then talked the minister into giving him five loaves of bread.

Then David said, "Are there any weapons around somewhere in the basement or a closet?"

"The only weapon in the place is the sword of Goliath, which you brought to the church as a souvenir."

"That is fine," said David, "give it to me as it is a real good weapon and I need one badly."

David then fled from Jerusalem for he knew that the soldiers of the king would be searching for him.

[1]Saul was not too good with the javelin [2]Men used to cry in those days

David figured he might be safe in another county so he went to an area controlled by Milton,[1] who thought of himself as a king.

The associates of Milton told him that they thought the stranger who had arrived was David, the great warrior about whom the number one song was centered, entitled, "Saul has killed his thousands, but David his tens of thousands."

As a result, there developed suspicion about David and what he was doing in Milton's country; so Milton had a tail put on him.

David discovered this and decided that he would pretend to be nutty; so he started writing crazy messages in the rest rooms, carving on trees, and drooling at the mouth.

Milton then decided that David had lost his marbles and he began to gripe at his aides for letting David hang around the area.

Chap. 22

As a result, David decided to depart before they put the hounds on him and he fled to Carlsbad Caverns[2] and began to make himself at home there.

As word of this began to spread in the area every man that was too deep in debt, or was having trouble with his wives, or was in some distress, began to come to the cave to join David, until he had a band of 400 men, all discontented.[3]

David then went privately to the Governor of Mississippi[4] and asked him to take care of his father and mother, as he was afraid Saul might use them for vengeance. David said that he would not forget his kindness.

One day a prophet of the Lord came by Carlsbad and told David that the Lord thought David should go to the area where the tribe of Judah lived. David did this, and arrived in the area known as the Black Forest[5] with his strange band of men.

Saul began to hear through the grapevine that David had been seen in a place or two and Saul was also having one of his depressive and self-pity moods.

Saul then sat under a tree with a large number of his soldiers around him. Saul was holding his inaccurate javelin in his hand, and Saul said, "Why do all of you favor David? Can he give you vineyards, or bestow government property on you, can he promote you and get salary raises for you? Yet none of you seem to sympathize with me or feel sorry for me. You never even told me about the agreement that Jonathan had with David. I am greatly disappointed in all of you."

"You are wrong, King Saul," said Fast Buck Otto,[6] "for I was just about to tell you something that I learned. It was just relayed to me that David went to the priest in Jerusalem, Father Peel,[7] and the priest gave him bread and the sword of Goliath."

[1]Achish   [2]Adullam   [3]A real leadership challenge
[4]Moab   [5]Hareth   [6]Doeg   [7]Ahimelech

"Send for Peel at once," said Saul, "and get his family along with him, and assistants."

When Peel arrived Saul said to him, "Why have you plotted against me, to feed and arm my enemy David, and you've probably arranged an ambush."

Then Peel said, "You aren't thinking very clearly. David is the most loyal of all your subjects. As far as I know, David is your son-in-law, free to come and go in the king's house, how in the world could I think that he was your enemy? I am absolutely innocent."

"I don't believe a word you say, and you and your family shall be executed."

The king then turned to some of the soldiers standing near him and said to them, "Kill Peel and the assistant ministers as well as Peel's family."

The soldiers, however, would not kill a priest of the Lord. Then Saul turned to Fast Buck Otto and asked him to kill them. As a result Fast Buck killed the priests that were present and then went into town and killed everyone he found with a reversed collar.

One of the local ministers managed to get out of town and went to the Black Forest and told David all that had happened.

David said, "I was afraid of something like this, because ole Fast Buck was at the church when Peel supplied me with food and Goliath's sword. Well, at least you might as well join me, as you'll be missed in Jerusalem and Saul will put you on the same wanted list on which I am."

Chap.
23

Word then came to David that a band of Fascists had been raiding the barns and warehouses around Junction.[1] David then prayed to the Lord and asked if he should take his more or less dirty dozen and go and fight the Fascists and save Junction. The Lord encouraged David to go.

When David announced his idea to his band of discontents, however, they were not happy as they reasoned that they were in enough danger living in Judah in fear of their own people without getting in trouble with the Fascists.

David prayed again, but the Lord encouraged David to make the effort and promised victory to David.

David persuaded his men to go with him and they fought the Fascists gang and defeated them, and in the process captured a lot of cattle, as well as saving the people of Junction.

Word of all of this came to Saul and he also learned that David and his men had moved into Junction and were living in the town. As a result, Saul was elated, for he figured that he could take a large army and surround the town and then demand that the people of Junction turn over David and his men to the king, or else Saul would wipe out

[1]Keilah

the whole community.

David, of course, heard of this through his wiretapping connections[1] and he sent for the priest and the two of them worshipped God and prayed together for advice. The Lord revealed to David that his information was accurate and also that the Junction people would turn against David and his men to save their hides.[2]

David then called together his band of men which had now increased to 600[3] and suggested that everybody leave town as fast as he could and it was an everyman for himself escape project.

David took to the hills and hid himself in the Blue Ridge Mountains[4] while Saul searched for him every day.

Jonathan was with the search party, which actually was almost an army but scattered about in patrol groups. Jonathan located David and encouraged him. Jonathan told David that he would help keep Saul from finding him and that one day he knew that David would be king, and Jonathan his chief assistant. They shook on this.

Then some of the Hatfields[5] who thought David had some Coy blood in him, came to Saul and told Saul where David was hiding. They suggested that Saul come with them and Saul thanked them heartily.

Saul then said, "Go and get a scouting report on him. Find out how he gets his food, who visits him, and then come and tell me and I'll take over from there."

David, needless to say, got word of all of this and he began to shift his hiding places. David had assembled again a band of discontents and this made hiding even more difficult. In fact, it became impossible, and finally Saul and his men had David and his men trapped on a hill.

At this very moment a messenger came to Saul saying that the Fascists had decided to take advantage of Saul's big chase deal and they had invaded the homeland and Saul, therefore, had to rush his army home at once.

David and his men, therefore, escaped, and they moved away to the area of Fort Knox,[6] a better stronghold.

Chap.
24

After Saul had handled the matter of the Fascists he took 3 thousand selected warriors and started out again for David, having already learned that he had taken refuge in Fort Knox.

It so happened that in camping and in choosing cubby holes and caves for spending the night, that Saul went into the very cave that David was in, though David was well hidden in the back with a few of his men. After Saul went to sleep, David slipped up to him and cut a part of his robe and returned to his men, telling them that he could

---

[1]Not as sophisticated as ours today.   [2]Think a little before criticizing Junction for this.   [3]Inflation and victory had helped.   [4]Ziph   [5]Ziphites
[6]Engedi

not kill his own king, who was the Lord's anointed, and he also restrained his men from doing this.[1]

The next morning Saul arose and left the cave and when he was a couple of hundred yards away David called to him and said, "Good morning, Saul, my king." David then bowed down to the king.

Then David said to Saul, "How did anyone convince you that I sought to ever hurt or harm you? Look, here is proof of my feeling toward you. While you were asleep my men thought I should kill you, but I assured them that I would not raise my hand against the Lord's anointed. Take a good look. Here is part of your robe which I cut off. I could have killed easily. There is no evil intent or malice in me toward you. The Lord can judge between you and me, but I will not raise my sword against you. What have you, the great king of Israel, come to seek? Are you looking for a dead dog or a flea? That's all the importance that I have. May the Lord judge and plead my cause before you."

Then Saul said, "Is this truly you, my son David?" Saul then wept.

"David," finally Saul said, "you are more righteous than I am. You have proven to me that you plan no harm, for if a man finds his enemy at a disadvantage, certainly he will not let him go. May God reward you for what you have done today. I also know now that you will succeed me eventually as king and the Kingdom of Israel will be established firmly under you; so promise me now that you will not eliminate my family, but that you will retain them in the kingdom."

David then took an oath to act accordingly. Saul then returned to his home and David and his men went back to Fort Knox.

Chap.
25

Samuel died and they buried him in Mo-Ranch.[2] David moved his camp from Fort Knox and pitched his tent in the area near Yellowstone Park.[3] There was a big rancher in the area who owned land in Wyoming[4] and Utah[5] and his name was Nabal and his wife's name was Sharon[6]. It was generally known that Sharon was a wise and beautiful woman and that Nabal was a wicked and embittered man, completely self-centered.

Now word came to David that Nabal, who was exceedingly rich, had just finished shearing his sheep and he was now richer than ever, with cash in the bank.

As a result, David sent ten of his young followers to call on Nabal, to give to Nabal David's greetings, and present Nabal with a brochure showing how much help David needed for his army and to seek a contribution, being very courteous and polite with the whole presentation.

When this was done and the men called on Nabal he said to them, "Who is David? There are often fellows on the loose, why should I

---

[1]This is true greatness   [2]Ramah   [3]Paran   [4]Maon
       [5]Carmel   [6]Abigail

take what is mine and give it to this nobody. Go tell the man that sent you that I'm not in the least interested."

The young men returned and reported the conversation to David. Needless to say David was indignant; so he ordered his men to strap on their weapons, every man with a sword, and David put on his sword, and with 400 men David headed for Nabal's ranch, with destructive intent.

One of the young servants of Nabal then went to Sharon and reported to her that the young men from David's camp had been courteous and friendly, and had not stolen so much as one sheep, but that Nabal had given them a crude rejection and the servant was fairly certain that David would come for vengeance. The servant apologized for bothering Sharon but he said that Nabal was such a son of the devil that he couldn't talk with him.

Sharon then hit the kitchen running and began to bake two hundred loaves of bread[1] and she got together fruit, and wine, and plenty of meat. She did not tell Nabal what she was doing, but she told her servants to take all the goodies and head down the ranch road and that she would follow as soon as she got a shampoo and set. When she had caught up with her servants, for she was on a donkey, she met David and his men.

David, in the meantime, had regretted that he had kept his men from stealing or pillaging the ranch of Nabal, and so he had come now to teach the ungrateful wretch a lesson. In fact, David said that it was his intention to kill everybody on the ranch who urinated while standing.[2]

When Sharon saw David she jumped down from the donkey and bowed down to him and spoke to him saying, "Pardon me for being so bold as to speak to you. Please do not let this man Nabal upset you. Actually, he is a sad sack, with a bad attitude. If I had seen the young men you sent there would have been an entirely different answer given. The Lord has encouraged you not to shed blood unnecessarily and so spare Nabal. Accept the presents which I have brought to your young men.

I know you are a great man and I know you will prosper for you fight the battles of the Lord, and you have a wonderful reputation.

The Lord will continue to bless you and he will curse your enemies, and they will disappear as if shot from a sling shot, and then you will be king in Israel.

It would be a shame for a man of your greatness and your future to spoil his record by avenging himself against an arthritic old sour puss. Also when you become king, remember me, and here is my phone number."[3]

"Thank the Lord for sending you to speak to me," said David, "for this is good advice and you have kept me from shedding blood

---

[1]She had the biggest kitchen in the county.　　[2]Probably meant all the men
[3]Words to that effect.

uselessly, and from vengeance. In fact if it were not for you, by tomorrow morning there would not be left on the ranch anyone who urinates while standing."[1]

David then accepted the gifts and told Sharon to return to her house in peace.

That night Nabal was having a big feast celebrating the selling of his wool and he finally passed out from over drinking; so Sharon did not tell him about David.

In the morning, however, Sharon told Nabal at breakfast how she had visited David and bowed down to him and talked him out of cleaning out the ranch. Nabal was so furious that he had a stroke, became paralyzed, and died in ten days.

When David heard that Nabal had died of a stroke he said, "Hurrah! The Lord was just seeing that Nabal got what was coming to him."

As a result David wrote a note to the widow Sharon and in the hand delivered note of sympathy he asked if she would consent to be his wife.

The messengers who came to Sharon with this note were well received and she washed their feet. Then she selected five handmaidens to go with her and she followed the messengers back to David and became his wife.

David had two other wives already, but he was one short of the three considered normal because Saul had made Greta leave David and marry another fellow.

Chap.
26

As time went by Saul had further periods of depression and the Hatfields came to him again and said that David and his men were in their area and that Saul should come and kill him as Saul would never have peace of mind as long as David was alive.

Saul then gathered 3,000 men and went to the Blue Ridge Mountains to look again for David. David's spies reported all of this to David, who was beginning to tire of this way of life.

David, who was a skilled woodsman by now, came near to the place where Saul was camped and saw where Saul and his bodyguard, Bouncer,[2] were stretched out, apart from the main camp. That evening the Lord caused a deep sleep to fall upon the two of them[3] and David then turned to J. Carson[4] and Flip Wil[5] and said, "Who will go down with me to visit Saul's camp?"

"I'll go," said Flip.

"I'll stay here and keep the fire going," said J. Carson.

As a result David and Flip silently slipped into Saul's camp and stood over Saul who had his untrusty javelin stuck in the ground by his side, and Bouncer was dead asleep on the other side of Saul.

---

[1] David liked this expression. I doubt if Sheila did.   [2] Abner
[3] With a boost from too much wine?   [4] Ahimelech   [5] Abishai

"God has delivered your enemy into your hands, David," said Flip. "Let me stick him through with my spear. One sticking is all I need."

"No, Flip," said David, "do not destroy him, for he is the Lord's anointed. His day shall come and he will perish no doubt in battle some day against the Fascists."

David, however, took the spear that Saul had stuck in the ground by his side, and he also took his canteen from the knapsack which was loosely tied to his waist, and returned to the safety of the hill.

Next morning David stood forth on top of a nearby hill and called out in a loud voice, "Good morning, Bouncer. How are you doing today?"

"What voice is that? Who is calling to disturb the king?"

"Are you a brave and careful watchman, Bouncer? Why don't you guard the king more carefully? Last night a couple of my people came to destroy the king. The king could have been killed. You ought to be killed yourself, for neglect, for you have not protected the Lord's anointed."

At this point David raised Saul's spear and held up his canteen for all to see.

"Take a look, Bouncer. These were taken from the king last night, and it could have been his life."

Saul was listening and he recognized David's voice.

"Is that you, David?" asked Saul.

"Yes, it is me, my lord and king," replied David. "Hear me now, my king. Why do you pursue me? What have I done that is wrong? If the Lord has stirred you against me, then let us make a peace offering jointly to the Lord, but if it be men that have caused you to turn against me, let them be cursed of God. This is silly for a great king like you to seek one man, who is only as a flea, or for you to hunt a man as if he were a quail."

"I have sinned again," said Saul. "I will do you no more harm. I have played the fool. I am sorry."

"Thank you," said David. "Now send one of your young men over here to get your spear.[1] May the Lord render to every man justice. Just as I had the chance to kill you and refrained because you are the Lord's anointed; even as I have spared your life may the Lord also spare mine."

Then Saul said, "Blessings on you, David. I foresee a great future for you, and I know that in the long run you will prevail."

After this Saul returned to his home and David left again for the hills.

Chap.
27

After David had a little time to think and review his knowledge of psychology, he realized that Saul would no doubt become depressed

[1] I think he kept the canteen, as he didn't have one.

again and try again to find and kill David. As a result, David decided that he had better leave the area and lose himself among the Fascists in Austin where he could easily lose himself on the drag. David took with him his six hundred men and his two wives Sharon and Susie.[1]

The word came to Saul that David was in Austin and Saul thought this was a good place for him so he quit worrying about him.

David then approached the Governor at Austin and asked him if he might be willing to give David a town, that was nearby, and then David and his men would not be in the way and the Governor wouldn't have to worry about David's presence.

This pleased the Governor very much and so he gave David the town of Dripping Springs[2] and David stayed there for nearly two years.

The inactivity began to get to David and his men so they decided to go north and make a raid on an old enemy of Israel that had not been properly handled. As a result David and his men went to Tulsa[3] and Oklahoma City[4] and they slaughtered the men, women, and children and took all the cattle and the loot they could carry, and returned by way of Austin.

The Governor of Austin said to David, "Where have you been? I heard that you had gone forth to war."

"We went south to fight against some of the Hebrews that have been giving me so much trouble."

This was told[5] by David so the Governor, who was a Fascist, would not know that David had attacked some of the Governor's allies. This is why he killed everybody; so there would be no one to report the matter. David stuck to this policy all the time. This fooled the Governor and made him think that David was totally estranged from his own people and would never be a threat to the Fascists again.[6]

Chap. 28

It was not long after this that the Fascists decided to get their armies together and invade Israel.[7] As a result, the Governor at Austin told David of this and said that he knew that David and his 600 men would join the Fascists in the war against Israel.

"Of course you know what I will do," said David.[8]

The Governor then said to David, "I expect you to be my chief protector."

Now Samuel was dead, and more or less in his honor, Saul had passed a law against fortune tellers, witches, mediums, or people using ESP.

When Saul, however, was told of the massing of the troops of Fascists, he became depressed and afraid, and his prayers to the Lord

[1]Ahinoam. I think he left one back in the hills.   [2]Ziklag   [3]Geshurites
[4]Amalekites   [5]not true, of course   [6]A nice place to stop and discuss
foreign policy.   [7]There was no TV, football, or much else to do.
[8]The forked tongue touch

did not seem to get off the ground. Saul longed for Samuel, but Samuel was dead.

Then Saul said to one of his servants, "Locate me a fortune teller or a medium that I may go and get some inside information."

One of the servants said, "Well, there is one I've heard about, the witch of Endor, who is doing black market business as a soothsayer."

As a result, Saul disguised himself and with two servants went to the woman at night and he said to her, "Bring to me a person from the spirit world. I know exactly to whom I wish to speak."

"Unfortunately," said the witch, "Saul the king has passed a law against this. How do I know but what you are an undercover agent who is laying a trap for me, to catch me, and have me executed?"[1]

"I take an oath that nothing will happen to you, and there shall be no punishment," said Saul.

"Who do you want me to contact?" asked the woman.

"Get me in touch with Samuel," said Saul.

Now when the woman understood that it was the dead Samuel that was wanted, she said, "You have deceived. You are Saul, the king. He is the only one who would seek Samuel." At this point the witch gave a pitiful shriek.

The king said to her, "Be not afraid. Tell me what you have perceived."

"I see various forms and one of them is an old man, and he is covered with the robe of a prophet."

Saul then decided that the witch was in touch with Samuel and he bowed his head to the ground.

Then a voice said, "Why have you disturbed me, Saul?"

"Because of the Fascists," said Saul, "and because God has deserted me, and there are no more prophets.[2] I have called on you to tell me what to do."

"Why call on me, if the Lord has left you, and I am with God?"

Saul remembered the very words of Samuel who had said when he was alive, "The Lord hath rent the kingdom out of your hands and given it to a neighbor, even to David, because you did not obey the voice of the Lord."

"Therefore hath the Lord done this thing to you," said the voice of Samuel, "and moreover the Lord will turn Israel over to the Fascists, and tomorrow you and your sons will join me in the next world."

Then Saul fainted. For one thing, he had not eaten all day, nor all night.

Then the good witch came to Saul and said, "I have obeyed your voice and trusted you with my life, and I have listened to your request, now let me feed you and give you strength, and get you out of here."

[1] You would think a Grade A witch would know.

[2] Saul had killed most of them

Saul, however, refused to eat, but the woman and the servants forced food into him, and finally he was able to sit up on the side of the bed. The woman then went to the kitchen and fixed some barbecued ribs, and a good meal and fed the men properly, and they left strengthened.

Chap.
29

Now as the Fascist army began to assemble and the thousands of soldiers passed along to the gathering place, David took his men and got behind the Governor and his men.

When the leaders of the Fascists met to plan their strategy, one of them asked about David and said, "What in the world are those Hebrews doing with our army?"

"These men are David and his men, and they have been with me a long time and I have found no fault with them."

The Fascists leaders were angry about this, however, and said, "Send this fellow back. We don't want him in back of us. We don't trust the Hebrews and he may decide to help Saul. David is a powerful man, and our enemy, for there was even a folk song about him saying 'Saul has killed his thousands, but David, his tens of thousands.' Those were Fascists that he killed."

Then the Governor sent for David and said, "You have been good to me and I trust you completely, but the other Fascists leaders don't agree, so I think the best for all concerned is for you to return to Dripping Springs and we will fight Israel without you."

"What have I done wrong? I am disappointed. I don't see why I can't be allowed to help."[1]

"I know you are right, David," said the Governor, "but the princes of the Fascists have out voted me and they say definitely that you shall not enter the battle with them. My suggestion is that first thing in the morning you and your men get up and go." This they did.

Chap.
30

When David and his men returned to Dripping Springs they found the place had been burned to the ground by one of the Fascist outfit, a group known as the Sooners,[2] that the mayor had been killed, the women taken captives, and all the cattle and valuables stolen. The wives and children of David and all of his men had been taken captive and all that David and his men could do that day was weep.

In fact, the people were so upset that they considered stoning David to death for having gone off to join the Fascists and leaving the homestead defenseless.

David then went into the church with the priest and stood before God with his problem, asking God if it were wise to pursue the

---

[1]Apparently David was going to sabotage the Fascists from the rear

[2]Amalekites branch

Sooners and attempt to recapture their families.

The Lord encouraged David to pursue and promised that the trip would succeed.

David and his six hundred men pursued the Sooners and finally came to the Red River.[1] About 200 of the men were too pooped to cross the river, so David continued the pursuit with only 400 men.

In their pursuit they found a wetback[2] walking in a field and the men brought him to David, and fed him, and gave him something to drink.

David said to him, "Who are you?"

"I am a wetback," said the man, "and I have been working as a slave to one of the Sooners, but I became sick and they left me behind. In fact, I was with them when they burned Dripping Springs."

"Can you tell me where I can find this bunch of Sooners?" asked David.

"If you promise not to kill me or to deliver me back to the Sooners, I'll put the finger on them."

As a result David, of course, gave his promise and the wetback led David and his men to the place where the Sooners were camped. When David and his men saw them, the Sooners were spread out over the valley, eating, drinking, and dancing, celebrating their good luck. David and his men interrupted their evening drinking and eating, and caught them completely unprepared and stayed after them all through the next day so that only 400 escaped, and these were young men who fled on camels.

David recovered the cattle that had not been eaten and also his two wives. In fact, David took control of everything that the Sooners had and declared immediate possession of the flocks, herds, and material things.

David then began to return to Dripping Springs, and when he came to the Red River the 200 men who had stayed behind came out to salute David.

Some of the men with David then said, "Since these fellows were not in the fight, we don't think they should get any of the spoils, except their wives and children which we bring back to them."

"No," said David, "we will not operate in this fashion. It is important to always have men left behind to guard our tents and equipment. Also we must remember that it is the Lord that gives the victory; so we will divide properly the profits with those that remained and guarded the equipment as well as with those who did the fighting." This then became a policy in Israel from that day.

Upon returning to Dripping Springs, David took some of the excess profit and he sent messengers to the various tribes in Judah and throughout Israel making valuable gifts to each in David's name

---

[1]Besor   [2]In this case an Egyptian

and as a notification of his victory.[1]

In the meantime, the Fascist army moved against Israel and the army of Israel was defeated and fled. The Fascist followed with great determination, particularly wishing to kill Saul and his sons who fought valiantly.

Jonathan and his brothers Bill[2] and Pete[3] were both killed in the battle. About this time one of the archers wounded Saul with an arrow and he could not continue to fight. Saul then turned to his armorbearer, who was by his side, and said, "Kill me with your sword. I do not want to be killed by the heathen Fascists and I know my end is close at hand."

The armorbearer said, "I cannot kill my king."

So Saul took his own sword and stuck the hilt in the ground and fell on his sword, killing himself. When the armorbearer saw what Saul had done, he did the same thing to himself.[4]

As soon as word of this defeat spread, the Hebrews across the Jordan, and the ones occupying the cities of Israel all fled to the various places in the wilderness and the remote areas. The Fascists moved in and took over Israel.

The Fascists found the bodies of Saul and his sons, and they beheaded them, and they took the head of Saul and sent it around the various cities on display and they took the armour of Saul and put it in the Smithsonian Institute.[5] Now the bodies of Saul and his sons had been hung on the wall of the Astrodome,[6] but these bodies were stolen in the night and taken to be burned and buried by friends.

[1]It is hard to realize that he had no PR man

[2]Abinadab

[3]Malchishua

[4]This is maybe taking loyalty too far

[5]Ashtaroth

[6]Bethshan

II SAMUEL

After David had been back at Dripping Springs for about two days a man came into town with his clothes all torn, dirty, and exhausted, and he found David and bowed down to him.

David asked, "Where have you been? What gives with you?"

"I have just escaped from the camp of Israel," replied the man.

"How did the battle go?" asked David.

"The people of Israel have fled and Saul and Jonathan have been slain," reported the man.

"How do you know this?" asked David.

"As I happened to pass by the area," said the fellow, "I saw Saul leaning on his own spear and the chariots and horsemen were coming down upon him. Then Saul begged me to kill him, so I did as he asked, for I could see that he could not live in his present condition anyway. While I was there, I took the head piece of the king from his head and the arm band marker of the king, and I have brought them to you."

Then David tore his clothes in anguish as did those others standing around and they mourned the passing of their king and his son, and for the whole house of Israel and its troubles.

David then sent for the man who had brought the news and asked him to identify himself.

"I am a Sooner," said the man.

"Why were you not afraid to smite the Lord's anointed, the king of Israel? No heathen has this right."

David therefore ordered that one of the soldiers should kill the Sooner who claimed to have killed Saul, for David said that the man had convicted himself by his own testimony.[1]

Then David composed a folk song of praise for Saul and Jonathan, and this song was to be recorded and sung thoughout Israel.

The Song

The beauty and glory of Israel is gone.
The great and mighty have fallen.
Mention it not among the heathen.
Let there be no rejoicing among them,
Better let the mountains have no dew,
Or the soft rain cease to fall
For the shield of the mighty Saul is gone.
The brave Jonathan is no more,
He never retreated in the face of the enemy;

[1]David obviously didn't believe that Saul would ask a heathen to kill him.

Oh! Saul and Jonathan were great in life,
It is fitting that they died together,
For they were swifter than eagles,
And stronger than lions,
Weep, girls, weep for Saul
For Saul clothed you in scarlet
And he trimmed your dresses with gold.
The mighty have fallen in battle.
Oh! Jonathan, Jonathan, how sad I am,
Even though you had a warrior's death,
How joyful and great was our friendship,
More enduring was our love,
A love more binding than other loves,
How strong a friendship we had,
How are the mighty fallen!
How sad this day for me and Israel!

Chap. 2

After everything had settled down a bit and the mourning period was ended, then David prayed to the Lord for guidance, and God encouraged David to return to Judah and to investigate the possibilities of some restoration.

As a result, David with his two wives and all his men and all their possessions were assembled and they moved into the area of Judah and settled in a town called Rochester[1]. The men of Judah came there and anointed David as king of the tribe of Judah. The men also told David about the fellows from the University of Louisville[2] who had come and stolen the bodies of Saul and his sons from the Fascist and had given them proper burial.

David then sent messengers to the University and extended his thanks and his blessings to those that had done this fine thing at great risk. David said also in the message that he would remember this and that their kindness would some day be amply repaid.

Bouncer, however, wanted to initiate the restoration through the line of Saul as he knew how he stood with David, so he took an older son of Saul who had not been in the Fascist battle and made him king over an area containing about five small towns and consisting of part of one tribe, but he felt it was a start. Shorty,[3] the king, lasted only two years.

During this time an interesting incident took place. Bouncer took a few of his young soldiers to a water hole and by prearrangement met Tuffy,[4] who was David's aide and who came with some of David's men.

Bouncer said to Tuffy, "Why don't we let our young men engage

[1]Hebron   [3]Ishbosheth
[2]Jabeshgilead   [4]Joab

in a contest, soccer or something, and we can watch."

"Great idea," said Tuffy.

As a result, twelve men from each side went together on the side of the pool supposedly for a contest, but it immediately broke out into a fight. Apparently they did not come to play as each man grabbed his opponent's head and stuck his sword in him and they were all killed. Then the rest of the soldiers joined the fight and the soldiers of Tuffy, David's men, defeated the soldiers of Bouncer.

Incidentally, they named the place Bloody Pool,[1] and placed there a historical marker.

One of Tuffy's brothers was named Lightfoot Harry,[2] for he could run like a deer, and he began to chase Bouncer.

Bouncer, while running, yelled over his shoulder, "Are you Lightfoot Harry?"

"You better believe it, man," called out Lightfoot.

"How about chasing one of the younger men who are running? I am about pooped out and I don't want to kill you. I can whip you, but I don't want to have Tuffy after me."

Lightfoot would not listen to him and he caught Bouncer, but as he reached for him Bouncer thrust a spear through him and killed him.

This made a bunch more people mad, and a group from the tribe of Benjamin met on a hill and organized a posse under Tuffy.

Bouncer then called out to Tuffy and said, "Let's call this thing quits before more people get hurt. Are we not all Hebrews? Why should we start a civil war that will just lead to more and more trouble?"

"You spoke just in time," said Tuffy, "for in the morning we were going to pour down on you."

As a result, Tuffy had the bugler blow recall and everybody went his own way in peace. Tuffy was satisfied to be able to report to David that they had lost only 19 men while they had killed 360 of Bouncer's.[3]

Chap.
3

This by no means settled everything for the supporters of David as the followers of king Saul's son were constantly on the warpath with raiding parties and the like. The men of David, however, seemed to increase in number and their success began to grow as the followers of the line of Saul became weaker and weaker.

David, in the meantime, had added four wives to his string, more in keeping with his prosperity, and the total of six wives brought him six sons in a fairly short span of time. The third son was one born to Trudy,[4] one of the new wives, and the boy was named Absalom, though his playmates called him Abby.

[1]Helkathhazzurim

[2]Asahel

[3]Bouncer had a good
reason for peace talk

[4]Maacah

Now Bouncer was asserting himself pretty strongly in assembling men to serve for Shorty and Bouncer made himself General over the forces of the son of Saul, and developed a real sense of self-importance.

Bouncer had decided to take for himself the former mistress of King Saul, a girl named Mame,[1] and King Shorty didn't like this.

"What are you doing fooling around with my dead father's mistress?" Shorty asked Bouncer one day.

"Don't talk to me that way. If it weren't for me you wouldn't be king. In fact, I control the army, and I could easily turn you over to David, and here you are squalling because I'm having a little pleasure on the side. If you aren't careful with me I'll turn the whole house of Saul over to David."

This hushed up Shorty real fast.

Bouncer then sent a message to David and said, "Let's make a deal. I will join with you to take over Israel."

"Not until you have the king return to me my first wife, the daughter of Saul, my true love, Greta."

Bouncer relayed the request of David to Shorty, who was scared anyway, and so he sent for Greta and packed her off in a hurry to David. Now Greta's husband was greatly upset and followed her down the road weeping and wailing until Bouncer had to order him home.[2]

Then Bouncer began to pass a message along to the elders of Israel saying that he knew that they had long wanted David for their king[3] and it was about time that this came to pass for it was common knowledge that the Lord had promised to save Israel by the hand of David, from the Fascist as well as other enemies.

After Bouncer had spread the word pretty well among the tribes he went to see David personally, taking with him only 20 men. David received the group graciously and had a big banquet in their honor.

Bouncer then told David that he would start gathering all the people of Israel together and get all the tribes to consent to accept David as king. As a result, David let Bouncer and his men depart in peace.

A couple of days later Tuffy returned to David's camp after a successful raid on a Fascist ranch, and Tuffy learned that Bouncer had been in David's camp.

"What did you do, David?" asked Tuffy. "How could you let that snake in the grass Bouncer come here and leave unharmed. You know that Bouncer is up to no good and that he is working some trick play to spring."

Tuffy, who was still properly sore at Bouncer for having killed his younger brother Lightfoot, sent messengers to Bouncer telling him to

---

[1]Rizpah   [3]Bouncer was cagy

[2]Greta must have been something else for real

return for a brief conference.

When Bouncer arrived at the entrance of Raleigh, where the headquarters of David was, Tuffy met him at the gate and said, "Step aside over here, Bouncer, and let me give you a little inside information before you go to see David again."

Bouncer then stepped aside behind the corner of the wall and the inside information that Tuffy had for him was a sword inside the fifth rib, which killed Bouncer on the spot.

When word of this came to David he did not seem to be in the least disturbed, but he did say, "As a matter of record, let it be known that this was not my doing, nor that of my kingdom, but a personal thing between Tuffy and Bouncer. I think also that Tuffy and his house should be blamed for this unsatisfactory settlement of an old feud."

David then called a meeting of the leaders of the people and said, "It is proper that we mourn for Bouncer and give him a decent burial, for he was a warrior, the protector of King Saul. It is great that he died as a warrior, not as one with his hands tied, or in chains."

David then said, "Let there be mourning in my house. I will not eat all day long for I will weep over the death of Bouncer. There has fallen today a prince and a great man in Israel."

All of this favorably impressed the people, and it became known far and wide that David was in no way responsible for the death of Bouncer.

Chap.
4

Now when Shorty heard that Bouncer was dead he knew the jig was up and he trembled. Lots of people in Israel became nervous, for they had been supporting Shorty's regime.

When Jonathan and Saul had been killed, the five year old son of Jonathan accompanied by his nurse fled to the hills and in running the child fell and became permanently crippled. The name of the boy was Sonny[1] and he remained hidden in the hills with his nurse.

Now Shorty had two young men who were captains in his army, one was named Mert[2] and one was called Hoot.[3] These two figured the kingdom under Shorty was a goner so they decided to get in good with David. During siesta time, therefore, they went into the house of Shorty and found him taking an afternoon nap and they killed him and cut off his head and slipped away without being seen.

In a couple of days they arrived at the headquarters of David in Raleigh and presented him with the head of Shorty, saying, "Here is the head of your enemy, and you are now avenged of all that Saul did to you."

[1]Mephibosheth   [2]Rechab
[3]Baanah

David then said, "Will you birds ever learn? When the man reported to me that Saul was dead the messenger thought he brought good tidings, but I had him killed for saying that he had put Saul to death. The nut thought I would reward him. I am not a man of blood and vengeance; so I had the messenger killed.[1]

"How much worse it is for wicked men like you to have killed a righteous weakling in his bed in his own house. Surely you do not belong on this earth."

David then commanded his soldiers to kill Mert and Hoot, to cut off their hands and feet, and hang the remains from a tree, but he ordered a decent burial for the head of Shorty.

Chap.
5

Then came all the tribes of Israel to David and told him how they had known all along that he would be their ruler, and they spoke of their close kinship and reminded him that they were all Hebrews, and then they anointed him king of Israel.[2]

David and his soldiers then went to Jerusalem which was at the time controlled by the Apache Indians[3] and David wanted to know if these people wanted to be taken under the new kingdom.

The Apache reply was to the effect that the lame and the blind among the Apaches could hold off all David's army without help from any of the warriors.

David was greatly insulted and he told his men to surround the city and crawl in under the walls through the gutters and the tunnels and to fight fiercely and make the Apaches eat their smart remarks. David's men took the city, and it became known as the city of David.

David continued to grow in greatness and he increased his possessions and the power of the Lord was with him.

As a tribute as well as good public relations, the king of Tyre sent a crew of carpenters and masons, along with a lot of wood and stone, and built David a fine house, with many rooms. David counted the rooms and realized that he did not have enough wives to put in all the spaces in the girls dormitory, so he recruited some of the best looking and most attractive girls in the area. It was not long before David had eleven more children[4].

Now the Fascist heard that David had been made king of Israel, and the Fascist as usual began to get organized and decided to march against David from Valley-Low.[5]

David, as his custom was, prayed to the Lord for guidance and decided that the Lord wished him to move against the Fascists and that the Lord would give Israel the victory.

David met the Fascists at a place called Custer's First Stand and

[1]Good place for discussion and dialogue

[2]David was always getting anointed. I think he liked it.

[3]Jebusites

[4]Since daughters were often not counted, there may have been more than listed.

[5]Rephaim

David and his men beat them so thoroughly that the Fascists fled in all directions like water spilling from a broken dam. David then changed the name of the place to Broken Dam.[1] The Fascists fled so rapidly that they left their flags and insignia, and David burned these.

The Fascist reorganized again, however, and again set up camp near Valley-Low. David prayed again for guidance and from his meditation came forth the plan to slip up on the Fascist by having his men move cautiously using mulberry branches and trees as cover. The ruse worked beautifully and David had another victory over the Fascists.[2]

Chap.
6

David, feeling that the Fascist matter was pretty well handled, assembled an impressive army of 30,000 men and set forth to march to Montreat and bring back to the city of David the ark of the covenant of the Lord.

Upon arriving at Montreat, the ark of the covenant was taken from the Assembly Inn and placed on a cart to be drawn by oxen. The trip back was really a big parade with the men playing all kinds of musical instruments, and various bands from the small towns joining the parade. One of the drivers of the cart was a fellow by the name of Jinx[3] and when nearing one of the resting places the cart hit a bump as it was being driven into the barn for the night; so Jinx reached forth his hand and touched the ark of the covenant to steady it, and he fell over dead, for the Lord had decreed that no hand but that of a priest conducting service should ever touch the ark.[4]

This incident scared David and he was afraid to bring the ark to his house or to his city, for David feared the Lord. As a result the ark was left in the house of a man named Moody.[5] The Lord therefore blessed the house of Moody greatly and the family became well-to-do and prominent in business as well as in the Lord's work.

David learned of this; so he decided that maybe the ark of the covenant should be in the city of David after all. As a result, David sent for the ark and it was brought into the city of David, and there was a proper sacrifice made at the gate, and David led the parade down the street. The parade was a wild one, with the men singing and dancing and playing all kinds of instruments. David led the parade and he danced himself into a frenzy, even doing the watusi.

It so happened that Greta, David's first wife and his favorite, looked out the window and saw David doing his thing, and she was furious.

The ark of the covenant was then brought into the tabernacle and

[1]Baalperazim

[2]Shakespeare picked up this item for his Burnham wood account

[3]Uzzah

[4]It was always loaded on the cart by pole lifters

[5]Obededom

proper offerings were made to the Lord. Then cake, cookies, and coffee was served to all the people and there was great joy and thanksgiving.

When David came home, however, Greta lowered the boom on him saying, "You made a jackass of yourself in the parade. Doing those crazy dances and throwing up your skirts to attract the attention of all the girls watching the parade. Shame, shame!"

"You are wrong, Greta," said David, "for what I was doing was part of the worship service. What is more, I am ruler of the people, chosen by God, and I'll probably do worse things than this. As for the girls, I hope I did impress them, for I go for girls pretty strongly."

Greta then refused to allow David to touch her for the rest of her life.[1]

Chap.
7

Things settled down in the city and all was quiet on the western front and David was having little to do but look for something to do. David sent for Nathan, the prophet of the Lord, and said to him, "I live in a big fine house and yet I notice that the ark of the covenant of the Lord is just in a little place shut off with curtains."

"As far as I'm concerned, David, if you want to do something about it, have at it," replied Nathan.

That night, however, the word of the Lord came to Nathan suggesting that he go and talk to David and tell him that the Lord did not want David to build a temple.

Nathan called on David and said, "The Lord says that the temple bit can wait. The ark of the covenant has remained without its own house for many years, in fact ever since it was built in the wilderness under Moses. There has never been any request from God for a temple for the ark.

"Tell David also, the Lord said to me, that I brought him from being a little runny nose sheepherder to be the king of Israel, that I have protected him and delivered him from all his enemies. Remind David that I will establish my people in my way in my own time. The Lord also has promised to see that the line of David is continued, and his son shall build a proper temple in the fulness of time. The Lord also will provide through the line of David a kingdom that shall be forever and not subject to defeat."[2]

Then David prayed to the Lord himself and said, "Who am I to be so greatly blessed? I am deeply touched. I know that thou art great, O Lord, that there is none like thee, nor is there any other God. What more could a nation ask than to have the Lord as their God, and to worship him?

[1] I think she was the first Greta to say "I want to be alone."

[2] Christ came through the line of David

As for the word about the line of David and the eternal kingdom, accept my gratitude. I know you are the true God, and the one Lord of all. Continue to bless this house of mine and may it be blessed forever, even as you have decreed."

Chap.
8

There developed a slack year or two in Israel so David decided to go and give his army a workout and to build up the treasury and extend his kingdom; so he started by attacking Naples [1] where one of the Fascist outfits were stationed. David took Naples without any trouble and then he decided to move against some of the places in Mississippi.

David captured several hundred of the men and made them all lie on the ground face down. Then David ordered the soldiers to kill two and skip one all the way down the line as he wanted to save a hundred or so as servants. [2]

David then went into Tennessee [3] and defeated the forces of Jimmy, mayor of Memphis, and he extended his territory this way to the Mississippi River. In this raid David captured one thousand chariots, 700 horsemen, and 20,000 footmen. David was afraid that the chariots might be used against him sometime so he had all the chariot horses' tendons cut so they would be lame, and he gave them to poor people for their farms.

The Syrians from Damascus then came to the aid of the mayor of Memphis and David and his men killed 22,000 of them before the rest decided to return home and tend to their own business. David then began to build forts in all parts of the land and in every place that he conquered, he left small bands of his men to rule these forts and to keep the peace.

The spoils of these little wars were great, and David brought great riches in brass and silver back to Jerusalem.

Now when Tito [4] heard that David had defeated his old enemy from Memphis he sent his son Joey [5] to visit David, to thank him, and to give him some very expensive presents of silver, and gold, and brass. David dedicated all of these spoils and gifts to the Lord.

David's fame spread greatly after defeating the Syrians and he returned a great hero. [6]

David reigned over Israel, with justice and fairness to all, and he made Tuffy commander in chief of the army under David.

Chap.
9

David still often thought of his friend Jonathan and he still grieved over his death and so he asked one of his servants if there was anyone left in Saul's family that David could help for Jonathan's sake.

---

[1]Methegammah   [2]David thought this easier than saying I want one-third of the men saved.   [3]Hadadezer   [4]Toi   [5]Joram
[6]But still no Greta reception

A man who had worked for Saul was located and he came to David and David asked him if there were any descendants of Saul left alive.

"Yes," replied the man. "Jonathan left a son who was crippled in an accident when he was a child."

"Where is he?" asked David.

"He is living in a little town in the hills called Woodsville."[1]

As a result David sent for Jonathan's son and when he arrived he fell on his face in front of David.

"Are you Sonny, the son of Jonathan?" asked David.

"I am," said Sonny.

"Do not be afraid, Sonny, for I have no thoughts but kind thoughts for you because of your father. I plan to restore to you the land that was your grandfather's and I expect you to live in a guest house here with me and to eat with me continually."

"I am greatly honored, for actually I am only as a dead dog, being crippled and no longer of any use," said Sonny.

Now J.P.,[2] the man who reported about Sonny, was a man with fifteen sons and twenty servants and David put him in charge of the old Saul place and told him to run the place and bring the profit to Sonny, but that Sonny would live on the palace grounds. J.P. was to get well paid, of course, for his work.

As a result, Sonny and his wife and young son moved into the guest cottage and Sonny was a regular guest at the table of King David, though he was still lame in both legs.[3]

Chap.
10

Not too long after this, word came to David that the mayor of Cleveland[4] had died and this his son Hubert[5] had taken his place. David remembered that the mayor had been kind to him one time and he thought of him as a friend; so he decided to send some of his young warriors to Cleveland to put some roses on the grave of his friend and show goodwill to Hubert.

Some of the city councilmen, however, were very leary of this and they told Hubert, who seemed to be the gullible type, that David was probably using this as an excuse to spy on Cleveland and to lay plans to capture it.[6]

As a result, Hubert ordered that half of each man's beard that David sent be shaved off and that they all be put in mini-skirts and sent home. The warriors were mortified beyond description.

When David heard of this he went to meet the men, and reassured them about themselves, and then told them to go to Chicago[7] until their beards grew again to full size.

David let it be known that when he faced in the direction of

[1]Lodebar   [2]Ziba   [3]It was unusual to help the handicapped in those days
[4]Ammon   [5]Hanun   [6]Suspicion is still an international troublemaker.
[7]Jericho

Cleveland he smelled a bad odor, and the people of Cleveland learned of his dissatisfaciton. As a result, Hubert made a deal with the Syrians to join them in battle against Israel.

David then sent Tuffy and all the array of mighty men that he had in the army, and when they arrived in the area, Tuffy saw that the Syrians were gathered on one side and the men of Cleveland on the other. As a result, Tuffy split his army, and took the best warriors from the army and put them with him, and the less experienced men he put under Abbie[1], his younger brother.

Then Tuffy said, "I will attack the Syrians and you attack the men of Cleveland. If I'm having too much trouble with the Syrians then you come and help me, and if you can't handle the men of Hubert, then I'll come help you."

When Tuffy and his crack troops stormed into the Syrians, the Syrians came right soon to the conclusion that the fight wasn't worth the money; so they began to flee. When the men of Cleveland saw that the Syrians were fleeing, they decided the war was not such a good idea after all, and they fled.

Then Tuffy returned to Jerusalem and dismissed the army for the time being.

The Syrians decided to do a little more recruiting and to try again with a larger army, and a man named Rumel[2] stirred up the people and moved with great confidence and great speed against Israel.

When David learned of this, he ordered the army to reassemble and then did a little extra recruiting also and David crossed the Jordan and met the Syrians at Bunker Hill.[3]

David and his men defeated the Syrian army again and the Israelites killed 700 chariot loads of Syrians and 40,000 cavalry men,[4] and also killed Howe,[5] one of the prominent generals.

As a result, the Syrians decided to make peace with David and they also decided that they would no longer try to help Cleveland.

Chap.
11

About a year had elapsed and it was time again for the winter games, which meant sending troops to worry the Fascist, locating any new Dalton gangs, and fighting the Mafia, if they could be located. David decided to sit this season out, and he remained in Jerusalem, but Tuffy directed the field operations in various sections of the country.

One day after his afternoon nap, David was walking on his rooftop in the sun as he often did, and he looked over the fence and saw an exceedingly beautiful woman taking a bath in her backyard.[6]

At supper that night, David asked one of his aides, "Who is the lady who lives next door?"

"If you are talking about the neighbor we think you mean, her

[1]Abishai   [2]Hadarezer   [3]Helam   [4]Counting in those days was not always accurate   [5]Shobach   [6]I think she knew what she was doing

name is Gina[1]," said one of the men.

"Incidentally," said one of the fellows, "she is married to an army man and he is out on maneuvers."

As a result David sent for her and she came over and spent the night with him, and returned home in the morning.

A few trips later and she remarked to David that she was pregnant, and that her baby would be the child of the king.

David then decided to send for her husband, Corps Happy,[2] and so the good captain Corps Happy came to the palace from the front line.

David said to him, "How are things at the front? How's Tuffy? How are the raids going?"

Corps Happy gave a good report.

David then said, "You'd better go home and wash your feet and get a good nights rest before returning to the battle lines."

David gave him a big box lunch to take with him. Corps Happy, however, did not go home, but slept on the floor in the king's palace. David was told of this the next morning so he sent for Corps Happy and said, "Why didn't you go home last night, especially after such a long journey?"

Corps Happy then said, "The ark of the covenant and my comrades in Israel and Judah are sleeping on the ground in tents, and some of them, even Tuffy, are sleeping in open fields, how then when my friends are having it so tough can I go to my house and eat and drink and lie down with my wife?"[3]

"Well, if you feel that way about it, stay around the palace today and tomorrow go back to the troops."

In the morning David wrote a letter to Tuffy, sealed it, and gave it to Corps Happy to deliver. In the letter, he told Tuffy to let Corps Happy lead the next charge against the Fascists, and then let the fellows around him back off and leave Corps to fight the Fascists by himself.[4]

Tuffy did his job well and he put Corps Happy in a place where he would charge the strongest point of the Fascist garrison. In this unnecessary attack a number of the soldiers of David were slain, and in the group was, as planned, Corps Happy.

Then Tuffy sent a messenger to David and told him of the attack on the strong garrison of the Fascists. Tuffy also told the messenger that David would probably criticize his strategy, and complain about getting so close to a strong point to attack, and he might even mention the case of the girl dropping the stone on Patton's[5] head. After he has complained a bit, then you say to the king, "your trusted warrior, Corps Happy, was also killed in the action."

The messenger came to David and said, "We had a rough time the other day. We pursued some of the Fascists and we came too close to

---

[1]Bathsheba   [2]Uriah   [3]Another good place for a heated discussion
[4]This has to be the dirtiest trick of the week   [5]Abimelech

the walls of the city, but Tuffy had told us to do this. As a result some of the archers began to get the ones in the front, and some of the king's soldiers are dead, and so is Captain Corps Happy."

David then told the messenger to return to Tuffy and to tell him not to be discouraged, but take his time and approach the city with more caution and in time conquer it.

When Gina heard of the death of her husband, she went into mourning. When the accepted mourning period was through, however, she was brought to the palace and Gina became David's wife and gave birth to a son.

The Lord, however, was greatly displeased with the thing that David had done.

Chap.
12

The Lord then sent Nathan, the prophet, to David and he spoke to David saying, "There were two men in the city and one was rich and one was poor. The rich man had plenty of sheep and cattle and the poor man had only one little ewe lamb, and it was part of his family, eating with them, and was greatly beloved by the poor man.

The rich man had an occasion when he needed to possess a ewe and he decided that instead of taking one from his many, he went and took the only one the poor man had."

The story stirred David's sense of justice and he said to Nathan, "That is awful. As the Lord lives, so help me, I'll find that rich man and have him executed, and he shall have to restore four lambs to one for what he has done."

Then Nathan said to David, "You are the man."

Nathan then proceeded to remind David that the Lord God of Israel had anointed him king and made him safe from Saul, and delivered to him great riches and many wives, as well as the whole house of Israel. The Lord would have done even more if it had been desired. Why then would David despise the commandment of the Lord, and do such an evil thing as have Corps Happy killed?

Nathan further said, "The Lord says that for this sin the sword shall be part of your house. The Lord will raise up evil out of your own house and he will see to it that some of your wives are unfaithful, and it will become public knowledge, for the same thing that you tried to do secretly the Lord will have done to you publicly."

"I have sinned against God," said David.

"The Lord will forgive you, but you will still be punished by the death of one of your sons; so you will know how God feels when one of his sons rebels against him."

As a result, the Lord caused the child that was born to Gina to be very sickly, and David and his servants prayed and fasted hoping to save the child's life. David was very distraught and on the seventh day the child died.

The servants and friends of David were afraid to tell him when the child died, for they felt that the news might cause David to have a stroke. David saw them whispering, however, and he knew then that the child was dead.

David then asked, "Is the child dead?"

"Yes," the servant replied.

Then David arose and took a bath and put on his robes and went to the church and there he worshipped God. After this David returned to his own house and began to eat again.

One of his friends then said to him, "What gives? While the child was alive you would not eat or sleep, and now that the child is dead you seem to be all right. We don't understand."

"Well, while the child was alive, there was some hope that I could implore God to save the child's life, but now the matter is done, and the child is now with the Lord."

David did the best he could to comfort his wife, Gina, for it was her firstborn that had died. David continued to keep Gina close to him and she became pregnant again and delivered another son, and they named him Solomon, and the Lord was delighted and blessed the new baby.

Tuffy continued the siege of Venice,[1] the city of waters, and he saw that success was close at hand, so at the suggestion of his PR man he sent for David and told him to come with reinforcements and get in on the big victory.

As a result, David and additional troops joined Tuffy and they captured Venice, and David took the crown from the head of the mayor of Venice and put it on his own head, and there were great valuables taken along with the city.

Although David spared the lives of most of the people of Venice, he made them yardmen and maintenance workers at low salaries.[2] Since this seemed to be a good idea, and since he had his army already all together, David did the same thing to two or three smaller cities on the way home to Jerusalem.

Chap.
13

With all the wives that David had who bore him children, the property of David held several houses and there were many half brothers and half sisters running around the palace. Absalom, David's favorite son, had a beautiful sister named Tamar and one of her half brothers, a fellow named Aubrey,[3] fell in love with her.

Since Tamar was his half sister Aubrey didn't know exactly what to do, though he had a friend who was ready with some poor advice. The friend was a high ranking army man named Flint[4] and he outlined a scheme for Aubrey.

Flint explained to Aubrey that if he could get Tamar alone and get her to go to bed with him, then Aubrey could tell King David

[1]Rabbah [2]Well before minimum wage programs [3]Amnon [4]Jonadab

about it and David would let them get married.

Aubrey followed the plan devised by the cunning Flint. Aubrey played sick, and when David inquired of him, he said that he thought he would get well if his half sister Tamar would come and nurse him and feed him in bed.

As a result, David sent for Tamar and she came and cooked some chocolate chip cookies and fixed some meatballs and came to feed Aubrey. Aubrey then asked all the rest of the help to leave and he propositioned Tamar. Tamar said it was not the proper thing to do and she would not get in the bed with Aubrey; so he raped her.

When the deed was done, Tamar said, "The only thing to do to keep me from shame is for you to tell the king and he will then let us get married."

Aubrey, however, was apparently no longer interested in Tamar and merely sent her home. Now Tamar was Absalom's full sister, and when he learned of what had happened and saw his sister Tamar weeping and in shame, he was mad as a hornet, but he kept his anger to himself.

David, however, was angry over the matter and probably cut Aubrey's allowance in half.

About two years after this Absalom sent word from his ranch that it was shearing time and he wanted the king, his father, and all the sons of David to come help with the shearing. David wouldn't go, but the rest of those invited, including Aubrey, went to the shearing, as Absalom had insisted that his father send Aubrey.

Absalom then instructed his soldiers, who were also ranch hands, to watch Aubrey, and when in the evening Aubrey was fairly full of wine, then to kill him, which they did. The other sons of David decided that they might also get similar treatment and so they fled on camels or mules or whatever they could find.

The grapevine reports that came to David were that all the king's sons had been killed by Absalom. David then went into mourning.

Flint, however, came to David and told him that only Aubrey had been killed and that this was in exchange for the way he had treated Absalom's sister.

Absalom knew that the king and many of his soldiers would be upset over this murder and so Absalom left the country. Shortly after this the king's sons began to straggle back to the palace and there was a big reunion, with much weeping.[1]

Absalom stayed away for 3 years and David his father was sad over this, as Absalom was his favorite son.

Chap.
14

Now Tuffy could see that David was sad and he knew that he longed to have Absalom back home; so Tuffy decided to use an indirect approach.

[1] Weeping for men was still in style.

Tuffy paid an actress to dress herself as a widow in mourning and come to David with a plea. The woman was admitted to the presence of the king and she told David a big story about her husband being dead and her two sons having a fight in a field and one killed the other. Then the people in town thought the other son should be executed for murder, but this would leave her without husband or sons, and she wanted the king to intercede in her behalf.

David immediately agreed to intercede and said that he would see that she and her remaining son were protected. David also said that there was no point in useless killing and vengeance.

Then the actress said, "Can I have permission to speak an additional word without being punished?"

"Permission granted," said David.

"Why don't you practice what you preach? Is there any reason why you should not let Absalom return here? The people need Absalom and a lot of folks are out of work with him gone. Use the same godly wisdom in dealing with your own son, and the same sense of justice as you have decreed for me."

"All right," said David. "Now I want to ask you a question, for this whole session seems to be a staged affair. Did Tuffy put you up to this?"

"The king is as wise as an angel of God, and surely nothing can be hidden from you. Yes, it was Tuffy."

Then David sent for Tuffy and told him to go and get Absalom and return him to his property, but not to bring him to the palace.

As a result, Tuffy made the trip to get Absalom and Absalom returned to his own ranch, but he did not get to visit his father the king.

Absalom was the most handsome man in all Israel and he was very popular and quite a playboy. Absalom went to the barber shop once a year and had two pounds of hair cut off his head.[1]

Now Absalom had been back home for two years and he still had not seen his father; so he sent a message to Tuffy asking Tuffy to visit him. Tuffy wouldn't come. Absalom wrote him again and Tuffy still wouldn't come.

It so happened that Tuffy's ranch and farm land joined Absalom, so Absalom had some of his cowpokes go when the wind was coming from the proper direction and set fire to Tuffy's fields.

Then Tuffy came to see Absalom and said, "What in the thunderation do you mean by setting fire to my field?"

Absalom said, "Well, I sent for you twice and you wouldn't come, so I thought this would bring you. I want you to arrange for me to see my father the king for I've been here two years and have not been invited to visit him. If my father thinks I'm a bad boy that should be punished, then let him judge me to my face and have me killed."[2]

[1] I have no idea why this is in the Scripture   [2] Absalom knew that his father loved him very much.

As a result Tuffy arranged for David to receive Absalom. When Absalom came, he bowed on the ground to his father and David embraced him and restored him to favor in the kingdom.

Chap.
15

Although David was getting old, Absalom decided he did not want to wait the extra years before he could make a bid for the kingdom, and so he began to plot in devious ways a revolution to overthrow his father's government.

One thing he did was to get 50 excellent horsemen, and a strong running escort, to go with him all around the city, and he attracted great attention and much admiration.

Also everytime people from another tribe would come to David with a complaint, Absalom would talk with them and tell them that if he were king he would be of more help. He also bribed strangers and travelers to spread the word throughout Israel and to put bumper stickers on their chariots saying "Absalom for King."

Absalom then came to David and asked permission to take a trip north toward the borders of Syria, saying that he felt called of God to make this trip. David consented, and Absalom went with some two hundred men, the men posing as civilians although actually they were the soldiers of Absalom.

Absalom also enticed Welby,[1] David's advisor, to leave David and join Absalom. The conspiracy against David was strong and many people began to gravitate to Absalom, for they thought that he was a winner.

Word came to David finally that the people of Israel had turned pretty completely against him and had gone over to Absalom's side.

David then took his servants and a fair number of his wives and family and fled from Jerusalem. Many people from the city joined David in his flight and went with him over the hill and across the river.

There came then the mayor of Atlanta to David and said that he and his men appreciated all that David had done and they wished to join him in his time of trouble.

David advised them to go back to Atlanta and stay out of his troubles as the future looked dim. The men from Atlanta, however, said that trouble was no stranger to them and they would stick with David, which they did.

The ark of the covenant was also brought on the trip and it was under the care of Sheen.[2] David told Sheen to take the ark back to Jerusalem and said that if the Lord blessed him that he would return in triumph, and if not, then David said that he would accept the Lord's will for his life.

David then said further to Sheen, "You are a prophet, are you not, and a holy man with vision? Return with your two sons Ned[3] and

---

[1]Ahithophel   [2]Zadok   [3]Ahimaaz

Fred[1]", and they did.

In the meantime, David had already learned that Welby had defected and when David said his prayers that night he asked the Lord to confuse Welby's mind so that his advice to Absalom would be poor.

As David was climbing a small hill where he went to meditate and pray, he encountered an old friend, Rollow[2] from Arkansas[3], and he found his friend depressed over the political situation.

"Actually, my friend," said David, "joining me here is no help, but if you will go to Jerusalem and join Absalom, then I will have a source of information to offset the presence of Welby next to Absalom. If you have any information at any time just pass it along to Sheen at the church and he will get Ned or Fred to bring word to me."

Rollow did as he was asked and went into the city where Absalom was, for Absalom was taking over Jerusalem.

Chap.
16

After this meeting David moved over the top of the hill and saw there J.P., the right hand man of Sonny, the son of Jonathan.

"What are you doing here?" asked David.

"Sonny sent me with bread and wine for you and all the people with you."

"Where is Absalom?" asked David.

"He is in Jerusalem," said J.P., "and he expects to take over your kingdom today."

"You and those with you are all that are left out of the supporters of Saul, I guess." said David.

"Yes," said J.P., "and I hope we will find favor in your sight."

About this time, one of the food bearers from the supporters of Saul blew his top and came out in front of everybody cursing David, calling him a bloody killer, denouncing him for letting Saul fall to the Fascists. The cursing man also said that the rebellion of Absalom was the punishment of God.

Then Al, a younger brother of Tuffy, stepped forth and said, "Why should this dead dog curse our king? Let me cut off his head."

"Let him alone and let him curse. If the Lord has told him to curse me, we shouldn't stop him, and if not, it doesn't matter. It is the revolt of my son which disturbs me, not the cursing of this nut. In fact, it may be that this cursing will suffice, and the Lord will then bless me again."

This encouraged the cursing fellow a great deal, and as he walked along the hillside he continued to yell curses and to throw stones at the army.[4]

In the meantime, Absalom came to Jerusalem with Welby and

---

[1]J. Abiathar   [2]Hushai   [3]Archite   [4]Some of his descendants are still living.

with all the host of Absalom and there Rollow joined the group. As Rollow came to Absalom he said, "God save the king, God save the king."

"Is this the way you treat your friend, my father. Why are you not with him?"

Then Rollow replied, "I go with the crowd. All the men of Israel have chosen you, so I am simply doing the same. What's more, should I not serve the son of my friend as I have served my friend? As I have been adviser to your father, so shall I be to you."

Then at dinner that night Absalom said to Welby, "Advise me what to do."

"What I think you should do," said Welby, "is go to your father's house in Jerusalem and publicly make free with his mistresses or wives that are left. Then all Israel will know that you have defied your father."

As a result of this advice, the men of Absalom put a tent on top of the roof of David's house and the public watched as Absalom would take one of his father's mistresses into the tent. Now Welby gave his advice as if it had come from God.

Chap.
17

The next day Welby came and said to Absalom, "I have some more advice. Let me select 12,000 of the best soldiers, and let me cross the Jordan and pursue David, who we know is old and weary. The small number of people with him will flee and I will kill only King David, and bring back all the rest of the people to join you, and the nation will be yours."

This sounded like a real good idea to Absalom and the local big shots sitting around him.

Absalom then said that he would like to hear what advice Rollow had and what he thought of the plan.

When Rollow came they told him of the suggestion made by Welby and then asked his opinion.

"I think it is a foolish plan," said Rollow. "You forget that your father is a warrior and he has a lot of strong and valiant men with him. Also David is as mad as a bear deprived of her cubs. As a result, you will encounter some real opposition and there will be much shedding of blood, while David will remain hidden in a cave or some safe place, as his loyal servants will protect him this way. Then the word will begin to spread around Israel that the followers of Absalom are blood spillers, and you won't have captured David either. My advice is that you gather together as great an army as you can and that you go forth in front of the city on the plains leading up to Jerusalem and challenge David and his army to come to you. You can lead this army, and then if you are victorious it will be understood, for it is proper to win a kingdom in regular battle. Then you can chase down all the men of David.

Your force will be so impressive that if David flees into a city, you can tie a rope around the city and drag the whole thing into the river Jordan."[1]

Absalom and all the big shots agreed that the advice of Rollow was vastly superior to that of Welby.

Then Rollow passed the word on the whole conversation to Sheen who passed the word to Fred and Ned, who did not try to slip out until it was dark. Even at that they were seen by a young fellow who passed the word to Absalom. Realizing that they might be caught, the two went to a friend's place near the edge of the city and the wife lowered the two into the well, then covered the well with a cloth and spread corn and shucks over the cloth as if she had been drying her corn.

When the search on the house to house plan developed, there came two to the place where Fred and Ned were hidden, but they could not find them. The lady said she thought she had seen them crossing the creek back of the house.

After the searchers left, the lady retrieved Fred and Ned from the well and they escaped to the camp of David and told him to get across the river and then decide what to do.

Now Welby was so upset over having his advice rejected, and since advisors had no advisors, Welby went out and hanged himself.

Absalom had, of course, fired Tuffy as chief of staff and Tuffy had slipped over to David's side.

Friendly people in the wilderness brought food and supplies to David and many valiant men and great warriors began to gather to fight for David, for he had built a great record of success and many people were loyal to him and had received great kindness for him.

David then organized his army.[2] He divided the army into three main sections, putting Tuffy in command of one section, dependable Al in command of another, and the third section was the group from Atlanta under the command of McDill.[3] David then said that he would also go into battle, in spite of his age and sore feet, as well as a touch of arthritis. The people would not agree to this, and they insisted that he remain on the wall of a small fortress and wait there for news of the battle.

David, the King, stood by the gate and blessed the people and their army, and they all heard him instruct the three generals to spare the life of Absalom.

The battle was engaged near the Vienna[4] woods and the three armies of David had trapped the army of Israel under Absalom in the woods, and the army of Absalom was badly beaten and more of his men were lost in the woods, running into trees, fleeing helter-skelter.

Absalom was riding a mule full speed[5] and Absalom's head became caught on a limb in the fork of the branches, and he was

---

[1] A wee bit oratorical at this point.   [2] David was truly a military genius.
[3] Ittai   [4] Ephraim   [5] This was a scared mule

hanging there kicking and asking for help. One of the soldiers of David saw the accident and came and reported it to Tuffy.

"Why didn't you kill him?" bellowed Tuffy. "I'd given you $500 for that."

Then the man said, "I would not have killed him for a million, for I heard the king say that he wanted Absalom's life spared. King David eventually learns everything that goes on, and it would have cost me my life to kill Absalom."

"O.K.," said Tuffy, who immediately went to the place where the soldier said Absalom was hanging and pierced his body with three short arrows, and then several other fellows who were there took an unnecessary hack or two at Absalom with their swords.

Then Tuffy had the bugler blow recall and he did not want to kill anymore Israelites, figuring that they would be needed in a couple of years probably to fight the Fascists again.

Tuffy and his squad of aides took the body of Absalom and buried it in the woods and covered it with a huge pile of stones.[1] Later the head stone,which Absalom had made for himself, was secured from his home and placed on the grave.

Then said Ned to Tuffy, "Let me go and tell David of the victory."

"Not today, Ned, for the king's son is dead and there will be no mail today," said Tuffy.

Then Tuffy turned to Owens and told him to go. After Owens left Ned then talked Tuffy into letting him go also.[2]

Ned took the shortcut which he knew and he arrived before Owens, and the watchman saw him coming and said to David, "A runner comes."

"If he is alone there is news. Just so it isn't the whole army running."

Then the watchman said, "There is another runner coming."

"He also brings news," decided the king.

"The first runner looks like Ned to me."

"He is a good man, so he brings good news," said David.

Ned arrived, panting, and said, "All is well. Blessed be the Lord God who has delivered our king and smitten the men that rose up against him."

"Is Absalom safe?" asked David.

"I don't know," said Ned, "there was a great tumult and much excitement over something, but I don't know what it was."

Then Owens arrived and began saying, "Good news, my king. The Lord has avenged us today of those in rebellion."

Again the king said, "Is Absalom safe?"

"He and others of your enemies are dead."

Then David went up to his room over the gate of the city and as he climbed the stairs he was heard in anguish saying, "O, my son,

[1]They didn't want an autopsy   [2]There's something here I don't quite get.

Absalom, my son, my son, Absalom, would to God that I had died instead of you! O, Absalom, my son, my son."

Word came to Tuffy and began to spread all through the city and among all the people of Israel that the king was in mourning for his son.

Instead of celebrating a great victory the people walked softly in the city. Then Tuffy came to David and complained that the king was embarassing his army and his friends because he was sad in victory and did not appreciate that his servants and his friends had saved his kingdom. Tuffy even suggested that David acted as if he wished Absalom had lived and all the friends and soldiers of David had died.

Then David arose and sat in his regular place of judgement and justice near the gate of the city.

Now following the battle every rebel in support of Absalom had fled to his own home and there was worry and strife through all the land.

David then sent for Sheen as well as Ned and Fred and suggested that they pass the word to the various leaders in all the areas of Israel and tell them that the king had forgiven their rebellion, that he considered all of them Israelites, and that he would greatly appreciate being invited to be their king again and to reunite the tribes of Israel.[1]

"Particularly get the word to General Carter[2] who was the chief of staff for Absalom, and tell him I will bring him back on equal rank with Tuffy," said David.

As this word spread, the peoples' hearts melted for David and they sent servants and gifts, asking him to return as their king.

J.P. came with his various vehicles to help David. The crazy nut who had cursed David also came and he fell at David's feet and apologized, saying that he was first of all the true sons of Joseph to come to David and he sought David's blessing.[3]

Al stepped forward then and suggested for the second time that he be allowed to cut off the guy's head, reminding the king that it was the man who cursed him. David, however, said that there would be no blood shed on the day of peace, for on this day David again became the king of Israel.

Then there came to meet him Sonny, the son of Jonathan, who had not washed his clothes since all the trouble began as a means of showing his sympathy to David.[4]

Sonny apologized to David for not coming to meet him in the wilderness, but he had no transportation and being lame he could not walk.

[1]And get anointed again.   [2]Amasa   [3]He still sounds crazy
[4]The first Hippie to make Scripture

David was understanding and restored the land to J.P., and
Sonny which they both had owned prior to the revolution. Sonny
said he was so happy over David's return that he wouldn't mind if
J.P. took all the land.

There was a grand old man of the times named Holmes, who
was one of the oldest men in the country, and he came to see that
David was safely transported across the Jordan.

David then said, "Come with me to Jerusalem and eat with me
in the palace."

"I'm sorry," said Holmes, "but I doubt if I have that much time
left to live. I can't taste what I eat, or tell what I'm drinking, I'm too
deaf to hear singing, so I'd just be in the way. I'll go with you a short
distance, then I'll turn back and die in my own city, in my own
house. I would appreciate it, however, if you would take my
grandson, Scott[1], with you and let him have the advantage of
growing up in the king's palace."

David was glad to do this.

When the entourage, consisting of the men of Judah,
approached Jerusalem escorting David, the men of Israel were jealous
and asked why they were not included in the big parade.

The men of Judah explained that they were already near to the
place where David was and that no offense was meant. There was
much discussion over the matter and loud talk, but the men of Judah
out talked the men of Israel.

Chap.
20

There came upon the scene at this time a devilish fellow by the
name of Adolph[2] who was fanatically ambitious and he made a big
noise, and gathered a throng on the courthouse lawn and said, "Why
do you Israelites let the men of Judah select the king? Why don't we
have our own king? I suggest that all the faithful Israelites return
home and leave King David with the tribe of Judah, and then Israel
can become organized under me."

As a result, the men of Israel pulled out, but the men of Judah
stayed with David.

In the meantime, David had been told about the scandal
involving the ten semi-wives that he left at the palace and whom
Absalom had publicly confiscated; so he built a small dormitory for
them and imprisoned them in it for the rest of their lives.

The king then said to General Carter, "Go gather together an
army of men of Judah and be back in three days."

General Carter didn't return in three days and David became
properly suspicious.

David then remarked to Al, "Adolph will do us more harm than
Absalom, for I'm sure General Carter has joined him. Pursue after
them before Adolph and Al have time to get organized and capture a

[1]Chimham   [2]Sheba

bunch of cities and fortify them."

Al assembled the army and Tuffy, chief of staff, led the mighty men in hot pursuit of Adolph and General Carter.

It was not long before the army caught up with General Carter, who in leaving had stolen Tuffy's coat and sword, with all the fancy and high ranking insignia.

Tuffy noticed this, and when he walked up to greet General Carter he said, "How goes it?" As if in friendly gesture he grabbed Carter by the beard,[1] and then took the sword he had in his hand and thrust it through the general. General Carter fell dead in the road, and Tuffy suggested that the pursuit of Adolph be resumed. With Tuffy and Al leading the way, the march continued.

So many of the people and soldiers stopped to look at the dead general in the road that finally one man dragged the body over in the bushes.

The word was passed everywhere as the march continued that all the people loyal to Tuffy and to David should join the march and help chase down Adolph and destroy his army.

The army of Judah finally caught up with Adolph and he was in the city of Nashville;[2] so Tuffy had the men build trenches and lay seige to the city. It so happened that there was a very influential woman living in Nashville and she was very wise.

The woman stood on the wall of the city and called out, "Tell Tuffy to come near enough for me to speak to him."

As Tuffy approached the woman called out, "Are you Tuffy?"

"I am he," said Tuffy.

"I've got something to say," said the lady.

"Say it," said Tuffy.

"I am one of the peaceful and loyal persons in Israel. You and I are both Hebrews, and yet you want to destroy a city and kill a bunch of people, including mothers like me. Why do you want to swallow up part of the Lord's kingdom?"

"I don't want to swallow up part of the Lord's kingdom. The trouble is that a man named Adolph has defied the king and wants to start a revolution. Deliver him to me and I'll leave the city alone," said Tuffy.

"All right," said the nice lady, "you just stay there a few minutes and I will throw his head over the wall to you."

The wise lady then turned to the people of Nashville and said that there was no point in a big bloody and losing battle, as the head of Adolph was all that was wanted.

In a few minutes one of the men brought the lady the head of Adolph and she threw it to Tuffy. Tuffy then had the bugler blow recall, and the army departed from around the city. On returning to Jerusalem David gave Tuffy a medal and a raise in pay and made a few other promotions in the army.

[1]This was a similar custom to our handshake   [2]Abel

The next item on the agenda in Israel was a three year drought, which meant a famine in the land. David, as his custom was in time of trouble, called on the Lord and the Lord explained that it was because of the useless bloodshed that Saul had managed to put on the Commanche Indians.[1]

David then sent for the chiefs among the Commanches and apologized for Saul and asked what he could do to make up for the trouble that had been caused them.

"We do not want silver or gold and we don't want you to kill any of the men of Israel as a balance."

"All right," said David, "what do you want?"

"Saul was the man that plotted against us and drove us from our watering places and hunting grounds, so we suggest that you turn over to us seven of his descendants[2] and we will hang them in a special sunrise service."

David said, "I will deliver them to you."

David did not permit Sonny to be one of them. David did arrange for five of them to be sons of Greta, Saul's daughter, but none that were David's sons, only the sons of another husband. The mother of the other two sent to the Commanches was Mame, who had been a mistress of Saul as well as Bouncer. Word came to David that Mame had gone into mourning and was also staying by the dead bodies of her sons, protecting them night and day from the vultures.

David then decided to locate the bones of Saul and of Jonathan and to put them in a proper and dignified burial ground with proper ceremony. This was done. After that it began to rain and the Lord again blessed the land of Israel.

It had been several years since the Fascists had caused any trouble and apparently David missed them for he took a company of soldiers and went into their area and fought against one of their smaller garrisons. David was getting too old for this type of thing and he fainted during the fight.

One of the Fascist, Big Roy,[3] saw this and came near to kill David. Big Roy was a giant of a man, and a high draft choice, but Al arrived in time to attack the big man and to kill him, saving David's life.

The company attacked three other garrisons and in each case one of the men of David's army killed one of the giants that was with the Fascists. The most impressive of these giants was one who had 6 fingers on each hand and 6 toes on each foot, and he could count to 24. A nephew of David's was credited with this kill.

Then David, realizing that his life was nearly spent and that the

[1]Gebeonites   [2]Saul had about 35, legitimate and otherwise   [3]Ishbibenob

Lord had placed him in great circumstances, in conjunction with a couple of local writers, composed his funeral service, in the form of a song.

The Song of David

The Lord is my rock, my fortress, my deliverer
I trust completely in God, who is my rock,
He is the shield and the horn of my salvation
He is my high tower, my refuge, my saviour.
I call on the Lord and he saves me from my enemies,
When the waves of death seemed near,
And the flood of ungodly men were on me
I called on the Lord, and he heard, and delivered me
The earth shook and trembled
Because God was shaking my enemies
The sight was one of smoke and fire rising
Coming up out of the earth.
Darkness he sent, and wind on wings
Thunder and lighting came from God
The lighting was like arrows on the enemy
The sea raged, the earth opened up,
From all of this he delivered me.
He delivered me from powerful enemies,
Enemies too powerful and numerous for me
The Lord saved me, for he approved of me.
The Lord rewarded me according to my goodness
For I kept the ways of the Lord[1]
I never departed from any of his commandments[2]
The Lord always shows mercy to the merciful,
He helps the afflicted and frowns on the snobs,
The Lord is my lamp, and he makes my path bright
Because of God's help I have defeated a troop,
I have even been able to jump over a wall
The Lord's way is perfect
The Lord is a strong support to those that trust him
For there is only the one God, and the one Rock
God is my strength and my power
God has made me swift as a deer,
He has trained me as a warrior, I am strong,
The shield of God's salvation protects me
My feet are steady because I trust God
I have pursued my enemies to their death
I've watched them lying at my feet
Anyone who rose against me was defeated

[1]With a few exceptions not for funeral service comment [2]I think the local PR men added this

The necks of my enemies were under my feet,
I was able to spread them like dust on the street
The Lord has also delivered me from my own people
Even strangers saw the power, and submitted to me
The Lord liveth, happy am I in my Rock
It is the Lord that does all things
Therefore I give thanks to the Lord,
I will even sing God's praises to the heathen
For he is a tower of strength,
A tower of salvation for his king
The Lord is merciful to David and his family,
Forever, and forever, Amen.

Chap.
23

After this song was composed David spoke to the people and explained that he was moved by the spirit of the Lord in his song and in his speaking.

David said, "The Lord has said that anyone who rules over men must be just and he must fear God. If the ruler does this he will be as the light from the rising sun, and he shall be welcomed as the sight of tender grass with the sun shining on it after a rain."

David went on to say that the Lord had made an everlasting covenant with him and his people, and always the people of God must know that the sons of the devil are as thorns and must be dealt with carefully, though eventually the wicked shall be burned.

David then called out the honor roll of mighty warriors and he told of some great feats that they reputedly had accomplished. David even said that York[1] had killed 800 men at one time with one spear, and he gave him, of course, a medal.

This occasion was quite impressive when David had the medal ceremony, naming and awarding outstanding warriors. In telling about 3 of the men David recalled the night that he had longed for a drink of water from the well in Bethlehem, but Bethlehem was in the hands of the Fascists. On this occasion, three mighty men crawled over the wall of Bethlehem and pulled a mission impossible, returning with a cup of water from the well in the city.

David was so impressed by this action that it was well remembered how he took the water and said that he, David, was not worthy of such loyalty and courage, that only God should receive such a tribute, and he poured the water on the ground as an act of worship.

Al was one of these men and it made such a tremendous impression on him that Al killed 300 Fascists over the next few years in his zeal to please King David.

One of the warriors was decorated for killing an Egyptian, who

[1]Adino

had a long spear. The man of David attacked the Egyptian, took the spear away, and killed him with his own spear.

Another warrior jumped down into a snow pit and killed a lion that was trapped and hungry, and then came out and killed two men from Mississippi who had come to see what was happening.

The names, tribes, and lineage of these men are listed in II Samuel 23:24-39.

Chap.
24

The people of Israel began to stray from following the Lord and the Lord was displeased and David was also displeased. David decided that he would punish them with a plan of his own, which was to put them to work; so he ordered a census.

Tuffy raised sand about the order saying that it didn't make any difference how many people there were as long as there were plenty of them. In fact Tuffy went so far as to indicate that all David wanted to do was to brag about the number. The captains tried to talk David out of the census also, but David wouldn't budge; so out went the teams throughout all Israel and counted Hebrews for nine months, all the way from Maine to California.

The report showed that there were 800,000 men able to draw a sword in Israel and 500,000 in Judah.

David then regretted what he had done for he felt that he had punished the people his way and had not gone to the Lord with the matter. David then prayed for forgiveness and asked for guidance.

The next day David's private prophet Billy Sun[1] came to him and told him that the Lord had provided three choices of punishment for the people.

The first was seven years of famine, the second was 3 months of fleeing from enemies, and the third was three days of pestilence. David was told that he could make the choice.

David said, "It is better to fall into the hands of God than in the hands of man, so we'll take the short one, the three days of pestilence."

As a result a plague fell upon the people and some 70,000 died before the Lord stopped the plague by using an angel to intercede.

David told the angel, "I have sinned, but why should so many of the people be punished?"

God then sent word to David to build an altar and to worship. As a result David bought a barn and converted it into a church and there he conducted a worship service and prayed in the presence of the Lord God of Israel, and the plague was stopped.

[1]Gad

David became old and had very little life left in him and so he was cold all the time. Blankets didn't seem to do any good and as a result one of the palace groups suggested that there be secured a beautiful teen-age girl who had a yen to serve her fellow man and she could wait on David some during the day and lie close to him at night and make like a hot water bottle.[1]

As a result there was staged a Miss Teen-Age Israeli contest and a girl named Susie Q[2] won the contest and was brought to the palace. The girl performed her services well and she kept the king warm, though David did not trifle with her at all.

There then arose an ambitious young man named Nap[3] who decided to see if he could take over the kingdom. The first thing he did was to get an escort of fifty men and a few chariots and began to make a show around town. Nap was a younger brother of Absalom and was a pretty nice fellow. When David did not criticize him for his activities, Nap decided everything was going his way. Tuffy and Al then both began to help Nap, as they knew David was near the end of his days.

Nathan, the prophet, the other priests, and many of the mighty men of war were still determined to be loyal to David until his death.

Nap then had a big outdoor bar-b-que and invited a lot of important people and he planned to announce his intentions of being king, but he did not invite Nathan, or Solomon, or any of the mighty warriors loyal to David.

Nathan then spoke to Gina, the mother of Solomon, and asked her if she knew what was going on, and if King David knew what was happening.

Nathan then said, "Let me tell you how to save your life and the life of your son Solomon. Go to David and remind him that he took an oath saying that he would see to it that Solomon became the king after David's death. Then while you are still talking with King David, I'll come and support all that you say."

As a result Gina went to the king, who was very old, and Susie Q was nursing him. Gina bowed to the king, and David said, "What do you want?"

"I want to remind you that you took an oath saying that Solomon would reign as king in your place and yet Nap is establishing himself. In fact, he is having a big bar-b-que as an announcement party, and he didn't invite Solomon. Tuffy and Al have joined Nap and so have most of your other sons. All Israel wants to know what you plan to do, for your silence has left the impression that you support Nap."

[1]No heating pads then. [2]Abishag [3]Adonijah

While Gina was still talking in walked Nathan, the prophet, and he said, "Is it true that you have approved of Nap as your successor? There is a big outdoor picnic being staged and all indications are that you don't mind. Tuffy and Al are saying 'God save the King' to Nap. Now Solomon, myself, and the local priests have not been invited. Have you approved this matter without consulting us? Who have you chosen to sit on your throne?"

Now Gina had left the room by this time and David sent for her and said in her presence, "As the Lord liveth, even as I took oath before, I do so again, saying that Solomon shall be the king in my place. I will tend to the matter today."

Then Gina bowed low to David and did him reverence and said to him, "May the king live forever."

David then said, "Call Sheen, and Nathan."

When Sheen and Nathan were present together David said, "Take my stoutest warriors as escort, put Solomon on my mule, and go to Montreat, and there let Nathan and Sheen anoint Solomon as king, and then blow loudly the trumpet and proclaim 'God save King Solomon'. Then follow him back here and immediately put him on my throne as king, for I have appointed him ruler over Israel and Judah."

Then Cosby,[1] one of the high ranking priests, said "Amen. The Lord God of the king says Amen also. As the Lord has been with David so will the Lord be with Solomon and the Lord will make the throne of Solomon even greater than the throne of David."

As a result, Nathan, Sheen, Cosby, and a group of warriors went with Solomon to Montreat and Sheen took the horn of oil from the tabernacle and anointed Solomon. Then was the trumpet blown in front of the tabernacle and the group shouted, "God save King Solomon."

This started a wave of celebrating and a huge crowd gathered and began to make a great noise blowing on various types of horns and instruments. There was so much noise that Nap and his guests heard it all while they were eating and Tuffy, who had heard the sound of the trumpet, said, "What goes on that causes all this noise?"

While everyone was wondering there came into the meeting a young priest named Jon[2] and Nap said to him, "You are a good man, tell us what good thing is happening."

Jon said, "Our lord King David has just made Solomon the king. There has been a complete and proper ceremony, and Solomon rode to the tabernacle on David's mule, and Sheen has anointed Solomon with oil, and Nathan was in the ceremony, and now the people of the city are rejoicing, and that is what the noise is that you hear. Furthermore, Solomon is already sitting on the throne, and the mighty warriors of David have visited him, and approved his action and they are determined to make Solomon an even greater king than

[1]Benaiah [2]Jonathan

David. King David has already given his thanks to God for enabling him to see the new king on his throne."

This broke up the picnic, as all the guests were afraid and each person went quietly to his own house.

Nap was also afraid and he went to the church and kneeled in front of the altar. The news of this came to Solomon and he said to tell Nap that he had nothing to fear as long as he was a good man, but if he was wicked he would be killed.

So Solomon sent for Nap and Nap bowed down in front of Solomon and acknowledged his kingship and so he was allowed to go home.

Chap.
2

David came to Solomon and said, "I am shortly going to die, for I will go as the way of the earth is, but I charge you to be strong, and be a real man, be sure that you keep the charge of the Lord your God, and walk in his commandments and follow his judgements and his testimonies as they are recorded in the constitution,[1] in order that you may prosper and that the Lord may continue his promise to me when the Lord said 'if your children watch their step, and walk before me in truth with all their heart, with all their soul, there shall not be a failure on the throne of Israel.'

"As for a few practical matters," continued David, "let me remind you that Tuffy has been a bloody man. You know what he did to Bouncer, and the two captains, what he did to General Carter, how he often shed blood in time of peace, and what a violent man he was. Deal with him according to your own wisdom, but don't let him die in peace.

Show kindness, however, to the people of Atlanta, for they helped me when I needed help, as did J.P. and his crowd. Invite them to be at peace in the palace.

You have also the problem of Foul Mouth,[2] the fellow who cursed me mightily and whose life I continually spared, for I promised not to kill him, but he should not go unpunished. I will leave the decision to you, but don't let him die a natural death."

Then David died and was buried in the city of David. Solomon was upon the throne and the kingdom was as well consolidated as it had ever been.

Nap then called on Gina and asked to see her. Gina said, "Do you come in peace?"

"Yes," replied Nap, "I come in peace."

"What do you want?" asked Gina.

"I want you to go to your son Solomon and ask him to give me Susie Q for my wife. I know that the king will say yes to anything his mother requests."

As a result, Gina went to Solomon and Solomon invited her to

[1]Deuteromic Code [2]Shimei

sit on his right hand and then he said to her, "Mother, what is it that you want?"

"Will you promise to say yes?" asked Gina.

"Tell me what you want and I'll grant it to you," said Solomon.

"I want you to give Susie Q, your father's bed warmer, to Nap for a wife," said Gina.[1]

"You must be kidding, Mother. Why don't you ask me to give the kingdom to Nap, since he is my older brother? What about Tuffy, do you want something for him, or Fred, the priest who joined Nap?"

Then King Solomon said, "So help me God, Nap has revealed his treason. As the Lord liveth and has put me on the throne of Israel, and established my house, I promise that Nap won't live through the day."

King Solomon then sent word to Cosby, his temple hatchet man, to kill Nap and it was done that very day.

The king then sent word to Fred, the priest, telling him to escape to his fields for Solomon was sparing his life for his work in bringing the ark of the covenant to Jerusalem. Then there was banished from the ministry the last of the descendants of Eli.

Word of all this reached Tuffy, who was getting a little old and creeky boned, and he was afraid for his life and so he went to the tabernacle and knelt in front of the altar.

The news of this came to Solomon and he sent word to his head hit man Cosby to have Tuffy killed.

Cosby came to Solomon and said that he had invited Tuffy out of the church to fight him in the street, but he wouldn't come.

"Kill him where he is," said Solomon. "For he is a man that has often shed innocent blood, and has brought violence into peaceful times. Did he not kill Bouncer without permission? And what of General Carter, and the two young captains? The blood of all of these and more is on the head of Tuffy. Let him have it!"

As a result, Cosby went into the church and killed Tuffy in front of the altar, and then let the family take the body home for burial.

Cosby was then promoted to General and Sheen was given the top spot in the church organization.

The king then sent for Foul Mouth and said to him, "Build yourself a house in Jerusalem and stay in it. You are not to leave the immediate area as long as you live, and if you so much as cross the creek you will be executed."

"Thank you," said Foul Mouth, "that is a fair arrangement."

About three years later, two of the servants of Foul Mouth went AWOL and left the city limits, figuring that Foul Mouth would not dare chase them.

Foul Mouth, however, figured the king might not learn of his

---

[1]I've never felt that Gina thought much of this Susie Q business.

leaving or that he may have forgotten the arrangement, and so he pursued the servants, caught them, and brought them home.

Solomon learned of this and he sent for Foul Mouth.

"Didn't I make you swear before God that you wouldn't leave the area?" asked the king. "Didn't I tell you that you would be executed if you left town? Didn't you say that this was a fair arrangement? Furthermore, you know your record of wickedness and how among other things you cursed my father. Your chickens have come home to roost."

Solomon then told Cosby to see that Foul Mouth didn't live another day, and so he was killed after he left the palace area. Then the kingdom settled down for a few weeks.

Chap.
3

Solomon's first plan in connection with protection for his people was to develop friendly relations with Egypt, which he did by bringing a daughter of the Pharoah to Jerusalem as one of his wives, and he kept her as testimony of his good faith during the entire time of his building a huge palace and the greatest temple ever constructed.

Solomon loved God and obeyed his commandments and he worshipped God in the high places in his kingdom and made sacrifices on various hills that had been designated holy places.

The Lord, on one of these trips of worship, appeared to Solomon in a dream and asked him to name the thing he would prefer to possess above all other things.

Solomon spoke to the Lord in prayer and meditation and he said "You showed great mercy in dealing with my father David who walked before you in truth and uprightness, and you gave him a son to sit upon his throne and I am that son. I seem to myself to be as a little child in charge of a kingdom, almost as if I do not know when to come and when to go.

Yet I am in the midst of a people that are too numerous to number, and so I would ask for an understanding heart that I may be able to judge the people justly and to discern between that which is good and that which is bad."

This presentation pleased the Lord, and God said to Solomon, "Because you have asked for what you did, and did not ask for riches or for long life or for the death of your enemies, but have asked for understanding, be certain that I shall give you such a wise and understanding heart that there had never been one like you and there will never again be one your equal in this capacity. I will also give you great riches, though you did not ask for such, and you will have honors, so that there will be no king like you as long as you live.

What is more, if you will walk in my ways and keep my commandments and my statutes, then I will also give you long life."

Solomon awoke and realized he had had this dream, and so he came to Jerusalem and entered the tabernacle and made an offering and praised God.

There came before the judgment seat of Solomon two women, neither of whom had official husbands.

One woman spoke to Solomon and said, "The two of us girls live together, and I had a baby son. Three days later this other girl had a baby son, and there were no other people in the house; so there are no witnesses.

Now this other girl's baby died in the night and while I was asleep she exchanged babies with me; so that in the morning I had the dead baby. I recognized immediately that the dead baby was not my child."

"That's not right, King Solomon. The living son is mine," said the second girl.

"You're wrong," said the first, and thus they continued back and forth.

The king then said, "Bring me a sword," and they did.

The king then said, "Take the sword and cut the baby in half, and give half to each woman."

Then the first girl said, "O, no, not that. Give the child to the other girl. I'd rather be deprived of my son than to have him killed."

The second woman, however, said, "I think dividing the child in half is a good arrangement, then it will be neither one of us who benefits."

Then Solomon said, "Give the child to the first woman. She is the real mother."

This account spread through all the countryside and the people developed a great respect for Solomon and his wisdom, for they perceived that the wisdom of God was in him.

Chap.
4

King Solomon began the first real organization of the kingdom of Israel. One thing that he did was to appoint rulers over various sections of the kingdom and to make them responsible directly to him. One of the neat things he did was to appoint 12 chefs for the palace, one for each month. The list of all the rulers and chefs are in I Kings 4:2-19.

Judah and Israel combined were really big by this time and there was much eating, drinking, and making merry under the wise rule of Solomon, for every man felt safe from any outside enemy.

The possessions of Solomon were quite impressive. There were so many people connected with the palace itself that 30 beef cows were killed daily to feed them, not to mention deer of various kinds, including the fallow deer.

Solomon had a stable with 40,000 stalls for the chariot horses, and men everywhere worked for the government to provide for all of these additions. Solomon's wisdom, his great gift from God, enabled him to rule wisely and his reputation was in itself a great protection to the people.

At one time or another, Solomon uttered 3,000 proverbs and wrote over 1,000 songs and he was knowledgeable about trees, animals, and fish. Kings and important people from all over the world came to visit Solomon to learn from him and to see the many tourist attractions that he added to the kingdom.

Chap.
5

Hiram, King of Tyre, who had been a friend of David's, sent greetings by messenger to Solomon, for Hiram was in the construction business.

Solomon sent word then to Hiram telling him that David, his father, had wanted to build a temple to the Lord, but that he had too much trouble with wars and internal enemies to do this, but that Solomon was ready to build.

Solomon said, "The Lord my God has given me rest from my enemies, and I plan to build a church in the name of the Lord my God, exactly as the Lord had told my father that I would. As a result, I want to place a gigantic order for timber, both cedar and other timbers."

Hiram rejoiced in this and blessed God for raising up such a wise son to David and Hiram agreed to fill the order. In fact, Hiram said that he would secure the cedars from Lebanon and float them down the Jordan to the nearest point of building. Hiram did the same thing with the fir trees which were needed.

Solomon paid Hiram a good price for this material and Hiram and Solomon made a permanent agreement of goodwill between them.

Then Solomon drafted 30,000 men of Israel as laborers rather than soldiers, and they went forth as wood choppers and transportation people, log rollers, and lineman, and Solomon appointed 3,300 foremen to supervise the work.

Then Solomon had great stones cut from the quarry and the stone quarriers and stone masons worked together, some of Hiram, some of Solomon, and they laid a foundation for the house of God.

Chap.
6

An intricate description of the building, with measurement details, material factors, and contruction plans. The summation — tremendous! It took eleven years to finish the building.

Chap.
7

In the meantime, Solomon was also building a new palace and this took thirteen years. Solomon built some other buildings also, furnishing one of the greatest employment plans ever devised.

The description of Solomon's house is concisely stated in I Kings 7:2-12. Solomon also built a special house on the grounds for Pharaoh's daughter, who was one of Solomon's wives.

Hiram then came from Tyre, for he was an artist in brass work and in decorating, and he worked on all the trimmings which are carefully described in I Kings 7:14-50.

After everything was finished, then Solomon brought into the temple the precious antiques of his father David. The silver things, and the gold things, and the artistic vessels and containers.

Chap.
8

Then Solomon assembled all the elders of Israel, and all the high ranking churchmen, and he had the ark of the covenant of the Lord brought to the temple and placed in the holy of holies. A worship service with proper sacrifices was conducted in the presence of the congregation. There was nothing in the ark of the covenant except the two tables of stone containing the ten commandments.

The glory and power of the Lord made a visible manifestation in the temple, and the priests even could not remain, for the cloud of God was thick in the temple.

Then Solomon spoke to the people saying, "The Lord said that he would dwell in privacy, and I have built for him a worthy place."

Then Solomon blessed the people and thanked them for their interest and help.[1]

Then Solomon spoke again saying, "Blessed be the Lord God of Israel who spoke through David, my father, and who has made good his promises. For the Lord called no city his own and no place his temple, although it was in the heart of my father, David, to build a house for the Lord, the Lord said to David 'It is enough that you desire to do this, nevertheless, it will not be you, but your son who builds the temple to the Lord.'

The Lord has performed his word and I have built the temple."

Then Solomon stood in front of the temple and spoke further saying, "There is no God like the Lord God of Israel, neither in heaven above or in the earth beneath. The Lord is the keeper of the promises, and he is merciful to those who follow in his commandments. The Lord has kept his promise to David, and may the Lord continue to do so, and keep the throne of Israel intact by providing righteous men, for sin brings destruction.

Yet how can man expect to contain God in a building, for his expanse is from heaven to heaven and to heavens, yet Lord, I pray that you will diligently watch this house day and night, and listen when the people pray facing this house, and forgive them when they sin.

Remember also, O Lord my God, to restore the people when they return after wandering from you, do not hold their sins against them for any length of time, and when they fully repent, please fully restore them.

When the people have sinned and are punished with a drought, and then they turn to this place and pray for help, hear their cry and

[1]Imagine getting a thank you from the IRS

give aid to their land, and forgive the people.

If there be pestilence, and disease, and mildew, or if enemies plunder and capture, hear then the prayers of those who face this place and seek your help.

Hear also, O Lord God, the prayer of the stranger who may come from a far country and face this place and pray in full belief. Answer the stranger's prayer so that all the people of the earth may know the one true God.

If the people of Israel go forth to battle and before the battle face this place and pray, hear their prayer, and support their cause.

If the people sin, and they probably will, and are captured and taken into strange lands, then if they repent and face this place and call upon the name of the Lord, hear their plea and support them.

Forgive thy people when they seek forgiveness, have compassion on them, for they are designated as the people of God. These people are chosen by the Lord to be delivered from Egypt and to have the special function of magnifying the glory of God. Let all of these things assist in making known that the Lord is God, everywhere, over every nation."

Then there were special services dedicating different parts of the temple and there were feasts, and all these things took eight days, and were all part of the dedication of the temple.

Chap.
9

Now it had taken Solomon many years to complete all his building programs. The Lord appeared to Solomon a second time and told him that God had heard his prayer and that the house that he built for the Lord would be blessed and that the heart of God would always be in his church. God then again remembered his covenant telling Solomon that if he would walk uprightly and not be diverted to strange gods, then the Lord would make the throne of the kingdom of Israel permanent,[1] but if Solomon or any of his descendants began to turn from God and seek off-beat idolatries, then the Lord said that he would cut Israel out of the land that was theirs, and the name of Israel itself would become the brunt of jokes.

When such a thing occurs people in the future who view the remains of the majesty of the temple shall be told that the calamity was because the people wandered from the Lord God of Israel, the keeper of the promises.

At the end of the building period of about 20 years Solomon paid the Hiram Building and Supply Co. for the materials and labor, and the price he paid was to give Hiram and Co. twenty whole cities in Galilee. Hiram, himself, came to view the cities and he was pleased with the price and desired to do more business with Solomon.

It was, of course, necessary for Solomon to raise taxes again for the payments as he needed to build replacement cities. Solomon

[1]Which I think he finally did in Christ.

began to tax all the people everywhere in every direction and he made bonded workers out of all people who were not Israelites, and made warriors out of all the able bodied men of Israel.

There were 550 men of Israel chosen to direct all the work camps, and all the reconstruction in the cities.

Pharaoh's daughter, the wife of Solomon, moved into her private home on the palace grounds.

Solomon went to church three times a year, as was required by the law of Moses.

Solomon then conceived the idea of developing a navy and a merchant marine, in order that gold and silver from faraway places could be brought to Solomon. Hiram Building and Supply Co. got the contract for building all the ships and Hiram supplied experienced seaman to sail with the men of Israel and train them.[1]

Chap.
10

Now the Queen of Sheba heard of the fame of Solomon, of his wisdom and his great tourist attractions, and so she decided to come and visit and see for herself.

As a result, the Queen of Sheba came to Jerusalem in an impressive fashion, with an escort of camels carrying rich spices, and much gold, and many diamonds.

Sheba met with Solomon and they had long conversations and she was tremendously impressed with his vast knowledge, and with the temple and the palace, and even with the fabulous foods which were served. She was also impressed with how well trained his staff was, how handsomely they dressed.

"It was a true report that I heard in my land about you," said Sheba to Solomon, "and I admit that I did not believe it. I was in error, for what I have seen is even more fantastic than had been told me. Your wisdom and your prosperity exceeds everything that I have heard. How fortunate are the people who know you and have the benefit of your wisdom. Blessed is the Lord your God for putting you on the throne to render judgements and to deal justly."

Then Sheba presented Solomon with many gifts, and chiefly were the gifts precious spices, for Solomon had everything else already.

Solomon then gave the Queen of Sheba all that she asked[2] and then Solomon added a big bonus from his own treasury.

About this same time Solomon had been told by Hiram of a special brand of tree known as an almug tree. Hiram said there were only a few in all the world and Solomon ordered everyone of them at a great price and he made beautiful posts, and there has never been another almug tree in the world.[3]

Solomon had an income of about 20 million a year direct,

[1]Hiram was an industrialist   [2]Which I bet was plenty   [3]I am suspicious of Hiram here. We still have some Hirams in the world, though no almug trees.

which did not include his cut on all the merchant marine, caravan taxes, and the protection game which he used on the Arab kings, as well as on all small-time rulers.

Solomon had such a gold problem that he made shields of gold, and targets of gold, and all of his cups, and plates were solid gold. To add to his splendour he had a throne made of solid ivory covered with gold and there were all kinds of figures of beasts around the throne.

Every three years the navy and the merchant marine came to port and brought Solomon gold, silver, ivory, apes,[1] and peacocks.

Kings and princes came from everywhere to visit Solomon, to seek his advice, enjoy his hospitality, and exchange gifts.

There was so much silver around that it became as worthless as stone and cedar boards became as worthless as sycamore planks. Linens were brought from Egypt and this also turned into a good business.

Chap.
11

Then the foreign women began to get to Solomon. Not only Pharoah's daughter, but the rulers of many different places began to send their prettiest girls, and Solomon added to his household wives from India, Persia, Mississippi, some gypsies, and as Solomon became older [2] the foreign women mislead him and Solomon, for their sake, began to worship strange gods such as Ash[3] and Totem[4] and Solomon began to neglect his own church and the one true God. Solomon began to build private temples for his favorite wives, and the Lord became angry.

The Lord then said to Solomon "Because you have forsaken me, I will take the kingdom away from your descendants. I will not do it in your lifetime because of my promise to your father David, but I will keep one tribe only for your son, and the rest shall depart from your family."

Along with his neglect of God, Solomon also began to neglect his kingdom and there came into power in Egypt a refugee from the land of Canaan, who had heard of the death of David and Tuffy, and this man, named Tom Nester,[5] began to organize an army and to harass the southern portion of Solomon's kingdom. Tom had made friends with Pharoah by giving him his sister-in-law and he was therefore supported somewhat by the Egyptians.

The Lord also stirred into action a fellow named Reo Villa[6] who began to organize an army in the north, and he took command of Syria and he began to raid the northern outposts of Solomon's kingdom.

Then Jerry[7], the son of one of the palace servants, began to organize a little against Solomon, almost right under his nose.

[1] I still don't know why he wanted apes. Maybe because he didn't have any.
[2] Probably late forties [3] Ashtoreth [4] Milcom [5] Hadad [6] Rezon [7] Jeroboam

Now Jerry was a mighty warrior and an impressive person and so Solomon put him in charge of the tribe of Joseph, not knowing that he was a potential defector.

It happened one day that Jerry left Jerusalem on a short trip and he was stopped in a field by L. Evans,[1] a prophet of the Lord.

Now Jerry had on a new flowing cape, and the prophet took it and tore it into ten pieces and said "Thus says God, the Lord of Israel, for you are to take the ten pieces as a symbol that you will be given ten tribes of Israel over which you are to reign. One tribe will be left for a descendant of David, because of the faithfulness of David, and one shall be left to care for Jerusalem, which is my city. I am doing this, God has said, because Solomon is worshipping strange gods and neglecting his own church and his kingdom. I will not do this, God has said, in the lifetime of Solomon, but his days are numbered, for he has burned his candle at both ends for too long. You will take over ten tribes and the son of Solomon shall have one."

"As for you," continued the prophet, "God says that you will be king of Israel, and if you observe God's commands and walk in his truth, then God will build for you a name and a lineage as God did for David."

Word of this leaked out[2] and Solomon sought to kill Jerry, and put out a contract on him. As a result, Jerry fled to Egypt and remained there as a guest of Pharoah until Solomon died. Solomon ruled Israel for forty years and then he was buried in Jerusalem and his son Roger[3] assumed the throne of Israel.

Chap. 12

There was then a great assembly called at Baltimore[4] in order to make Roger king of Israel. In the meantime, the people had sent for Jerry and a great group of people joined Jerry in appearing before the new king and asking about his policy.

The spokesman for the people said, "Your father Solomon really hurt us with his taxes and we have decided that if you will lighten our tax load, we will all support you as king."

"Come back in three days and I'll give you my answer," said Roger.

Then Roger called to him a group of wise and experienced men and he asked these older men what they thought he should do with the request.

The men replied "Agree to cut the taxes. If you will let up a bit on these people they will be grateful and you will be a respected and beloved king over all the tribes."

Then Roger called to him a group of his young friends, who were inexperienced and also eager for their own benefits as friends of Roger. These young men advised Roger to reply sharply to the

[1]Ahijah [2]Leak outs in church work are still common. [3]Rehoboam [4]Shechem

people and deny their request, and to raise their taxes, just for bringing the matter to his attention.

Three days later Jerry and the representatives of Israel appeared before King Roger for his answer.

Roger had decided to follow the poor advice of the youth group and he spoke sharply to the people as they had suggested saying "My father treated you lightly compared to what I plan to do. My little finger will seem as big to you as my father's leg. I will add to the yoke my father placed upon you and where he beat you with whips I'll do it with scorpions."

When the tribes of Israel saw that the king paid no attention to them, the people then said, "What have we to do with you? We are not in the tribe of Benjamin as David was, we don't have to recognize you as king, and you can go jump in the lake."

As a result every man of Israel returned to his home. The Israelites in the tribe of Judah and the small group of the tribe of Benjamin remained under Roger.

When Roger sent his tax collector to start work in Israel, the people stoned him to death. Roger then retreated to Jerusalem, for he feared for his own life.

As word spread regarding this, and as the news was out that Jerry was back from Egypt, the people of the ten tribes called Jerry into a big meeting and made him their king.

When Roger returned to Jerusalem he immediately began to recruit an army from the men of Judah and Benjamin to go and fight their fellow countrymen of the ten other tribes of Israel.

Then the word of the Lord came to Stewart,[1] a spokesman for God, and told him to go to Roger and to all the people of Judah and Benjamin and to tell them that the Lord was against their moving to fight the other tribes and that the Lord was commanding them to go home.

The people listened and they dissolved the army by each going to his own home.

Now Jerry was a plotting type and basically insecure, so he began to worry about the times that the members of the ten tribes under his rule would go to Jerusalem for their worship occasions.

It occured to Jerry that these people would come under the influence of Roger and might desert Jerry.

As a result, he decided to build two worship places of his own, that were readily accessible to his people. At each of these selected places Jerry had golden calves placed on display and he told the people that these calves delivered the Israelites from Egypt and that worship in these places would save the trip to Jerusalem and still count as church.

This was a great sin in the eyes of God, and Jerry made it worse by placing men not of the priestly line of Levi in charge, and

[1]Shemaiah

designating thereby his own priests.

Jerry worked out some sacrifices and an order of worship and led in the idolatry. It was an all-laymen church.

There came then a man of God out of Judah to one of the idol worshipping places, the one at Vegas,[1] and he spoke against the idol worship in the name of the Lord, and he prophesied saying, "From the line of David a child shall come to rule named Josiah and he will burn men on this altar. This shall be the sign, that the altar shall split in two and the ashes shall spill forth."

When Jerry heard these words he put forth his hand over the altar and ordered his men to seize the prophet.

When Jerry thrust his hand over the altar, his hand withered, and he could not move it, for it became paralyzed. Then the altar was split in two and the ashes poured forth as the Lord had decreed through his prophet.

Jerry then said to the man of God, "Pray for me. Ask the Lord to restore my hand."

The prophet interceded in prayer for Jerry, and the paralysis left his hand.

"Come home with me," said the king, "refresh yourself and I will also give you an honorarium."

"If you would offer me half of all you possess," said the prophet, "I will not go with you, for the Lord told me to eat no bread and drink no water, nor to vary from my path home, being careful to return by a different route."

Now there was an old prophet living in Vegas who heard of this and since his two sons had seen the road down which the real prophet had departed, he got on a donkey and went after him.

When he found the true man of God he spoke to him, as the prophet was sitting under an oak tree, and said "Are you the prophet that came from Judah?"

"I am," the prophet replied.

"How about coming home with me and having a meal?" asked the Vegas soothsayer.

"I cannot do it. I am under direct orders from God not to eat bread or drink water or turn aside until I have returned to my home church."

"Well," said the Vegas prophet, "it so happens that I am a prophet also, and an angel came to me just a short time ago and told me to tell you that your instructions were cancelled and you could return with me." Of course, the Vegas man lied.

As a consequence, the prophet of Judah returned to Vegas and ate bread and drank water and refreshed himself. The Vegas prophet knew that the Lord would not allow such disobediences and he

[1]Bethel

envisioned that the man from Judah would not have a safe trip back home.

After the meal was over, the prophet of Judah got on his donkey and as he was enroute home a lion attacked him and killed him and stood by his body.

Men on the road saw what happened and they saw the lion standing by the body and they reported this in Vegas.

When the Vegas prophet heard this, he thought surely it was the prophet from Judah who disobeyed the direct word of God.

Then the Vegas prophet got on his donkey and went to get the body. The lion was still there and ran off when the prophet came. The Vegas prophet took the body and brought it to Vegas and buried the man in the place he had fixed for himself saying, "Alas, my brother is dead. When I die just put me on top of my departed fellow prophet for surely he was a true prophet of the Lord and his words at the altar will be found to be accurate."[1]

None of this had any effect on Jerry as he continued his evil ways and his violations of worship, and the sin of all he did was disastrous to his whole family.

Chap.
14

Shortly after this Tab,[2] the son of Jerry, who was but a small boy, became ill. Jerry then said to his wife, "Disguise yourself, so no one will know that you are the king's wife, and go to Montreat,[3] and visit there with the prophet L. Evans, who told me I was to become King, and ask him about our son and if he will get well, and take the proper fee and also a sacrifice for the altar."

Jerry's wife did as she was told and she came to L. Evans, who was now blind in his old age. The Lord, however, revealed to L. Evans that Jerry's wife was there to see him[4] and the Lord inspired Evans so that he knew what to say.

When L. Evans then heard the sound of the woman's feet approaching him, he said, "Come in, wife of Jerry. Why try to disguise yourself? I have bad news for you. Go tell Jerry that the Lord God of Israel exalted him and made him king over the people of Israel, and took the kingdom away from the house of David, and yet Jerry has not followed my commandments as David did, but has done evil in the sight of the Lord. The Lord, therefore, will bring evil against the house of Jerry, and will cut his son off from the line of the kingdom. The Lord will take away the remnants like a farmer cleaning his barnyard. The descendants of Jerry will die in the fields or in the streets of a city, and their bodies shall be left for the vultures and the jackals, and the dogs. When you leave here and return, your son shall die as you enter the city.

Because this young boy was blameless he shall be an exception, and Israel shall mourn his death, and he is to be given a proper

[1]This little account baffles me a bit [2]Abijah [3]Shiloh
[4]God sometimes used helpers to pass information, I think.

funeral.

Because of the sins of Jerry, and the sins of the people in following him in the worship of idols, the Lord shall scatter Israel and the Lord will depart from Israel."

Then Jerry's wife arose and returned and as she entered the child's room, the boy died, and all Israel mourned, and the boy was given a proper funeral.

Jerry reigned in war and wickedness for 22 years, and then he died.

In the meantime, Reo Villa was king in Judah and he also did wickedly and led the people in idol worship. The people began to buy and sell graven images, and to adopt the evil ways of the heathen neighbors who lived near them.

In the fifth year of the rule of Reo Villa, the king of Egypt, Clyde[1] came to Jerusalem with a troop of warriors and captured all the treasures of the temple, the gold shields, and the many valuables of David and of Solomon.

After this was done, Reo Villa had imitation shields and cheap ornaments made to replace the valuables stolen by Clyde.

There was also continuous strife between the people of Reo Villa and Jerry. Reo Villa died and was buried in the place of Kings, and his son reigned in his place. Huff,[2] the son of Reo Villa, did evil as his father did, and continued the wickedness of the kingdom and the strife with Jerry's people.

Chap.
15

For the sake of his faithful servant David, however, the Lord allowed the reign to continue through Huff's son, Asa.

Now Asa was a fine man and he did that which was right in the eyes of the Lord and he launched moral campaigns, and fought crime, and tore down all the idols that had been erected by his father. Asa went so far as to remove his mother from having the status of queen because she had made an idol and placed it in the woods. Asa had the idol destroyed.

Asa also began to bring gifts of silver and valuables back into the Lord's house.

There was continued strife between Israel and Judah, and Baldy,[3] king of Israel set up his army on the border of Judah and stopped all traffic and all trade to the outside world in that direction.

Asa then took the treasures which he had accumulated and he sent them with messengers to Robinhood,[4] king of Syria, living in Damascus.

"Robinhood," the messengers said, "Asa would remind you of the treaty that has existed for many years between our nations. He is sending a valuable gift in gold and silver. He wants you to declare war on Baldy and smite Israel and relieve him of the pressure he is under."

[1]Shishak [2]Abijam [3]Baasha [4]Benhadad

Robinhood thought well of this, and he and his men'went to Israel and destroyed many cities and gathered a great amount of spoil. When Baldy heard of this, he removed the great road block he was building in the form of a fort and he fled. Asa then took the materials from the fort and built a small town.

Asa was a good man and did many fine things, but in his old age his feet hurt terribly,[1] and he died and was buried in the place of kings with honor.

To get back a bit chronologically, Baldy had become king of Israel by getting a bunch of warriors together and fighting the wicked Theo,[2] who had taken his father Jerry's place as king. Baldy killed Theo and took his place. In fact, Baldy sought out every descendant of Jerry and had each one of them killed, as L. Evans had predicted.

Baldy, like Jerry and Theo, was also a bad boy.

Chap. 16

The word of the Lord then came to a man named Jay[3] and the word was that the Lord was displeased with Baldy and he would do to Baldy's lineage what he had done to Jerry's.

While Asa was still king in Judah, Baldy died and his son Simbo[4] took his place. Now Simbo had a warrior named Zulu[5] who was in charge of half the chariots, and Zulu developed some big ambitions. As a result, when Zulu knew that Simbo was getting stoned at a friend's party, he entered and killed him, and declared himself king.

The first thing the new king did was to kill all the male descendants of Simbo, as well as all of his close friends and kinsmen. This is exactly what Jay said would finally happen.

Apparently Zulu did this killing very promptly, for he was king only 7 days.[6]

When word of Zulu's conspiracy and the murder of Simbo went around the country, the men of Israel didn't like it, and they appointed Rowan[7] to be head of the troops and to march against Zulu. When this occurred, Zulu became terrified and fled into the king's house, set fire to it, and burned himself up as well as the house.

Then the people were confused as they had no king, and half wanted to make Rowan king and half wanted a man named Martin.[8]

The people who favored Rowan finally won out and so they buried Martin.

Now Rowan was king for 12 years. The first six years he lived in the San Fernando Valley,[9] but then he decided to live on a hill. As a result, he bought a whole hill and built his palace on the hill and called the place Samaria.

[1]Phlebitis, no doubt [2]Nadab [3]Jehu [4]Elah [5]Zimri
[6]Hardly worth the trouble [7]Omri [8]Tibni [9]Tirzah

Now Rowan did everything evil that Jerry or Baldy or any of the others had done, and then he added some new twists of his own. Rowan also caused the people to sin and set an example of wickedness and he provoked the Lord to anger against Israel.

Then Ahab, the son of Rowan, took the throne after his father's death, and Ahab broke all the records for wickedness. The worst thing he did in the sight of the Lord was to marry Jezebel, a mean heathen woman, and to begin at once to worship Baal, who was the idol that Jezebel advocated. Ahab did more to provoke the Lord than any of the other kings.

During this time, however, the city of Jericho was rebuilt by a man named Zachry.[1]

Chap.
17

The Lord raised in North Carolina[2] a great prophet named Elijah and he appeared before Ahab and told Ahab that there would be no more rain in all the land until Elijah asked God to send rain.

Then, following the inner voice of God, Elijah left the area and camped by a small spring fed stream, and there he was fed by the ravens who robbed area ranches and brought Elijah food.

Finally, the terrible drought in the land caused the spring to run dry and the inner prompting of the Lord told Elijah to go to Ashville, N.C.[3] and that there he would find a widow who would care for him during the remainder of the drought.

As Elijah approached Ashville he saw a woman gathering sticks and he said to her, "Bring me a cup of water."[4]

As she was going to get the water he called after her and said "and while you're up, bring me a sandwich also."

"So help me God, fellow," said the woman, "I don't have but one handful of flour left in the last barrel, and I'm gathering sticks to build a fire, bake one roll for my son and me, and lie down and die of starvation."

"Don't panic, now" said Elijah, "but bake me a roll and bring it to me, then you will find that there is still plenty left for you and your son, for the Lord God of Israel will see to it that you are never without flour and cooking oil as long as the drought lasts."

The widow woman did as Elijah said and as a result Elijah moved into her house and there was always food available for the woman, her son, and Elijah.

Some time after this the son became very ill and he fainted, and was not able to catch his breath.

"Why did I ever let a man of God into this house? You have come to punish me for my sin by taking the life of my son."[5]

"Hand me the child," said Elijah. Elijah took the boy to his room and gave him artificial respiration and he prayed to the Lord

[1]Hiel [2]Tishbite [3]Zarephath [4]It was polite to order women around in those days.
[5]Here you get to fill in your own sin.

for the child's life, and the Lord heard Elijah and breath came back into the boy and he revived.

Elijah brought the son to his mother and the woman said, "Truly now I know that you are a man of God, and the word of the Lord which you speak is true."

In the third year of the drought the word of the Lord came to Elijah and urged him to visit Ahab. There was, of course, a great famine now in the land.

In the meantime Ahab had called Dean Dusk,[1] his secretary of state, and told him to search one half of the land while Ahab searched another half to see if they could find anyplace to put their cattle and mules for grass and water.

Now Dean Dusk was a man who was upright and who respected God. In fact, when Jezebel had made a purge of the land in her style by having all the priests executed, Dean had helped 100 ministers to escape and he had been sneaking them food as they were hidden in a couple of big caves.

As Dean was searching his half of the land he met Elijah, and recognizing the prophet, he bowed to him, but to make certain he said, "Are you not Elijah?"

"I am. Now go tell Ahab that Elijah is here."

"What have I done to deserve such trouble? Ahab will kill me! Didn't you know that wanted posters are in every post office in the land on you, and every town has had to swear that you were not hiding in the town? Now you say, 'Tell Ahab Elijah is here.' Then as soon as I go to tell Ahab, the Spirit of the Lord will cause you to disappear again, and he'd kill me. Have a heart, Elijah. Haven't you heard of my hiding the preachers from Jezebel? Now you're pronouncing doom on one saying 'Tell Ahab Elijah is here."

"I am determined to appear before Ahab, as the Lord liveth; so get with it."

Dean then went to Ahab and told him that Elijah was here, and Ahab went to meet him.

When Ahab came to Elijah he said, "Are you the cause of all the trouble in Israel?"

"No, I am not," said Elijah, "but you and your household are. You have forsaken God and taken to the worship of Baal, and caused the people to worship Baal."

"Now listen to this," continued Elijah, "get word to all the people to come to the Yankee Stadium,[2] as many as can get in, and then assemble all the priests of Baal from everywhere, and we will have a great contest."

Elijah then began speaking to the people that he met telling them that the time for decision was come, either to follow the Lord

[1]Obadiah [2]Mt. Carmel

as God, or Baal. The people did not say anything as they were afraid.

"Apparently, I am by myself, yet Baal has 450 prophets. We will have a contest. Build an altar around second base in Yankee Stadium, and put sacrifices on the altar, and place the wood beneath, but set no fire to it. Then let the priests of Baal call upon Baal and I will call on the Lord God of Israel, and whichever sends fire to consume the altar, then let him be recognized as God."

All this was done, and beginning about nine in the morning all the way to noon the priests of Baal called on Baal for fire, the priests even began jumping up and down on the altar, but nothing happened.

Elijah was in the dugout and about noon he began to heckle the priests saying, "Cry louder. Maybe your god is talking to someone, maybe he's asleep, or he may be off golfing somewhere!"

The priests then called louder, and began to cut themselves with knives and let their blood spill on the infield grass, and still there was no response.

About three o'clock the priests were pooped out, and Elijah came out of the dugout and told the people to watch him closely as he rebuilt the altar which the priests had broken.

Then Elijah took twelve stones, representing the 12 tribes of Israel, and he built a new altar and he dug a trench around it, and he placed a sacrifice on the altar and he poured 4 barrels of water over the altar.[1] Then he had the helpers do this three times until the water had run down into the trenches.

Then Elijah called for silence and he raised his voice in prayer saying, "Lord God of Abraham, and of Isaac, and of Jacob, let it be known this day that you are the true God of Israel, that I am your servant and that I have done these things at your command. Hear me now, that these people may know that you are the Lord God, and that you are ready to receive the people again."

Then the fire of the Lord came flashing down and struck the altar and consumed it with fire.

When the people saw this they fell on their faces and said, "The Lord, he is God, the Lord is the true God."

Elijah then turned to the crowd and said, "All right, but don't let a single one of the 450 priests of Baal escape."

As a result, the people took the 450 priests and carried them down to the edge of the Hudson River[2] and killed them all. [3]

Elijah then spoke to Ahab and said, "Go somewhere and eat, for it is going to rain, can't you hear the thunder?"

Ahab went to eat, and Elijah climbed up to the top of the Press Box and bowed his head, and then he said to his servant, "Climb on the roof and tell me if you see rain."

"There is no cloud in sight," reported the servant. Elijah sent

---

[1]Some cynics have said this was kerosene [2]Kibron
[3]Losing really hurt in those days

him up seven times, and after the seventh trip the servant said, "I see a small cloud that looks no bigger than a man's hand."

Elijah then told the servant, "Go tell Ahab to get in his chariot and get out of here, for it is going to rain bull breetches."

In a few minutes the sky was black and the rain began to fall and Ahab raced in his chariot back to his palace at Jersey City.[1]

Elijah got a ride on a faster chariot and beat Ahab to Jersey City.

Chap.
19

Ahab immediately went to Jezebel and spilled the whole story, and he put it on pretty thick about the killing of the 450 priests of Baal.[2]

As a result Jezebel sat down and wrote a letter to Elijah saying:
Dear Elijah:

May the gods do to me, and even worse, than you did to my priests if by this time tomorrow you are not as dead as my priests.
Love, Jezebel

Elijah, accompanied by his servant, fled in terror.[3] When Elijah got as far away as Denver he left his servant and went a full day's journey into the wilderness by himself.

Finally he came to a juniper tree and sat under it and greatly depressed he prayed saying, "Lord, take my life. I'm no improvement on the previous generation."[4]

Then Elijah fell asleep, as he had been running all day, and when he awoke he found that an angel of the Lord had brought him supper. Elijah looked at the meal and went back to sleep. The second time the angel stirred him and said, "Arise and eat. You're pooped from your journey."

Elijah then arose and ate and was strengthened. After staying in the wilderness for forty days, Elijah climbed a nearby mountain and took refuge in a cave.

The word of the Lord then came to Elijah saying, "What are you doing here?"

"Well," said Elijah, "I have always worked for the Lord and have been busy in the church for years, but the people would not listen, and they destroyed your ministers and broke your covenant, and they seek my life, for I am the only good man left."

"Step out of the cave," said the voice, and Elijah did.

The Lord then manifested himself and caused a mighty wind to blow, and then an earthquake, and finally a flash of fire, but the Lord was not in any of these natural happenings. Then as Elijah stood in the entrance of the cave there came a voice again saying, "What are you doing here, Elijah?"

"Just like I said before," said Elijah, "I have been a good minister but the people would not listen and now they seek my life,

[1]Jezreel [2]Jezebel cansidered [3]Not a bad idea [4]A terrible feeling for a young man

for I am the only good man left."

"You're way off, Elijah," said the voice, "for there are more than 7,000 in your own country who have never worshipped Baal. Now get on the road and get to where the action is. First go to the wilderness around Damascus and anoint Billy the Kid[1] as king of Syria and then anoint Jay king of Israel, and anoint Elisha as your successor. It will come about that the enemies that Billy the Kid doesn't handle, Jay will, and those that Jay doesn't get, Elisha will."

Elijah then departed and he found Elisha plowing in a field with 12 oxen and Elijah cast his cloak over him as a symbol of selection and appointment.

Elisha then followed Elijah and said, "Can I go and kiss my folks good-bye?"[2]

"Sure," said Elijah, "don't make such a big deal of this. Being a prophet is hard work."

Then Elisha returned, killed all the oxen, had a big dinner party for the friends and neighbors,[3] and then left to begin his apprenticeship under Elijah.

Chap.
20

Sometime after this Robinhood, king of Syria gathered an army together in his neighborhood and he signed up thirty-two kings to join him. As a result there was assembled a large but rather poorly organized army, and they went and laid seige to Samaria.

The King of Syria was impressed with his mighty numbers of chariots and men and so he sent a messenger to Ahab and told him that if he would pay a large fee in silver and gold, plus surrendering all his wives and children[4], then the Syrians would not attack his area.

Ahab sent word back to him that it was a deal. Then Robinhood decided that Ahab must be easy pickings so he sent another message saying that the price of protection had risen and that he was going to send his men to go through the palace and all the houses of the city and take anything they saw and wanted.

The king of Israel then called the city council together and said to them that he thought the king of Syria was a troublemaker.

The leaders of the city then told Ahab not to agree to the terms. As a result, Ahab sent word to Robinhood that he would still go with the first offer, but that the second one was out of order.

This brought another message from Robinhood by chariot express telling Ahab that the Syrians had the biggest army in history gathered, even more men than there were grains of dust in West Texas.[5]

Ahab then worked up a sharp reply suggesting that the time to

[1]Hazael [2]Elisha was ready to quit plowing right then.
[3]Farm work came to a screeching halt.
[4]I don't know why he wanted all the children. [5]Samaria

boast was after a battle not before it.

This last message came to Robinhood while he was doing some heavy drinking with his aides, and so he jumped up and yelled, "Let's go get them!"

There appeared then before Ahab a prophet of the Lord and he said, "The Lord says that he will deliver you from this Syrian horde and you shall know that the Lord is the one God."

"By whom shall we be delivered? Who shall lead the army?" asked Ahab.

"Select the young men from the area to lead the fight, and you are to be at the head of the army."

All Ahab could find was 220 young men, and there were 7,000 other people who were halfway willing to go along behind the young men.

It so happened that by noon Robinhood was pretty drunk in the big tent with the 32 kings, who were also drunk. Someone came and said that there were a small group of men approaching and Robinhood said that they should be invited to join the party.

The 220 young warriors began to kill the members of the drunken Syrian army and the 7,000 followers jumped in as the Syrians began to flee. Robinhood escaped on a horse, but there was great loss of life and materials on the part of the Syrians.

The prophet then came to Ahab again and suggested that he get organized for the next year for the Syrians would surely return mad.

Now the advisers to the king of Syria told him that the trouble was that the god of Israel was a god of the hills, and that next time Robinhood should fight Israel on the plains that were not under their god's control.

Another thing, the advisers said, is to get rid of the 32 kings as leaders, and put warriors instead of drinking politicians in charge of the army. Finally, they suggested that the king assemble an army as big as the one that he had before as it was better to have a big army than a little one.

Next year, sure enough, there came on the plains of Israel ole Robinhood with his tremendous army.

The children of Israel looked like a drop in the bucket compared to the vast size of the floods of Syrians.

Then the prophet came to Ahab and said, "The Lord is angry because the Syrians have said that he is Lord only of the hills, and so God will deliver the Syrians again into your hands, and you shall again know that the Lord is the one great God."

The two armies camped in sight of each other for over a week before the battle began.[1] The children of Israel fought soberly and well and killed 100,000 Syrians in one day.[2] A bunch more of the Syrians fled and all climbed up on a high wall and the wall fell with

[1] I think the Israelites were waiting for the Syrians to get good and drunk again.
[2] According to a press release from Ahab's place.

them and killed 27,000 more. Robinhood escaped along with a few friends,[1] and hid in a room in a nearby city.

The friends had a conference and agreed that Ahab had a reputation for mercy and that if they went to him and surrendered they might have their lives spared.

As a result, Robinhood and his group put on old clothes, tied bands around their heads, and tried to look dirty and humble, and then they presented themselves at Ahab's camp. Ahab was standing in his chariot and one of the men said, "I have a message from Robinhood."

"Is he still alive?" said Ahab. "We are brother kings together."

When they heard this brother Robinhood bit, they all shook themselves and Robinhood stepped forward and said, " I am Robinhood."

"Get up here in the chariot with me, brother Robinhood," said Ahab.

Then Robinhood said, "The cities which my old man captured from your old man I will restore to you. I will name a bunch of streets for you in Damascus.

"It's a deal," said Ahab, and he sent him home.

There was a certain man in the area who was descended from the prophets and he went to a neighbor and said, "In accordance with God's wishes, sock me in the jaw." The neighbor refused.[2]

The prophet then said to the neighbor, "Because you have refused to obey the word of the Lord, as soon as you leave me a lion will kill you."

Sure enough, that's exactly what happened.

Then the prophet found another man and he said to him, "Sock me one."

The man then knocked the stuffing out of the prophet and wounded him pretty badly.

The prophet then waited by the side of the road for the king, disguising himself as a wounded soldier. When the king came by he called out saying, "I was in the middle of the battle and a soldier brought me a prisoner and said for me to keep him, or it would be my life for the prisoners. Now I got busy in the battle and first thing I knew the prisoner was gone."

"You've condemned yourself," said Ahab.

Then the man took off his disguise and showed Ahab that he was a prophet, and then the prophet said, "The Lord says that because you let the man go, the king of Syria, whom the Lord delivered into your hands, it will be your life for his, and your people for his people."

Ahab returned home from his victory then feeling depressed and displeased.

---

[1] They left the fight a little early. [2] It does seem to be a nutty request.

It so happened that there was a rancher living on the outskirts of Jersey City just beyond the king's palace and he had a beautiful vineyard.

Ahab wanted the vineyard and so he went to the owner, a man named Naboth, and he said to him, "I want your vineyard. I will either give you a better vineyard for it or else I'll pay you what its worth in money."

"No, thank you, Ahab," said Naboth, "this vineyard was my father's and I want to keep it."

Ahab came home depressed and pouting, crawled up in bed, faced the wall, and wouldn't eat.

"What in the world is wrong with you?" asked Jezebel, his wife, "you must really hurt if you won't eat."

"The trouble is, Jezebel, that I tried to buy the vineyard from Naboth and I offered him money or another vineyard, and he still wouldn't sell," moaned Ahab.

"Aren't you the king? Come on, get up and eat like a big boy and I'll go get your little vineyard for you," cooed Jezebel.

As a result, the next day Jezebel wrote some letters and forged Ahab's name to them, put the king's seal on them, and sent them to the city council.

In the letter she suggested that the city have an appreciation dinner for Naboth and make a big affair. Of course, they complied.

Jezebel then bribed two crooks to attend the banquet and publicly accuse Naboth of blasphemy against God and treason against the king.

The banquet was scheduled and the crooks arose on the occasion and accused Naboth of blasphemy and treason. Since two witnesses were all that were required at a public gathering for conviction, the two crooks took Naboth outside the city and stoned him to death.[1]

The crooks reported to Jezebel that the mission was accomplished. As soon as the news reached Jezebel she said to Ahab, "Get up and go. Naboth is dead and you can possess his vineyard by just moving in and taking it."

Ahab then arose and started to the vineyard.

The word of the Lord came to Elijah and suggested that he go to Naboth's vineyard and encounter Ahab and prophesy his doom.

When Ahab saw Elijah, Ahab said, "My old enemy has found me."

"You better believe I have, " said Elijah. "I have found you because of the evil that you have done in the sight of the Lord. The Lord has decided to take away your posterity, and all your male heirs, and to clean you out like he did Jerry and Baldy, for you have provoked the Lord to anger."

[1]This revised the appreciation banquet.

"Also," continued Elijah, "the Lord is unhappy about Jezebel and the dogs of Jersey City shall clean the bones of Jezebel and none of your children will have a proper burial. All of this is because you have worked wickedness, and followed idols, and listened to Jezebel, and worshipped Baal."

When Ahab heard these words he went into a deep depression, and he fasted, and he walked quietly, and stood in awe of God.

Then the word of the Lord came to Elijah and said, "See how Ahab has humbled himself? Because he has humbled himself, I will not bring all this evil in his lifetime, but in his son's lifetime."

Chap.
22

There were three years of peace between Israel and Syria.[1] In the third year, Fatso,[2] king of Judah, came to visit the king of Israel. During the conversation, Ahab said, "Will you and your army join me in trying to recapture a city from the Syrians?"

"Consider us one outfit, my people and your people, my horses and your horses."

Then Fatso said, "Inquire about how the Lord feels about this plan."

As a result, the king of Israel gathered together 400 prophets and asked them saying, "Shall I go to conquer Buffalo[3] or not?"

The prophets all said, "Go, for the Lord will give you the victory."

"Is there not a prophet of the Lord that is not a member of this union, that we might ask him?" said Fatso.

"Yes," said the king of Israel, "There is an independent prophet named Fosdick,[4] but I don't like him because he always prophesies against me."

"You are imaging things," said Fatso, "let's hear what he has to say."

As a result a messenger went for Fosdick. Ahab and Fatso each sat on a throne, side by side, and they put on their kingly robes, and the various prophets came before them and did their thing.

One, a witch doctor type, made horns of iron and said, "Thus saith the Lord, with these horns shall you push the Syrians out of existence."

The big pep rally continued with all the various speakers saying, "Go, for you shall win!"

The messenger that came to get Fosdick told Fosdick that all the prophets had told the kings to go to battle and he suggested that Fosdick do likewise.

"I will say whatever the Lord wants me to say," said Fosdick.

Fosdick then came to the kings, and the king of Israel said to him, "Shall we go and try to capture Buffalo or not?"

[1] One of the longer peace times. [2] Jehoshaphat [3] Ramoth-gilead [4] Micaiah

"Go and prosper, for the Lord will deliver it to you," said Fosdick.

"Aren't you pulling my leg? Tell me the truth, Fosdick."

"The truth is that I see Israel scattered all over the hills as sheep without a shepherd. I see them each returning to his own home at the Lord's suggestion."

The king of Israel then turned to the king of Judah and said, "Didn't I tell you that he would prophesy evil for me?"

Fosdick then continued, "I saw the Lord sitting on his throne and all the assistants in heaven standing around, and the Lord said, "Who will persuade Ahab to go and attack Buffalo? One suggested one plan and another suggested another plan. Then one came forward and said, 'I will persuade Ahab to shuffle off to Buffalo.'

The Lord said, "How will you do this?"

'I will go as a lying spirit and enter the tongue of the prophets, telling them to say go, man go.'

Therefore, you see, the Lord has approved a lying tongue to lead you to destruction."[1]

Then the prophet with the iron horns came forward and slugged Fosdick. The smart elec witch doctor said, "What spirit was that that went from me to you?"

"You'll know one of these days," calmly said Fosdick, as he was getting back to his feet, "when you are hiding in terror."

Then the king of Israel said, "Take Fosdick and take him to jail, put him in solitary confinement on bread and water, until I return in peace."

"If you ever return in any fashion, then I have misunderstood God," said Fosdick, "and I want you people listening to remember this."

Then the two kings approached Buffalo. As they drew near, Ahab said to Fatso, "You dress as a king, but I'm going to disguise myself, because they will be looking for me for sure."

Now the king of Syria instructed his 32 leaders to look for the king of Israel, telling them that the death of Ahab was all that mattered.

Of course, when the chariot leaders saw Fatso dressed as the king they took after him in a bunch.

Fatso yelled, "I'm a sucker for sure," and he turned and headed for the hills. The chariot leaders soon saw that this was not Ahab, so they quit chasing Fatso.

One of the Syrian archers was behind a rock just shooting his arrows in the air[2] and one of the arrows happened to enter the chariot of Ahab and killed him. Some of the men brought his body to Jersey City and he was buried there. One man washed the chariot, and blood ran in the street and the dogs licked it, as the prophet had

[1]This ruined the pep rally [2]Lots of soldiers operate this way in every war

said would happen.

Fatso was 35 years old when he began to reign and he ruled Judah for 25 years. Fatso worshipped God and he fought wickedness all his days, and cleaned out a lot of the evil in Judah.

Fatso went into ship building, and built a small fleet to go get gold from Africa, but all the ships sunk.

Then Thumbs[1], the son of Ahab, suggested that Fatso get some more ships and let Thumbs furnish half the sailors, but Fatso had had enough of Ahab's family.

Thumbs lasted only 2 years as king and he did evil in the sight of the Lord, and he followed in the muddy tracks of his father and mother, and like Jerry he caused his people to sin in worshipping Baal, and he provoked God to anger.

[1]Ahaziah

After the death of Ahab, Mississippi revolted and began to cause
Thumbs, Ahab's successor a lot of trouble.

Thumbs had a household accident and fell through the lattice to
the ground floor and suffered internal injuries.

As a result, Thumbs ordered a couple of messengers to go to
Seattle[1] where they worshipped the god Gull[2] and to ask the god
there if there was any chance of recovery.

The angel of the Lord then came to Elijah and told him to
intercept the messengers, which he did. Elijah stopped the
messengers and said to them, "Is it because God is not recognized in
this country that you go elsewhere for a god? For this neglect, tell
Thumbs that he will not recover from his fall."

The messengers turned back and came to Thumbs who asked,
"Why are you back so soon? You could not possibly have made it to
Seattle."

"We were intercepted by a man who told us to turn around and
go and tell you that it was because there was no recognition of the
true God in our country that you had to go elsewhere for help. Also
the man told us that you were going to croak, right where you are."

"What kind of looking man was it that said this?" asked
Thumbs.

"He was a hairy man," said one of the messengers, "and had a
belt around his waist made of leather."

"It's Elijah," said Thumbs, "the fellow from North Carolina."

Thumbs then ordered a captain to take fifty men and go and get
Elijah. When the captain and the fifty men approached Elijah they
found him on a hilltop.

"Man of God," called out the captain, "the king wants to see
you."

"If I am a man of God, then fire from heaven will come down
and wipe you out," said Elijah. Immediately a ball of lightning hit in
the crowd and cleaned them out.

The king then sent another captain with another fifty men and
the same thing happened to them.

Then the king sent a third captain and fifty men[3], and this time
the captain bowed down in the presence of Elijah and said, "O man
of God, please spare my life and the lives of my men. We know what
happened twice before and it seems silly to keep this thing going.
Save us, please."

The angel of the Lord then said to Elijah, "Go on with them,
for they will not harm you."

When the group arrived at the king's place Elijah spoke to

[1]Ekron [2]Beelzebub [3]All this reminds me of an attempt to take
a hill at Okinawa

220

Thumbs and said, "Is it because there is no God in Israel that you sent to Seattle? For your faithlessness you shall die in bed."

Shortly after this Tumbs died in bed from his fall. Since he had no son to take his throne, Spiro[1], his brother, became king.

The time arrived for Elijah to die and Elisha had been with him as an apprentice for about 2 years. The two men went to Norfolk[2] and Elijah told Elisha to remain there while he went to Vegas.[3]

"I will not let you go by yourself," said Elisha.

When they came to Vegas some of the congressmen there said to Elisha, "Isn't it true that your leader is about to be taken away by God?"

"It is true," said Elisha, "but just don't get in a stir about it."

Elijah then said to Elisha, "Stay here in Vegas while I go to Jericho."

"No," said Elisha, "I'm going with you anywhere you go."

When they arrived at Jericho the group of up-to-date leaders there said to Elisha, "Don't you know that your leader is about to die?"

"Yes," said Elisha.

Elijah then spoke to Elisha and said, "The Lord wants me to cross the Jordan here by Jericho, so you stay in the city."

"I'm going with you," said Elisha, and the two went toward the Jordan together.

Now fifty men stood on the wall of Jericho and watched the two men go to the banks of the Jordan.

When Elijah and Elisha reached the Jordan, Elijah took his mantle and hit the water with it, and the waters parted and the two crossed on dry ground.

As soon as they reached the other side, Elijah said, "My time has come. Ask me what you want from me before I am taken by God."

"I would like to be twice as capable as you are," said Elisha.

"That's a mighty big asking," said Elijah, "however, if you see the Lord take me, your request will be given, and if you don't, it won't."

As they were talking there came down from the sky a ball of fire in a whirlwind and blew them apart from each other and the whirlwind took Elijah up to the heavens, and Elisha saw it and he cried, "My father, my father, the chariot of Israel has taken you."

Then Elisha tore his own clothes to pieces as a sign of mourning, and he took the mantle which Elijah had left and went back and stood by the Jordan River.

Elisha then took the mantle of Elijah and struck the water saying, "Where is the Lord God of Elijah?" Then the waters parted

[1]Jehoram [2]Gilgal [3]Bethel

and Elisha crossed the Jordan on dry ground. The fifty men from Jericho witnessed this and they came to Elisha and acknowledged him as the chief of prophets.

The men said to Elisha, "There are fifty of us and we saw the whirlwind take Elijah and perhaps his body is in the hills, or smashed against the rocks, and we will go and try to find him and give him a proper burial."

"There is no point in it," said Elisha. The men kept insisting, however, and Elisha finally told them to go but that it was a hopeless task.

The fifty men went across the Jordan and searched for 3 days, but they could not find the body of Elijah.

When they returned to Elisha he said, "I told you so."[1]

"We have a problem, Elisha," said the men of the city, "for we have a nice and beautiful community but our water is bad that comes from the spring, and so our grass won't grow."

Elisha then took some salt and put it in the source of the spring and said, "Thus says God, that from now on this water will be pure, and the grass and diarrhea problem will no longer occur."

Elisha then left Jericho and returned to Vegas wearing for the first time the mantle of Elijah and appearing as a true prophet of the Lord.

As Elisha came near to Vegas some young hoodlums and kids came out and began yelling at him, saying, "Hi, there, you ole slick top, and here comes Baldy, ole hairless top."

Elisha then turned and pronounced a curse on them for their indignities, and in a few minutes two female bears came out of the woods and began to attack the youngsters and wounded forty-two of them before they could get back to the city.

Chap.
3

Now Spiro, the brother of Thumbs, and the son of Ahab and Jezebel did evil in the sight of the Lord during his reign as king of Israel. Spiro was not evil like his mother and father and did not worship Baal, but his morals were bad and he had little concern for his fellowman.

Now the governor of Mississippi had been paying a protection fee to Israel for a number of years in the form of sheep and wool. After Ahab died the Mississippi governor decided there wasn't much protection left and so he quit paying the fee. Thumbs was king too short of a time to get involved, but Spiro decided to try and collect.

As a result, Spiro sent a message to Fatso, king of Judah, and suggested that they join forces against the Mississippi group.

Fatso gave his usual agreeable reply, "Count me as being with you, my people with your people and my horses with your horses.

---

[1] As far as I can find this is the first time this phrase is used-not the last.

Which way shall we go?"

Spiro suggested that they go by way of Alabama[1] and get the governor of Alabama to join them so that there would be 3 rulers and 3 armies to one.

By prior arrangement, the 3 rulers and their armies met on the border of Mississippi and there was no water for their horses or for their cattle.

Spiro immediately panicked and said, "We're ruined. The Lord has decided to destroy us all at once."

"Not necessarily," said Fatso, "Isn't there a real prophet of the Lord to whom we can turn and ask for advice?"

"Yes," said one of the servants, "there is a prophet of the Lord named Elisha."

As a result, the three rulers called on Elisha. Elisha immediately jumped verbally on the king of Israel saying, "What have I to do with you, you godless one? Go to some of your strange gods if you want help."

"Not so fast, Elisha," said Spiro, "it appears to us that the Lord God himself is preparing to deliver us to the heathen, all three of our armies."

"All right," said Elisha, "but I am prophesying only because of Fatso, the king of Judah, who is a God fearing man."

Elisha then prepared himself to meditate and communicate with God, beginning first with some music. While the music was being played the spirit of the Lord came to Elisha and he understood what he should advise the kings.

"In the morning," said Elisha, "take all your men and let them dig trenches[2] and then though there will be no wind the trenches will be filled with water which will provide for you, your cattle and your horses. This type of thing is no trouble at all for the Lord to do, and he will also deliver the Mississippi group into your hands. When God does this, you are to destroy as many of the towns and cities as you can, cut down all the trees you see, and plug up all the water wells, and put stones in the fields so they can't be plowed."

In the morning, flood waters from Alabama came into the area and filled the trenches.

Now the governor of Mississippi had gathered together a small army and he led his army to the place where the three kings were camped. Just as the sun was rising the Mississippi group looked toward the enemy camp and the waters in the trenches appeared to them as blood on the land, for they did not know about the trenches and the water.

"Look at the blood!" said some of the men. "Surely the kings have quarreled among themselves and there is not much left of any of them. Let's go and gather the spoils."

When they arrived, however, they found 3 armies waiting for

[1]Edom   [2]What's an army without a trench?

them, and they were greatly surprised, disorganized, and soon badly defeated.

The men of Israel, Judah, and Alabama then did as the Lord had told them to do and they destroyed cities and towns, and ruined fields with stones, cut down good trees and plugged water wells. The sling-shot experts handled Biloxi.[1]

When the governor of Mississippi saw that things weren't going his way, he took 700 men and tried to break through the battle to kill the ruler of Alabama, but he could not.

The governor of Mississippi then took his own son and offered him as a burnt offering on an altar in front of everybody, and this disgusted the men of Israel so much that they quit fighting and went home.[2]

Chap.
4

A daughter-in-law of one of the local ministers came to Elisha and asked for help. The woman said, "My husband has had an untimely death and the creditors have come to me to claim my two sons in payment for what is owed."

"What do you have in your house?" asked Elisha.

"Not much of anything, just one small container of cooking oil."

"Go borrow as many empty jars and containers as you can," said Elisha, "then take them into your house with your two sons and shut the doors and begin to pour oil from your container and you will be able to fill all the vessels that you have borrowed."

The woman did as she was told and when she had filled all the vessels with oil she came back to Elisha and told him that she had plenty of oil now in the house.

"Go then," said Elisha, "and sell all that you need to pay your debts and keep the rest to live on until your sons are old enough to work and support you."

One day Elisha came to a small town called Midway[3] and there was living there a wonderful woman named Betsy. She was impressed with Elisha and she invited him to dinner. After that, everytime Elisha came through Midway he stopped and had dinner with Betsy and her husband.

One day Betsy said to her husband, "I have decided that the prophet whom we have often invited to dinner is truly a man of God and a very holy man. I think we should build him a small room on the wall and put a bed, a table, a stool, and a candlestick in it, and then he can stay here overnight anytime he comes this way.[4]

This was done and on a later occasion when Elisha was staying in the guest room he said to his assistant, a fellow named Billie So,

---

[1]Kirharaseth   [2]It had been a long day anyway.   [3]Shunem   [4]This was probably the first guest room ever built specifically for this purpose.

"Call Betsy, I want to talk with her."

In a few minutes, Betsy came and Elisha said to Billie So,[1] "Tell Betsy that we appreciate this guest room and the nice meals, and that I want to know what we can do for her. Would she like for me to say a good word about her to the king or to the commander-in-chief of the army?"

"I live with my own little group and have no interest in politics," said Betsy, and she left the room.

"What can be done for her?" Elisha asked Billie So.

"She has no son, and her husband is getting old," said Billie So.

"Call her back," said Elisha.

Then Betsy came again and stood in the door.

"In the proper time of about nine months, you shall have a son," said Elisha.

"You shouldn't lie to me, for you are supposed to be a man of God," said Betsy.

As Elisha had said, however, she became pregnant and in the normal time gave birth to a son.

When the boy was somewhat older, though still a child, he went to watch his father who was cutting grain in the field. In a few minutes the child said, "Daddy, my head is hurting something awful."

"Go to your mother at once," said the father.[2] Another boy, one of the workers, then carried the child to Betsy.

Betsy held the boy on her lap until he ceased to breathe. Then she took the child and placed him on Elisha's bed in the guest room and she called out back to her husband, "Send me one of the workers to saddle a donkey for I'm going for Elisha."

"Why do you want him today? It is not one of the regular times," said the husband.

"Just do as I say," said Betsy.

Betsy then kept telling the donkey driver to keep pouring it on the donkey as speed was important. She came to the man of God who was at Yankee Stadium preparing for services.

Elisha saw Betsy coming in the distance and said to Billie So, "Run and meet Betsy and ask her if all is well with her, and with the child."

She told Billie So that all was well, but she headed straight for Elisha and fell at his feet. Billie So tried to drag her away but Elisha said, "Leave her alone, for obviously something is wrong, though the Lord has not revealed any problem to me."[3]

"Did I ask you for a son? Didn't I tell you not to deceive me?" moaned Betsy.

"Here, Billie So, take my staff and don't turn aside to even speak to anybody until you have placed my staff on the child."

[1]The indirect approach   [2]Still standard first aid treatment
[3]Some odd thinkers say his ESP was broken.

"Elisha, I am going to stay with you. I doubt if the staff without you is any good."

Elisha then started to Midway with Betsy, but Billie So was already long gone, and he placed the staff of Elisha on the boy, but nothing happened.

Billie So met Elisha and Betsy and said, "The child has not moved."

When Elisha came to the house he found the child breathless and he entered the room, closed the door, prayed to the Lord, and then gave the boy oral resuscitation.[1] Breath began to return to the child and Elisha warmed the boy's body with his own body, and then the child sneezed seven times and opened his eyes.

Then Elisha called to Billie So, and said, "Call Betsy."

When Betsy came into the room Elisha said, "Take your son."

Betsy first bowed herself at Elisha's feet and then took her son and departed.

Elisha then came to the area around Kansas and there was a great drought in the land and there was nothing much to eat.

There was a men's conference scheduled and Elisha was to be the speaker but there was no food. Elisha then told the men to go out and gather what herbs they could and they would cook a big pot of soup. The men did, and they gathered various things for the soup, but one of the men, being partly ignorant, brought toadstools and put in the soup.

As the men began to taste the soup one of them cried out that the food was poison, and he said to Elisha, "There is death in the pot."

Then Elisha said, "Bring me some meal." When they did, he tossed it into the soup.

The soup became all right then and the men could eat, and so they could have their conference.

One of the men who came late to the conference was from Missouri City[2] and he brought some bread and fruit for the group and he said, "Serve it to the men."

The fellow in charge of the dining hall then said, "How can I put this small amount in front of 100 men?"

"Give it to the men," said the donor, "for the Lord has blessed it and there shall be enough, and some left over."

And that's just the way it was.

Chap.
5

General Naaman was head of the Syrian army and he was a man highly regarded by the king and he was also a very honorable man, and very courageous. In fact, the Lord had given success to Syria because of Naaman, but he contracted leprosy.

[1]The first account of this of which we know.   [2]Baalshalisha

There was a young teen-age slave girl of Israel working in the Naaman household and she said to Mrs. Naaman one day, "I wish General Naaman would get with the prophet of the Lord who lives in Samaria for he would heal him of his leprosy."

Mrs. Naaman had this word passed along to the king. The king then sent a messenger with a gift of money to the king of Israel saying that he was going to send General Naaman to Samaria to be healed of leprosy.

The king of Israel immediately began to climb the wall and groan saying, "Does the king of Syria think I am God to kill or to make alive? He knows that I cannot heal leprosy, and he is just looking for an excuse to raid my kingdom again and take off a bunch of slaves."

Elisha heard about this and he sent a message to the king of Israel saying, "Why are you so disturbed? Send the fellow to me and I'll show him that there is still a prophet in Israel."

As a result, the king of Syria sent Naaman with his horses and chariot and he arrived at a little place in Samaria where Elisha was staying.

When Naaman stopped in front of Elisha's place, Elisha sent word to him by Billie So that the great General was to go and take a real good bath in the Jordan river.

Naaman was really burned up about this message and said, "What kind of a nut is that prophet? Certainly he could have come and prayed over my hand, and done something. This 'take a bath' bit is crazy. I could have bathed at home where we have clear water, a sight better water than the old Jordan has." Then Naaman started away in a great rage.

One of the aides of Naaman, who wasn't ready for another 70 mile chariot ride, said, "General, if the prophet had asked you to do something very difficult we know you would have done it; so why not do something that he asks that is simple?"

This reasoning made sense to Naaman and he went to the Jordan and took a real good bath, and when he had finished bathing he was no longer a leper.

The General returned to the place where Elisha was, accompanied by his official escorts, and he said, "There is no God in all the earth except in Israel. Please, Elisha, accept a big fee for this great healing."

"As the Lord liveth," said Elisha, "I will accept no fee." Naaman urged the prophet to accept, but Elisha continued to refuse.

Then Naaman said, "As I return I will take two mule loads of earth from this place as a sign of my faith and I will never worship or sacrifice again to any God except to the Lord God of Israel. In fact, even when I am required to accompany the king when he worships at the altar of Rimmon, in my heart I will be bowing to the true God."

Elisha said, "Go in peace."[1]

Now Billie So was not too happy with this deal and he mumbled to himself, "My boss has let this Syrian General go without accepting a red cent; so I think I'll go chase him down and put the bite on him myself."

Billie So then chased after Naaman and when Naaman saw him and recognized him, he stepped down from the chariot and said, "Is anything wrong?"

"All is well," said Billie So, "but my boss sent me to catch you for two young men from Union Seminary just came by and they are looking for some scholarship help. A little silver and a couple of suits of clothes as a morale factor would be appreciated."

"Fine. In fact, I'll give you twice as much as you asked," said Naaman. Then he ordered two of his servants to take the gift back to town. Billie So then returned to his work as receptionist and aide to Elisha.

"Where have you been for the last couple of hours, Billie So?" asked Elisha.

"Nowhere in particular," lied Billie So.

"Don't you know that I felt it in my heart when you chased Naaman down. Is it right for you to act this way, to receive money, clothes, cattle, servants, vineyards and the like? You have been stealing secretly for a long time, and so the leprosy which I took from Naaman I will bestow on you."

Billie So turned white at these words, and he became a leper.

Chap.
6

Elisha had gathered a few students who wished to learn to become ministers and he had a small seminary in operation.

A committee of the students came to Elisha and suggested that living under his constant supervision was a little too much for them and they wanted to build a small dormitory about a half a mile away on the banks of the Jordan river.

"That is fine with me," said Elisha.[2]

"Will you go with us and help us with advice?" asked one of the students.

"Sure, I'll go along," replied Elisha.

When they arrived at the Jordan they began to cut down the wood but as the one with the axe was swinging on one tree the axe head flew off and fell into the Jordan river.

"Woe is me," said the student. "I borrowed that axe, and I'm in for it now."

Then Elisha asked, "Where did it fall?" The student then showed Elisha the exact point of the splash. Elisha then took his knife and cut a stick and tossed it on the spot and the axe head

---

[1]It is not certain if he used the finger sign or not.   [2]He was a little tired of supervising, too.

floated to the top.

"Now just pick it up," said Elisha and the student did.

The king of Syria decided that it was about time to initiate a few raids against the king of Israel and so he instructed his chief officers to set up a couple of secret camps and ambush the king of Israel and some of his men.

Elisha, informed mysteriously through God about these camps, told the king of Israel and warned him to stay clear of the areas, which he did.

The king of Syria was irked about his ambush not working and he asked his officers what was the trouble or where was the information leak.

"There is only one leak, O King," said one of the officers, "and that is Elisha the prophet, who apparently knows what you say even in your bedroom."

"That does it," said the king. "Find out exactly where this prophet bird is living and then bring him here."

"At present, sir, he is living in the little town of Dothan," volunteered one of the officers.

As a result, the king of Syria sent a troop of horses, chariots, and men and they came in the night and surrounded the town of Dothan.

The next morning, Elisha's new assistant, looked out the window and saw that the city was circled with soldiers. Terrified, the young man said to Elisha, "What shall we do?"

"Don't worry," said Elisha, "for we have more going for us than they do."

Then Elisha prayed to the Lord that his young assistant might see visions of many soldiers on his side, to comfort him, and then he asked the Lord to send a blinding dust to strike the eyes of the men surrounding the town. The Lord then smote the Syrians with blindness.

Then Elisha went out of the town to the blinded soldiers and said that he would lead them to the place they needed to go to find the man they sought, and so they blindly followed Elisha who led them into Samaria close to the headquarters of the army of the king of Israel.

When they arrived Elisha prayed to the Lord to relieve their blindness and their eyes began to clear and they saw where they were.

The king of Israel then said to Elisha, "Shall I kill all these Syrians while I have such a good chance?"

"No," said Elisha, "Would you kill prisoners? These men I led in here as captives. Feed them, be kind to them, and send them back to their master."

So the king prepared a big meal for the men and when they had finished eating and drinking they returned to Syria and were no longer interested in trying to pull anymore raids in Israel.

A year or so later, however, Robinhood gathered together a pretty big army and decided to lay siege to Samaria. The siege cut off all transportation and prices became unbelievable in the isolated town, dove leavings sold for $10.00 an ounce and the head of a dead donkey was worth $8.00.

As the king of Israel was walking on the wall of the city a woman cried to him saying, "Help us, O king, help us."

Then the king said, "If the Lord doesn't help, where can help be? The barns are empty and the wine is gone. What is your particular problem?"

"We are starving to death. My next door neighbor has suggested that we turn cannibal and eat my son today and hers tomorrow."

When the king heard this he was greatly distressed and stood on the wall and tore his clothes and mourned for his city.

Then the king said, "At least I can do something. I'll kill Elisha, because he has not secured help for us from God."

In the meantime Elisha was sitting in his house discussing matters with some of the older men when the king sent a messenger to summon him.

Elisha turned to the men and said, "This son of a murderer, the king, has sent a messenger to summon me to my death. When he comes don't let him in, and then in a few minutes the king will come himself and I'll deal directly with him."

The messenger came and then the king who said, "This trouble is of the Lord, why should I wait any longer to do something about it?"[1]

Chap.
7

"Now hear what the Lord has to say about all this trouble," said Elisha. "By this time tomorrow inflation will be ended and the price of flour will be reasonable."

"Yeah," said an aide to the king, "I doubt if this could be if the Lord made windows in heaven and lowered the food down."

"You will see it with your own eyes," said Elisha, "but you will not get to enjoy it."

There were four lepers about to enter the gate of the city to beg and one of them said to the others, "How stupid can we get? This city is starving. If we go in here we will only die with the rest of the people."

"Well, we surely will die if we just sit here at the gate, too." said another.

"Why don't we go to the camp of the Syrians? If they feed us fine, if they kill us, we'll just die, which we are going to do anyway," suggested another.

[1]In those days if things didn't go right you killed the preacher.

As a result they went to the camp of Syrians to beg for food and they found no one home. The camp was completely deserted.

What happened was that the Lord had sent a storm, with roaring hail, and hearing it in the distance the Syrians thought that the noise was chariots and horsemen and a great army coming and they said to one another, "The king of Israel has gotten the Eyptians and a Green Beret[1] army and they have come to wipe us out, let's get home before we get killed."

As a result they fled in panic, even leaving their tents and many of their pack animals, and provisions.

The lepers finding this situation first ate and drank their fill and then began to take various articles that were left behind and hide them.

One of them soon said, however, "This is not a good thing to do. Today is a day of good news and we should not keep it to ourselves, but let us go to the city and tell the king of Israel."

As soon as they came to the entrance of the city they told the gate keeper what they had found, and he told two bell hops, and they sent word to the king.

The king immediately got out of bed, for it was night, and he took a dim view of the report saying, "It is a trick. The Syrians have just gone and hidden in nearby fields and when we come to their camp they'll ambush us, figuring they will then have the city all to themselves."

"Just in case it isn't a trick though," said one of the hungry servants, "why don't we send some fellows on the five horses that are left alive in the city."

"All right," said the king, "but we will only risk two horses and they can pull a chariot."

The two messengers in the chariot trailed the Syrians all the way to the Jordan and found many garments and weapons dropped along the way by the Syrians who fled in a panic from the roaring storm.

The messengers returned and told the king and the people poured out of the city and gathered great quantities of food and clothing and other spoils from the deserted Syrian camp. As soon as the people returned with ample provisions, inflation was ended and the price of flour returned to normal.

The king had appointed the man who was to kill Elisha to be in charge of the gate of the city and the people stomped him to death pouring into the city at night with all their free goods. [2] Just as Elisha had said, the man saw the price of flour drop, but he never got to enjoy it.

Chap.
8

Some months after this Elisha was at Midway and he told Betsy

[1]Hittites [2]It never did pay to tamper with Elisha.

to take her son and leave the area for there was going to be a seven year drought and famine. Betsy did as Elisha suggested and moved her household into the Fascist country a long way from Midway.

At the end of the seven years drought, Betsy returned and went to the king and wanted her house and land back. Now Billie So had recovered from his leprosy[1] and he had been telling the king of all the mighty and wonderful acts of Elisha and that Betsy was very special to Elisha. As a consequence, the king restored to her the land and house that had been hers.

Elisha made a trip to Damascus and he was told there that Robinhood was sick. Robinhood was also told of the arrival in the area of Elisha.

The king then said to his top gun, Billy the Kid, that he should go visit Elisha, take him some presents, and ask him if Robinhood would get well.

Billy the Kid then drew expense money from the treasury of about $1500 and called on Elisha.

"I have come from the king," said Billy the Kid, "to ask if he will recover from his illness."

"Go tell him that he will get well," said Elisha, "however, privately the Lord has shown me that he will die, but don't tell him." Then Elisha became very sorrowful.

"What's wrong?" asked Billy the Kid.

"I am sad because I know all the evil that you will do in Israel. You will raid their towns and villages and set fires, you will kill the young men, and even children, and you'll violate and kill the women."

"Do you think I am some kind of a dog that would do such things?" asked the Kid.

Elisha then only said, "The Lord has revealed to me that you will be king of Syria."

Billy then returned to his king who said, "What did Elisha have to say?"

"He told me that you would recover," said Billy the Kid.

The next day Bill the Kid took a wet blanket and held it over the king's face and smothered him to death. Then Billy the Kid announced that he was the new king of Syria.

During this period several sections of the smaller tribes in Israel revolted because of the evil reign of Spiro in Judah and they were never reconciled.

Sprio's son, Thumbs, came into power, as has been previously mentioned, and he was wicked. Thumbs did, however, get with Jo Jo and went to war against Billy the Kid. Jo Jo was wounded and went to Jersey City for recovery. Thumbs visited Jo Jo in Jersey City when he was sick.

---

[1]I guess Elisha took pity on him.

Elisha sent for one of the seminary students and told him to get ready to travel. Then Elisha gave him a box of holy oil and told him to go to Buffalo and locate Jay.[1]

"When you find Jay," said Elisha, "he will no doubt be with some of his army group; so call him out and privately anoint him with the oil and tell him the Lord wants him to be king of Israel."

The young man found Jay eating with a bunch of army captains and he said, "I have a message for you, captain."

"For which one of us," asked Jay.

"For you," said the young man.

Captain Jay then arose and went into the room with the young man and the messenger from Elisha poured the oil on Jay's head and said, "The Lord God of Israel has chosen you to be king of Israel. You are to wipe out the house of Ahab as part of the penalty for what Jezebel did to the Lord's ministers. The Lord has said that he will make the house of Ahab as vacant as the house of Jerry and the dogs shall eat what is left of Jezebel in the streets of Jersey City."

As soon as he finished speaking, the messenger ran away as fast as he could go, for he was obeying Elisha and was not interested in being involved in a revolution.

When Jay returned to the table where the other captains were, one of them said, "Is everything all right? What kind of a nut was that who came in here?"

"You know who that was and what he had to say," said Jay.

"Cross my heart, man," said one of the captains, "we have no idea what that was all about."

"In short," said Jay, "the messenger anointed me king of Israel."

"Hurrah!" they shouted. Then they took a trumpet and sounded it in front of the restaurant and yelled, "Jay is king!"

Now Jo Jo[2] was king of Israel, but he had been wounded fighting Billy the Kid's outfit and was recuperating in Jersey City. Jay said then to his cohorts, "Seal the city here in Buffalo. Don't let anyone leave to go to Jersey City and report the revolution."

Jay then organized a small force and drove his own chariot in the lead and headed for Jersey City. Now Thumbs was in Jersey City visiting Jo Jo, and Thumbs was king of Judah at the time.

The watchman on the wall at Jersey City saw the Chariot group approaching and sent word to Jo Jo. Then Jo Jo suggested that messengers be sent to meet the group and ask if they came in peace.

The messenger came to Jay and said, "Are you come in peace?"

"You'd better join us, fellow," said Jay and the man did.

The watchman then reported to Jo Jo that the messenger didn't return.

[1]Jehu   [2]Joram

"Send another one," said Jo Jo.

The second messenger arrived and the same thing occurred.

The watchman then told Jo Jo that the second messenger did not return. The watchman said that the way the chariot took the corners on one wheel, he thought that the driver was Jay.

Jo Jo then limped out to his chariot and Thumbs got in his chariot and with their escorts they rode out to meet Jay.

When Jo Jo saw Jay he said, "Do you come in peace?"

"How can there be peace with a whore like your mother Jezebel running things?"[1]

Jo Jo decided that things looked bad, so he called to Thumbs and said, "There is treachery here!" Then Jo Jo turned his chariot around and started to leave, whereupon Jay shot him in the back and the arrow came out through the heart and that ended Jo Jo.

Then Jay told Plummer[2] to throw the body in an open field as the Lord had decreed this to be done in punishment for the way Naboth and some of the ministers had been treated.

When Thumbs saw all this, he also fled, but some of Jay's soldiers caught him going around behind a hot house and wounded him so that he died on the way to the hospital in the next town.

When Jay came storming into Jersey City Jezebel heard of it, and she put on her makeup and curled her hair and looked out the window from the second floor.

When Jay entered the city she called out, "Did Zulu who killed his boss have peace?"

Then Jay looked up and yelled forth, "Who is on my side? Anybody for me?"

Then two or three semi-fellows who were with Jezebel looked out the window also.

Jay called to them, "Throw her down." The three eunuchs then threw Jezebel out of the window and Jay ran over what was left of her with his chariot. As had been predicted, her blood was left for the dogs of Jersey City to lick.

After Jay had taken the city and had a good dinner he suggested that the remains of Jezebel be found and that she be given a decent burial because she was the daughter of a king.

Only the skull, feet, and hands were left and they reported this to Jay. Jay then remarked, "This is just as the prophet of the Lord said when he told us there wouldn't be enough left of Jezebel to recognize her."

Chap.
10

Now Ahab had about seventy male descendants left in Jersey City anyone of whom might become a king, so Jay sent a letter to the city fathers and suggested that they select the best from among the seventy and make him king.

---

[1]This was intended as an insult, though true.   [2]Bidkar

The city fathers thought about this and remembered that the two previous kings had simply brought trouble and so they wrote Jay and said that since he was the powerful ruler in the area they would rather serve under him than select a king from among Ahab's relatives.

Jay wrote back and thanked them and added a postscript saying that if they meant what they said he would become their ruler in exchange for the lives of the seventy relatives. The seventy were present when the letter was read and the city fathers immediately had the local police execute the seventy and they sent the 70 heads in baskets to Jay.[1]

When the heads arrived Jay had the baskets placed on either side of the entrance to the city and in the morning Jay went to the place and spoke to the people gathered there saying, "I admit that I killed my boss in order to become king, but I did not kill these 70 men. This represents the punishment of God which was promised to Ahab for his wickedness."

Then Jay departed for Samaria and was eating at Sheep's Inn where they served hamburgers when the associates of Thumbs, king of Judah, entered also to eat.

"Who are you?" asked Jay.

"We are associates of Thumbs and we are on the way to pay our respects to the king and queen."

Jay then instructed his soldiers to sieze the men, disarm them, and then take them out in the back and kill them in the sheep pit. There were 42 men killed this way.

As Jay was traveling that afternoon he ran across Little Red.[2]

"Hello, Red," said Jay, as he stopped his chariot. "Are you as much for me as I am for you?"

"You'd better believe it, sir," said Little Red.

"Then take my hand and get in the chariot with me," said Jay, and Little Red did as he was told, for he had no real choice.

When Jay arrived in Samaria and had finished killing everybody he could find that had supported Ahab, he made a speech in the court house square, "As you know, Ahab followed in the way of a little worship of Baal, and I expect to double all he did. Call to me then all the priests of Baal and everyone who is devoted to Baal, for I wish to make a public sacrifice."

Jay did this as a means of getting all the Baal crowd in one place.

Jay then announced a great assembly of all Baal worshippers and sent through all the land passing the word about the time and place.

The day of the assembly found the auditorium packed with worshippers, and each was given a name tag on which was written, 'We worship Baal.'

---

[1]Apparently there were no postal inspectors   [2]Jehonadab

Then Jay and Little Red went through the crowd and passed the word up and down the pews to make certain that there were only worshippers of Baal present.

Then Jay ordered his crack soldiers to get outside the auditorium and as soon as the service of worship started he ordered the soldiers to enter the auditorium and kill every worshipper. The soldiers did as they were told and they also took the images of Baal and burned them. In this manner, Jay destroyed the religion of Baal in the land.

Jay was no purist, however, and he did not bother to tear down some of the remote idols. The Lord, however, was pleased that at least he cleaned out the Baal worshippers, whether the method was right .or not, he had carried out the Lord's plan for the house of Ahab. Jay did not walk carefully in God's commandments, but followed some of the violent and sinful tendancies of Jerry.

Because of this, the Lord did not support Israel entirely and Billy the Kid began to make successful raids again, particularly along the coast of Judah.

Jay died after a violent reign of 28 years and his son Little Jay[1] became king in his place.

Chap.
11

Now when Reba, the mother of Thumbs, saw that her son was dead she was furious and ordered all the young descendants killed. Lucy, however, stole one of the young children and hid him with his nurse at the temple, for Lucy was the daughter of Jo Jo and had temple privileges as well as a place of her own. The young son of the king, named Bing,[2] was hidden in the temple for 6 years while Reba ruled the kingdom harshly.

Matt Dillon[3] was priest of the people at that time and in charge of the temple and the temple guards.

At the end of seven years of Reba's cruel reign, Matt Dillon called together the leaders of the people and the captains of the temple guards, put them under oath of secrecy and showed them the king's son, their rightful ruler. Dillon then explained to them the plan and issued to each man weapons from David's private collection in the temple.

From that time the young boy was under careful guard until each of the assembled leaders had time to recruit others and wait for the appointed day, which was to be the first sabbath when the people gathered to worship. On this occasion, Dillon brought Bing, a seven year old boy, before the people and announced that he was king, and he put the crown on him, and gave the proper affirmations, and anointed his head with oil. The people and all the leaders clapped their hands and shouted, "God save the King."

When Reba heard all the noise and the shouting she came to the

---

[1]Jehoahaz   [2]Joash   [3]Jehioada

temple and when she entered she was amazed to see the seven year old king, with guards around him and the people rejoicing; so she began to tear her clothes and yell, "treason, treason."

Matt Dillon, however, in his quiet way ordered one of the deputies to take her out of sight of the temple and execute her, as he did not want a killing in the temple. The men took her out by the barn and killed her.

Then Matt Dillon made a promise and an arrangement between the Lord, the king, and the people that they should be the Lord's people, and he also made an agreement of service between the young king and the people.

As a result, the people left the temple and went into the house of Baal and tore it down, destroyed the graven images, and killed the high priest of Baal, a man called Lazy Dan.[1]

Dillon then arranged for the young king to move to the palace and to be given all the rights of a king and so Bing began to reign at the age of seven.

Chap.
12

Bing reigned for 40 years and he did that which was right in the sight of the Lord according to the instructions of Matt Dillon.

Bing said to the priests one day that all the offerings and all the tax deductible gifts that were brought to the church and the priests should be used to repair all the church buildings in the area and restore all the sacred things.

At the end of 23 years Bing noticed that this had not been done and he called Matt Dillon and the other local leaders together and demanded that the churches be repaired. As a result, all future offerings went to carpenters and masons and the various houses of the Lord were repaired. The only offerings that were not used were the sin offerings, which were kept for the use of the priests.

There was no accounting made for all the church repairs as the superintendents were all honest and faithful men and no contracts or records were necessary.

Then Billy the Kid began to cause trouble again with his raids and he captured Gath and began to rob and pillage various villages and threatened to come to Jerusalem. As a result, Bing took all the gold he could find around the palace, and all that was left at the temple, and all the beautiful pieces of jewelry and valuables that were left in the kingdom and he sent them to Billy the Kid as protection, and Billy the Kid stayed away from Jerusalem.

Two disgruntled servants named Bonnie[2] and Clyde[3] went on a spree one day and killed Bing, and so his son, Greg,[4] became king.

Chap.
13

During part of the time that Bing was king of Judah there came

---

[1]Mattan　[2]Jozachar　[3]Jehozabad　[4]Amaziah

to the throne of Israel the son of Jay, a man named Jason and he did evil in the sight of the Lord and followed the sins of Jerry.

The anger of the Lord was again kindled against Israel and Billy the Kid and his son Robinhood the Second both made successful raids against Israel and caused much trouble. Finally Jason sought help from God and the Lord heard the cry and delivered them, but the people still did wickedly and their leaders were still not dedicated, God-fearing men.

Finally, Lester,[1] the son of Jason became king and he continued the evil ways of his father.

In the meantime, back in Judah, Elisha became ill and the good king Bing of Judah came to visit him and lamented over the illness of the mighty prophet.

"Open the window," said Elisha, "and shoot an arrow." Bing shot an arrow.

"That is the arrow of the Lord's deliverance from Syria," said Elisha.

"Take the remaining arrows," said Elisha, "and beat the ground with them." Bing did this three times.

"That's not enough," said Elisha, "for you shall now smite the Syrians only three times and you need to do it five or six times to really wipe them out."

Bing was impressed and moaned over Elisha and said, "O my great father, you who are the chariots and the horsemen of Israel, you are our great strength."

Then Elisha died.

The next year a band of raiders from Mississippi were in the area and one of their number died. About this time the group saw some of the natives coming over a hill and they threw the dead man aside and his body fell on the bones of Elisha, and the man came to life and stood on his feet.[2]

Billy the Kid died and Robinhood the Second, his son, took his place and three times Bing moved against him and three times Bing won victories, and recovered some of the places previously lost.

Chap.
14

While Greg was king of Judah he did that which was right in the sight of the Lord, not as well as his ancestor King David, but he did as well as Bing.

One thing that he did promptly was have Bonnie and Clyde executed for killing his father, but he did not have their children killed as the book of the law of Moses containing the commandments of God said that fathers should not be put to death because of their children nor children killed because of their father's mistakes.

Then Greg sent a message to Lester, king of Israel, and suggested a confrontation for Greg was fresh from a great victory

[1]Jehoash   [2]I think everybody fled the scene then.

over the Colts.[1]

Lester sent a message back in the form of a fable saying, "There was a thorn in Lebanon that went to a cedar in Lebanon and said give thy daughter to my son for a wife. A wild beast passed by and stomped on the thorn. That is what will happen to you. You are over-elated over your victory over the Colts, but you'd better stay at home and not come to meet me. You will fall and lose Judah also."

Greg would not listen to this reasoning and he took his army and confronted Lester and Greg was defeated and the men of Judah fled to their tents.

Lester then went to Jerusalem and tore down a large portion of the wall and took as spoil all the treasures of Jerusalem.

In time a conspiracy developed and a group found Greg and killed him and his son, Elmer,[2] who was 16 years old, was made king of Judah. Elmer did some restoration work for Judah.

In the meantime, Jeb,[3] one of the sons of Jason began to reign in Samaria. Jeb did evil in the sight of the Lord, but because of his promises to Abraham and to David, the Lord had pity on the children of Israel and their plight and he used Jeb to save them from complete destruction.

Chap.
15

Zeke,[4] son of Jeb, became king of Israel.

Greg's son Elmer became king of Judah at the age of 16 and he did that which was right in the sight of the Lord, although he failed to abolish the idolatry practiced by the people in the hill country. Because of this, the Lord caused Elmer to contract leprosy and he was forced to live in isolation during part of his reign. Because of this, Don, the son of Elmer did most of the active work for his father while his father lived in isolation.

Meanwhile, back in Israel, Zeke reigned for only six months, as he did evil in the sight of the Lord and a man named Ringo plotted against him and killed him in public and assumed the throne of Israel. Ringo lasted only one month as king because Link[5] came down from the north and killed Ringo and took the throne of Israel.

Link reigned for ten years and he killed the people of Long Island Sound[6] because they would not give him proper social recognition and during his reign he continued to do evil in the sight of the Lord.

Then Cagey,[7] a leader from Assyria, threatened to destroy Link and take over his operation so Link began to pay him protection money. Needless to say, he raised this money by taxing the people. Cagey took the pay and left Link alone.

[1]Edomites [2]Azariah [3]Jeroboam [4]Zachariah
[5]Menahem [6]Tiphsah [7]Pul

Then Greg Peck,[1] son of Link, became king and he also did evil in the sight of the Lord and Mitch[2], one of the more ambitious soldiers in the employ of Greg Peck plotted against Peck and killed him while on a pleasure trip to Samaria, and made himself king.

Mitch ruled for twenty years and continued the pattern of doing that which was evil in the sight of the Lord.

Finally, a man named Hooty[3] decided to become king so he killed Mitch and took the throne.

In the meantime Don was the king of Judah and he did that which was right in the sight of the Lord, except that he too failed to destroy the idols and burnt incense worshipping in the hill country. When Don died his son Ahaz became king.

Chap.
16

Ahaz immediately adopted the wicked ways of most of his predecessors and even sacrificed his own son on an altar in accordance with a heathen practice that had been condemned by the Lord.

The king of Syria and the king of Israel declared war on Ahaz and besieged Jerusalem but they were not able to take the city itself. Ahaz considered his plight to be great, however, and he sent a message to Tiger[4], the Assyrian king, and offered him a big price to attack the forces besieging Jerusalem or to divert them by attacking their other bases.

Tiger liked the idea and he first captured Damascus and created enough other diversions to draw the armies away from Jerusalem.

Ahaz later visited Tiger in Damascus and while there he observed an altar that he thought was exceptionally beautiful. As a result, he instructed his home priest at Jerusalem, Marvin,[5] to make an exact copy of the altar for him in the temple at Jerusalem and to take the old altar and put it in a special place for the private use of Ahaz.

All of this was done as a further sign of the heathen and idolatrous inclinations of Ahaz. When Ahaz died he was buried in Jerusalem and his son Hez became king.

When Hooty began to reign as king of Israel he did evil in the sight of the Lord but he was not as bad as some of the previous kings.

One of the things Hooty did was to pay protection to Assyria, but on the side he conspired against the Assyrians with the king of Egypt. The king of Assyria learned of the matter and put Hooty in chains. Consequently, the Assyrians were encouraged to further conquests and besieged all of Samaria and finally captured the people

[1]Pekahiah   [2]Pekah   [3]Hoshea   [4]Tiglath-pileser   [5]Urijah

of Israel and took them as prisoners and scattered them in many strange and remote places.

This was actually God's punishment to the people for their continued failure to worship God and walk in his commandments. Although the children of Israel sometimes made a show of worshipping God, they secretly did many things displeasing to God and they continued the practice of placing idol markers and graven images on some of the hill tops for the worship of strange gods.

The Lord had often sent prophets and sometimes wise kings who instructed the people in the ways of the Lord, but the people did not listen, and they hardened their hearts and would not submit to the simple discipline of the one true God, Jehovah. The people repeatedly worshipped idols and joined the strangers in their heathen worship and they forsook God.

The people even went to the extreme of sacrificing their children on the altar of fire as a worship service and they did many things to cause the anger of the Lord to rise against them.

The tribe of Judah sinned also and followed the wickedness of Israel and the Lord rejected Israel and he delivered the people to the spoilers. As a result, Israel was carried away out of their own land into the vast areas of Assyria.

As a result, the king of Assyria brought men from strange and faraway places such as Lima,[1] Honolulu,[2] and Lisbon.[3] When these people came to dwell in Israel they did not know or fear the God of Israel and so God sent hungry lions to attack them and terrify them.

As a result, these people called on the king of Assyria to help them and the king was advised that the trouble was their ignorance of God, who ruled Israel. The king then sent a priest selected from the captives and he was dispatched as a missionary. The priest came and stayed in Aspen[4] and tried to teach the people about the God of Abraham, Isaac, and Jacob.

The various nationalties, however, began to devise gods of their own and to erect statutes and to place idols in various prominent places. Along with all the many weird gods they worshipped the people also tried at times to give some amount of token recognition to the Lord God of Israel, but they never ceased to continue their strange idolatries.

In spite of being amply reminded that the Lord God of Israel was the one God, and that there should be no other god served, and in spite of the clarity of the commandments of the Lord, and the assurance that faithfulness would be blessed and that unfaithfulness punished, the people, even though they stood in some awe of God, continued to worship idols and violate the commandments.

[1]Cuthah   [2]Ava   [3]Hamath   [4]Bethel

In the meantime, during the 3rd year of Hooty, as king of Israel, before he was captured, Hez became king of Judah. Hez was 25 years old when he became king and he was more of the type of his ancestor David, and he did that which was right in the eyes of the Lord.

Hez even had the idols destroyed, the hidden places in the groves removed, and he trusted completely in the Lord his God. As a result God was with him and he prospered him and as a result he did not pay protection money to Assyria. Hez was also successful in attacking the remnants of the Capone gang.

During this time the king of Assyria captured Israel but he did not attack Judah. Some ten years later, however, a new Assyrian king gathered together a tremendous army and the new king, whose name was Big Hun,[1] came down upon the country of Judah and began to take all the towns and villages. Hez did not want war and he offered to pay Big Hun to go home.

Big Hun said that for $1,500,000 he would go home. Hez tried to pay this with golden doors and various ornaments. In spite of the gifts, Big Hun brought his army and camped with his tremendous numbers in sight of Jerusalem and demanded a conference with Hez.

Hez sent a committee and stayed at home to hear the result. The committee consisted of Senator Fulbright,[2] Wilbur Mills,[3] and Harry Truman.[4] The spokesman for Big Hun made a bombastic type of speech to them, full of threats and sarcasm, saying, "Big Hun wants to know why you all are putting up such a brave front. You indicated that you have strength for war, but on what is this based?

We have been told that you are counting on help from Egypt. In the first place Pharoah is a double-crosser and he'll join the strongest side.

Maybe you trust in God? This is a big laugh. In fact, just for kicks, Big Hun has said that he will give you for free 2,000 horses if you have enough soldiers to ride them, just so we can have some sport.

As for the Lord, it might interest you to know that Big Hun says the Lord is the one that told him to come and capture Jerusalem."

"Look here, sir," said Fulbright, "can't you speak in latin so our people on the wall can't understand what you are saying? We can understand a little latin, and we don't want our people to hear all this big talk."

"Not a chance," shouted Rickles,[5] "what I have to say is for

[1]Sennacherib [2]Eliakim [3]Shebna [4]Joah [5]Rabshakeh

everybody. They are the ones that are going to starve to death in the city and die of thirst with the food and water supply eliminated."

Then Rickles stood on a little mound and shouted to the people on the wall of Jerusalem, "Don't let ole Hez fool you. He can't deliver you. Don't let him sell you on that ole line about God delivering his people. Big Hun says that all you need to do is pay enough and you will be left alone to enjoy yourselves and remain in your own homes. Later next year we will move you back to Assyria to some real good country there and put some other people here in Jerusalem in accordance with our transplanting policy, but you will get to live in a land rich with corn, and the biggest thing is that you will get to live.

You think God will deliver you? Where are the gods of the people of Samaria and some of the towns of Judah? Did the moon gods, or the sun gods, or any of the others save anybody from Big Hun? How do you figure that this small-time Lord of yours will save Jerusalem?"

The people on the wall did not say a word, however, as Hez had already instructed them not to answer the rabble-rouser.

Then the committee of Fulbright, Mills, and Harriman returned with their mouths down, their clothes dragging the ground, and they were shredding Kleenex in their misery.

Chap.
19

When Hez heard all this he was miserable and he went into the church to pray.

Before going, however, he told the committee to report to Isaiah, the prophet of the Lord. The committee said to Isaiah, "This is a sad day, one of difficulty, and one of blasphemy against God. It may be that the Lord heard the speech of Rickles and that the Lord is angry and will help what few of us are left in all this holy land."

"Well, you go tell Hez," said Isaiah, "not to be afraid of words. Also tell him that I will arrange to have a rumor spread in the camp among the soldiers of the Big Hun, and he will worry over the rumor, and return home, and get killed in the process."

Big Hun had already heard of a rumor of trouble from Ethiopia and so Rickles sent a written message to Hez repeating his speech and defying the Lord God of Hosts.

Hez took the letter and read it and then went again to the church and in the place of prayer he spread the letter in the presence of the Lord.

Then Hez prayed to the Lord saying "O Lord, Thou art the one true God, the God over all the kingdoms of the earth. You have made the heavens and the earth, listen now, and also Lord take a look at our predicament, and consider the big boasting of Big Hun. The Assyrians have demolished all the idols and defied all the gods they have faced, now, Lord, please save us from the Assyrian, in order that all the kingdoms of the earth may know that you are the one true God."

Shortly after this, Isaiah sent word to Hez saying that the Lord had indicated to him that the prayer of Hez had been received.

Isaiah then said that the Lord had authorized him to talk back to the Big Hun and say "You are despised and just a big laugh to the Lord. How dare you defy the holy one of Israel? You have even reproached God with your big lip messenger. Don't you know that God is above the tops of the mountains, that God blows down the tall cedars of Lebanon, and that God can dry up a river by stepping in it? Haven't you heard of these things? You have pushed around some small communities and taken advantage of weak people, but you are beginning to smell, and I've seen enough of your cruelty; so I will just put my hook in your nose and my bridle in your big mouth and turn you around and head you back to the north.

The Lord will save a remnant of the people of Jerusalem and their roots will grow deep in the land, but you ole Big Hun, shall not come into Jerusalem, nor even shoot an arrow over the wall, much less organize an attack. You will simply return by the way you came, for God affirms that he will defend this city for his own sake, and for the sake of his servant David, and in answer to the prayer of Hez."

And it so happened that night that an angel of the Lord passed through the camp of the Big Hun and a virus smote the soldiers so that they vomited most of the night and some died and many felt like they were going to die or wished to die by morning.

Big Hun then returned with his sick and straggling army. When he approached one of his home villages two of his relatives thinking that the straggling, weak army had been defeated, killed Big Hun and placed his son Little Hun[1] on the throne.

Chap.
20

Hez became old and sick and Isaiah made a sick call on him.

"You should make out a will, Hez," said Isaiah, "and get all your affairs in order for I don't think you have long to live."

Isaiah departed and Hez turned his face to the wall and prayed to the Lord and mentioned that he had been faithful in word and deed and asked the Lord to extend his time on earth.

Before Isaiah had time to leave the palace grounds the word of God came to him and as a result he returned to Hez and said "The

[1]Esarhaddon

Lord has heard your prayer, Hez, and he will heal you and in three days you'll be well enough to go to church.

The Lord also says that He will defend this city during your lifetime for his own sake and for the sake of his servant David."

The trouble with Hez physically was primarily an infected boil and Isaiah took a ripe fig and placed it on the boil and the poison began to go into the fig and leave Hez.

Hez was greatly pleased with the word that Isaiah brought but he wanted a sign and proof that the word concerning the deliverance of the city was accurate.

Isaiah then asked the Lord to back up the shadow on the sun dial 10 degrees and this happened and Hez became happy and reassured.

The king of Babylon, Diamond Jim,[1] heard that Hez was sick and so he sent Hez a get-well card and several nice gifts. This pleased Hez and so he foolishly invited the messengers to see all his treasures, his antiques, and the jewelry in his vault.

A few days later Isaiah came to see Hez and asked "Who were the big shot visitors that you had the other day?"

"They were visitors from Babylon," said Hez.

"What all did they see here in Jerusalem?" asked Isaiah.

"Everything," said Hez. "I even let them look in my vault."

"You really blew it, Hez. They merely were here to case the joint and God says they'll come some day after you're dead and steal everything you showed them and probably take some of your sons as captives."

"I am sorry," said Hez, "but if this is the will of God then I am satisfied."

Hez, known widely for his conduit system of bringing water to Jerusalem, died fifteen years after the boil trouble and his son Lurch[2] reigned in his place.

Chap.
21

Lurch was 12 years old when he became king and he apparently responded to wicked advice for he began to do evil in the sight of the Lord. One of the things he did was to restore idols in the high places in the hills and he placed altars in the wooded areas to Baal and generally patterned his behavior after that of the wicked king Ahab.

As Lurch grew older he also grew worse and he sacrificed one of his sons and spent a great deal of time encouraging witchcraft and fortune telling industries. Lurch even erected a graven image in the house of David which had been built to the glory of God.

[1]Berodachbaladan   [2]Manasseh

Lurch led the people away from the one true God and the people forgot the promises of God and the faith of their forefathers.

The Lord spoke through his representatives that were left among the people and the Lord promised to bring trouble to Jerusalem and on the tribe of Judah and the Lord stated that the enemies of Judah would arise and capture the people and the people would become a prey and spoil to their enemies.

Lurch further aroused the anger of God by shedding innocent blood and creating a condition of violence in the city of Jerusalem.

Lurch died and his son Amon became king at the age of 22. Amon was also wicked and he served the false gods that his father worshipped.

Then one day the palace workers organized and killed Amon. This made the people of the city angry and they banded together posse style and hunted down all the palace workers and killed them and made Amon's son Jose[1] king.

Chap.
22

Now Jose was eight years old when he became king and he was blessed with good influences and he began to do that which was right and proper in the eyes of the Lord.

One of the things that Jose did was to authorize the high priest to use the offering collected at the church to pay for the repair and remodeling of the temple of God.

The high priest did as he was told and he reported later to Jose that one of the workers had found the book of the law of Moses and the messenger brought the book to the king and read it to him.

Jose was tremendously impressed with the words of God as contained in the law of Moses and he expressed great concern that the people and the nation would be punished as God had promised for the sins of worshipping false gods and failing to follow the laws of God.

Jose requested that the high priest seek a true prophet of the Lord and that the prophet be told of the book that had been found and told of Jose's concern .

It developed that the best qualified prophet was a coed at Jerusalem University and she was told by the high priest of all that Jose had read and also for his request for clarification.

The prophetess at the university said, "Go tell the king that the Lord will bring evil and destruction on this place in accordance with the words that are in the book, because the people forgot God, and burned incense to false gods, and sought their own pleasures."

[1]Josiah

"Tell the king, however," continued the lady, "that the Lord is impressed with the spirit of Jose and pleased at his efforts to restore the worship of God, and that because of this, the Lord will delay the punishment of the people of Judah until after the death of the king; so that the eyes of the good king will not witness the scattering of his people."

Chap.
23

Then Jose called an assembly of all the people at Jerusalem and he read to them the words of Moses, the commandments of God, and the words of the covenant which God had established between him and his people.

After reading this, Jose publicly proclaimed his intention of worshipping God and observing the laws of Moses. Jose told the people that the commandments of God would be the commandments of the kingdom of Judah. The people joined Jose in making this covenant.

As a result of this a mammoth cleanup campaign was initiated which took many years. All the idols, the symbols, the hill top shrines were all burned by fire. All the heathen priests were located and executed. The places for the sacrificing of children were completely destroyed.

The various statutes, such as the horses dedicated to the sun god, were all destroyed. As the various heathen shrines were destroyed, they were converted into burial plots and the bones of the dead were placed there, being all the bones of those who had worshipped false gods, as well as many bones of unidentified people.

The bones of the prophet of the Lord who had predicted that this would eventually occur were found and the bones of this prophet were not moved to the condemned area but left in their place as a memorial to the prophet who had been destroyed by a lion.

In the eighteenth year of the reign of Jose, after all the false gods had been denounced and the law of God was rather firmly established in the kingdom, Jose called for the greatest passover celebration of all time. This was used as a tremendous religious program and was the greatest passover feast ever staged or celebrated.

Following this, Jose began to remove the soothsayers, gamblers and deceivers of the people and to establish a solid reign of law and order under God.

Jose studied continuously the law of God and there had never been a more devout king in the history of Israel. Because of this, God delayed his punishment to Judah, but the Lord did not forget his anger with Judah and he merely postponed the punishment promised during the evil reign of Lurch.

After thirty-one years as king of Judah, Jose was killed in a battle against a raiding army from Egypt. After the death of Jose his son, Jed[1] became king of Judah and he lasted only 3 months, and he did evil during the 3 months of his rule. The Egyptian general didn't like the way Jed did things and so he captured him and sent him to Egypt, placing a half brother of Jed's by the name of Dru[2] on the throne. Dru agreed to pay the general the proper fee for protection, which money he raised by taxing the people. Dru reigned for eleven years and he did that which was evil in the sight of the Lord.

Chap. 24

There came into power in Babylon a king named Big Ned[3] and he caused the Egyptian army to return to Egypt and he forced Dru to begin to pay tribute to him instead of paying to Egypt. The Lord during this time was causing the people of Mississippi, and the gypsies, and Assyrians to rise against Judah and to desire to capture the whole of the promised land.

Following the death of Dru there came on the throne his son Sad Sack[4] who had a brief reign of 3 months. During that time Big Ned arrived on the scene with a large army and lay siege to the city of Jerusalem.

Sad Sack surrendered promptly and turned himself, his family, and all the treasury over to Big Ned. Big Ned then took all the strong men of Jerusalem, and all the skilled craftsmen, and blacksmiths and took them back to Babylon as captives. Big Ned then selected a young relative of his named Harpo[5] and left him in Jerusalem as king. Harpo, of course, followed heathen ways, and did evil in the sight of the Lord. With the taking of the captives into Babylon the Lord had finally destroyed the kingdom of Judah in punishment for their sins.

Some years after this, however, Harpo wearied of paying tribute to Big Ned and he revolted against him.

Chap. 25

As a result, Big Ned came back to Jerusalem during the ninth year of the reign of Harpo and he brought a big army with him and he lay siege to the city.

As a result, Harpo fled in terror and was captured on the plains near Jerusalem and what was left of his army left in the night through an opening in the wall, and remnants of the army were also

---

[1]Jehoahaz   [2]Eliakim   [3]Nebuchadnezzar   [4]Jehoiachim   [5]Zedekiah

captured.

Then MacArthur[1] who was a young captain in the Babylonian army led the storming of the walls and captured Jerusalem. The priests of the temple were captured and brought to trial before Big Ned, who had them all executed. Only the very poor and lowest grade workers in the vineyards were left to live in Jerusalem. This was the final carrying into captivity in Babylon of the people of Judah.

The small remnant that was left in Jerusalem were told by Big Ned that Gabby[2] was to be their king. Gabby told the people when they were assembled that all would be well with them if they would serve the king of Babylon faithfully and place themselves in subjection to the men of Babylon.

Seven months later a group of unhappy Jews got together and raided the palace and killed Gabby, but then they fled to Egypt for fear of reprisals from the Babylonians.

In the meantime, back in Babylon, Big Ned began to feel sorry for Sad Sack and he released him from prison and put him on a pension for the remainder of his life.

[1]Nebuzaradan   [2]Gedaliah

I CHRONICLES

The names of the people of God with the genealogies of selected families.

The genealogy of the tribes of Judah and Israel with particular emphasis on the lineage of Saul and David and the names of people associated with them.

When the ark of the covenant was finally brought to the city of David and proper rejoicing was had, then David gave to each person present a loaf of bread, a piece of meat, and a bottle of wine.

On the first day after the presence of the ark of the covenant and after David had appointed special priests from the tribe of Levi to minister to the people from the place of the ark, then David composed a psalm of thanksgiving to God in the general manner as follows:

"Thanks be to God, spread abroad the name of God, call upon him, tell people of the mighty acts of God, sing praises to the Lord and mention frequently his mighty works for man.

"Let anyone that praises God do so joyfully, seek the strength of the Lord, remember his great works, his mighty judgments, and the words of his mouth.

"You children of Israel, you descendants of Jacob, be certain that He is the Lord our God, his authority covers the whole earth, and he has a covenant with his people, commandments that are made to last thousands of years and the Lord is the one promising and He is the keeper of the promises. The promises that he made to Abraham and Jacob are still good.

"God said that he would give the land of Canaan even though you were but a handful of people, but God cared for you his people and he protected the children of his Israel for the sake of his promise.

"So sing to the Lord. Declare his glory. Proclaim his might. The Lord is to be praised and He is an awesome god. Gathered around the Lord is glory and honor as well as strength and gladness.

"Not only should you give glory and honor to God, but bring offerings to his temple and worship the Lord in the spirit of beauty and holiness. Encourage men everywhere to say that the Lord reigns over the earth and the heavens, for this is surely true.

"The roar of the sea is an acknowledgement of God, and ripe fields testify to his goodness, and the wind in the woods sings of the glory of God, announcing the presence of God.

"Be grateful to God, for he is good and his mercy endureth forever.

"Pray that God will deliver you, that he will save you from the ungodly nations and that he will gather you together as a nation so that as a united people you may worship the Lord and glorify his name forever."

Then the people shouted, "Praise the Lord!"

The assembly was then dismissed and everyone returned home and David returned to the palace and the ministers of the tribe of Levi were left in charge of the ark of the covenant.

Chap.
17

One day David was talking to Nathan the prophet and said, "Nathan, it has occurred to me that I live in a mighty beautiful and fancy house while the ark of the covenant of the Lord is simply stuck behind some draperies."

"God is with you, David," said Nathan, "and if you want to correct this situation I'd say have at it."

During the night, however, the word of the Lord came to Nathan telling him that it was not God's will for David to build a temple and Nathan visited David and repeated to him the message he had received from God, saying, "David, the Lord has revealed to me that you are not to build the temple we were talking about yesterday."

"In fact," continued Nathan, "the Lord would remind you and everyone else that no dwelling has been erected for God since Israel left Egypt, but the ark of the covenant, the symbol of the presence of God, has been shifted from tent to tent.

"God never requested from any of the leaders of his people a house of cedars. The Lord would remind you, David, that he took you from a small boy, acting as a sheepherder, and made you ruler over all the children of Israel."

"The Lord reminds you, David, that he has been with you and he has handled your enemies and made a great name for you among all peoples. The Lord has also determined that he shall provide a place for his people and the Lord has promised to increase your power, David, and to provide from you a great descendancy. In fact, David, God promises to raise up children and grandchildren and one of the children will be given the privilege of building a great temple to the Lord."

"I will bless this boy and not depart from him and I will show him great mercy."

After hearing this, David went into the place of prayer and knelt in the presence of God and prayed saying, "Who am I, or what have I done to deserve such a great blessing? Your promises may seem to be a small thing to you because of your greatness, but to me they mean everything. How can I thank you?"

"O, Lord, there is none great except you. What one nation in all the earth is blessed as is Israel? It is wonderful that the people of

Israel are your people, and that you have made them great, and that you are their God."

"May your name be magnified forever. Surely the Lord God of hosts is the God of Israel as well as a God to Israel. May you also bless my family as you have said that you would and may the lineage of David always be worshippers of the true God. Bless my house, O Lord, and may it always be faithful to you."

Chap.
18

In uniting the tribes and establishing the kingdom of Israel David found it necessary to subdue the Fascists, who had captured Gath and some of the other towns previously held by the Israeli. David also made war on Mississippi and these people then befriended David by bringing him expensive gifts, which actually amounted to tribute money.

David also took his army north toward Syria and conquered Hap,[1] king of Zobah, and in the process captured a thousand chariots and a great number of soldiers.

When the Syrians heard of this they were afraid that David was getting too close for comfort and they sent an army to fight David near Zobah, but David defeated their army and began collecting tribute from these people also. The Lord was with David and the real cause of his success.

Among the many valuables captured by David were many solid gold shields, and David brought these back, to Jerusalem and placed them in the church treasury.

Now when word of all David's greatness and success reached the ears of Big Toe,[2] king of Harvard,[3] he sent his son, Little Toe,[4] to visit David. Little Toe came to David and congratulated him on his great success and he brought David many presents of gold and silver. David added all this loot to the church treasury, which was, of course, under David's control.

David ruled Israel wisely and with justice and he served the Lord. David organized his government and delegated authority, naming Tuffy,[5] Commanding General of the Army.

Chap.
19

About this time Nahas, the king of Annum, died and his son Hanun became king. David heard of this and he decided to send a visiting committee to call on Hanun and express sympathy to him because of David's friendship with his father.

The committee of young men called on Hanun and conveyed David's messages.

Some of the advisers to Hanun, however, told the king that they thought the committee was a spy group and that David was seeking information rather than sending condolences.

---

[1] Hadarezar   [2] Tou   [3] Hamath   [5] Joab   [4] Hadoram

As a result, King Hanun became very upset and took the members of the visiting committee, shaved their beards off, cut their hair, cut the seat of their pants out, and sent them out bare tailed and clean shaven.

David heard of this and knew the committee was ashamed to be seen; so David sent word to the men to stay in Jericho until their beards and hair grew and also he told them to get some new pants.

Word of all of this came to Hanun and he realized he had been wrong and that in David's opinion he was an unappreciative stinker; so Hanun gathered together a great sum of tax money and signed up an army of paid soldiers from the surrounding areas and paid these soldiers to declare war on David.

When David heard of this, he sent for Tuffy and told him to get the army together and handle the situation.

Tuffy did this, but when he saw that the invaders were divided among themselves, the Syrians being in one group and the men of Ammon in another, then he divided his army and put one section of it under his brother's command, a man named Flip Wil.[1]

Tuffy explained to Flip Wil that while he attacked the Syrians Flip would attack the Ammonites, and if Tuffy needed help Flip would come to his rescue and if Flip needed help, then Tuffy would come and help him. Tuffy then invoked the blessing of God on the whole procedure.

When Tuffy and his crowd approached the Syrian mercenaries they decided that they had already earned their money and so they began to flee. When the children of Ammon saw the Syrian army fleeing they decided the jig was up and so they fled also.

Hearing all this, David decided to put the lid on the Syrians for good and so he took the combined armies and sought the Syrians and defeated them, making them surrender numerous people as servants and paying great tribute to David in the form of gold and silver. David always enjoyed receiving tribute. The Syrians also agreed never to make another deal with the children of Ammon.

Chap.
20

After a year of inactivity it was time to give the army a work-out; so Tuffy took the army on live maneuvers in the land of the Ammonites. David did not go on the trip but enjoyed receiving some of the spoil, particularly the heavily jeweled crown which was removed from the head of the Mayor of Rochester.[2]

The prisoners taken from the city of Rochester were worked long and hard with saws and axes to discourage any further trouble.

Trouble soon arose again also from the Fascists around Austin and one of the group was a giant who was killed by one of David's warriors who was quick as lightning and known as Sly Mike.[3]

---

[1]Abishai   [2]Rabbah   [3]Sibbechai

Later in the year another champion from Austin began to talk big as he was also a giant and carried a spear that looked like a vaulting pole. Again one of the trained warriors of Israel, this time a man named Sharpy,[1] fought the giant and killed him and the disturbance died down a bit.

Finally, a giant who was great in stature, but a bit freakish in having 24 fingers and toes challenged the people of Israel and one of David's nephews[2] named Delli[3] met him in combat and killed him. This ended the season on a winning note.

Chap.
21

There was now an idle time for David and the devil in the form of vanity suggested that David might take a census to learn how mighty a king he was and how many people he controlled.

As a result David called Tuffy to him and said, "I want you to be in charge of taking a census as I want to know how many people are in the kingdom."

Tuffy, who was a warrior not a census taker, said to David, "Why count the people? All the people are under your control so why worry about how many? Why cause all this stir and trouble?"

David, however, insisted on the census being taken and so Tuffy grudgingly went to work. Finally Tuffy returned to Jerusalem and reported that there were 1,000,000 men of draft age in Israel and 470,000 in Judah. The figures, however, did not include the tribes of Levi or Benjamin as Tuffy had gotten disgusted with the matter and didn't count them, thinking no one would know anyway.

God was displeased with David's vanity and with the counting of the people without the Lord's blessing.

David soon realized that he had sinned and he asked the Lord to forgive him.

The Lord spoke to David's religious advisor, a man named Oral[4], and told him to tell David that since he had repented then the Lord would give him a choice of three punishments.

Oral came to David and said, "The Lord offers you a three year famine for the land, or three months of trouble from the enemies of Israel, or a three day run of sickness in the land. Take your choice and I will relay your decision to the Lord."

David then said, "Oral, any way I decide is tough, but I would rather be at the mercy of God than left at the hands of enemies; so I'll take the three days of sickness for Israel."

As a result there was great sickness in the land so that about 70,000 people were stricken.

God also was so displeased that he sent an angel to destroy Jerusalem, but God then decided against this and stopped the angel who was standing in front of the barn of a man named Deere[5], who

[1] Elhanan   [2] He had hundreds   [3] Johathan   [4] Gad   [5] Ornan

was the leading grain thresher of the area.

David saw the angel of the Lord and he appeared to have the sword of destruction in his hand and David and the leaders of Israel who were with him fell on their knees in front of the angel.

David then prayed to God saying, "It is all my fault, Lord, why punish the people? I had the nutty idea of counting everybody. Punish me, and my family, but do not punish the people any more on my account."

The angel of the Lord then spoke to Oral and told him to tell David to build an altar and make a sacrifice in Deere's barn.

Now Deere and his three sons looked out and saw the angel with the sword and they hid behind a threshing machine until David entered the barn, then Deere came out to speak to the king, and bowed down to David.

Then David siad, "Deere, may I have a corner of the barn to use as a place for an altar in order that I might make a sacrifice to God? I will pay you a proper price."

"Anything you wish," said Deere, "but it is not necessary to pay me. I will even furnish the meat, the wood, and anything that is needed. It is a pleasure."

"No, Deere," said David, "I wish to pay the full price. It is not proper to make an offering that is not mine."

As a result David paid Deere about $4,500 for the equipment and the space.

David then made the proper sacrifice to the Lord and the angel put his sword away.

David then continued to use the place for his regular worship instead of going to the tabernacle which was at this period of the year in the hills. David was also still a little nervous about the angel with the sword and he felt at ease in Deere's barn.

Chap. 22

Now David felt that there should be constructed a magnificent temple, a great house for the Lord, a proper place for the offerings of the people to be received and for the altar services and worship services of the people.

David then ordered that all the non-Jews be conscripted for work if they were able to labor or had skill as masons or carpenters.

David began to purchase construction supplies, iron for nails, and brass for fittings, and great quantities of cedar.

Since David realized that he did not have much time left to live he concentrated on preparing plans and equipment so that Solomon, his son, could build the temple. David then sent for Solomon and instructed him and charged him with the responsibility of building the temple.

"My son," David said to Solomon, "It was in my mind to build a house to the Lord, but the word of the Lord has forbidden me, for

I have shed too much blood and made too many wars. The word of the Lord, however, has promised me a son who should be a man of peace who will be protected from his enemies. The son will be Solomon and he will build a house for the Lord and the Lord will carefully look out for him. Now may the Lord bless you, Solomon, and prosper you. You must, of course, build the temple. I pray that God will give you wisdom and understanding and I pray that you will observe the commandments of the Lord.

You will succeed, Solomon, if you observe the laws of God. Be strong, son, and of good courage, and do not be impatient or discouraged.

As a practical matter, I have saved and set aside well over two billion dollars in gold bullion, about two million dollars worth of sterling silver, and so much iron and bronze that we haven't even been able to weigh it, as well as enough timber and stone for all the walls. Already you have enough on hand for a good start.

There have been assembled and organized innumerable workers, hewers of wood, stone masons, skilled craftsmen of all kinds, with great abundance of gold, silver, brass, and iron for ornamentation. All you need to do is get with it!"

Then David gathered together the main leaders of the house of Israel and he spoke to them saying, "You are to help Solomon. The Lord has prospered you and protected you. There is peace in the land, direct your heart and soul on the Lord, work together, and build the temple to the glory of God. When the temple is finished, bring the ark of the covenant into it and all the holy vessels consecrated to the Lord."

Chap.
23

David had become very old and so he made Solomon king in his place, and David retired. David had also just before his retirement made a survey of the tribe of Levi and set apart 24,000 of the priestly tribe to supervise the building of the temple, some to be foremen, some to act as guards, and some to furnish music to soothe the workers while the building was in progress and to praise God.

The specific division of the tribe of Levi by name and duty is recorded for scholars in I Chronicles 23:5-32.

Chap.
24,25,
26

Further divisions of the tribe of Levi by name and duty for the building of the temple.

Chap.
27

The Israel army was organized on a basis of 12 regiments with 24,000 men to each regiment. Each regiment was called up for active duty one month out of each year. The names of the regiments and their leaders are recorded in I Chronicles 27:2-33.

Chap.
28

David, old and near death, called a convention of all the leaders of Israel, the heads of the tribes, the army leaders, the mighty men of valor and he caused them to be assembled and David made the keynote address to the convention saying,

"As most of you know, I have desired greatly to build a temple to the Lord, but I have had to be a man of war and have shed too much blood, but the Lord has blessed me with the privilege of uniting the tribes of Israel and establishing the kingdom of Israeli. The Lord has also blessed me with sons, and the Lord has told me to appoint my son Solomon as king in my place and he has told me that Solomon is to build the temple to the Lord.

God has further promised to make the kingdom strong and durable, provided the people adhere to the commandments of the Lord.

In the presence of God and in the sight of the leadership of Israel I charge you all to keep the laws of God, adhere to his ways and his judgments. If you do this, you will keep this land."

Then David turned to Solomon and in the presence of the leaders of Israel, he said to him, "Solomon, my son, worship the Lord God of Israel, the God of your fathers. Serve him with a willing heart and an active mind. Seek God and you will find him. Forsake him and he will cast you aside. Be exceedingly careful, for the Lord has chosen you to build his temple."

David then made a public presentation to Solomon of all the blueprints and plans for the temple, all the contracts, a list of all the supplies, the equipment, all the specifications, even to the size and style of the candlesticks, the altar table and all the decorative touches. David told Solomon that all these things had been planned and blessed by God.

Again David impressed on Solomon the need to be strong and courageous, dedicated to his work, and he again reassured him of the availability of money, materials, and labor.

Chap.
29

David turned again to the assembled leaders and said, "Solomon, my son, whom God has chosen, is young and green, and the job he has to do is immense, for this building is not for a man, but for God. Now I have done the best I could in gathering together all the material and working on plans and letting contracts. I have also raised plenty of money through conquest, and gifts. I have also shown my own zeal by making a gift of about $100,000,000 in gold and silver as my personal donation.

"Which ones of you are now willing to pledge his service to the accomplishment of this wonderful work?"

The leaders of Israel responded to David with enthusiasm and pledged their time and interest. In support of this they also made great contributions, amounting to over $145,000,000 plus a great quantity of jewelry. The people found great happiness in their giving, and their generosity and sincere interest brought a deep joy to the old king David.

As a result, David praised the Lord, and offered a prayer of thanksgiving saying, "Blessed is the Lord God of Israel. Praise ye the Lord."

Thine is the true greatness, O Lord, and power and glory and majesty are yours, for all that is in the heavens and on the earth is yours.

All riches, all power, all honor has its beginning in God. We thank you, God, and give you all the praise and all the glory.

It is humbling to stand in your presence, to willingly pledge ourselves to your work, when we know that all things, and all people are yours anyway. Man, in a way, is insignificant, for we are merely temporary visitors on this earth, and our lives move like shadows and are gone.

It is interesting to note that all that we have gathered for the building of this house of the Lord is just stuff, that has been yours all along anyway. I know you examine the hearts of people and it is a great joy to give so willingly to this temple and to behold my people giving so willingly.

Now, O Lord God of Abraham and of Isaac, and of Jacob, prolong this inspiration, keep our hearts in strong dedication to you, give Solomon a perfect heart, help him to keep your commandments, to follow your statutes, and to properly build the edifice which I have so carefully planned. Amen."

David then turned again to the assemblage and said, "Bless the Lord!"

Then the whole group bowed their heads and prayed to the Lord.

Following this there was a great feast and the offering of sacrifices to the Lord and great gladness and abundant joy on every hand. Solomon was again anointed as king and Solomon arose and sat upon the throne in his father's place and all Israel obeyed him.

There then came before Solomon all the mighty men of Israel, the leaders of the tribes, also Solomon's brothers and they all pledged allegiance to him.

This was the beginning of 40 years of the reign of Solomon and he died in his old age, full of honor and great riches, and his son took the throne after his death.

Now all the acts of the great king David are recorded in the books of Samuel, and in the book of Nathan, and also in the book of Gad, with many details.

Solomon, the son of David, was strengthened in his kingdom and the Lord his God was with him and encouraged his development.

Solomon spoke to the leaders of Israel and invited them to accompany him to Westminister Abbey where the ark of the covenant resided and there Solomon worshipped God and offered sacrifices in accordance with the liturgical commandments of Moses.

That night the Lord appeared in spirit to Solomon and inspired Solomon to pray. As a result, Solomon prayed and said, "O Lord, you blessed greatly my father and now you have chosen me to take his place. Continue the promise you made to David, my father, and since I must rule over a multitude of people grant to me wisdom and understanding that I may be competent to rule and judge this mighty nation."

God was greatly pleased with this prayer and because Solomon had not asked for wealth or power for himself, but had asked for wisdom and knowledge that would be beneficial to others, the Lord not only granted the request of Solomon but added to the blessing of Solomon wealth and honor in excess of any that anyone had ever had.

Solomon returned from this place of worship and reigned over the people of Israel. Solomon instituted a great activity program and he gathered horses and chariots and specified certain cities for the training and maintenance of the chariots and crews, and Solomon promoted so much business around Jerusalem that gold was as plentiful as stone and cedar trees were like scrub oaks.

Solomon imported horses and linen yarn from Egypt, purchasing all things at wholesale prices and selling them at a great profit.

Solomon then set forth to build the temple of God, designed by David, but destined to be built by Solomon.

Solomon then sent a message to Hiram, the king of Tyre, and reminded him of all the purchases arranged by David and he asked Hiram to continue to work this time with David's son, until the great temple was completed. Solomon reminded Hiram that he was building a house in honor of the one great God of all, that it was to be a place for worship and for observing all sacred feasts and customs. Solomon then humbly mentioned to Hiram that he was in great need of a true craftsman, a master builder, a man exceedingly gifted in decorative detail, skilled in the use of gold, silver, and brass. In addition, Solomon requested a contract for more cedar trees, fir trees, and algum[1] trees. The need for timber experts, log rollers, and

[1] I think Hiram found a substitute wood in this case

other laborers was mentioned. Solomon offered Hiram a tremendous sum for all these things, including 20,000 sacks of grain, 20,000 barrels of olive oil, and 20,000 barrels of wine.

Hiram was greatly pleased to receive such a fat contract in the mail and wrote Solomon by return mail as follows:

Dear Solomon:

Surely the Lord loves Israel to provide such a wise king as you. I, myself, bless the Lord God of Israel, who made heaven and earth, for he has given my friend David such a wise and understanding son that he might build a suitable house for the Lord.

For this reason, I am sending Crafty Wright,[1] who is an exceedingly talented artist as well as a knowledgeable builder and decorator. All you need to do now is send the payment to me. Incidentally, we will cut the cedars in Lebanon and float the logs down to Tel Aviv[2] and you can have them easily transported to Jerusalem.

Hope to see you soon,

Sincerely yours,

Hiram

Solomon then initiated a vast conscription enterprise and drafted into a giant labor battalion all the men living in Israel who were not Jews and were able-bodied. There were over 150,000 such in the land and he made 70,000 of them common laborers, 80,000 loggers, and 3,600 he appointed as foremen to supervise the work.

Chap.
3

At last, in the fourth year as king, Solomon actually began the construction of the temple on the mountain of Moriah, an area chosen by David because this was the area of the threshing floor of Mo Ranch where the Lord appeared to David through one of his angels.

The central foundation of the temple was 90 feet long and 30 feet wide with the roof 180 feet high. There was a covered porch attached, the ceiling and inner walls of which were covered with solid gold.

The main portion of the temple was paneled with gold beaten into the wood and then plated with gold and engraved with many figures and artistic renditions. Jewels and various precious stones were also inlaid into the wood.

The Holy of Holies, which was 30 feet square, was overlaid with solid gold and bejeweled. It was estimated to be worth over $15,000,000 unfurnished. Various other ornamentations were placed in and around the temple and two huge pillars reaching over 50 feet in height were placed in front of the temple.

[1]Hiramubi   [2]Joppa

A bronze altar was constructed 30 feet square and 15 feet high. A huge tank was forged that was 15 feet in diameter and 7 and ½ feet deep. This water tank was placed on the backs of two rows of oxen, all the oxen made in one cast. There were 12 oxen made all in one piece, with 3 oxen facing in each of the four directions. The tank itself was about 5 inches thick and was made to bulge out like a water lily, and the tank could hold 3,000 barrels of water.

There were 5 vats constructed on each side of the tank as the priests were to use these vats for washing of offerings.

All manner of tables, lamps, pedastals, and other fixtures were made and Crafty Wright made shovels and various devices and utensils used in working the sacrificial offerings.

At last Crafty Wright completed his work, having used polished bronze to construct the two pillars, the vats, the bases for the vats, the huge tank, the oxen, the fleshhooks, shovels, pots, the 400 pomegranates hanging from the chains around the tops of the pillars, as well as the tops of the pillars.

In the temple itself, only gold was used. Solomon commanded everything in the temple proper to be solid gold, the main door of the temple, the inner doors, the lamps, basins, spoons, even the candle snuffers — everything solid gold.

When the temple was finally completed Solomon had all the treasures saved by David brought into the temple and then he had a meeting with all the leaders of Israel to plan for the transfer of the ark of the covenant. As a result, the chief priests of the tribe of Levi took the ark and brought it to the temple and Solomon and the people sacrificed on this occasion with offerings too numerous to be recorded.

The ark of the covenant itself was placed in the Holy of Holies and only the supports of the ark could be seen by members of the congregation, for only the high ranking priests were allowed to enter the place of the Holy of Holies. There was nothing in the ark but the two tablets of Moses, and at the time of the writing of these Chronicles the ark was still intact in the temple.

There gathered then a great choir of the priests in pure white robes and they sang and played instruments to the glory of God. The singers sang a song saying "The Lord is good, and his mercy endures forever."

Then the glory of the Lord filled the house and it seemed as if the glory was a cloud that filled the temple and the priests left the temple for the glory of the Lord was so intense.

Solomon prayed then saying, "Lord, you will no longer have to dwell in darkness or be homeless, for I have made a temple for you, and may you live forever."

Then Solomon turned to the gathering of people and said, "Blessed be the Lord who has kept his promise to David, for he told David that he had postponed choosing a place for his temple until the people were united and Jerusalem was accepted as a holy city. It was in the heart of my father David to build the temple and the Lord assured David that it was satisfying to him that David had this great desire, but God would not let David build his temple, but left it to me, his son, to do. The Lord has kept his promise, for I have taken my father's place and have built the house for the name of the Lord, and in it have I had placed the ark of the covenant."

Solomon was standing in the presence of the people on a platform which had been built in front of the temple for such a purpose. Solomon then kneeled down and again voiced a public prayer in the presence of the crowd of people saying "There is no God like the Lord, in heaven or on earth, for God is the keeper of the promises, and he is merciful to all that turn to him. Even this day we witness the promise of the Lord to David being kept. For my father David's sake, keep the throne of Israel intact as you have promised if the people walk in the law of the Lord. Verify here today your promise.

"Yet I know that God is too great to be confined to a temple, for his dominion includes all of heaven and earth, yet listen, O Lord, to the plea of your servant. Always hear the prayers that are made in this temple, look down now and bless this building and make it holy.

"When we are here and seek forgiveness, hear our prayer, O Lord, and forgive.

"Let the innocent find a place of comfort and acquittal here and let the guilty be punished by you.

"If the people of Israel sin and forget you, and are defeated by their enemies, and then they come here and pray for forgiveness and help, hear their prayer and restore them.

"When skies are closed and there is great need of rain because of the sins of the people, hear their prayers when they come here to find you. Forgive them and teach them what is right.

"If sin produces poverty and hunger, if there are crop failures, and insect problems, let the people come here to pray, and hear them, O Lord, and heal the land. Give to each man that which he deserves, but forgive them and heal them.

"May our people always reverence the Lord and walk in the ways which you have directed.

"Even in the case of foreigners who come from strange lands to see your temple and to pray, hear them and answer their prayers, then all men everywhere will begin to know that you are the one true God.

"If our people of Israel go forth to war and pray here at your temple before going, grant to them victory over their enemies.

"If the people sin and forget you, Lord, and as a result are captured and scattered in various nations, and then repent and face toward this temple and pray, I plead with you to forgive them and restore them.

"Be constantly, O God, mindful of all the prayers offered in this place.

"Now, Lord, enter your temple, and let the priests of the Lord be clothed with understanding and righteousness, and let all men rejoice in goodness. Remember, Lord, your love for David and turn not aside therefore from me, your anointed one. Amen."

Chap.
7

After Solomon finished his prayer, fire descended and consumed the sacrifices and the glory of the Lord was meaningfully present. The glory and the smoke was such that the priests did not even feel competent to enter the temple, and all this so impressed the people that they bowed down and worshipped God, saying aloud "The Lord is good and his mercy endureth forever."

Solomon donated a tremendous amount of beef for this occasion as he was very rich and there was held one of the most impressive outdoor church bar-b-ques ever recorded. The skilled musicians from the tribe of Levi brought guitars and furnished music for the occasion, using the special guitars made by David for the church. Solomon participated in further services, dedicating each part of the temple to the glory of God.

The observing of these ceremonies lasted a full eight days and at the end of the time the people returned to their homes and to their tents full of joy, and hope, and bar-b-que.

This marked the completion of Solomon's plan to build the greatest of all temples to the glory of God.

The Lord then appeared to Solomon in a dream and said to him "I, the Lord, have heard your prayer and I have chosen this temple as the symbol of my presence, and a place of sacrifice. If I close the heavens so that there is no rain, or if I send pestilence to devour the land, then if my people who are called by my name, and who know me, if they will humble themselves, and turn away from their evil ways, and pray to me, then I promise that I will hear and will heal their land. My eyes shall be open and my ears particularly attentive to the prayers made in this holy place, for this is my chosen place, and I shall be related to it forever."

"As for you, Solomon," continued the Lord, "if you will conduct yourself as David your father did, and observe my statutes and my commandments, then I will establish the throne of your kingdom and there will always be a Jew available to rule my people. If, however, you turn away from me and serve strange gods and follow weird customs, then I will remove my people from this land which I gave them and I will cause the land to be abused by other people, and people of strange origins will ask why the great temple was destroyed and the people scattered, and it shall be told them that the people deserted God, and were unfaithful to the one Lord who brought them from Egypt, and for this reason they were punished."

Chap.
8

The building of the great temple and the completion of the palace and related buildings all took about twenty years, and then Solomon turned his attention to rebuilding the cities which had been given to him by Hiram and he placed many of the children of Israel in these cities in positions of authority.

Solomon built Phoenix[1] in the desert and Tampa[2] in the swampland and also he built Fort Knox[3] as a city of storage, and he also built places like Little Rock[4] and North Little Rock.[5]

Solomon also used all the immigrants, foreigners, and non-Jews as forced laborers, and others who were not Jews but who had always lived in the land and were natives, these Solomon taxed heavily.

The children of Israel, however, were never used by Solomon as servants, but they were made warriors, or horsemen, or white collar workers.

Solomon then moved one of his wives, who was Pharaoh's daughter and not a Jew, away from the holy city Jerusalem and put her in a country palace near the city. Solomon stated that he did not want his pagan wife to live in touch with the holy places and the holy objects in Jerusalem.

Solomon continued to strictly observe the proper religious practices and he appointed various priests to handle various obligations of the church and he devised a wise and orderly manner of religious practices.

After all this was done, Solomon took a trip to San Francisco[6] and there he met with the representatives of Hiram who had a fleet of ships. Solomon arranged for some of his own men to sail with the men of Hiram and they went to the Klondike[7] and returned with great quantities of gold for Solomon.

Chap.
9

The Queen of Sheba became curious about all the reports she had heard about Solomon and so she decided to come to Jerusalem to see for herself, bringing a great caravan of gifts and many evidences of being rich herself.

Sheba and Solomon had many talks and she was tremendously impressed with his wisdom and appalled at the wealth and the cultural advancements so obvious in the temple, the palace, and all

---

[1] Tadmor   [2] Hamathzobah   [3] Baalath
[4] Lower Bethhoron   [5] Upper Bethoron   [6] Eziongeber   [7] Ophir

around the city.

"All the things I heard about you are true, Solomon," said Sheba, "and the reports are not even equal to the real thing. You are greater than I had imagined and your possessions more abundant than I thought possible."

After this Sheba prepared to leave and presented Solomon with many magnificent gifts and received from Solomon everything she desired and more than she asked was added to the loot she took home.

After this Solomon had a period of making some very expensive things, including 300 solid gold shields, worth about a quarter of a million dollars each, plus some smaller versions, worth in the neighborhood of 15 million dollars all told. Solomon also ordered a new throne and considerable new equipment of unbelievable expense. Solomon even decided to have all the dinner plates, salad dishes, coffee cups, knives, forks, and all dining room stuff made of solid gold.

Every three years ships returned from Africa and the Klondike with gold, silver, apes, and peacocks.

Solomon also encouraged all the neighboring kings to bring him riches from their countries in exchange for protection and trading favors.

Solomon built 4,000 stalls for horses and he established regular chariot cities for the training of the horsemen. The king's handling of the finances of the country was so astute that silver became commonplace as cedar trees. Solomon reigned for a total of 40 years and then died and was buried in the city of David his father, and his son Roger became king.

Chap.
10

Roger then went to Baltimore where the leaders of the people had gathered to make him king. Jerry, who was in Egypt at the time, heard of this so he came back to Israel to attend the gathering.

Jerry and the other leaders then handed Roger a petition which read "Your father went too strong on the taxes and the burden that he put on us was too fierce, but if you will agree to a policy of easing up on us a bit we will loyally serve you and recognize you as king."

"I'll think about it," said Roger, "and you can come back in three days for an answer."

Roger then called for a small group of wise, experienced men who had been associated with Solomon and explained the request to them and asked them for their advice.

The old, experienced men then said to Roger, "If you will be kind to these people, ease up on them a bit, and speak good words to them, then they will support you as long as you live."

Roger then summoned a group of his own cronies and asked their advice and they said to Roger, "Tell the people that the taxes and work load imposed by Solomon was nothing compared to what you will do to them. Tell them that your little finger will seem bigger to them than your father's legs, and where your father beat the slothful with whips you will beat them with scorpions."

When Jerry and the leaders of Israel returned the third day Roger spoke to them roughly and answered them in the identical manner suggested by his young cronies.

As a result of this, all the members of the tribe of Israel refused to acknowledge Roger as king and each man went his own way, and Roger found himself only king of the tribe of Judah.

When Roger sent a tax collector to Israel the people stoned him to death and refused to support Roger in any way or to pay the taxes. Roger had to flee to Jerusalem, the stronghold of Judah, for Israel rebelled against this portion of the house of David.

Chap.
11

When Roger was safely in Jerusalem he began to organize an army from among the men of Judah and Benjamin in order that he might make war on Israel and see if he could obtain control of the entire kingdom.

The word of the Lord, however, came to Stewart, a man of God, and he was inspired by God to go to Roger and tell him not to start a civil war. Strangely enough, Roger listened and refrained from declaring war on Israel.

Roger did, however, decide to begin building up the cities in his area, fortifying them, and making them strong against attack.

At this time there also began to gather in Jerusalem and place themselves under the administration of Roger a large number of priests of the tribe of Levi, for Jerry had abolished them and no longer used the trained priests of God. Jerry made some of his own friends priests and put them in charge of strange rites and let them lead in the worship of pagan gods.

The kingdom of Judah was further strengthened by the arrival of many refugees from Israel who did not wish to worship strange gods, but wanted to worship and serve the one great Lord of all. These people had a good influence on Roger and for about three years he walked uprightly and acted more nearly like the great kings, Solomon and David.

Roger was a great ladies man and he desired many wives and so he married a great number of girls, but he apparently loved Marjorie,[1] the daughter of Absalom, more than any of the others. Roger also began to re-locate his children in other cities, and to strengthen thereby his relationships in many different communities.

Chap.
12

Roger, having organized Judah and strengthened his position,

---

[1]Maachah

became careless and started wandering from the law of the Lord, and he no longer properly worshipped God, and the people followed him.

Because of this the Lord allowed Clyde, an Egyptian leader, to make war on Jerusalem and Clyde had with him a large and impressive army. Clyde captured the neighboring towns and then laid siege to Jerusalem.

Then the prophet of the Lord, Stewart, spoke to the king and the people and told them that the trouble was their neglect of God. Upon hearing this, the princes and the leaders of the people recognized that it was true, and they fell on their knees and humbled themselves before God.

When the Lord observed this, then He spoke to Stewart and told him that because of the people's good attitude the Lord would not totally forsake them, and that even though they would suffer losses and be punished, the Egyptians would not sack the city of Jerusalem.

After this, Roger made a separate peace with the Egyptians and agreed to let them take away many people as servants and workers and he let them take many valuables in the form of gold and silver.

Since the shields of gold of Solomon were taken by the Egyptians, Roger had shields of brass made and he then went into the house of prayer and repented to God. As a result, the Lord preserved Roger and the main body of the people of Judah and the kingdom began to become organized again. Roger reigned for 17 years and he died in Jerusalem after a fairly evil and disruptive reign, involving constant war with Israel and wandering from the worship of God. Tab, the son of Roger, then became king.

Chap.
13

Tab reigned for three years and spent most of the time at war with Jerry. Tab gathered a large army and defied Jerry and the people of Israel. Tab stood on a hill top and spoke to Jerry and the people of Israel saying,

"Didn't you know that the Lord God of Israel gave the kingdom to the sons of David? Why is it that Jerry, the son of one of Solomon's warriors, has rebelled and is causing so much trouble? In fact, he has assembled a lot of mercenaries, and evil men, as well as pagans. Now you think you can defy God, who is on our side.

"You are a great multitude, you are also infiltrated with idol worshippers, you have dismissed the ordained ministers of God. The Lord, however, is with us, we have not forsaken him, and we conduct regular services and as a result we consider God himself as our ruler and the leader of our army. I warn you not to fight against the forces of God."

Jerry, however, had decided to trick the men of Judah and the army of Tab with an ambush, and had large forces slip around in back of the army of Tab so that they appeared to be surrounded.

When the soldiers of Judah saw there was an army in front of them as well as one behind them, they called on the Lord for help, and the priests sounded the trumpet, and the men of Judah charged with a great shout and the Lord was with them and discomfited the enemy, and delivered the enemy into the hands of Tab. There was a great slaughter on that day, but the children of Judah won because of their faith in God.

Tab and his army pursued Jerry and captured many cities. Jerry fled to the point of exhaustion and was never able to recover his strength. As a result, Jerry died. Tab reigned in a fine manner, but did not live very long.

Chap.
14

Tab's son Asa became king and he was a righteous man and he did right in the eyes of the Lord and the kingdom was quiet and prosperous for ten years. Asa had all the false idols removed from the land and he implored the people to turn to God and to obey the Lord's commandments. The Lord encouraged Asa and gave him rest from his enemies during these times.

During this period Asa introduced a public works program and began to rebuild cities and strengthen those that needed attention. Asa also organized a regular standing army that was well trained and it discouraged most plans for invasion.

There came from Egypt, however, a leader of an Ethiopian group whose name was Highly[1] and he attempted to invade Judah. As a result, Asa took his army and when they were near to the Ethiopian army Asa spoke loudly through a megaphone, praying for the benefit of all to hear,

"Lord God of hosts, it is of no consequence to you whether there are few or many on your side, we know your power, help us, O Lord, today, for we are depending on you as we battle this foreign multitude. You are surely the Lord God, and don't let a bunch of heathen men defeat you."

The Lord heard the prayer of Asa and the men of Judah had a mighty victory and pursued the defeated Ethiopians and completely routed them. While they were at it, they captured a great number of cattle and took much spoil and brought home captives and many valuables.

Chap.
15

Elmer, a prophet of the Lord, moved by the spirit of God, called on Asa and said to him, "You must remember that the Lord is with you as long as you are with him. If you search for God, you will find him, and if you forsake him then he will forsake you.

"Now Israel has gone a long time without the true God and worship has been sadly neglected. The people have tried to live

---

[1]Zerah

without law and without the leadership of the priests. Israel has always found, however, that when they do turn to God, then He is prepared to receive them and to help them.

In the midst of all these things there inevitably is trouble and confusion, and jealousy between nations, and enmity between cities, but you be strong and persist in the work of the Lord and your efforts will be rewarded."

After hearing these words, Asa was encouraged and he initiated a great clean-up campaign and conducted an impressive type of 'mission to the nation.'

As a result, the people began to renew their worship and to offer sacrifices to God and the people shouted and blew trumpets and made great promises re-affirming their faith. Their enthusiasm went to the point of decreeing the death penatly to anyone who did not serve the Lord and the entire tribe of Judah was joyful. As a result, the Lord gave the people rest from their enemies.

Asa even demoted his mother from being honorary queen because she was found with an idol which she had made and placed on the patio. Asa had the idol destroyed. Asa also returned to the house of God the precious vessels of gold and silver that had belonged to his father, and peace settled on the land and with the people.

Chap.
16

During the 36th year of the reign of Asa in Judah the neighboring king of Israel, called Baldy, decided to create some problems; so he built a blockade on the major access point to Judah and wouldn't let anybody come or go without his permission.

Asa then decided to buy some help in Syria and so he sent a large sum of money to Robinhood who was living in Damascus and entreated him to start a war with Baldy and relieve Asa of the problem he was having.

Robinhood liked the price and so he sent various ones from his merry band to start hacking away at the borders of Israel. Just as Asa thought, word of this came to Baldy and he quit trying to blockade Judah and Asa sent some of his men to tear down the blockade which Baldy had constructed.

Along came Criswell,[1] however, a fortune teller, and said to Asa, "You really blew it! You decided to rely on Robinhood, a pagan, to help you in your troubles and you should have come to the Lord God of Israel. What happened to your faith? It was certainly strong when you withstood the Ethiopians and relied on the Lord, and the Lord delivered you. Didn't you know that God wanders over the earth day and night keeping in close contact with all that goes on everywhere? Because of your lack of trust, you shall be plagued with

[1] Hanani

a bunch of petty little wars as long as you live."

Asa didn't like to hear this word at all and so he had Criswell put in jail and he also began to get tough with some of his workers, all because he had gotten up tight over being reprimanded.

Asa died not very long after this, probably from phlebitis. Because he had in general been a very good king he was given an exceedingly elaborate funeral, even putting flowers and all kinds of spices in the casket with the body prior to cremation.

Chap.
17

After the death of Asa, Fatso,[1] the son of Asa, became king and he immediately began to develop the army and resources of Judah as a threat to Israel. Fatso did this by fortifying the more vulnerable cities and placing armed garrisons in strategic locations.

Now Fatso served the Lord and walked carefully in the commandments of God, and he did not turn to Baal, but followed the Lord of his father and also took David as an example. The Lord, therefore, strengthened Fatso and as a result people seeking his favor and protection brought him valuable gifts and he gained in honor and in wealth.

Fatso not only did away with the constantly recurring sin of the people in the weird rites conducted in the groves, but he actually sent missionaries to instruct the people in the ways of God. These wandering missionaries taught the law of the Lord. As a result, the fear of the Lord came upon all the bordering nations and they were afriad to attack Judah.

Even the people from Mississippi brought gifts and sent cattle and sheep to Fatso as a sign of friendship. Fatso became a very powerful ruler and began to build new towns and to promote business, but he kept the army in Jerusalem. In charge of the various divisions were mighty men of valour and skilled generals, like Stonewall Jackson,[2] Douglas MacArthur,[3] and Pershing.[4]

Chap.
18

Fatso in time acquired more wealth and influence and he brought about a truce with Ahab by sending a daughter to marry into Ahab's family. Sometime after this Fatso visited Ahab and was entertained with bar-b-ques and special feasts.

Ahab succeeded in promoting Fatso to join him in a venture against the city of Buffalo and Fatso said to Ahab, "I am with you, and my people and my army are at your disposal."

Fatso, however, was a man of faith and he said to Ahab, "Let us ask of God about this matter."

As a result Ahab sent for the various ministers of all groups including his own fortune tellers and he said to them, "Shall we attack Buffalo?"

[1] Jehosophat   [2] Aduah   [3] Amasiah   [4] Elradaa

"Go, man, go," they said, "for God will deliver the enemy into your hands."

"Ahab, I'm not too certain about this group. I didn't recognize any of the ordained ministers or any of the genuine prophets of the Lord."

"Well, Fatso," said Ahab, "there is one, but I don't like him. In fact, he never says anything good to me. His name is Fosdick."[1]

"You are imagining all that, Ahab. Send for Fosdick."

As a result Ahab turned to the sergeant at arms and said, "Get Fosdick for me on the double."

The two kings then sat side by side on separate thrones and awaited the arrival of Fosdick. While they were waiting, some of the fortune tellers and public relations representatives of the sword manufacturers began to put on some acts and make like a pep rally.

One of these men, Big Bird,[2] had secured a piece of iron shaped like a steer's horns and began to shout "Hook 'em, horns! This is the way you will push the Buffalo crowd out of the stadium."

The other prophets and associates all supported this and kept yelling, "Go get 'em."

The messenger, in the meantime, came to Fosdick and said, "The king wants you to come and give him the word. Let me suggest that for a change you agree with him, as all the other representatives are for the invasion."

"I'll go with you, Mac," said Fosdick, "but I will speak only the truth as revealed to me by the Lord."

When Fosdick stood in front of Ahab, the king said to him, "Shall we shuffle off to Buffalo or not?"

"Go," said Fosdick, "and everything will work out fine."

"Now Fosdick, don't pull my leg. I want the truth," said Ahab.

"The truth is," said Fosdick, "that I see your forces scattered as sheep without a shepherd and as a result, having no leader, each one returned to his own place."

Ahab then turned to Fatso and said, "See, I told you that I would only get a bad word from Fosdick."

Fosdick then spoke again saying, "In my vision I also saw a committee before God and God asked who would induce Ahab to go against Buffalo and various suggestions came from the committee members. Finally, one of the committee turned to God and said, "I have a plan to entice him."

"I will go down on earth and put a lying spirit into the mouths of the so-called prophets and they shall encourage Ahab to go to Buffalo."

"As you can witness," continued Fosdick, "this is exactly what has happened."

[1]Micaiah   [2]Zedekiah

This infuriated Big Bird so much that he ran up and socked Fosdick on the jaw and as Fosdick was getting up Big Bird yelled, "Which committee member proposed that?"

"All right, Big Bird, you will learn the source of such when you are trying to hide and your conscience begins to work on you."

Then Ahab said, "Take this man Fosdick to the Federal Prison in Atlanta, put him on bread and water, and leave him in prison until I return in peace."

"If you return in peace, a winner, Ahab, then I'll admit I no longer speak for the Lord, but I want everyone here to be a witness to my prophecy."

In a few days Ahab and Fatso and their armies headed for Buffalo.

"I am going to disguise myself," said Ahab, "and I will dress as an ordinary soldier and you, Fatso, wear the king's robes and the symbols of authority."

In the meantime, the commander of the Syrian force from Buffalo had given his men the game plan saying, "Do not worry about ordinary soldiers, but go only to kill the king or one of the leaders, as this is the quickest way to victory."

As a result, when the armies approached each other the chariot captains of the Syrians spotted Fatso in the king's robes and made a direct attack on him.

Seeing this, good ole Fatso called forth loudly, "God save me!"

As a result, the Lord enabled Fatso to find an opening and to flee at full speed. The chariot men in pursuit soon recognized that Fatso was not the king for they knew King Ahab was slim; so they quit chasing Fatso.

In the meantime, one of the ordinary soldiers who was behind a rock shooting arrows in the air accidentally hit Ahab who was riding disguised in a chariot.

"I'm shot," yelled Ahab to the driver. "Get me out of here."

The battle lasted all day and Ahab remained in the chariot badly wounded, and died about sundown.

Chap.
19

Fatso returned to Jerusalem and was met there by a fortune teller who came to sound-off publicly and the fortune teller yelled, "You have been helping the ungodly, that worthless Ahab, and God doesn't like that kind of thing, and so he is probably irritated with you. Of course, you have some good points, for you have destroyed the idols in the groves and you yourself are God-fearing."

Fatso soon began to promote a revival of religious interest and he also began to consolidate the kingdom.

One of the things Fatso did was to appoint judges to rule for him in the various towns and villages and he instructed them when appointed, saying to each, "Remember, you are judging not for man's sake, but for God's. There is no iniquity with God; so you must be just and blameless in your decisions. You must make no distinction of persons and you must not accept gifts."

In Jerusalem Fatso organized the ministerial association and placed the ministers in charge of controversies, telling them to make their decisions faithfully and in accordance with the will of God.

Fatso said, "When cases are appealed to you, be certain and examine all the evidence and rule without prejudice as part of your responsibility. I have placed Peter Marshall[1] over you in all matters pertaining to God. Be courageous, and God will be with you."

Chap.
20

Somehow or other a bunch of men from the Mafia[2] got with an armed group from Mississippi[3] and decided to join together in an attack on Fatso and his kingdom of Judah. When this was reported to Fatso he called a gathering of the leaders of Judah and as many people as wished to attend and he told them the news.

On this occasion, which was held in front of the main church in Jerusalem, Fatso called on the people to kneel while he publicly prayed to God.

"Lord God of our fathers," prayed Fatso, "You are the ruler in heaven and on earth, in your hands there resides all possible power. We know you are responsible for us being here in the first place. We also know that when we stand here in front of your church you will help us when we have a great need. You have always delivered us when we have prayed properly in this place.

"Now we are in a big jam. It is reported that a big army of men from Mississippi along with a large group of outlaws and Mafia boys are headed our way and they plan to move against us and here we are with our wives and children and we don't know how to handle a tough outfit like this."

The spirit of the Lord then moved in one member of the congregation, an outspoken type of fellow named Big Ben[4], who was an ordained priest, and he said, "Listen, everyone of you, and also the king, don't be afraid! The forthcoming encounter is not yours, but it is God's. Tomorrow when these armies approach go down to meet them, but be certain that God will get the job done, for these people are defying God. You won't even have to do much fighting, if any, yourselves. You can be spectators. You will witness the deliverance by God, for God will be with you."

Then Fatso and all the people bowed down to the Lord and worshipped.

Early in the morning the people arose and in a great throng proceeded out of the city and marched toward the area where they expected to see the visiting armies. The ministers of the churches led

[1]Amariah [2]Ammon [3]Moab [4]Jehaziel

the march and led in the singing of the Battle Hymn of the Republic.

In the meantime, the Mafia group and the Mississippi combine had encountered a large group of Kentucky mountaineers and had begun to kill them in a bloody battle. Shortly the Mafia group and the Mississippi bunch began to fight among themselves over the spoil and a great slaughter took place, which resulted in such disorder that those who weren't dead or wounded soon went home. The men of Fatso then came and took all the spoil that had been gathered by the invading armies and considerable wealth was brought back to Jerusalem. In fact, it took three days to get all the cattle, jewelry, and miscellaneous valuables back to Jerusalem.

When all the spoil was safely stored or divided, then there was a big celebration, with much singing and dancing.

The word also went out that it didn't pay to try to attack a nation that was under God; so Fatso began to have another period of peace and quiet. Fatso continued to serve God as his father had done.

Sometime after this Fatso made a deal to join Thumbs, King of Israel, in buying a fleet of ships to make money, but Thumbs was an ungodly man and so one of the local ministers forecast the doom of the project. In fact, not too long after this a storm hit the fleet and most of the ships were blown into the rocks or cracked up by the storm.

Fatso died after a successful reign of some 35 years.

Chap.
21

Spiro, the oldest son of Fatso, assumed the throne and he was 32 years old at the time, and mean. One of the first things that he did was to have all his brothers and half-brothers killed so there wouldn't be any mumbling in the family about who would make the best king.

Spiro had married a daughter of the wicked Ahab and she took after her father apparently and influenced Spiro to pursue the ways of evildoing.

Since Fatso had left each of his sons a nice nest egg, Spiro acquired considerable wealth when he had the other sons killed and absconded with their property.

The Lord did not destroy the wicked kingdom because of his promise to David, but he began to cause the people and their king a lot of trouble.

For one thing, the people of Alabama[1] revolted and to this day[2] they are not at ease under restraint or outside control. Georgia[3] also pulled out from under Spiro and revolted.

Spiro also instigated some heathen observances and encouraged the people in public and obnoxious orgies.

[1] Edom   [2] As of this writing   [3] Libnah

Not long after this the postman brought Spiro a letter and when he opened it he read as follows:

Dear Spiro:

The Lord God of David, your noble ancestor, has instructed me to tell you that you have refused to follow the good example of your father and your grandfather, but have followed the evil example of Ahab, even to slaying your own brothers, and so the Lord says that he will smite your people with a plague, and there will be a great outbreak of diarrhea and there will be an awful time for everybody.

Yours truly,
Elijah, the prophet.

About this same time also the Fascists became active again and troops from Ethiopia decided to stage a few raids and they came into the land of Judah and plundered, and took away the wives of Spiro and his sons, all except Jed[1] who was a teen-ager. Spiro was too sick to be moved and he was stricken with cancer and died in two years.

Spiro reigned for eight years and he died and no one mourned his passing. Spiro was buried in Jerusalem, but they did not bury him in the sepulchre of the kings.

Chap.
22

Apparently the kingdom was up for grabs for awhile, but by the time Jed was old enough to vote, the people made him king. Jed was under the influence of Reba, his mother, who was a wicked daughter of Ahab, and Jed followed the evil advice which she gave him.

For one thing, he joined Thumbs in making war unnecessarily against Billy the Kid and he was wounded at the battle of Buffalo. Jed returned to Jersey City and checked into the hospital there. Thumbs came to visit and Jay used this opportunity to get both of the potential threats to his revolution at one time, and he managed to kill them both at Jersey City, as the Lord had spoken against the descendants of Ahab.

When Reba learned of the death of Jed she went on a mad spree and had all the posible heirs to the throne murdered.

Florence,[2] a nurse of one of the boys, took the small boy Jap[3] and hid him so that he would not be killed. For six years the nurse kept him hidden in the church while Reba ruled the kingdom with an evil and violent hand.

Chap.
23

After Reba had been reigning wickedly for over seven years Matt Dillon[4] decided that it was time to act. Dillon was in charge of the tabernacle and head of all the priests and ministers.

First, Dillon quietly sent word to all members of the ministerial alliance[5] in the entire area and he assembled them secretly at the

---

[1]Jehoahaz   [2]Jehoshabeath   [3]Joash
[4]Jehoiada   [5]This has to be the trick of the week

church. Dillon explained to them that young Jap was now old enough to be at least a teen-age king. Dillon distributed many of the valuable weapons of the time of King David and arranged for separate groups to guard each entrance to the temple.

The plan was put into effect the first full worship Sunday and when the people gathered in the temple, there they saw Jap standing in the king's spot, flanked by the armed members of the ministerial alliance. Dillon explained to the people that Jap was the legitimate king and the people began to shout, "God save the King" and to sing, dance, and generally create a disturbance.

Reba heard all the shouting and singing at the palace and so she hurried down to the temple to see what was happening. When Reba arrived she was amazed to see Jap, who she thought was dead, standing in the king's place.

"Treason, treason," she yelled and began shredding her Kleenex.

Dillon then stepped forward and quietly said to the army captain present, "Seize this woman. Take her to the stables and kill her."

After this was done, Jap was escorted to the palace and officially declared king, with Dillon as his chief advisor.

Dillon made a brief speech declaring that the people would now serve the one true God and that they would again be God's people. Whereupon he led them in a mission to destroy the places for the worship of Baal, and the people tore down the idols and destroyed the pagan ritual images and for good measure killed the priest of Baal in charge of the idols.

Matt Dillon then re-organized the church and there was a big celebration, and the king was praised and all the people rejoiced and peace descended on the area.

Chap.
24

Jap was seven years old when he began to reign, but he operated largely on the advice of Matt Dillon. When Jap became older, Matt Dillon arranged for Jap to acquire two wives and as a result he began to have sons and daughters.

Jap then decided that the church building needed a lot of repairs as the maintenance program had not been doing very well. As a result, he instructed the members of the ministerial alliance to put on a fund-raising drive and secure money for the rebuilding program, and to do it in a hurry.

The priests did not get into action fast enough to suit Jap and so he sent for Matt Dillon and said, "Are you getting too old to be tough, Matt? Why haven't you been riding herd on the building fund drive? Don't you know that the sons of the wicked Reba had damaged the church and stolen the valuables from it? Anyway, I hereby command that offering plates be placed in the form of cedar chests and I want the people to bring their offerings and get with it on this program."

The leaders and the people responded to this command and brought offerings until the needed amount was secured. Then the work started on the remodeling and the excess of funds which continued to come in were used for special vessels and ornaments.

Not long after this Matt Dillon, who had become very old, died and was buried in the plot reserved for kings, because of all the great things he had done in Judah.

After the passing of Dillon, some of the leaders of the people decided to return to the worship of material things and to act selfishly, forgetting the Lord and the promises made to observe his commandments and to worship him. As a result, the Lord became angry with the people.

The Lord inspired some of the ministers to preach to the people concerning the error of their ways and their forsaking of God, but they would not listen.

Finally, the spirit of the Lord descended on Zeke, [1] the son of Matt Dillon, and he began to admonish the people and denounce their leaders. As a result, some of the leaders secured the consent of the king and then had Zeke stoned to death. Jap, the king, sinned in permitting this.

As punishment, the Lord supported a small band of Syrians in their move against the people of Judah. The Syrians destroyed the leaders of the people and made away with many captives and a lot of loot.

The Syrians also left Jap severely wounded and so some of the associates of Jap who didn't agree with the stoning of Zeke decided to finish Jap off, and so they killed him while he was lying in bed.

Following the death of Jap, his son Greg became king.

Chap. 25

Greg[2] was 25 years old when he began to rule and he attempted to observe the commandments of the Lord, but he did not have the compassion of David or the understanding of Solomon. The first thing Greg did was to have all the men killed that had been involved in the plot against his father, though he did spare the lives of their children.

Greg also did a thorough job of organizing Judah, and he secured 100,000 mercenaries to handle any unpleasantness that might arise from his neighbors.

A prophet of the Lord then came to Greg and advised him against the use of mercenaries and told him that the Lord would fight his battles if necessary and furthermore the prophet suggested that if Greg led the mercenaries into battle he would get killed. As a

[1]Zechariah   [2]Amiziah

result, Greg disbanded the group and sent them home. The mercenaries left mad and bitter.

"What about the money I paid them?" asked Greg, "Is all that wasted?"

"The Lord will make it up to you, Greg," said the prophet, "but for the time being the money is blown."

Greg then led his own army of his own people to fight a troublesome group of guerrilla warfare fellows who were doing some hijacking and robbing in the north. Greg defeated them thoroughly and returned with a great deal of spoil.

In the meantime, the mercenaries decided to go it alone since they had all sharpened their swords anyway, and so they laid waste a city or two in West Texas and cleaned out the banks and jewelry stores.

Greg had captured some of the images of the gods of the guerrilla group and brought them home and began to worship them instead of going to the tabernacle to worship the Lord God of Israel.

It was not long after this that a prophet of the Lord called on Greg and said, "Why have you started the worship of strange gods? In the first place, they are the gods of the losers."

"Who asked you to speak to me?" snapped the king. "In fact, you should be executed for criticizing your great leader."

"All right, I'll quiet down, but I know God has decided to destroy you for your wickedness."

After this Greg began to worry and so he sent for Jap and suggested to the king of Israel that they have a big battle, winner take both kingdoms.

Jap wrote a note back to Greg saying:

Dear Greg:

There was a thorn which asked the cedar tree for his daughter in marriage, but a wild beast came and stomped the thorn into the ground.

In short, just because you've won one tiny little battle, don't get the big head or you'll get clobbered. You'd better stay at home and cool it.

Cordially yours,
Jap

Greg was not influenced by the letter, however, and gathered his army and marched to battle Jap and the army of Israel.

As Jap had suggested, Greg and his army was defeated and Jap took his outfit even into Jerusalem and sacked it, taking away spoil and captives.

Greg was left with a poor and unhappy kingdom over which he reigned another 15 years. Some of the local men finally became dissatisfied with Greg and they had him killed, but they did give him a proper burial.

The people then decided to make Wayne,[1] the 16 year old son of Greg, the king of Judah. Wayne had a long reign of 52 years and he attempted to do all that was right in the eyes of the Lord. As a result, the Lord blessed Wayne and encouraged him.

Wayne did a fine job of organizing the kingdom and he built fine defenses for the cities and the Lord prospered him as long as he was faithful.

Wayne was a very active king and provided good equipment for his soldiers. Wayne also sent the troops forth in separate bands at different times with adequate rest periods and so he kept his soldiers content and yet vigorous.

Wayne finally became so successful, however, in his later years that he became arrogant, even to the point of thinking that he did not need the priests of the Lord to conduct worship services. Wayne, in spite of the long standing commandment of God, usurped the place of the priest in the burning of incense and began to do this himself.

As a result of this action, Wayne was asked to leave the tabernacle and he was furious over this. In fact, he raised a burning incense holder aloft in defiance of the priests, and on this occasion he was struck with leprosy. Consequently, he was banned from polite society and spent the rest of his days in seclusion.

Don,[2] the son of Wayne, then became king and he attempted to do that which was right in the eyes of the Lord, but he would not go to church for fear of being struck with leprosy. As a result, the people of Judah did not take their worship seriously and soon became corrupt in their ways.

Don was a successful king, however, for he was conscientious himself and he faithfully adhered to the commandments of God as well as he understood how to do so.

Ahaz was made king after the death of his father and he was 20 years old at the time. Ahaz immediately pursued evil ways and turned his back on the ways and admonitions of the Lord. The principle sign of the wickedness of Ahaz was the worship of Baal and the encouragement of strange services to strange gods.

The anger of the Lord was kindled by this and as a result the Lord permitted the Syrians to smite Judah and to carry many people into captivity. Then later the remainder of the people were overcome by the warriors of Israel.

The Israelites acquired many captives and great spoil and returned to West Texas with loot and captives.

Then a prophet of the Lord, a man named O.J.[3], stood before

---

[1]Uzziah   [2]Jotham   [3]Oded

the assembly and said to them, "You have overdone this thing. The Lord was angry with Judah and therefore delivered the people into your hands, but you went forth in anger and overdid the violence bit. You are even now planning to make slaves of the people of Judah. This is too much. The Lord is angry. You should return the captives."

Then some of the local leaders who had not been drafted chimed in saying, "Yea, man. Don't bring all those people in here. We are already in dutch with the Lord and now this will make things a devil of a lot worse."

As a result, the warriors walked off and left all the captives standing around in front of the civic group.

The men who had opposed receiving the captives then organized a small Salvation Army unit and they clothed the captives and fed them. Those that could not walk were put on donkeys and the others were all escorted back to Jericho, a city of palm trees, where their own people could attend to them.

Shortly after this, Ahaz contacted some of the Assyrian leaders in the hopes of getting them to join him and help rebuild the reputation of Judah, for the Capone gang, the Mafia, even the Daltons were raiding Judah as the kingdom was almost defenseless.

The Assyrian group came to Ahaz and in spite of the protection money which Ahaz gave them, they did not do anything for Ahaz, for God was punishing him. Instead of repenting, Ahaz began to denounce God and praise the gods of the Assyrians. Ahaz even destroyed the worship places where the faithful still went to serve the Lord. Ahaz was such a wicked king that after he died he was not permitted burial in the regular cemetery.

Chap.
29

Now Hez,[1] the 25 year old son of Ahaz, became king and he immediately initiated one of the greatest reform movements of all time.

The first thing that he did was to repair all the churches of the living God and he restored all the properly ordained priests from the tribe of Levi.

Hez reminded them of the failures of the previous generation, and of the loss of life and wealth that had resulted and he spoke to the ministers saying, "It is in my heart and is my basic plan to make a covenant with the Lord God of Israel and seek to cool his anger to us. Do not be negligent of your duties as ministers of God, for you have been historically chosen by God to lead us in worship."

The ministers responded wonderfully to this pronouncement and they immediately began to put the churches in order and they reported later in the year to Hez that all things were ready for the

[1]Hezekiah

proper worship of God.

For the occasion of launching the great reform, Hez had a great feast prepared and many sacrifices to God made ready. There was a great deal of singing and eating and celebrating for it was a great day of revival and renewal in the church and therefore an appropriate time for rejoicing.

Hez and all the people rejoiced and it was a great occasion on the earth.

Chap.
30

Hez, the next year, sent messages to all the worshippers of the true God throughout all the land, to all the places in Israel and Judah and the surrounding country, and invited the true believers to all come to Jerusalem during Passover week.[1]

This occasion was a tremendous success and so many more people came than the tourist bureau estimated that there were major housing problems and not everyone could properly prepare in order to meet the various liturgical requirements. Hez encouraged everyone to participate in the passover and Hez prayed to the Lord that those who did not follow the book would be forgiven, and they were.

The Lord heard Hez, and he healed the people and he blessed the occasion. There was great joy in Jerusalem that rivalled even the days of David and of Solomon.

Chap.
31

Following this renewal of the church, the men of Israel went out and destroyed all the places of idol worship and tore down the temples of Baal.

The Lord blessed the people and they began to bring gifts to the church and they again began to tithe and worship God regularly. Hez entered with enthusiasm in the development of the kingdom and in the worship and service for God.

Chap.
32

A year or so after all this had been happening, Big Hun, an aggressive leader of the hosts of Assyria, decided to go on a big raid, acquiring land, cities, and captives.

When Hez realized that Big Hun would not wait too long before storming Jerusalem, he ordered a lot of work to be done. One thing, of course, was to strengthen all the fortifications of Jerusalem and he also constructed conduits to handle the flow of water so that the attacking Syrians would not have access to any stream.

Hez reorganized the army and then he called for a public meeting and he spoke to the army and to the people saying, "Do not be afraid of Big Hun and his great multitude. Be strong and courageous. Big Hun has an army of flab, but we have the Lord our God to fight our battles."

---

[1] Years later this week was the one during which Christ was crucified.

The people relaxed after this and were comforted.

Big Hun at the time was besieging another city but he sent messengers to Jerusalem to tell the people there that Jerusalem was next on the list.

The messengers brought some leaflets which they posted around Jerusalem and on the leaflets was a message from Big Hun saying,

"Has ole Hez talked you all into dying or starving to death? Has Hez not taken away all your gods but one, and you are putting all your eggs in one basket?

"Check my record! I have destroyed everything and everybody that got in my way. You're next!

"Don't count on any god. I've been destroying gods by the dozens; so why should you figure that your God will be any different?

"Don't let ole Hez out-talk you!

"Surrender while you can!'"

The men who came and nailed up the posters and leaflets were even more boastful in their talk.

On top of all this, Big Hun sent a number of hecklers who stood outside the walls of Jerusalem and taunted the people, and they denounced the Lord God of Israel.

Hez and Isaiah, a mighty prophet of the Lord, prayed to God over the matter.

The Lord sent an angel through the camp of the Assyrians and they became violently ill, and many died, and the others began to return home in miserable shape.

In fact, when Big Hun returned home a couple of his cousins killed him and took command. There was not a single arrow shot over the wall into Jerusalem.

The Lord saved Hez and the people of Jerusalem and there was again great rejoicing in the city and the people brought many gifts into the house of the Lord.

Hez became sick for awhile but the Lord extended his time because of the plea of Hez. Hez lived to build many fine things around Jerusalem, and the water conduits were among the best of the things he did.

When Hez died he was buried in honor in the place with King David and Lurch,[1] his son, took his place as king.

Chap.
33

Lurch was only 12 years old when he became king and naturally he had to have a little guidance for awhile. The guidance counselor was a baddie and Lurch pursued evil ways, forsook the church and the worship of God, and re-established idolatry and pagan worship.

Lurch even put an idol in the tabernacle at Jerusalem. The Lord

---

[1]Manasseh

sent prophets and ministers to teach and warn Lurch and the people but they did not heed their words.

As a result, the Lord permitted the Assyrians to invade and capture Lurch and many of the people. Lurch was bound with chains and carried captive into the city of Babylon.

While in captivity, Lurch repented and humbled himself before God, and remembered the God of his father Hez, and he prayed earnestly to the Lord.

The Lord heard the prayer of Lurch and provided a means of escape and Lurch repented and humbled himself before God, and remembered the God of his father Hez, and he prayed earnestly to the Lord.

Lurch immediately went to work and did a number of things, for he had learned a lot of lessons. One thing he did was to restore the altar in the church and he commanded the people to serve God. Lurch also began to fortify Jerusalem and all the cities of Judah and to train a proper and dedicated army.

The reform movement of Lurch was not as successful as that of his father, as many of the people began to worship God but also retained their relationship to the idols in the hills.

When Lurch died his son, Brad, who was 22 years old, assumed the throne and he immediately began a reign of wickedness, forsaking the worship and recognition of the Lord God of Israel.

Brad's rule was so evil that those working close to him murdered him. The people then had the murderers executed and placed Jose on the throne. At this time Jose was only eight years old and not quite ready to run a kingdom.

Chap.
34

Jose[1] was under good influences, however, and when he was 16 he began to study for himself the laws and statutes of God. By the time he was twenty, Jose initiated great reforms and started another renewal within the church.

Jose also began a great remodeling program of all the churches and many of the cities. In the process of remodeling, one of the priests found the original laws of Moses and these were returned to their proper place, but not until Jose had spent a great deal of time studying the law.

After reading the commandments in their original form, Jose was tremendously impressed and greatly penitent for the unfaithfulness of his people.

Jose was truly terrified that the wrath of God would consume them and he sent priests to seek the word of God. The priests returned from visiting a prophet who turned out to be a female, and also a coed in Jerusalem U.

[1]Josiah

The young lady told the priests to tell Jose that the Lord was indeed angry with the people for their years of neglect and that all the curses and punishments written by Moses would be placed into operation.

"However," the young lady said, "tell Jose that the Lord is pleased that he has humbled himself and that he has studied the word of God and the Lord therefore will allow Jose to complete his reign in peace and he will not punish the people during the lifetime of Jose."

Upon hearing this, Jose called for a day of compulsory chapel and he made a public confession of his own faith and urged the people to be faithful to the laws of God and to worship the one true God.

Jose kept the passover feast each year and he worked diligently on the reform movement and the Lord blessed his work and prospered him. The annual passover feast of Jose was the greatest of all, and the word was that this year was the biggest event of all and the people felt that there had never been in the past nor would there ever be in the future, passover feasts in the same class as those provided by Jose.

During the later years of Jose, a leader from Egypt brought a marauding group to fight some of the neighbors of Jose, primarily seeking captives and jewelry.

The leader of Egypt asked Jose to remain neutral as he did not wish to have any trouble with Judah and its army.

Jose agreed not to send his army, but Jose was a brave man and he felt he should support his neighbors and so he disguised himself and fought against the Egyptians. During the skirmish a stray arrow caught Jose in the chest and he was transferred to a Red Cross chariot and returned to Jerusalem where he died.

There was great mourning for the passing of Jose, and there were several days of singing and lamenting, and a whole new bunch of folk songs and ballads came into existence.

Jeremiah, the prophet, led the services of mourning.

Chap.
36

The people then declared that Jed, the son of Jose, was the new king. Jed did not last three months, as he was captured by the leader of the Egyptian forces and he was taken prisoner to Egypt.

The king of Egypt placed his own man on the throne of Judah and declared his name to be Sad Sack. Sad Sack did evil in the sight of the Lord, as might have been expected, and it was not long before Big Ned came down and captured Sad Sack and took over the kingdom.

Dru, who was eight years old, was made king and lasted only three months. In fact, he never really learned that he was a king.

Anyway, Big Ned sent for him and with the usual touch of

patronage put one of his half brothers in charge of the kingdom, a man named Harpo, who ruled the kingdom poorly and wickedly for 11 years.

Although Big Ned had made Harpo promise before God that he would be loyal, Harpo decided to rebel. The people continued to wander from God and to worship idols and the prophecy of Jeremiah, echoing the words of the years, warned the people of the wrath of God.

The people were then captured and taken into Babylon and surrounding areas as captives.

Cyrus, king of Persia, then made a famous decree and published abroad a great statement, saying, "The Lord God of heaven has given me control of all the kingdoms of the earth, and he wants me to rebuild his house in Jerusalem. Who is there among his people who will go and do this thing?"

EZRA

In order that the word of the prophet Jeremiah might be made valid, the Lord moved the spirit of Cyrus, the king of Persia, so that he made a proclamation and then had bulletins posted in public places throughout his kingdom saying, "The Lord God of Heaven has supported me in worldly conquests and He wishes me to acknowledge Him by having a church built again in Jerusalem. Who is there among the believers who will do this job?

The man who undertakes this job will have my support and I expect the people of the land to support him. Everywhere this man stops with his helpers en route to Jerusalem, I expect the people to make a free will offering of gold, silver, beasts, or whatever possessions may be available. This is the order of mine, and I am Cyrus, king of Persia."

When this notice was posted many of the leaders from the tribes of Judah and Benjamin, and many of the priests descended from Levi, were encouraged and full of the spirit of God and they were determined to return to Jerusalem and re-build the house of the Lord. The people responded with gifts and Cyrus made several large contributions as well as giving the group some of the valuables originally stolen from Jerusalem. The total gifts from Cyrus were in excess of a million dollars.

The names of most of the families involved in this undertaking are listed in Chaper 2:1-63.

The total number was in excess of 42,000, not counting the servants, maids, folk singers, popcorn vendors and other miscellaneous travelers. There were 736 horses plus 245 mules and 435 camels as well as some donkeys.

This great caravan returned to their previous places of residence in the area of Jerusalem and after seven months of getting moved into new dwellings and adjustments, the people turned to the matter of the construction of the house of the Lord.

Even before the foundation of the church was poured, an altar was built in order that the people might worship God, for the people were afraid of the unfriendly natives who did not desire the return of the refugees to Jerusalem. The people felt that only God's blessing and help would protect them and so they worshipped God faithfully.

After two years time, under the strong leadership of J. Newton[1] the work on the church began with the laying of the foundation. It was a tremendous occasion when the foundation was laid and the singing and the shouting of the people could be heard for miles.

[1]Zerubbabel

There were many laughing and singing for great joy and there were some old timers crying because they could remember the days of the great and glorious temple of the early years.

Chap.
3

The building of the temple was such a stimulating and exciting activity that the pagan natives came to J. Newton and asked to join in the project and be part of the great job of construction.

"You are not really interested in serving God," said Newton, "but you only wish to get in the business and be part of the success." Newton refused to employ any of these people and as a result they began a program of sabotage and the creation of many difficulties for those laboring.

The native objectors were employed agitators to relay distorted accounts to King Cyrus and to complain and criticize.

After Cyrus died Artie[1] became king of Persia and no sooner was he on the throne than the aggravated group around Jerusalem wrote a letter and had a bunch of people sign it.

The letter said: 'Dear King Artie: A great number of us who support you in your kingdom want you to know that the Jews that were sent here from your kingdom instead of building a church are building fortifications and preparing a big revolution. We want you to know that if Jerusalem is rebuilded you'll never get it again. These people are troublemakers, and we want you to do something about it.

Sincerely yours,
Nader[2] and others.'

The king then wrote an answer. Dear Nader:

The letter which you sent has been read and I have checked the history of Jerusalem and you are right in noting that it has a history of defects and revolts. The record also shows that there have been some great kings and rulers in Jerusalem and this is a dangerous thing.

You have my permission to put a stop to all the work being done, until you hear from me further.

Cordially yours,
Artie (The King)

This letter and the authority it represented brought the building program and the public works to a sudden halt, and the condition remained until a new king came to the throne in Persia, a man named Darius.

Chap.
5

Again J. Newton, encouraged by the urging and preaching of Zig[3] and Zag[4], organized his work forces and started the restoration of the temple a second time. There was a new head of the puppet

---

[1]Artaxerxes   [2]Rehum   [3]Haggai   [4]Zechariah

government in the next county under a man named Spot[1] and he came to J. Newton and the workers and wanted to know if they had permission to build and who were they anyway.

Nothing came of this conversation and the work continued; so Spot wrote a letter to the new king, Darius.

Dear Darius:

Peace to you! As a matter of information, a bunch of us went into the province of Judah to do some sightseeing and we saw the Jews there rebuilding the temple to their God. The work is progressing rapidly and well.

We asked the leaders who gave them permission to do this work and they said they were working for the God of heaven as they were his servants.

They also said that the original temple had been built by one of their ancestors before Big Ned had come and carried the people away captive into Babylon. The leaders also reported that Cyrus, the Great, had commissioned the Jews to return and rebuild the temple and they even said that Cyrus had donated to the cause.

Since then J. Newton, who says he was sent by Cyrus, is still trying to rebuild the temple and he may succeed at the rate he is going.

Would you be kind enough to check the files and see if all this is true, and then tell us what in the devil to do about this problem.

Yours truly,
Spot and Friends.

Chap.
6

Then Darious the king ordered one of the secretaries to check the files and some months later a scroll was found which had been misplaced in a Highway Department folder and the scroll contained a record of the order of Cyrus even to the point of including mention of the plans and specifications.

In the scroll was also an admonition to the neighboring county commissioners to help and not hinder the project, helping primarily by staying out of the way.

The penalty, mentioned in the scroll, for tampering with this order was fairly stiff, stating that any man who stood in the way of this project would be hung and his home be destroyed and turned into a garbage heap.

Darius then took the words of the scroll and the penalties and endorsed the writing and sent the order over his name back to Spot and his friends.

As a result, the elders continued to work and the temple was completed and the children of Israel dedicated the temple with great joy and with a great celebration.

[1]Tatnai

The priests organized proper worship services and the people joyfully worshipped God, and were grateful to God for their deliverance from captivity and for the fact that God had melted the heart of the king of Syria so that he supported the Jews in their rebuilding of the temple. The people kept the passover and observed the proper and appropriate services.

Chap.
7

The most influential spiritual leader in the entire program of re-building the temple was a man named Ezra, who was a scribe of the Lord, a dedicated church leader, and one who had been appointed by Artie to select as many volunteers as he could find among the captured Jews and to return to Jerusalem with them.

King Artie gave Ezra a letter of authority granting to Ezra the right to employ people and Artie also gave Ezra a letter of credit to the tax officers in the neighboring counties which amounted to something over $200,000.

King Artie in his letter and decree mentioned that he did not want any trouble with the God of Israel and that the commandments of the God of Israel were to be respected. King Artie also declared all the ministers to be tax exempt. Ezra was also instructed to establish a system of courts and to punish with death any Jew who failed to observe the laws of God.

Ezra then said, "Blessed is the Lord God of our fathers who has put such a plan and such thoughts into the mind of the king. Fortunate am I to be strengthened by the support of God and to be given this wonderful opportunity of leadership."

Chap.
8:1-20

List of the leaders who helped lead the people from Babylon.

As the end of the journey neared and the area was near where robber bands and thugs were apt to rob a caravan, Ezra debated what to do. Having proclaimed to the king the belief that God would protect his people, Ezra hated to ask for an armed escort. As a result, Ezra dispatched the ministers with the money to go on a different route to Jerusalem and Ezra went the regular way with the main body of refugees.

The Lord delivered the caravan safely to Jerusalem and also protected the priests as they made their way.

Ezra, a descendant of Aaron, rejoiced in the success of the trip and he praised God.

Chap.
9

After all this was accomplished, the temple restored, and the regular worship services of the people put back on a regular schedule, then Ezra began to receive unfavorable reports about the activities of the people of God. It was reliably told to Ezra that the people were chasing the foreign women, neglecting the church, and attending worship at pagan rites.

When Ezra heard these things and was convinced that they were true, he wept openly, tugged at his beard, and pulled on his own hair. Ezra then called for an assemblage of the people and Ezra sat in silent meditation until the people were gathered in his presence.

When the people were quiet and ready to listen, Ezra spread his hands in a sign of prayer and with all the people listening he said, "O God, I am ashamed and I blush to even pray to you for we are a sinful people who have done evil and who are acting wickedly. All of us have sinned and fallen far short of the expectations for the people of God.

In spite of all our wickedness, we have been given the great privilege of restoring your temple, or escaping the captivity in Babylon. We know that even in our bondage the Lord God did not forsake us and extended mercy to us, even to softening the heart of the Persian king.

What can we say? In the face of all your kindness we have forsaken your commandments. You told us not to mix with the strangers who served weird gods and observed shameful practices. Yet you have not punished us in proportion to our sin else we would have all been consumed and there would be no remnant left.

In the face of all of this we can only say that you are the essence of righteousness and understanding and we stand before you today acknowledging our sins and we are deeply ashamed."

Following this prayer the people wept and confessed aloud their sins.

Then a man named Wilson[1] arose and spoke to Ezra in the presence of the people and said, "You are right in all that you prayed. Let us now make a promise to God that we will do away with all the additional wives that we have added from among the pagans and to send all the children of these wives away to school in the mountains."

All the leaders agreed and a great pledge was made before God to do this very thing.

Ezra went into a period of mourning and fasting and meditation for he was grieved over the sins of the people and he was grieved for the pagan wives and children who were suddenly cast-offs with no visible means of support.

A great convention was then announced so that all the men who were not present at the first meeting could attend. It was a three day convention for repentance and the people at this convention also agreed to separate themselves from all their pagan attachments.

The practical matter of providing for the separation and all the arrangements were placed in the hands of the leaders and a time began of dealing with the problems, for there were many people and many arrangements to be made.

The leaders sat in council and the men of the nation were

[1] Shechaniah

required to report and to pay a fine for each pagan wife and to agree on plans for dismissing her. A list of some of the men who came before the council and declared themselves to have an excess number of wives from among the non-Jew population is recorded in the book of Ezra, chapter 10:20-43.

NEHEMIAH

My name is Nix[1] and this book is an account of my activities,
thoughts, and prayers.

At the time of this writing I am recalling the circumstance of
my being in good standing in Babylon with King Artie, as I was one
of his favorite friends and consultants.

One day a fellow and a few of his friends came to me and said
that he had recently been to Jerusalem and I asked them about the
conditions of the remnant of the Jews that had escaped, and also
about the city itself.

"There is nothing but bad news. The remnant of the Jews that
are left are not doing well and also are being abused by their neighbors.
The walls of Jerusalem are torn down, the gates to the city are
burned, and there is nothing going for Jerusalem," said Hoby,[2] the
leader.

When I heard this I just sat down and cried.[3] After sneezing and
putting the Kleenex in a wastebasket, I then prayed to God saying,
"O God, the keeper of the promises, yet full of mercy particularly
for those who obey your commandments, hear my prayer, which I
expect to repeat almost day and night because of my distress. First, I
confess that all of us are sinners, our people have not observed your
commandments. I have sinned and so have all my family. We have
not been good, but corrupt.

You remember, God, that you told Moses that our people
would be scattered if we were disobedient, but you also said that if
we turn to you and begin to keep your commandments, and
genuinely reform, you will enter the picture again, restore us to our
land from widely scattered places. Remember, please, that these
people are your redeemed people.

Grant, O Lord, mercy and guidance to me today and be with
me tomorrow when I call on the king, for I will need courage."

Always when I was with the king I was a happy, pleasant person
and this was one reason the king enjoyed having me around socially.
On this occasion, however, I was intentionally sad and was truly
down in the mouth.

"What's eating on you?" asked the king. "You're not sick; so
you must be carrying some grief."

"I am sad, O King," I said, "because my hometown is in
trouble. The place where I was reared and my parents are buried is in
pitiful shape. The walls of the city have been torn down and even the

---

[1]Nehemiah   [2]Hanani
[3]Remember, this was men's fashion in those days.

gates have been burned to pieces."

"All right, Nix, what do you want me to do? Do you have a request?"

At this point I made a quick, silent prayer to God saying "help."

"If I'm in good standing, King, and you really want to help why don't you order me to go home and rebuild the city of my fathers," said Nix.

The queen was sitting by the king while this conversation took place and the king asked, "How long will the trip take and when will you return to Babylon?"

To make a long story short, the king decided to send me and I agreed to set a time for returning. The king gave me his Master Charge card to use for purchasing materials for the wall and for a house for me, and the Master Charge also was useful in showing the various government representatives the support of the king. The king also sent an armed escort to provide me safe conduct to Jerusalem.

Not everybody was happy with this arrangement as Sandy[1] and Toby[2] did not approve of any relief for the Jews and I was immediately made aware of this when I came to Jerusalem.

After being in Jerusalem three days without making myself known I decided to do some sightseeing or inspecting on the sly; so I selected two or three trustworthy men and went out in the middle of the night to see the city. I found the walls completely torn down as reported and also the gates burned to ashes. None of the fountains were working and there were no pools for watering animals, and I found all Jerusalem in ruins.

Now I had been careful not to let any of the rulers or leading citizens know of my plans or what I was doing in town, but now I was ready to call a meeting, which I did.

When I had a good, representative group assembled for a town meeting I made a stirring talk to them, telling them that I was inspired of God, authorized by the king, and determined to lead the people in the restoration of Jerusalem.

As a result, a great enthusiasm for the project arose and the people shouted, "We will build the wall."

Sandy and Toby heard about this and they were red hot about it and began to make fun of the project. In fact, they began to taunt those of us interested and even intimated we were rebelling against the king.

"God will help us," I told them, "for we are servants of God. We will arise and build, but you lip artists will do nothing and you will leave no memorial for yourselves."

[1]Sanballat   [2]Tobiah

Chap.
3

Everybody seemed interested in getting into the act. A group of ministers, for instance, started rebuilding the old sheep gate and various groups began to restore areas or sections close to them or in which they were particularly interested. The King James version of the Bible lists all the names of the people and families involved.

Chap.
4

Sandy and Toby shortly heard news of the building of the wall and the remodeling of the old business places and they got real hot about the matter.

In fact, Sandy stood in front of a band of his soldiers and shouted, "What goes with these feeble Jews? Do they think they can protect themselves with a wall? Do they think that something can be accomplished by some magic prayer, or do they really have the idea that they can build something from the pile of rubbish and ashes that was Jerusalem?"

Then Toby put in his two-bits worth saying, "Yeah, man, some wall they'll build from that rubbish. If a fox crawls on it during the night it will tumble down."

Then I prayed to God upon hearing this and said, "We are despised, O Lord, in the eyes of these strangers. Do something about it. Turn the reproach back onto them. Surely they have provoked you as well as those of us who are building."

As a result, the workers became even more interested in building and the wall was soon joined all around the city.

When Sandy, Toby, and their associates learned that the wall was joined together and that even the personal openings were being closed and fortified, the gang decided to band together and fight against Jerusalem and prevent any further accomplishment.

As a result, we set watches day and night and the long hours and constant need for alertness began to weary the builders and they became discouraged.

Also rumors began to spread among the workers to the effect that their enemies would come into the city quietly and begin to kill the Jews one by one. Word also came that the workers would be mugged and killed on the way home at evening time or on the way to work early in the morning.

Because of all of this I stationed special guards as lookouts and I saw that every man and every family was armed and I told the people not to be afraid. I reminded them that God was with them and that God would support them as they fought for their homes, their families, and their friends.

When the neighboring gangs heard of all the preparations for resistance they became discouraged and the workers returned to full time labor on the walls.

To continue the precautions, however, I decided to let half the workers all the time stand by as an armed guard, with spears, shields, and big clubs, and this was impressive and very comforting to the laboring group. Every worker carried a knife or a sword on a belt around his waist and the whole look was formidable.

As a further exercise of care I announced that I would have trumpets placed at regular intervals around the wall and if the enemy appears at one place the trumpet will be blown and our forces will converge on the spot.

Furthermore, I ordered the men to no longer reside outside the walls of the city, but to stay in motels, apartments, tents, or private homes so that going and coming to and from work would be within the security as established.

As for myself, my associates as leaders, and our special administrative helpers, we never took off our clothes during this time except to take a bath.

Chap.
5

Everything went well for awhile until it developed that some of the greedy-minded among the Jews began to take advantage of the situation. Certain motel owners raised their rates, and food costs arose for those supplying the needs of their families outside the city. The bankers also raised the interest rates, and many of the workers had had to mortgage their lands and vineyards in order to pay the taxes due to the king.

In fact, many of the workers claimed that their children were being used as servants because of their debts and that their own Jewish businessmen were responsible.

When I heard all this I really blew my cool. After thinking the matter over carefully, however, I called a meeting of the rulers, the bankers, and Chamber of Commerce group and I spoke to them saying, "You are taking advantage of your friends and neighbors. I join them in being against you completely for this.

"What do you think you're doing? After we have redeemed the captives from Babylon you are making bondsmen of them yourselves. Will you sell your brothers? Will we have to buy brothers from brothers?"

There was nothing they could say to this forthright talk and they had no answer to the charges.

Then I decided to add a few more things to my speech saying, "Don't you fear God? You are acting like the heathen who is our enemy. Did it ever occur to you that I could have been getting a rake-off as well as some of the foremen, but we haven't. Now, shame on you.

"Furthermore, I urgently request you to restore what you have taken. Do it today! Return the mortgages and free the bonded servants and as much of the money, corn, wine, and oil that was an excessive charge."

The men did as I suggested. Then I called the ministers of the churches together and made a promise of all this in their presence. Then I took the apron which I had on and shook the cookie crumbs out in every direction saying, "May God be a witness, and may God do to any man that fails in his promise as I have done to the cookie crumbs."

Then the people who were witnesses shouted "Amen!" Then the people praised God.

All of this work on the wall took 12 years and even though I was the governor appointed by King Artie I did not eat the fancy food allowed a governor, nor did I collect anything from the people for myself, for I respected God and observed his commandments.

I didn't even buy any land although I knew that when we finished the wall the values would rise, but it was not for profit that I was acting as governor.[1]

Not only did I observe such ethics, but the 150 members of my administrative staff also followed my example.

Then I prayed to God and said, "O Lord, think well of me for my actions and bless all that I have done for the people."

Chap.
6

Ole Sandy and Toby began to plot again, and this time they brought Jocko,[2] an Arab terrorist, into the picture. As a result of the meeting they sent a messenger to me at Jerusalem suggesting that we have a meeting at Joe's Bar and Grill about 10 miles out on the road.

I sent a messenger back to them saying that I was too busy with the work of rebuilding and fortifying Jerusalem and there was no profit in stopping a full day just for some beer and a grilled cheese sandwich. I knew, of course, that their invitation was just a plot to get me killed.

This didn't seem to discourage Sandy and his henchmen as they sent messengers four times with the same request, and each time I sent the same answer.

Finally Sandy wrote me a letter and had it delivered by hand. The letter stated that the word was being spread that I was plotting a revolution and that the building of the wall was to protect me when I declared myself king.

It is also reported, the letter said, that you have contracted with a P.R. firm to glorify your name, even to the point of having the ministers preach an occasional sermon supporting all that you do. It would be unfortunate for you, the letter said, if the king heard about this; so Sandy suggested a private meeting.

I then wrote a letter in reply.

Dear Sandy:

Thanks   for   your   letter,   but   you   are   completely

---

[1] A governor or so like this today would be a blessing.
[2] Geshenn

misinformed or you've made up a bunch of lies for your own purposes.

Yours truly,

N-

After this the word came that the mugging and sneak attacks would be renewed and many of our people became afraid again. Then I prayed again for strength from God.

One of the local leaders felt we should have an emergency meeting and that it should be held in the temple and that the doors there should be bolted and guards stationed as a security measure.

Then I said, "Am I the type that runs at every sign of danger? What man in a position as governor such as I am would go into the temple to save his life and escape danger? I will not go!"

It turned out that all this had been contrived as a threat sponsored by a bribe from the Sandy camp. The idea was to make me look bad before the people and to sin by worrying about God's ability to protect me.

"O God," I prayed, "Think about what Sandy and Toby and a few irresponsible ministers have been doing and fix them for me, Amen."

As a result the wall was completed in every detail and when all our enemies heard of it and the non-Jews around us saw what had been done, they were greatly impressed and they understood that all this was the work of God.

Not everything was rosy, however. There were many nobles who didn't care for me and the methods of fair business practice that I enforced, and they wrote letters frequently to Toby, who had married into a Jewish family, and they then expounded to me on the greatness of Toby and tried to intimidate me. Even Toby wrote me a threatening letter or two, which I just put in file 13.

Chap.
7

Now when everything was completed, even the doors properly hung, there were appointed the proper people for supervision, the singers named for the church choirs, and the ministers given their assignments.

Then I gave my brothers Bobby[1] and Teddy[2] complete charge of the palace and all Jerusalem and I instructed them saying,[3] "Don't open the gates of the city until the sun is well up, and even when the gates are closed keep them guarded. Furthermore, train every man to be alert as a watchman at his own home or business."

At this time, the city was large but there were not too many people living within the walls and re-building of homes was just beginning.

God then moved me to make a record of the families and the

---

[1]Hanani   [2]Hananiah   [3]I still don't care for nepotism.

names of the people who would be called "charter members of the new Jerusalem."

I did this and they may be found recorded in Nehemiah 7:6-65.

There were numbered 42,360 not counting servants, horses, and the 245 members of the Jerusalem Singers Association. From all these were received offerings to pay for the materials used in reconstruction and for the work of the church.

Chap.
8

On one occasion, most of the people gathered in a great assemblage on the street and Ezra, the scribe, who was responsible for keeping the books of law, arose and read to the people from the book of laws compiled by Moses.

Ezra started reading at 9 a.m. and read straight through to twelve noon. Some people didn't stay for the whole thing, but many did. There were a number of prominent people who were on the speakers platform, and none of them could leave, and they heard all the law.

At the end of the reading I stood up and announced that this day was to be considered a holy day and that the meeting counted as attending church. Also I told the people to leave the meeting in a joyful frame of mind, thankful to God, and to go forth and do something in God's name for someone else. Take food to someone who is in need, and let the joy of the Lord be your strength.

That evening there were a whole bunch of private parties and social gatherings.

On the second day the ministers began to review the reading of the law of Moses and they arranged for the institution of the seventh year of forgiveness to be reviewed, and for the establishment of booths for people by families and by groups for merchandising, as was the way of the wilderness. The law was periodically read for the next seven days and at the end of the eighth day the celebration ended.

Chap.
9

Toward the end of the month a day was set aside for special service and at this time the children of Israel stood apart from all the non-Jews and they spent part of their time worshipping God and part of the time confessing their sins, and then they also used a good bit of time confessing the sins of their fathers and grandfathers.[1]

At the end of the service the ministers began to bless God and to praise him, and each doing a part, they recounted the summary of God's relationship with the people.

"There is only God, the one God," the summary started, "and the one God made the heavens and the earth and all things everywhere, and the whole host of heaven worshipped God.

[1]This came real easy

"God chose Abe and brought him from Palm Springs and gave him the land of Canaan, and Abe was faithful to God. As a result, God promised to establish the lineage of Abe as his people. God heard his people when they were in bondage in Egypt, and he heard their cry from the Red Sea, and after impressing Pharoah with signs and wonders, God opened the Red Sea and destroyed the army of Pharoah as a stone disappears in deep water.

"God also provided food, and meat, and water for his people, and in spite of all of this the early day Jews of that time were stiff-necked and hard-hearted.

"When the people made a golden calf and went wild with a big party, God forgave them and sustained them for the forty years necessary in the wilderness, as a penalty and a preparation for entering the promised land.

"God gave the Jews kingdoms, and fields, and vineyards, and fruit trees, and they were disobedient again, this time in a day of prosperity. Ultimately this led to the downfall of the people and the Jews fell to their enemies and were scattered abroad, and then again the Lord heard the cry of his people and a remnant was restored, and we are that remnant, again in the holy city of Jerusalem.

"We are servants today in our own land, under a stranger king who lives a long way from here, and we are under a foreign jurisdiction. We, therefore, make a great promise, to which we all ascribe.

"We agree to walk in God's law and to observe the commandments of the Lord our God.

"We will not intermarry nor allow our children to intermarry to those who do not serve the one true God.

"We will not conduct our regular business practices of buying and selling on the Sabbath day and we will observe the seventh year of repentance and forgiveness of indebtedness.

"We will bring a proper offering to God on a regular basis as well as special gifts for special occasions.

"We will agree to the system of drawing names out of the hat for those who will do the gathering of wood and the management of chores in connection with the work of the church.

"We agree to tithe, and this tithe shall be ten percent and it is to be paid before we do anything else with our profit.

"We agree to support the ministers, and the ministers are to be responsible for the conducting of the worship services."

Chap.
11

After this was presented as a covenant before God, it was explained that one out of every ten families would be required to live within the walls of Jerusalem and the families were selected by lot and the people blessed particularly those families who volunteered to do this service.

A list of these volunteers is recorded in Nehemiah 11:3-12:26. _{Chap. 12}

I failed to mention earlier that in the dedication of the wall of Jerusalem I divided the leaders in two great companies; so that there would be thank expressions properly presented on all portions of the wall; so everyone would be a part of the celebration. I led in all the thanksgiving along with the other rulers and it was a great occasion.

Another thing that happened that day was that in the reading of the law mention was made of those particular groups that had failed to help the children of God in the wilderness and so a separation from these people was decreed.

This brought to my mind the fact that when I came to Jerusalem from Babylon I found that the Jewish leadership was in decay, and I had Toby thrown out on his ear, and I brought the ministers back into action, and I helped reorganize and renew the church.

There was great sin among the people when I first came to Jerusalem. I found Jews working in the winepress on the Sabbath day, and I testified against them, and against the men of Boston[1] who brought fish for sale on Sunday. I closed the gates of the city on Sunday and made the Blue Law work. I threatened to physically throw off the wall any merchants who tried to sell on Sunday by climbing the wall.

I recall the horrors of those early days when I saw so many of our young people marrying into anti-godly families and having families that couldn't speak Hebrew or read the word of God.

I gave them a fit. I admonished them, I pulled some of them by the hair, and I knocked some of them in the head.[2] One of the head ministers had a son who married an anti-godly woman and I chased him out of town.

My prayer is that God remember this, remember the evil that these people have done, and remember the offerings that I have brought and all the good things that I have done.

[1] Tyre   [2] A real active evangelist

There was a king by the name of Aha[1] who ruled an extensive kingdom, covering an area from India to Ethiopia, comprising 127 satellite nations.

During the third year of his reign, Aha staged a huge celebration, bringing representatives from all over his widespread domain to behold his glory, and to be entertained. Aha exhibited his riches in the form of beautiful tapestries, reclining couches of red, white, blue, and black marble, as well as beautiful linens, with some bedspreads made of fine woven gold and silver threads.

After the distinguished guests had spent many days viewing these wonders, Aha provided a seven day feast period. Royal wine was served in abundance in gold cups, although the drinking was done by law, which simply provided for abstainers, as the law merely stated that a person could not be compelled to drink.

At the same time the queen, an exceedingly beautiful lady called Vash[2] was entertaining all the wives and girl friends in a similar manner.

By the seventh day of this, many of the men and certainly the king were overly merry because of the wine and the king began to brag about the beauty of his queen, and decided to send for her in order that all the princes and the people could admire her beauty. The king therefore appointed a committee of seven men to go to the queen's palace and bring her for display. The queen had been belting a few herself and certainly did not want to appear without getting a shampoo and a set; so she refused to come.

When the committee returned and reported that the queen had rejected the order of the king there was great consternation. The king asked his advisors for counsel. The chief aide of the king, a man named Mem[3], spoke eloquently on the subject.

"The queen has not only wronged the king, but the whole kingdom, every prince and every married man from India to Ethiopia has been wronged. For certainly this great act of disobedience will be noised abroad unto all women and we will have a woman's lib movement. In fact, the ladies of Persia and Media shall refuse to obey their husbands and their boy friends, and all men shall be held in contempt."

There was much murmured agreement in the assemblage; so old Mem continued, "I therefore recommend that the queen be displaced, that this be an irrevocable ruling, and that another lady be chosen to take her place." The motion apparently passed unanimously, and so the king sent letters to all the provinces, with bulletins to be placed in all public places ordering every man to rule

[1]Ahasuerus   [2]Vashti   [3]Memucan

his own house.[1]

Some few days later, after Aha had sobered up and recalled the banishing of Vash, he asked his advisors for a plan to select a new queen.

The plan proposed was very simple, as it only called for a beauty contest. The idea was for each province to select its own beauty and send her to the palace at Shushan and there all of the finalists would be carefully screened and a winner selected by the king. This meant that every province had a chance to provide the girl who would be Miss Syria and then the Queen of the land.

This action was initiated and some months later all the contestants were assembled at Shushan and put under the care of Birt Perks[2], the Dean of Women.

Now it so happened at this time that there was a Jew named Mort[3] who had been captured by a previous king, and who had brought with him into captivity his much younger cousin, and since she was an orphan, Mort had reared her as his own daughter. Esther turned out to be an exceedingly beautiful young lady.

Esther won the local beauty contest very easily and was taken to the palace where she immediately made a big hit with Perks; so that he gave her the best room in the women's building, and also helped her with her cosmetic selections. Esther had been careful, however, not to let it be known that she was Jewish, and brought to the area as a captive.

Now Mort, who apparently did not have regular employment, checked daily on Esther and her progress and hung around outside of the palace a great deal, and often sent messages to Esther.

Each finalist spent one night with the king and then was referred to the girls' dormitory for boarding and availability should the king decide to send for one of the girls for an additional interview. Esther's time to be with the king came in October, over three years after the contest started. Esther obtained great favor with the king and he was so completely delighted and entranced with Esther that he assembled all the finalists and proclaimed Esther the Queen and placed the crown on her head and published the news in all the provinces.

Mort, for lack of anything else to do, always sat outside the palace gate and kept in touch with the news and gossip. Mort learned one day that Black John[4] and Mike the Mouse[5] were planning to assassinate the king; so Mort slipped the word to Esther, who told the king, giving credit to Mort. The king investigated the matter and learned that the report was true and he caused the two hoods to be

[1]I cannot help but wonder about the percent of compliance.

[2]Hegai   [3]Mordecai   [4]Bigthan   [5]Teresh

arrested and hung. The matter was recorded in the king's diary which his secretary faithfully kept.

Time marched along and the king promoted a man named Heyman to be the general manager of the kingdom and relieve Aha of most of his duties; so he could have more time for play. Since Heyman was quite an egotist, the servants and others around the palace began to bow to him, as this pleased Heyman very much.

Mort, however, who was always hanging around, would not bow or reverence Heyman, and the others thought it looked bad for them to be bowing and Mort, a self-confessed Jew, to remain aloof; so they reported Mort.

Heyman was infuriated to learn that he was not properly revered by a Jew, but he felt it beneath his dignity to deal with the matter personally. Heyman determined to use an indirect approach.

When in counsel with the king one day, Heyman said, "There is a people scattered abroad throughout the land that are known as Jews. These people do not obey the king's laws and their own laws are different from ours. I propose that we set aside one day, the 13th of December, and let it be an open season on these people. On this day let all the real natives destroy, kill, or cause to perish all Jews, both young and old, women and children, and to rob them of their possessions. From this day I will collect enough to pay $100,000 into the king's treasury, and we need the money."

The king then published the decree, and sent it to all the provinces, and had it posted on all public bulletin boards, using the words of Heyman. The people were perplexed and most of them wondered what brought on this nutty announcement.

Now when Mort read the bulletin he howled like a stuck pig for he knew what was back of it and he knew that the whole plan was simply a way of legally getting him killed. Mort put on his hippie type clothes as an expression of mourning and since such clothes could not be worn around the king's gate, Mort began hanging around only at night.

There was also great mourning among the Jews throughout the provinces as there seemed to be no way of escape. The Jews, as captives, had no means of resistance and sadness was everywhere.

Esther was told of Mort's hippie clothing and she sent a new suit to Mort to cheer him up, but he refused to wear it and continued to lament. Esther then sent messengers to Mort to learn of the details and Mort relayed the whole business, his refusal to bow, the planned vengeance of Heyman, the plight of the Jews. Mort urged that Esther go immediately to King Aha and make a plea for some help.

Esther sent a message then to Mort reminding him of the peculiar office arrangement devised by Aha to keep down the number of visitors. The arrangement was that the king sat on his throne and unless you had been previously invited by the king, you took great risk in appearing. If, for instance, you appeared and the king was feeling good and wanted to see you, he would hold forth the golden sceptre, but if he didn't, you were immediately executed, without further trial.

The reply of Mort to Esther was some truly great wisdom. Mort said, "In the first place, you are a Jew, and for all you know someone in the palace might take the notion to kill you. Ultimately, of course, God will himself deliver his people, but you and I might go in this purge. Speak up! Go to the king. How do you know but what you were born for such a time as this?"

Esther replied by messenger saying, "I will go to the king, and if I perish, I perish, but pray for me, and ask all of God's people everywhere to fast and pray for me."

Chap.
5

Three days later Esther put on her best purple outfit, went into the king's house and stood in the inner court, looking her very, very best. The king looked upon her and held out the golden sceptre and Esther advanced and touched the top of the sceptre, as the custom was.

Then the king said, "What is your request, Esther? I'll give you about anything you want."

"I have come to invite you to dinner, and I would like for you to bring Big Cheese Heyman with you."

"Send for Heyman," said the king, "and we will dine with Esther."

During the cocktail time before eating, Aha asked Esther further about her request as he knew that something was behind the entertainment approach. Esther told Aha that she would tell him the next night, if he and Heyman would come again for dinner.

The next day found Heyman beside himself with joy, until he noticed Mort at the gate and Mort did not so much as look up when Heyman paraded. When Heyman came home later in the day, however, he assembled some of his friends, his wife and family and he spoke in his bombastic fashion saying, "I've got it made! I am rich, I have many children, I have been promoted by the king, and I am the only man who has ever had dinner as the guest of the queen in company with the king and eaten a meal prepared by the hands of the queen. What's more, I'm invited again tomorrow. Yet as long as old Mort sits at the gate, my ulcers act up and I'm despondent."

Then some of the friends of Heyman suggested that he build a gallows and he prepared to hang Mort in the palace yard on the morning of December 13. The idea excited Heyman so much that he caused a gallows 50 ft. tall to be erected the first thing the next morning.

For some reason, however, the king had insomnia that night and so he decided to catch up on back matters and read the diary of the kingdom for the last few preceding months. In reading this he was refreshed in mind about Mort saving his life by reporting the assassins.

The next morning the king asked his servants what had been done to honor Mort, the man who had saved the king's life. The servants told him that nothing had been done.

"Where is Heyman?" asked the king.

"He is standing in the courtyard," was the reply.

"Get him," said the king.

When Heyman appeared, the king said, "What would be a good thing to do for someone that I would like to honor?"

Now Heyman, of course, thought the king had Heyman in mind; so he replied, "I would suggest that the royal apparel that the king normally wears be brought, and the king's horse, and the king's crown, and let the man to be honored put on the king's apparel and ride the king's horse down Main Street, and have an announcer with a megaphone going in front saying, 'The king is honoring this man.'"

Then the king said to Heyman, "Make haste and do as you suggested, and get Mort the Jew and array him, and put him on my horse, and don't omit a single detail."

When this had been done, Heyman returned to his home mourning, with his hat pulled way down on his head. After telling this to his friends and his wife, the gathered company sympathized with Heyman, but expressed the belief that the signs indicated the fall of Heyman. About this time the escort came to take Heyman to dinner again with the queen.

Again during the drinking time before the meal the king asked Esther, "What is your big petition? Just name it, and I'll do it."

Esther then said, "If it please the king, spare my life and that of my people." Esther explained about the open season and the bad day of December 13th.

The king said, "Who is responsible for this terrible thing?"

Heyman was terrified. The king went into the garden to think over what he had heard and Heyman prostrated himself by the couch on which Esther was reclining and was begging her for mercy. When the king suddenly returned, he saw Heyman kneeling by Esther and thought that he was making a pass at her. The king shouted for the bodyguards who immediately put the clamps on Heyman.

Harry,[1] one of the bodyguards, suggested that since there was already a gallows just finished in the courtyard that it could be used to hang Heyman; so they hanged Heyman on the high gallows.

[1]Harbonah

As an expression of appreciation, and by authority of the king, Aha then cancelled Heyman's will and gave all Heyman's property to Esther. The king gave Mort one of his rings and Esther made Mort the overseer of all Heyman's property.

Esther came again in a few days to the king and when he held forth the golden sceptre, she advanced and asked the king to do something about Dark Monday, December 13.

"I know," Esther said, "that you cannot change an irrevocable law of the Medes and the Persians, but why not pass a new law, giving the Jews on the same day the right to defend themselves."

"Brilliant idea," said the king. "Let the writers prepare a letter and a law, let it be put on all the bulletin boards, and spread abroad through all the provinces, taking the message by horseback, by riders on mules and camels, and young dromedaries and let the law and letter say, 'The king grants to the Jews to gather themselves together, to stand for their lives, to destroy, to slay, to cause to perish anybody who assualts, both little ones and women, and to take any spoil they can."

And so it was done and it was published at Shushan, the palace. Mort left the palace in a flashy blue and white suit and a cloak of fine purple linen, and the city rejoiced and the Jews had gladness, and joy, and were respected by the people. The Jews throughout the provinces rejoiced and had feasts and many of the people of the land became Jews, figuring that if you can't beat them, join them.

As the day approached, the Jews began to have some pep rallies, to gather themselves together, and organize for resistance. Most of the public officials began to act favorably toward the Jews because of the high position of Mort, who was in high standing with the king and managing most government contracts. When the day came, there was much fighting but not as much as anticipated. There were some 500 killed in the capitol. The queen petitioned the king the next day to have the ten sons of Heyman hung and he gladly obliged. There were reported some 75,000 persons slain throughout the entire area from India to Ethiopia. The days following the one big day of fighting were days of feasting and celebration. This time became a national holiday by the decree of Mort and he published this information throughout all the provinces.

A name was given to the holiday, the name of Purim, because the day was picked by lot, and the word for lot was Pur. The two days of feasting following the December 13 uproar were therefore made national holidays.

To make the whole matter official, Esther wrote a letter to the same effect.

There is much recorded about King Aha, his taxes upon the

land, and upon the isles of the sea, and many versions of his power and also his declarations about the greatness of Mort, for Mort was second only to the king. It was noted that Mort was accepted by the multitude of his brethren and that he worked seeking wealth for his people and he spoke words of peace to all his followers and descendants.

There was a man from Utah[1] named Job and he was a God-fearing, righteous man, law-abiding and opposed to evil.

Everything in connection with him seemed to be ideal, and he represented the American dream. Job was rich, he had more sons than daughters, plenty of servants, a huge ranch, good health, friends who didn't live too close, and his only worry seemed to be that his children would not follow exactly in his footsteps.

When Job was at his peak there appeared one day before the Lord in heaven the spirit of evil, old Satan, or the Doubter, and told the Lord that he had been traveling on earth.

"Did you see my man Job, in Utah?" asked God. "Job makes me glad that I created man."

"Sure I saw him," said Satan, "and he is mighty righteous but who wouldn't be at the price he's getting? You have put him in the lap of luxury so why shouldn't he worship you. You start causing him trouble, though, and he'll quit you quick."

"I think his faith is sound, but to prove it, I will let you bother him. You can do anything you want to do but you are not to touch him personally. No arthritis, backache or the like," said the Lord.

Shortly after this one day Job was having dinner. During the meal a messenger came bursting into the room all out of breath and shouted, "Job, there's big trouble. The West Side gang[2] attacked the ranch, killed all the ranch hands but me and then drove all the livestock away with a well run rustling job."

No sooner had he finished than another runner came and said, "Job, there's big trouble. I've just come from the sheep ranch and lightning has struck the sheep and killed the shepherds. I'm the only one left."

In a few minutes another messenger came charging in and yelled, "Job, the camel corps is gone. The Pittsburgh Pirates[3] divided into three teams and came pouring down on us, captured all the camels and killed all the helpers except me, and I'm scared half to death."

Before Job could absorb all the news another messenger appeared and said, "Job, I've got bad news for you. All your sons and daughters were having dinner together enjoying wild turkey when a tornado came and struck the house, tore it down, and killed all your sons. In fact, I'm the only survivor."

Then Job went through the proper procedure of mourning, which in his day was to shave his head and tear his clothes to shreds. Then Job worshipped God and prayed, saying, "I was born naked and

[1]Uz   [2]Sabeans   [3]Chaldeans

I guess I'll die naked. I was born broke, and I guess I'll die broke. Sometimes the Lord gives, sometimes he takes away, but blessed is the name of the Lord."

In no way did Job blame God or refute him.

Chap.
2

Sometime after this the various angels began reporting to God and old Satan came along with the crowd and God said to Satan, "What are you doing here?"

"I've been traveling around on your earth," said Satan.

"What did you think of my man Job?" asked the Lord. "Didn't you notice that he stood fast under adversity and did not fold or turn against his creator?"

"Yeah, man, old Job is pretty tough and a good one, but man is basically selfish and he can in time of stress stand anything as long as it doesn't physically bother him. You let me mess with his digestion and such and he'll turn bad."

"All right," said God, "You can test him, but you will not be permitted to kill him."

As a result, Satan headed for Job full speed and socked him first with boils. Job was immediately miserable, as there was no penicillin or good medication and he sat in hot ashes.[1]

Job's wife came to him then and said, "Why don't you quit, Job? Curse God and die.[2] That will relieve you of your miseries."

"You speak like a poorly informed female. Don't you have any reasoning ability? God is in charge of everything, both good and bad, and sometimes He dishes out one and sometimes the other, and who are we to say He doesn't know what He is doing?"

Word, of course, of all Job's troubles spread around and some of his cronies from neighboring ranches and towns heard of his problems and some of them got together and decided to visit Job and offer their sympathy.

When Job's friends approached him they hardly knew him for his sad condition and they were shocked to the point of tearing their clothes, putting ashes in their hair, and generally putting on an act.[3]

The three visitors, friends of Job, sat down with him for seven days and seven nights and no one said a word.[4]

Finally Job broke the silence and spoke to his friends saying, "It would have been a great help if I had never been born. How nice if the day of my birth could be cancelled. I wouldn't be here.

"No more birthday parties for me. Every time I think of my birthday I will cry and groan.

"It would have been a real break if I had been born dead. I could then have slept instead of living.

---

[1] Recommended by a neighbor   [2] Job had good insurance policies
[3] No longer stylish   [4] The early orientals didn't rush things

"In fact, it would have been great if I had been born in prison and killed on birth as is the custom under these conditions. Now all I can do is long for death, and it does not come. Why should I be living when I want to be dead? Great trouble has come to me, everything I didn't want to happen has happened. In spite of being in good shape, I have been stricken with awful ailments."

Chap.
4

"Now Job," said Vince,[1] "I hope you don't mind an opinion or two from a close friend. I know you have been a source of great strength to many people and that you are a highly respected citizen. You are hit by trouble yourself for a change, and you can't take it.

"As little as I like to mention it, I feel I must remind you that the innocent never suffer. Trouble comes to those who deserve trouble. It is God's punishment that you suffer.

"I know these things because of a clear vision from God. God surely is not going to make it tough on the righteous.

"It occurs to me that God cannot completely trust his angels, let alone man. Man lives briefly and then his life is snuffed out, why should you think you are above all this?

Chap.
5

"A person can get by a little while without God, but not for long. God gets to a fellow and misery comes to punish a man for his sins.[2] Man sins very easily, we understand that.

"My advice to you, Job, is to confess your sins. God might change everything for you. He certainly can, for He controls the rain, and helps the poor, and attends to sufferers. God constantly wars with the crooks. In fact, He makes the crooks act like men who can see no better in the day than at night.

"The poor have hope, for God will look out for them. Actually, you are honored to be afflicted by God and you should be pleased with the attention. For when you sin and then confess, God heals and He will help protect you from further sins. God will protect you from starvation, and war, and gossip,[3] and you will be safe from wild animals and thieves and your sons will become leaders and so will your grandsons. I know from experience that all this is true; so admit your sins."

Chap.
6

"You know what I wish?" said Job, "I wish that there were some scales to weigh my troubles. I believe my troubles would outweigh one thousand seashores.[4]

"The Lord has struck me down with poisoned arrows. Everything and everybody is against me.

"If all was well I wouldn't be howling, for surely a jackass

---

[1] Eliphaz   [2] I'm glad this isn't true
[3] Only God can do this   [4] You've got to believe he hurt

doesn't bray unless his food is gone. A man gripes when there is no salt on his potatoes. To me now nothing has any taste and I can't stand the thought of eating.

"All I ask of God is death while I still acknowledge him. Why am I strong enough to live? I am helpless, I feel there is no hope, but I seem to be as tough as brass, and I can't die.

"On top of this you accuse me of sin, without any facts. What kind of a friend are you? Don't you fear God yourself? You are proving to be highly unreliable.

"Any hope I had of help from you is gone. I feel like a caravan that has stopped at an oasis and found that the well was dry. You act as if you are ashamed to be my friend.

"Tell me now, Vince, what have I done that is wrong? Give me a reasonable answer. You are wrong about me. I am still a righteous man. You have no basis for your accusations. I know the difference between right and wrong, and if I were wrong I would gladly admit it.

Chap.
7

"I know a lot of things. I know life is long and hard and man often yearns for the day to end. Just like it must be for a slave who works hard and only looks ahead for the week-end day of rest. I realize I have been allotted months of frustration and long and endless nights.

"When I go to bed at night I long for the morning and when morning comes I wish it was already night. My skin is infected, it aches and it itches. My boils fester and are painful, my life is passing by, and I fight for breath. Maybe I'll die soon, I certainly think so.

"When I die I shall disappear as a cloud and be gone so let me sound off a bit here at the end.

"Oh God! What's wrong? Am I some grim monster that you must torture me all the time? Even when I finally get to sleep I have nightmares.

"I wish someone would choke me to death. God, please leave me alone and let me die in peace. Why spend so much time with a mere man? Let me alone, God, even if it is just long enough to spit.

"How did I get to be your big target? If it is a sin, why don't you pardon it and let me be whole again? It is only a matter of a few years anyway; so why not take me now?"

Chap.
8

Then one of Job's friends called Short-stuff[1] spoke saying, "How long will all this windy talk keep going? What a lot of guffaw! The matter is simple. If a man is righteous God blesses him, and if he is wicked he gets in trouble. If you were forgiven and righteous again you would be made well again.

[1] Bildad, the Shuhite

"Isn't this the history of man? Hasn't this always been the rule? Granted that the wicked may prosper like a growing weed for a short time but the wicked are consumed just as a weed withers. That's life, man!

"The wicked have it tough in the long run. There is no security for them. God will not help evildoers nor will he desert a righteous man. When you are laughing and well again then you will be considered righteous and then the wicked will envy you, but now you are just one of them."

Chap.
9

"What you say," said Job, "sounds reasonable, but how can mere man be reasonable with God. Would you get into a question and answer game with the Lord? I agree that no one can eventually prosper who challenges God.

"God removes mountains, causes earthquakes, orders the sun to rise, and has put the stars on a definite schedule.

"In fact, God controls the winds, and all the weather and other wonders too numerous to mention. In fact, God comes passing by and he cannot be seen. God does as he pleases. Who can say to God, 'Why are you doing thus and so?'

"This being the case, surely you don't expect me to argue with God. No one could be righteous enough to argue with God.

"I admit that God is dealing me the real miseries. I can't catch my breath though I've never smoked. If I attempt to justify myself before God, advocating my own course would be a sin in itself. Even if I were absolutely perfect I could not be expected to understand my own soul.

"I am convinced that God knows everything and is in charge of everything. God destroys good people and bad people. It is only with God's permission that the wicked run everything.

"There are a lot of crooked judges and politicians[1] and God apparently lets them be unfair. It's got to be God that allows this. Who else could it be?

"My time on earth disappears swiftly, the years swish by like an eagle diving on a pigeon, or as a ship drops over the horizon. I wouldn't dare forget my troubles and act as if nothing were wrong or God would just crack down on me with even worse ailments.

"God has it in for me for sure. I don't know why, but being innocent isn't the answer. I don't think there is any use in my trying.

"If I made myself spotlessly clean, and used the best cleaning soap, God would just push me into a muddy ditch.

"My situation is terrible. I can't defend myself against God. If God were a mere man we could settle our differences by arbitration, or call on an official of some kind to make a ruling. Not so with God.

[1]Who said the Bible was out of date?

It must all be his way.

"Would to God that he would ease off of me long enough for me to recover, and maybe I wouldn't be so intimidated and I would say to God that I am innocent and not deserving of all this misery."

Chap.
10

"Woe is me. I am weary of life and sick inside as well as outside. Listen to me, Lord. Is this really a good plan, to give so much trouble to a good man and to let the wicked prosper?

"You know that I am not wicked. You made me, why are you trying to destroy me? You set a mold for me and poured me into it as if I were milk and curdled cheese, you put flesh on me and hung me together with bones and sinews, you breathed into me life.

"What is your secret plan? If I do any tiny little thing wrong you whack me down, and yet if I'm upright and law-abiding I get it in the neck even worse. What goes on? Why was I born? I know I don't have long to live for no one lives very long; so how about just leaving me alone for a while? Let me have a little breather here at the last before I go into the great unknown."

Chap.
11

Then Godfrey,[1] another of Job's friends, began to speak and he said, "All those big words and long speeches of yours ought to be answered. I can't let you get by with false statements.

"You have said that your thoughts and actions are good, but I bet anything that God knows about some sins of yours that you haven't mentioned to us. In fact, you probably deserve more punishment than you are getting.

"What's more, you can't figure out God. Don't you know that he is higher than the sky and deeper than hell. God can do anything and he knows everything. God doesn't have to read the morning paper to learn of the sins of man.

"In fact, insignificant man has as little chance of reasoning about God as a wild horse's colt has being born tame.

"You say you are ready to turn to God and reason with him, then the first thing you better do is confess your sins. You aren't really puzzled, you just don't want to admit that you have privately been a bad boy.

"After you have done this, then everything will come clear, you will have hope again, you will be able to sleep, and you will recover a feeling of security."

Chap.
12

"Nuts to you," said Job. "You leave the impression that when you and a few others die there will be no wisdom left on earth. Well, I know just as much as you birds do. Furthermore, you haven't brought out anything new. Your comments have been often

[1]Zophar

discussed.

"What I am saying is that I have called on God for help and the result is that I am suddenly a big joke to my friends. My argument is that I know some rich people who despise the poor and who have no sense of mercy and they are well and happy, yet I have always been kind and I am in a mess. I know robbers who are doing well and I have never stolen a thing and yet I am suffering terribly.

"I know God does everything. I just don't know why. There's nothing great in knowing this. Every animal knows, the birds know, the earth knows, all nature obeys every wish and follows every plan of God. I know that the soul of every person and the life of everything is in the hand of God.

"This is not hard to understand. Just as I can tell good food by the taste glands around my tongue so my mind can tell the truth by the taste of what I hear. At my age, experience has made this possible.

"God can destroy and God can restore. God can cause floods or bring on a drouth. God is all strength and all wisdom, and all people, good or bad, are under his authority.

"God is able to control judges, make or break kings, overthrow the mighty or raise up the poor. God can confound a man's mind and often introduces senility into the aged. God builds up some nations and destroys other nations, and sometimes he confuses the leadership of a nation so that the people wander around without direction as if they were a bunch of drunks. I know all this. I've seen it, and heard it, and I believe it."

Chap. 13

"Actually, you birds coming here to advise me don't know any more than I do. You are flops as doctors. Certainly I would be pleased if I could talk this whole thing over with God. If you want to be helpful the best thing you could do would be to shut up.

"How about listening to my reasoning and my pleas. I'm the one in trouble. You talk as if God has given you inside information, which I seriously doubt. Dare you speak for God? Aren't you afraid of God? The talk you have been giving is worth less than ashes and your attempt to defend God is ridiculous.

"Risky as it may be, I am going to empty my mind, and take the consequences. I realize God may take my life because of what I am going to say, I must speak as I feel. You see, even if he kills me, I still trust him, and that is why I am going to speak my piece, for I trust God.

"I only ask you, my friends, to do two things. One is to take your cotton picking hands off me, and the other is not to appear so imposing and seem to be so shocked.

"Basically, my affirmation is that I am a good man. I defy any of you to name sins that I have recently committed, although you talk to me as if I were still a kid stealing watermelons. Man is a fragile creature for he is born, lives a little while, and then dies.

"Actually, he comes on the scene like a flower unfolding and disappears as a shadow fades.

"No one is pure. God knows that. How can one born impure be pure. Man is not a plant, nor is he like a tree. A tree can be cut down and then sprout new growth and new trees even where it falls, but man dies and is gone until the heavens disappear and an arrangement is made.

"It would be nice if I was in the grave now and forgotten, only to be remembered and called forth for judgment at a set time. I am willing to die and wait for the great change. You all are among those that make everything hopeless. You notice every little error, you gossip, and go great guns with nit-picking. You do to man what water does to a stone as it gradually washes it away. You talk as enemies of man, who insist on making him old and wrinkled before his time, and then dying a miserable death."

Then Spock[1] spoke saying, "It is strange to me that a supposedly wise man like you should utter such nonsense. Actually, you are being crafty and plotting under the guise of prayer, attempting to hide your sins.

"It is not mine, but your own testimony that gives you away. You talk as if you were the first man born and that you have been with God from the very beginning. Were you here before the hills, or do you know the secret of life? You don't know anything that we don't know. Yet you seem to argue with God and act very much like a know-it-all.

"No man is clean. How could he be and be born of woman? You swallow sin as if it were water, and what greater wrong is there than this?

"Now as for me, I know the truth. I learned it from my elders, it has been handed down, and the truth is that the wicked suffer just like you are suffering. Trouble, anguish, and hunger follow the wicked and finally the wicked are terrified. The bad people finally are separated and live lonely lives, and they also lose all their money.

"The people who attempt to deceive as you are doing are hypocrites and real phonies and God sees to it they don't have anything but troubles like you are having."

"A miserable bunch of comforters you fellows are. You make me feel worse," said Job. "I could make pious and objective statements myself if I were in your shoes, but I think that my

[1]Eliphaz

approach would be to attempt to give you strength and encouragement.

"Worn out and tired as I am, you come and make things worse. Even though I know I am innocent I receive no help. God is crushing me as if he were angry, my friends chide me, and my enemies take advantage of my sickness and my trouble. I am completely miserable.

"Yet I know that I am innocent. It is not sin that has caused all the trouble that has come my way. I still am turning to God in prayer and I am pleading with Him. I don't have long to live and all I'm asking is a little peace and ease as I near my end.

Chap.
17

"Here in my sad condition my friends are making fun of me. I think God has actually prevented my friends from understanding my situation. I am a complete mess. People who used to know me don't recognize me when they see me.

"Nevertheless, I know that in the final analysis, the righteous will prevail. Good men gradually gather strength over the years, strength of spirit.

"But I have had it. I am weary. Please all of you leave. None of you have helped or made sense in any of your talk. There would appear to be no help for my condition. I must just hang on as best I can and hope to die. There is no other hope for me."

Chap.
18

"Now wait a minute, Job," said Short-stuff. "We are not animals, and we aren't so dumb, either. All this moaning and groaning and tearing your clothes doesn't cause the earth to shake or the wind to blow. The old time truth is still correct, and that is that the wicked are punished and the righteous prosper.

"If you are having such a bad time it is because you deserve it. The wicked will always catch it. Life will constantly deal the evil people a load of trouble. Finally, the wicked should be thrown into everlasting darkness, alone and lost. That is exactly what happens to sinners and to those that reject God."

Chap.
19

"You keep harping on the same theme. You've called me a sinner umpteen times. All right, name one of my sins. What has actually happened is that God has forsaken me, though I have not forsaken God. God has deprived me of everything and left me with absolutely nothing.

"My wife and brothers don't even recognize me. I call my servant and he doesn't come. My best friends have deserted me. Please have pity on me. Can you not see that God is inflicting all manner of torture on me? Why add to my torture with your own criticisms?

"Oh, how I wish I could write what I know so that it would always be read. I wish I had an iron pen that would write on a big rock, then I would write for all to read forever. I would inscribe on the rock the assurance that in spite of everything I know that my redeemer liveth and that when all is said and done, He reigns, and He will reign forever. After I die I expect to see God, and then God will be with me, and I will not be forsaken. In fact, I will see God not as a stranger, but as a friend.

"How do you dare continue to pick at me, one who sees such a glorious hope even in despair. You act as if I were a condemned man and I am not, and you had better watch for yourselves, for your attitude will get you in trouble with God."

Chap. 20

Then Godfrey spoke forth and said, "I can hardly wait to answer your charges. I heard you and my own good sense calls on me to reply.

"In the first place, don't you know that from the very beginning the plan of God has been for the wicked to prosper only a short time. Even though a wicked man may rise to great heights it is a short trip with him and he will disappear as an overnight dream. Even though he might outwardly seem to enjoy his wickedness, even then he suffers inside and is fearful. The wicked may get rich quick, but God will soon take it all away. This is done as punishment to the wicked ones who have been selfish and ignored the poor and the needy.

"God will definitely give it to him here on earth. God will strike him while he is enjoying things the most and he shall be reduced to misery and poverty. That is exactly what happens to the wicked."

Chap. 21

Job said, "Hear me once again, and then you can mock me to your heart's content. I have no complaint against man. You are going to be astonished at what I am going to tell you, for I even tremble myself that I say these things.

"I observe the wicked. Some of them grow old, still rich and in power, some of them dance all the way to the grave. They defy God. They even say there is no need of God for them. I have never been influenced by such evil men. I know they are struck down in death, and then if not before they will taste the wrath of God.

"No one teaches God anything. Everyone dies in his own time as God wills it. Some die quietly, some in suffering, and some in bitterness. Don't you think for a minute that everything is settled on this earth. The wicked die, sometimes in the height of glory and wealth, but they will be summoned from the grave at a proper time to face the judgment of God.

"You are no comfort to me, for you are misinformed about the ways of life."

Chap. 22

Then Vince spoke again and said, "You are wrong about man

being worthwhile to God. God couldn't care less. What is one fellow to Him, whether he is wise or foolish?

"Do you think that it is important to God that you claim to be a good man? You are bound to be wicked somehow. You have welched on a bet, taken clothing from the needy, failed to provide bread and water to the starving, or stolen some little old ladies social security check. God is high in the heaven and He looks down and He sees you do things that we don't see or know what has happened.

"What you need to do is to confess and repent. Return to God in humility and He will restore you. In fact, if you are sincerely penitent you will no doubt get rich again and all will be well with you. Once you have fully repented you will be able to pray again and your relationship with God will be satisfactory."

Chap.
23

"I still say I'm getting worse treatment than I deserve," said Job. "My condition is so bad that my feeble attempt to find God fails. If I could just sit down and talk with God all this business would clear up promptly.

"I just can't find God. I look ahead and He is not there, I look behind and He is not there, right and left I search, but I cannot find him. God will find me though. God knows where I am and where I go. When He is through testing me, I will be all right. God knows I try to be a good man and faithful. God knows what He is doing and He won't be persuaded to change His plan. For this, I am afraid. For I know God knows about me and my problem, and He knows my thoughts. For some reason God is keeping me alive, weak, helpless, blind, and miserable, but alive.

Chap.
24

"The bad people do not think this way. These people mistreat God's creation, they pollute the waters, erode the soil, and shamelessly destroy God's creatures.

"The wicked care only for themselves. They never leave grain in the field for the needy and they pay no attention to the lonely, the poor, the naked, and the starving.

"The bad people take advantage of the ignorant, they cheat the people who work for them, and they take advantage of minors, yet God doesn't stop them at once or bring their activities to a screeching halt.

"Many of the wicked are only concerned to see that man does not catch them stealing, or falsifying reports, or committing adultery. All these people try to do is to avoid being caught by man. They do not consider that God knows all that happens.

"One thing for sure, though, the grave catches the wicked like a hot drought catches the snow. The wicked may rise in great power and with great show for a little while, and then they tumble. Who thinks now that I am not telling the truth?"

Chap.
25

"Aren't you terrified of God?" asked Short-stuff. "How can man justify himself in the sight of God? God orders the stars, commands the moon. Do you think that God concerns himself with man, who is really just a worm in his sight?"

Chap.
26

"What a brilliant bunch you birds turned out to be," sneered Job. "You have brought me no comfort and you think you are wise while all the time you tell me stupid things.

"Have you never really thought of the majesty of God, how He stretches the north over the empty place and hangs the earth on pure relativity, not to mention the marvelous arrangement of carrying the rain around in clouds. God made everything from the highest heavens to the tiny little crooked snake. There is no way of understanding all of God.

Chap.
27

"Even though God himself is responsible for my troubles, I promise you I will not speak evil or act deceitfully, as I will retain my faithfulness. I am not a bad man and I am not going to be one. I will not succumb to pressure and if you don't believe me you can hardly be considered friends," continued Job.

Chap.
28

"Men know how to do a lot of things. They know how to mine for silver, they build dams to contain streams, they find treasures in the earth, and they plant and sow, but man cannot discern the deep wisdom of God. Only God knows where complete wisdom resides and only God reveals this knowledge as it pleases him. To stand in awe of God, that is what God says is the key to wisdom, it is where man begins his search.

Chap.
29

"Of course, I long for the good old days, when I was healthy and well to do, a respected member of society, surrounded by friends, and certain that God was helping me every step of the way.

"I was really something in the good old days. Young men stood aside for me, my opinion was sought by the highest council, I was even named Citizen of the Year, and enjoyed a fine reputation.

"I had even figured out that I would lead a long, fruitful, helpful life and then die a respectable death in my old age. It is hard to realize how successful I actually was.

Chap.
30

"Now I am nothing. Young men spurn me, stupid young fellows with strong backs and weak minds. These young upstarts constantly make fun of me, they sing silly limericks about my sad condition, and my status is gone. No one respects me. I am despised and pitied.

"I can no longer sing or play the guitar, and I cannot sleep at night. Everything seems black and dismal to me. I know my end is death but I thought it would be a dignified arrangement.

"I helped the poor, I was always doing good things for others, and so I expected that good things would happen to me, but instead only trouble came my way. My heart is troubled and I am afflicted. All of my joy and gladness has turned to sadness.

"You keep wanting me to admit to something that isn't true. I have been careful about women and have even refrained from looking at pretty girls so that improper desires would not arise within me. I know you fellows think I've been tom-catting around on the side, but it is not true. God knows it isn't true, even if you don't.

"You think maybe I've taken advantage of someone's wife, but that isn't true. If it were true, I'd want someone to take advantage of my wife. I insist that you think of me as a fair and decent man.

"You all may think that I have been unfair in dealing with the servants, but this is not true. I am fully aware of the fact that a servant is as much a creation of God as I am, and I have always treated my servants with this mind.

"Furthermore, I have not been unmindful of the poor, or the widows, or the orphans. I have earnestly tried to see that my success has not gone to my head, but in all things have acknowledged that everything has come from God.

"My problem is that I am baffled. I wish God would speak up and tell me what is wrong. It would be even better if the causes of my trouble were put in writing and I could begin to cope with them, but as it is, I only know I suffer, and I do not know why. Woe is me."

Apparently listening to all this exchange between Job and his three friends was a young man named J. Namath.[1] When all was quiet, Namath spoke, "I can't stand listening to all this tripe any longer. I may be young, but I'm not stupid. Not every rich and famous man is wise, and as you have just proven, being old doesn't necessarily make you wise, either.

"It was obvious that none of the three of you got anywhere with Job, and you surely didn't make much of a case against him. Now the time has come for you all to listen to me.

"I speak with no authority of title, except that I am a child of God, and I'll speak for him as nearly as I can. You say, Job, that you are righteous and that God is punishing you without cause. You are accusing God of being unjust. Let me remind you that God is greater than man, and the justice of God cannot always be understood by man. Why do you keep arguing with God? God is not accountable to anyone.

"You sit back and listen now to a little good, common sense, Job. God does not enter into philosophical debates with man. Now

[1]Elihu

listen carefully, fellows, for the ears can taste the truth, but you have to be really listening.

"Now Job should be called Absorbine Jr. for all that he has had to soak up from his friends. Yet he continues to declare his righteousness and asserts that delighting God does not necessarily bring any reward.

"Get this straight first, God does not initiate torment and he will not divert justice just for kicks.

"It is not proper to say to a king that he is wicked nor to top rulers that they are worthless, so how much less proper is it to accuse God of neglect?

"Everyone is the same in God's sight, rich or poor. God made them all, and no one lasts very long on this earth, whether they be weak or mighty. God sees everything and knows everything. There is no hiding from him.

"You have got to admit that God is fair. God knocks over the wicked in their time, He brings peace when He so desires to do so, whether it be to a person or a nation.

"As for you, Job, if you have committed no other sin, you are guilty of rebellion. The least you can say is that God is right and that you have deserved all your trouble. You can't possibly say that God is wrong.

"Think a little deeper, Job," continued J. Namath. "Do you think it makes a great deal of difference to God whether a man is good or evil? You have got to learn to accept God as He is. You are trying to make a gigantic case out of one little man. Do you think variety is a way of approaching God? You are just wasting words!

"Just keep quiet. I haven't finished yet. I haven't gotten to the part where I speak for God. You must understand that God is all powerful and the one mighty ruler. In the final analysis, he blesses the good and curses the wicked. It is just that simple!

"Are you aware of how great God really is? He makes the tiny little drops of water, and also the whole sea. God has covered the bottom of the sea and spread clouds in the heavens and he arranges for light to come and go on to earth. God roars in the thunder and crackles in the lightning.

"God has arranged for the snow, the light rain, and torrents. God sends the animals into caves to hide when He brings the hurricane from the south, and the clouds respond to the wishes of God, for watering the earth or for punishing the people with floods.

"Now, Job, you just stop a minute and think about the majesty and the power of God. How smart are you? Could you weigh a cloud? Were you working with God when He made the universe? The cloud covers the sun until the wind of God blows the cloud away and man has light again. Man can do nothing else but fear God, and arguing with God is unthinkable."

Then God began to come through to Job and Job heard the reasoning of God, for Job understood God to say, "Where were you, Job, when I began creation? Where are the foundations of the earth and how is it suspended and held in place? Who enclosed the seas as if in traps, or arranged for morning to arrive on schedule every day?

"Have you walked the bottom of the sea to learn all the secrets there, and do you know about death, and its meaning? What is the origin of light? Do you know all about hail? Did you know that I am even reserving a lot of hail for a big battle some day?

"What about rain in desolate places where there is no man. Who is responsible for this? Do you think rain has a father and a mother? What about the stars? Does any man have any say-so about the course of the stars or the stability of the North Star?

"Did a man arrange for water to cause clods in a dusty place, or did man teach the lion to hunt food for the cubs?

"What about lambing and calving? Do you think the 4-H Clubs decide on these matters? What about the wild horse? Did man free him?

"Do you think that man can train an animal to plant seed, harvest corn, cook, baby-sit, or can a man create a memory for the ostrich who has a hard time remembering where she has laid eggs? God deprived the ostrich of widom and there is nothing man can do about it.

"Have you ever tried to build a horse? What about the hawk and the eagle? Did man teach these birds to fly? Are you responsible for making the eagle blood-thirsty?

"Do you now have any argument with me, Job," said the Lord.

"All I know now for sure, O God, is that I am nothing. I have nothing to say for myself."

"Face matters, now, Job," said God. "Are you wishing to question my judgment? Do you wish to appear righteous at my expense?"

"Maybe, Job, you don't realize your own inadequacy. Can you drag a whale ashore with a simple hook? Are you responsible for the strength of an ox? Are you the one who made the mountains provide food and shelter for the animals?

"How can man expect to contend with God when man cannot create or completely control creation. It just isn't reasonable! There is no limitation to the power of God and there are none who can contend with Him or stand against Him.

"You are absolutely right, O Lord. I know you can do anything," said Job. "I have talked too much, and blabbed too much that I didn't understand. I have always heard you, O Lord, but now I can really begin to understand a little about you. I repent and bow down in shame and humility."

God then moved the friends of Job to be remorseful for their treatment of Job and they came to Job with food and gifts seeking forgiveness and affirming their friendship.

Job prayed to God in behalf of his friends and this pleased God and He returned to Job all of his glory and wealth and health and He blessed him so that he was in better shape after his sad experience than he had been formerly.

PSALMS

Blessed is the man who does not seek the advice of the wicked, nor hang around all the time with sinners, nor join in with bitter critics, but whose delight is in the law of the Lord, and much of his time is spent in thinking on God's law.

Such a man shall be strong like a tree planted by a good stream of water, that regularly bears fruit, and whose leaves do not wither. Whatever such a man does succeeds.

The ungodly are not so, but are as undependable as chaff which the wind blows away, therefore the ungodly will not be able to survive judgment, nor will sinners be allowed eternally in the company of the righteous.

The Lord blesses the way of the righteous, but the way of the ungodly shall perish.

Why do the heathen make such a racket and in rage defy God? Often great rulers get together and work against the Lord's plans and his workers, thinking they will be able to rule everything and everybody.

The Lord sitting in his heaven shall laugh and be amused at their folly. Then God will also act to confound them.

God has declared his own ruler in Jerusalem and God will place the heathen under his control. God warns the wicked that they shall be broken with a rod of iron and smashed like a piece of pottery.

If the rulers and the judges are smart they will begin at once to serve the Lord with great respect, and to bow down before the Son lest he be made angry. Happy are those who completely trust in Him.

Lord, there seem to be more and more people objecting to me. Some even write me off as hopeless, but I know, Lord, that you are my shield and my defense. When I cried unto the Lord, he heard me, and so I will not be afraid if 10,000 line up against me for God delivers, God will smite my enemies and break their jaws, for salvation is in the hands of God, and His blessing is upon his people.

Hear my prayer, O Lord, as you have helped in the past, have mercy on me again.

How long will men be vain and make shame of the glory that is mine in the Lord? God will hear those whom he has set apart for his work.

Stand in awe and sin not, be quiet and think about God. Offer to God your goodness for his use, and trust him.

There are some who think God is not interested. Show me your light and put gladness in my heart and I will then be able to go to bed and sleep in peace.

Hear another prayer from me, O Lord. This is a morning prayer.
I know the foolish will perish and that you have no use for
workers of iniquity, particularly those who are violent and deceitful.

As for me, O Lord, I will come to you asking for mercy and in
wonder will I worship. Lead me in the paths of righteousness because
my enemies work against me, show me the correct path to follow.

There is no faithfulness in the wicked, they flatter and mislead,
please destroy them, Lord. Let all those that trust in God rejoice and
shout with happiness, bless the goodies, Lord, protect them as with a
shield.

Lord, please don't blow your cool and punish me. Have mercy
on me. I am weak and I ache, my soul is disturbed, save me, please,
for I am afraid to die, or at least I'm not ready yet.

I am weary, Lord, with groaning and I cry all night.[1]

Tell my enemies to leave me alone. I feel suddenly that the
Lord has heard my prayer and I am confident my enemies will
retreat.

I put all my trust in you, O Lord. Save me. If I had done
anything wrong it would be different, but my enemies are stomping
me without cause. Settle a quick judgment on them, O Lord.

Lord, judge the people now, including me. Judge me according
to my righteousness and my integrity. Put an end to the wicked. I
know God helps the righteous and hates the wicked.

I know the Lord is fully prepared to handle the wicked. God
arranges for the wicked to fall into their own pits and to receive the
very trouble they intend for others.

Therefore, I praise the Lord because of his righteousness and I
sing praises to the most high God.

O Lord, how excellent is your name in all the earth. Your glory
exceeds the glory of the heavens, you have even managed to let
babies be more powerful than those who oppose them.

When I think about your heavens, the work of your fingers, the
moon, the stars, the planets which you made, it makes me marvel
that you have taken such an interest in man. You have really blessed
man and made him a wonderful creature, almost as glorious as the
angels. You have given man control of the earth, you have granted
him the job of managing the sheep, the oxen, and the wild game, the
fowl of the air, the fish of the sea, and all the creatures of the sea.

How excellent is the name of the Lord in all the earth!

[1] Definitely the back ache

I will praise God with all my heart and acknowledge all his wonderful works.

My enemies will be defeated by the presence of God.

God has always supported me, God has rebuked the wicked, and reduced them to nothing.

The day of the wicked is a short one. The Lord is a righteous judge and he will administer judgment on the people.

The Lord will always be a refuge for the oppressed, and God will support those who put their trust in him.

Sing praises to the Lord and declare to all the people the wonderful things that the Lord continues to do.

Have mercy on me, O Lord, and consider my troubles with my enemies. I will rejoice in the salvation of the Lord. The heathen are sunk down in a pit of their own digging.

The wicked, and all the wicked nations will be turned into hell.

The needy will not always be neglected and the poor will not be without help forever.

Be active, O Lord, scare the willy-nilly out of the evil persons, and let men be reminded that they are merely human.

Why do you so often seem remote, O Lord? The wicked are getting by with persecuting the poor. The wicked are even boastful about their success, and they disdain God.

The wicked think they are self-sufficient, they curse, deceive, they lie, and plot and cheat, they sneak up on the innocent and uninformed. Arise, O Lord, and whack them good.

God, you know how the wicked defy you, how they boast, please at least break a few arms here and there.

The Lord is king forever and forever, and the heathen shall perish. God will help the fatherless and the oppressed, and bring justice into being on this earth. Amen.

I put my trust in God. Why would I want to flee to the mountains or seek some escape?

The wicked are at work. Their arrows are constantly being directed to the righteous. Sometimes it seems as if law and order have collapsed.[1]

Don't worry, the Lord is in his holy temple, God is watching all the time, and the Lord enjoys the view of the righteous but the ways of the wicked are irritating.

Eventually the wicked will catch hell from the Lord, and God will smile on the righteous.

Help! Help! We need help, God. The righteous are having it

---

[1]So that's where the expression originated

tough. The wicked are undermining the good people with flattery and lies and talk of big profits.

The Lord will finally hush up the lip artists and bless the poor and the oppressed.

The word of God is sure, it is also pure as refined silver, O God, please preserve and protect the good people from the vile and evil persons who are everywhere, and who often are made rich and famous.

Chap.
13

Do you remember me, O Lord? When will I get a little relief from my enemies and comfort for my sorrows?

Lord, brighten my life a bit. You certainly don't want my enemies to get the best of me. I have trusted in God, though, and I know God's mercy. I will praise God, for God has been good to me.

Chap.
14

Only a grade A nut has said in his heart that there is no God. Such persons are no-good fools, who do abominable deeds. The whole crowd of them are a bunch of dirty bums.

You'd think they would know something, but they don't even say a blessing before the meal. They should be terrified, for the Lord is associated with the righteous.

What a great day it will be when the people of God are restored and the goodies rule the world under God.

Chap.
15

Lord, who do you want around you? I'm sure you wish a person who walks uprightly, who does good work, and thinks truthfully.

You certainly prefer a pleasant speaking person and not one who complains about his neighbors, or acts mean to his neighbors.

You desire, of course, someone who stays away from evil relationships, but loves and respects the righteous.

God also wants around him a person who tells the truth even if it penalizes him to do so, a person who loans money at a fair interest rate, and a person who does not take advantage of others.

There's a stable man for you!

Chap.
16

Protect me, O God, for I trust fully in you.

I know it will go hard for those people who seek strange religions and observe strange rites. I am most fortunate to have been reared in a godly environment. I will therefore continually thank God.

My heart is glad and my spirit is bright for I am dependent on the Lord. I know that God will keep me from hell, and will save my soul from torment. I know that the righteous way is far more pleasant and God will continue to guide me.

O Lord, check my record. See if I have not made every effort to adhere to your requests and to obey your commandments.

Make me secure. Hide me from the wicked. The evil ones are waiting for me like hungry lions. Arise and deliver me, Lord.

Save me from the wicked men around here, the fat, prosperous, power-mad, money-hungry scoundrels. As for me, I can go to sleep seeing the protective God over me all through the night.

The Lord is my rock, my strength, my deliverer. I will always call on the Lord, and he will save me from my enemies and deliver me from the flood of troubles, the sorrows of hell, and the snares of men.[1]

When I explained to the Lord about the evil ones, God heard my prayer and he shook the earth, he stirred things plenty with thunder, lightning, smoke, and fire.

God used hail and all types of natural powers to discomfort my enemies. In the midst of all the confusion, God delivered me, he made me stand in a safe place, he did this because the Lord was pleased with me. The Lord rewarded me according to my righteousness and in accordance with the cleanliness of my hands.

God did this because I have observed his laws and worshipped him. God shows mercy to those who show mercy. How simple it is.[2]

God has given me great confidence and I have the feel of success. All of this is a credit to God. It is not me, but God who acts and blesses. God has protected me, has strengthened my life, and enabled me to walk with confidence.

God has delivered me in battle and enabled me to be victorious. God has made it possible for me to be the ruler of a mighty kingdom, within which are many evil men. God delivers, and so I give thanks to the Lord for he has given great deliverance to his king, to his anointed one, to David, who is me.

The heavens exhibit the glory of God and all the expanse of sky testify to his handiwork.

Everything carries a message about the glory of God; the darkness of a silent night, the noise of day, the sun appears as if arising each morning from the tabernacle of God, the sun bursts on the world like a bridegroom on his honeymoon, or a great athlete being announced just before a game. The sun is marvelous on its rounds, there is nothing hidden from the heat of the sun. It is testifying to the glory of God.

The law of the Lord is exact and a real challenge to a man's soul. The statutes and regulations of God are right and pure, and makes man see life more clearly.

The respect for God is a clean and wholesome feeling and God's

---

[1]Sounds like he had been a dormitory supervisor   [2]Try it — you'll like it

judgments are always absolutely correct.

Life is really sweet to the one who obeys God and learning of God is much more to be sought than silver and gold. The standards of God are good guides and there is great reward for observing them.

Lord, protect me from the sin of thinking too much of myself, and so let me be a righteous person.

Let the words of my mouth and the meditations of my heart be acceptable to you, O Lord, my strength and my redeemer.

Chap.
20

I am confident that the Lord will hear me in time of trouble. We will all rejoice in the salvation God provides for the righteous. Yet God must do as God sees fit.

I, for one, know for sure that the Lord cares for those who trust him. Some people trust in chariots, some in horses, some in planes, and some in banks, but most of us trust in the name of the Lord.

The wicked fall, the righteous are risen, hear us when we pray, O God, the Lord of hosts.

Chap.
21

As king, I rejoice in the strength of God which is available for me. You have given the king everything he wants.

You have done everything for the king; a beautiful crown, long life, glory, honor, and majesty have been made a handy thing for him. The king trusts in God, and God willing, the king will not change.

The enemies of the king shall finally be swallowed up and disappear as if thrown into a fiery furnace. The enemies of the king were always plotting evil, but God was always watching.

Blessed is the Lord God, and we will sing his praises and recognize his power.

Chap.
22

My God, my God, why have you neglected me? I have been crying day and night and nothing has happened. O holy God, our fathers trusted in you and it worked. Make it work for me.

I am in trouble. The people boo me even before I get to bat. They make fun of me and call me a Bible thumper. They say, he trusted God, why doesn't God deliver him? I pass it on, why not help me? You are responsible for my being here in the first place.

My opponents are really organized. I feel as if I am surrounded by hungry lions. I feel weak, my strength is gone, my tongue sticks to my mouth, and the worst part is my back hurts.

Please help me. Deliver me from this sorry pack of human dogs. Be certain that I will praise the name of the Lord in public.

In fact, I tell everybody now to praise God. The Lord delivers, he never turns his back on those that trust him, always God knows and God cares.

Eventually, all the ends of the earth shall praise the Lord, all nations shall worship God, for all the kingdoms forever are the Lord's, everything is God's, from the smallest seed to the mightiest mountain, and from One shall come the word that shall cause a new kingdom of God's making to encompass the earth.

Chap.
23

The Lord is like a shepherd to me. I never need anything. God leads me by still waters for drinking and refreshment, he guides me along a good path in order that I might honor the name of the Lord. Though I face death or uncertainty I am without fear, for God is with me, he is ready to protect, I am at ease so that I can eat without worrying and I have a full life. I am respected, and I find goodness and mercy around me all the days of my life and I look forward to dwelling in the house of the Lord forever.[1]

Chap.
24

The earth is the Lord's and everything in it, including all the people. God built the earth. Who do you think he wants around him?

A man with clean hands and a pure heart, one who is no phony, such a person will receive the blessing of God.

The King of Glory appears. Who is the king of glory? The Lord strong and mighty, the conqueror of all, the Lord of hosts, he is the king of glory.

Chap.
25

I trust in the Lord. O Lord, don't let me down. Whack away at the wicked.

Lead me in a plain path, show me the truth, remember all thy mercies of old and make them presently available, forget my sins as a youth.

Teach all who need guidance, Lord. Those who fear God and seek him are in need of learning. Bless them all, Lord.

God will reveal his promises to those that trust him.

I am always praying to the Lord for it seems that I am always in trouble. Just like now. My enemies are many and they are plotting all the time. Deliver me, O God, and be certain that I trust in the Lord. Keep me on a straight path, and while you are saving me, Lord, save all Israel.

Chap.
26

Judge me, Lord. I've done absolutely the best I could. I have avoided phony people, I have kept your loving kindness before my eyes, I have stayed away from the wicked. I am really not a bad guy.

I don't mind speaking out in church in your behalf and telling of all your wonderful works. I enjoy being in your temple and associating with nice people and I really detest going with a crummy crowd. Redeem me, Lord, be merciful to me. I will witness to your greatness before the people.

---

[1] I definitely prefer the King James version of this psalm.

The Lord is my light and my salvation, whom shall I fear? The Lord is the strength of my life, of whom shall I be afraid?

When the wicked headed my way they stumbled and fell. I'm not afraid any more regardless of the numbers on the other side. I am not even worried in war.

My main goal is to live as close to God as I can, always trying to learn more. I know when trouble does come that God will protect me and shield me, and that I will finish way ahead of my enemies.

Hear me, Lord. Have mercy on me. Hide not your face from me, Lord, and put me not away in anger. Never forsake me, O God.

Even though my father and mother give up on me, the Lord will take my part. Teach me, Lord. Lead me in a plain path. Cheaters and liars have risen up against me, so much so that I would have fainted unless I had believed to actually see the goodness of the Lord in the land of the living.

Be patient. Serve the Lord. God will strengthen you, just serve God.

Hear me, Lord. Answer me. If you don't speak I will be as desolate as a fellow deserted in the pit.

Prevent me, Lord, from falling for the soft talk of those who would lead me astray. Punish those characters. See that they get theirs.[1]

I know God will finally destroy them. Blessed is the Lord who has heard my pleas.

The Lord is my strength and also the strength of all who trust in him. Bless your people, Lord.

Give glory to God. The voice of the Lord is powerful, his word controls the waters, the storms, the acts of nature, controlling fires, producing calves and fawns, the Lord is the king, the God of all, in charge of everything.

I will praise you, Lord, for all your goodness to me. You have given me birth and kept me alive. Sing, everyone, to the Lord and be grateful to him.

The anger of God is never very long and as weeping vanishes in the night and morning comes; so is the joy of the Lord.

Be helpful to me, Lord. Don't let me get killed, for if I'm dead I can't write songs of praise. I will always give thanks to the Lord who has turned my mourning into rejoicing.

I put all my trust in the Lord. The Lord is full of mercy. Ease my pain, O Lord. At present I am in great distress and I am full of

[1] Imagine a pit stop and no help

grief. I am getting old and creaky boned, people don't like to look at me, there is much slander out against me and some are plotting to take my life.

Save me. Brighten my life. Put the quietus on the liars.

Blessed is the name of the Lord who has shown me such kindness in his beloved city. Love the Lord, all you believers, be of good courage and God will strengthen your heart. Hope in the Lord.

Chap.
32

Happy is the man whose sin is forgiven and whose life is purified. I remember when I was burdened with sin, how miserable I was, I felt clammy, my bones hurt. Then I confessed my sin and God forgave me.

Don't be stupid like a beast and have to be guided by reins. Trust in the Lord and let him guide you. Be happy and shout for joy, for the goodness of the Lord is real.

Chap.
33

Praise the Lord. Rejoice in the Lord for the earth is full of the goodness of the Lord. It is amazing to consider the majesty of God's creation.

Let all the earth stand in awe of God. God spoke and creation came into being. The Lord confounds the wicked. Blessed is the nation that recognizes God and worships him.

No king is saved by numbers, no man saved by his own strength, all things are controlled by the Lord. God is our help and our shield and the more we trust in God the happier we get.

Chap.
34

O magnify the Lord, let us all exalt his name. I searched for God, and then he found me. A poor man cried and the Lord saved him even as the Lord delivered me. Taste and see that the Lord is good.

Depart from evil and seek good. Keep your tongue from evil and your lips from speaking guile, seek peace and pursue it.

God responds to calls. God is close to those who are contrite and he mends the broken-hearted.

The wicked finally wind up killing each other, but the Lord redeems the soul of the righteous and no one that trusts in the Lord will be lonely.

Chap.
35

Lord, listen to my plea. Get to work on my enemies. Blow them away like chaff, turn your angels loose on them, hound them to pieces for they are a great nuisance to me, always plotting my downfall.

When you have trapped them, Lord, in their own snares, then will I rejoice and praise your name.

It is really provoking to me that the men who slander me and make all kinds of false accusations are the very people that I have helped the most.

Judge me, O Lord. See for yourself that I am innocent. Don't give that bunch of crooks any satisfaction. Put them down fast. Confuse them and shame them and then will the name of the Lord be truly exalted and I will witness daily to the power and righteousness of God.

Chap.
36

The wicked really puzzle me. They act as if they have no fear of God. On the other hand I see the Lord, the originator of righteousness, the ruler of man and beast, how outstanding is the loving concern of the Lord. All real pleasure stems from God and God's blessing goes to those who trust him, God is a fresh fountain to them.

Protect me now, Lord, from myself, from the pitfall of pride and conceit, and while you are at it, sock it to the wicked.

Chap.
37

People, don't worry about evildoers and certainly don't envy the workers of iniquity.

Trust in the Lord and he will provide for you. Stick with God and his program. You must be very patient and do not worry about the flash success of the evil ones. Suddenly one day the wicked will be gone and there will not even be a historical marker to note where they had been.

The patient and the understanding shall inherit the earth and shall enjoy peace. While the wicked are plotting against the just and denouncing them God is merely laughing at the futility of their efforts.

The wicked prepare to shoot their arrows at the innocent, but the arrows will fall back on the wicked. The arms of the wicked will be broken and the righteous will be at peace. It is a promise that will some day become reality.

The law of the Lord resides in the heart of the righteous, so be patient. I have seen the wicked in great power, spreading themselves as a giant green bay tree, yet they disappeared and could not be found.

The man of peace is upright and he will witness the collapse of the wicked. The Lord is the strength of the righteous and he is their salvation. The Lord will help them, and deliver them, because they trust in God.

Chap.
38

Don't criticize me any more, Lord. I know I have sinned. I am truly sorry. I smell bad even to myself because of my sin.

I am feeble and groaning. I hurt all over. Nobody will have anything to do with me and I don't blame them. Everyone is plotting against me.

Actually, I am trying to be deaf to all the complaints, for I put my hope and my trust in you, O Lord.

I am penitent. I am ready for a new life. One mistake and all the tongues started wagging against me. Forsake me not, O Lord, be my salvation and my help.

Chap.
39

I determined to keep my mouth shut. I never said a word, but my insides shook, and my heart burned.[1]

Heal me, Lord. I have had a mild stroke, I can only mumble. What is in store for me? Am I near death? Refresh me, God, draw near to me. I feel deserted; let me have my strength return. Hear my prayer, O Lord.

Chap.
40

The Lord has heard my plea and rescued me from the depths of despair and from the infirmity of my flesh. I sing now as with a new song. Blessed is the Lord and happy is the man who trusts in him.

There is no way of recounting the wonderful works of the Lord. Offering sacrifice or paying the church pledge has no great meaning unless a person gives of himself. So I am ready to be used. Surround me, Lord, with your goodness and your loving kindness. Make haste to help me and hurry to confound my enemies.

Bless those who seek you, Lord, and may they all together praise the Lord. I am weak and in need, O Lord, and you are my only help, but please hurry. Amen.

Chap.
41

Blessed is the person who is concerned about the poor. The Lord will preserve such a person for God has real use for him.

I pray, Lord, that you will have mercy on me and heal me, yet my enemies are pulling for my death and can hardly wait. The baddies are really plotting together against me. They are passing the word that I will never get out of bed again.

I know you are with me, Lord. Heal me. This will reassure me about your power. Nevertheless, I continually say, Blessed is the Lord God of Israel forever and forever. Amen.

Chap.
42

As a young deer pants for the water in a fresh running stream, so pants my heart for the Lord. My soul thirsts for further knowledge of God.

Yet here I am crying in bed, unable to arise. I can remember the great day of dancing and parading as we took the ark of the covenant to the temple.

Then I say to myself, why are you depressed, why is your soul in low key? I will hope in God for I will yet again be able to arise and praise him in his temple.

I admit my boat is swamped. The waves and waters of trouble

---

[1]This was before Alka-Seltzer

have washed over me, but the feeling of the presence of God, day and night, that is a great comfort.

My enemies keep taunting me. They say, 'Where is your God?' Again I say, my hope is in the Lord.

O Lord, brighten my day a bit. All I hear is the complaints and plots of my enemies. Send out thy light and your truth, let them lead me, let them bring me to a good understanding. When that happens, I can again declare the glory of God in his temple.

We know the record, O Lord. We know all you have done in the past. Our fathers did not capture the promised land by their own swords, but only through the power of God. Praise the Lord, and let us boast in the name of the Lord.

You have now, O Lord, let us get in bad shape. We have a poor image with other nations. Everybody picks on us. It is confusing. The enemies seem to be increasing, and yet we continue to declare your majesty.

You have really put us to the test. Judge now, O Lord. Haven't we stayed by you and continually declared thy name as Lord of hosts?

For your sake, O Lord, we are picked on all day every day, we are like sheep lined up before the slaughter pens. Wake up, God. Save us! Deliver us from our enemies and all our woes, and redeem us for your mercy's sake.

A Song About King David

You are indeed a handsome man, and you have a friendly spirit. Put on your sword and ride majestically. Your presence will intimidate your enemies.

God has blessed you. God has wanted you on the throne of Israel, for it is God's throne. David, you are a righteous person, seeking to improve; so God has given you the crown.

You are really well fixed with a wardrobe full of up-to-date clothes and with a bunch of beautiful daughters. Everybody loves the king, even strange girls from foreign lands fall for David on sight.

It is a beautiful sight to see a wonderful daughter with her companions coming to pay homage to her father. What is more, God has promised to make the name of David a good name, to be treasured generation after generation.

God is our refuge and strength, an immediate help in time of trouble, therefore we will not be terrified even if the earth seems to be in the act of moving, or mountains shake and suddenly slide into the sea.

Just remember that there is a place of eternal refuge, where a river flows by the throne of God, and God is ever present.

The heathen rage, God utters his voice, and the earth melts. It is good that the Lord our God is with us.

Take a look. See how God sometimes destroys and makes desolate, and then how suddenly he makes wars end, doing away with weapons and the implements of war.

Think about it. Know that the Lord he is God, he will be exalted in the heavens, he will be exalted in the earth, the Lord of hosts is with us, the God of Jacob is our refuge.

Chap.
47

Get excited! Isn't it thrilling to know that the Lord is a great king over all the earth? God plans everything that's necessary.

Sing praises to God, for he rules over all the earth, he reigns over the heathen as well as the people of God. God is greatly to be exalted.

Chap.
48

Great is the Lord and greatly to be praised. Particularly should this be the case in Jerusalem, for it is God's city.

Great rulers have often been terrified when they viewed the power and might of the Lord.

Let us declare the rule of God throughout the whole city, tell everyone you see, have the men in the towers to shout it to the passersby, for God is our God forever and forever. Amen.

Chap.
49

Now hear this, everybody, whether you be educated or not. I will teach you now with a parable. A rich man who depends on his wealth is in trouble, for none of them can buy a favor from God.

God deals death to the wise and the foolish, the rich and the poor. Often a rich man thinks he can leave arrangements to perpetuate his house or his wealth, but it can't be done. Time erases too much. No one can take his wealth with him, either.

Therefore, I place my soul in the hands of God, knowing that the praise of man perishes, but the favor of God is eternal.

Chap.
50

God has spoken and God shall continue to speak. Assemble the people, get a big crowd together and hear God.

"I have an announcement," said God, "for I am your God. I don't need all your puny little gifts. Are not all sheep mine anyway? If I were hungry I could eat anything, for everything in the world is mine.

"Come to me with thanksgiving in good times and I will come to your aid in time of trouble.

"I have also observed the wicked. They do not read my word. They encourage crookedness, they are those that commit adultery, they are deceitful and speak with an evil tongue. I know you, wicked ones. You thought you were getting by with all this, but you were wrong. I plan to fix you plenty! To those who praise me and who obey my laws, to them I will show salvation."

Have mercy upon me, O Lord, according to thy tender kindness and the multitude of your mercies, please blot out my transgressions. Wash me thoroughly, cleanse me from my sin.

I admit my sin. It is horrible for me to think about it.[1] My sin is truly against you, and you only.[2] I guess I am just a natural born sinner.

You want the truth, and the truth I'll give. Please clean me out but good, maybe even with Lysol. Let me again start to feel right about life. Don't discard me, Lord.

If you will let me speak, I will again speak your praises. I know you are not interested in my church pledge, or else I would double it,[3] but I know that what really appeals to you is a broken and a contrite heart.

Be good to Jerusalem, Lord. None of this was their fault. Bless the people and I am sure they will respond.

A Song about a Tattletale

Why do you boast about being a blabbermouth? You just prefer evil to good. God will fix you for this. God will destroy you, he will take you away from home and have you banished.

The good people will get a laugh out of this, even though it be a terrifying thing. They will say that that is what happens to a fellow who turns against God.

As for me, I feel safe. I am under God's protection, and I trust in the Lord. I will praise God forever, I will serve under the banner of God, and I will set a good example.[4]

The fool has said there is no God. They are corrupt and they think everybody else is. God looks down and sees evil everywhere, so much so that there is no completely pure and righteous man in sight. I can hardly wait for God to stir the people who trust in him so that they will become super active and committed to God, and then be able to rejoice in glorifying his name.

Save me, O God. Hear my prayer. Strangers and oppressors are rising up against me. They are really after me. I will sacrifice to you, O God, in a proper way, I will praise God's name for he has delivered me.

---

[1] It didn't do Uriah any good either   [2] I still think Uriah got a dirty deal
[3] I've always thought he should do this also
[4] This was probably written when David was a fugitive from Saul and pretty young

Hear me, Lord, as I moan and groan and complain. I am sick and weak and afraid of dying. I wish I had the wings of a dove, then I would fly and hide in the wilderness.[1]

There is such violence in the city, muggings every night. Wickedness is everywhere, strife and terror, but all these things I could face, but now it is you, Lord, you are indicating that my time of death is near, and I am afraid.

I still trust in you, Lord, I will pray day and night, and please deliver me now as you used to deliver me in battle.

God shall surely punish the wicked. Fellows with butter-smooth words but evil thoughts are not likely to deceive God.

I know that anyone who will cast his burden on the Lord will find support, and the righteous shall never be trodden under foot. I know the wicked will be cut short, while I will continue to trust in the Lord.

Be merciful to me, O Lord. I have many enemies,[2] but when I face terror I know you are with me and I will not therefore fear what any man threatens to do to me.

The fascists are working on me, every day, changing my words, trying to trap me. Why don't you trap them?

I know that God is for me, that if I had saved my tears there'd be at least a ten gallon jar full of them. I put my trust in the Lord, I will not be afraid of man, I will continue to praise the Lord, for it is only reasonable that as the Lord has delivered my soul from death he will certainly deliver my feet from falling and permit me again sometime to walk publicly in the view of everyone, with God's blessing.

Be merciful to me, O God. Help me. I am a fugitive from Saul, send guidance to me, O Lord, and look kindly on my predicament.

Although I am in great personal danger, I still can envision the greatness of the Lord. Let your glory, O God, encompass the earth.

A net is prepared for me, and a pit dug, but I perceive the diggers are even now falling in their own hole. My own heart is at peace, for I praise the name of the Lord.

Continually will I praise you, O Lord, even now as I strum on my guitar. I sing of your great mercies, I will sing of you in the presence of all nations, so let thy glory be over all the earth.

The wicked are truly a bad lot. Some of them almost seem to be born bad. Let them melt away, O Lord, for we have had enough of them for awhile.

It would be nice, O Lord, if you adjusted your system so that

---

[1]But not during dove season   [2]Everyone that was a fascist

the righteous would get all the good breaks. Then men would say that it paid to be good.[1]

Chap.
59

Lord, I am in hiding again. Saul's men are trying to catch me. They can't wait to capture me. Save me, please, God. Arise, O Lord, and whack away at the wicked, not missing a single one.

They are like a pack of dogs barking at each other, signalling and making all kinds of threats. Laugh at them, God. Show them who is the real boss. Scatter them, bring them to their knees, condemn them for their cursing and lying, burn them in your wrath, and show them that you are the Lord God of Israel.

No matter, even if they continue running around the city like mad dogs, I will still praise the Lord, I will speak of your power and praise your mercy, for you have always been my strength, for you are both my God of defense, and my God of mercy.

Chap.
60

Father, the battle is not won and we have not been doing well. This means that you are not with us. It looks as if at times you are even helping the enemy.

You are our only help. Help from man is useless. Through God, and only through God can we conquer.

Chap.
61

Hear me now, Lord, as I pray. I will always be praying, when I am discouraged I always turn to the rock that is higher than I am.

Always have you, Lord, been a tower and a shelter to me, I am at ease in your temple. I am blessed in being born in a line of church people. I will always remember to praise the Lord ever day.

Chap.
62

My soul rests at ease because of my faith in God. He is my rock and my salvation.

The wicked will not last very long. Learn to trust in God, people, for he is all that I say he is. Don't be influenced by circumstances, whether you are rich or poor, educated or not, all power belongs to God and all mercy. God blesses each person in the exactly proper measure; so don't be up tight, trust God.

Chap.
63

O God, thou art my God. I will continually praise you. As long as I live I will praise you, whether I be thin or fat, hungry or full.

At night as I lay in bed and think of you I am comforted, for I know that those plotting against me haven't a chance with you as my protector. Those that support me shall be blessed, and I know that those that tell lies about me shall be punished.[2]

---

[1] This is an example of unanswered prayer
[2] Just so God didn't have to do it all, David punished some himself.

Lord, I am praying again for protection. Be a secret place for me, O God, for my enemies are putting their fat lips out against me. They say everything you can imagine. Bounce it all back on them.

Would that all men would fear God. Surely the righteous shall be glad of their faith and the upright in heart shall find peace.

All the people praise you, O Lord. Some day all will turn to you in prayer. Particularly fortunate is any person called of you and inspired to serve under your care.

Let us learn to be satisfied to worship. We recognize that you have the power to calm seas, to quiet down people, to make the wind cease, you control the sun and the moon and their schedules, you control the rain, and all nature responds to your control. May we join nature in songs of praise.

Make a joyful noise to the Lord, everybody, serve the Lord with gladness, let God know how impressed you are with his power, come and see the works of the Lord.

Don't you remember how God opened the sea? God watches everything. Please, God, don't let the wicked prosper.

Bless the Lord, everyone. As for me, I have been through great strife, but I declare the Lord to be my salvation and I make public witness to the glory of God and I testify as to what God has done for me.

I prayed to the Lord and though he was a little slow, the Lord answered me, God showed mercy to me, and I bless his name.

God be merciful to us and bless us and cause his face to shine upon us, in order that we might recognize that there is help on earth through the Lord.

Would that all the people would praise God. Would that the nations would be glad and shout for joy, for God has judged the people fairly. Come on, everybody, praise the Lord!

Then shall the earth yield its full amount and God, even our own God, shall bless us, and all the ends of the earth shall fear him.

Let God arise and scatter all his enemies. I wish God would blow evil away like smoke or melt it like wax.

Praise ye the Lord. God is all powerful. God breaks the chains of the prisoners, he shakes the earth, he sends rain, he helps the poor, he defeats the kings.

The chariots of God are innumerable and wonderful to behold, God has led captivity itself away into captivity, bless the Lord who daily provides our needs.

God is surely the God of salvation, the ruler of rulers, and the Lord of all. Put an end to war, O Lord, and let all the people turn to praise the Lord our God.

Save me, O God, for I am depressed. My eyes are wet and my throat is dry as I serve God, hoping for some help against my enemies. I have more enemies than I have hairs on my head.

All that I have done, I have done for the sake of the Lord. I have endured shame, I have been a fugitive, and a rebel. All this for your sake.

Now, God, come to my aid. You know all about all my troubles. I have had to eat gall and drink vinegar.[1] I am heavy-hearted because of what I have done wrong and even more so over the things of which I am accused and am yet innocent.

Please do a little fixing of my enemies. One suggestion is the stomach ache. Try this on some of them. The troubles that you have brought on me I deserve, but not the extra punches of the wicked. Why not just take them completely out of the land of the living, particularly the ringleaders who plot so against me.

As for me, I will praise the name of the Lord, and I am certain that this is more desirable than sacrifice or a big plate offering.

The Lord will in time bless the needy; so let heaven and earth praise God, let all the people of God praise him, and may the name of the Lord be a sacred treasure handed down from one generation to another. God will provide an eternal place for his people.

Hurry, O God, with deliverance. My time is really crowding me. Let the people who seek the Lord prosper and let the wicked get it in the neck.

I am poor and needy,[2] O God, please no delay, just deliver me now.[3]

In thee, O Lord, do I put my trust. Deliver me from the unrighteous and the wicked. You have been with me from the very beginning, God. Some people admire my bravery, but I know it is because you are with me.

The talk is that the wicked are spreading, that God has deserted me and that now would be a good time to run me off the throne. Hurry with some help!

Confound and confuse my enemies. I continue to hope, and to praise your name. I move daily in the strength of the Lord. Stay with me, Lord, I know I'm old, but I need you all the more.

Praises continue to come from me. I sing to the glory of God, and my tongue tells of the righteousness of the Lord, but please bring quick confusion to my enemies.

---

[1] This is slightly exaggerated, but he made his point.
[2] He meant poor and needy in spirit.   [3] A spear had just come close.

God bless my son Solomon. Grant that he may judge the people fairly and with mercy and encourage him to help the needy and the disadvantaged.

Give dominion to Solomon, that he may increase the expanse of the kingdom, spread his name abroad in every direction.

Grant that Solomon may be widely respected and that many kings will come to him to acknowledge his greatness.

Make the name of my son Solomon memorable so that as long as there is history his name will be remembered. Let Solomon be a blessing to all nations, and may these things also be a means of glorifying the Lord God of Israel.

May the whole earth be full of the glory of God, Amen, Amen, as prayed by David the son of Jesse.

I know that God is really good to his people, but I was slipping. I had gotten where I was envious of the wicked and I resented their success. It just seemed that the wicked were always better off than the good boys.

The wicked wear coats of pride and breeches of violence, they are also usually fat and rich. They are corrupt and they defy God.

For instance, they ask how God knows anything. How can God see and not be seen? These are really an ungodly bunch. As for me, I behave myself, go to church, and I'm having a terrible time with backache and arthritis.

The only help I get is when I go into the sanctuary and pray.

I guess that you will suddenly put an end to all their wickedness just as a dream vanishes when a person awakes.

You are all I have, Lord. I am depending entirely upon you. My flesh and my courage are at a low ebb, but you come on strong as the strength of my life.

It is refreshing for me to draw near to God, it is stimulating and encouraging.

How long are you going to be angry with your people, O Lord? Remember us poor church people, for we are having trouble, right in our own congregation. There are some bigmouth people urging the doing of wicked things. They are doing crazy things in your sanctuary, even having a bar-b-que.

The church seems to be deteriorating. We no longer have great dedicated preachers and none of us seem to know how long the wicked will prosper.

How about doing something? You divided the sea, created the mountains, dried up rivers, started floods, made summer and winter, so why not do such a little thing as crack the heads of the wicked.

Save me, God, don't let the wrong crowd rule the church. Act now, for the baddies are on the increase.

Thanks be to God. Promotion or prosperity does not come from man, but from God. Only the Lord is able to render proper judgment.

The Lord prepares the wine for the righteous and the wicked get the dregs, so let me praise the Lord for he will bring justice to the earth.

The name of the Lord is greatly respected in Judah. God destroys the weapons of war, and demolishes the chariots of the wicked. When God is aroused there is no standing up to him, for God is fierce, he rules the earth. He will trim down unruly leaders to size, and he will save the humble.

I cried to the Lord in my day of trouble and he heard me. I'm glad I remembered to pray. I admit there are some puzzling matters.

Why does God often seem so inactive? Has God forgotten how to be merciful and helpful?

Surely there is no god like our God, and I will think of the wonders of the past, the dividing of the waters, the floods, the fire, the voice of God's thunder, the lightning, the storms at sea. I will remember and be comforted, for you have a record, Lord, of leading your people.

Let me remind everybody and let us tell our children about the commandments of God and his statutes. God's law is to be handed down from generation to generation. Teach the children to set their hope in God and forget not his commandments.

Tell the children to be an improvement on their parents. God has done many marvelous things and yet the old timers failed to obey the Lord.

Help us, O God. Forget our shortcomings, deliver us, and purge us for your name's sake.

Listen, Lord, to the pleas of the prisoners and balance the books with the wicked, and then we your people will give you thanks and we will show our appreciation down through the years.

Turn to us again, O Lord, bless us and restore our power. How long do you plan to be angry?

We were a great people, escaped from Egypt, and we began to cover the Promised Land as a vine and spread as branches of a tree. Then all of a sudden every beast of a heathen began to gnaw away on us and we are next to nothing.

Look down from heaven, Lord, and check on us. We need some help at once. Inspire us, renew us, and bless us. Let us seek your face again and then we shall be saved.

Sing to the Lord, make a delightful song to praise his name. The law of God was blessed in Joseph who controlled the land of Egypt when he didn't even know the language. God has been tested and we know that he delivers.

The Lord has declared that he is God and we have failed to listen. If the people will return to the Lord and obey his commandments then God's blessing will again reside with his people. If only the people had obeyed, then God would have long ago devoured their enemies.

God is the judge of all the earth. How long are you going to let the wicked get by as they do, O Lord?

Why don't you defend the poor and the disadvantaged? These people are in trouble and they don't understand. Get with it, God. Start your action!

Don't be quiet, God. Speak out. Your enemies are raising hell everywhere and saying all kinds of weird things. Some of them are saying there should be no nation of Israel.[1] In fact, they have organized a group of nations just to wipe out Israel.

Fix some of these people like you did the Moscow Muggers and the Capone Gang. Blow them around like chaff in the wind, burn them like kindling, terrify them, make them ashamed, humiliate them so that all men may know that your name is Jehovah, most high ruler over all the earth.

How pleasant it is to be in your church, O Lord. Often I yearn just to be in peace, quietly sitting in the sanctuary.

Just like the sparrows find a place to nest and the swallows a chimney down which to swoop, so it seems as a sanctuary to those of us who come to worship in your house.

Happy is the man whose strength is in you, a person who going through a difficult situation digs a well so the next person coming that way may be refreshed.

All such godly people finish their life in the presence of the Lord.

A day in your presence, Lord, is better than a thousand elsewhere and I would rather be a menial servant in a hut of yours that to dwell in the glamour suite of the Waldorf-Astoria.

The Lord is a sun for light and a shield for protection, the Lord gives grace and glory, and no good thing does the Lord withhold from those that love him and who obey his commandments. Happy is the man who trusts in God.

---

[1] Some of them are still saying it

Lord, you have been good to Israel and restored our unity, you have forgiven our sins, continue to be merciful to us, inspire us, and grant us salvation.

Certainly the Lord speaks of peace to his people and salvation is offered to those that fear him. Surely a new day is coming full of righteousness and peace and the Lord will bless our land and we shall glory in praising God.

Hear me now, O Lord, for I am in great need. Protect me, and encourage me. I know the Lord is good and ready to forgive. Have mercy on me, Lord.

Always when I am in trouble I call on the name of the Lord, for I am confident that God will help me. There is no other god except Jehovah and the words of God testify to his greatness.

Teach me continually your way, O Lord, and I will continue to praise you, and always will I depend on your mercy, for I know you are compassionate and considerate. It would be greatly helpful, Lord, if you would do something extra nice for me now, Lord, so that my enemies might be able to see that you support me.

The city of God is set upon a high hill and the Lord favors this city over all others. Many glorious things are spoken about Jerusalem.

I hear fellows brag about being born in Egypt, or the South, or California, but some day persons will be bragging about having been born in Jerusalem. Jerusalem shall some day be the key word in great songs widely sung throughout the world.

Continually, O Lord, do I find myself praying to you about all manner of things. Now I'm asking for relief from my troubles.

I find myself getting old and nearing death, my hearing and my sight are fading, and I feel that you are leaving me in the dark.

Don't wait too long, O Lord. There is no point in healing me after I'm dead as I'll be in the cemetery. I want some healing now.[1]

O Lord, don't you realize that I cannot praise you from the grave, nor from that dark hole can I tell of your loving kindness and mercy. I am really in bad shape and of no use to my friends or my family. Please heal me. Just a quick miracle, O Lord.

The time has come for us to sing of the mercies of God so that all generations forever will know that the Lord is good, that the throne of David will remain intact year after year, and the heavens shall carry the story of the wonders of God in the shifting clouds and twinkling stars.

[1] David's back was really hurting

The strength and power of the Lord is visible on the sea, and blessed are the people who recognize the power of God and who rejoice in praising him.

God is the strength behind David and the Lord will bless his works and strengthen his arm and the followers and descendants of David that serve the Lord will be blessed.

All these things being true, it is hard to understand why David becomes old and suffers, as if you had deserted him. At such times as this we wonder where the loving kindness of the Lord is, for is not his servant David in great distress? When will help come?

Nevertheless, blessed be the Lord forevermore.

Chap.
90

Lord, you have been a central concern in all generations. Before the mountains were formed or ever you had created the earth, always you were in existence, even from everlasting to everlasting you are the one God.

A thousand years seem but as a day to you from your scale of observation, it passes as if it were a half-time show.

Everything is under your careful control, you know everything, we daily face the tribulations caused by our own errors, and yet one whole lifetime passes as a story told around a campfire.

We are basically limited to 70 years anyway, give or take a few, and we never know all about your wrath or the use of your power, so teach us to try to make every day count, and daily bring us closer to you.

Have mercy on us. At least balance our hard times with good times.

Let the graciousness of the Lord be reflected in our lives, bless the work we do, and make it durable for your name's sake.

Chap.
91

Anyone who loves the Lord is able to live in the shadow of God's majesty, and so I think of the Lord as my fortress, for I completely trust in God.

Think of the Lord as a giant bird that will cover you with his wings and deliver you from the traps and the snares of life. There is no need then to fear the bullet that flies by day nor the violence abroad at night, for the Lord will protect as he pleases.

A thousand might die very close to you, but the Lord is able to save you, no evil will come to you, sickness or misery except with the Lord's permission.

It is really quite simple, for the Lord merely assigns a couple of angels to watch over his chosen ones, and they can even keep you from stumping your toe.

God responds to those that love him, he provides deliverance and honor, and the life of those who love God is a full life.

It is a good thing to give thanks to the Lord, to sing his praises, to comment on his lovingkindness and his faithfulness.

How great and wonderful are the works of the Lord. Brutes and fools can't see this, and they perish because of it.

The enemies of the Lord in time will be consumed, but those that love the Lord shall be refreshed and flourish as a well-watered tree. The Lord is my rock and there is no error in God.

The Lord reigns. The throne of God is established forever. The Lord is above the floods, above the mountains, above the noise and strife of even the storms at sea. The words of the Lord are true and holiness is the name of God's house.

Now, Lord, I think it is time for you to take action against your enemies. How long do the wicked get to do their thing? How long will you allow them to brag, to take advantage of widows, to murder? Did you know, God, that they think you aren't keeping in touch?

I know the brutish and cheaters are going to be punished, but they don't think so.

The Lord knows even the thoughts of man. Fortunate is the man that God teaches, even though God uses hardship and suffering as a means of teaching. Eventually all will be properly adjusted.

From my own experience, I know that I would have been lost if all I had depended upon was the help of some friends, but I trusted in God, and the Lord has supported me. The Lord is my rock and the Lord will destroy my enemies in his own way and in his own times.

Come, let us sing to the Lord, let us really belt it out in praises to the rock of our salvation.

The Lord is a great god and a great king above all gods, in his hands are everything, the deep places of the earth are his, the seas are his, for he made them, and God's hands formed the dry ground; so come let us worship, let us kneel before the Lord our maker.

Surely he is our God and we are the sheep of his pasture. I have been imploring you hard-headed people for forty years, please now turn to the Lord and depend on him.

Sing a new song to the Lord. Declare his greatness, describe his wonders to everybody. Honor, majesty, and strength all belong to the Lord our God.

Give to the Lord the glory due him, honor him properly, tell the unbelievers about God, witness to the power of the Lord, then watch the heavens rejoice, the sea roar, the field applaud, and the whole earth be glad, for the Lord will come to judge the world, to see that righteousness rules and that God's word is supreme.

The Lord reigns. There may be clouds, and darkness may seem
to cover the earth, but God will go forth with fire from his mouth
and consume his enemies.

Confused and baffled will be those that serve false gods, who
worship money or science, for the heavens will declare the power of
God in lightning and natural disasters, but the Lord will deliver from
fear those that love him; so rejoice in the Lord, be grateful that God
is holy.

How about even another new song? The Lord has done some
marvelous things. The Lord has declared his salvation, he has
remembered his promises of mercy; so let us make a joyful noise to
the Lord, crack out all the musical instruments, let the sea roar and
the waves clap their hands, for the Lord comes in great righteousness
to rule the world in fairness.

God reigns. Let the wicked tremble and the righteous stand in
awe. God is the king that loves justice, exalt the name of the Lord,
for he is holy.

Moses, Aaron, and Samuel praised God and when they called on
the Lord he responded. God replied with a cloud and a pillar of fire,
for when they sinned they repented, and they observed the laws of
God.

Exalt the Lord our God and worship him.

Make a joyful noise to the Lord, everyone; serve God
cheerfully, realize that he is God, that it is God that has made us, we
are not self-made, we are his people, so come with thanks to God and
bless his name, for the Lord is good, his mercy is everlasting and his
truth endures forever.

I will sing praises to God and bless the Lord for his mercies. I
will no longer go to the girlie shows and associate with brawlers. I am
definitely going to give up all wickedness. When I hear gossip start I
am going to just walk away.

My concern and my interest will be with those who are faithful
and I shall gather around me as helpers those that are honest and
godly.[1]

The liars and the deceitful are not to be tolerated and I plan to
clean up Jerusalem.

Hear me now, Lord, for this is one of my trouble times. I am
too upset to eat. Groaning and not eating have caused me to lose

---

[1] Wish Nixon had done this

weight and I just sit around like a pelican, doing nothing.

I feel like a lonely sparrow on a rooftop with all the B.B. guns pointed at me. I cry in my beer.

God, you lift me up, then cast me down; but it is great to know that you endure forever. I look to the day when the heathen shall all fear the name of the Lord, when the kings of the earth shall see your great glory, and the kingdom of God will prosper.

For generation after generation shall the Lord look down from heaven and he will hear the prayer of the lonely and the destitute, he shall release the prisoner, and gather all the kingdoms of the world together in peace.

I wish I could live to see all this. I know God does not plan these things in my lifetime, but I know that the generations to come will behold his glory and the children of God shall be well established in the earth.

Chap. 103

Bless the Lord, O my soul, and all that is within me, bless his holy name, and never forget all that God has done for us.

God forgives errors, he heals diseases, he equips believers in loving-kindness and tender mercies, he makes food taste good, and refreshes a person so that even the advanced in years feel young and spry and seek to fly like eagles.

The Lord has provided a basic system of justice. God revealed his plan to Moses and his activities were witnessed by all the people of Israel. The Lord is merciful and gracious, slow to anger and plenteous in mercy. God will not always be scolding nor will he always remain angry.

God has never punished us in relation to our sins nor rewarded us on a basis of what we really had coming. As high as outer space is above the earth, so tremendous is his mercy to those that worship him. As far as the east is from the west, that's how far God has separated us from our mistakes. Just as a loving father cares for his children, so the Lord cares for those that serve him.

God knows us. He remembers that originally we were a pile of dust. A man is really a lot like grass or a flower in the field, he grows up and then suddenly the wind blows him away, but not so with God's mercy, for it is from everlasting to everlasting, and his righteousness spreads from generation to generation among his followers, those that keep his agreements and remember to obey his laws.

The Lord rules over all the earth and all the kingdoms of the earth.

Bless the Lord. Let his angels that do his errands bless the Lord, let the ministers bless the Lord, and let all the good things that are being done in all the earth be a sign of the blessing of God. Praise God again and again.

Bless the Lord. Acknowledge the goodness of God and the greatness of God. God is clothed in light and God stretches out his creation like a curtain. Do you know who made all the seas?

What about the clouds and the winds? They are God's playthings. The Lord has angels for special work and also ministers to preach his word.

Creation is a marvelous thing. Imagine making something as permanent as the earth. Yet God separated the water and the land, furnished a little thunder for sound effects, and produced mountains and valleys. Then God put boundaries on all creation. Just think of all the details. The spring, the birds transplanting seeds, grass for cattle, herbs for the wild game, fields for food and wine to nourish mankind, oil for cosmetics and bread for body building. God thought of all these things.

Trees made so the sap may run, also providing a place for birds to nest, high hills for goats and rocky places for black squirrels, the moon to tell of the seasons and the sun to keep track of the days. God arranged for a period of darkness so the subtle creatures like coons could steal corn and lions could stalk young deer. When the sun rises the animals go to bed and man gets up and goes to work. I just can't imagine such wisdom and such planning.

The sea is a fabulous creation with all kinds of little things swimming around under water and man rowing a boat on top. The playful whale is a sight in itself.

Yet God continues to rule. When God so decrees all is well and when God decides otherwise, he complicates matters. The glory of the Lord is surely forever and the Lord shall rejoice in all his creations.

Now and then God looks hard at one place and causes an earthquake or he tumbles a mountain top and starts a volcano erupting. For all these things, I will worship God, I will sing songs of praise to him. I am satisfied with my belief in God and I also know that the wicked will in time be eliminated. Bless the Lord, O my soul.

Give thanks to the Lord and tell everybody about his wonderful works. Be glad to be one of God's people, search for the Lord, be mindful of all his wondrous works. Surely the Lord is God and his judgments are to be exercised all over the world.

God has made a number of promises, some to Abraham, some to Isaac, and some to Jacob, and God keeps all his promises. It never mattered to God whether his people were few in number or many, he protected them. God appointed prophets and leaders, he sent Joseph ahead of time to prepare a place for his people, and God always blessed his people.

God sent Moses to deliver his people, he gave Moses great

powers so that the Egyptians saw the waters turn to blood, the hail, the locusts, all the plagues were testimony of the power of God.

The Lord led his people in the wilderness with a cloud by day and a pillar of fire by night and he fed the people with manna from heaven and quail from a special migration.

God remembered his promise and finally the people crossed the Jordan with great singing and much pleasure as they came to claim the land of Canaan.

Praise the Lord for he is good and his mercy endures forever. Blessed are the good, for they can appreciate the mighty works of the Lord.

God, help our people. Inspire them. None of them saw the miracles of Egypt, and even our ancestors that saw these things forgot about them when confronting the Red Sea, yet God delivered them and swept away the Egyptian army in a flood.

Even after this, though, the people soon forgot about the power of God and his willingness to protect his people, and they disobeyed God and pursued the lusts of the flesh.

The whole history of the trip through the wilderness is a record of sin, repentance, and deliverance, then sin again. The patience of God is without measure. Time and again God delivered, and time and again the people rebelled.

Save us again, O Lord. Gather us together as one people. Blessed be the Lord God of Israel from everlasting to everlasting. Amen.

Give thanks to the Lord, for he is good and his mercy endureth forever. Certainly those that have been delivered by the Lord should give thanks for he preserved them in the wilderness, he has helped the hungry and thirsty, God has saved so many. Would that all men would appreciate the Lord and bless him.

God fills the hungry soul with goodness, and I wish mankind would continually praise God for his goodness and for his wonderful works to the children of men.

God has even delivered fools who have rejected him until they are at death's door, but even then God responds.

Some men are impressed, of course. Certainly those that go down to sea in great ships and travel on the great waters, for they see the power and majesty of God. These men learn of God in the raging storm when the seas are tumultous and the ships are tossed to and fro. At such times men call on the Lord and he delivers.

How I wish men would praise the Lord for his goodness and his wonderful works for the children of men.

The church people should also praise the Lord. Surely they observe the Lord turn a drought area into a lush green pasture, the fields are blessed, the land prospers. The Lord often helps the poor and the church people know this, so let them rejoice, and those who are wise should learn from this that the Lord is good and his loving-kindness is a working matter.

Chap.
108

The time has come for me to sing, to glorify God, to take my guitar and sing first thing in the morning.[1]
God is merciful and to be praised. God always speaks in holiness and God has promised me success against the enemies of Israel. The Fascist[2] dogs will get it for sure.
Who else could guarantee such victories except the Lord? Help us now, Lord, and lead us in our battles. Although we are brave, it is only because we know that the Lord is with us.

Chap.
109

Lord, it's time for action. The wicked are going full speed and they are mouthing about me something awful. I have tried to be considerate of my enemies, even praying for them, but they are worse than ever. Please smite them.
There are several things you could do, Lord. One is just shorten their time of life, cause them to lose their jobs, or let their children become instant delinquents. Another way is to let them start blackmailing each other.
Most of these wicked men seem to enjoy cursing others, how about encouraging others to curse them?
Deliver me, Lord, because of your mercy and because everyone knows that I trust in the Lord. Save me. Do it in such a way that everyone will know that it is done by your hand.
Continually do I praise the Lord, trusting in him, and being assured that God will always help the needy.

Chap.
110

The Lord has spoken to the Savior who is to come, who sits on the right hand of God,[3] and has promised that under the Messiah will the world grow in righteousness and the wicked gradually be removed.
The Lord has promised the Messiah. He shall judge the heathen, he shall be the glorious high priest over the one great church idea under his direction. Someday he shall be the real king of kings.

Chap.
111

Praise the Lord. Note his wonderful works. The Lord is gracious and full of compassion, he has fed his people when they were hungry, the works of his hands are true and his commandments are upright. God has provided a means of redemption for his people. The Lord is holy, reverence the name of God, and stand in awe of the

---

[1]Neighbors were not allowed to complain about kings
[2]Philistines
[3]This interpretation seems quite clear to me

Lord, for this is the very starting point of wisdom. The peace of God endures forever.

Happy is the man who respects God and observes his commandments. Such a man is blessed in himself and his descendants make a contribution in life.

Such a man as is godly considers himself rich, life is enjoyable to him and interesting, he is compassionate, he gives freely, he conducts his affairs with great integrity, and he shall not worry over bad news, for he trusts in the Lord.

A good solid Christian citizen gives to the needy, stands unafraid in the community, is honored by his peers, and the wicked observe him and are jealous.

Praise the Lord. Blessed be the name of the Lord from morning until night. The Lord is truly the Lord of all, he is in charge of everything, he is concerned about the poor, he sometimes relieves a barren woman so that she starts having kids, and he often elevates the lowly to a high place.

Long ago Israel made a break with Egypt and the promised land was waiting, the Red Sea opened to let God's people through, mountains and hills proved to be no barrier. Stand in awe, everyone, for the God of Israel brought water from rock and made the earth tremble.

Let all the glory go to the Lord. The gods of the heathen are really pitiful for they are made from metals by men's hands, they have eyes but see not and mouths but they can't talk. They have hands that do nothing and feet that don't take them anywhere.

O Israel, trust in God. The Lord has been great in our past and will bless our future. Blessings come to those that worship God. Let us bless the Lord while we are alive for it will be too late when we are dead.

I love the Lord because he has heard me. When I was sick and dying, when I was in great trouble, I called on the Lord and he delivered me; so naturally I praise his name and trust in him.

How can I possibly repay God for all that he has done for me. At least I can publicly witness to my belief in God.

Precious in the sight of the Lord is the death of his saints.

I am your servant, Lord. I will pay my church pledge and in the presence of the people I will praise the name of the Lord.

Praise the Lord for his merciful kindness, praise him all the nations, for the fact of God is an eternal truth.

Give thanks to the Lord for he is good, let all Israel say that God's mercy endures forever. I called on the Lord in time of great distress and he came to my assistance.

It is a lot better to trust in God than to depend on man. Even though I become surrounded by a multitude of nations, yet I will trust in God.

The Lord is my strength and my song. I shall live and declare the works of the Lord, even though he punished me, he did it for my own good.

The very stone which the builders refused has become the head of the corner. This is the Lord's doing and it is marvelous to behold.

This is the day which the Lord has made, let us rejoice and be glad in it. Along with this good day, Lord, please send some instant prosperity.

The Lord is my God, and I will exalt his name. Give thanks to the Lord for he is good and his mercy endures forever.

Chap.
119

Blessed are those who walk in the ways of God. God has told us to obey his laws and I wish I could do this, then I would never be ashamed. I will keep trying, Lord, please don't forsake me.

How can a young fellow clean up his life? It's simple, just follow the word of God. Blessed are you, Lord, teach me your laws again and again. I really rejoice in your word, I meditate, and I will not forget your instructions.

Deal generously with me, Lord. Open my mind so that I can understand better your word. I need more information. I don't understand everything you do. People argue with me, but I still insist on advocating your way.

Help my understanding! I would like to be able to comprehend more of your ways so I could speak more fully in your behalf. Stay with me, Lord, even as I am staying with your regulations.

Give me a better understanding and it will be easier for me to keep your laws. I need to be influenced more to good and to enjoy good things more than I do. Protect me from conceit, and strengthen me in righteousness.

Be merciful to me, Lord, so that I may talk back to my enemies and demonstrate to them your support. I will enjoy your laws and I will tell other kings of you and your goodness.

My great comfort is the word of hope which you have given to me. I have been comforted by remembering your mighty acts of old, for I have plenty of enemies who talk constantly about how they despise me.

Have mercy on me, Lord. I have considered my plans and determined that I will follow your suggestions. The wicked have taken advantage of me, but I have clung to my faith. I try to associate with good people. I know that the whole earth is full of your mercy.

You have done well by me, Lord. Teach me more, though. I went astray, but I returned. You are good, and it was helpful to me to go bad and then reform. I would rather have possession of your law, O God, than to accumulate silver and gold.

I know your judgments are right. Let the proud be put to shame, but protect me from wandering from your law.

My soul sometimes begins to feel weak because your word seems scarce. I can't see clearly, and my mind becomes like a bottle of smoke. My problem is that I can't wait for you to punish my enemies.

Help me now, Lord. Show me your will clearly.

The faithfulness of God has been firmly established. This knowledge has pulled me through my troubles. I have seen that everything is perishable except your word.

I really enjoy your laws. I meditate on them all the time. Studying your commandments has made me wiser than my enemies, and I even know more now than most of the preachers. I even know more than the old-timers, for I am obeying the law of God.

How comforting are your words and they taste better than honey.

Your word is a lamp to my feet and a flashlight on my path. Please accept the praises of my lips. I am determined to obey your laws all my life.

I have grown to hate evil and to love good. Your word, Lord, is like a shield for me, or a hiding place. The Lord plans to put away all the wicked as if they were litter. It scares me to think of the power of God.

It is time to get with the program, though, Lord, for the wicked are getting mighty active and prosperous.

I love to read your word. It is hopeful, it gives light, it directs and teaches. I sometimes sit and cry because of all the wickedness that I see.

My enemies are getting right important, and I seem small and unimportant, but I still cling to your word.

I cried with my whole heart to God for help. I was so miserable and prayed so long that morning seemed as if it had been postponed. Hear my cry. The wicked are at work. Control them promptly, please.

My enemies are numerous. I know your mercy is great, O Lord, and I surely need some of it now. I know your word is true, and it really hurts to see these monkey heads making fun of you.

Great peace comes to those that love the Lord and observe his word. I keep such things fresh in my mind by having my devotionals seven times a day. Hear me now, Lord, and lend me a helping hand. I know I went astray, but I am back now in the fold.

In my trouble I called on the Lord and he heard me. Protect me now from the damage done by the lying lips of gossipmongers, help me. I am a man of peace, and yet all my advisers want me to declare war.

I lift up my eyes to the hills. From where does help come? My help comes from the Lord, who made heaven and earth.

He will not let you be knocked off balance, for He is a keeper that neither slumbers nor sleeps. God protects you, so that in the day the sun does not get you, nor will you get in trouble on a moonlight night,[1] but the Lord is able to preserve you, God will watch your going out and your coming in, from now on, and forever more.

I was delighted when they said it was time to go to church, particularly in Jerusalem. Jerusalem is a well built city and here the tribes of the Lord gather to give thanks to God. It is here that the thrones of Israel have been established.

Pray for the peace of Jerusalem. I pray that peace and prosperity may be found in Jerusalem, for the sake of the people, and because the great house of the Lord is in Jerusalem.

As the eyes of a servant looking toward the master, as a player to a coach,[2] as a girl to her hairdresser; so we look to God for instruction and help.

Have mercy on us, Lord, for we are fed up with seeing the proud, fat cats live at ease and scorn God.

If it had not been that the Lord was on our side, our enemies would have swallowed us. We would be desolate if it were not for the Lord. Blessed be the Lord who has enabled our souls to be free as a flying bird, for our help is in the name of the Lord, who made all things.

Those persons that trust in the Lord will become as stable as a mountain. The Lord surrounds those that trust him just as the hills surround and protect Jerusalem. God will prevent the good from being in the position of being forced into wickedness.

The Lord will guide those who turn aside from evil and peace shall finally come to Israel.

When the Lord freed us from captivity we became a people full of laughter and singing. We sang of the great deliverance and we praised the Lord for saving us.

---

[1]It ain't easy all the time   [2]Such as Lombardi

We are a happy people, for we went forth in sorrow and returned in great joy.

Except the Lord approve, those that build even a house are doing so in vain, and unless the Lord is keeping a city the watchman is wasting his time.

It is silly for a man to be so restless that he arises early and stays up late, for the Lord expects a person to sleep and to be free of worry.

A man with a family of kids is fortunate, for he is busy, and his children join in standing by him in time of need.

Blessed is everyone that really worships the Lord. Things will go well with such a man, he will enjoy eating, his wife will be a help to him and will produce children. A good man enjoys seeing his children grow and he particularly delights in his grandchildren.

Things have often gone hard for me, but the Lord has pulled me through my problems.

I would like to see all those that hate the people of God consumed by fire as if they were dry grass, and may they never receive the normal blessing of 'peace be with you,' or the like.

Out of the depths have I cried to the Lord. Listen, God, to my case. I know you believe in forgiveness or there would be none of us left. My soul waits for reassurance from God, even more anxiously than those who watch for the sunrise.

I am confident that the Lord will redeem all of Israel.

Lord, I do not think too highly of myself, nor do I aspire to accomplish things beyond my abilities or my opportunities. I am becoming very sensible. Let all the people of God see hope in the Lord.

Lord, remember David. He is the one who took an oath not to sleep or rest until there was a proper place for the ark of the covenant to dwell, a place which the Lord might consider home.

Bless the ark of the covenant, the church, and those who minister there. Remember your promise, Lord, to keep the throne of David intact, as long as the people worship you and obey your commandments.

God has chosen his people and his church. Jerusalem is the center. God has promised to clothe the ministers and priests with joy and to bless the people of the fellowship in the Lord.

The enemies of David will come to shame, but David shall prosper.

Chap.
133

How pleasant it is to be in a church where the people get along well together. It is like cool oil on hot, dry skin. It is refreshing as the morning dew on the mountain of the Lord.

Chap.
134

Bless the Lord all those that serve him, particularly those that guard the Lord's house. May the Lord bless you in return.

Chap.
135

Praise the Lord, for he is good. The Lord has chosen Jacob and Israel for his special attention and I know that the Lord is great and that he is the Lord of all.

When the Lord created the heavens and the earth, he did everything exactly as he wanted. God set up the clouds, the lightning, the rain, the wind and the fogs.

The mighty acts of God are historical facts. God smote the first-born in Egypt, he sent plagues, he smote many nations who opposed the advance of Israel.

The Lord will judge his people and will separate them from those that serve gods made of silver and gold, for these gods are useless, they have mouths and don't speak, eyes that don't see, and ears that don't hear.

Bless the Lord. Serve him all you who are descended from Aaron or Levi, or any who recognized and worshipped the Lord God of hosts. Praise ye the Lord.

Chap.
136

Give thanks to the Lord, for he is good, his mercy endures forever. It was the wisdom of God that caused the waters to be divided, that made the great lights of heaven, that delivered Israel, that opened the Red Sea, that overthrew Pharoah and overcame many kings.

God remembered us when we were down and out, he redeemed us from our enemies, and he fed us.[1]

Chap.
137

We sat down and cried by the rivers of Babylon, we hung our guitars on hickory limbs, for we had been carried away captives, and they made fun of us, daring us to sing our favorite hymns in a heathen land.

How can we sing the songs of home in a strange land? It's easy! It would be easier to forget that I had a right hand than to forget the good ole days.

If I ever forget the joys of Jerusalem I hope my tongue clings to the roof of my mouth.

Be sure and remember, O Lord, what the Gestapo[2] did to our families in Jerusalem, and so bless the man who wipes out the Gestapo and kills them dead.

---

[1]The Israelites were greatly interested in eating   [2]Edomites

I will praise the Lord with my whole heart. I will face the temple in Jerusalem and praise the loving-kindness of the Lord. All the kings of the earth shall finally praise the Lord.

Great is the glory of God, and even though the Lord is high and lifted up, yet he is greatly concerned with the lowly, and God spearates himself from the haughty.

Though I walk in the middle of trouble, the Lord will be with me, he will strike my enemies. Continue to do your mighty acts, O Lord, for you are a God of mercy.

O Lord, you have had a good look at me. You know when I get up and when I lie down. There is not a word I speak that you don't hear. You are everywhere.

Just to think this way is really too much for my feeble mind. Surely though there is no way for me to be apart from God.

If I ascend to the clouds, you are there, if I go into the depths of the earth, you are there, if I take the wings of the Continental[1] and dwell on some island, you are there to guide me, and if I think I can hide at night from you I am wrong, for you make light out of darkness.

I will praise the Lord, for I am intricately made. It is appalling to consider the human body.

Yet you knew all about the body before it was made, you had it on the drawing board before man came into being.

How impressive it is to think thoughts, yet they come so much that they cannot be numbered.

One thing again, Lord. Surely you are going to get rid of the wicked. I want you to know that I'm against anybody that is against you.

Search me, Lord, try me, examine my thoughts and see if there is any wickedness in me at all,[2] then lead me in the way everlasting.

O Lord, deliver me from evil and violent people. There are too many people with sharp tongues who are always trying to stir up some strife, particularly against me.

I have publicly declared the Lord to be my God, strengthen me then in my time of need and protect me in the day of battle.

As for my enemies, it will suit me fine if their heads become exposed, if you send burning stones to whack them, let some of them be thrown in the fire and others in deep pits.[3] Surely the Lord will support the righteous and stand behind the afflicted.

Lord, hear my prayer. Protect me from saying some of the bad

---

[1]Golden-tailed bird   [2]I'm not quite as ready as David for this
[3]David disapproved of violence?

things I think. Don't let me be influenced by evil thoughts, and don't let me fall for the sins of the flesh.

If anybody is to correct me, let it be a righteous man who corrects with graciousness and is not offensive.

Constantly I look to the Lord for help, please save me from the daily snares of the wicked. Let the wicked fall in their own nets and let me escape.

Chap.
142

I cried to the Lord and I complained about my troubles. In the first place, I am deserted. No one seems to care for me. I have no men rallying to my cause. Naturally I cried to the Lord for the Lord is my refuge.

I am really down and my spirit is at a low ebb. Encourage me, Lord, bring my feelings out of the prison-like despair I feel, and then I can enthusiastically praise the Lord.

Chap.
143

Hear my prayer, O Lord. My enemies have laid me low. I am depressed and deserted.

I remember the good ole days, and I think back on the times of your mighty acts. Stimulate me, Lord, so that I will no longer think I am dying.

Reveal to me a new attitude so that I may start the day with freshness and vigor.

Destroy my enemies and raise my spirits for I am your servant, Lord.

Chap.
144

I will praise the name of the Lord every day forever and forever. Great is the Lord and greatly to be praised.

One generation shall pass along the information to the next generation concerning the mighty acts of God.

Really, what is man that you should pay any attention to him? Certainly he is just like a shadow that passes.

Get with the action again, Lord. Cause earthquakes, volcanoes, or floods and deal harshly with the wicked.

Then I will originate a new ballad and it will be like a hymn to be sung to the glory of God, for the Lord is good and his tender mercies endure forever.

Chap.
145

All the works of the Lord testify to his glory and his saints add their praises, for they tell of the power of God's kingdom, they speak of the mighty acts of God, and they proclaim that your kingdom is an everlasting kingdom and that it will endure through all generations.

The Lord supports the weak and looks out for the disabled. The Lord is righteous and opens his hand to make all the provisions of the world.

The Lord is near to all those that call upon his name and the Lord makes the life of the believer a full life.

The Lord will save those that love him and he will destroy those that don't.

My mouth will always praise the Lord, and may all people bless his holy name.

Chap.
146

Put not your trust in leaders[1] for they are not dependable, they are also short-lived as other people are; so trust God. In trusting the Lord there is happiness.

The Lord is the creator of all things, he controls all things, he releases the prisoner, and provides food for the hungry. God is a great humanitarian.

The Lord shall reign forever and forever. Praise ye the Lord.

Chap.
147

It is good as well as pleasant to sing praises to the Lord. God has gathered together the outcasts of Israel, he has healed the broken-hearted, he has relieved the wounded.

Great is the Lord. God even knows the names of the stars,[2] his power is great; so sing to the Lord.

Be thankful to the Lord for he is the one in charge of the rain,[3] he also causes the grass to grow on the hillsides, he feeds the birds and the animals.

God, however, is not particularly interested in track meets.[4] Praise ye the Lord.

Praise the Lord, for he is a strength to his people, he is a peacemaker, he issues orders to man and nature, he sends snow, and he sends freezing, icy days, and then he eases all this in the spring, and the snows melt and the waters flow.

God has revealed his truth to his people, and only to those that seek him. Praise ye the Lord.

Chap.
148

Praise the Lord. Praise him all the angels, praise him all the people, let the whole earth praise the Lord.

Fire, hail, snow, dragons, golfers, winds, mountains, valleys, beasts, cattle, birds, kings of the earth, disc jockeys, anchor men, pretty girls, let them all praise the Lord for his name is excellent and his glory above heaven and earth. Praise ye the Lord.

Chap.
149

Let all Israel rejoice. Let all those that worship God rejoice. Sing to the Lord.

Let the people dance[5] and sing before the Lord, praise God

---

[1] You can say that again   [2] Even the ones in Hollywood
[3] El Paso, Las Vegas, Oklahoma City
[4] That's what the Bible says!   [5] You mean in church?

with musical instruments,[1] and understand that God enjoys his people.

Let the believers rejoice and sing, even on cold, dark nights, for the Lord will punish the enemies of God, their kings shall be cast down, and the saints will be honored.[2] Praise ye the Lord.

Chap.
150

Praise ye the Lord. Praise him in the church, praise him in the great outdoors, praise him for his mighty acts, praise him with the trumpet, with the guitar, with castanets, with dancing, praise him with great orchestras, let everything that has breath praise the Lord. Praise ye the Lord!

[1]Even the saxophone?   [2]Maybe some day in New Orleans

PROVERBS

Solomon, the son of David and the wise king of Israel, composed and collected a series of proverbs or thoughts for the day and even a few bumper sticker sayings. Here they are.

To become truly wise, so that even justice is clear, to adhere to fairness, to treat all men with equity, to be wise enough to teach young people, to be open-minded, to be able to distinguish between good and poor advice, and to clearly understand wise comment, a person must first stand in awe of the Almighty God. Fools disregard this.

Young people, listen to your fathers and mothers, for much of what they have to tell you is good.

Don't let evil doers snare you into joining them. If they tell you that they know any easy way to get a few fast bucks by taking advantage of someone, do not join them. Leave them entirely alone.

These types are always ready to shed blood, they are greedy, and finally the very net they spread catches them.

Wisdom and good sense often have no listeners and good words are often lost in street sounds.

God has offered wisdom, and those who refuse to take it will call in vain upon the Lord when calamity comes. It will be real terror to finally call on the Lord and hear nothing. Do not refuse to worship God and respect Him, or you will be left to yourself when trouble comes.

The work of fools and of evil men is self-defeating, but those who seek the Lord and call on his name shall find a real security.

People, if you will listen to God's word and meditate on his commandments, and truly seek to learn that which is right, so that you seek goodness as if you were searching for silver or gold, then you will begin to understand God and find a comfortable place in his presence.

The Lord grants real wisdom to those who seek him. God gives these people a very genuine type of protection.

As a person grows in wisdom, then understanding becomes pleasant, and discretion enters into a person's life, and a person begins to learn how to refrain from evil associations.

The judgments of the person seeking righteousness will cause him to depart from evil associations, to be leery of wild women, particularly one that flirts and flatters. Following such is a sure path to death.

Eventually the righteous will gradually begin to prosper and evil persons will be deprived of eternal life, and their pleasures will only be short-lived and transient.

Observe the law. This will result in a full life, and not one full of miserable worries.

Let mercy and truth be a definite part of your character, and you will be respected by both man and God.

Trust in the Lord. Do not let your own judgment oppose the law of God.

Do not think of yourself as being wise, but acknowledge that wisdom is of God.

Be generous and honor the Lord with your willingness to give, giving from whatever you first earn, not waiting to merely give what is left over. The Lord will look out for you.

Don't get upset when God teaches you by means of trouble. This just means that God is interested in you.

Happiness is really only finding wisdom through complete trust in God. This is a better possession than silver and gold, it is more precious than rubies, and more to be desired than anything.

Wisdom found in trusting the Lord means peace and happiness, a sense of fullness of life.

It was the wisdom of God that founded the earth. God in his wisdom created the heavens, the clouds, the dew. Don't forget that.

The only safe way to walk in this life is in the full trusting of God.

When you have a chance to do good, don't hold back or wait. Don't tell a neighbor that you'll help him later when it is more convenient.

Don't be quarrelsome.

Don't envy bullies, even though they may seem successful. The blessing of God is with the righteous, and God's curse is with the wicked.

God has no use for snobs, but he blesses the humble; God gives eventual glory to those who praise the Lord but shame shall come to the fools.

Chap.
4

Now listen to the good advice of an experienced father. I will tell it to you like it is. I learned these things from my father and my mother, and they were successful people.

Seek to understand life. Learn the truth of life, stick with the truth and the truth will stick with you.

Understanding is the key. Get wisdom, of course, but with it get understanding, a knowledge of how to apply wisdom.

If you observe the above, you will find life to be full and honorable.

Walk the straight and narrow. Continue to learn, never stop pursuing knowledge. Don't run around with goof-offs. All they do is live on trouble and they will involve you in it.

The path of the righteous is clear and bright, but the wicked are always stumbling around in the dark.

Don't fall for every pretty face. Avoid carefully the company of girls that kiss anybody anytime. Don't be a constant girl watcher. Keep your eyes on the road, particularly when you're driving.

In the search for wisdom you will find discretion. Stay clear of wild women. They look good and talk mighty cozy, but an evil woman will lead you to death and hell.

Listen, young people, don't gravitate to scoundrels. They merely seem attractive. If you defile yourself with wicked companions you will wind up sick and you will begin to degenerate.

Drink your own water that you know is safe. Don't have children by other women, but be faithful to your chosen wife. Why do you think you need to go to some woman other than your wife? The Lord keeps up with you, anyway. Those who wander from God's ways will be punished.

Don't go around endorsing just anybody's note. Be responsible for your own credit. Look at the ant. There's a good example. Each ant does its own work and is responsible for its own share of the common load.

Do you think you can get somewhere just sitting on your can? Get to work!

Have you noticed what a wicked man is like? He lies all the time, he uses signals in playing bridge, he cheats at poker, he starts arguments, and he will suddenly come apart all at once.

There are seven things that the Lord doesn't want to see. A man who is a snob, or a liar, a murderer, a crook who plans his sneaky crimes, a fellow who enjoys doing bad things, or a perjurer, or one who is always creating discord.

Son, follow the teachings of your father and mother and you will find these teachings a great comfort and a helpful companion.

The commandments of God are a lamp, and the law of God sheds light.

I seem to be harping on this, but please, son, stay away from prostitutes and loose women. There is nothing but trouble here.[1]

Actually a whore will just gradually get all your money and if you are cheating with another man's wife you just might get killed. It isn't worth it!

People will be right understanding of a thief who steals to keep from starving, but even in this case the fine is usually enough to bring starvation.

The man who commits adultery is really a fool. When the husband learns and seeks vengeance there will be no way of paying

---

[1]Solomon had 1,000 wives and concubines so he was speaking from experience, I guess.

him off.[1]

Study the commandments. Learn them so well that they are
constantly at your fingertips. Think of righteousness as your sister.
Be daily acquainted with her.

Let me tell you about something I saw. I was looking out the
window and I saw a fine young man, full of life, walking down the
sidewalk. It was just about dark and I saw a pretty woman move
toward him. She was dressed with a low neck blouse and a split-skirt.
The man should have run!

The woman smiled and said, "How fortunate! I am delighted to
find you."

"Thank you, Ma'm," he said.

"I am celebrating, and I'm so glad you are here," she said as she
pressed against him and kissed him.

"Come to my house," she continued. "My husband has left
town with a bundle of money and I know he won't be back for a few
days. I need a man very much, and you are just the one."

"I don't know if I should do that," said the fellow.

"Come on. I have put on clean sheets, and even perfumed the
room. It will be an experience you can't forget! We can spend the
whole night in great pleasure."

As a result, the man went with her, just as a steer heads for the
butcher, or a bird to a snare.

Please, kids, don't fall for that way of life. It just isn't the fun it
sounds to be. Lots of good, strong men have been reduced to nothing
this very same way. If you want to find hell on earth, then that
woman's house is the door to it.

Wisdom, which is really righteousness, is to be seen everywhere
if you would look for it. Actually, it is just commonsense.

Listen to the truth. Wickedness just doesn't make sense. Learn
the truth. It is better than getting silver or gold, in fact there is
nothing to be compared to wisdom.

Wisdom encompasses good judgment. One way of showing
wisdom is to stand in awe of God and to hate evil. Wisdom gives
strength to kings and enables judges to make fair decisions. An
interesting thing about righteousness is that those that seek
righteousness find her.

A search for righteousness makes one rich in a sound and
enduring fashion, as wisdom enables a person to grow in stability and
strength.

Wisdom was in the beginning a part of God. Before fountains or
mountains, before the earth existed, wisdom was present. Wisdom

[1]Solomon really must have had plenty of girl trouble.

was there when God laid out the plans for heaven and earth, when God established the clouds, defined the sea, and when God created the earth. Wisdom joined in the pleasure of the creation of man.

Blessed are those who follow the words of wisdom. Blessed is the man who hears God's word and observes the teachings. The person who finds wisdom and righteousness finds God, and God blesses them, but those that despise the word and hate God shall only find death.

Chap. 9

Wisdom is a well established fact. Wisdom has its own attraction, it has its banquet scene, its delights, it has some good girls working for it. They call to the uninformed and invite them to become righteous, the good girls would have men set aside their foolishness.

There are some interesting observations in life. If you explain something to a phony, he gets irritated, but a wise man will thank you for the instruction. This is how a wise man becomes wiser.

Respect of God is the beginning of wisdom and the appreciation of holy matters is the start of understanding.

Wisdom is self rewarding and if you make light of wisdom or disdain it, then it is your loss.

It is not hard to tell a bad girl. She is usually loud and pushy, she approaches men, some of whom are busy attending to business. She says such things as "stolen fruits taste sweeter, or stolen drinks are more enjoyable." Then she entices the men to follow her. What she fails to tell them is that those who have previously heeded her are already halfway to hell, at least on earth.

Chap. 10

A righteous son brings great happiness to his parents, but a wicked son is a heavy burden to bear.

The treasures of the wicked disappear at death, but the righteous take their treasures with them.

The Lord will always be concerned with the righteous, but the wicked can't count on his help.

A lazy man gets a poor return for he doesn't work, but a hard working man gains in life.

A wise man is alert to his opportunities and is not a victim of procrastination.

A just person is generally respected but a wicked man is very apt to get socked in the teeth.

The memory of a just man is very lasting, but the wicked are forgotten in short order.

A wise man will listen, while a fool prattles all the time.

An unright person can walk with confidence, but the wicked are always looking around nervously.

It is worthwhile listening to a righteous man, but it is a waste of time to listen to the wicked.

Hate causes trouble, while love smooths over anything.

A righteous man begins to accumulate wisdom, while a wicked person just gets lashes on the back or his credit card destroyed.

Sometimes the only thing a rich man has is his wealth, and sometimes riches is the only thing a poor man lacks.

A righteous working man has a full life, while all the wicked can do is pile up their sins.

A man is a fool who tries to deceive people and to hide his true feelings.

Beware of talking too much. With a lot of talk you are bound to say some of the wrong things.

The words of a good man are really worthwhile, but the words of the foolish are cheap and easy to come by.

God's blessing is a rich thing to receive and he doesn't add a penalty either.

Mischief is funny to a fool, but a wise man doesn't participate.

Fear usually catches up with a wicked man, while the righteous man usually has his hopes fulfilled.

The wicked will disappear as if blown away by the wind, but the righteous have eternal life.

A man who employs a loafer feels just as if he took a swig of vinegar and put his teeth on edge, or as if he got smoke in his eyes.

Respect for God gives life fullness, but the wicked are always running out of time.

The righteous man can look forward hopefully and gladly, while the wicked must know that only death awaits them.

The Lord will support the upright, but not the wicked. Eventually, the righteous shall prevail, and the wicked shall no longer have the use of the earth.

The word of the just is permanent, but wicked sayings will eventually all perish.

The upright man speaks good things, but the wicked are all negative and only criticize.

Chap.
11

Lack of fairness is greatly irritating to the Lord. God expects a person to give full value for what is received.

A man who begins to think he is self made or a great personal achiever is headed for trouble. The Lord blesses those who are humble.

The integrity of the honest man is a safe road to travel but cheaters have a pitfall awaiting them.

When the day of judgment comes it will be righteousness, not material possessions, that will be the pay load.

Righteousness provides a plain path but the wicked have to travel at great risk.

When a wicked man dies, he's a goner, but the righteous man continues to live.

A hypocrite attempts to destroy with his mouth, but the just man can survive underserved criticism.

A community enjoys two things, the success of a good man and the death of a bad one.

A fellow who doesn't know about life jumps to conclusions about his neighbors, but a smart fellow does not form snap opinions.

A good man keeps a secret, but a talebearer can't stop running off at the mouth.

A community that has no one living there to advise people is in bad shape. In fact, the counsel of many good men is better than the counsel of one.

A man who endorses notes for people he doesn't know is nutty, and he will suffer for it.

A gracious woman is honored and so is a man who knows how to handle financial matters.

A man full of mercy is always improving but a cruel man gets worse, and finally hurts himself.

Wicked men practice deceit, but righteousness brings its own reward.

The Lord doesn't care for a brassy person, but God delights in the upright citizen.

Even though the wicked organize into the Mafia, they will still be punished, but even the children of the righteous will receive a blessing.

A beautiful woman who is well behaved is like a precious gem.

Righteous people have good intentions, but the wicked are always planning trouble.

It is possible to be a giver and be better off after being generous; while a money grubber becomes poor because he thinks of himself as being poor.

People appreciate the person who makes his crops and goods available at a fair price, but the people learn to despise those that hold their goods for a price rise.[1]

A diligent person that looks for the good finds it, but the mischief maker gets caught in his own mischief.

A foolish man is always rationalizing in his own behalf, but a person who listens and learns becomes wise.

A fool blows his top while a wise man keeps his cool.

A wise person speaks and brings comfort while a fool injures with his big mouth.

Joy is the reward of the peace maker, but deceit accompanies the mischief minded.

---

[1] Pretty modern talk

A foolish man vainly displays his foolishness, but a wise man does not try to make a show of his knowledge.

A lazy man has to depend on someone else for his food, but not so with the diligent person.

There is no death along the road of righteousness, for it leads to eternal life.

Chap. 13

It is smart to listen to the advice of those of experience.

Control of the tongue is a mighty accomplishment.

A good man has no use for falsehoods, but the fool doesn't care.

It is possible to be rich in worldly goods and have nothing, and it is possible to be broke and have plenty.

A poor man never has to worry much about being kidnapped.

False pride creates controversy.

Wealth acquired improperly usually disappears, but riches secured by hard work will stick with a person.

Life rewards those who observe the commandments of God, and the respect for such laws is refreshing.

A sensible man plans ahead while a fool admits he doesn't care.

A reliable messenger is of great value for clear communciation is a real problem.[1]

A person that isn't interested in learning is headed for poverty and shame.

Everyone enjoys seeing plans work, but a fool continues with his plans even when it is obvious they are no good.

A wise man finds wise companions while a bunch of fools are usually seen heading for destruction together.

Righteous people are blessed, while wicked men are cursed.

Grandchildren profit from the inheritance of a righteous man, but the government usually takes all that a sinner leaves.

Injustice often prevents the poor from making a good living.

If a man loves his son he will correct him and not spoil him rotten.

A fool seems to live just to eat, while a wise man eats to live.

Chap. 14

A wise woman tries to make a home, while a foolish one is indifferent.

It is easy to keep an empty stable clean, but if you have no cattle you're a poor rancher.

A good witness tells the truth and a poor one lies.[2]

An interested learner has no problem while the smart alec finds wisdom elusive.

[1]You certainly can't count on tapes
[2]Lots of recent information on this

There is not much point in hanging around a foolish and deceitful person.

Fools make light of sin, but the wise think this is a serious matter.

Joy and sorrow can only be measured by the person concerned.

There are some things that seem pretty good to a person, but the end result is disaster.

You can cover sorrow or disappointment with laughter, but the sorrow is still there when the laughing ends.

The careless man becomes bored, but the righteous man sees a purpose in life.

A wise man doesn't believe everything he reads or sees.

A bright person is truly afraid of evil, but a nut thinks he can cover evil with rage and cursing.

A person with a short fuse is always getting into trouble.

Foolish people are called goofy while a wise man is respected.

People are more inclined to be friendly to the rich than to the poor, but blessings on those who do try to help the poor.

Mercy and truth are the companions of good people.

Work is a good thing, but just talking about it won't help.

Standing in awe of God creates strength and God offers protection to such persons and to their children.

A king measures his success by the number of people he rules.

It is wise to be slow to anger but a hasty temper invites trouble.

Envy will get you nowhere.

To the wicked the trip to the cemetery is the last ride, but to the righteous it is a road to a new life.

Righteousness is elevating to a nation, but sin drags a country downhill.[1]

A person who takes advantage of the poor is attacking God, so we should support those who show mercy and concern.

A ruler appreciates good help and doesn't care for lazy people.

Chap. 15

A calm answer cools wrath, but a haughty spirit makes things worse.

A wise person knows when to speak and what to say, while a fool is a pop-off.

God is always watching!

A righteous man is rich in peace while a wicked man accumulates trouble.

The Lord despises the attempts of the wicked to buy him off, but the Lord appreciates the worshipful gifts of the good people.

A person who will not accept constructive criticism is doomed.

God knows all about heaven and hell, how can you think he

[1] Our crisis is not energy, but sin

doesn't know what goes on inside of you?

You can always spot a scornful person as he thinks he knows it all.

A happy person has his happiness reflected in his face.

It is better to be poor and love God than to be rich and headed for hell.

It is better to eat squash with a heart full of love than to eat sirloin steak with a mind full of hate.

A wise son makes his parents happy but a foolish one is a source of sadness.

An indifferent person has a thorny life while an upright man walks in a plain path.

Silly things are fun to a silly person.

It is wise to listen to the advice of more than one person.

How helpful it is to say the right thing at the right time.

The anti-godly are in trouble with God, but a righteous widow has a real good thing going for her.

Greed brings trouble.

A wise man thinks before he speaks, but the fool never waits.

The fool hasn't much chance in prayer for he is wicked, but the righteous are in communication with God instantly.

Everybody enjoys seeing beauty and hearing nice things.

The first step toward wisdom is respect for God, and humility is the first step toward success.

Chap.
16

God is responsible for the outcome of everything, even though we may do the planning.

Most people can justify anything they do, but the Lord decides on the basis of intent; therefore a person should commit his life to God.

God is in charge of everything and everybody.

It won't do the wicked any good to get organized against God.

The best way to avoid evil is to think constantly of God.

When God is pleased with a person, the Lord even causes his enemies to think well of him.

When we make plans we should ask for God's guidance, and rulers would do well to do this particularly, for a ruler can only be fair with God's help.

A ruler can get good help from truthful aides.

A wise man will help calm down a king, for a king can cause a whole lot of trouble.[1]

It is better to become wise than rich.

You are better off to be sweating it out with the poor than sitting around dividing profits with evil rich people.

---

[1] Somebody needed to calm down Henry VIII for sure

Righteousness is like a fresh water fountain in a man's life, but evil makes a man stagnant.

An ungodly man is always digging up trouble and starting dissension, spreading gossip, taking advantage of his neighbor. Such a man sits around thinking up bad things to do.

A good, honest old man with white hair is worth much — listen to him.

If a person has learned to control himself he is more successful than a man who has control of a government.

Man can take all the chances he wants, but God is in charge of everything and doesn't leave anything to chance.

Chap.
17

It is better to have a poor meal in peace than a seven course dinner during a big argument.

A wise servant should take advantage of his bosses' sons if the sons are no good.

You can purify silver and gold with fire but only God can purify the heart.

Wicked people and liars enjoy dirty jokes and malicious gossip.

God punishes those who laugh at other people's misfortunes.

A father glories in his children but the grandfather enjoys them the most.[1]

It is not proper for a leader of men to be untruthful and so you rarely find a fool talking straight.

A bribe often works, but it is a shame.

Nobody likes to be nagged.

Correcting a wise man once is better than whipping a fool a hundred times.

An evil plotter is always stirring up rebellion, and eventually it gets stirred up against him.

You are better off encountering a mad she bear with cubs than a fool on a binge.

A person who repays kindness with malice gets to keep the malice for a long time.

Starting trouble is like opening a watergate; so be careful when you start.[2]

The Lord has no use for those who justify the wicked or condemn the innocent.[3]

It is a waste for a student to pay to go to school who has no intention of learning.[4]

A good friend will stand by you anytime and a brother is usually ready to help in time of trouble.

---

[1] I thought I was the only one who knew this
[2] Once is enough   [3] Watch out, lawyers!
[4] I was never much on compulsory education

A troublemaker is usually boastful and looking for trouble.

The father of a fool has a hard life.

A joyful attitude is real good medicine, while a gloomy spirit makes your bones ache.

It is bad to offer bribes.

A fool is always seeking some weird and far away goal while the sensible man has a good purpose in life.

It is not good to punish the just, and it is wrong for those in authority to ask for kick-backs.[1]

A knowledgeable man rarely runs loose at the mouth and so often a fool with his mouth shut is mistaken for the wise.

Chap.
18

A self-centered person twists everything around to suit himself.

Along with wickedness you will find indecency and contempt as companions.

The words of a man's mouth usually reflect the depth of his thinking.

A fool is always arguing, and if he is a golfer he always wants you to give him strokes.

The words of a gossip are malicious and deeply harmful.

A goof-off and a spendthrift are closely kin.

A righteous man receives strength in the safety and sureness of the name of the Lord.

Often a rich man uses his wealth to separate him from life and to build conceit.

There is no use talking to a man who has a closed mind.

When a man loses his courage he is reduced to nothing.

Proper use of a man's talent will often bring him into important circles.

Hearing only one side of a story is not enough, for one must hear both sides to be fair.

Often a touchy argument can be settled by the toss of a coin.

When you offend someone in your own family the damage is extremely hard to repair.

Being able to give good advice is as much fun as eating.

The tongue can really get you in trouble, especially when you say the wrong thing at the wrong time.

Finding a good wife is a real blessing.

Often when the poor seek help the well-to-do offend them and refuse.

There is no one any better for a person than a real good friend.

Chap.
19

It is better to be poor but honest, than to be affluent and a fool.

[1]Somebody should have read this in 1973

Being intentionally stupid is not an asset. It is also wrong to blame everything on God.

Wealth brings easy friends, while the poor aren't so popular.

Fasle witnesses and liars get theirs some day!

A ruler or a rich man are always being approached for favors or money. The poor man is neglected, even by his own friends.

If a person searches for the good it will be found.

It strikes me as being a shame when I see a fool as a ruler or an incompetent person head of a business.

A good man overlooks a lot of other people's faults.

When the king is angry he can cause terrible trouble, but when he likes a person he can make life easy for that one.

A foolish son and a nagging wife is about the worst thing that can happen to a man.

A man might inherit a house and a rich business, but if he gets a good wife he can thank the Lord.

Laziness is a real drag.

Keeping the commandments is the same as preserving one's soul.

When a person gives to the poor he is giving to the Lord.

Correct your son while he is young enough to be impressed.

A fellow with a hot temper is going to have a hectic life.

There are all kinds of thoughts in the mind of man, but attempt to discover which is of God.

Kindness should be instilled in everyone. Respect God and live.

A real lazy person is one that won't even feed himself.

A son who teases his mother and wastes his daddy's money is no good.

An ungodly witness doesn't care at all about justice.

Fools and scoffers are either criticized or given a beating.

Chap.
20

Wine and liquor lead to false courage and brawls and it is nutty to be mastered by strong drink.

It doesn't pay to make a king mad.

It is honorable to avoid strife.

A lazy man won't plow when it's cold and so he will go hungry.

It is unusual to find a truly faithful man, though there are plenty that say they are.

A good man is an asset and his children are fortunate.

A judge should consider all the evidence before rendering a decision.

No person can claim to be sinless.

The Lord doesn't care for any type of unfairness.

Even a child knows right from wrong and should be held accountable.

God made the ears and the eyes; so listen and look for the good things of God.

Don't sleep your life away. Get with it, boy!

A buyer acts as if he were getting gyped then brags to his friends about his bargain.

The words of wisdom are more precious than rubies and fine gems.

Again, don't make loans to strangers.

Deceiving a person may be fun at the time, but it won't work for happiness.

Don't declare war just on your own opinion.[1]

Be careful not to associate with a gossip.

Persons who turn against their parents will live in a dark world.

Inheriting a batch of money is no good unless you go to work with it.

Let the Lord punish the wicked, don't take it into your own hands.

A good ruler works against the wicked.

God's spirit is like a flashlight in a man, illuminating the reality of his life.[2]

A fair and merciful ruler is apt to last a long time.

Young men enjoy the strength of youth and old men have to be content with gray hair.

Effective punishment will often get rid of evil.

Chap.
21

The Lord directs the thoughts of leaders just as easily as water is used for irrigation.

God would prefer that a man be just and merciful than that he just make a big pledge to the church.[3]

A conceited attitude is a sin.

Hard, steady work is more productive than overnight speculation.

Ill-gotten gains will finally make you sick.

Crooks robbing crooks is a laugh, as it goes unreported.

A man is better off living alone in a tiny closet than living in a mansion with a talkative woman.

A good man learns a lot from watching the wicked catch it in the neck.

A person who will not listen to the pleas of the poor will some day find his own requests unnoticed.

Nothing calms and pacifies like sending someone a nice gift.

The wicked like to destroy and the righteous enjoy building.

---

[1] At least ask Congress   [2] That's a conscience
[3] It's the ones who do neither that are irksome.

A man who loves only pleasure, wine, and sauna baths won't last very long.

A fellow is better off living in the desert alone than in a fine palace with a contentious and angry female.[1]

A wise man doesn't spend everything he has at once.

The pursuit of righteousness results in the finding of life and honor.

Wisdom conquers anything.

A false witness must perish.

There is nothing that works successfully against God. It doesn't matter how prepared a person may be, God is still in charge of everything.

Chap.
22

A good reputation is rather to be chosen than great riches, and loving friends are better than silver or gold.

The rich and the poor have one thing in common; God made them all.

A smart fellow sees evil coming and gets out of the way.

The combination of humility and respect for God results in a man being rich in every way.

Train a child properly and when he is grown he will remember it.

The rich rule over the poor and the lender over the borrowers.[2]

An evil person becomes vain, and then he gets it.

Giving bountifully is a wonderful blessing to a person.

Rulers are always seeking the support of upright men.

The pessimist thinks that every time a circus comes to town he will be eaten by a lion.

A fellow who falls for the enticement of a wicked woman has just jumped over a cliff.

Kids are at times very foolish, but wise use of the paddle will straighten these things pretty quick.

Trust in the Lord, that is the secret to life.

Don't take advantage of the poor or the handicapped, for the Lord is especially interested in them.

There is no point in joining an angry man for fear you too will get angry.

Don't loan your money foolishly.

Leave the historical markers alone.

Do you know a real hard-working, honest man? Watch him. You will find around him the best people.

Chap.
23

If a rich man invites you to a special dinner don't eat like fury

---

[1]I keep remembering that Solomon had 1,000 wives and concubines
[2]Sad, but true

or believe everything he tells you. Surely he wants something from you.

Don't work just to get rich. Riches can easily disappear. Don't set riches up as a goal in life.

If evil men will offer you opportunities, turn them down. It is all a snare.

A man is no better than he thinks in his heart.

Don't waste a lot of wise advice on a fool with his ears closed.

Don't take advantage of orphans or others who have no protection. God is back of these people as a father.

It won't hurt to whip a child as a correction. A little whipping won't kill them, and it might save them.

Try not to envy sinners. They aren't as happy as they try to appear.

Don't be a heavy drinker or a glutton.

Don't rob the poor, or demand money for your advice from people who can't pay.

Stay away from prostitutes. They just wait for one unfaithful husband after another. They take your money and your soul.

Do you know what happens when you drink a lot of intoxicants? Well, you get red eyes, a babbling mouth, you become depressed, and you think the world has turned agaisnt you. I tell you, intoxicants are just like a snake bite.

When you've been drinking you get the notion to chase women, and you finally find yourself worn out, with a hangover and sick at the stomach. Phooey on that!

Chap.
24

Don't be envious of the evil ones. They really have nothing, while a wise and righteous man grows in strength and honor.

People who are always working up something bad get the reputation of being mischief makers.

You are not very strong if you let little setbacks discourage you.

If you have a chance to stand up for the innocent, don't keep quiet. There are no excuses for holding back.

Wisdom does the same thing for your person that honey does for your body; it gives strength and sweetness.

Evil men are always causing trouble for the righteous, but the good men can take it and bounce back.

Don't be pleased with the misfortunes of anyone. Never say happily, "Well, I see he got his."

My son, respect God and the law, and don't be an obstacle to those who would encourage change. No one is wise enough to know everything.

It is wrong to whitewash the wicked, but rebuke sin openly. People like straigthforward statements.

One day I passed by the field of a lazy farmer and I saw the weeds and the careless maintenance. I learned a lesson. If you sleep too much and work too little your possessions will begin to disintegrate.

Some of the graduate students in the days when Hez was king copied down some of the proberbs of Solomon. Here they are.

God can keep as many secrets as he wishes, but a ruler should keep the people informed. You can't possibly know all the king knows, either. Finding out things is the king's business.

If you can get rid of the defective men working close to the king you will do for the kingdom what is done for silver when the dross is burned away.

Don't force yourself on important people. Let them ask for you.

Don't jump into a controversy without full knowledge. After learning all about a matter you may be able to offer some helpful advice.

A wise advisor is like a golden ear ring to a good listener.

A faithful messenger who tells it like it is arrives as refreshing as a brief snow storm on some hot laborers in a wheat field.

A person who claims to be able to do something he can't do is like a cloud that doesn't produce rain.

If you find an enjoyable pleasure don't over-use it or it will finally be tiring and make you sick.

Don't pester your neighbor. He can easily get enough of you.

A man who tells lies about his neighbors is worse than a swordsman gone berserk.

Trusting a man who is not dependable is like eating peanut brittle on a broken tooth or trying to race with a leg out of joint.

Singing giddy songs to a person stricken with grief is wrong, it is worse than snatching an old man's coat in the winter or putting vinegar on vanilla ice cream.

If your enemy is hungry give him food and if he is thirsty give him something to drink, for this will get to him, and the Lord will in time reward you.[1]

A sharp reply is as sure to cause anger as a north wind drives away rain.

Good news to people living in seclusion in the country is better than fresh water.

When a good man joins an evil outfit it is like a clear stream getting muddy.

Living to obtain glory for yourself won't work.

A man who has not learned self-control is like a city that has no walls and a crooked city council.

[1]Christ quotes this

Fools are no more associated with honor than snow with summer or rain with winter.

There is a reason for everything, for the bird migrating, the swallow flying, and the salmon going upstream.

A whip for the horse, a bridle for the donkey, and a paddle for the fool's tail all have the same purpose.

There is no point in arguing with a butt-headed fool.

There is no profit in trying to send messages through a foolish messenger.

A parable is no more help to a fool than bad legs to a crippled man.

If you honor a fool, you are just loading his gun and he'll soon shoot somebody.

Explaining something to a fool through a parable is as useless as sticking a thorn in a man dead drunk.

God will handle all the rewards and punishments.

The only thing worse than a fool is a man wise in his own conceit.

A real lazy man doesn't even turn over in bed very fast and he hates to feed himself, and yet he thinks he knows it all.

It is as foolish to stick your nose in other people's business as it is to grab a strange dog by the ears.

A man caught in a lie who says he was just teasing is as dangerous as a fellow on the loose with knives and guns.

When there is no one around to gossip, strife ceases just as a fire goes out when the wood is gone.

Pretty words are able to cover a wicked heart just like porcelain on a jar.

Beware of the man who speaks with the forked tongue. He is two-faced.

People who are always trying to trap others will eventually get trapped, and a person who throws stones is surely going to get hit.

Flattery is a wicked device and helps make a phony world.

Don't boast about all you are going to do. Let someone else praise you, don't push yourself.

A rebel is harder to carry around than sand or stone and envy is as difficult to confront as wrath and anger.

Open rebuke is sometimes better than secret love.

It is better to be wounded by a well intentioned friend than praised by a devious thinking enemy.

The hungrier a man is the less choosy he is about what he wants to eat.

A wandering man is like a bird lost from the nest.

A good friend makes life sweet, just as perfume helps a room.

In time of trouble it is better to seek help that is close at hand from friends of your own or friends of the family, than try to go to a brother in a distant land.

Don't wake your neighbor at daybreak yelling "Good morning." He won't like it!

A contentious woman and a droopy, gloomy day are just alike. Stopping a complaining woman is like trying to pick up something with oily hands, or blowing back against the wind.

A good worker is rewarded and blesses his employer.

A man can look at his heart just as he can view his reflection in a mirror.

Man is always looking for something new.

A fool is hard to cure.

Keep up with what you have and use it. There is no telling how long you'll live or how long you'll own the ranch. If you are careful, you will have enough food to eat, clothing for your family, and a place to live. Just don't think this will necessarily always be the case.

Chap. 28

A wicked man jumps and runs at every sound, but a righteous man doesn't have to worry.

When there is moral rot in a nation, the government is insecure and is always changing and confused.[1]

When the poor turn against the poor it is like a short shower that runs off and doesn't do anybody any good.

Law-abiding people usually stick together and the crooks are always working to free each other.

Wisdom comes to those who seek the Lord.

A law-abiding son is a great delight, but one who runs with shameful men is a sadness to the father.

Men who take advantage of the poor and then get rich will eventually have all their possessions taken over by charities.

Woe to the ones who cause the innocent to fall.

A rich man is apt to become a self glorified person while a poor man begins to learn about the real life.

No one enjoys seeing the wicked prosper, but it is pleasant for everyone when a good man makes a killing.

A person who confesses his sins and errors and apologizes comes out fine.

Happy is the man who always stands in awe of God.

A good king is apt to have a long and happy reign, but a wicked ruler is always being investigated.

Do not protect a man who has committed a crime of violence.

A man who works at his job will be far more content than a fellow looking for easy money.

To become rich quick will usually cost a man his integrity, and

---

[1] We know it! We know it!

it is not worth it.

There is no place in life for prejudice.

It is better to tell a man the truth than to lie to him in flattery.

A person who steals from his father and mother and uses as an excuse the idea that some day the possession will be his, is a Grad A rogue.

When the wicked are ruling good men are hard to find, but when a righteous man arises then good men can flourish everywhere.

A man who resents correction is doomed.

A good king is helpful, but one who is involved in graft ruins a nation.

Righteous people are concerned with the poor, but the wicked act as if the poor didn't exist.

A man who flatters his neighbor is just spreading a net in which he himself will be caught.

Wise men are peacemakers while fools are always trying to start fights.

Violent men hate the upright, but the righteous seek to save the souls of all.

A corrupt ruler usually secures corrupt aides.

The Lord makes no distinction in sending daylight for the rich and the poor.

A righteous ruler has it made, for God is with him.

Correction is a good thing for a child, for if you leave a kid on his own you get real trouble.

The wicked may multiply and evil increase, but in time the righteous will see all this change.

Where there is no vision, the people perish.

Sometimes words are not enough, but you must instruct by penalty.

A person who has someone work for him all his life and treats him properly will find that he has a son.

A man who is partner to a thief becomes accustomed to evil and doesn't even notice cursing.

A really good man is sorely hated by the wicked.

There was a man and his name was Aggie[1] and he made a profession of his philosophy and a confession of his own faults.

"I am a stupid brute," said Aggie. "I have no secular knowledge or any holy knowledge. Who knows the heavens? Who created the earth and gave it shape? What is the name of the maker of everything?

"It is God. Everything connected with God is pure. God is a

[1] Agur

shield to all those who trust him.

"Let no one add anything to the words of God. Two things I ask of God. Removal of lies and vanity. Let me be neither rich nor poor. I'm afraid if I was real rich I might think I didn't need God. Yet if I was very poor, I might be tempted to steal.

"There are some generations that do not respect their parents, that think they know it all, they go around filthy, they take advantage of everyone.

"There are four things that are never satisfied; the grave, a barren womb, earth without water, and fire.

"Those that don't respect their parents will be punished.

"There are four things that I can't understand. They are too wonderful for me to grasp. One is the way the eagle soars so effortless in the air, another is the way a snake crawls across a rock, the way a ship rides on the surface of the sea, and the way of a man with a maid. I might add another thing I don't understand, how can a prostitute entice a married man and then say, "What's wrong with that?"

There are four things that are not tolerable on this earth. A worker who takes over without authority, a fat fool, an unfaithful wife, and a maid who runs off with the husband.

"There are four things on earth which are small but quite wise. The ants are small and not strong, but they work all summer preparing for the winter. Cliff badgers are another. They live in the rocks. I don't see how they do it. Locusts are another. They have no leader, yet they divide into groups and organize in a marvelous fashion. The spider is another. The spider goes even into the king's palace. I don't understand how they string their web.[1]

"There are four important animals, as I see it. The lion, the king of the beasts, a greyhound, unbelievably fast, and a goat. Add to this a human animal, a king who rules in peace.

"Finally, keep your big mouth shut as much as possible. Just like churning stirs up the milk and makes butter, or the twisting of a nose brings blood; so angry talk causes strife."

Chap.
31

Now we have the words of Lem, things taught to him by his mother.

Don't waste all your energy on women. A good king is better off without wine and strong drink for the drinking might bring a poor decision or a bad judgment of a case.

If anybody should drink, it should be someone burdened with sorrow or someone who is in great pain and who may die.

As king, help those who cannot help themselves. Take the side of the needy and the poor.

[1] I don't either, Aggie

It is hard to find a really virtuous woman. She is worth a lot more than riches. Her husband can trust her. He doesn't need to constantly give her gifts. She will do him good and not evil all the days of his life.

She sews. She searches for good food. She gets up before day[1] and fixes breakfast for the family. She may buy some property if she sees some that is real good. She doesn't mind working in the garden. She stays in shape.

She looks out for the poor. She doesn't worry about cold weather for she has already made warm clothes for the family. She decorates her home herself. Her husband is greatly respected for she even sews enough to sell some of her things for the family income.

Strength and honor are hers, and she will some day be rewarded. She speaks wisely and kindly, she does not gossip. She never loafs. Her children love her and her husband loves her, and they are all proud of her.

Many girls have made good, but none like the one I've described. Beauty can be deceiving and a charming personality misleading, but a woman who trusts God shall be praised.

Let her share in what she has done. She has a right to profit.[2]

[1] Daylight Saving Time
[2] There you are, Libs. It's in the book!

ECCLESIASTES

Editorial Comment: Solomon is the recognized writer of this book. Solomon had everything: money, power, wisdom, good health, and off and on he had a case of the Blahs. I think he wrote this book during some of his attacks. — A.E.

There is nothing to life. It is all one round of vanity, seeking and finding, and to what purpose? One generation comes, then another, and life goes on, repeating itself. Why? The sun rises, the sun sets, then circles to be ready to do the same thing again, the wind goes south, then turns back and goes north, the rivers all run into the sea but the sea never gets full because of evaporation, clouds, and then back to the rivers.

Everything is always active. Man's eye never sees enough nor does his ear ever hear enough. History just keeps repeating itself. There is nothing new under the sun.[1] Anything man discovers he then learns has pre-existed in some form. Yet it doesn't seem to matter. No one even seems to care if it has happened or if it will happen again.

"Just look at me," said Solomon, "I am the king and also I am the preacher.[2] I set out to learn everything about everything. I have seen everything, I have nothing to which to look forward, I've got the Blahs.

"That which is crooked can't be corrected and that which doesn't exist cannot be numbered.[3] I looked at myself and realized that I was real smart, in fact smarter than anybody who has ever been to Jerusalem. I devoted my life to learning. I even tried to learn of madness and folly. I decided that the more you know the sadder you get.

"So I said to myself that I would dispel my sorrow with glee. As a result, I kicked up my heels and made merry. I was soon tired of laughing and joking, it all seemed silly.

"I tried drinking. I thought this might teach me that there was something helpful in being a fool. It didn't work.

"The next thing I tried was super activity. I put on the greatest building program ever conceived. I built buildings and houses, I planted vineyards, I planted all kinds of fruit trees, I made swimming pools everywhere and used the water for irrigation also. I accumulated a tremendous number of servants, I bought cattle until I was the biggest baron of them all, I collected silver and gold,[4] I organized a men's chorus, an all-girl singing group, as well as an

[1] He should have lived to see the Brooklyn Dodgers
[2] Mixing Church and State is a no-no, Solomon
[3] You left some of us behind on this one, Solomon
[4] Solomon was also the IRS so this didn't hurt him

orchestra with multiple types of instruments.

"O.K.; so I was great. I never lost my understanding doing all this. Anything that I saw which I wanted I bought. I tried everything that sounded like fun and gave it a whirl, but after all was said and done I was back where I started, frustrated, nowhere to go, nothing to do. I felt blah!"

"Then I began to study by the comparison method. On this basis I concluded that it was much better to be wise than to be foolish, just as light is preferable to darkness. The wise man walks in light, the fool stumbles around in darkness. Yet they both wind up with arthritis; so what gives? The wise and the foolish both wind up in the same way — dead. History makes very little distinction between a prominent wise man and a prominent fool.

"Why then should I live? For what? I regretted all the fine work for which I was responsible because I would die and all the fine things would be used by people coming after me that I don't know, many of whom have not yet been born. How do I know if the person who takes my place in life will be a wise man or a fool? So I despaired again.

"What good does it do to work anyway? Life is full of sorrow and disappointment.

"From watching the handiwork of God I decided that a man should eat, drink, and enjoy his work, directing it for good. God blesses such a man with wisdom and joy. The sinner receives inner disturbance from God. But both of these situations come from God; so what difference does it make?

Chap.
3

"To everything there is a season and a time to every purpose; such as, a time to be born, a time to die, a time to plant, and a time to dig up what's planted,[1] a time to kill and a time to heal, a time to tear down and a time to build, a time to weep and a time to laugh, and a time to be mournful and a time to dance, a time to embrace and a time to refrain from embracing, a time to get and a time to give, a time to rip and a time to mend, a time to keep silent and a time to speak,[2] a time to love and a time to hate, a time for war and a time for peace.

"Wherein does hard work profit for a man? God has made such a beautiful world, but God limited man so that man cannot see the whole thing. I conclude then that a man should make the most of the time he has, eating, drinking,[3] enjoying himself and the results of his efforts. All things are made possible by God; so enjoy yourself, man, if you can.

"Whatever God does that is it. There is no change with God.

[1] I get this one mixed up sometime
[2] This is a real toughy   [3] Orange juice?

God is in complete charge of the past, the present and the future.

"There is a lot of crookedness in the world, and injustice, there even being politics in the church courts, but God will judge all these matters. Nothing escapes the scrutiny of God.

"I have decided that God lets things go along like they do to try men out, and see if they are any better than plain animals. Men live, beasts live, men die, beasts die; all the bodies disintegrate. Does anyone really know that a man's soul departs his body and continues while not so with a beast?

"As a result, I advise men to work at something they enjoy and get something going for them in this life.

"Well, I continued studying, this time turning my attention to the people who had real hardships. A galley slave has a tough life and no one to comfort him. The powerful ruler who works the slave doesn't have a comforter either. They would both be better off dead. In fact, I sometimes think the best thing to do is not to get born.[1]

"Then I observed that the motive for work was usually to simply outdo the fellow next door. To that I would say, so what? Yet a man is a fool to be lazy and work just enough to stay alive, thinking that since it is all going to end in death why should he work himself to death.

"I have observed some other rather odd conditions. One is the case of a man who has no dependents, no heirs, and yet he works tirelessly trying to accumulate riches. Why? There is no one to leave it to and he can't take it with him.[2]

"It is better for two people to be working together than one, for one might have a heart attack and the other could help him. It is also better to sleep with someone, rather than by yourself, for it is warmer with two.[3]

"In case of being attacked in Central Park it is better to have two together to resist and even better with three.[4]

"It is better to be a poor but wise teen-ager than to be an old and foolish king.[5] In fact, a poor but wise teen-ager might be born in a ghetto and get to be President.[6] Such a person attracts help and becomes an idol and everybody shouts his name, and then a couple of generations pass and he's forgotten. So it still makes life seem to me to be like chasing the wind.

"When you go to church, keep your ears open and if possible your mouth shut. Be real careful if you do say anything in church,

[1] You've lost me again, Solomon
[2] It's true. I know of a test case.
[3] So he knew about the energy crisis, too
[4] I'd be willing to go to four
[5] Some of these were bumper stickers on Solomon's chariots
[6] Please hurry!

for it is God's house. You can usually tell a fool by his being a lip artist.

"If you make a promise to God get with it at once. Don't delay a minute in fulfilling a promise to God. You'd be better off not taking the pledge if you don't intend to keep it. You can't talk your way out of the same thing you talked your way into.

"A lot of dreaming and yakking will get you nowhere. Stand in awe of God. That's a good way to do in church!

"No doubt you will see many injustices in life, with the strong taking advantage of the weak, and the rich pushing around the poor. Don't let it panic you. God is watching and in his time there'll be a real judgment.

"The earth is for everyone and it is necessary. The king has to eat, so the field is essential to him. A strange thing in life is that a person who loves money never gets enough. That's why I say life is like chasing the wind.

"A hard worker enjoys his sleep at night, the employer always wants more money so he wakes the guy up early for work.[1]

"I've seen a lot of trouble. I've seen rich men go broke. A man suddenly set back where he started. Then he usually becomes a frustrated grouch.

"That's why I say a man should eat and drink, enjoy his activities as much as he can while he is alive, and use the gifts that God has given him and be grateful. Such a fellow doesn't have to look back and groan, for the joy of the Lord is in him.

Chap.
6

"There is a terrible thing that I have observed occasionally, and that is a man working hard, acquiring good wealth and position, and then he loses his health and is not able to enjoy the fruits of his labor. I think that's a shame!

"If a fellow lives a mean life, even if he leaves a hundred sons,[2] when he's dead and gone and left nothing constructive behind him, why was he born in the first place? He would have done better not to be born! Never having lived, never having had a name is better than living two thousand years in waste. What's the difference?

"Wise men and fools both scramble for a living, but the wise man enjoys the scramble.

"Just wishing for things will get you nothing, you must work for what you get. This, too, is chasing the wind.

"God has always known what was in store for each man. Why buck it? What point is there to all this? That is what bugs me. How does a man know what is best for now or what the future will bring?

[1]And this was before DST!   [2]Pretty mean, I'd say

"A good reputation is better to have than money and the day of your death is more to be celebrated than the day of your birth.[1] It is more satisfying to attend funerals than to go to banquets, for you should concern yourself with the problems of death more than the problems of life.[2]

"Sorrow is more productive than laughter, for a solemn face doesn't get wrinkles quick; so a wise man is serious and fools laugh all the time.

"A person is improved who listens to criticism from a wise man instead of listening to a stream of musical groups. Praise from a fool vanishes like tissue paper in the fire and there is no value remaining.

"Attempting to bribe a good man makes the man angry and disgusts him with life.

"Finishing is more satisfying than starting and patience is more valuable than pride. A quick temper is no good, and makes a fool out of a person.

"Don't always be harping on the good old days. Your memory has just gone caput.

"Observe nature. Work with the way things are, for wisdom is a good protection, and so is money, but wisdom is a lot the better of the two.

"You can't improve or change what God has done or planned; so be happy when things are going good and be thoughtful when things are in poor shape. Actually God has built into life a balance of good and bad.

"Don't overdo anything, certainly don't be too wise or too foolish or you'll just burden your life with misery. I've seen good men die young and bad persons live a long time. The key to life is to learn to stand in awe of God.

"No one is perfect, but try to be good, for a city is in better shape with a good, wise man in it than if it had ten mighty powerful fools.

"Another thing, don't go around listening to other people's conversation. You are bound to hear some unpleasant things about yourself and it will also cause you to say unkind things about others.

"I determined to be completely wise, but it is impossible. I wanted to know why about everything, particularly wickedness and foolishness.

"Avoid a conniving woman. She is all snares and trouble, and the man inclined to sin is sure to get caught. In all my searching I have found a good man occasionally, about one out of a thousand, but I have never found a good woman.[3] In my opinion God made

---

[1] Who does the celebrating?
[2] Solomon may have been having a touch of the flu with the blahs
[3] Imagine being rich enough to talk like this

man all right, but women are always trying to ruin what God did.[1]

"A man who has learned something about living has it reflected in his face. A person should be a law-abiding citizen. Do your duty even if it means getting drafted. You do have some obligations. There is power in government. A wise man recognizes law and order.

"There is a certain amount of time set aside for misery; so learn to accept it, but you can't anticipate it; so don't worry about it.

"No man has control of death. It is coming to the just and the unjust. The unjust die and it is soon forgotten about how bad they were. Just because God doesn't punish people promptly for their sins many begin to think that it doesn't matter whether you are good or bad.

"There is much I don't understand for I see good men suffering and undergoing hardship and I see the wicked often having it easy. Life really puzzles me.

"For this reason I advise people to eat, drink and enjoy their work and let the chips fall where they may.

"I assure you that there is no way of learning all there is to know about life. Even if you could search and inquire day and night, without sleep, you could never probe all the mysteries of God.

"I tried to work on the theory that God looks out for the good and the wise. It doesn't work that way. God provides the same for everybody, the sun, the earth, the whole thing is equally available to good and bad alike, to the cursing sinners and to the righteous saint. It just doesn't seem fair.[2]

"Stay alive. There is always hope for the living. A living dog is better off than a dead lion. Since we don't know what happens after death, I suggest we stay alive. As far as we know death takes away all feelings; so don't risk it. Live and enjoy it. Wear clean clothes, use after shave lotion, stick with your wife, and whatever you decide to do give it all you've got. There is no knowledge, work or skill in the grave; so use all you have while you're alive.

"Another thought I had was that everything is left to chance. The race is not always won by the swiftest, nor the battle by the strongest, nor do the wise and good always get rich. Man never knows how long he will live, anymore than a fish knows when he will get caught in a net.

"I observed something one time that impressed me. There was a tiny rural village with only a few men in it and a powerful king with a strong company of soldiers came and laid siege to it. In the little village was a poor but wise man who devised a clever trick to save the

[1] I imagine a lot of good ladies dodged Solomon
[2] Hint to Solomon — "My ways are not your ways, saith the Lord"

city.[1] A few years later nobody could remember the name of the man who saved the village.

"Obviously, wisdom proved to be better than strength, but the wise man may be shortly forgotten. Anyway you cut it, though, a quiet word of wisdom is better than a lot of foolish shouting, and wisdom is always superior to weapons. I admit that a bad man, though, can cause a lot of trouble.

Chap.
10

"A dead fly can cause a stink in a bottle of sweet odor, just like a little evil can ruin the whole reputation of a good and wise man.

"A good man is always planning good things while an evil man is cooking up mischief. A mischief-maker gets where he can be identified by the way he walks around the town.

"If the man for whom you are working blows his top you keep your cool. This is good advice.

"I have seen a lot of things in life that just don't seem proper. I've seen people in authority misuse their power, I've seen nuts given great recognition while a man who has become rich by his own skill is snubbed, I've seen a hard-working man digging a well and then fall in and break his back, or a person loading a truck let the load fall on him. Life is tough. Sometimes a person working hard building a wall gets snake bit. Try to be smart in your work, such as sharpening your axe so you won't have to swing it so hard.

"Just as a snake bites without any reason so does a blabbermouth speak forth without cause. A wise man speaks graciously, but a fool shows himself to be a fool by starting out with trivia and ending with a bad suggestion. Just thinking about work bothers a fool.

"Pity the nation with a playful kid as its ruler and whose selected leaders are already drunk in the morning. Happy is the land that has an honest ruler and whose leaders eat and drink for strength to do the work of the nation.

"Laziness and indifference will cause a building to be poorly constructed.

"A party is lots of fun and wine makes a person merry, but if you are rich you can have these things anytime you desire.

"Don't always be criticising the people over you or the government, or complaining even privately about the rich people, for somehow word of what you are saying leaks out and you'll get in trouble.

Chap.
11

"Just do good for goodness sake, and goodness finally finds its way back to you. Don't hesitate to be generous.

When the clouds get full they empty themselves with rain, when

---

[1]Probably posted a smallpox sign

a tree falls it falls, whatever will be, will be; so don't procrastinate, waiting all the time for everything to be just right. Just as it is difficult to understand the way God arranged for a child to grow in the mother's womb; so you don't know all about life. Get to work. Sow your seed, for you never know how much will grow or which seed will prosper.

"It is good to wake up in the morning and see the sun and know you are alive. Enjoy the good days, for there will inevitably be bad days. It's God's way.

"Enjoy being young, but don't forget that God is watching and you will be held accountable for your actions. Be as happy as you can, but remember, young man, that you may have many years ahead and there is plenty of grief and pain to come.

Chap. 12

"As a young man think about God and store up treasures of truth for the day will come when the fun of the young will be gone. It will be too late to try to find God when you are old and blind, when your brain is addled and your body is miserable. Old age doesn't have much to offer. You may be able to hear a quail, but you won't be able to whistle, you can't climb a ladder, or even go to the top of a hill, small noises like a cricket makes or a faucet dripping will be very irritating and your sexual desires will be gone.

"Remember God while you are young and able, for soon everything snaps, you can't drink from a cup without spilling it, you can't draw water from the well or even wait on yourself, and then you die and return to the dust from which you came. Why? I just don't understand why, and I was the Preacher.

"I was a good preacher. I taught the people good things, I wrote out a lot of proverbs and thoughts for the day, I used words carefully to nail down important truths. Good students listened and learned.

"In conclusion, young man, let me tell you that there is no end to people writing books, and studying hard is a tiresome affair, but the whole business centers on one thing, stand in awe of God, keep his commandments, for this is the whole purpose of man, for God will bring every work into judgment, even the very secret matters,[1] and God will judge whether it be good or whether it be evil."

---

[1] even tapes

SONG OF SOLOMON

Editorial Comment: It is not for me to try to justify this book being in the Bible. It is written for a purpose, for some day and age. It doesn't do much for me, but at least try it — it might be just the thing for you. A.E.

Chap. 1

This is a song written by Solomon or written for Solomon or sung for entertainment during his evening meals.

"Let Solomon kiss me, for his kisses are more stimulating than wine," sang the lady singer, "and he smells good; so that even the very young girls fall for him at once.

"It is good that King Solomon plans to take me into his bedroom and make love to me, for I will rejoice, and it will be a memorable time.

"I know I am very dark-skinned, not like the local girls, but I am beautiful and I have been touched by the sun, for my family made me do all the dirty work outside, laboring daily in the vineyards.

"Tell me, Solomon, what is your program today? Where are you going? Let me join you, I don't want to hang around the palace all day with the rest of your crowd.

"I tell you what you do," replied Solomon, "just pack a lunch and follow my sheep. You are some woman! You have impressed me more than a group of Pharoah's best horses. Your cheeks are like rubies and your neck is golden, and we will get you additional jewelry of silver and gold to go around you."

"The king as he eats lying on the dinner lounge is enchanted by my perfume, which I have coming from a sachet between my breasts," sang the siren.

"You are a beautiful girl," chanted Solomon, "you are pleasant, a pretty sight as you recline on green grass, in the shade of the cedar trees, and look at me with eyes of the dove."

Chap. 2

"Call me the lily of the valley," sang the girl.

"You are like a lily among the thorns when I see you with other girls. You are like an apple tree among scrub oaks when I see you with young men," chimed in Solomon.

"How much is my delight in being close in the shadow of my king. Solomon lets me eat with him and sit close to him. I am really lovesick. What a thrill when he places his hand under my head and with the other hand holds me in an embrace. Then the king goes to sleep, so keep quiet or get out, all you serving girls, don't dare awaken the king."

"Sometimes I can hear my beloved king coming," sang the girl,[1]

[1] Same song, second verse

"and he seems to me to come leaping forward like a young deer, for I saw him looking for me out of the window, I could see him moving through the lattice work. Then he called to me and suggested that we get going, for it is a delightful day and the rain has stopped, spring is here, the birds are singing, and the voice of the turtle can be heard.[1] The fig tree is turning green, the grapevines are smelling good, come on, he cries, come let's get away to some private place.

"How nice everything is. The foxes are eating the grapes, my lover king is mine, all is in order. Come stay with me, my king, all the night, and act like a young buck.

Chap.
3

"One night I awoke and Solomon was no longer by my side," sang the girl,[2] "and I went everywhere looking for him. I went into the city and searched the streets. I found the night patrol and asked them if they had seen my lover. Not long after this I found him myself. I took him to my own home. Be quiet, everyone, particularly giggly girls, for my king is asleep and is not to be disturbed."

Then the girl chorus came on the program singing, "What is the big show we see coming? Who is the person who smells so good, who comes on like a cloud of smoke. It is Solomon![3] There are sixty mighty men around him, the greatest bodyguards in Israel, they watch carefully over Solomon day and night,[4] they have mighty swords, and Solomon is riding in a special chariot made of the cedars of Lebanon, a real Mark IX, trimmed in silver and gold, painted purple. Come on, all the girls of Jerusalem, look at this tremendous sight, King Solomon, dressed in all his finery, wearing his jeweled crown, and in a good humor."

Chap.
4

"How beautiful is a beautiful girl!" spoke Solomon.[5] "Sweetie, you have the eyes of a dove. Your hair is more desirable than mohair. Your teeth, when you smile, look like a hillside of white sheep, freshly clipped, your lips are like a scarlet thread, your speech is soft, your temples are made to appear as pure as split pomegranates, your neck is as stately as the tower of David, a classic fortress, and your breasts are matched like twin fawns. You are super beautiful and you make the night a sweet smell and I long to spend that time with you, you are perfect, there is no blemish on you.

"Let's take a trip to Lebanon together. Let us climb a mountain together and see the sights, watch the leopards and the lions, and wild beasts frolic. You have really stolen my heart. One look from you makes my heart spin, and a glance at a part of your neck

---

[1] Not for ordinary listeners   [2] She had lots of songs. The pay was good
[3] Solomon really liked to hear this kind of song
[4] He slipped away once we know
[5] This could have been a talk to his regular Sunday night supper group

exposed makes me thrill to my bones. I love you so much, you are better than wine, and your perfume smells better than food. Your lips are sweeter than honey, being close to you is stimulating. Your smell is as pronounced as the fresh cut cedar of Lebanon.

"You wonderful girl, you are like a private garden, a secret spring, your very gestures are beautiful and fill my every need. You are like an artesian well, like a bounteous table decorated with the tasty things of life. Let the wind blow me to you and let me take advantage of all the glorious joys that are available through you."

Chap. 5

"I tell you people," chanted Solomon, "I really enjoy being in my garden. It smells good. I enjoy eating fruit here, drinking wine or milk with chocolate chip cookies. Join me. I like having a bunch of girls around. Eat and drink all you want.

"One night I lay dreaming," sang the lead girl singer, "and I thought I heard the voice of my king, then a knocking at my door, and it was the king wanting to get in, saying that the dew was heavy and he didn't have on his raincoat.[1]

"I told the king I was undressed and had gone to bed, even that I had washed my feet, and my clothes were not handy. My lover tried to open the door but it was latched on the inside. I couldn't stand it any longer, I longed for him, so flipping on a little perfume as I went, I unlatched the door, but the king was gone. I called for him and searched for him, but he was gone. I went out into the streets of the city searching for my love, the cops pushed me around for I was a nuisance. O girls, you cuties with the Jerusalem chorus, if you see my loved one tell him that I am lovesick."

"Tell us, beautiful, sunburned girl," sang the chorus, "what is so exceptional about this one you love. Describe him to us."

"My loved one," sang the soloist, "is ruddy complexioned, he would be easily selected from a crowd of 10,000, his head is like solid gold,[2] he has black, bushy hair, black as a raven, his eyes are like the eyes of doves reflected in clear water, his cheeks are rosy, his lips as soft as lilies and dripping honey, his hands are covered with jeweled rings and he wears a fantastic belt of ivory studded with sapphires, his legs are solid marble, he wears golden shoes, he is as impressive as the cedars of Lebanon, and his mouth is enticing and lovely. That's the man, that's our King Solomon![3]

Chap. 6

"Where has your lover gone, O beautiful singer, where shall we look for him?" sang the chorus.

"He has gone to one of his gardens, or perhaps to feed his sheep, or maybe to pick some flowers. I am so in love and I know he

---

[1] or some such excuse   [2] She meant well
[3] Solomon enjoyed listening to his singers

loves me," warbled the soloist.

"You are a beautiful woman, my beloved one, more beautiful than Jerusalem and more impressive than an army parading with its banners," chanted Solomon. "Don't look at me, as I melt under your gaze, you with your better than mohair hair, you with the sheep white teeth, and your skin like peaches. There are 60 wives available to me, 80 concubines, and no telling how many willing young girls,[1] but my love is only for you. You are the only girl that has ever been born as far as I am concerned.

"Everyone loves and admires my beautiful one, even my wives do.[2] You wonderful creature, you are like the morning in brightness and brilliant as a Mardi Gras parade."

"I went wandering along the garden, among the flowers," sang the soloist, "and as I observed the fruit and petals I became homesick."

"Don't go away. Come back to us," sang the chorus of girls.

"What do you see in me, a poor little girl from Atmore, Alabama?"[3]

Chap.
7

"You dance so wonderfully," chanted the king. "Your feet are super. Your hips were made absolutely perfect, and your navel is as inviting as a full glass of wine. Your waist is as trim as a wheat field bordered by lilies and your breasts are matched as twin fawns. Your neck is like a tower of ivory, your eyes as clear as two fish pools, your nose is as straight as the tower on the gate of the city of Lebanon, your head sits straight like the top of Mount Carmel and your hair holds the king in captivity as if it were a purple robe.

"What a joy and delight you are, my love. You are beautifully built, tall and slim, with lovely breasts, stately like a palm tree, and I would greatly desire to hold that tree, to receive your kisses, which will bring new life to me, quicker than can be done with wine."

"I give myself to my beloved, and my lover comes to me, let us go away together, let us walk the fields and visit the nearby towns, let us go inspect the vineyards together early in the morning. We will make love in the vineyard and we will eat grapes and other fruit."

Chap.
8

"How I wish we could go about as brother and sister so people wouldn't gossip about us," continued the songstress. "Then I could kiss you, lover, anytime I wanted, and I would take you to Mama who would know how to fix your drink.

"You would put your left hand under my head and embrace my body with your right. He's asleep now, girls; so don't awaken the king."

"Who is this that we see coming from the distance, leaning on

---

[1] Solomon was still young and hadn't secured his 1,000 wives yet.
[2] This is slightly exaggerated   [3] Shumanite girl

her beloved?" sang the Jerusalem girls chorus.

"I have loved my lovely doll ever since she was born under the apple tree," chanted Solomon.

"Seal me in your heart, my king, just as you would bind something to your arm, for my love is as strong and sure as death, and jealousy is a deep emotion also, burning one inside like the fires of hell. Nothing can quench the fires of love, no flood can drown it, and it cannot be bought, even if a person sold everything to raise the price."

"What happens to a little girl that is unattractive? What shall we do if someone wants to marry her?"

"We will devise and use all types of cosmetics and equipment to help her,"[1] chanted Solomon.

"How fortunate I am. I am slim and tall and beautifully shaped," sang the sunburned lead girl. "How lucky I am. Solomon had lots of property and for most of his places he leased for $10,000 a year, while I received mine free and sub-leased it.

"How wonderful, great lover, that so many have the privilege of listening to your voice. Please let me hear it also. Then come quickly to me, my lover, like a young buck frolicking on the hillside," sang the tall and beautiful girl.

[1] Actually Solomon apparently recommends silver falsies

ISAIAH

My name is Isaiah and I have had a vision which has revealed to me the generalities as well as a few specifics in the past, present and future of Israel.

Animals such as the donkey and the ox show more recognition of the Creator than do the children of Israel. Israel is now a sinful nation, full of evil, and a nation that has forsaken God. I am even afraid that matters will get worse before they get better.

The whole land is in ruin. The people are taken into captivity and the remnant that remains are a disadvantaged minority.

Let me urge you, you people of Israel, to hear what God has to say. The Lord of Israel wants to know why you waste time and substance with occasional offerings of rams and fresh beef. The Lord doesn't need such sacrifices. In fact, God is not interested in such silly attempts to appease God and cover your sins. The Lord wants you to abandon your evil ways, to be concerned with helping the poor and the needy. This is the type of offering to bring to God.

When you begin to do these things God says that though your sins be as scarlet He will make them white as snow. If you will obey God, the Lord will restore your land, but if you continue in your evil ways you will be destroyed.

The leaders of Israel are selfish and seek their own interests and Jerusalem itself is a contaminated city. God will restore his people and provide good leadership, but first He will purge the land of the transgressors and those that have forsaken the Lord will be consumed by their own greed.

The revelation of God which has come to me always indicates that at some far away time God shall be exalted on the earth, and people from everywhere will desire to come to Jerusalem and gather around the lofty mountain of the Lord, to hear His instructions. International law shall come from a meeting of nations at Jerusalem and the Lord shall be responsible.

As a result of this gathering, there shall be the voluntary surrender of all armaments and men shall be determined to make farm implements and household gadgets out of the weapons of war, and peace will come on earth.

At the present time, however, the Lord is not supporting his chosen people for they have sinned and rebelled, the people of Israel have turned to fortune tellers and strangers for their guidance. The people of Israel have contaminated themselves with possessions, and the people are fascinated by their own inventions. A nation cannot survive this way and in time the people will throw away their possessions and hide in caves or storm cellars because God will terrify them with his power. Be certain that the time will come when the

Lord will assert his power.

You people had better believe that the Lord means to act. Jerusalem and the holdings of the tribe of Judah will disappear. God will not accept being ignored by the chosen people. The Lord disapproves of the way the leadership has taken advantage of the young and the poor and the Lord intends to punish the nation and take away its many possessions and leave its people scattered.

In fact, times will get so bad that women will be pursuing men shamelessly just in hopes of getting something to eat. Then there will come a purging of the people and when the people seek again sincerely the Lord, the Lord will bless the land and the Lord will bless the people.

The Lord considers Israel as if it were a vineyard which had been well planted and properly nourished, but a vineyard which began to bring forth wild grapes instead of the proper grapes for marketing. God insists that He did everything for His people, and yet they were unfaithful and wandered from His very plain path.

God warns people and declares that they are foolish to let the thirst for property cause them to build too many houses and develop too many businesses. The Lord further warns against drinking liquor all day, and the indulging in fruitless social gatherings full of wasted time. It is this very type of thing that has caused the children of Israel to go into captivity. This type of conduct and foolishness only increases the number of people who will reside in hell. Be sure, though, that in time the Lord will be exalted.

The Lord issues a warning for various types of people, to those that demand immediate action from God, to those that pass off evil for good, and good for evil, to those that consider themselves wise, to those that ruin their judgment with too much drinking, to those that complain all the time and criticize people trying to do good, such persons will not be able to stand before God. The anger of the Lord is aroused easily against such persons.

Yet God will always make himself available to those who will respond, to those who repent and seek him, and the people who turn to God shall find him, their steps will be certain and they will not stumble. These are the people who will truly inherit the earth.

The next vision that I had came to me the same year that King Uz died. In this vision I could see the Lord high and lifted up, and the whole scene left the impression of power and mystery, with smoke and odd figures of the type you see in dreams, and all of the visionary creatures worshipped God and called forth "Holy, holy, holy is the Lord of hosts, the whole earth is full of his glory!"

I said to myself, "Woe is me! I have had it! I realize that I am a man of unclean speech and I associate with people who are just like me, yet my eyes have seen the glory of the Lord, I'm certain I will be struck dead."

Then one of the flying creatures in the vision came to me with a live coal in his hand, which he had taken from the altar with tongs, and he placed the burning coal on my mouth and he said, "Now that this hot ember from the altar has touched your lips you are free of sin."

Then I heard what I am certain was the voice of God saying, "Who will be my representative? Who will go out and witness for me?"

Then I said, "I am here, and I am willing to go."

Then the voice said, "Go. Tell them all you know of me, but they will not hear you. This is all right. Let them ignore me, let them sin and get fat in corruption, for they have never been a people who would understand and learn except under great pressure."

"How long, O God," I asked, "will this condition continue?"

"It will last until the cities of Israel are captured, the people led away, and then there will be a tenth of the people left, a sound hard core minority, and in them will reside the strength of Israel."

Chap.
7

The Lord then instructed Isaiah further saying, "Go to Ahaz and encourage him. Tell him that all the threats from Syria are at present not worth his worry. The plot to go against Judah will fail this time."

Later the Lord spoke again for the benefit of Ahaz and said, "Would you care for a sign, ask for anything from bottom to top, and I will exhibit my power."

"I'm not going to get caught in the matter of questioning the word of God. I don't need a sign," said Ahaz.

Isaiah then said, "There is no way of pleasing you people. As a result the Lord will give you a sign anyway for a virgin shall one day in Israel give birth to a son and his nickname shall be 'God with you.' From the very first the child shall know the difference between good and evil and he shall always choose good. This will not occur during the reign of any of the present kings.

"Before this great blessed event your land shall be laid waste. The Egyptians and the Syrians shall plunder unmercifully and the people of Israel shall be desolate."

Chap.
8

The Lord then spoke to Isaiah again in another revelation and the Lord said, "Write this down, Isaiah. I am going to give you a son. You are to call him Victor."[1]

---

[1] Nahershalolhashbaz

Immediately I sent for two reliable witnesses and they saw me write this prophecy.

Then I summoned my wife and took her to bed and nine months later my son Victor was born.

The Lord informed me that before Victor was old enough to speak distinctly the conqueror from Syria would come and invade.

The Lord spoke to me, Isaiah, again and said, "Tell the people to beware of making all kinds of weird confederations and alliances. Tell the people to stand on their own and trust their Lord. Advise them not to turn to mediums, or radical leaders with fancy plans, but to trust God.

"It is a shame for these people to stand in awe of Syrians or Egyptians when they should stand in awe only of God."

Israel and Judah refused to trust God, however, and there will be great trouble for them, including persecution, separation of families, loss of homes."

"Isaiah," God said, "write all these things down and protect the manuscript, seeing that it is handed down from one worthy and God-fearing man to another on through generations to come in order that mankind may know the Lord and understand his ways.

"I know that the only hope is in the Lord. I wish all the people of Israel and Judah felt as I feel. The Lord has left us some names, the names of hope in the future, and the names are Victor[1], and God Saves,[2] and God Cares[3].

It seems strange that the people cannot see the bright prospects in the coming generations. It is so stupid to guess about the future and depend on man's mind and man's own limited ability."

"Just check the so-called wise sayings of man," said God, "against my word. If the word of a man is different from the word of God then you know that the man is wrong. It is just that simple! The result of this foolishness of following erratic leaders will be poverty, desolation, captivity, and trouble. Undoubtedly my people will be scattered everywhere because of their failure to observe my law and follow my statutes."

Chap.
9

"Nevertheless," said God, "this sad account is not permanent and the feeling of loneliness, despair, and darkness shall be broken. For the people that dwell in darkness shall see a great light, and even those under the shadow of captivity and oppression, the light will even shine upon them.

"The people of God shall be restored. Again they shall be a great people, broken from the chains of oppression, full of joy at harvest time, again operating as a great nation.

"Eventually there will be peace. There will be no need for

[1]Nahershalolhashbaz   [2]Isaiah   [3]Shearjashub

weapons of war, or bloody uniforms, or military funerals, or medals for killing.

"The reason for this peace will be started with a child who will be born to us. The one true government shall be on his shoulders. The years shall add to his titles and he will be called such names as Wonderful, Superstar, Mighty God, Everlasting Father, and Prince of Peace.

"The spirit of the Lord will see that the type of kingdom that he establishes shall increase and it shall gradually encompass the earth. This will be no secret king. Nations all over the earth shall begin to notice this kingdom.

"The people of Israel will not believe and follow in this kingdom at first. The leaders of Israel shall be poor leaders, and the people will be scattered and persecuted. The divisions among the Jews themselves will be their undoing, for in forsaking God the Jews lose their point of common worship and brotherhood. The strife between tribes will increase and families will be divided. These things are the normal consequence of corruption and greed. Always, however, God leaves an outstretched hand for his people!"

Chap.
10

Isaiah reports that in his vision, which vision was a revelation from God, he saw the judgment of God placed on the offending people of Israel. The people had forsaken God and now they had no one to whom to turn in the days of stress and difficulty. God will continue his punishment of his people until they thoroughly repent.

God plans to send a heathen force from Assyria to act as a punishing instrument for God, to take spoil from the people, and to kill many of the people. Why shouldn't God act this way? God allowed West Texas[1] to be captured and also Las Vegas[2] because of the worship of idols; so why shouldn't God do the same to Jerusalem and its people who are now worshipping idols.

The forces of Assyria will also in time be punished even though the Lord allows them to be victorious for a while as God's means of punishment.

The time will also come when a remnant of the people shall repent and place their trust in God, the Almighty of Israel. The people of Israel must suffer under the power of the Assyrian army, but God will accept the pleas of repentance from his people and the Lord will strike the Assyrians as surely as he struck the Egyptians. The small remnant of the Jews that repent and call upon the Lord shall return to the Promised Land and the Lord will bless this action.

The Lord will exercise his control in the day of repentance and the mighty shall be humbled before him.

---

[1]Samaria   [2]Hamath

Another portion of one of the visions of Isaiah reveals the announcement of the coming of a new type of king, a descendant of the line of King David, and the very Spirit of the Lord shall be upon him. This new king will not be fooled by outward appearances, but he will be capable of looking into the heart of man.

This new leader shall judge the people fairly and he will seek to arrange for equality among men. The weapon which this king will use will be words and his own life shall be above reproach. As a result of his teaching, there shall gradually develop an attitude of peace, so that even the animal kingdom will cease to fight among themselves for food. The whole earth will then become full of the knowledge of God.

This descendant of the line of David shall provide a symbol for the people,[1] and the symbol shall be accepted by the Gentiles.

Again the Lord will provide for a return of the people of Israel and they shall come from all over the world to establish themselves in the land of Canaan. The whole earth shall begin to recognize the sign of the cross and even the tribes of Israel will set aside their jealousy one toward another and they shall work together under one government.

The Lord will also destroy the opening of the Nile[2] and it shall be split into a number of smaller streams and the mouth of the great river shall be spread so wide that a man can walk across it, for it shall be shallow.[3]

When all this occurs, the Israeli people will praise God and they will say, "Now that your anger against us no longer exists, we welcome your comfort. We will no longer fear, for God is our salvation. We will draw water from the wells of the understanding of God, we will shout praises to the Lord, we will sing to the Lord in praise for the wonderful things that he has done for us, and we will proclaim the Lord as the Holy One of Israel."

The plan of God ultimately calls for the destruction of the wicked. Babylon, symbol of evil and treachery, is doomed by the Lord. All these things were revealed to Isaiah in a vision, and other matters also.

There will definitely be a Day of the Lord and at that time the Lord will gather all his forces from the far ends of heaven and the purpose of the Almighty will be the destruction of evil. This will be a time of great fear and all people everywhere will be impressed and many will groan as a woman in labor and the power of the Lord will

---

[1]My guess is that this refers to the cross
[2]I consider the Nile the "tongue of the Egyptian Sea"
[3]This, apparently, is yet to happen

be reflected on the faces of the people and God will destroy all the sinners.

The stars at this time will refuse to shed light and the sun will not show itself nor will the moon reflect the light of the sun. On this occasion the proud will be humbled, the wicked punished, and the arrogant shall be brought low.

God plans to shake the earth at this time and the earth will lose its place and terror will be everywhere. This will be the Day of the Lord. People will witness horrible destruction and torment and evil armies shall pillage and kill without concern for women or children.

Babylon, now a great city of evil, will be in its time reduced to rubble and no one will be able to rebuild it. The city will be a dump, a heap of ruins and furnish shelter for wild animals, but Arab people will never again reside within its old walls. Shepherds will no longer bring their flocks to the great city, but owls shall abide in the ruins and all kinds of strange animals shall use the old city as a dwelling place.

Chap.
14

God will in time show mercy to the line of Jacob and the children of Israel shall grow to the point some day of ruling over those who had previously ruled over them. The Jewish people will be brought together in Israel from many strange lands and the Lord will bless their return and they will be free from hard bondage and great fears. There will be great rejoicing when this occurs.

On such an occasion, evil will be reduced to the grave, and the devil himself, who weakened many nations, will be tossed into a permanent grave. The devil and the evil that he represents has long bragged about the success of the wicked and has proclaimed himself to be superior to God and to the ideas of goodness. The devil will be reduced to nothing and cast into a hell of his own making. While other people will have a place in eternity, dwelling in God's kingdom, the devil and his followers will not even have a grave in which to reside.

Particularly will there be the destruction of Babylon, for there will be nothing left except rubble and some mud holes where the city once stood. God promises to destroy the evil ones that shackle and torment his people.

The destruction of the evil regime of Babylon is just a beginning, for there will be other evil people and evil nations to rise, but they too in time will recognize that God has laid a strong foundation upon which the righteous can build, and the poor and the needy will find help in the Lord.

Chap.
15

The time will come when those who do evil will be a target of the Lord, whether the people be in China, Mississippi, New Jersey, Siberia, or anywhere. The misery of these people will come primarily from such natural disasters as floods and drouth, as the whole world will suffer because of the evil that many men will do.

I, Isaiah, foresee that the day will finally come when the extortioners, the oppressors of the poor, the money mad, the perpetrators of evil shall have had it. The Lord plans to bring all such to a miserable doom.

All the shallow pleasures of the wicked shall be taken away, and the miserly people who have created so much trouble shall have to live without joy, or water, or good lands, and there shall be no singing for them. The evilly inclined shall even try to call upon such false gods as force or money, but to no avail. The land of Moab where so much is evil at present shall last only three years, but it is a symbol and an illustration for what is in store for wicked people and evil localities or nations.

Damascus is a good illustration. Because it is now a place of wickedness, of slave trading and idolatry, Damascus will in time be levelled to a dung heap. The same fate is in store for any city or nation that continually despises God and seeks its own salvation.

The Lord rules, even though a nation be as far away as Ethiopia. These people also are under the will of God and when they rise up to discomfort God's people and move toward the promised land, their fate is sealed. These people cannot succeed and finally, after many conflicts, even these people shall come to Jerusalem with gifts and with a request for peace.

The land of Egypt will not be spared from the wrath of the Lord. In Egypt there shall be continuous internal strife and civil war. Accompanying all this shall be drouth and famine and water shall be a crucial need.

As a result of all this, the people of Egypt will finally stand in terror of all Israel.

God has sent foolishness into the minds of the advisors of Pharoah and as a result the program of Egypt is as poorly designed as the path of a drunk. Egypt shall finally be a nation that is a weakling, afraid of every threat. Conditions will actually reach a point that many Egyptians shall begin to praise God and seek to worship Him.

The forces of Assyria shall overcome Egypt and lead a great number of its people away as captives. After all these things have occured, there will be a religious movement in Egypt and the people shall seek the one God. As a result, many will turn to Jehovah and God will heal the land and bless it. As a result, there shall be three great leading nations in the Middle East; Egypt, Palestine, and Assyria.

The Lord spoke to Isaiah and told him of the immediate difficulty facing Egypt. The Lord spoke through Isaiah saying, "The king of Assyria will lead away the people of Egypt and Ethiopia, just as Isaiah is going around preaching barefooted; so shall the captured people be when they have fallen to the Assyrians."

The Lord intends to destroy Babylon. Babylon has been a destroyer of others and so the Lord will destroy the destroyer, which is always the way.

It staggers my mind to see the vision of the terrible destruction of Babylon. It will be a sudden thing. One moment everyone will be eating and partaking of a big banquet, and then the next moment there will be destruction.

The Lord suggested that I place a watchman on the wall and this I did. The destruction of Babylon is a solemn message from God to the wicked.

"Watchman, what of the night? When will all this happen?"

"Judgment Day is every day with God. Turn to God now, before it is too late. Seek the Lord first, then come and ask your question again," said the watchman.

God also has a warning to the people of Arabia. God will scatter the people and leave only a few, for this is God's way and His will.

God has a message for Jerusalem. The Lord wants to know why everyone has gone looney. The people are in great tumult and distress, and well they should be for God is no longer protecting Jerusalem from the plague or from invading armies.

Your trouble is that you think you are self-sufficient. You have great plans for mending the walls and providing a reservoir of water, but you have not asked for God's help or for his blessing.

The Lord expected you to worship and to practice self-denial and self-control, but instead of that you celebrated with big feasts and ornate parties. Your philosophy is eat, drink, and be merry for tomorrow we die, and the Lord will not overlook this sacrilege.

Because of this the Lord will see to it that you are taken away into captivity. You will be scattered and discarded as if you were litter.

However, the Lord says that there shall be a savior of the people, one who comes from the line of David, and he shall be given all power so that he may open or close everything, at his own discretion. This savior shall be as a nail thrust into a sure place and all the glory of all time will hang upon him, and all other nails will become as nothing. God has ordered that it be done in this way.

The Lord has turned his eyes on Tyre and God is displeased. Tyre is a wicked city, a prosperous city, and its merchants and rulers are great leaders, but the city is a place of slavery and God is displeased. The sea itself does not care to continue to behold the wickedness of Tyre.

The Lord has commanded that Tyre be destroyed. At first it shall simply be forgotten for seventy years and neglected by the men of commerce. Tyre shall revive, but the revival itself will be a renewal of wickedness, and so God shall command that the city be totally destroyed.

Chap. 24

The land of Judah will also suffer because of the sins of the people. The Lord will make the land desolate and scatter the people of Judah in far away places. There shall be no distinction made between clergy and laity, between men and women, master and servant, or mistress and maid, the seller will go as well as the buyer, the one who pays usury as well as the one who demands it, and so the land shall be laid to waste, for this is God's will and God's judgment.

The story will be the same in every city, but always there will be a remnant spared.

Finally, it will seem as if all the world has gone bad with treachery, and hate, and malice. The earth will shake itself as if it were drunk, and then shall come the punishment of the Lord. The wicked leaders will get it first. Then all that are left shall be assembled as if they were prisoners, and the moon and the sun shall in shame hide their lights. Then the Lord and his saints shall reign in glory.

Chap. 25

As for me, O Lord, I am a prophet that praises God and I will continue to praise thy name for all the wonderful things which you have done.

I have observed your power, how simple it is to reduce a mighty city to complete ruin. The most important people on earth are bound to recognize your greatness for you are a champion of the poor, a strength to the needy, and you put the quietus on noisy strangers.

Some day Jerusalem will be the headquarters for peace and the Lord shall prepare a great dinner for the celebration. At this time fear and death shall be abolished, and God will wipe away all tears from the eyes of his people.

On this occasion the people shall say, "The Lord is our God. We have waited for him and he has come. We are unbelievably happy in his salvation."

The wicked shall at this time be punished and their pride in their accomplishments shall be a frustration to them, and every form of protection or rationalization for the wicked shall be destroyed.

Chap.
26

In that final time of victory for the righteous there shall be fantastic rejoicing. Salvation and peace shall be as walls for the city. The gate will be open to all the righteous from everywhere, without distinction. There will be perfect peace for those who have completely trusted in God, for God is everlasting strength.

The proud, the vain, the oppressors of the poor and the needy, they shall be brought down from their lofty positions. This is a day and a time worth waiting for, and even though in times past man has followed strange and inadequate gods, at this time there will be no name mentioned but that of the Lord God of Hosts.

For the Lord has gradually blessed the righteous people of the earth so that as if they were a nation unto themselves they have gradually taken the name of the Lord across the whole earth.

The people of God have prayed in time of distress as a woman cries before the delivery of a child. We, the people of earth, have not been able to develop a perfect kingdom. As a result we must face trials and tribulations, but in the end the Lord will come forth and declare his power and his justice.

Chap.
27

The Lord will destroy evil and all its ugly manifestations. The anger of the Lord toward Israel will cease and again the Lord will bless the vineyards of his people, and Israel will prosper.

Israel has been punished for its sins, but not as much as the enemies of Israel. At times as the people of God are scattered it will seem as if they are forsaken, but when the great day draws near the Lord shall return them, small numbers at a time, from all over the world, to the land of promise to be near the holy city Jerusalem.

Chap.
28

There is trouble for Samaria as it has become a place for God's people to revel and seek to escape God. The armed forces of Assyria shall come down on the city and destroy it and the glorious beauty of the place shall be destroyed by a heathen horde.

As always there will be a few of the faithful and they shall receive strength from the Lord. The leadership of Jerusalem at this time, however, is weak and sinful, with drunken judges and priests.

The people shout at me, "Who do you think you are, Isaiah, to keep telling us such things over and over again. We heard you the first time."

"It is because you won't listen," I told them. They still did not listen and the only language which they are capable of hearing is punishment, and God will speak this way to a wayward people.

As anxious as the Lord is that his people turn to him, the Lord has spoken now against them.

"You think you have made a deal," says the Lord, "to save yourselves when the evil ones come. This is a foolish plan. Man cannot save himself. Your only hope is to build on the solid foundation which I have laid down in plain language for the people of God. I know that you will have to suffer, but finally the truth will dawn on many of you.

"You see, you have made a bed to lie on that is too short and the cover is inadequate. Don't make fun of these sayings or else the Lord might deal even harder with you than he plans.

Remember that the Lord is a great teacher. The Lord has taught the farmer to plant as well as plow, and to use different seed in different areas at different times. This is the wisdom of God and He is trying to teach you.

Chap.
29

God has pronounced difficulty for Jerusalem in payment of the sins of the people. The Lord will allow the enemies of Jerusalem to sack it and strangers shall come and go in the streets.

This is not for always, for God will bless the remnant and the repentant and the righteous. Because of them, the enemies in time will be blown away as if they were chaff and the Lord will thunder upon them and shake them with earthquakes.

You are dumb not to believe the promises of God. You had just as well be a staggering drunk as to hear of these things and believe them not. It is a shame that you are so concerned with yourselves and selfish matters that you do not have time to consider these words of truth.

Of course you can't hide from God. There is no such thing as doing something in secret. Don't you realize that the potter knows everything there is to know about the jar he makes; so it is with God who has made you.

The day will come when the land of Israeli will be full of fruit and then shall the people begin to understand the truth of the blessing of God. The wicked shall begin at this time to taste of the defeat which will in time be forthcoming. This will be an occasion of repentance and renewal.

Chap.
30

"What a shame," says the Lord, "that the people of God are not content to trust in the Lord. Rather than come to me for help or advice my people foolishly turn to worldly authorities, such as going to Egypt with vast sums to buy support.

"Egypt is not capable of delivering you nor are they willing to be of great service. The same is true of other powers. Why do you not trust in me?" asks God, "for I am willing and able to do anything."

"Now listen to this," says the Holy One, "Because you don't trust in God, but choose to trust in man, great calamity shall befall you. Because you close your ears to the prophets who speak my truth in my behalf, you shall be broken as a potter drops and breaks a vase.

"You do not have the necessary faith to calmly stand firm in the face of mounting 'difficulties. Still the Lord always stands ready to receive you when you return to him and call upon his name. Even though the Lord will place adversity on you because of your sins, there will always be teachers left among you to help restore your faith. These good men are guides for the Lord and will influence you so that eventually you will realize the difference between material values and spiritual values.

"Once the Lord begins to heal the repentant people and the repentant nation, there will be great natural blessings given in good harvests and productive weather.

"You must remember, though, that the Lord acts with great shaking of the earth and mighty thunder when he is angry. God also will sort out the wicked nations and pour his wrath on them, but the people of God will be able to rejoice, and a deep happiness shall fill his people.

"As the Lord has spoken against Assyria and as His voice declares the downfall of these people so also does His voice declare the end of war and those who pursue such things.

Chap.
31

"The Lord does not appreciate people seeking help from men, particularly ungodly men, when all the time the Lord is available," said Isaiah. There is no point in turning to the Egyptians, for instance, simply because they may have access to good military equipment. There is no deliverance in this type of arrangement as the Lord will in time destroy both those who help and those who unfaithfully seek help on a practical or material basis."

In a way, the Lord is similar to strong lions who don't care whether they are confronted by one shepherd or a dozen. The Lord plans to defend the holy city Jerusalem as skillfully and as easily as birds fly.[1]

"My advice to you is simple, turn to God, serve him, and worship and then you shall see the destruction of the Assyrian as well as any others whose ways come in conflict with the Lord."

Chap.
32

"You can safely look for better days for the Lord will in time bring a righteous ruler with some inspired helpers. The happening shall be similar to a safe cave for a man on a windy day, or as refreshing water in a desert area, or a shady place in the heat of the day. The lives of men will begin to change and understanding will come to men who were accustomed to being short-tempered.

"This new approach will begin to change values, so that no longer will the violent and the wicked be heroes, for their falseness and their phony front will be obvious. In that day shall the goodness

[1]Some scholars consider this a prophecy of air support for Jerusalem. Quien sabe?

of the generous be a blessing and a strength, and will not be considered a weakness.

"This change in values will also affect women. Look out, girls! No longer will you be allowed to sit around, as some of you do, lazy and pampered by men just because you are girls, for you will be expected to do your part. You, too, will be expected to do good works, and be busy at the Lord's request.

"The end of all these things shall see the arrival of justice and peace. Calmness will come with comfort, and the people of God will dwell in safety under the protection of the Lord of hosts, who will bless his people abundantly.

Chap.
33

"Let me again and again warn the sinners and the enemies of God. There is no way to defeat the Lord. As long as you are wicked you are doomed, but for those who live righteously and speak truthfully to help their fellow man, for them God has prepared blessings. Jerusalem shall some day symbolize the safety of the children of God, for it shall be a quiet place, a holy place, and completely stable.

The Lord shall be as a vast expanse of water around his people so that no enemy might attack or torment the righteous.

Chap.
34

Again let me remind you that the Lord is opposed to evil, and God is opposed to those nations who act with evil intentions. These nations shall enter pointless wars and there shall be much blood shed, and it is God's way of expressing his disapproval, for it will leave finally every thoroughly wicked nation destitute and barren.

Chap.
35

On the other hand, God shall abundantly bless the righteous in his way and in his own time. The blessing will be an obvious matter, and there will be a great flowering in the desert and the hearts of the sad shall be made glad, and the discouraged shall see a new hope.

Man once again will be free to walk the streets and the highways with no fear of being attacked, and the songs of the people shall be songs of joy and gladness.

Chap.
36

Now in the fourteenth year of the reign of Hez, Big Hun came from Assyria with a gigantic army and he began to capture all the cities in the whole area.

As his custom was, Big Hun[1] sent his mouth-piece, a man high in the diplomatic corps, to intimidate Hez and the people of Jerusalem.

Standing in front of the wall at Jerusalem, the spokesman for Big Hun yelled to the King and the people, "My boss thinks you all are fools to think that Egypt will come to your rescue. The Egyptians have never been dependable, and have always been inclined to stab you in the back. Why deal with them? You merely

[1]Sennacherib

invite disaster. Fooling with Egypt is similar to leaning on a sharp stick.

"Maybe, however, you people are those foolish types that 'trust in God.' This is a laugh. One of your own kings defied your God and worshipped idols. How does that grab you?

"Big Hun, my leader, is a sport, though, and a gambling man. In fact, he has authorized me to bet you that you don't have 2,000 men ready to ride. Big Hun says that if you'll furnish 2,000 riders that he will furnish 2,000 horses. Even then you couldn't make a dent in a small fraction of the army that we have assembled.

"Finally, as a matter of information to you, the Lord himself has commanded us to conquer you. Now how about that?"

Then Fulbright and Harriman and Mill said to the speaker, "Don't talk to us in Hebrew, but speak Aramic. We can understand Aramic and the people can't and we don't want our people to know what you are saying."

"That's tough," called out the mouth-piece, "for Big Hun wants all the people to hear what he has to say. He wants the people to know that if you don't surrender that we'll lay siege, cut off all water and food supplies, and let all of you die a miserable death.

"Now hear this you people on the walls of Jerusalem," shouted the speaker, "don't let ole Hez fool you. Don't listen to his promises that the Lord will deliver the city and save you. Make an agreement with me and we will have a peaceful settlement. You will be fully protected until we can move you to some other country to live where you will have a nice easy life. Don't let ole Hez talk you out of this agreement, for it is either that or a sure death for each of you.

"Look at the record," the speaker continued, "and read the papers. Don't you know how we have laid flat Rome[1] and Athens[2]? What about their gods. Where were they when this happened? Have any of the gods saved any of the cities? What makes you think that your God will save Jerusalem?"

The people listened but they said not a single word for they loved and respected Hez and he had told them to stay silent.

Chap.
37

The details of all of this were immediately reported to Hez and he went into meditation and was greatly troubled. Hez then sent Fulbright, Harriman and Mills, his foreign policy people, to Isaiah with a message saying, "This is a time of great trouble and distress as if the nation were a woman in labor and yet unable to give birth to the child. Pray for us, Isaiah. Perhaps God heard the blaspheming of the Assyrian. I'm sure if God heard him that he won't let him get away with such talk. Pray for us, Isaiah."

When Isaiah received the message he spoke saying, "Tell King

[1]Hamath   [2]Arpad

Hez that God says don't worry about the big boasting of the Assyrian lip-flapper. For one thing, a rumor will start in the camp that will cause Big Hun to head for home fast, and when he gets there he will be killed."

Now the big mouth ambassador returned to Big Hun and reported and then Big Hun put his threat in writing and had it delivered to Hez at Jerusalem.

The letter contained all the threats that had been made orally and so Hez took the letter and went into the house of prayer and spread the matter in the presence of the Lord.

Then he prayed to God saying, "O Lord, I know you are the God of all creation, open your eyes and hear our problem and listen to our difficulty. The Assyrians have wiped out other cities and other nations, and we are next.

The Assyrians have thrown the gods of the other peoples into the fire, for of course they were gods made by the hands of men. Now, O God, deliver us from this monster so that all men everywhere will know that you are the one true Lord of all."

Isaiah then sent word to Hez saying that God had heard the prayer and that God despised Big Hun. Furthermore, the Lord reported that He was aware of the success of Big Hun and how he had been successful against small cities and weak nations, but now he had defied God and would be punished.

It is the will of God, that Big Hun will not get to so much as shoot one arrow over the wall at Jerusalem but he shall return home as if he were turned around by a bridle like a horse. God says that he will defend Jerusalem for his own sake and for the sake of his servant David.

That night the angel of the Lord went forth and passed through the camp of the army of Big Hun and smote the army with a sickness and in the morning many were dead and many were too sick to move or march. As a result, Big Hun departed the area and began to journey toward home and he was killed en route by cousins who wished to rule in his stead.

Chap.
38

A few years after this Hez became sick and his minister, Isaiah, came to call on him.

"The Lord has suggested to me," said Isaiah, "that I advise you to get your affairs in order for you are about to die."

This did not do much for ole Hez; so he began to pray to the Lord saying, "Lord, please remember that I have been as faithful as I could and I have really tried to live properly, and I'd like a little longer time to live."

Not long after this the Lord inspired Isaiah to call on Hez again and tell him that the Lord had heard his prayers and would give him about 15 more years to live. The Lord also revealed to Isaiah that

God would defend the city against the Assyrians while Hez was alive. As a sign from God to validate this promise the Lord would cause the sun dial to lose six minutes by the Lord holding back the sun for this amount of time[1].

As a result of this experience Hez became a little poetic and composed some lines in celebration of the occasion that went something like this:

> Things looked mighty dark to me
> Facing death so early
> No more would my friends I see
> No wonder I am surly.
> Delirious I chattered as a bird
> Mourning also like a dove
> Praying, praying, yet not heard
> Knowing my boil came from above.
> But heal me, Lord, heal me quick!
> Thank you, Lord, I needed that
> I know you're wise to make me sick
> But now I'm well and getting fat!

Praise God — He heals — He healed me and I will praise him forever.

To assist with the healing let it also be made known that Isaiah had instructed the servants to put an open fig on the boil and it drew the poison out. Praise the Lord.

Chap.
39

When Cannon,[2] king of Babylon, heard that Hez was sick he sent him a get well card. Hez was greatly pleased to get the card which was delivered in person by a number of Cannon's helpers. As a result, Hez escorted the visitors around and showed them all his antiques and even took them into the vault and let them see his treasures.

Isaiah came over to visit Hez in a few days and inquired about the visitors that had been noticed.

"What were those fellows doing here, Hez?" asked Isaiah. "What did they say, and from where did they come?"

"They came from a far country," replied Hez.

"What did they get to see?" asked Isaiah.

"Everything. I showed them the works," said Hez.

"Now hear this, Hez. You have really blown it. These fellows will some day get organized and come here and take everything they saw back to Babylon. In fact, God has revealed to me that they will even take your sons into captivity," said Isaiah.

"All right. I made a mistake, but at least I won't be alive when this happens, and for this I am grateful," concluded Hez.

[1]Science reports some missing time and here's 6 minutes of it!
[2]Merodachbaladan

"God has some encouraging words for His people," said Isaiah. "The people have been amply punished and have suffered sufficiently."

"I seem to hear a voice," continued Isaiah, "shouting from the wilderness and saying 'Prepare for a manifestation of God. Make a straight road for the emissary of the Lord, for in the coming of the one God will send equality will be established, the crooked shall be made straight, and the full glory of the Lord will be revealed. Everyone will see this for the Lord has planned that this shall be the way."

A voice spoke to Isaiah and said, "Speak out!"

"What shall I say?" asked Isaiah.

"Tell the people that they are like grass and flowers. The flesh of man grows and blooms and then it withers and dies as the breath of God blows and His spirit wills. The word of God, however, is undamaged and it is permanent.

"Tell the people, however, that there is good news. God will come with a strong hand and His arm shall rule for Him. The hand of the Lord shall be capable of rewarding and shall also initiate a great work. When He comes He shall feed His people as a shepherd feeds his lambs. He shall protect them in his everlasting arms, and He shall lead His people gently.

"Have you ever considered the majesty of God, the Creator, who measured the waters of the earth, whole oceans, in the palm of his hand, the One who placed the mountains, and balanced them delicately with the hills? Do you think God had to consult engineers?

"Nations must seem to God as drops in a bucket or dust on a scale. How then can you describe God, for there is no way of comparison.

"It is ridiculous to attempt to reduce God to a skillful image of gold made by an artist. Don't you know anything? Haven't you heard, were you not always told, don't you know that from the very beginning of the foundations of existence that there is only One that sits on top of everything? The creator, who spread the heavens as easily as a woman spreads a sheet, and set the earth like a tent in which man could live.

"God rules. God makes and breaks princes and judges. To whom then can the Lord be compared? To no one, for there is none like Him.

"Wake up. Take a look at the majesty and power of God. Who dares to think that anything can be hidden from God.

"Have you not heard, have you not known that the Everlasting God, the Lord, the creator of the ends of the earth is never weary, nor depressed, nor is there any way of equalling His understanding.

"God sometimes chooses to grant strength to the weak. It is also noticeable that even the young people with their vigor and freshness become tired and lose their force, but the people, young and old, who serve God have an inner strength from the Lord, and they shall continually be refreshed by the Lord, they shall often have their spirits soar as if borne on the wings of an eagle. They shall run and not notice their weariness, and they shall walk and feel no faintness."

Chap.
41

"Be quiet a minute," spoke Isaiah, "and listen to what God has to say."

"Who makes history?" asks God. "I make it. Often have I blessed a righteous man and led him to victory. I also planned the system of generations and placed within man the seeds of cooperation so that the carpenter would encourage the goldsmith, and the various skills of various people would work together in order that buildings might be constructed. This is part of the plan.

"Also remember," says God, "that I have chosen Israel as my servant and Israel is not to be afraid. In due time I will strengthen Israel and I will confuse those that strive against the servants of God.

"Do not fear. I am the Lord. I will give you strong support. I will make of you, the servants of God, more effective than a threshing machine and those who oppose you will be scattered like dust and disappear in the wind.

"I will also be helpful to the poor. Their cries will be heard and I will make new springs for them for their thirst, I will cause trees to be planted in desert places, and I will enable the people to secure irrigation and make orchards in the desert. These things I will do in order that the people may know that I am the Lord, the Holy One of Israel.

"What about some of the idols made by hands that you have worshipped? Can they tell what has happened in the past or can they look into the future? No, but I the Lord can do these things.

"What about Cyrus? Did I not tell you that one would come from the north at my bidding? None of you or your idols, or soothsayers knew of this.

"Was I not the first to tell Jerusalem that help was on the way? Don't you see that your idols and your various little hang-ups are foolishness and a waste of time?"

Chap.
42

"What is more, I am sending to you my very special servant. I shall place my own spirit upon him and he will come for the benefit of all nations and shall reveal real justice.

"My chosen one shall not be a loud mouth, a ranter, nor a great warrior, but He will be gentle and careful, not a harmful person. He will open up the barrel of truth, He will be completely successful, never discouraged in spite of difficulties, and his law shall spread over the whole earth.

"I am the Lord, and I will bless my chosen one, and I will give him complete rigtheousness and I will present him to the people as part of my promise. The chosen one shall be a shining light for all the world, for he shall enable the blind to see, and he will liberate men from prisons that are real as well as imaginary. I am God, and I will not share my glory with idols. In fact, the idol bit has had it. There is a new program on the way.

"As I announce my chosen one also I announce new ways and new thoughts for men. Begin to sing a new song to God, even you sailors. Sing a joyful song. Let the mountain people sing with joy and the wilderness folk.

"Let everyone give glory to God. I have waited long enough," says God. "Now I will go forth as a mighty man. When necessary, I will destroy. Sometimes I will use drouth and make water scarce. I will do wonderful things, providing all kinds of things for the blind, and I will straighten out many crooked problems for my servants.

"Many who have blindly worshipped idols shall repent, and many who have not listened to my voice will begin to hear. Often the worst offenders are my own people who refuse to see and who will not listen.

"Man is responsible for his own troubles for he refuses to hear God, or to behold his majesty and he brings calamity on himself. When will you learn? Even these miseries that man brings on himself are merely my way of trying to teach man to repent," says the Lord.

Chap.
43

"Again I say to you, Israel," says the Lord, "You have no cause for fear, for I have redeemed you, and named you, and claimed you. I stand with you in times of trouble.

"Some day I will gather you when you have scattered, and I will reassemble you from all over the world. I will protect you because you are called by my name.

"No one can testify or witness about their meagre gods as you can witness about me, the One Lord. You know what I have done. You know as a matter of record how I destroyed the Egyptians in the waters of the sea and how you were delivered from the menace of the great horde from the north.

"Remember, you are my witness that there is no other God but me. I am your Holy One, the Creator of Israel. What is more, I have great plans for the future, involving the reclamation of desert lands. In spite of all this, you have not properly worshipped me. You do not bring a fair portion to the house of the Lord, and you have wearied me with your sins and your errors. Because of this, I have caused people to think poorly of your priests and your judges. Yet I am still the Redeemer, and I continue to blot out your transgressions for my name's sake."

"I have declared myself again and again," says the Lord. "I am the one Holy One, I am the first and the last, and there is no God beside me. You are to be witnesses to this fact.

"The people that make graven images, and worship material things, they are in for it. There will be no peace in their minds, their downfall is assured.

"You remember me, you servants of the most high God. You are to be my witnesses. I have blotted out your sins and forgiven your errors. Therefore you are to testify in my behalf to all the world.

"Remind people that I am the Lord God of hosts. I am capable of confusing the liars, disproving the soothsayers, and making the highly educated seem to be fools. I can do all things. I will dry up rivers when necessary, and will use men like Cyrus and cause him to decree that the temple of the Lord be built again in Jerusalem."

"The Lord has announced," reported Isaiah, "that He has chosen Cyrus, a man who does not know God, to carry out the wishes of the Lord. The Lord will tear down the gates of the cities that resist Cyrus, and Cyrus will obtain hidden treasures to finance his conquest.

"The Lord is using Cyrus in order that everyone under the sun will know there is but one God. The Lord will use Cyrus to subdue Egypt and Ethiopia and then Cyrus will release the captives of Israel and encourage them to return to Jerusalem and to rebuild the temple. The Lord plans all these things for his own glory.

"To His people Israel the Lord orders them to look to Him for salvation for the Lord is a great God and a just God. The Lord has also decreed that eventually every knee shall bow and every tongue confess the righteousness of God and the availability of His salvation.

"It is a laugh the way the idol gods of Babylon fall off carts and can't stand being moved from one place to another. If these gods can't even help themselves, how can they possibly help anybody else?

"Would you be interested in comparing the Lord God of Israel, the creator, with a god made by a craftsman? Ridiculous, for there is only one true God, the Lord. In fact, He expects to bring his salvation to Israel, and to personalize his salvation among his chosen people.

"Babylon, you've had it," says the Lord. "You will be uncovered and shown to be as corrupt as you truly are.

"I let my people come under your rule because of their sin, but you mistreated them and you'll pay for it. You have flaunted your success and considered yourself to be the Queen of the kingdoms, but you will be degraded. You will lose your following. The astrologers, the stargazers, the soothsayers, the magicians, none of these can save you. You will be destroyed as a kingdom and you will be crushed by too much advice and by wickedness itself.

"In a way, you are lucky, you descendants of Jacob," says the Lord, "for I am going to deliver you for the sake of my own name and for my glory. I have long told you of creation and also of things planned in the future so you would not be tempted to attribute anything to some graven image which you devised overnight.

"Remember that I am the Lord of all. I control the Babylonians as well as the children of Israel. I have never been shy about declaring that I am God, who rules all the earth and all the people. I have redeemed Israel as simply as I caused the water to flow for the people in the wilderness. Furthermore, have decreed that there will be no peace for the wicked.

"Listen to me," says the Lord, "for I am sending one called from birth to pronounce my words and declare my glory. It is sad that my own people, of whom my servant is one, will not receive him, but the Gentiles will and He shall be a light to them. Kings and princes shall in time come to worship my anointed one.

"I will send my representative at a proper time and he shall be similar to a covenant for the people, so that those in darkness may see some light, prisoners may be freed who are unjustly held, and the prince that I send will lead in a gentle manner.

"This shall be the beginning of great joy and a great time of singing for the Lord will show mercy on his people. Those who have been forsaken because of their sins will be restored. Freedom will again be your prized possession.

"In spite of how sad and desolate the area may seem to you now, it will some day be crowded with people and prosperous. You wonder how these things shall be? I will see to it that the gentiles restore you themselves, they will provide transportation for your descendants to return. The gentiles will be concerned with your welfare and the great leaders among them shall be considerate and will bring things to you as if they were your servants.

"What is more, I will be against anyone who turns against you. This should be a comfort and a challenge to you. In time, every living person shall know that I am the one true Lord of all.

"Do you know what caused you to be led captive in the first place?" asked Isaiah. "Well, it wasn't the weakness of God, for He can do anything, but it was sin and disobedience. God is always capable of anything, for he can fill the desert with water or dry up the seas.

"The Lord has blessed me with the wisdom of words and the Lord reveals to me what I should say. I am dead set on this matter and no one will stop me from speaking what God has told me to say.

"The people who try to stop me become enemies of God and they disappear as completely as an old sweater gets eaten by the moths. Trust in the Lord, even if you are in deep despair, trust in God, for God delivers. Those who try to tough it out for themselves and attempt to live without God will be miserable and their sorrows will increase.

Chap.
51

"Listen to me, those of you who seek to live a righteous way," says the Lord, "recall that I have encouraged you from the start. You are descendants of Abraham and I blessed him and I will bless your land for in time it shall change from a barren country to one that is fruitful and yields abundance.

"Those who are my people and seek my righteousness do not need to worry about being few in number or encountering difficulties. The wicked and their evil ways are perishable, but my salvation is eternal. Be sure that the righteous shall have their day, their times of great joy, for this promise is mine, and I am the Keeper of the Promises.

"Why should a righteous person be afraid of any man, for are not all of them short-lived, and nothing they do can impede the will of God. I have declared you to be my people, rejoice in that announcement and obey my laws.

"You have suffered enough for the time being. You have deserved it, but I am planning to bring you great relief.

Chap.
52

"Now get with it. Get up and get to work. I am with you always. My people need to remember that I am God and that I care for my people.

"How beautiful upon the mountains are the feet of them that bring good news, that speak of peace, and announce salvation. There is no greater shout than the refreshing words 'God reigns!'

"This will be no secret, but everyone in all the world will know of God and his offer of salvation. You are going to be properly released from captivity and God shall be your guide.

"My very special representative shall appear among you and he shall astonish the lowly and the mighty, even kings shall be dumbfounded by his teaching. He shall be physically abused, but even then shall he be an astonishment, for he shall speak wonders and declare new ideas.

Chap.
53

"Who is this servant of the Most High God? Well, he will grow up like anyone else, a root out of the ground, a tender plant, and he shall have no great physical characteristic that shall set him apart from ordinary people.

"He will, of course, be despised and rejected by men, a man who knows sorrow and has felt grief, and many people will ignore him. Yet the sorrows that he shall bear are our sorrows, and many of us will just think he is a nutty teacher, even though he will be wounded for our sakes, and beaten because we have sinned, and still his very scars shall be signs for our healing.

"When he is oppressed he does not blow his top and he appears as innocent and harmless before his tormentors as a lamb before the shearer. We are the ones who have gone astray, not him. Yet the Lord allowed him to accept the iniquity of us all.

"He will be taken from prison to judgment, for the sake of all of us poor sinners, he will die with the wicked and be buried with the rich, yet he committed no violence himself and he had not deceived anyone. It was God's will that he must suffer, and he shall understand that he does this for a worthy cause."

Chap.
54

"Now is a time for celebration," said Isaiah, "for great things are beginning to happen. Jerusalem can rejoice at this opportunity, and the great messages entrusted to Israel shall be made available to the people of the world. All of this is because God is Lord of the whole earth, and not just a part of it.

"At times it seems as if God has momentarily forgotten his people, and in his anger over the way men do things God sometimes seems to hide his face, but God returns with great mercy. For God has said that though the mountains and the hills might disappear, the kindness and the love of God will never cease.

"Let all the children be taught about God and in this manner they may attain his peace. What is more, when people organize against the followers of God, they shall not be successful. Remember, I have created the ones who destroy as well as the ones who build and I assure you that no weapon ever formed by man can do away with my people against my will. This is what comes of being a follower of God!

Chap.
55

"Are you thirsty or hungry?" asks God. "Well, come to me and be refreshed. I am willing to make an agreement with you as I did with David, and he is an example of how I deal with my people. Nations and people will seek you because they too want to be under the Lord God of all.

"Seek the Lord at once. Call on God while you have the chance. Tell the wicked to quit his evil ways, and encourage the unrighteous ones to even do away with evil thoughts. God stands ready to receive the repentant.

"This is because God's ways are not similar to our ways and His thoughts are different from ours and are higher thoughts than the heavens are higher than the earth.

"The word of God is like the rain as it comes down to water the earth, and causes the earth to bring forth plants and flowers, that it may provide seed for the sower and bread to the eater. This is the way of God's word, it shall not return to God unproductive, but it shall accomplish his will, and it shall fulfil his purpose.

"Because of this you shall learn to go out with great joy, and live in peace, the mountains and hills shall seem to be full of the sound of music, and the rustling leaves shall sound like applause. Where you were accustomed to seeing thorns you will see a fir tree and where there were briars you will see a myrtle tree, and these are to be everlasting signs marking the glory of God, and nothing can change this plan.

Chap. 56

"In God's name, I plead with you to do justly, for the revelation of God is close at hand," said Isaiah. "Blessings on those who refrain from evil and who pay proper tribute to the Lord on his holy day.

"Non-Jews have no reason for alarm. The Lord is ready to receive strangers, eunuchs, deformed, retarded, for God has prepared a place for everyone that calls on His name. God's house is a house of prayer, and it is a house for people. The Lord will gather to him all those that seek Him.

"Not so with those whose lives are a succession of selfish pursuits. Greedy people, looking out only for themselves, and ruining their minds with strong drink.

Chap. 57

"Why is it that often good people die young and long before they are old? Let me assure you that God often takes them to deliver them from evil days that might lie ahead for them. Remember, the godly who die surely rest in peace.

"Those who forsake God, and seek gods of their own, who pursue their own pleasure, and build altars for themselves on lofty places, there is no help for them. Their whole program is self-defeating.

"God has placed a limit on the idol worshippers and self-seeking people. The High and Holy God has a place for the humble and the contrite, but no place for the arrogant. The wicked shall be like a choppy sea whose waters turn up dirt and mire and there is no peace for the wicked, but there is peace for the righteous, for God heals and God bestows his peace.

Chap. 58

"God has instructed me," said Isaiah, "to speak frankly to you. You enjoy coming to church on Sunday and making the appearance of devoutness, but you continue to hate and despise people, to quarrel, and to seek material things. God is not impressed.

"God says that if you want to impress Him you should be concerning yourself with feeding the hungry and clothing the naked. God would have you free people from oppression. When you do these things, your own life will change, and you will shine as a fresh morning star and the glory of the Lord will be an escort for you. Try it, you'll like it! The Lord will see that you are uplifted in spirit and His joy will abide in you."

Chap.
59

"The big trouble with you people," continued Isaiah, "is that your sins have built a wall between you and God. You have trusted in vanity and mischief, and you disregard justice. Your feet run to evil and you think nothing of shedding innocent blood. Your very wickedness stands in the way of your peace, you walk in darkness and keep yelling for a light. Anyone who tries righteousness is scorned.

"God saw your plight and so he is sending a Redeemer, one who has righteousness strong as an armor and salvation like a helmet. The Redeemer will lay down the law, he will cover the earth like a flood, and he shall bless those who believe in him. Those who recognize him shall be filled with the Holy Spirit of God and they shall learn to love good and to hate evil.

Chap.
60

"Rise and shine! The time is coming for the glory of God to be revealed. All the peoples of the earth shall seek the new light that comes among you.

"There is a great future in store for you. Presidents and kings shall help you, transportation shall be furnished you to bring your relatives from distant lands, and foreign aid shall see to the rebuilding of your cities. Jerusalem shall again become the Glorious City. Peace and righteousness shall again some day be restored and violence shall disappear from your land. Your key words shall be salvation and praise and the glory of the Lord will shine to such an extent that the sun and the moon will almost go unnoticed. Your people will become good people and greatly beloved, for the Lord himself shall arrange this."

Chap.
61

"The spirit of the Lord has come upon me," proclaimed Isaiah, "and I am inspired of God to preach good news, to heal the broken hearted, and to liberate those who are oppressed in body or mind. I am prepared to exchange beauty for ashes, soothing oil for mourning, and praise for the neglected, and to thereby change people into trees of righteousness.

"Those who are so touched by the spirit of God shall become priests and ministers, and workers of good deeds. The Lord will reward you for all your trouble, and everlasting joy shall be your innermost possession. The Lord will cause the earth to break forth in righteousness in a manner similar to the budding of flowers and the beginning of spring."

"The Lord has told me" said Isaiah, "that for the sake of his people the cause of righteousness shall prevail and people of all races and nations will have the opportunity of knowing the righteousness of God and they shall accept a new name for all those who follow the revealed righteousness of God. [1]

"No longer will you be despised and a new holiness will come to Jerusalem. The Lord also has planned that there shall be an end of the world, a day of judgment, a time for the full glory to the righteous. The righteous shall then be truly called a holy people."

"Who is this that I see now in my vision?" called forth Isaiah.

"It is I, the Lord. I am announcing salvation and declaring that I am come to save."

"Why are your clothes so red, O Lord?" asked Isaiah.

"It is the blood of the enemies of God. I will stamp out evil in my fury. I sometimes crush whole nations because of their evil. I am capable of executing all necessary judgments."

"I will tell your people, O Lord, of your loving kindness to those who understand and your great goodness to your people of Israel. Surely God has become a saviour. He has redeemed his people in love and because of his pity for those who are afflicted. Those who rebelled and rejected him, they had to be treated as enemies."

"Now, Lord, hear my prayer. Remember your promises to Moses, remember how you made a glorious name by leading your people through the wilderness. O Lord, you are still our deliverer, you are still our father. It is not Abraham or some earthly father, but you are our Father. We confess that our hearts have been hardened and we have sinned, but return to us. Restore to us our name and our place.

"It would be great, O Lord, if you would open the heavens and come down and be with us. This would make a great impression on all the earth and man could see the mountains melt and the waters boil as a sign of your presence and your power.

"We need a revelation. No eye has seen nor ear heard the thing you have prepared for the righteous. In the meantime, we find ourselves a wicked people living in sin. Take us, Father, like the potter takes the clay, and make us worthwhile. Everything is in a mess. Come help our world, O Lord, please come. Amen."

"People who never showed any interest in me are now calling

---

[1] I think this is a prophecy of the name Christian

on my name," says the Lord. "I am glad for them. My own people, however, continue to reject me, even though I have extended my arms and sought them. My people continually turn to material things and worship prices and such commercial matters. Yet these very people disdain from associating with those they consider inferior persons. This just makes me smell smoke! I will not accept this kind of thing, and punishment is sure to come.

"I will not destroy all my people because there are some who still worship me properly and who seek righteousness. For their sake I will bring forth a saviour who will make provision for them.

"As for those who have forsaken me, you have had it. I will cause you inner discomfort. Food will not satisfy your hunger, nor will drink satisfy your thirst. While my servants shall be full of joy, you will be perplexed and uncomfortable. Your name will fade and a new name will be assigned to my followers."

"In the final times I will create a new heaven and a new earth," said the Lord. "All former things shall be forgotten and a great and joyful newness shall be everywhere. There shall be no more young and old, but all shall be ageless. There shall be houses and vineyards, but these shall be ceaseless. No one will build and then others enjoy the building, for a man will continue to live. No work shall be in vain and there shall be such a sense of peace that the wolf and the lamb shall reside together and there shall be no hurt nor any harm in all the holy mountain of God where I, the Lord, will dwell eternally with my people."

"Now hear my final words," says the Lord. "Heaven is my throne and earth is my footstool. You can't match that with a temple. My love turns to the humble and contrite man, who acknowledges that I, the Lord, rule over everything.

"To those others, however, who reject me and make fun of me, I will send massive troubles to them. Let them make sport for awhile of you who are my followers, but not far off is the sound of their destruction, for I will destroy them myself. I will punish them and the world with fire.

"In the middle of all the tumult there will be missionaries throughout the world proclaiming my name and publishing the good news. These persons shall have great success and shall win many to the cause of righteousness. These carriers of the gospel shall be considered by me as my representatives.

"When the time comes for my new heaven and new earth, my people will have a new eternal name, all worship shall be a regular matter and my people will realize that I have punished all the wicked and the wicked will be a pitiful sight to see."

JEREMIAH

Jerry,[1] an ordained minister from El Dorado,[2] received a number of messages from God and these are recorded here.

"I have known you a long time, Jerry," said the Lord, "for I planned that you should be born for a mission and I prepared you to be a prophet."

"I am overwhelmed by this news, God. I really am surprised for I seem to be very ordinary and certainly no great speaker," replied Jerry.

"Don't think of yourself as being ordinary or like a child for I intend to be with you and I will inspire you when you speak. Don't get mike fright, either, for remember that I am sponsoring you and as always I am willing and capable of delivering you at any time," said the Lord God.

The Lord then touched the tongue of Jerry and put words into Jerry's mouth.

"Bear in mind," said God, "that I have put you over nations and kingdoms, to pull down in some places and to build in others, and in some places to merely plant ideas."

God then said, "What do you see in your mind now, Jerry?"

"I see a hickory switch."

"Good. That is simply a sign of my intent to punish the wicked. What else do you see?"

"I see a pot boiling and the front of the pot is facing north."

"That is accurate. I am preparing the armies of the heathen people of the north and they will come south and march against Jerusalem. This is being done as punishment to my people who have forgotten me and who have turned to false gods and gods made by the hand of man."

"Don't be afraid to tell the king and all the people about this. They won't like to hear it, but they will not harm you for I will be at your side and I will see to it that nothing happens to you."

"Listen, you people of Israel, hear what God has to say," spoke Jerry.

"I remember well your history, you Israelites," said God. "I remember how eager your ancestors were to serve me in the wilderness, and how excited the people were who viewed the miracles of those early days."

"Now you've blown it. You and your fathers have wandered into strange ways and adopted many of the customs of the people you have conquered. How stupid can you get? You have changed

---

[1]Jeremiah   [2]Anathoth

426

gods, when you were prospering under the only one true God.

"My words and my commandments were like containers full of living water and you have exchanged this for broken pitchers. You should be ashamed like a thief caught in the act. Incidentally, now that you see disaster coming from the north and the peril of invasion at hand, where are your icky little gods? Can they help you?

"It amazes me how you have forgotten me. A bride never forgets the wedding gown, but you have forgotten me. You have even shed innocent blood for profit. You even try to picture yourself as innocent and intimate that you were a victim of circumstance. Hog wash! You cannot deceive the Lord, your maker."

Chap.
3

"There is an old law," said Jerry, "that says that if a man divorces his wife and then she marries someone else, the wife cannot return to her first husband because she has been corrupted. God knows that Israel has forgotten the Lord, departed to other gods, and deserves no consideration, but the Lord is still willing to receive again a penitent Israel.

"Your wickedness and your pursuit of strange gods has caused the Lord to withhold the spring rains. The Lord has spoken to me about such things."

"Do you know what God said to me? He said, 'Have you observed the evil that is being done by backsliding Israel? It is unbelievable how wicked Israel has become.'

"God also spoke about your sister tribe, Judah. You would think that Judah would learn from the experience of Israel, but such was not the case. Judah built graven images as fast as she could find the stones, and it is a rocky area.

"God has asked me to plead with you, Israel, and beg you to return to God, to acknowledge him and to worship him. The Lord has told me to remind you that He is merciful and that He will not keep His anger forever.

"Salvation doesn't come down like water flowing from the mountains, but it comes from God. God assures all of you people that if you will repent and call upon His name that He will receive you again.

"God promises that He will send wise leaders for you, that you will prosper, that you will recover your land, and that all the people of Israel and Judah will be as me. All you have to do is call God your father and walk in His ways.

Chap.
4

"The opportunity is here," said Jerry to the men of Israel and Judah. "All you need to do is turn to God, to call upon the name of the Lord and declare the Lord God to be your true ruler. If you would only do this, God would make of you a blessing and a leader among the nations of the earth.

"But look out, you people of Jerusalem. If you can run you'd better get with it, for you have failed to repent and because of your sin a great army is forming in the north and it is coming down fast. It is still not too late to repent, but if you turn to God you must do so instantly, for your doom is on the way.

"It is a sad thing for me to behold the ruin of the people, but you asked for it. The Lord is going to allow the northern horde to destroy this land and make it a desolate place, but there will at least be a small remnant saved. This is the way and the will of God. In my vision," continued Jerry, "I can see the people in distress and I can hear their gasping cries of frustration and pain.

Chap.
5

"It would be great if you could point out to me one fine, honest, God-fearing leader of the people, then the Lord could work through him and God would be willing to save the people. Unfortunately, there is no such person at present.

"You people are bull-headed and stiffnecked beyond description," said Jerry. "The leaders in government are the same way. All are doomed. There is no peace for the wicked. The Lord has definitely declared his judgment.

"God cannot overlook such defiance. Many of the people go so far as to say that God would not dare punish His own people. Well, you'd better believe it, for the Lord is a jealous God, and the Lord plans to bring a nation from a long distance, a nation with a strange language, and this nation shall consume and destroy.

"Some of you are dumb enough to ask why the Lord allows such a thing as a foreign people to capture Jerusalem. Well, it is because of the sins of the chosen ones. The ministers are preaching their own ideas and the judges rule on a basis of their own ideas, and the people are content to let this occur."

Chap.
6

"Now listen to me, you people of the tribe of Benjamin," said Jerry, "you had better get ready to split, for the forces of the north are coming against you. You are in bad shape because of your sins. Actually you are as helpless as a young and delicate girl surrounded by a bunch of hot blooded shepherds."

"I wish you had sense enough to repent at once, but to whom can I speak? You people have put plugs in your ears, and you will not listen to the word of the Lord.

"Actually I am as steamed up as God is in connection with your sins. The whole city is consumed with graft and evil doings, included in the wrongdoers are most of the judges, educators, and priests. These crooked people call forth 'peace, peace,' when there is no peace. What is more, the people and their leaders are not ashamed.

"As a result God has planned to punish you all with many problems and great dismay shall come your way.

"A cruel people from the north will descend on you and you shall be terrified long before the north men arrive in armored array. You have sinned and not repented, and so the Lord has cast you aside as damaged silver, no longer fit for use."

"I have also a word to the tribe of Judah," proclaimed Jerry, as he stood on the top steps of the temple. "Change your ways. Begin to deal fairly with each other and with strangers, take an interest in helping the sick and the elderly, care for the widow, and God will preserve your place here in this fair land.

"Yet you steal, murder, and commit adultery during the week and then on the Sabbath day you come into the temple, which is known as God's sanctuary. and disregard all the evil which you continually plan. You have made God's house a den of robbers. God will do to this house, which is called by God's name, even as he did to the Westminster Encampment,[1] simply because of the evil you do.

"Don't you know what goes on at Jerusalem? Haven't you seen whole families working together to gather an offering to some strange god? This is not only a way of stirring God's anger, but it is a cause of confusion among the people.

"God is angry. The people have contaminated the church. There is sure destruction in store for the people and there shall be a great slaughter with no proper burials involved.

"The invaders who come will be a mean bunch. In fact, they will dig up the bones of the prophets and the king and spread them in the sun. Times will be so difficult that the people who survive will envy the dead. One would think you would know better. The stork knows when to travel, so does the turtle, the crow, and the swallow, and yet you don't seem to understand the judgment of God.

"There are some so-called modern teachers among you who do not know enough to obey God, and they will go down the drain for sure. They will lose their wives and their possessions. Yet these same teachers have often said that everything was all right, yet they could easily see the sin and injustice that existed all around them.

"Bad times are close ahead, and when you look for peace, you will not find it and when you seek health you will find only new ailments.

"You people have no idea how grieved I am. I know what is going to happen and how you could save all this with great repentance, but there is no way to ease my pain, for the Lord is angry and vengeance is on its way."

"I wish I could tie my body onto an artesian well so that I could cry all day without running out of tears.[2] I even wish I had a

[1] Shiloh [2] Jerry is really pouring it on here

little cabin in the back woods where I could get away from it all. The people around will bend their tongues and shoot lies as arrows, but they will not take a bow and arrow to defend their country. The people have wilfully separated themselves from God.

"One of the worst things that has happened to you people," continued Jerry, "is that you lie to each other and deceive each other so much that the whole nation is in decay.

"The Lord will not let this condition remain unpunished and so Jerusalem shall be reduced to ruins, predators shall have dens in the city, and the communities of Judah shall be left desolate and uninhabited.

"The punishment that I have planned for these people is harsh, but they deserve it. For one thing, bitterness and a complaining attitude shall be part of their existence, and the people will be scattered throughout the world in many nations and in strange and far away lands they will be mistreated.

"You might as well alert the best moaners and groaners among your loudest women, for there is going to be plenty cause for loud wailing. You might as well pick out a wall for it now and get with it. Your ladies might teach your daughters how to wail, too, because there is going to be enough trouble to spread over more than one generation.

"The Lord suggests that the intelligent person should not think that he can make it on his own brain, nor the mighty warrior survive by his own strength, nor the rich man buy his way free, but let everyone turn to the Lord, and glory in God's name, and recognize the righteousness, the loving kindness, and the judgment of the Lord. The Lord has definitely decided to punish the wicked, regardless of race, color, creed, or national extraction."

Chap.
10

The very essence of ignorance is to go into the forest, cut down a tree, bring it into town, decorate it with silver, nail it so it cannot move, and then worship it as a god. How stupid can you get, you who serve such man-made gods.

The Lord is a true God, a living God, one who causes the earth to tremble, and no nation can withstand the displeasure of the Lord. The Lord God is the one who made the earth and all existence, the Lord utters his voice and it rains, and lightnings and winds are at His command.

The Lord has decided to eject from the land the people who turned against him. The Lord is greatly disappointed that the people have misused his church, and God is disturbed that the ministers and leaders of the church have polluted the worship in the sanctuary.

"Please, Lord," prayed Jerry, "ease down a bit on me. Do not be too harsh on me, for already I am in great trouble. Pour some of your anger on the wicked invaders who are making a wasteland out of our country."

"Now listen, Jerry," said God, "and pass this word to the people. I made an agreement with the fathers and forefathers in all Israel, and the arrangement was that the children of Israel would obey my commandments and I would bless them, and be with them, and protect them.

"What happened is very simple. The people ceased to obey my commandments and they sought strange gods and pursued evil and now they will be punished. Now Jerry, there is no point in your praying to me in behalf of these people because the evil is done and the punishment is on the way. It is because of the wickedness of the people in worshipping Baal that I am bringing great trouble on the people."

The Lord then revealed to me that among other things the leaders of the Jews were planning to kill me, and I was being set up as a lamb for slaughter. The Lord enabled me to understand that the leaders were worried over my prophecies and my messages and planned to stop these by killing me.

When I learned all this, and that the group that planned to kill me was known as the Black Shadow[1] Gang, I encouraged the Lord to deal with them justly. As a result, the Lord promised to punish the gang, and to see that they died by the sword or by famine, and other punishments would come until there were no remnants of the group to carry on their evil ways.

"Now, Lord," prayed Jerry, "I know you are righteous and wise but there is one thing that really bugs me, and that is the prosperity of the wicked. It seems obvious to me that the hell raisers are all happy and I am always in trouble. I would like to suggest a change in strategy. Why don't you just line the wicked up and have them march into the slaughter pens.

"The wicked really are doing us no good. They pollute the land, kill off all the game without observing the game laws, and they pooh-pooh the idea that you will do anything about it."

"All right, Jerry, now listen carefully to what I'm saying," said the Lord. "If you can't stand running with men, such as watching a few evil men prosper, how will you do when you must race against horses? If you can't keep the faith in a place where there is peace and quiet, what will you do when the Jordan overflows or other disasters take place?

"You do have troubles, Jerry. Your own family tells lies about you. Just don't depend on them or believe what they say. You can trust me, though, Jerry. What you must first understand is that I have abandoned my people for the present because of their sins. My people have trod upon my name and defiled my house.

[1]Anathoth

"Because of this my sword of destruction is already determined. The whole land shall be scorched and violated by the enemy. I will also punish the pagan neighbors and they too shall be taken into captivity. On the other hand, when my people repent, and if they call upon my name, I will in time restore the people to their native land and I will bless them. Again I say, over the long haul, the wicked will perish and the righteous shall enjoy the land.

Chap.
13

"Let me give you an illustration," said the Lord to Jerry. "Go and buy yourself a new pair of underwear. Wear it for a few days and then go hide it in a rock."

Jerry did as God said. About a month later the Lord moved Jerry to go and get his dirty underwear which he had stuffed in the rock. Jerry retrieved the clothing and found that it was ruined with mildew and general dirt and decay.

"Now, Jerry," said the Lord, "that is a good illustration of what is in store for Judah and Jerusalem. The people who follow strange gods and neglect to worship the Lord will end up just like dirty, shredded, worn-out underwear."

Jerry then turned to the people of the land and said, "Every bottle shall be filled with wine."

"That doesn't make sense," they replied, "for everybody knows that. So what?"

"It is God's way of saying that all of you with your wicked leaders shall be full of wine and you will be smashed against each other like bottles and your destruction is near," spoke Jerry.

"Why don't you shape up?" continued Jerry. "Give glory to God before it is too late, and He encloses you in darkness and despair. Tell your king and queen to humble themselves. As things stand now, the government will be overthrown and Judah will be taken captive. What then about your beautiful herds and flocks? When this destruction comes you will no doubt wonder why it is happening to you. I am telling you now. Your own evil and neglect of God has brought this whole trouble down upon you. In fact, you have become so accustomed to doing evil that changing to good all of a sudden would be almost like asking a leopard to change his spots."

"Because you have forgotten me," said the Lord, "and trusted in falsehood and your own selfish ways, you are doomed. I have watched your meanness and your self-centered evil and as a result Jerusalem will be destroyed. I wonder how long it will take you to repent."

Chap.
14

The word of the Lord came to Jerry and told him that there would be a terrible drought and famine in the land. The time would come when the head of the household would send the young men for water and they would return ashamed with empty canteens. The farmers would be ruined and the ranchers would lose their cattle.

"O Lord," prayed Jerry, "There is no doubt about our being a sinful nation, but for your own sake and your own reputation don't let strangers see the terrible trouble which you have promised. We are your people and this is your land; so please cancel the drought and famine."

"The people have rejected me, Jerry," said the Lord, "so don't waste your breath praying for them. I have planned to see that they are punished by the famine and also by military aggression."

"There are a lot of preachers, Lord," said Jerry, "that are telling the people that everything is going to be fine."

"They are preaching lies, then," said the Lord, "and I have not instructed or inspired them to speak this way. In fact, I will see to it that the famine and the sword shall make an end to these phony preachers. Also the people who listen to them will be punished and they will die in the streets of Jerusalem, some from famine and some from the sword of the enemy.

"This ungodly outfit can let their tears flow, for they are going to have plenty about which to cry."

"We confess our wickedness and the wickedness of our fathers[1], and now we plead with you to remember us. Do not disgrace your record of saving us. Where else can we receive help? Is there some other god on whom we can depend for rain? We will serve you, O Lord, for we know that all things are in your hands and under your care.

Chap. 15

"I am sorry, Jerry, but even if Moses and ole Sam asked me I would not change my mind about socking it to these people," said the Lord.

"What is more," continued the Lord, "if her people ask you what to do you can tell them of their four choices, one is just drop dead, another is to get a sword and fight back, another choice is to starve to death, and the fourth is to be led away into captivity.

"My plan is to see that my people who have forsaken me are led away into captivity. I will continually create difficult problems for them. There will be widows by the hundreds and the mothers will cry bitterly for all their sons will be dead."

Then Jerry spoke to himself saying, "Woe is me. My own dear mother must be sad for she has brought into the world an unsuccessful sad sack. Everybody hates me, even though I owe no money and nobody owes me any. I have prayed to you in their behalf and the people still curse me."

"Trying to change these people is like trying to break iron bars," said the Lord, "and so I will deliver them and all their wealth

[1] This has always been easy

to their enemies."

"Now, Lord," prayed Jerry, "I would like to say a few kind words in my own behalf. I have suffered terribly because of my faithfulness. I have been living on your words and speaking constantly in your behalf. When the others made fun of you, O Lord, I sat alone in your defense. Your help to me has been very spotty, a little here and a little there, but no real deliverance from all the people that persecute me."

"Don't be so touchy now, Jerry," said the Lord. "Your job is to speak for me to the people. You are not to be overwhelmed by them, but you are to overwhelm them with your sure words which I give you in my name. The people won't like it and they will try all kinds of things against you, but I am with you and I will watch carefully over you, for I am proud of you, and I will in time save you."

Chap.
16

The Lord continued to speak to Jerry and told him not to get married and have children for such would merely bring grief for the Lord was going to punish the Jews and there would be death and shame. The Lord reminded Jerry that the peace of the Lord was going to be withheld at this time from the Jews. All joyous sounds of the people, such as occasioned by a wedding feast, and all mirth and laughter would come to a halt, for God reminded Jerry that the punishment for the people who had turned their back on God was sure and terrible.

God told Jerry that when all this was told by him to the people that they would not believe it. In fact, with some indignation they shall say, "What have we done?"

"When this occurs, Jerry," said the Lord, "tell the people it is because their fathers have forsaken the Lord and followed other gods and that the present generation is even worse. Tell them again that I will have them driven out of this land and scattered. The conditions will be awful.

"However," continued the Lord, "the great day will come when the living Lord will again be honored and recognized, but this time it will be for bringing people back to the promised land.

"In the meantime, however, I will see that your enemies fish you out of watery hiding places, and hunters search you out of caves and canyons, and I will double your punishment for defiling my land."

"Lord, my strength and my fortress," prayed Jerry, "I am sure that people from everywhere will begin to say how foolish their fathers have been, knowing that it is silly to think that a man may make a god with his own hands."

"Then, Jerry," said the Lord, "when the people come to me with the right attitude I will demonstrate my power and let them see that I alone am the true God."

The people of Judah sin as if it were a law to follow, one that was written with an iron pen or the point of a diamond, and so the people of God shall be punished and forced to live on foreign soil.

The Lord has said, "Cursed is the man who trusts in mankind and disregards the Lord. Such a man will be like a desert traveler seeing mirages, and yet he shall continue to remain in a parched and barren land.

"Happy indeed is the man who trusts in God. Such a man is like a tree planted by everflowing waters, a tree whose leaves stay green and whose roots do not have to worry about periodic droughts.

"A man's heart is a deceitful thing. Only God can really search and see the heart. One way of seeing the heart of a man is to give him freedom and see how he does on his own. Some people secure riches, but those that secure riches improperly are eventually as unproductive as a quail that sits on a nest and never hatches anything. A man is a fool then to secure riches improperly."

Then Jerry spoke forth saying, "Lord, you are the only hope of Israel, and I know that everyone who forsakes you has had it. Heal me, though, Lord, then I know I will be well, save me, and then I know I will have security.

"Lord, did you know we have some smart alecs who say, 'Where is God's word? We don't see anything happening.' Thank goodness, that's not me. I do the best I can and I minister as well as I know how to do. Continue, Lord, to be my hope and not my terror. Pour it on those that persecute me, though. Don't let me be discouraged, but let my enemies be discouraged. In fact, give them the old double whammy."

The Lord then instructed Jerry to take a stand by the common gate to Jerusalem through which gate the kings and the people of Judah have historically come and gone.

Jerry then began to teach the people in accordance with his inspiration from the Lord.

"Mend your ways," said Jerry. "One thing you can start on is the proper observance of the Sabbath. You are not to be using the Sabbath for unnecessary manual labor, but the Sabbath is a time to rest from your labors and to worship God.

"Your fathers didn't do this," continued Jerry, "but they turned a deaf ear and became stubborn and self regulated. If you, however, will listen and will worship God properly and observe his day, then once again the kings and princes of Judah will come and go through these gates, riding in style. People from all the rural areas will then come to worship and bring their gifts to God, coming to the tabernacle in Jerusalem.

"If you don't respond to this plea, however," emphasized Jerry, "the Lord plans to bring ruin of the worst kind on you all."

Jerry then went down to watch the potter as he turned his wheel and made his pots, for Jerry was inspired of God to do this to learn a lesson.

While Jerry was watching the potter a fault developed in the vessel which the potter was making so he threw it down and made another vessel.

"Do you get the lesson, Jerry?" asked the Lord. "The people are as clay in my hands even as the clay is to the potter. I will deal with people and with nations as the potter deals with the clay.

"Now, Jerry, go tell the people everywhere about this. Tell the people I am planning to cast them aside. I tell you all that I will make the land a pitiful place and people will wonder what has happened to Israel. I will scatter the people and I will hide my face from them."

The people listened to all this and became angry with Jerry and the people began to criticize him behind his back and to agree not to listen to him any more.

Jerry then turned to God saying, "Do I receive evil in exchange for all the good I've tried to do for these people? I pleaded with you in their behalf, and now they turn around and want to hang me. All I can say now, Lord, is let them have it! Kill them in battle, let their children starve to death, don't forgive any of their sins, and deal with them when you are at the peak of your anger."

The Lord then led Jerry with his spirit and moved him to go to Watergate[1] and to take with him a vase and then having arrived at Watergate accompanied by a group of curious spectators and some members of the press, Jerry spoke to the people, being inspired by God to do so.

"Now hear this," said Jerry. "That word goes for the king as well as the people, rich and poor alike, the Lord is pronouncing doom on this nation because it has forsaken the God of truth and the Lord of honesty. In place of serving God, the people and their leaders have decided to serve such gods as power and wealth, and therefore instead of a refreshing sound, the name Watergate shall be a stench in the nose of the people.

"The Lord will not allow the leaders and responsible parties to prosper for long who cause such problems and obviously relegate the Lord to a secondary power. I will see to it that the offenders turn on one another and consume each other with their own bitterness."

Jerry then broke the vase which he was carrying and said, "Even as I have broken this vessel; so shall the Lord break this nation and destroy all those who have worshipped strange and man-made gods. The Lord has pronounced this judgement on those who consistently

[1]Tophet

refuse to do his will."

Now Pete[1] was Chief of Security for the city of Jerusalem and when he heard all that Jerry had said he had Jerry put in chains and exhibited on the court house lawn.

The next day Pete had Jerry brought to his office for questioning.

"Let me tell you a thing or two, Pete," said Jerry. "In the first place your name is no longer Pete, but your name is Mud.[2] The Lord is planning to make you a real terror to everybody around you and you will even begin to hate yourself.

"The king of Babylon will come and take this whole city and lead the people away captive. In addition, the invaders will steal everything in sight. You will be led into captivity yourself and you will die there, for the Lord will not allow you to escape."

Later that day Jerry prayed to the Lord in anguish saying, "Lord, you haven't helped me a dime's worth yet. I am hourly taunted, threatened, and accused. I spoke frankly to the people, telling them all the bad things in store for them, just exactly as you told me to do. I certainly can't keep quiet when your word is burning in my heart. The people are fed up with hearing me denounce them. I have not said a kind word to them yet, for you have given me none.

"In spite of everything, I am still sticking with you, Lord, and I guess some day things will get better. At least let me live to see some of your vengeance on these people. That will help some. Yet I still praise the Lord, for I know he will deliver the unfortunate in his day and in his way."

"At the same time, I wish I had never been born. I feel like cursing the man who brought word to my father that I was born.[3] In fact, curses on anyone who was standing around with a sword and didn't kill me while I was a baby. It would have been much better for me if I had been born dead. Since I've come into this world all I've seen is labor and sorrow.[4] All I do now is live in shame."

King Z,[5] who ruled over the area which included Jerusalem, had
been told that Bad Ned[6] was preparing to declare war and invade and so he asked the Chief of Security, ole Pete, to check with Jerry and find out if the Lord was going to deliver them from their prospective trouble.

Jerry turned to Pete and said, "You go and tell King Z that the Lord is going to be on the other side. In fact, the Lord is angry enough to fight against you himself and he will not help you in any

[1]Pashur
[2]Magormisabib
[3]Jerry is pretty depressed at this point
[4]Jerry is really feeling sorry for himself
[5]Zedekiah
[6]Nebuchadre

encounter against anybody.

"You can also tell King Z that he will be captured along with all his family and his servants. In fact, you have only two choices to offer to the people. One is to go out of the city and surrender and be led away into captivity and the other is to stay in Jerusalem and die by either famine or the sword.

"All of this, the Lord reminds you, is because you have forsaken God and neglected to obey his commandments."

Chap.
22

Jerry was then inspired of the Lord to go to the house of the king of Judah. When Jerry arrived he spoke to the king and to others who were present and would listen.

Jerry said, "I have a message from God. The Lord says to begin to deal justly with everyone, to advocate righteous living, and perform all business in an honest manner. Be kind to the poor, deliver the unfortunate from his oppressor, and be fair in dealing with strangers. If you obey these words then prosperity and peace will return, but if you don't, God will cause the defeat of this nation."

"In fact, the Lord warns you all that people will pass through this country and marvel at its desolation and they shall comment to one another that this is the type of thing that happens when God's people are unfaithful.

"People who have built huge buildings and paid low wages or none for the building, just like the king did for his palace, these places shall be destroyed. Do you want to hear about King Jay Jay?[1] He doesn't have a chance because of his wickedness. No one will mourn for him when he is killed and dragged out of the city like a dead jackass.

"The Lord warned you plenty during all your affluent years, but you wouldn't listen. Well, Bad Ned is going to get you, each and everyone. The throne of Jerusalem has been contaminated and the Lord doesn't want a king in Jerusalem again."

Chap.
23

"The Lord has said that the blame rests primarily on the unrighteous leadership," continued Jerry, "for the leaders have failed to teach the people and have not visited the people and instructed them. God will correct this some day and God has revealed that in time there will come from the line of David a righteous teacher, his name shall be Lord of Understanding, and in his name shall restoration begin and a new day started.

"God is presently sick at his stomach over the corruption in government, the flagrant violations of moral law, all this business of everyone doing as he pleases without regard to morality or the

[1] Jehoiakim

convenience and concern of his fellow man.

"The prophets are for the most part not speaking for the Lord. The prophets are pleasing their own selfish desires, walking in lies, committing adultery themselves, encouraging evil people. The Lord will destroy these people as simply as He did Sodom.

"These prophets have been so bold as to tell the people that wickedness is acceptable. That God is not a God of punishment. This is pure nonsense!

"God is aware of what the prophets have been doing. Claiming, for instance, that every dream one of them has is a revelation of God. These prophets can't tell the difference between a dream and a direct revelation of God.

"Because of all these things, for the wicked leadership and the encouragement of permissive sin, the Lord has turned against his people, and punishment is a sure thing. Consider yourselves as of now, separated from God.

Chap.
24

In order that there should be no misunderstanding on Jerry's part, the Lord told Jerry to observe a pile of figs, some being good figs and some being evil.

God then revealed to Jerry that the good fig represented the people who surrendered and were taken into captivity, for in time these people would return and be part of the restoration program in times to come. The bad figs represent those who continued to defy God and they are those that shall be scattered throughout many countries and they shall perish by pestilence, and by the sword, and by famine.

Chap.
25

"It has been thirteen years," spoke Jerry to the people, "since I first began to tell you of my messages from God. Other prophets through the years have also carried the same messages from God, but you have refused to listen to them either. The result is that the anger of the Lord is risen against you.

"The Lord is going to use a pagan king, Big Hun, and he will come with a mighty conquering army and he will represent the fury of the Lord. As a result there will only be gloom and sad cries of anguish and despair for the Jewish people. The people will be led away from Jerusalem and the surrounding area as captives and shall remain in captivity for 70 years.

"After the passage of the 70 years then the Lord will punish the pagans of Babylon and they shall suffer for their sins and for their mistreatment of the Jews. Actually the Lord will in time reward all the nations and all the people in accordance with their deeds.

"The Lord has commissioned me to go to the leaders of various nations, such as Babylon, Egypt, Alabama,[1] Mississippi,[2] the

[1] Assah   [2] Moab

Moscow Muggers,[1] and Massachusetts,[2] and tell them that they shall have to drink of the cup of the fury of the Lord, and so will the English,[3] the Americans,[4] the Japanese,[5] and any nation that at any time shows great prejudice and is wishy-washy in the acknowledging of God as the Lord of all nations. There is no way for a nation to successfully renounce the Lord or fail to grant Him the rightful place of honor among all nations.

"The Lord will use natural forces such as storms and fires and there shall be great trouble throughout all the earth, and it will all be the manifestation of the fury of God because of man's disobedience."

Chap.
26

Once again Jerry came to the temple of the Lord and for his sermon on Sunday morning he spoke in a straightforward manner, with emphasis on the errors of the people, and Jerry told them that if they did not repent at once they would be destroyed.

The people became indignant that Jerry would use the pulpit to denounce them in such a forceful manner and immediately they began to mumble among themselves and soon they decided that the simplest answer to the problem was to execute Jerry.

The other members of the ministerial alliance were greatly alarmed and disturbed and they added their influence to the movement to execute Jerry.

Jerry then spoke again to the unruly assembly and said, "The Lord sent me to tell you the things that I have told. It is not my doing. Again I remind you that you can repent and mend your ways and return to an orthodox worship of God. As far as I am concerned, of course, you can kill me or do with me as you wish, but I warn you that you will be shedding innocent blood and you will bring even worse things upon yourselves, for I am a representative of the Lord God of Hosts."

A great argument arose then among the people. Some members of the ministerial alliance defended Jerry on a basis of his speaking forth for God and that it was asking for it to punish a man for speaking for God. Others did not agree and one man began to tell of the time years before when a prophet predicted the fall of Jerusalem and the king sent all the way to Egypt for him just to have him executed. However, the protection offered by Cardinal Cushing[6] was enough to save Jerry from the angry mob.

Chap.
27

Not long after this another message came to Jerry from God and as a result he made some miniature yokes, of the type that tie oxen to a cart, with the thongs, and he sent a set of these to each of the leaders of Alabama, Mississippi, Massachusetts, and a few selected

[1]Philistines   [2]Ekron   [3]Dedan   [4]Tema   [5]Buz   [6]Ahikam

others, and he wrote to each a note saying, "The Lord has arranged for Big Hun, the leader of Babylon, to take over the Hebrew nation, and the Lord has instructed me to tell you to submit to the rule of Big Hun, because the Lord is with him at present and there is no way you can successfully resist. If your prophets tell you otherwise, they are grossly misinformed. In fact, the Lord will punish any nation that will not submit to the yoke of Big Hun.

"If you agree to the demands of Big Hun and submit to Babylon, the Lord will see to it that you retain your homeland. It would be foolish not to submit, for the Lord will destroy with pestilence, famine, and the sword, the nation that does not submit.

"The message from God also says that the valuable altar ornaments, and precious vessels for communion shall not be hidden, but should be taken into Babylon along with the captured people. The Lord himself shall see that after the captivity the sacred vessels will be returned to Jerusalem."

Chap.
28

There came into prominence then a modern, loud talking prophet named Hank Guru[1] and in a public demonstration he broke the wooden, symbolic yoke which Jerry was wearing and the new prophet told the people that things were going to get better, that the Lord was going to allow the captivity to exist for no more than two years, and that the power of Big Hun would soon be crushed.

Following this big meeting, Jerry departed and the Lord spoke again to Jerry. The Lord told Jerry to go to Hank Guru and tell him that the breaking of the wooden yoke was child's play, for the yoke which the Lord had provided was made of iron. The Lord reminded Jerry that the Lord had placed a yoke of iron on the faulty nations and that such was not easily broken.

As a result, Jerry went to Hank Guru and said, "The Lord did not send you. You are a fake and a liar, and you are simply trying to please the people, and to win friends. The Lord has decided that because you have done this terrible thing and misrepresented matters to the people, you shall die this year, as punishment for your rebellion against God."

Seven months later Hank Guru died.

Chap.
29

Now by this time Big Hun had captured the Hebrew nation and had taken many captives[2] into Babylon. Jerry wrote a letter to these captives and it was xeroxed and distributed among them.

Dear Captives:

The Lord has instructed me to write you a letter and tell you how to conduct yourselves while you are in captivity. Get to work! Build houses, plant gardens, start fruit orchards, get married, build

[1]Hananiah   [2]All who surrendered

families, and cooperate with the authorities in the city where you dwell. If you live in peace with those around you, then peace will come to you.

Don't let your prophets or your rabble rousers disturb you. The Lord has decided that you are to remain in captivity for 70 years, so any rebellion at present will just simply get you killed.

The Lord has great plans for you and God will consider your case after the 70 years of punishment is terminated. Serve your term well and the Lord will then listen to your prayer in regard to returning to Jerusalem.

After you have served your time, and repented, then the Lord will lead you out of captivity and he will bring his people from all the various areas to which they have been scattered. Your punishment is deserved and you absolutely must fulfill your time in captivity.

The wicked leaders among you, the dishonest prophets and judges, the immoral politicians, all these will the Lord punish in His way and in His good time.

Yours truly,
Jerry

There was another man whose name was Cosell[1] and he decided to get into the communication business. As a result, he wrote a circular letter to all the people in captivity and proclaimed to them that he was the authorized representative of God and that all his pronouncements were accurate, and that anything he said superseded anything that Jerry had to say.

The people then began to call Cosell and write him letters saying that Jerry had told them to cool it for 70 years and they suggested Cosell get to work on Jerry.

Cosell then visited Jerry and read some of his fan mail to him.

The word of the Lord then came to Jerry and comforted him by assuring him that Cosell did not represent God and just to prove the point the Lord would see to it that Cosell had no male children and that he would not live to see the good days which the Lord had in store for his people.

Chap.
30

Another message from God then came to Jerry, and this was a message of hope.

"The Lord has promised," spoke Jerry, "that the day shall come when the captivity of the people will be ended and the Jews will return to Palestine. Now the Jews live in strange countries, in fear and trembling, but the Lord will break the yoke and the Jews shall again serve the Lord and a new king will be born from the line of David.

[1]Shemaiah

"Just have patience, for God must do His thing. It is necessary that adequate punishment be given for the sins of the people. When the penalty has been paid, then the Lord will punish the people who are now punishing you.

"The Lord also has promised the rebuilding of Jerusalem and the restoration of the Promised Land. The Jews will prosper and will increase in numbers and in importance. Once again you will be the people of God. God's anger against the wicked will not fully be shown until near the end of the world."

Chap.
31

Jerry again spoke to the people and reminded them of the long time promise of God that Israel would be fully restored some day and that again it would become a great nation. The restoration of Israel, however, would always be conditioned on the people's acceptance of the Lord and their attitude toward His commandments and His statutes.

Jerry reported that the Lord had said, "I will bring the people from the north country, from the coasts, women and children, blind and lame, and they shall be joyful and there shall be singing again in the land of Israel."

"The Lord knows," continued Jerry, "that the weeping of his people could be heard in Berlin, in Moscow, and even occasionally at Miami Beach, and the weeping was the sobbing of Rachel as she cried for her children. All this will pass, and the Jews will be given their land again, for it is ordained of God that this be done.

"There will even be a new twist added as Israel will seek the Lord for a change. There will even be leadership from the women of Israel and they shall do their bit.

"The Lord has further declared that in time in Israel a man shall be accountable for his own actions and he shall no longer say that because his father ate sour grapes his own teeth are on edge.

"The time will come also, the Lord has said, when there will be a new agreement between God and man, and the law shall be written in the hearts of men and it will not be necessary to teach the young people about God, for they shall know the Lord first hand themselves.

"These promises come from the Lord who made the heavens, and set the course of the sun and moon, and hung the stars in their appropriate places. Great things are in store and even the boundaries of Jerusalem shall be extended."

Chap.
32

King Z became so furious at Jerry for telling the people that Big Hun would capture Jerusalem that he had Jerry put in jail. The Lord spoke to Jerry when he was in prison and prepared him for a visit from his cousin Burl.[1]

[1]Hananeel

Sure enough, Burl came to Jerry while Jerry was in jail and offered to sell him a piece of land.

"The land is cheap now, Jerry," said Burl, "because everybody has listened to your big talk about Big Hun capturing everything and everybody. The people are also dubious about your talk of the return of the Jew to the promised land and so I am willing to sell my land cheap and must, of course, offer it to my next of kin first."

"All right, Burl, I'll buy it and pay the fair market price. I want witnesses, and I want everything legal, for the Lord of Hosts has plainly stated that houses and fields shall be bought and sold again in the promised land."

Following this transaction Jerry then prayed to the Lord saying, "O God, I know you are in charge of everything and everybody, but getting me to buy land when the invading army is already storming the walls has got to be a shaky proposition."

"There is nothing too difficult or impossible with me, Jerry," said the Lord. "Big Hun and his army shall capture the city because of the sins of my people, for my people turned to Baal and to strange gods. Again, Jerry, I remind you, that though I provide destruction as a means of punishment, I also restore, and I do plan to restore Israel in future years. Just as I have brought hardships on my people because of their sins, when they return to me and repent then I will bring blessings more significant than the hardships."

Chap. 33

"It will be a great joy to me when the repentance of my people will enable me to restore them and to bless them. The cities of Israel shall again prosper and joyful sounds shall some day be forthcoming from all areas of Israel. This is my sure promise to my people," said the Lord.

Chap. 34

During the height of the siege of Jerusalem King Z had a conference with Jerry and again Jerry told him that disaster was ahead and that the king would be led away into captivity and that the king would die in peace and receive a decent burial.

Following this conference, King Z published a decree freeing all the Jews who were bonded or in slavery and the people obeyed the decree. This did not last long as very soon men began to secure slaves and servants again. This displeased the Lord greatly and again the Lord renewed his promise of punishment. Because of this and other sins the Lord renewed his promise of supporting Big Hun in his conquest.

Chap. 35

The word of the Lord then came to Jerry and Jerry was instructed to go to the Puritans[1] and to speak to the Puritans in the

[1]Rechabites

presence of some of the leaders at Jerusalem.

In accordance with the instructions of God, Jerry assembled a council of the Puritan leaders along with several of the rulers of Israel and Jerry placed an assortment of wine and strong drink before them, and he invited them to start drinking.

"We don't want to offend you, Jerry," said the Puritan spokesman, "but our grandfather and former leader, Miles Standish,[1] told us to beware of getting too civilized and he made us all take an oath not to drink, not to live in houses, not to be farmers, or ranchers, and so we live in tents,[2] we don't drink, and we just wander around and make out as best we can with our cruising herds.

"We wouldn't be here in Jerusalem now if it wasn't for Big Hun and his army. As soon as this cotton-picking war is over we are going to move our tents outside the city walls and start living again."

Then the Lord spoke to Jerry and told him to speak to the people of Israel and use the Puritans as an example.

"Tell the people," said God, "that although I sent prophets and messages, you disobeyed me and you will be conquered because of this, but the Puritans will be blessed for their faithfulness and as long as the earth lasts I will see to it that there is always a Puritan living and as such he shall have access to me very readily."

Chap. 36

During the fourth year of the reign of Little Jay[3] as king of Judah, the Lord suggested to Jerry that he write down all the sayings of the Lord concerning the capture of the Jews by the army of Big Hun and specify what they must do to avert such a disaster.

As a result, Jerry wrote down the words of God, naming the sins of the people, and assuring everyone that under the present administration and with the failure of the people to observe the commandments of God there would be a time of captivity as punishment from God.

After Jerry had completed this document, he sent for Laughlin[4] and he asked Laughlin to take the document, saying to him, "Laughlin, you are the best reader in this area, and though I'm pretty good myself, I am also in jail and can't go to church. I want you to take this document to church Sunday and read it to the congregation for me."

Laughlin complied with Jerry's request and read the document.

Attending church that day was a man named Whisper,[5] and the first thing Monday morning Whisper went to the palace during the coffee break and told the leaders exactly what was said in church.[6]

The advisers to the king decided that it would be wise to secure

[1] Jonadab   [2] For some today this is reason enough to drink
[3] Jehoiakim   [4] Baruch   [5] Michaiah
[6] It has always been hard to get leaders in church in person

the sermon and have it read to the king so Laughlin was asked to appear and to read the word to the advisers. Laughlin did this and the certainty of the statement dealing with the fall of Jerusalem disturbed everyone. Laughlin was told to leave and hide and to keep his mouth shut about the sermon and to tell Jerry to do the same.

The advisers then hid the sermon, but the king learned of it[1] and sent for the word. By the time the king had heard the first few pages he was plenty mad and had the reader throw the whole thing into the fire.

The word of the Lord then came to Jerry and instructed him to write the sermon again and to add to it a few lines telling Little Jay that burning the Lord's word was dangerous and that as a result the Lord would punish Little Jay and everybody close around him.

Chap.
37

Now there was a local newsman named Earl Wilson[2] who had heard of the words and the prophecy of Jerry telling of the forthcoming captivity and of the invasion of Jerusalem and he made this information available to the cabinet members of the king.

The cabinet members then went to King Z and the spokesman said, "O King, this man Jerry is ruining us. He has stated that under the authority of God, he has declared the doom of your city and this has lowered the morale of the army.[3] What we would like to do is get rid of Jerry."

"It is out of my hands," said King Z, "and you can do with Jerry as you wish."

"As a result of this statement, the cabinet members had Jerry seized and they put him in a deep dungeon, without food or water.

Now Ears Black[4] kept the king informed on local matters and he reported to King Z that Jerry had been put in an old well, over 30 ft. deep, and that Jerry was stuck in the bottom of this old well. Ears explained to the king that Jerry would die of hunger or thirst[5] and Ears wanted the king to take action.

As a result, King Z gave Ears a rescue permit and Ears along with a few of his cronies tied a bunch of sheets together and lowered the sheet rope to Jerry and rescued him. Jerry was then smuggled into the king's private prison.

Later the king sent for Jerry and asked him for the real inside on what was going to happen.

"I will tell you what is going to happen if you promise not to have me executed," said Jerry.

"I will protect you, Jerry, but you must agree not to let the advisors to the king learn of my intentions," said King Z.[6]

---

[1] They had stool pigeons in those days also
[2] Shephatiah
[3] The old army morale problem again
[4] Ebedmelech
[5] Kings have never had time to think about such details
[6] King Z was a real sad sack

"O.K., King. Now here is the deal. If you resist the siege of Jerusalem the city will in time be captured and burned to the ground, but if you will surrender, you will have your life spared and you will be led away peaceably into captivity."

"I am afraid of what the Jews will do to me, Jerry, if they learn that I have been getting secret advice from you," said King Z.

"Don't worry. The Lord will see that you are kept intact," said Jerry.

"Well, just in case some of the cabinet members hear you are on the palace prison list and they begin to inquire about our relationship, don't tell them that we have been talking."

As a result of this arrangement Jerry stayed in the general confines of the palace prison until the Chaldeans captured Jerusalem.

Chap. 39

In a year or so the siege of Jerusalem by Big Hun became so intolerable that the army of the Jews in Jerusalem escaped from a door in the wall of Jerusalem during the night and so did King Z. The next day the patrols of Big Hun began to chase down those fleeing and one patrol captured King Z. Big Hun decided to spare his life and take him to Babylon as a captive, but he had his eyes put out and he had his sons executed in his presence before he was blinded.[1]

At the order of Big Hun, however, Jerry was freed, and was left in Jerusalem with a remnant of the Jews, consisting of the poor and the disadvantaged.

The word also came to Jerry that the Lord was going to save Ears Black because of his faithfulness and his kindness to Jerry.

Chap. 40

Now J. Edgar,[2] who was chief of security in charge of the prisoners for Big Hun, had taken Jerry along with the other captives to San Diego.[3]

J. Edgar sent for Jerry and said to him, "Now I know that the Lord has brought all these things to pass, and I know that you are the one who said that it would happen this way; so you are free. You can return with me to Babylon and be at ease there, or you can go back to the Jerusalem area and try to tough it out with the poor and the small remnant left there."

J. Edgar gave Jerry some food and spending money after Jerry had decided to return to Jerusalem. Jerry returned to Notre Dame[4] where a remnant of the refugees had gathered.

It so happened that Big Hun had appointed a man named Fast Katz[5] to represent him and to rule as a satellite prince over the people left in the promised land. When the people and their leaders came to Katz he encouraged them to learn to live under the Chaldean

[1]It didn't pay to lose a war then   [2]Nebuzaradan
[3]Ramah   [4]Mizpah   [5]Gedaliah

rule, to pay their taxes, and to adjust to controlled conditions. Katz explained that he planned to do as best he could and to work well under the Chaldeans.

Word of all this began to spread and many of the Jews who had hidden in the hills returned to start planting their vineyards again, for many had gone and hidden in the hills during the Chaldean invasion.

Some men came to Fast Katz and told him that there was a contract out on him and that one of the kings had employed Spear-Point[1] to kill Katz. Katz thought that this was a silly report as he could not think why anyone would be interested in killing him. In fact, one of the friends of Katz offered to kill Spear-Point before he could get to Katz, but Katz thought the whole thing sounded silly.

Chap.
41

Some months later, Spear-Point and his ten henchmen visited Katz and Katz invited them to dinner. After dinner, Spear-Point and his ten men attacked Katz and killed him, gangland style. Some of the servants of Katz came into the room, hearing the noise, and they were killed also.

About this time a small group of men came to the city to call on Fast Katz and Spear-Point and his men met them and invited them into the palace. When the men were inside, Spear-Point and his crew killed these men also.

Spear-Point had a big pit dug and threw the dead bodies in the pit, and then he took the people remaining who were alive and well and made captives of them. When word of this began to leak out, a warrior by the name of Sam Bass[2] gathered a small band of fighters and went to get Spear-Point and free the captives. The captives were freed, but during the fighting Spear-Point escaped and he made it safely across the border to Laredo.[3]

Sam Bass then led his small force and all the captives south toward Bethlehem in preparation for a flight into Egypt, for he expected more trouble than he could handle.

Chap.
42

Sam and a few of the top warriors then came to Jerry and asked him to pray to the Lord in their behalf as they were poorly armed and very short on food. Sam also wanted some advice on the next move.

"I'll do as you ask," said Jerry, "but remember, I will tell you exactly what the Lord advises and you may not like it."

"You tell it like it is and we will listen. We want the straight stuff," replied Sam.

Ten days later Jerry sent for Sam and his group and spoke to the whole gathering saying, "The Lord wants you to stay put here in this land. The Lord will bless you if you will try to tough it out. You

---

[1]Ishmael   [2]Johanan   [3]Land of Ammonites

are not to be afraid of Big Hun, for the Lord will protect you.

"However, if you say no to this and try to escape to Egypt, thinking there will be peace and security there, then you will have nothing but trouble. The war which you flee will catch you, and the famine that you fear will also find you in Egypt. All the men who make a move to Egypt shall die by the sword, or famine, or pestilence.

"The Lord says that as surely as His anger was turned on Jerusalem for the disobedience of the people, it will also be turned on you if you refuse to listen to this warning. Don't go into Egypt! That's exactly what God is saying. When you asked me to pray you promised to observe the answer, and now you have the answer, stay here and live under God's blessing, endure the hardships, or go to Egypt and die."

Chap.
43

Then one of the associates of Sam, a man named Sloppy Joe,[1] spoke forth saying, "You are not telling the truth. You have been bribed by Laughlin to get us to stay here and be captured and sent to Babylon as slaves. We are going to go to Egypt."

As a result, Sam Bass and all the gang gathered together the remnant of the Jews and left for Egypt. Jerry went with them.[2]

After arriving in Egypt, the Lord inspired Jerry to go and place some stones in a secret place near the entrance to Pharoah's house. The Jews were witnesses to this action and then Jerry spoke, "The Lord has decided to send Big Hun down here to conquer Egypt and he will build his royal pavilion over the top of these stones. When Big Hun comes he will kill some and capture some and he will burn houses and make a great destruction in Egypt, destroying many of the false gods."

Chap.
44

Then Jerry spoke to the Jews who had left Judah under Sam Bass and who were residing in Egypt saying, "You really blew it. God told you not to come to Egypt. You apparently did not learn anything from the example of your fathers who disobeyed God in Jerusalem. Now you are in Egypt and you are burning incense to the queen and you are worshipping strange gods.

"You are right, Jerry," one of their spokesmen replied. "We figure we have a better chance of surviving in Egypt by serving their gods and burning incense to their queen."

"God is going to punish you for this," said Jerry. "You will be killed, and die of famine or the sword. All of you who stay in Egypt shall perish. The Lord plans evil for you and not good, for you have forsaken the Lord. As a sign of the power of God, be certain that Pharoah will be conquered and you all shall be destroyed, that is all

[1] Azariah   [2] Where the congregation goes the preacher goes

of you who stay in Egypt."

Jerry then sent word to Laughlin reminding him that God was going to punish him also and that added to his grief and multiple troubles would be the destruction of buildings and the destroying of crops. Jerry wrote a denunciation of Laughlin, telling him that no matter how he sought to save himself, there was to be only misery and restlessness for him the rest of his days.

The word of the Lord then came to Jerry concerning the plight of Egypt. Jerry spoke forth in a public address and said, "Get your army in shape, O Egyptians. Sharpen your swords, brace your shields, call your best men into service, but none of this will do you any good. You are doomed.

"Assemble the best forces you can gather, even getting expert help from Ethiopia and Libya, but none of this will do any good. Get your entire strength together and go to meet the Big Hun from the north, but you will be defeated, for the Lord is going to punish Egypt and God is using the force of Big Hun to effect his decree.

"The only people to be delivered will be a small band of Jews who are faithful to God and we will seek to return to Jerusalem. The small remnant shall be blessed and restored in the Lord's time. God has promised that although many nations may be totally destroyed, the remnant of the Jews will be preserved and will be blessed."

The word of the Lord then came to Jerry and in God's name Jerry denounced the Moscow Muggers.

"You Moscow Muggers," said Jerry, "You will be destroyed by floods. The Lord will cause mighty waters to roar and there shall be great panic and distress. The wicked cities of Tyre and Sidon shall be cut off by floods for the Lord will spoil the land.

"The Lord will go forth with great destruction against the wicked and nature shall work at God's command."

The word of the Lord then came to Jerry and he was inspired to prophesy against Mississippi.[1]

"The land of Mississippi is doomed," said Jerry. "People will cease to speak well of Mississippi. It would be a good idea to leave Mississippi and go somewhere else to live.

"Mississippi has had it too easy for too long. Strangers will move into Mississippi and contaminate it. Shed some tears, for Mississippi is doomed. All kinds of miseries shall come upon the land, for it is no longer interested in God and there are too few unselfish people left.

---

[1]Moab

·You have never seen such sorrow as shall come to the land. This is God's way with any wicked area. Success seems so sure, but evil is self-destructive and the Lord in time punishes, and so Mississippi is a goner.

"There is no escape. If a man runs to avoid a pit he will be caught in a trap. The Lord has already arranged for the punishment of Mississippi. Still, in the latter days of the world, Mississippi will be restored and will again turn to the Lord."

Chap.
49

The Lord, according to Jerry, authorized him to speak and make pronouncements concerning some of the existing cities and nations.

"The Lord has decided to eliminate Laredo," said Jerry, "and to burn it to the ground. The town of Ai will be conquered also. Do you want to know about Edom? Well, they have grown stupid. The wander-curse of Esau will come upon them. The people will attempt to hide, but no one can hide from God.

"The Lord is arranging for some of the heathen nations to be God's instrument for punishing many of the wicked places. There is no way to escape from God. You cannot hide in caves or ascend like eagles, the Lord must in time be confronted. Edom is definitely doomed by the Lord's order, for He will cause the mighty men of Edom to become faint-hearted.

"Damascus is also in trouble. It will be a seething place, filled with internal disorders. Damascus shall be destroyed, for the Lord has so decided.

"Other areas, like Massachusetts,[1] that have failed to follow the Lord and to obey his commandments, these places are put on the expendable list. The Big Hun shall come and make a desolated place of this area.

"As for Hollywood[2] it shall be dismantled. It will finally reach a point where no one will agree to spend the night in the city. Other wicked places shall in turn receive similar treatment.

Chap.
50

"The word of the Lord is also against Babylon," said Jerry. "The Lord used Babylon and the area people to punish the Jews, but in time the Lord will avenge himself on the Babylonians.

"Fierce people from the north, with unbending arrows, shall attack and they shall make Babylon a desolate place. The vengeance of the Lord shall cause the walls of Babylon to fall, the crops to fail, the people to be killed or captured.

"Through all these things, the Lord has not forgotten His promise to protect and preserve the faithful remnant of Israel. In the time of the restoration of Israel, there shall be a recovery of worship,

[1]Kedar   [2]Hazor

and the people will become faithful to the Lord and devout in their worship.

"The Lord has also planned the destruction of the neighboring allies of Babylon. Archers shall rain arrows on Babylon. The vengeance of the Lord will be thorough for Babylon shall be rewarded in accordance with her wicked works. Babylon has defied the Lord God of Israel, and the punishment of Babylon will be intense. The young and the old shall be slain in the streets, the proud shall stumble and fall, and fire will gut the city.

"The Lord God is the Redeemer, a strong and mighty ruler, and God will care for the faithful and confuse the wicked. The sword of the Lord is set against the rulers of Babylon, against its liars, against the treasures of the city, and the very waters of Babylon's existence shall be dried. Finally the wild beasts of the desert and the predators from the islands nearby will come to stay in Babylon, and the city will become similar to a haunted house with the owls making it their home. Babylon shall never be inhabited again as a testimony to the sureness of the acts of God. Babylon will exist no more, even as was the case with Sodom and Gomor.

"The destruction of Babylon shall arise from cruel people of the north who shall come with many horses and the warriors shall shout like mad. As the noise of the storming of Babylon is heard the king of Babylon shall know a deep fear, and all the nations of the earth shall hear of the cries and know that the Lord God of Israel is at work.

Chap.
51

If there is any chance to flee, be sure and get out of Babylon. Winds shall rip through the land, and many shall be slain by arrows and by spears. Be certain that this is a sign that Israel has not been forgotten by the Lord of Hosts.

"The Lord used Babylon and its prosperity in the manner that a golden cup full of wine is used to make men drunk; so Babylon has made nations drunk with power, but now she is doomed.

"Let everyone that would seek a righteous way of life flee to his own country and worship the Lord, recognizing that all of this history that is being made is of the Lord.

"It doesn't matter how well Babylon seems to be prepared, how adequate its watchmen may be or its defenses, for the Lord has proclaimed its doom. The enemies of Babylon will seem to be as thick and numerous as a migration of caterpillars.

"As punishment for all the evil that Babylon represents the Lord will act as a battle axe and will break into pieces nations, separate horse and rider, come between a man and his girl, scatter the flock and lose the shepherd, smash rulers and captains for such is the power of God.

"The Lord is against Babylon, and it will look like a black

mountain when God has finished with it, and there won't be enough stones left to start a new building. Every purpose of the Lord will be fulfilled; so already the men of the north are assembling, and the land is beginning to tremble in anticipation of the destruction.

"The men of Babylon shall turn chicken, they will burn their own homes, and doom shall be reported from one messenger to another, even before it happens. Babylon is similar to a threshing floor of ripe grain, the time is at hand for the threshing.

"Big Hun has defied God for the last time. The Lord plans to dry the springs and the wells, to remove the sea, and the desolation of Babylon is set. The city will be a place where people passing will make snide remarks and marvel that it no longer exists.

"The warriors of Babylon shall be full of wine and too drunk to fight back so that most of them will die without drawing a sword. A great storm from the sea shall in time come and wash away all that is left from the fire and from the pillage.

"Please let the captives of Israel who serve the Lord be impressed with this prophecy and let them make every effort to escape immediately. Think of Jerusalem and the power of God to restore the Jews. There is no way that Babylon can prevent her defeat or be delivered from her fate.

"The enemies of Babylon from the north shall come and find the leaders, the princes, the warriors, drunk and in no condition to fight. All last minute efforts shall fail, and fire and arrows shall begin the destruction."

Now all these sayings were written in a book by Jerry and he sent the book with a reader to Babylon to warn the Jews. The reader was also instructed that after reading the book to the people, a rock was to be bound to the book and it was to be cast into the sea. At this point the reader was to announce that the same thing was going to happen to Babylon that happened to the book.

Chap.
52

Now King Z had never been a good king during his reign in Jerusalem and he did evil in the sight of the Lord. It was under King Z that Jerusalem revolted and it was under his reign when Big Hun conquered Jerusalem. King Z was captured as were most of the men of the army, all of whom had tried to flee from Jerusalem.

It was on this occasion that Big Hun became responsible for burning the house of the Lord in Jerusalem and most of the city as well as tearing down all the walls.

The tribe of Judah was carried away captive into Babylon, all except the poor and the indigent, who remained under the surveillance of J. Edgar. All of the brass vases and items of liturgical worship, and all the treasures of the house of the Lord were taken to Babylon. Many of the church leaders were condemned to death, but 3,023 Jews were spared and brought to Babylon as captives.

Over thirty years later the king of Babylon brought Little Jay out of prison and released him, giving him some authority in the land, feeding him well, and Little Jay ate his meals in his latter days with the king of Babylon.

LAMENTATIONS

How can I help but mourn when I see the condition of Jerusalem? A beautiful city teeming with people, now reduced to a grim reminder of the sins of the people of Judah. The people who really cared for Jerusalem have been taken into captivity and they dwell now in a heathen land.

The small remaining group of the people of God are sad for no one comes to church anymore, her family night suppers are dismal failures, and the ministers are greatly discouraged.

The enemies of God's people are a prosperous bunch, however, and this makes the affliction of the people seem to be even worse. About all that is left is the memory of the good old days, but they are gone, for enemies came and captured the city and its people and no one came to help.

Jerusalem became a sinful city and now she is paying for her excesses. The city seems barren and almost naked, the enemies have taken everything. The heathen have shown no respect for the church and they have contaminated all the things of God.

Jerusalem has really been discarded. There is no sorrow comparable to the sorrow of forsaken Jerusalem. The people that were taken into captivity are begging for bread and have already turned in most of their treasures to the pawnbrokers.

The Lord has done all this as punishment. The mighty men have been trampled under foot, the city and its people have been crushed as if they were placed in a winepress. No wonder there is this great sadness. There is apparently no comfort to be found, and Jerusalem has even reached the point of being of no use to her enemies.

Yet the city must cry out saying, "The Lord is righteous. The punishment which is received is justified. Behold, O Lord, our condition. We are desolate. Our enemies of the years have heard of our troubles and they are glad. How about giving our enemies a dose or two of the medicine we are receiving? We are distressed, our groans are real, our hearts are discouraged."

I am a prophet of the Lord, Jerry of El Dorado, and I have witnessed the collapse of Jerusalem. The Lord has certainly revealed his anger and let his wrath be as a cloud over Jerusalem, and the Lord has not even spared His church in His anger.

The Lord has done all these things. The Lord has destroyed the strongholds, corrupted the leaders of Judah, and the Lord did not contend with the enemies of Israel.

In fact, the Lord has treated Jerusalem as if it were an enemy, and the Lord destroyed all the beauty of the city. The Lord has broken down the churches, and ended all the pleasant assemblies of the people. The Lord has even allowed the heathen, the enemy, to come into the church and make all kinds of weird noises and strange

455

sounds.

The elders of the city are grief stricken. They sit mournfully together with ashes on their heads and eyes staring into the ground. The young ladies are solemn and dejected and they are not bubbling with joy as they should be. The youngsters call for food and then they fall in weakness on their mothers sobbing, and the mothers have no help for them.

I wonder if there has ever been such sorrow as there is now in Jerusalem?

Most of the prophets have been selfish and misleading, they have lied to the people and failed to warn the people of the consequences of sin.

Everyone makes fun of Jerusalem. The great, beautiful, wonderful city is gone. The enemies of Jerusalem jeer at the city and remind everyone they see of how easy it was to swallow up Jerusalem.

All of this is simply the fulfilling of the will of God. The Lord has always told the people that the consequences of sin were dreadful.

The people have finally wept in the presence of the Lord. The tears of the people have created a wailing wall and it is in use day and night. I know the people need to repent, pray day and night, to lament before God in real sincerity.

The people need to cry to God and remind him that these suffering people are His people. Ministers are dying in the church and starvation is bringing the people almost to the point of cannibalism.

The dead lie in the streets. The young warriors were killed by the swords of heathen enemies, but all this was God's doing. The Lord has done a complete job of letting his anger fall on the sinful people.

Chap. 3

The Lord has really done it to me also. I have witnessed all of the destruction. The Lord led me into darkness and not into light. God is apparently against me also, for my bones ache and my skin is getting wrinkled,[1] my flashlight battery no longer works, and God has hemmed me in so that I cannot escape to do my own thing.

When I pray I don't seem to be getting through to God at all. The Lord has jumped on me as if He were a bear or a lion, and he has torn me to bits. The Lord caused me to be a source of derision among the people and small boys threw stones at me. The Lord has caused me to be bitter and the fillings have dropped out of my teeth. I can't even remember being prosperous and content. I will always be ashamed with bitter memories of tragic years.

There is only one small ray of hope. The Lord is basically

---

[1] It happens to everybody, Jerry.

compassionate and the Lord is good to those who serve him if they will be patient, for a man must hope and he must wait on the Lord.

It is very good for the young to learn about discipline, to sit quietly during adversity. It is a known thing that the Lord will not withhold his favor forever. Although the Lord causes grief, the Lord will also bring relief.

The Lord does not enjoy punishing his people nor inflicting on them all kinds of grief. It is not for man to question the judgment of God. Let us examine ourselves and let us return to the Lord. Let us lift up our hands and our voices to God.

We have sinned, but as yet God has not pardoned our sin. The Lord has had some of us tortured and others slain, and the Lord has apparently not been available for our prayers. Our enemies have overcome us, fear has come to us, desolation and destruction is everywhere, and our tears make streams of water.

I have personally even been put into a dungeon where I would not see the light of day. As I cried and lamented for the city and for the people of the city, then I called on the Lord out of my dungeon saying, "Lord, hear me. You told me once not to fear, you have always encouraged me, you have redeemed my life, but listen now to my case.

"You have seen all that has been done to me, you have heard all the denouncing of me. The people have criticized me so much that the words have been put to music.

"Take a whack at my enemies, O Lord, and reward them in accordance with all the bad things they have done. Give them the full treatment, Lord, and let your anger be strong against them."

Chap.
4

It is really pitiful to realize what has happened. Our most valuable possessions, even the gold trims from the altar in the temple, have been stolen or stomped in the dust. Our youth, our treasure for the future, they are starved, many of them are already dead without having had a chance to live.

Those accustomed to riches and fine food are in wretched condition. The Lord was kinder to Sodom, for He destroyed Sodom with one deadly blow, while we perish an inch at a time.

The lucky ones are the ones that were killed by the swords of the enemy in the street. It is much easier to die by the sword than to starve to death.

Some years back no one in the world would have believed that Jerusalem would be levelled to the present condition. Sinful prophets and sinful priests, they are part of the cause of the death in the streets. These same men are blindly wandering in the streets today, contaminating everything they touch. The Lord will not help these men for they persecuted the few prophets and priests who were faithful to God.

Those of us who are left are doomed. Our lives are in danger every hour. We had hoped for help from friendly nations, but it hasn't come and it is not likely to come. Actually our days are numbered. Our king was captured, and that meant another thin hope was gone. There was a time when we thought that under our king we could withstand all the nations of the earth.

As for the people who take advantage of our condition and who sponsored our defeat, you are doomed. Israel will one day be restored, but not the enemies of God. You have had it!

Chap.
5

"O Lord," prayed Jerry, "remember all that has happened to us. Our homes, our nation, our city are full of strangers and we are apparently orphans in our own land. We have to buy water and we pay exorbitant prices for even the necessities of life. We are forced to work under painful conditions and we are constantly humiliated.

"We find ourselves begging for food, from Assyria to Egypt. Actually, it was the generation before ours that sinned, and yet we are getting the punishment.

"The people who formerly worked for us are now our rulers and we work for them. This hurts! Our skin shows how poorly we are doing.

"Our women aren't safe. It is no longer a crime to rape a Hebrew woman. Our princes are hung by the neck and our elders are treated as if they were little boys.

"There is no longer any music among our people. The teenagers don't even feel like playing a guitar. We are in deep distress, and we know it is the result of sin. The mountain of the Lord is so desolate that the foxes walk on it.

"Yet again we proclaim that thou, O Lord, are the everlasting God, thy throne from generation to generation. Please don't forget us for such a long time. Renew our spirit, O Lord, let us return to you, let us have the good old days back again. Yet it looks from here as if we have been utterly rejected and that you are still angry with us."

EZEKIEL

Among the many Jewish P.O.W.'s living as captives in the land of the Huns[1] was a man named Ezekiel, the son of a minister. This book is his testimony.

Ezekiel reports that when he was about 30 years old, living as a captive, he had a vision.

"The vision which I had," reported Ezekiel, "was too fantastic and impressive to adequately describe, what with the fire, the lightning, the shining brass, the retractable wheels, the roaring noises, the harmony of four wings with changing faces. The vision brought me to my knees."

The vision seemed almost to describe a UFO or a formation of four team flying jets. The wheels which had spokes were retractable and in the vision were sucked up by the four vehicles. The sound seemed to Ezekiel as the sound of roaring water and Ezekiel was certain that he was seeing a glimpse of the glory and majesty of God, and so he fell on his knees and listened for the words of the Lord.

"Son of man," came the voice from the glory of God, "stand on your feet and I will speak to you."

"The spirit of the Lord then entered me," reported Ezekiel, "and I stood on my feet and heard the message of God."

"Zeke,[2] I am sending you to the children of Israel," said the voice, "even though they are a rebellious nation, and even though their fathers have sinned and forsaken my way, and I realize that they are a stubborn outfit, but I want you to go to them and tell them that I sent you. Whether they will listen to you or not is not the point, but I want them to know that I am sufficiently interested to send them a prophet.

"Now Zeke," continued the voice, "don't be afraid or discouraged. I know it will be similar to living among thorns, but stick to your job. Disregard their verbal objections and their attempts to intimidate you. Speak my words to them, and whether they listen or not is not your problem.

"Now you are not to be rebellious as these people are, and I want you first to get a good dose of my word."

Zeke then looked and there was suddenly at hand a scroll and on it were the admonitions of God, his promises, his commandments, and his punishments.

The voice then said to me, "Take the scroll and eat it."[3]
I did as I was told and I absorbed the word of God which was

[1] Chaldeans   [2] Ezekiel
[3] Trying to play God we still say "I'll make you eat it!"

459

written on the scrolls and I began to feel better about things and a sweet taste came to me.

God then spoke to me and told me to go to the house of Israel that was in captivity and to speak to them about the word of God. The Lord reminded me that I was not a foreign missionary going to a strange land and encountering people of a different language, but that I was going to my own people and we had no barriers of language or custom between us.

The Lord reminded me, however, that I had a tough job for the captive people of Israel were stubborn, resentful, pig-headed, and hard-hearted. The Lord encouraged me somewhat by reminding me that I was made of the same stuff, and the Lord had made me as hard-headed as any of the Israelites.

The big thing, of course, was for me to learn the message of God for myself, to know His word, and to trust God completely before I began teaching all these things to others.

Again I was moved by the spirit and again I heard the noise of the mighty wings and the noise of wheels, and even though I moved reluctantly, I realized that the hand of God was upon me. The spirit moved me to Aspen[1] where a segment of our people were camping and in captivity.

After seven days here feeling as if I was in a trance, the word of the Lord came to me saying, "Zeke, I have decreed that you are to be as a watchman to Israel, and I want you to listen to me and then relay my word to the people.

"You really have quite a responsibility, Zeke. For instance, if I tell you to tell a wicked man that he shall surely die for his sins and you do not properly warn him to change his way, even though the wicked man shall die in sin, you will be held responsible.

"If, however, you warn the wicked as you should and the wicked men continue their wicked way, the wicked shall die, and you will be cleared of any responsibility.

"Let me give you another illustration. Suppose a righteous man ceases to be righteous and death comes to him, if you have failed to warn him, the responsibility is yours. If, however, you have properly preached to him, you are in the clear."

The spirit then moved me to the plains area and the glory of the Lord was there as surely as it had been at Aspen. The spirit then sent me into a house and there I remained confined by the Lord and realizing more certainly every hour how minutely I was under the guidance of God.

Chap.
4

"The next thing you are to do, Zeke," said the Lord, "is to take a large, flat piece of tile and begin to draw on it a picture of the siege

---

[1]Tel-a-bib

of Jerusalem. I want you to include all the details, with the battering rams and other siege devices. Encircle the entire model with a band of iron as a symbol to the house of Israel that the siege is total.

"In further preparation, in order that you might really impress the people, you will be paralyzed so that you will lie for about a year only on your left side. To prepare for this bake plenty of bread and arrange for water. You are to mix the bread dough carefully. You are to leave your right arm exposed as a symbol of attack and the days of your lying on your left side should represent the years of punishment to Israel. Then you will lie for a little over a month on your right side, and this shall represent the years of punishment to Judah.

"In making your bread dough, include ample vitamins by using wheat, barley, beans, millet and sage. Eat a small portion of meat regularly and drink water on a regular and measured basis.

"When you bake the bread use human dung as a covering, and this will be a sign to the children of Israel of the defilement of their bread because of the non-Jews who will be their conquerors."

"Wait a minute, please, Lord," said Zeke, "how about my using something besides human dung?[1] I wasn't raised on this kind of cooking."

"All right," said God, "you may use buffalo chips.[2] All this shall signify what is ahead for the people of Jerusalem, for there shall be such a shortage of food and water that rationing will be done in the most careful manner."

Chap.
5

The Lord then spoke to Zeke again and said, "Give the people of Jerusalem a prophecy and use visual aids in teaching. Take your hair and cut it off, and cleanly shave your beard, taking the hair from your head. You are to burn one third of it, destroy one third with a knife, and scatter a third to the winds, then the hair which has stuck to your robe you will destroy by burning your robe.

"Then you can tell the people of Jerusalem that all this is a picture of what is going to happen to them, for my people have disobeyed me, and have not walked in my statutes, but changed my laws to suit their own desires.

"Furthermore, my people have shown no restraint in controlling their population and have married any and everybody, and so I am against my people and I will punish my people in a worse manner than I have ever punished any nation.

"Suffering and famine will become so intense that strong family ties, such as between father and son, shall be completely disintegrated. Because my people have contaminated my church,"

---

[1]There was no foil then
[2]It is possible that the first chip throwing contest originated here.

continued the voice of God, "I will punish without pity. A third of
the people will die of pestilence and famine, a third shall perish by
the sword, and a third I will scatter to the four winds. I will pursue
even these with violence, and then the people will know that I am
the Lord God.

"As an additional stinger I will cause the nations of the world to
feel unfriendly toward my people and it shall be generally known
that I am angry with my people. You can expect famine and the
sword, persecution and peril, evil beasts and blood diseases, for all
these are part of the penalty.

Chap.
6

The word of the Lord then came to me[1] telling me that I
should warn all the hill country people of Israel and tell them of
God's anger. The hill country people have built graven images and
placed them in beautiful groves in the hills, and the people have
worshipped their own pleasures, and the Lord plans to destroy all
this.

The people will be slain by the thousands and their images
destroyed and treasuries stolen. The land shall be made desolate.

The Lord plans to leave a remnant of the people, but they shall
be scattered, and carried away captives, and they can then testify in
foreign lands as to the power of God. The people shall hate
themselves for having forsaken me and they shall know again that I
am the Lord God.

The Lord has instructed me to tell you these things forcibly,
and that is why I stamp my foot and shake my fist, for the Lord has
told me to preach in this manner.

When the hill country people see their men slain in their
favorite pleasure haunts and their land made desolate then they will
know for sure that the Lord is God of all.

Chap.
7

The word of the Lord continued to come to me and the Lord
told me to announce to the land of Israel as to their fate and I spoke
again saying, "You people of Israel, the time is short. The anger of
the Lord is upon you and evil is about to come to you.

"The time is short as the coming of a morning, the day of
trouble is very near, and the fury of the Lord is about to descend
upon you.

"The trouble for Israel will make no distinction between buyer
and seller, for no one will profit. Those that go forth with the sword
shall perish with the sword, and those that remain behind shall be
victims of pestilence and famine. There will be no relief. The people
will try to buy off their enemies, but the Lord has prepared
exceedingly wicked men to attack, and they shall kill and take

[1] Still Ole Zeke

everything as spoil, and money will be useless. Punishment will be given everyone from the king on down, and finally the people will know that the Lord is God."

Some time after this I was sitting in the presence of some of the elders of Judah and I went into a trance. I saw some weird images in my trance, and I seemed to be lifted up by a man of fire who held me by my hair[1] and in my trance I saw visions and had insights into the sins of the people of Jerusalem.

It was revealed to me the evil thoughts of men in church, and then I was taken in my fancy to a wall and told to dig, and I dug in the wall[2] and finally found a door. I opened the door and saw all the evil and wickedness of men in high places who thought they were concealed from the eyes of the world, and even from the Lord.

Then the man of fire led me to behold representatives of the women of the city and I saw that they were privately burning incense and worshipping a strange god of fertility. Finally, the man of fire showed me a group of men who had turned their backs on the church, and they worshipped only each day as it came into being and called forth to the sun as if to a god to give them prosperity.

The man of fire then said to me, "Now you have had a glimpse of what God sees, who can see into the hearts and minds of people. It is for these things that God is furious and there shall be no pity coming from God and the cries for mercy shall not be heard."

God then ordered me to summon the special seventy men that the Lord had provided for the city of Jerusalem. There were six of them and they came to me and one of them had writing material available. At the time, I was standing in the temple and the glory of the Lord filled the place and the spirit of the Lord was present.

"I want you to go through the city," said God to the warrior with the writing material, "and I want you to take a Gallup poll. Every person, man, woman, or young person, must be asked if he is sad because of the sins of the people, and those that are regretful are to be marked by you on their foreheads with the pen which you carry."

Then the Lord spoke to the remaining warriors and said, "Now you go through the city after the writer has had a chance to mark the people, and you are to slay with the sword all men, women, or young people who are not marked on the forehead. You are to begin with the church staff."

The warriors killed some who worked in the church and then many more throughout the city.

While this was happening, I fell down on my knees and prayed

[1]It had grown back by now
[2]Maybe a Watergate type of digging

saying, "Are you angry enough to destroy all of Israel?"

"The evil that has arisen in Israel and in Judah is great and the land is full of violence and injustice. The people think that the Lord has quit supervising the earth and I am reminding them that the earth is mine," replied the Lord.

It was not long before the warrior with the pen returned and stated that he had finished with his marking.

Chap.
10

Then as I stood at the entrance to the temple I beheld a strange vision, for a vehicle appeared out of the sky, and it had wheels, and it was capable of going in any direction. The strange contraption appeared to have eyes on each side, and as it landed the man clothed in linen, who I think was the writing material holder, walked under the shape and had in his hands a red flashlight.[1]

The vision was wondrous, and the sight of wheels within wheels[2] was amazing. The noise was the sound of mighty thunder and made me think that God was speaking. The whole scene was fantastic[3] and I was keenly aware of the presence of the glory of God.[4]

Chap.
11

As I stood in the temple then the spirit of the Lord led me to look toward the east, and there meeting in a corner were all the leading politicians, most of them prominent men, and the Lord spoke to me and said, "Zeke, do you see that bunch of fellows? They are selfish men, they seek to control everything, and they are telling the people that Jerusalem is as safe as Fort Knox and that now is the time to pass a big bond issue and rebuild the city. I want you to prophesy against them."

Then I went near to the men and spoke loudly, saying, "I know what you are thinking and plotting, and I know what you have done, for the Lord has revealed it to me. You have caused violence to be widespread in Jerusalem. You have been afraid of the sword that might come against you, and so God is going to arrange for such a sword to move against you.

"Some of you shall be taken into captivity and some shall die in battle, and these things will occur to remind you that God is the real ruler. God plans to judge you and there is no hiding from him.

"You have violated his law and failed to obey his commandments, and you have chosen to follow the customs of the wicked and godless people in your area."

When I said these things, one of the men, a fellow named W. Gate,[5] had a stroke and died on the spot.

---

[1] Burning coals, no doubt
[2] The first time he ever saw spokes
[5] Pelatiah

[3] Sounds similar to some UFO reports
[4] For better description read King James version

Then I prayed to the Lord earnestly for I wondered if all the people of Israel would be destroyed by God.

"Cool it a bit, Zeke," said God, "for the remnant that is still in Jerusalem have been saying that the exiles were the sinners and that the ones left behind in Jerusalem were saved by me. That is not so. Even though I arranged for the captivity of many of my people, yet I will constantly be available to them wherever they are. In time, I will reassemble my people, and bring them from the various countries to which they have been sent.

"When my people eventually return they will be a united people, and will no longer be divided into tribes, but will be a nation. There will be a new spirit in them, I will bless those that walk in my way and worship me sincerely. I will still be a means of punishment, however, for those who reject me."

Then the space ship, or what appeared to be a space ship, took me up and carried me to the people who were in captivity and I delivered God's message to them. Afterwards, I guess the space ship, which was used by the spirit of God, brought me back, for once again I was back in the city, ready to preach and teach again.

Chap. 12

The spirit of the Lord then brought to my mind the sure knowledge that I was dealing with a stubborn and rebellious bunch of people and that even though the truth was spoken to them, they paid no attention. Then I was inspired to attract their attention and possibly teach them something by using the visual aid method.

Inspired by God with the idea, I then began to move my clothes and all my possessions out of my house in the daylight, so that all the people would notice and begin to wonder what the prophet was doing. Then I began to dig a small hole in the wall of Jerusalem, and then I took my baggage and all the belongings that I could carry and in late evening I went through the hole and disappeared from the city.

The next day I returned to the city and the people immediately began to ask me what in the world had I been doing, packing my things, digging a hole in the wall, and disappearing in the darkness.

"I'm glad you asked," Zeke replied. "I was simply demonstrating what is going to happen to you. Your top ruler shall dig a hole in the wall and escape in the night, covering his face so that he will not be identified. The Lord will see to it that he is captured by the Babylonians and he shall be blinded. The rest of you will be a big scramble, some being pursued by men with swords and some being captured and scattered through many lands, and then you may begin to know that God is the Lord of all. Of course, God will spare a few who shall be able to witness and testify to the power and majesty of God."

Another little touch of visual aid teaching came into being when I publicly began to eat bread with trembling hands and to ration water to myself. When the people asked why I was doing this, I replied, "God told me to do this to remind you that captivity means eating in fear, and living on rations."

Then the Lord spoke to me and expressed his great displeasure at the word that was being passed around Israel indicating that the prophets didn't know what they were saying, for the days kept going by and none of the predicted disasters had happened.

The Lord then spoke to me and full of his spirit I spoke to the people saying, "The Lord has decided to change your conversation. The new saying is 'The time is at hand.' There will be no more postponement of punishment and the last chance for repentance is now."

Chap.
13

The Lord then reminded me that there were a lot of teachers and preachers trying to soothe the people and simply tell people what they like to hear.

As a result, I spoke to the General Assembly and said, "Pooh-pooh on you who speak from your own head and who do not speak from the inspiration of the spirit of God.

"O people of Israel, what a shame that you listened to these vain men. Listening to them is the same as expecting a fox to build a wall instead of burrowing under it. The Lord will fix these false preachers. They shall not be on the roll of the blessed.

"They have cried peace when there was no peace and they have given you nothing substantial but have constructed a wall and left out the mortar. Of course, all this will come tumbling down when adversity arrives and the storms of life begin to bring hail and wind. The Lord definitely intends to break down all the phony front that man devises. This is the fate of those who claim to see visions of peace, when there is no peace, and there is no vision."

"The Lord has instructed me also to denounce a bunch of women preachers, who are misleading the young, and who are offering to save souls by selling fancy arm bands, or pillows with sacred words sewn upon them. These people are profit makers, they are fakes. The Lord condemns these people, they shall finally fail, and God will deliver the innocent from them."

Chap.
14

A committee then called upon me, all being elders in the realm, men of position, men who put up a false front, for they were wicked at heart. I really didn't want to meet with them, but God told me to tell it to them like it was.

"Now hear this," said Zeke, "for the Lord has instructed me to tell you that the Lord is going to make every phony answer directly to Him. Your only hope is to repent at once. You have come to God's prophet for some approval or to make a show of righteousness, but it won't work. Repent or you've had it. If you think I am wrong, then you are thinking God is wrong, for the Lord has told me to tell you these things.

"The Lord is doing these things and warning you in the hope that Israel will not go astray. Yet the Lord is prepared to punish the land with famine and with wild beasts. Even if Noah, Daniel, and Job were alive and living in Israel, the Lord would still punish, though these three would be spared.

"If the Lord uses a sword on the people of the land, even if Noah, Daniel, and Jonah were alive in Jerusalem, there would be great slaughter, though of course these three would be spared.

"The same with pestilence. If a plague began to spread through the land at God's order, not even Noah, Daniel, or Job could stop it, though if they were alive they would be spared.

"God is prepared to send the four judgments on Israel, famine, wild beasts, the sword, and the plague, and yet even after all these have taken their toll, a remnant will be left to testify to the power of God. There will be pleasure in the small remnant, for they shall rear their children in the knowledge and fear of the Lord, and they shall know that the destruction of the Lord was not done without good cause."

Chap.
15

The word of the Lord came to me again and revealed to me that the Lord likened Israel to the branch of the vine tree. The branch is not big enough for timber or strong enough to hang clothes on, and so it is used for fuel and is burned in the fire. The same with sinful Israel.

The Lord plans to throw Israel from one fire to another and this is being done to cause the people to return to God. The Lord will make the land desolate as a sign to the people that God is active.

Chap.
16

The history of Jerusalem is interesting. Actually there was no city of Jerusalem, but a stage coach stop for the changing of horses. Then the Lord adopted the city and blessed it. The Lord agreed to do wonderful things for the city and its people, and it was understood that the people were to worship God.

Jerusalem grew. The buildings of the city were beautifully designed, the people began to dress in high fashion, and jewelry was worn by everyone. The trouble was that shortly the people began to think that these things were the result of their own ingenuity and skill and they did not glorify God or worship him.

The marvelous food that was available and the good wine and honey, all these things were soon attributed to man's ability and no longer recognized as gifts of God. The people were willing to do anything for money, even using their own children to help produce greater profits. The people have completely forgotten how Jerusalem was before God became interested.

To make matters worse, the people began to substitute material concepts to worship instead of God. It is amazing what the business people of Jerusalem did just to make a profit. It didn't matter whether a person was a native or a stranger, the men of Jerusalem were out to cheat him.

Because of all this wickedness and the worship of material things, the Lord has pronounced a judgment. The people that have been cheated all these years are going to get together and revolt, and the Lord will help them destroy Jerusalem.

Sodom was a wicked city and the Lord destroyed it, but it wasn't as wicked as Jerusalem is today. Samaria was a land of sin, but not half the sinner that Jerusalem is, and God caused the Samaritans to be conquered. The Lord is terribly angry with Jerusalem and his wrath will soon be poured on the city.

The poor people of Sodom and the unfortunate of Samaria will receive help before the people of Jerusalem do. The Lord has promised to deal harshly with Jerusalem in accordance with what it deserves, nevertheless the day will come when Jerusalem will be ashamed and will repent. At this time, the Lord will establish a new covenant, it will be God's, not yours, and this shall come to pass when the Lord is pacified again concerning Israel and its people.

Chap.
17

The Lord then revealed a message to Zeke through an analogy in vision form. Zeke saw a huge eagle, with great long wings, and it flew to Lebanon and broke off the top branch of the biggest cedar on the highest mountain and carried it to the city. The eagle also transported some of the seed of the land and planted the seed in far places near great waters, and the seed grew and became great vines with many branches.

Zeke then saw another eagle and the vine reached forth toward the second eagle, but the vine couldn't do it, and the vine withered when the east wind blew upon it.

Being instructed of the Lord, Zeke then explained these visions to the people of Israel saying, "Do you know what those visions mean? Well, it means the king of Babylon is coming to capture the king of Israel, and the mighty men of Israel, and will transplant them in Babylon. The king of Israel, who violated the covenant with God, will die in Babylon.

"Furthermore, the attempt to arrange for the king of Egypt to help will fail. The followers of the king of Israel shall be caputred, and these things are done so that the people may know that God is the Lord.

"The Lord will take a tender cutting from a young cedar and place it on the highest mountain in Israel and there it shall grow and prosper and it shall be a witness to what the Lord has done to his people because of their sin."

Again inspired by God, Zeke taught the people saying, "There is an old saying that you use 'Our fathers have eaten sour grapes and our teeth are on edge." This is stupid. You cannot blame your troubles on the sins of your fathers. God is just, and has said that all souls are accountable. The father is responsible for his soul and the son for his. The soul that sins shall die.

"For example, if a man is just, lawful, and has not served alien gods, nor tampered with another man's wife, nor taken advantage of the poor, and one who has not been violent, but completely fair in his dealings with others, and tried to follow the commandments of God; such a man is just, and he shall surely live.

"If such a man has a son who is a robber, a violent man, an adulterer, an oppressor of the poor, such a son shall not be saved, he shall die, and it is his own fault.

"If there is a son who has a wicked father, and the son sees all the sins of the father, and decides to live justly himself, and he doesn't oppress the poor, or tamper with his neighbor's wife, such a son shall be saved, for the wickedness of his father is not the son's fault.

"Why is this? Well, the soul that sinneth, it shall die. The soul stands on its own, it does not take its associates along. If the wicked, however, decide to repent, and change from bad to good, forgiveness is available, and such a soul shall be saved. In fact, the past wickedness will not even be mentioned to such a repenter in the world to come.

"When a righteous person, however, turns wicked, he shall die for his wickedness and his past record won't help him. That doesn't sound fair? Well, you don't understand the justice of God. Be sure of this, people of Israel, each of you will be judged on his own merits. Repent now, and turn away from sin, and your sin will be forgotten. Throw away evil, and start a new way of life. Why do you choose to die? The Lord has no pleasure in your being lost. Repent and live is the plea of God."

I, Zeke, mourn the passing of Israel and lament that she is a goner. At one time Israel was like a wonderful lioness who raised some cubs. When one cub grew he became powerful, and began to destroy, and he was captured in a pit and taken to Egypt.

Then the lioness encouraged the second cub, and this cub also became powerful and exerted a great influence, and he too became destructive and violent. Finally, they put him in chains and took him to Babylon.

The mother Israel was also like a vine, growing, with many fine branches, but she was plucked up and transplanted, the east wind dried her, and she withered away. Now she is surviving in the desert, the fire and the enthusiasm has left her branches, and she is no longer a ruler. Woe is us! How sad, how sad.

A few months later, I had a committee of elders of Israel come to me and ask me about God and what I thought was in store for the people of Israel.

"Some nerve you have," I said, "putting on a show of turning to God. You know as well as I do what God has done and what God expects of his people. God realizes you boys are phonies.

"In God's name, though, let me remind you that God delivered the children of Israel from Egypt, out of the house of bondage, and God insisted then that the people worship the one true God and set aside the idols of the Egyptians.

"God gave the people statutes and commandments, declared for them a day of rest and worship. God punished the people in the wilderness for disobedience and prolonged their conquest of the promised land, and then again God re-asserted His commandments to the next generation and delivered them into the promised land.

"The same routine again occurred. The people sinned and God punished them. No nation can succeed for long without the blessing of God. Yet the Lord continually returns to plead with each new generation to turn to God and to obey His voice, and observe His statutes and His commandments.

"As for you fellows, God says to quit polluting His church with your phony righteousness. You have a choice, either turn to the foolishness of idol worship or sincerely turn to God and follow His commandments. No matter which choice you make, in time you will surely know that truly God is the one Lord.

"The Lord has also instructed me to tell you that the south area of Israel will be burned by the fire of God. When you see this, then you will know that the Lord He is God."

The Lord then instructed me to turn my attention to Jerusalem and to go about the city moaning and with bitter sighing. Naturally this made the people ask me what was wrong.

"I'll tell you what is wrong. It is the tidings that I receive from God. For God has drawn his sword against the city, against all of us, good or bad. Israel has sinned and punishment is near.

"The sword of the Lord is ready to be used. As I go about the city and occasionally stop and smite my hands together; so shall the sword of the Lord be. It will smite in all places in the city. The rich and important leaders will feel the sword, and so will the poor and ignorant, for all of Israel has sinned.

"The Lord has also revealed to me," spoke Zeke, "that trouble will come on two fronts. The army of Babylon will divide itself and one portion will attack the city and another will attack the countryside of Judah.

"The king will surely lose his crown for the anger of the Lord is sure, and the sword of the Lord will bring dire and dreadful punishment to Jerusalem and all the surrounding area. There is no escape.

"As for the Alabamians,[1] the Lord has sent his sword against them. Even though they were used of God to punish Israel, their lies and wicked ways will be punished. The sword of the Lord is against them, they shall be utterly destroyed and as a nation they shall be completely forgotten. This is the Lord's decree.

Chap. 22

"Again I must speak against the city of Jerusalem," said Zeke. "The city has defiled itself with violence, with crime, and with the worship of material things. Because of this, the Lord will reduce the city to a mockery. It will become a shell of its former self.

"Let me remind you city people of some of your sins. You make light of marriage, you take advantage of visitors or strangers, you violate the Sabbath day, you are constantly plotting to make money, and you think nothing of shedding blood.

"There are all kinds of wicked practices being used. Many of you seem to think nothing of going to bed with your neighbor's wife, or even sometimes your daughter-in-law, you seem to think practicing of nudity is good sport, you make contract for people's lives, and you charge excessive interest rates if you think you can get by with them.

"God has had enough of your continuing to acquire dishonest gain. The Lord plans to have you captured, some of you city people will die by the sword and some will be taken into captivity. Hard and severe treatment by your conquerors will teach you a thing or two and you will know that the Lord reigns.

"God says that he will gather you people like the metal smiths get together gold, copper, iron and lead and toss them in the fire. You all will melt in the fire of the Lord. Just as silver is melted in a furnace.

"Furthermore, the Lord is aware of the false preaching that has been taking place. The ministers themselves have violated the holy laws. Many of these so-called leaders are just wolves in the barnyard, soothing the people, and rationalizing away their wicked ways. If there had been enough good men to influence the nation the people might have been saved, but there was no one to stand as a strong godly leader in the political leadership in Israel. As a result, God will bring on the people the very type of treatment that the people have used on the strangers and the unfortunate."

Chap. 23

Inspired by the Lord, Zeke then attempted to teach the people by an allegorical treatment of their history and the consequences.

"Let me tell you the story of two sisters, Moll[2] and Doll.[3] The

---

[1] Ammonites   [2] Aholah   [3] Aholibah

two lived in Egypt and they were in the line of those whose God was the Lord. The two girls turned wild, however, disobeyed God and became as prostitutes, selling themselves in any way for profit.

"Moll primarily made herself available to the Assyrians, enticing them in every possible manner, impressed by their brashness and expensive tastes, and Moll deserted her God and became completely materialistic.

"As a result, the Babylonians took advantage of her, wore her down to nothing, discarded her, trampled her under their feet, and she was left a hopeless captive, and she had even separated herself from God.[1]

"The same thing applies to the case history of Doll. Like her sister, she was influenced by all the proferred delights of the heathen, and the opportunity for riches and great possessions swayed her and she also turned to prostitution. There was nothing that she would not do for a profit.

"As a result she also sold herself to the Babylonians and the Lord has decreed that the very people to whom she gravitated with great greed would be the ones who destroyed her.[2]

"The Lord has told me," continued Zeke, "to denounce you for your wickedness and for your greed for material possessions. For this, God plans to punish you and God will use the Assyrian hordes themselves to do this. God will punish and the land will be brought low and become destitute, and this will be so that you will know that the Lord is God."[3]

Chap.
24

Almost a year later, the word of the Lord came to Zeke suggesting to him that at that very moment the king of Babylon was laying plans to conquer Samaria and Jerusalem.

"God has instructed me," Zeke said to the people, "to illustrate to you in Jerusalem what is in store for you."

As a result, Zeke took a dirty, rusty pot, filled it with water and built a fire under it. Then Zeke killed a lamb and put all the choice pieces of meat in the pot, along with all the bones, and he let the meat cook until it had fallen away from the bones. Then Zeke took the meat out and the bones and spread them upon nearby rocks and poured out the water, and the pot remained barren, dirty, and rusty. Even the scum remained in the pot.

"Now get the message, Jerusalem. You are a city of murder, violence, and money grubbing. You are like the pot. Even the good that is put in you does not change you. Even the heat of persecution and trouble does not cleanse you and you insist on sticking to your evil ways. The Lord wanted to cleanse you, but you refused and so

---

[1]He is speaking here of Samaria   [2]Referring to Jerusalem
[3]This chapter should be read by our Foreign Policy makers

you are doomed."

Then the Lord told Zeke that God was going to take Zeke's wife and spare her the tragedies ahead. The Lord also explained to Zeke that even this loss was to be used as a means of teaching.

"You are not to weep and wail at the grave," said God to Zeke. "You may sigh a bit but don't follow the custom of the times and don't even eat the food brought to you by friends."

The next day after Zeke's wife had died the people came to Zeke and inquired about him, wondering why he did not follow the normal customs of funerals and post grave activities.

"God has used my wife as a means of prophecy. Even as my beautiful wife has been taken from me so shall the beautiful temple of God in Jerusalem be destroyed. You will do as I have done. You will not get to wail aloud and eat bountifully. All these things are signs to you, and when they happen you will know then that the Lord is God."

God then comforted Zeke somewhat by telling him that when all these things came to pass the Lord would provide some eye witnesses to escape and come to Zeke and tell him of all things that they had witnessed.

Chap.
25

The Lord then told Zeke that there was punishment coming to some of the hecklers in the stands who rejoiced over the plight of Israel.

God became very unhappy with some of the people on the Riviera[1] for they cheered when they heard of the destruction of God's temple in Jerusalem and they rejoiced when the news of the capture of the Jews was reported. Because of this, the Lord plans to have the Riviera gradually infiltrated by people from other places, many from up east, and they shall make many changes unpleasant to the natives. The Lord is doing this simply because many of the people clapped their hands and stamped their feet in joy when word arrived that Jerusalem had fallen to the wicked. When this happens, you all should know that God is the Lord.

The Lord has also some other plans for Mississippi[2] and Detroit[3]. This is being done because many of these people, when hearing of the troubles in Judah, said, "The whole outfit are a bunch of heathens." Because of this, the Lord plans some labor problems for Detroit, and the city of Memphis will be in Tennessee and not in Mississippi where it belongs.

The Lord has also said that punishment is due to France[4] and God will make many occasions of desolation there for they too were not sympathetic to God's people.

As for the Moscow Muggers,[5] the Lord will take vengeance on

---

[1]Ammonites   [2]Moab   [3]Seir   [4]Edom   [5]Philistines

them, for they continually took advantage of God's people. Over the years the Lord will wreak a terrible vengeance on these types of people and they shall finally know that the Lord is God.

Chap.
26

The Lord is also unhappy with the city of Tyre. Tyre was jealous of Jerusalem and rejoiced over its destruction, for Tyre thought it would get all the business that had been going to Jerusalem.

The Lord does not plan things to work this way, for Tyre is a wicked city and every conceivable evil is there. Because of this, Tyre will be completely destroyed, and it will be scraped clean so that it will be left only as a place for the spreading of fish nets to dry in the sun.[1]

The Lord will cause the king of Babylon to fall upon Tyre and destroy it completely. In fact, the king of Babylon will tear down the walls and there will be so many horses stomping around that the city will be reduced to dust.

Finally the Lord has promised that the city will be left as a flat rock and it shall never be rebuilt.[2] There will be a lot of mourning for the good old days of Tyre, but it will never recover. The Lord plans to let Tyre be an example, a terror to remind man of the power of God. Often will attempts be made to rebuild Tyre, but none of the attempts will succeed.

Chap.
27

The eulogy over the death of Tyre makes interesting reading. Tyre was a beautiful city, the builders constructed many magnificent edifices going down to the very edge of the sea. The ships of Tyre were the best in the world, being built with cedar from Lebanon and oak from California. The seats on the ships were made of ivory from Africa, and the upholstery was all of fine linen.

Tyre had secured the best seamen in the world for captains of its ships and trade was at its very best. The city itself was well protected by highly paid warriors all carefully selected from the best of the NFL teams,[3] and the sharpest merchants in the east lived in Tyre and aided its prosperity. Tyre had trade connections everywhere, with Damascus, Jerusalem, Rome, New York, Tokyo and Moscow. The Chinese traded here and also men from England, France, and Germany. It is truly amazing, the scope and influence of Tyre. All this will collapse, because Tyre decided to laugh at God. The moans for Tyre will be heard all over the world.

Chap.
28

The Lord then encouraged Zeke to contact the leaders of Tyre

---

[1]This has happened!
[3]Persia, Lud, and Phut

[2]Finally the sea has even cut off the old rock foundations from the mainland and today fishermen spread their nets on the rocks.

and to speak to them. Zeke did and he spoke to them saying, "God is angry with Tyre and the leaders there. You have become so important and so sure of yourself and your power that you think you are gods yourselves.

"You think you are wiser than Daniel, and that you have everything under control. You think you control all wealth, and all trade, and that you are protected by a highly paid army. Well, God has planned an invasion for your benefit. How will you feel when there is a strange sword at your throat? Will you think you are a god then? You will die, for God has decreed this.

"What about your king? He is spoiled rotten. He sits on a throne of beauty and power, and lives as if he was in the garden of Eden. Materialism has gotten the best of you. You have been overcome by prosperity, for prosperity has introduced violence and evil.

"The Lord will cause Tyre to be destroyed by fire and invasion. The destruction of Tyre will be a great astonishment and in time it will completely disappear and it will never be rebuilt.

"Zidon will get it also. It is not as important or as prosperous as Tyre, but it is wicked. God will destroy Zidon by disease and internal revolution, and there will be great trouble for Zidon. No longer will Zidon be a thorn in the flesh of Israel. Eventually, long after the people of God have been scattered over the whole earth, when they have eventually repented, and when God gathers them again to Jerusalem, then shall they build houses and vineyards, they shall live safely, and then they shall know that the Lord is their God.

Chap.
29

Then the word of the Lord came to Zeke and he was inspired to testify against Pharoah.

"Now Pharoah," said Zeke, "it is necessary for me to tell you that God is against you. You have decided for some strange reason that the Nile is yours, as if you had made it.

"When Israel called on you for help against the Babylonians, that was your chance, and you blew it. God is going to punish Egypt for this failure, and then you will know that God is the Lord.

"God plans to make Egypt desolate and a trouble spot as long as it thinks the Nile is its own. During one period of about 40 years Egypt will be practically deserted and worthless. This is just a sign from God.

"During this forty year period God will cause the Egyptians to be scattered all around the world, but eventually God will bring them back to Egypt. The importance of Egypt will be diminished and it will no longer be considered one of the most important or powerful nations in the world."

Not long after this, the word of the Lord came to Zeke telling him that God was using Big Ned[1] to conquer Tyre and effect the punishment of God and that therefore Big Ned would be rewarded by God in that God would allow him to also conquer Egypt.

God also told Zeke that eventually the glory of Israel would be restored and the people of Israel would again worship God, and know that God is the Lord.

Chap. 30

"The Lord was displeased when Egypt failed to aid the children of Israel, even though such was God's punishment. The Lord plans to bring long and monstrous trouble on Egypt," said Zeke.

"What is more," he continued, "all the piddling little countries that joined Egypt shall catch it in the neck also. God is quite certain that Egypt will eventually know that God is the Lord.

"The Lord plans to do most of this through Big Ned, who is very careless about lives and property. The Lord wants the people to know that all of these things are part of God's control of history.

"The Lord is plenty burned up with Pharoah and God will destroy his strongholds and embarrass his whole program. God will accomplish this by making Big Ned powerful and allowing him to conquer Egypt and to scatter the Egyptians. Big Ned will also destroy all the idols of the land."

Chap. 31

The Lord then spoke to Zeke during the eleventh year of the captivity and told Zeke to address himself to Pharoah.

"The Lord has a message for you, Pharoah," prophesied Zeke. "You and yours are going to get it. Actually, you have acted just like the Assyrians, and you have exalted yourself and you have indicated that your power and your importance is great. Well, your time is drawing near for punishment. The Lord is not going to permit you or any other nation to place itself above God or to attribute godly powers to its ruler.

"About all I can say is that the fall of Egypt will be big news. The Lord is going to bring you, Pharoah, and your followers to a point that is comparably as low as you have exalted yourself. Other nations shall see you all tumble and will say, 'What a pity for such a great nation to come apart at the seams.'"

Chap. 32

Almost a year later the Lord inspired Zeke to produce a funeral lamentation for Egypt, for the fall of Egypt was almost at hand.

"Woe, woe is Pharoah," cried out Zeke. "Pharoah is like a fish caught in a net and thrown out on the land to flop and die. That is what God is going to do to Pharoah and Egypt.

"As a fitting sign of what is happening to Egypt the Lord has arranged for an eclipse. The Lord has also arranged for the king of Babylon, the meanest man on earth[2], to devour Egypt. When the

---

[1] Nebuchadnezzar   [2] An early day Don Rickles

terrible destruction of the Babylonians has levelled Egypt, then the people will know that God is the Lord."

"Pharoah will finally learn one thing though, and that is that the Lord in His own time plans to get around to all the baddies. The Babylonians will have a big time conquering Egypt, but they themselves will in time be destroyed.

"There shall arise new men of wickedness, and their days will also be numbered. It should slightly comfort Pharoah that he shares the darkness of the grave with some important has-beens[1]."

Chap. 33

Still later, inspired by God, Zeke made another speech.

"Now hear this," said Zeke. "The situation is not completely hopeless. My preaching is like a warning trumpet blown by the watchman on the wall. The people who hear what I say and repent shall be saved. If the watchman doesn't blow his trumpet, the watchman is penalized, but I am telling everyone now, the terror of the Lord is close at hand!

"Again I speak to the house of Israel and implore them to repent. God doesn't enjoy getting rid of the wicked and punishing them. God's preference is that the wicked repent and the wanderer return to God.

"God has said that the wicked shall eternally die, but if the wicked repent, return anything that is stolen, and make what restitution they can of other sins, and then begin to walk uprightly in the statutes of God, then these wicked ones will not die but will live eternally.

"The people often criticize this system and accuse God of being unfair, as a wicked man who repents receives the same eternal reward as a righteous man who remained righteous. It is your warped sense of justice that is wrong."

The Lord then spoke to Zeke and reminded him what a tough job he had preaching. The people would come and listen and seem interested and nod their heads, but they would not change their lives.[2]

Chap. 34

Then the word of the Lord came to Zeke and he was inspired to prophesy some more, this time to the leadership in Israel.

"You leaders of Israel are a miserable outfit," said Zeke. "You look out for yourselves real well, but you completely neglect the people. The Lord is plenty hot about this matter. You leaders were so busy with your own pleasures that you let the people go astray.

"God plans to look out for all the ones you have neglected. God will find the lost and to each will be given an opportunity for

---

[1]Hitler, Alexander the Great, the Kaiser, & Capt. Bligh
[2]How modern can you get?

restoration.

"God's plan is to provide one shepherd for the sheep, one leader for all of God's people throughout the whole earth. I will bless all the people who follow the shepherd that I send, the chosen one from the line of David.[1]

"The followers of this new leader will learn to feel safe in any land, for they shall know not to be afraid. They shall know that the Lord their God is with them and that they are His people."

Chap.
35

Another message from God concerned the people that lived around Mount Seir. These people were strong and mighty warriors, and most people always said, "Yes, Seir" to them.

The Lord, however, took a dim view of the wicked way that these people treated others and the Lord felt that they were so bad that they should be discontinued as a people. The Lord would cause these people to be completely overwhelmed as a nation and their country would never be revived.[2]

Chap.
36

The Lord again inspired Zeke to prophesy, this time a word of encouragement to the people of Israel.

"God would remind you, Israel," said Zeke, "that you are His first chosen people and that even though you have been scattered for your sins, you will be restored some day and your land will again be yours.

"God is always for his people, and in proper time there shall be an increase in the number of God's people, and the cities of Israel shall again be inhabited, and the waste areas will be reclaimed. Your situation will be better than it was when you first came to Canaan.

"These things will be done in order that God's name may be glorified, not because the people deserve this. The punishment which God sent, this was deserved. God had pity, though, on his people. Again God reminds you that the restoration of Israel is for the sake of God's Holy Name, and not a reward to the people.

"The Lord will gather Israel from all the nations and bring you again to your own land. God will put a new heart and a new spirit within you,[3] and you will choose to observe the laws of God and walk uprightly. At this time also God will multiply the success of those who plant grain and fruit orchards.

"People will be amazed at what happens in a land known for its desolation. These things God will do, for the sake of his Holy Name."

Chap.
37

Not long after this Zeke had a strange experience. While walking

---

[1] Obvious prophecy of Christ   [2] There are no Seirs
[3] I think the Christian spirit

in the area where the dead were casually buried in open graves, Zeke began to think that he saw the dry bones move. Then Zeke saw the ankle bone begin to connect with the knee bone, and so forth. Then skin formed over the bones and all the dead of Israel seemed to rise as a great and mighty army. The wind had blown spirit and life into the whole cemetery area and Zeke was scared purple.[1]

God then cooled Zeke down by informing him that this was a vision and that it signified God's intent to restore Israel and to eventually see that the people of God were in control of the earth.

God then inspired Zeke to try a little visual aid in teaching the people. As a result, Zeke took two sticks. On one of them he wrote Joseph, and on one he wrote Judah. Zeke then joined the sticks together by grafting or splicing.

"Do you see what I have done?", asked Zeke. "Well, this symbolizes the joining of all of God's people everywhere some day, and they shall no longer consider themselves tribes, but shall all serve one master.[2] God will then make a new covenant of peace with his people, and they shall be a new outfit. The spirit of God will be with them and they shall be God's people. The wicked and idolatrous shall then know that God is the Lord."

Chap.
38

"Now God has a word for a bad bunch from the North.[3] The Lord knows that you have been a constant nuisance for centuries. Everytime you thought Israel was weak and her cities poorly fortified, you descended on Israel.

"One of these days, many, many years from now, you are going to do this once too often and you are going to find all of a sudden that the weak cities and desolate rural areas are defended by God, and it is strictly curtains for you when this time comes. This is God's way with the wicked. It is slow, but it is sure!"

Chap.
39

"God has told me to emphasize the fate of the North Birds. God says that knocking you Northers is going to be as swift as snatching a bow from an archer and throwing his arrows on the ground. It's coming, boys! God says then you fellows will know that the Lord is God!

"Just to give you a fearsome idea of how complete the destruction will be and how great the loss of life, the Lord says that it will take seven months to bury the dead.[4] In fact, tourist groups will assist in this burying.[5]

"The slaughter of these people is going to be so great that the Lord wants me to alert the buzzards as the land will need plenty of

[1] This should have caused a halt to his prophesying
[2] I think this is a reference to Christ as head of the church
[3] Not necessarily Yankees   [4] Well before burial insurance, of course
[5] "Everyone out of the bus now for burying detail!" yells travel agent

them.[1]

"All these things will witness to the power and glory of God, and the heathen shall be astonished. Again God reminds his people that when they have repented and returned to the Lord, when the new shepherd has come, then God will no longer hide his face, but will pour forth his spirit on the people and Israel shall come into being again."

Chap.
40

Fourteen years after Jerusalem had fallen Zeke had a vision, and in this vision he seemed to be transported to the top of a mountain and from there he could behold a great city. There was present in the vision a man who shone as if he were made of brass and he instructed Zeke to look carefully at what he saw and report it to the Israelites who were still in captivity.

The vision of the city was seemingly quite accurate, with specific measurements for vestibules, rooms, the temple, and other buildings. Primarily the measurements concerned the inner and outer portion of the temple.

Chap.
41

More minute measurements and details of the vision of the temple seen by Zeke.

Chap.
42

After all the careful examination of the temple, the brass man took Zeke toward the eastern part of the temple, and the glory of the Lord of Israel became manifest. The vision was the same as with the earlier vision of the vehicle with wheels and wings, and the glory of the Lord filled the entire temple.

Then God spoke to Zeke in this vision and said, "Zeke, here are my headquarters. I have come to stay. I will not allow my temple to be continually contaminated. Tell the people to put away their idols, for I the Lord have come to stay."

The Lord then in the vision told Zeke to describe all that he had seen, particularly the temple. "If the people repent, let them have all the tiny details," said God.[2]

Chap.
43

Then God made available the details.[3]

Chap.
44

In the vision, then God closed the east gate and decreed that no one should enter it, for here had passed the glory of God. Only the priest of God could be near, and he will sit near the gate and eat bread.

Then was Zeke transported to the north gate and here reminded that the children of Israel had sinned in allowing strangers and

---

[1] Ezekiel was a natural born buzzard alerter.   [3] Read Ezekiel 43: 13-27
[2] Somebody repented for Zeke has all the details

plunderers to pollute the temple of God. There must be a real housecleaning in the church. Even though the regularly ordained ministers were wrong and have sinned, yet they must return and run the sanctuary. These ministers must observe the statutes assigned to them.

There are some ministers who never strayed nor were persuaded to follow strange cults and tangents. Let these ministers know they are welcome again as keepers of the house of God.

These ministers must be properly and unobtrusively dressed, and they must be robed when conducting regular services. These men are not to let their hair grow long, nor are they to drink, and if they marry they must marry maidens and not widows, unless the woman be a widow of a minister.

The ministers shall teach the people the difference between the holy and the profane, and in cases of dispute, the minister must render judgment. The ministers shall obey the laws of God and see that the sabbath is observed.

The first portion of the gifts that the people bring to the church shall go to the minister.[1] The ministers must remember not to eat anything dead of itself; so don't bring sick sheep as part of your church pledge.

Chap.
45

The vision also outlined the need of setting aside a certain amount of land to be considered church property. This should include a place for the minister's house.[2]

The Lord also suggested that Zeke remind the rulers that justice was needed, and also fairness. A standard for weights and measurements was recommended and the rulers were urged to see that there was no cheating of the people by the merchants.[3]

The remainder of the chapter tells about paying your church pledge in livestock and only the principle is presently applicable. Giving to God is still emphasized as basic to worship!

Chap.
46

Ordinances are set forth here instructing the ministers on how to prepare a family night supper without blemish.

Chap.
47,

The brass man from God then let Zeke look out of the east gate again and there he showed him a river beginning with waters joining waters until a great stream was created and flowed forth into the mighty sea. The vision was explained to Zeke indicating that as the waters expanded the power and truth of God would also go forth. Each tribe and each nation would be assigned an area suitable to their habitation.

---

[1] We all know that the preacher has to be paid

[2] Small lots were often selected
[3] Keep trying!

The land was to be divided first among the tribes and the area with bounds for each tribe was described and is recorded in Chapter 48. There would be set aside an area for a great city and this great city shall be called The City of God.

DANIEL

When J.J.[1] had been king of Judah for only about 3 years, Big Ned[2] came and declared war against Jerusalem. The Lord, in accordance with His plan of punishment, gave Big Ned the victory and J.J. was carried away captive to Babylon. Also Big Ned confiscated quite a number of the antique vessels and beautiful altar pieces from the church and had these valuable symbols placed in the pagan church in Babylon.

Big Ned then ordered his executive vice president, Aggie[3], to select the outstanding teenagers from among the captured people and to enroll them in the Big Ned University. At the college, the students were to be taught the language of the Northers,[4] general science, some psychology, political science, and palace manners.

One feature of the college was the training table. All the youngsters were to learn to eat rich foods, such as caviar and cherry jubilee. Among the teenagers were four named Daniel, Slim,[5] Tommy,[6] and Pablo[7].

Daniel, somewhat of a rebel anyway, decided that he would not eat all the rich food at the training table. Daniel had already made friends with the Dean of Student Life[8] and was therefore free to talk and reason with him.

"Dean," said Daniel, "I'm just not going to stuff my gullet with all that high chloresterol food you serve."

"Now, Daniel," said the Dean, "it is not a simple matter. If I don't feed you what the king has ordered and you get thin, then the king will have me beheaded."[9]

"Well, give us a try. Slim, Tommy, Pablo and I have agreed that if you feed us steak, milk and potatoes for ten days and we are not healthier than those who eat souffle' and eels, we will go with your system," suggested Daniel.

"That's a fair deal," said the Dean.[10]

At the end of the ten days Daniel and his friends looked much better than most of their carousing compadres and so the Dean put them completely and permanently on steak, potatoes, and milk.

God particularly blessed these young men and they grew in wisdom and stature, and Daniel was given an extra ability in the area of visions and dreams.

When graduation time arrived, the Dean brought the four young men to the king as his top graduates. The king asked them some

---

[1]Jehoiakim [2]Nebuchadnezzar [3]Ashpenaz [4]Chaldeans
[5]Shadrach [6]Meshach [7]Abednigo [8]Melzar
[9]Almost like working for a school board
[10]Probably the first decent offer the Dean had had from the students

questions and they replied in exemplary fashion and the king decided
that they were more intelligent than the consultants that the king
had been paying.

Some months after this the king had a bad dream and he awoke
in the middle of the night, tormented by his dream. To make matters
worse, all he could remember was that he had been having a bad
dream, though the details escaped him.

As a result, the king sent for his consultants and told them of
his problem.

"Just tell us the dream, Sir King, and we will tell you what it
means."

"The problem is," replied the king, "that I don't remember the
dream. If you will tell me the dream and what it means then I will
give each of you a big bonus, but if you don't, I'll have all the
consultants in the county executed."

"Nobody can do that," wailed the head of the magician's union.

"You are just stalling for time," said the king. "I've long
suspected you all are phonies, telling me only what I wish to hear.
Come up with the answer, or it is death to all of you."

Daniel heard about this, as he was one of those considered a
consultant, and knew his head would go also. In fact, Clothes-Line Sid,[1]
who was in charge of head-hunting, came to Daniel and Daniel went
to the king and asked for a little time to come up with an answer.

"If you can get the answer, fine," said the king, "and we will
postpone the executions for a few days."

Then Daniel went back to the apartment and he told Tommy,
Pablo, and Slim about the matter and they immediately formed a
small prayer group.

As a result of their prayers to God, Daniel received a revelation
concerning the dream of the king.

"Thank you, God" said Daniel. "Blessed is the name of the
Lord, for the Lord is in charge of all the earth, God changes the
seasons regularly, wisdom and power are all of God, and God
controls history, putting kings in power and taking them away.

"God knows," continued Daniel, "what is in the darkness and
God is responsible for all light. I thank God for the wisdom which
the Lord has given to me, for I know it is God's wisdom. Amen."

Then Clothes-line Sid escorted Daniel into the presence of Big
Ned and introduced him to the king.[2]

"Are you able, son, to tell me the dream that I have dreamed
and also the interpretation of it?

"You better believe it! The consultants, the magicians, the
astrologers are no help to you in this because only God knows and

---

[1] Arioch   [2] Big Ned couldn't remember names

only God can decide to reveal, for your dream tells of the future.

"First, the reason I know about the dream is simply because God has chosen to reveal it to me, and not because I am smarter than anyone else.

"In your dream you saw a great figure; it stood before you, shining with a terrible brightness. The head was of solid gold while the chest and arms were of silver, with the belly and thighs being of brass. The legs of the figure were of iron, and the feet were part iron and part clay.

"All of a sudden, the iron, clay, brass, silver, and gold were all busted into fine grain like dust and the wind blew it all away. The stone, which was just suddenly on the scene, and which had smashed all the figure to pieces, then became a great mountain and filled the whole earth. That was some dream you had, O King!"

"Now let me tell you what all that means," said Daniel. "You are a great and powerful king, for God has arranged it to be that way. God has put you in charge of the known world. You are represented in the dream by the head of gold."

"After you shall come an inferior kingdom, then a third kingdom, represented by the brass which is still more inferior, but it shall rule the earth. Then comes a strong kingdom, strong as iron. It shall break things in pieces and shall rule with ruthless power. The kingdom, however, shall become divided, as you saw the iron and clay mixed, so the kingdom will be partly strong and partly weak.

"At this point in time, God shall begin a new type of kingdom that shall never be destroyed. This new type kingdom shall gradually encompass the earth, not by action as a kingdom, but by different parts and different people gradually taking the word of the new kingdom throughout the earth.

"God has chosen to reveal to you this glimpse of the future." Daniel then sat down and mopped his brow.

The king was overcome with the speech. Immediately he ordered a new Mastercharge card for Daniel and a box of candy.

The king then said, "Surely, Daniel, your God is a God of gods, a Lord of kings, a revealer of secrets. Blessings on you, Daniel."

Then the king made Daniel a great man, gave him many gifts, and appointed him Governor of governors. At Daniel's request, the king then made Slim, Tommy, and Pablo assistants to the Governor of governors.

Chap.
3

Big Ned one day decided that he had had a great idea[1] and as a result he caused to be constructed a huge figure, covered with gold, that stood about 5 stories high. Upon the completion of this huge edifice there was, of course, a necessity to have a ribbon cutting and

---

[1]Actually it came from the suggestion box

dedication service.

All the government workers were invited to come through a memorandum from the king which made it clear that attendance was not optional. As a result, the princes, governors, sheriffs, judges, city managers, fire chiefs, chariot supervisors, consultants, and disc jockeys were all assembled on a set date for the big service.

One of the speakers at the dedication suggested that in honor of Big Ned a law be passed to the effect that when the palace orchestra began to blare forth on all the varied instruments of music, that this be a signal for everyone to bow down and face the new gold image, and worship this great creation of the king.[1] The penalty suggested for failure to obey this law was being thrown into a fiery furnace.

The law was passed by voice vote of the king and Big Ned gave the signal to the orchestra and all the local musicians blew it as best they could.

Some of the Chaldeans, however, noticed that some of the Jews didn't bow.[2] Two or three of these stool pigeons came to Big Ned and said, "It was a great ceremony, but we saw three guys who didn't bow, and it ruined the day for most of us."

"Ye gods and little fishes!" roared Big Ned, for he was terribly angry. "Go get the men and bring them here at once!"

This was done and the three turned out to be Tommy, Slim, and Pablo.

"Is it true that you kids failed to bow to the image and to worship as I had ordered?" asked Big Ned.

"It is true," they replied.

"Well, we'll give you another chance. I'll signal the orchestra again and this time bow or it's the fiery furnace for you all!" sternly said Big Ned.

"Mighty king, we can save you a few toots from the orchestra, for we are not going to serve or acknowledge any image, for we worship the true God. In fact, our God is able to deliver us,"[3] spoke Slim for the three.

At this point Big Ned had turned a deep purple and screamed at the furnace committee to throw another log on the fire. The king also ordered the security police to bind the hands of Slim, Tommy and Pablo, and to leave them in their clothes, even leaving their hats on their heads.

When the furnace had become seven times hotter than was normal for people throwing, Big Ned gave the order to the stokers to throw the men into the furnace.

---

[1] Actually he just paid for it with tax money

[2] I've always been puzzled by the ability of people with their heads bowed to see those that aren't.

[3] Of course, they realized God might decide not to deliver them

The flames were so intense that the stokers were burned to death getting close enough to throw the three in the fire.[1] Tommy, Slim, and Pablo then fell down with their hands tied into the flames.

Suddenly Big Ned rose in wonder and yelled, "Did we not throw three men into the furnace?"

"Yes, sir, that is right," replied the two nearest vice-presidents.

"But I see four men loose, walking in the flames, and they are not hurt, and the form of the fourth is like the Son of God," said Big Ned.

Then Big Ned came as close to the furnace as he dared and said, "Come on out, Slim. You, too, Tommy and Pablo."

The three came forth and all the many witnesses saw that they were unharmed, that not a single hair was singed, and there was not even the smell of smoke upon them.

Then Big Ned stood up and said, "I hereby make a decree, that anybody, in any nation, that ever says anything bad, in any language, about the God of Slim, Tommy, or Pablo, shall be cut to pieces and their home torn down, for there is no other god anywhere that can do the type of thing that I have seen today."

Following this, Slim, Tommy and Pablo were all promoted to sergeant.

Chap.
4

Then Big Ned went about his business as usual. Sometime later, however, he came out with another of his all-points bulletins, which were posted everywhere for everyone to see.

"Peace be unto you. I have decided that it is good to pass on to the people the things that the true God has made available to me through his wonderful signs. The kingdom of God is an everlasting kingdom and the dominion of God is from generation to generation.

"Now here is the way it happened. I, Big Ned, was at rest in my house and living it up, for things were going my way. Then I had a dream and I saw visions and I could not figure out the meaning. My consultants, magicians, and even my shrinks were of no use to me.

"However, Daniel, the smartest sidekick I ever had and one in whom God confides, came to me and offered to interpret my dreams.

"Well, Daniel, in my vision I saw a tree of great height in the middle of the earth, and the tree grew and finally it seemed to reach almost to heaven. The leaves were pretty and there was plenty of fruit for everybody, all the beasts of the field could reside in the shade and the birds of the air could perch on the limbs.

"Then a watchman came down from heaven and ordered me to chop down the tree, cut off the branches, shake off the leaves, scatter the beasts, and shoo away the birds. Yet I was supposed to

---

[1]It was difficult to recruit replacements also.

leave a stump, with the roots still firmly in the ground, surrounded by grass that would catch and hold the dew from heaven.

"Then I was told to transplant a beast's heart into the stump in place of a man's heart,[1] and then let there be time for adjustment to the new heart. The watchers were doing this so that the living might know that God reigns over man and gives rule to whomever God chooses. Now tell me, Daniel, what in the thunderation does all that mean?

"I want to report to the people," said Big Ned, "that Daniel went into shock for about an hour, but then he began to speak to me and he said, 'The dream applies to your enemies. The tree which reached to heaven, with the great shade and the mighty branches is you. You have become a great and powerful king and your greatness extends throughout the known world.[2] Unfortunately, however, the cutting down of the tree, the heart transplant and all this signifies what your enemies are going to do to you.

"Actually, they will drive you crazy and you will be a mental case, getting down on your hands and knees and eating grass with the oxen.[3] You will soon, however, acknowledge the power of God and as a result you will be permitted to retain your kingdom.

"My suggestion to you, Great King, is to reform at once, cease your life of sin and repent. Begin to show mercy to the poor and God may then lengthen your period of peace.'

"As King then I took the matter under advisement, but twelve months later I was still postponing reform.

"Then one day a voice from heaven was heard by me saying, "You've had it, Big Ned. You never took the advice. Your kingdom is a goner."

"That same hour I went nuts and was driven from the palace and went out in the fields and began to eat grass in competition with the oxen.

"Then I let my hair grow until it was as awful looking as Tiny Tim's and also I let my fingernails grow into claws.

"Sometime later I began to come to my senses and I lifted up my eyes to heaven, I blessed God, and acknowledged that the kingdom of God is the one kingdom that is forever, and that the dominion of God is forever. Then my recovery became complete.

"I returned to my palace and placed the kingdom back in operation, and now I, Big Ned, make this witness to the true God of heaven, all of whose works are truth, and be sure that those who walk in pride can be easily cut down to size by the true God.[4]"

---

[1] Just an ordinary heart transplant
[2] A PR man couldn't have done better
[3] A bad situation in an election year
[4] Not long after this Big Ned died

Sometime after this the son of Big Ned became king in his father's place and he mainly went into high social living. After a rather brief period of being king, Huey,[1] the new king, gave one of the biggest, most ornate banquets every staged. Huey even served the wine in the gold and silver vessels which had been taken from Solomon's temple in Jerusalem.

The whole crowd, consisting of princes, wives, go-go girls, and one or two party crashers all got to drinking expensive wine from the costly containers and they all became roaring drunk.

When the party was at its peak, suddenly the fingers of a man's hand appeared and wrote on the wall. The king saw the hand and the writing, and he turned pale, and his knees began to knock, for he was scared silly.

The king then howled for the magicians, the consultants, and even the local astrologers, and Huey spoke to them and said, "Read this writing. It is in a strange language. Whoever is able to translate this will get a new suit of clothes, two matching ties, and will be named third vice-president of L.S.U."

All the smarties looked on the wall, but none of them could translate the words. Huey then became greatly depressed and the party came to a screeching halt.

Now Ann Landers, the queen, had remained sober and she turned to Huey and said, "Don't be so down in the mouth. There is a man in town who can translate this. The man's name is Daniel and he was always bailing out your old man when he was stuck with a problem that the consultants or magicians could not handle. Just send for Daniel and let him do his thing."

Then was Daniel brought into the banquet hall and Huey spoke to him and asked, "Are you Daniel, the captive from Judah, who Daddy brought here?"

Daniel nodded.

"Well, I've heard of you," continued Huey, "and I understand that you have special insights and great wisdom. Well, my own staff of wise men have flunked out, and they cannot read the writing on the wall. If you can read the message you get two suits of clothes, two ties, and you'll be third vice-president of L.S.U."

"First, Huey, you can forget the gifts. Particularly the vice-president deal. I will, however, read the words to you," said Daniel.

"Almighty God gave your father glory and honor,[2] and because of this all nations and people trembled and were afraid of the power inherent in your father's rule. When your Dad thought somebody needed killing, he had them killed, or if someone needed to be

---

[1] Belshazzar
[2] Excuse Daniel for being a little eloquent, but he hadn't been on a program all year.

demoted, he also did that.

"In fact, your father became such a big shot that pride took the best of him, and God struck him down, so that he lost his glory, and he went nuts, getting out on the lawn and eating grass with the oxen. When he finally began to recognize God and call upon the name of the Lord, he was restored in power.

"You knew all this, yet you started out from the first with no humility, and you have lifted yourself even above God, stooping to use the priceless vessels taken from the temple at Jerusalem as a means of holding wine to get all the princes, the wives, the go-go girls, and the visitors all drunk.

"You have been toasting each other, and you have been toasting the gods of wood, or stone, or gold, or brass, or whatever. Yet you have not mentioned in any way the God of all, the one who furnishes life and breath.

"As a result, God has written you a note on the wall and the note says 'God has pulled the card on your kingdom, you are weighed yourself in the balances, and you don't measure correctly; so your kingdom is being given to the Medes and Persians."

Huey was greatly impressed, and immediately gave Daniel two suits of clothes and two neckties, and announced that Daniel was third vice-president of L.S.U. whether he liked it or not.

That night, Huey was killed and a young man named Darius claimed the kingdom. Darius was a Mede.

Chap.
6

Darius immediately re-organized the government.[1] First he appointed 120 princes, and over them he appointed a Board of Directors of three men, and Daniel was named one of these and then made Chairman of the Board. The new king figured that Daniel would then be able to run the kingdom and the king could spend more time at Camp David.

It developed that the other two board members and the princes didn't care for this as Daniel was honest and would not allow them to pad their expense accounts. In spite of employing a private investigator, the group could not come up with any dirt on Daniel.

The group was always meeting over the matter, however.

"I tell you what," said one of the board members, "we aren't going to find anything crooked about Daniel so we had better attack his religion."

As a result, a plan was devised. Representatives, including the two board members, called on Darius and said, "We have a law that we would like to pass," said the spokesman. "As an honor to you, we want the law to say that for 30 days no one shall petition or ask anything of any god or man except you, or be thrown in a den of

[1] I think this type of thing is still going on.

lions."

"Well, it appeals to me more than simply being made Jaycee Man of the Month," said Darius.

"Fine, mighty king. Now write out the law in accordance with the code of the Medes and the Persians, so that there can be no alteration or amendments," continued the spokesman.

Darius did as they suggested.

Daniel, of course, learned of this shortly and he merely went about his usual custom of kneeling in prayer to the Lord God of Israel as he faced Jerusalem. Daniel did this three times a day at an open window.

Needless to say, the men who designed the law arranged to catch Daniel. As soon as they had documented their case with eyewitnesses, the group came to the king and charged Daniel with breaking the law. They even mentioned that Daniel did this three times a day.

Now the king became very peeved with himself for he realized he had been had. At once Darius began to check if there was a legal way out of his jam and he worked all day on the problem, seeking a loophole in the law.

The group assembled again before the king the next day and said, "We hate to keep mentioning this, king, but there is no way of altering the law of the Medes and the Persians."

The king then ordered that Daniel be thrown into a den of lions. The king tried to console Daniel by saying, "Daniel, even though I can't do anything your God who you religiously serve will deliver you."

Then Daniel was put in the den with the lions and a stone was placed to seal the den, and the king's private lock was placed on the door to make sure there was no escape.

The king went to his palace and passed up the evening meal, even making the servants cut off the stereo. The king spent a sleepless night worrying about his friend Daniel.[1]

The first thing in the morning the king ran down to the lions' den and began to call, "Daniel, Daniel! Was your God able to deliver you from the lions?"

"You better believe it, King!" said Daniel. "My God shut the mouths of the lions and they have not hurt me. This was done because I am innocent of any wrong."

The king then was very happy and ordered the immediate release of Daniel. Just to make sure, Darius had one of his medics check Daniel, and there was no mark on him.

The king then decided to celebrate the safety of Daniel by arresting the originators of the law and throwing them into the lion's den. Since it was togetherness week, the families were thrown in with the men.[2]

[1] Daniel went to sleep probably after the lions did   [2] This law has been revised

Then King Darius published an all points bulletin which was released to all the media stating, "I make a decree that in every area of my kingdom men tremble and stand in awe of the God of Daniel; for He is a living God, and steadfast forever, and His kingdom that which shall not be destroyed and his rule shall be unto the end of time.

"The God of Daniel delivers and rescues, He works signs and wonders in heaven and on earth, He delivered Daniel from the power of the Lions."

Signed by hand
Darius, the King.

Chap.
7

The remainder of this book of Daniel consists of a record of prophetic dreams and visions which came to Daniel. The first of these occurred during the reign of Huey.

Daniel in reporting the vision stated that there appeared to him the impression of the four winds of heaven all blowing on the sea at once.[1] The commotion was so great that four sea monsters came to the top. The first monster looked like a lion with wings. All of a sudden the wings disappeared and the lion was forced to stand up like a man, and a man's heart was put into the beast.

The second beast appeared to be a big bear with somebody's ribs[2] in his mouth, and the bear was instructed to launch a big people eating program.

The third monster was like a leopard with four wings, and it also had four heads.[3]

The fourth monster was really hideous, very strong, with iron teeth, it was really mean, and it had ten horns, and suddenly there grew forth a little horn and it ate up three of the regular horns. The little horn had eyes like a man and it spoke like a politician.

The dream continued until all the thrones of the beastly rulers were destroyed and the Lord himself appeared on the throne of judgment. The throne of God looked like a flame itself and it had fiery wheels. All the people of all time stood in God's presence before the throne. I plainly saw the destruction of evil.

In the vision also there appeared the Son of man and he was in great glory before the throne of God. God gave him dominion and power over all the nations and all the kingdoms, and the kingdom given to him was the kingdom that cannot be destroyed.

Daniel, naturally, was a mite confused by all this, and so in his dream he stepped forward and asked one of the ones close to the throne to explain.

---

[1] As an old time sailor I promise you that made things tough
[2] The origin of spareribs
[3] Daniel was no doubt ready for Alka-Seltzer here

The answer was that the four monsters from the deep were four kings that would come to power, but that eventually the believers in the eternal kingdom would triumph.

When Daniel in his dream inquired further, asking in particular about the fourth monster, the informer explained that the fourth monster was different from and worse than the others. The establishment of this fourth kingdom shall be on a world-wide basis. Later ten kings shall arise from this mess, and then one small king shall arise and destroy three of the other kings. This upstart shall speak against God and shall give the saints a hard time. This evil king and his kingdom shall attempt to change all laws, even the matter of time,[1] and he shall be successful for awhile, but the judgment of God will get him and his kingdom, and the whole kingdom of the earth shall be given to the believers in God, and all people will serve under the head of the church of God.[2] Daniel awoke the next morning with a headache.

Chap. 8

A couple of years later Daniel had another weirdo of a dream. In the vision Daniel saw himself in a mansion overlooking Lake Susan.[3] There appeared on the edge of the lake a ram with two horns, and one horn was higher than the other, although it started growing last. The ram was taking charge of everything westward, northward, and southward.[4] The ram did as he pleased and became really the king of the mountain.

While Daniel observed this, an odd looking goat with one horn between his eyes came from the west and traveled without touching the ground.[5] The goat came to the ram and immediately attacked him. The goat whipped the ram thoroughly.

The goat then became king of the mountain and overlooked Lake Susan[6] with haughtiness. The goat grew stronger and his horn broke off, but in its place came forth four other horns. Out of one of the four horns then came a little horn which became very prominent and became interested in the land of the free.[7] This particular horn magnified itself tremendously and in spite of defying the hosts of heaven, the little horn prospered. The worship of God was outlawed and evil reigned.

Then there entered the dream two saints of old and one of them said, "How long do you think evil will be in control?"

"Two thousand and three hundred days," replied the other.

The dream seemed to fade and Daniel seemed to see in the

[1] There is that daylight saving deal!   [2] I believe this is a reference to Christ
[3] Ulai   [4] The Lake was probably eastward   [5] Amtrack?
[6] There have been some notable goats at Lake Susan
[7] America? Sicily? Monaco?

vision the appearance of a man.[1] Daniel then heard the man as he stood by Lake Susan speak to the angel Gabriel and say, "Gabriel, you are chairman of the End of Time Committee, tell this fellow Daniel what the dream means."

When Gabriel approached, Daniel trembled, even in his dream.[2]

"Try to understand what I am telling you, Daniel," said Gabriel, "for it has to do with your vision concerning the end of time."

At this point Daniel fainted.[3] Gabriel then held some smelling salts under Daniel's nose and stood Daniel on his feet.[4]

"I will tell you, Daniel," said Gabriel, "about the last days of trouble and struggle. The rams with the two horns are the kings of Media and Persia. The goat is the kingdom of Greece. Finally this empire breaks into four pieces of lesser importance and then a really, truly baddie comes along. The power of this guy is terrific[5] and he kills, conquers, deceives and makes a mess of everything and everybody, including God's people in Israel. God will handle him simply.[6]

"In your vision, Daniel, you heard about the 2300 days. That is an exact figure, but all this is so far off from your day that you might as well forget it. In fact, there is no point at present in your blabbing this all over town. Write it down for future scholars."[7]

When Daniel awoke the next morning he had a tummy ache. In fact, Daniel stayed sick for several days. The next week, however, Daniel was back on duty, advising the king, and entertaining everyone at the coffee breaks with his astonishing dreams.

Chap. 9

Another year passed, and Daniel in sincere prayer and meditation spoke to God and said, "Father, our people have sinned and fallen short of obeying the commandments. The people have been rebellious, have not been good about attending church, and when they did go they didn't listen.[8] Father, we are confused because we have wandered from the faith and have not found a proper way of life. We are sinners, and we have not repented, and we have turned to you, Father, as we should.

"All Israel is guilty. We know that evil has come to us because of our sins. We know that you, O Lord, directed the evil so that it would affect us, and hopefully bring us repentantly back to you.

"Father, take the heat off us now. We have sinned, we admit it. We have been punished; so ease up on us, and let your face shine upon us and listen to our pleas. We plead not on a basis of our

---

[1] This was another dream or the continuation of the present dream. So what?
[2] Daniel could no doubt see the trumpet   [3] I don't blame him one bit
[4] He couldn't steady his knees, though
[5] Alexander the Great? Antioches Epiphanes? Onassis?
[6] Alexander drank himself to death at 32   [7] So they can fuss, fuss, fuss
[8] The old, old story

righteousness, but on a basis of your mercies.

"Forgive us, O Lord. Remember Jerusalem, for it is called the city of God, and remember the Israelites, for we are called the children of God."

While Daniel was praying and in deep meditation, ole Gabriel arrived again.

"All right, Daniel," said Gabriel, "I have come to give you a little inside information. You are in real good standing with the Lord and God has permitted me to pass on to you some information.

"There will be 490 years more of trouble and disappointment, but at last the people will learn to serve God. At the end of this time the everlasting kingdom of God will begin to form on the earth. From the time the order is given to rebuild the temple until the first coming of the Messiah shall be 483 years.[1] The Messiah shall live only briefly, but he will die for the sake of others.

"After this there shall come a king with an army and he will destroy Jerusalem and defy God, even defiling the sanctuary of God.[2] God in the time and manner of His plan shall destroy this evil person, and God's judgment will be against him."

Chap.
11

Daniel, having received visions and insights, appeared before Darius at various times and reported to him; so he could share in Daniel's glimpses of the future.

"Know something, Darius," said Daniel, "there will be three kings in Persia, then a fourth that will be greater than any of the three ahead of him. This king will even attack Greece, for the king will have great strength and great wealth.[3] This king will be overthrown and his kingdom divided, but not among his sons.[4]

"Sometime after this shall arise a king in the south with a great following, but he will lose out through internal problems. Some years later an Egyptian ruler will form an alliance with Syria by giving his daughter in marriage to the king of Syria. This didn't work, as the girl didn't make a good wife.[5]

"Later, however, when the girl's brother becomes head of Egypt, he will organize an army and declare war on Syria. The brother will be successful and will bring many captives to Egypt.

"First thing you know, though, the sons of the defeated king of Syria will grow to manhood and they will decide to seek vengeance on Egypt.[6] There shall be much fighting back and forth for years, many shall be killed, and nothing much solved. In fact, the marrying a king's daughter stunt will be tried again and it will fizzle.

[1] Good scholars can explain the apparent 7 years discrepancy
[2] Probably Titus in 70 A.D.   [3] Xerxes? Quien Sabe?
[4] Xerxes forgot to write out his will   [5] That's what the king said
[6] The Middle East still has a few problems

"Some of the kings get killed in battle and some die of ulcers. One king will try sending a tax collector into Israel to collect a surtax, but the collector and the king both will die mysteriously.[1]

"Also in times to come in the middle east turmoil there will arise a Robin Hood type of king, who will declare war on all the rich and divide their land and their money with the poor. This king also dies, and the city slickers get the land and money again like they are supposed to do.

"Often two kings will sit at the conference table and plot against each other even while they are sitting there.[2] All these things are under the plan of God. Wickedness, hate, deceit, all these continually plague the world, but such is life, and all still is under God's scrutiny.

"As these kings down through the years fight back and forth Jerusalem and Palestine catch it coming and going. All this is God's process of purifying and punishing. None of these God-defying kings last long, though, as they die like everybody else."[3]

When the time comes for the consolidating of God's kingdom, Michael, the angel in charge of God's executive branch, shall attend to the deliverance of everyone recorded in the Lord's book of life.

Those who have already passed from this life shall be awakened, some to everlasting life, and some to everlasting shame and contempt.[4] Those who died in the Lord shall shine in great brightness and those who influenced others for good shall shine as bright as stars on a dark night.

"That's enough, Daniel," said Gabriel. "The book is closed. Don't add any more to it. There is going to be a lot of coming and going between now and the end of time."

About then in the vision Daniel saw two figures, one on each side of Lake Susan. One of the men turned to the other, who was actually already standing in the lake up to his ankles and said, "How long will it be before these things happen?"

Then the other man answered and said, "It shall be times, time, and a half. It will be after God has scattered the believers all over the world and all of God's plans are set."[5]

Daniel heard this, but he didn't understand it.[6]

Then Daniel asked, "What, O Lord, shall come about, and what will happen?"

"Sorry, Daniel, but it is none of your business. The information is top secret. You can be sure, though, that many will reform, that

---

[1] End of this plan   [2] How did Roosevelt & Stalin get in the scriptures?
[3] Alexander, Kaiser, Stalin, Hitler, Ptolemy, Antiochus — all dead! Good show!
[4] Surely Hitler is in this group   [5] Even less definite than a weather forecast
[6] I'm with you, Daniel

the wicked will continue to be wicked, and they won't understand. The searchers for God and his righteousness will understand what life is all about, though.

Anyway, from the time that the daily sacrifice is taken away[1] and the abomination that maketh desolate[2] is taken away, there shall be one thousand two hundred and thirty-five days.

"The people who are actually alive on the last day will really get to see a show, but you go on about your business for you won't live to see the day. You will be in your place, though, Daniel, at the end of the world."

[1] Whatever that is
[2] The Income Tax Law? The 55 mile speed limit? Alimony

HOSEA

Chap.
1

The people of Israel had departed from the ways of the Lord and had become completely materialistic, doing anything for money. Now Hosea was inspired by God to attempt to learn about God and also to do something about the conditions.

Hosea felt that the Lord wanted him to learn by first marrying a girl who was a prostitute, and an example of the evil that was flagrant in the land. As a result, Hosea selected a girl named Marlene[1] who was beautiful and desirable, but who was a prostitute working for the church.[2]

The marriage went fine for awhile. First there was born a son and the Lord told Hosea to name the boy Victor[3] for he would be a conqueror someday to restore Israel and defeat Steve McQueen.[4]

Next there was born a daughter and the Lord said name the girl Miss Clean[5] for she will be a symbol of my cleaning up Israel, but I will deliver Judah and have mercy on this tribe for they are not as bad now as the others.

There was born then a third child, a son, and the Lord said he should be named Split[6], for I am separating myself from this ungodly outfit.

However, God, the Keeper of the Promises, also said that the numbers in Israel would become great as God had promised Abraham, and that when repentance came God would forgive and unite the tribes again. Hosea didn't understand this at the time.

Chap.
2

Marlene began to stray again, however, and she started working part time as a prostitute for the temple.

Hosea then went to his kin people and even to his children and said "Some of you talk to Marlene. Plead with her to give up her wild ways and selling her body. In fact, if she doesn't reform, I plan to take all her clothes and possessions from her and place her naked in the street, and I will also desert the children for having been born to her."[7]

Hosea then began to plan to see if he could do something. In fact, he began trying to lock her in the room, then chain her to a fence post while he was away. If she gets on the loose I will pay fellows to block her path, he said to himself, until finally she will figure it a better deal at home with me, than the wild life whoredom was giving her. All this time, however, in spite of the threats, Hosea because of his love for Marlene paid her Temple percent and saw that

---

[1]Gomer   [3]Jezreel   [4]Jehu   [5]Loruhamah   [6]Loammi
[2]The Church or Temple in Israel was truly money mad at this time.
[7]At this point, Hosea was pretty angry.

498

she received corn, and wine, and the necessities of life.

At other times Hosea would become so frustrated that he would consider spying on her and catching her in the act with one of her lovers and then put her out of business with bodily harm if necessary and put an end to all her joy, and mirth, and celebrations. "What is more, I will steal all the profits of her prostitution," he mumbled to himself.

Hosea began to see that his feeling toward Marlene was the same as God's feeling toward the wayward people of Israel. For the Lord began to enlighten Hosea and to say that first He would speak quietly to his people to bring them back, and that through his word the Lord would persuade Israel to repent, and God will then destroy Baal and the false gods, and God will again bestow his love and mercy, for God is a forgiving God, for the Lord has promised mercy even to those who deserve no mercy, for the love of God is a forgiving love, it is a healing love, and boundless love, and God will plead continually with his people through his word to repent.

Chap. 3

Hosea then began to understand why God had moved him to marry a whore. Through the experience of his relationship with Marlene, Hosea began to understand a new theology, the forgiving love of God.

As a result, Hosea said to Marlene "You are forgiven. You may return to my house and be my wife. You will be faithful to me and I will be to you. This is the way it will be with the children of Israel, who have strayed from God and wandered off in other pursuits. The children of Israel shall suffer and be separated from God, but Israel shall return and seek the Lord their God, and they shall be united under God through David their king, a servant of the Almighty God."

Chap. 4

Having learned this great lesson and filled with the wisdom of experience, Hosea began to preach and teach the wayward people of Israel.

In his first sermon Hosea said to the people "The Lord is unhappy with his people. There is no truth among you, there is no mercy, and there is no seeking to learn of God. Most of you are swearing and lying and killing and committing adultery, and bloody violence is in the land. As a result the land will become polluted and the fish of the sea shall die with a red tide, and even the innocent will have to suffer because of the sins of the many.[1]

God says that since you seem to have forgotten the law of God, the Lord will just forget you. The former glory of Israel shall turn to shame. The people will be punished and will be rewarded in

[1]Who said the Bible wasn't relevant today?

accordance with their evil deeds.

The people will eat, but will never seem to get enough. There shall be recipe books by the thousands, but the people will still not be satisfied.

Constantly chasing wild women, and drinking wine incessantly shall affect the people in every way. The people will be disatisfied with the stock market and shall ask the experts what is the matter with the economy, and the answer is simply that Israel has forsaken God.

Your daughters and your wives shall run off with strange men, but I will not punish them says God because you have driven them to it with your greedy way of life.

"Judah, praise God, is still reasonably faithful, but not so with some of the other tribes, and the Lord will blow the winds of storms on them and create for them many difficulties."

Chap.
5

After this Hosea was asked to come and speak as a guest lecturer at a gathering of ministers and priests.

"Part of this trouble must be laid at your feet. The Lord is determined to punish his people. Even Judah will suffer because it has tolerated the sins of the other tribes. You preachers have found excuses for yourselves and for your people, but there is no excuse. God will punish."

Chap.
6

"That is the bad news. Now the good news is that we can return to the Lord. What God has torn, God is willing to heal. After two days will he revive us, and the third day shall he arise in our sight.[1] Then shall we know the Lord in a new way and it shall be as refreshing as the gentle rain."

"The trouble is that the goodness of so many is like the morning dew, it shortly fades away, or an early morning cloud that the first wind blows away. The people have the idea that as long as they drop a decent sum in the collection plate and learn the 23rd Psalm that God is pleased, but God wants to see action in the form of mercy, not just liturgy. I lay a lot of this blame on you priests and preachers. You have not laid it down tough enough to the people. Take Southern California,[2] the greed and sin, the Lord will now and then shake the earth under such, and other places."

Chap.
7

The Lord stands ready to heal. It is never too late for anyone. The Lord forgives. I, of all people, understand this at last. But the people do not hear. They do not listen to reason. They are like the baker who leaves his oven on all night and worries not, though in the

---

[1] A prophecy of Christ and the resurrection. I doubt if Hosea really understood the significance.   [2] Gilead and Ephraim

morning his bakery will be burned to the ground.

"So many of the people do not even learn anything as they grow older. They refuse to see the grey hairs, they do not see the signs of decay of the nation and that they need to turn to God.

The Lord is angry over this. The Lord will spread his net and it matters not whether you fly to Egypt or Switzerland,[1] the Lord will bring them down as a bird shot out of the sky.

It is strange, the Lord has said to me, that after all I have done for them, and all the goodness I have shown them, that they spurn me and give me only casual recognition."

Chap.
8

On another occasion, Hosea spoke at a Men's Conference sponsored by the Tribe of Israel. It was poorly attended, but Hosea said "Israel has cast away goodness, and calls on God only in emergencies. The enemies of Israel will eat her and pursue her.

Israel has elected princes and rulers that are not godly people. The rulers are greedy, they take bribes, and they worship material gods, it is just a rehash of the golden calf occasion. The Lord is angry and plans to punish Israel.

The Glad Sam Club[2] is in trouble also. It is just a snobbish way of looking out for a special group. They are sowing the wind with their big, boisterous noise, but they shall reap the whirlwind.

The tribe of Israel will be swallowed up by the Gentiles, the people of Israel act like a wild horse, they have discarded the bridle of God.

Some of the tribes have simply sold themselves to godless nations in exchange for good business, but the godless nations shall bring them only grief and deception.

The Lord has written his law to all the tribes. There is no excuse for ignorance.

Israel has forgotten the Creator the Lord God Almighty, and Judah has built some fenced in cities, but the Lord will destroy these with fire."

Chap.
9

On another occasion Hosea spoke again entreating the people in one breath and denouncing them in another, urging repentance and forecasting disaster.

"Rejoice not," said Hosea, "You people of Israel. The abundance of your riches shall not save you. Even when you interrupt your evil for a feast day to God, you use the occasion for profit. Your prophets even have lost their zeal, there is no sense of unity in the church, you divide among yourselves for money and for glory. Your leaders are phonies.

As for the people of Southern California,[3] the Lord will make

---

[1] Assyria   [2] Samaria   [3] Ephraim

gypsies out of you, wandering from one place to another, searching for you know not what, all because you have forsaken the Lord God of Hosts."

Again Hosea addressed himself to the people of the tribe of Israel saying, "You are like an empty vine. You keep your gains all for yourself. You have no benevolent program.

You will find all kinds of excuses for your difficulties. You will even say you have no king, when all there is that is needed is a return to God.

The Glad Sam Club is doomed. The worthy grand master of this crowd will be cut off as easily as foam on the water.

There will be no more easy living for any of you. You will have to tread corn, and plow, and work your own fields, for you shall be as servants rather than as owners.

If you would but sow righteousness, you could reap mercy. If you will but seek the Lord, you shall find him and his understanding. If you plow wickedness, however, you shall reap disaster, and Israel shall be overcome and dishonored.

Again Hosea spoke to the tribe of Israel saying "The Lord remembers well when Israel was as a child, and God loved Israel and delivered Israel from Egypt. "I blessed the people of Southern California also," the Lord has said, "in many ways, I gave them fruitful places for a dwelling. In spite of all my goodness, these people and others of my people have turned against me and worship many strange material things."

"The Lord, however," continued Hosea, "has said that he will exercise the fullness of his anger, for the Lord is God, not man, the Lord is the Holy One, and he will remain holy. Yet the Lord will sometimes roar like the lion and the cities shall shake in terror, but the tribe of Judah is still reasonably faithful with many saints, and the Lord shall bless Judah."

"There is no tribe or people that is sinless," continued Hosea, "but the Lord is particularly displeased with the money mad groups. The Lord even remembers the trickery of Jacob, but the Lord accepted his repentance, and the Lord knows there is wickedness in California, and Paris, and in Reno, and little villages, and the Lord waits for the people to repent."

Hosea then quoted God, "Remember that I am the Lord thy God, that delivered you from Egypt, and you shall have no gods before me. I will watch your activities as a leopard or a lion watches from the grass.

Israel has already destroyed itself, but I am still willing to help and deliver. How sad the people of Southern California do not stay in one place long enough to raise their children in a home, yet I will even ransom them in time from the grave and offer even to them redemption. The Good Sam Club crowd shall become desolate and they shall be slaughtered for their wickedness."

Finally, at a later time, Hosea pleaded again with the people saying, "Return to the Lord. It is never too late. Pray to the Lord for strength to overcome sins. There is no gain in praying to Buddha or to the Labor Relations Board, for help comes only from God.

God is ready to be as a fresh dew on the ground for Israel, the Lord is ready to spread his beauty as a giant tree, and his smell as the sweetness of the cedars of Lebanon. Those who turn to the Lord shall be under his protection and shall flourish. Even the people of Southern California shall call upon him, and forsake their greed, and he will make them as a green fir tree.

It is difficult to understand all of these things, but the ways of the Lord are right and those that walk in His ways, walk in safety, while ultimately the transgressors fall into deep pits."

JOEL

A message came to Joel from the Lord and Joel related it to the people saying, "Listen, you old codgers, in fact everybody should hear what I have to say, for God is planning some rough times for you all.

"You had better wake up, you bunch of heavy drinkers and goof-offs, for your wine is going to be gone. Tough times are really coming, for anything that the army worm leaves the locust will eat, then the cankerworm will eat what the locusts skip, and the caterpillar will bat clean up for the cankerworms. When this outfit finishes there is going to be nothing left of the vineyards.

"A strong nation with teeth like a lion will come and destroy the land on which you live. You had better start crying now, and you can weep like a high school girl who has had her steady killed in a chariot wreck.

"In the midst of all this the church will go broke. The ministers will moan to high heaven because the gifts to the church become very slim.

"The farmers will all be in trouble and all they will be able to do is howl and howl.[1] The crops of wheat and barley will be no good, and the fruit orchards will be chopped down.

"The whole ministerial association needs to go into mourning, to gather in groups and put on old clothes, and plead with the Lord, for the people will have nothing to bring to the church.

"I would suggest calling special services, organizing prayer groups, and bringing the people into the house of the Lord to plead with him and ask God for help. Destruction is close and there is very little time. I am warning each and every one.

"Unhappiness is everywhere, for desolation and depression are both at hand. The seeds are turning rotten in the ground, the barns are collapsing, and the corn is withered. The cows are perplexed. The wild beasts don't know where to go for food, the sheep are hungry and just stand around bleating.

"I, for one, am praying urgently to the Lord, for I see the brown fields and the burned pastures. The beasts join me in my cry for there is no water."

"Blow the horn, screech the siren," said Joel, "sound general quarters, for the punishment of God is at hand! No wonder it is cloudy and the day is dark, the world's atmosphere seems stifling. The enemies prepared by God are running roughshod over the land

---

[1] I have a feeling that the farmers are still howling.

and desolation is everywhere.

"The enemy seems to run like horses and yet to make noises like the sound of chariots on cobblestones — it is frightening! The people will naturally be terrified.

"The advancing army shall be the best trained outfit you ever saw, every man in his place, the lines straight, the advance ruthless, and the men will be so tough that sword wounds will seem to be scratches. All the heavens shall furnish a proper background, with the moon and the sun blocked out by clouds, and there will be no visible stars.

"Who can stand to be alive and face the appearance of the wrath of God as the army designated by God shall begin to handle the punishment for God.

"Again, however, God assures his people that it is never too late to reform and repent. Blow the trumpet again! Call for special evangelistic services, or at least some thanksgiving recognition.

"Let the ministers become very active, holding special services, leading the people in prayer. It would be a shame for the brethren to see the plight of Israel and then ask 'Where is their God'?

"When the people have repented and the Lord observes this, then God will have mercy on His people and He will see that they get food and clothing.

"God says that when the repentance takes place, then God will disperse the northern army, and the army will cease to be, leaving only a distasteful smell among the people.

"Don't you worry one minute! The Lord will do wonderful things. The land will take on new life, the beasts of the field will begin to find good pastures and the fruit trees will have good seasons.

"Rejoice, you people of Israel, for at this time the Lord will regulate your rain so that it falls moderately. As a result, there will be a great wheat crop.

"The Lord promises to make up for the time the army worms took over and the caterpillars wrecked havoc. Then will you know that God is in the midst of Israel, and the people of God shall no longer be ashamed.

"The spirit of the Lord will become active again, and the sons and daughters shall prophesy, your old men shall dream dreams, and the young men shall see visions.

"The working class of people shall be particularly blessed at this time, and God will demonstrate many wonders in the heavens,[1] there will be an eclipse of the sun, and the moon will turn real red. Let this remind you that the day of the Lord is then close at hand.

"Anybody who calls on the Lord at this time shall be saved, for the Lord has promised to deliver those who trust in him, those who

[1]UFO's?

know there is a city of God. There will always be that remnant of the people that shall be saved.

"The Lord has assured us that when Judah and Jerusalem are back in business and doing well, then the Lord will see that the enemies of God are gathered like an army trapped in a valley. This crowd is those that have bought and sold people as if they were cattle, sometimes selling an unfortunate girl for a drink of wine, or losing a slave in a poker game.

"The wicked cities of Tyre and Sidon are tremendously in debt to God, but even if they tried to buy themselves into God's good graces it would be useless. God remembers that the gold and silver vessels were stolen from his sanctuary and used for drunken parties.

"God remembers the selling of the Israelites. God suggests that the wicked get as organized as possible and prepare for any type of warfare they think will work, but it is to no avail. Let the heathen take their plows and make swords of them, and turn their harpoons and pruning hooks into spears. Get all the mighty men of the wicked all steamed up, but it is to no avail.

"Let all the heathen gather, trapped in a valley, for the Lord will sit in their presence and pronouce judgment. The valley is the last chance, it is the final valley decision. The sun is to be darkened and the moon will quit shining, the stars will also not be seen, and then the Lord will roar at the heathen,[1] but God's people shall know that the Lord is their hope. The Lord will want everyone to know then that God is with His people, that Jerusalem will then be a holy city in reality, and only the people of God will be allowed in the city.

"When that day comes everything will be hunky-dory. The mountain streams will flow with wine, some of the hills will flow with milk,[2] and the river Jordan will flow with water,[3] and the spirit of God shall excite the whole area.

"Egypt will be desolate because of its bad attitude toward Israel in the early days, and so shall the land be of all those who have persecuted the innocent. The children of God, such as those of Judah who have been faithful, and the believers everywhere, from Jerusalem to the fartherest corners of the earth, will be cleansed by the blood,[4] and God shall surely dwell with His people forever.

[1] Hurrah! At last!
[2] For us teetotalers
[3] For the health-kick people
[4] The blood of Christ

AMOS

Amos was a sheep herder living in Pecos and he had lots of time to sit and meditate as he sat and watched his sheep graze. On some of these occasions he began to have visions from God and one day, after several years of visions and meditations, he went to the city and stood on the temple steps and preached to the people of Israel as well as visitors concerning what God had revealed to him.

"The Lord has roared like a lion," spoke Amos. "Jerusalem itself shall hear, the shepherds shall learn from the drouth, the roar of the Lord has meaning.

"There is trouble in River City![1] The people of River City have sinned again and again and their wickedness will not go unpunished. Sometimes God will burn places like Chicago[2], wicked kings in the Middle East shall be greatly tormented, and many of the Assyrians shall become captives.

"Paris[3] is another place of sin. I will punish Paris. God will turn His hand against Moscow[4] and Peking.[5] The old Moscow Muggers gang shall be completely destroyed.

"Tyre will get it also. Tyre has long been a wicked city and its punishment is coming pretty soon.

"The Lord is going to punish England[6] also for the way it treated the Irish, and Rome[7] will burn because of its madness and sinning, and the palace of Nero will go down in flames.[8]

"The Lord will also punish areas of New England[9] because of the way some of the people have mistreated women. God will not tolerate this type of sin very long in any place. God will also use fire to punish places like Rio[10] and God will send wind to help fan the flames. The responsible leaders in such places shall have to go into captivity.

"God has roared against Moab. The sins of the land of Moab are various, including unreasonably harsh treatment of their enemies. Moab is a goner.

"Judah is also in trouble with the Lord. In spite of the preaching of some good men, Judah has refused to obey the laws of God. God will arrange for fire and pillage to work over Judah and make a shambles of Jerusalem.

"Israel has been just as bad or worse, even dealing in slavery and contract kickbacks. The wickedness of Israel has truly been terrible, disregarding the plight of the poor, ignoring the rights of good,

[1]Damascus   [2]The place of Hazael   [3]Gaza   [4]Ashdod   [5]Ashkelon   [6]Edom   [7]Terman   [8]Bozrah   [9]Land of Ammon   [10]Rabbah

wholesome people, and deteriorating to the point where a man and his grown son both used the same whore house. Some of the Israelites have come to church in stolen clothes and have drunk wine that was dishonestly acquired.

"God is particularly mad at the chosen people, for the Lord paved the way for their conquest of Canaan, defeated the powerful and impressive army of the Coassacks,[1] delivered the people from Egypt, and God even reared prophets and preachers from among the children of Israel to instruct you. Actually, you even influenced many of them to evil.

"You Israelites are going to be punished. The Lord will make you groan like a wooden wagon full of bricks, your swift warriors shall fall all over themselves, and your strong men will be weakened by viruses. Your bravest men will get scared to death and run for their lives, not even waiting to put on their pants or their track shoes.

Chap.
3

"God is really hot about the way you all have acted," continued Amos. "God specifically chose you and so you will be punished more than the others. You cannot walk with God using a different path than His. Do you think God roars without a reason? Not any more than a lion roars unless it is seeking a prey, for even a young lion roars only for a reason, such as hunger.[2]

"A trap is not sprung unless it is stepped upon. You are caught. Your punishment is justified. I am sounding the alarm like a trumpet. It is time for you to be afraid. God is arranging to punish you.

"God has sent prophets to warn you. This was done long ago. Now I am telling you like it is! The lion has roared. God is at work!

"I am calling on the leaders of Egypt and Assyria to witness. Let them take a look at the armies of Israel. The Lord knows that the people have forgotten what it means to be moral. Even the homes of the people are stuffed with ill-gotten gain. The Lord has decided to send enemies to destroy the beautiful homes, after first tearing down the forts of the cities.

"There will be a remnant left of the Jews, but it will be only as if the shepherd had saved a bone and a hank of hair from a lion's mouth.[3] Not much left. That is the message God has for Israel.

"At the same time that Israel is being punished so shall the temples of the false gods fall and the affluence of the rich will be reduced to nothing. All the fine homes and comfortable chariots will be destroyed. God is going to teach his people not to build their lives on material possessions.

Chap.
4

"God has a word to say to a small bunch of rich women," said

---

[1] Amorites   [2] All sheepherders know a lot about lions
[3] I keep thinking Amos had a lot of trouble with lions

Amos, as he continued his sermon. "God calls you 'Fat cows', you hound your husbands for more money, more money; so the stupid husbands raise rents, oppressing the poor, and charging usury interest rates on their money.

"The Lord has decided to snatch you all up like the fisherman snaps a tuna, and you will be tossed out of a hole in the wall as if you were a bucket of trash.

"God dares you to keep on as you are doing. Just continue idol worship, going through the motions of supporting some church or other, all for show, even making gifts for your own benefit and glory. Just keep at it, your time is at hand!

"God is tired of trying to teach you. For awhile you didn't need to brush your teeth because there was no food, then there was a drouth, then there was rain in one place and none in another, mildew hit your storage barns, still you did not return to God. Then the Lord tried pestilence, then some of your sons were killed in war, and your horses died in such numbers that you could hardly stand the smell. Still you did not return to God.

"Even when God tried taking isolated areas and punishing just them, this didn't seem to teach you a lesson. Because of all of this, Israel, you have had it. Prepare to meet your God!

"Be certain that he that formed the mountains, created the wind, created the mind of man, the one who made the extra darkness just before dawn, the one who overlooks all the earth, is surely the Lord, the God of Hosts is his name."

Chap. 5

"Now, Israel, hear this song of grief, for beautiful Israel is dead, thrown upon the ground, and there is no one to help her. Poor Israel! Where there were a thousand Jews there shall be a hundred, and where there were a hundred there shall be ten.

"The Lord continues to call. 'Seek me, and you shall live', says the Lord. Don't try idols, seeking help with Buddha[1] or some Guru.[2] Seek the Lord and live, or else Israel will be destroyed as if by fire. Change your ways. Begin to be just in dealing with the poor and the disadvantaged. Seek the Lord, for he is the one that put Orion's belt in the heaven, the one who changes death into life, the one who can darken a day or brighten a night, the one who put the waters in place on the earth. The Lord is his name.

"God helps those that attack the strongholds of evil, while you careless people have no use for an honest judge or a righteous leader. You sorry outfit, you who have taken advantage of the poor and the weak, who have made money unfairly, you have homes and fine chariots, you have fine vineyards and good corn crops, but you will not get to enjoy them. The Lord knows all your sins. God knows

[1]Bethel [2]Beersheba

how you accept bribes and disregard real needs of poor, but honest people.

"Seek good, and not evil. That is your only chance to survive. Be fair and be generous, then maybe God might ease up a bit. There will be some tall wailing at Wailing Wall. The crying shall be so great and often that the cries will become quite professional. There will be wailing in the country as well as in the city, for the Lord will tend to it.

"Be careful about praying for the end of the world, for that will be a time of judgment, of great darkness, of terrible confusion. You will be in the predicament of a man who runs from a lion and runs into a bear, or the times will seem as troublesome as if you went and in weariness leaned your hand against the wall and a snake struck you. God is thoroughly disgusted with sinful Israel.

"You cannot bribe God. Coming to church occasionally or mouthing a few pious phrases will not get the job done. God doesn't want to hear any of your silly music, either. You people are headed for captivity, and God doesn't mean just next door. That is what the Lord, the God of Hosts, has said.

Chap.
6

"God has a word also for a bunch of resort dwellers. You go from luxury to luxury, thinking only of your own pleasure. You keep putting off doing anything about a few good intentions.

"You eat well, I'll say that for you. Nice ribeyes, good lamb roasts, juicy filets, you also drink well, stretched out on ivory lounges you guzzle Scotch and rye, you listen to folk singers and walking guitarists, and you don't worry a bit about what God expects of you.

"It might interest you to know that you will be the first to go. God is fed up to here with such stuff. The men will die so fast that the family itself can't keep up with who is left. The big house will the Lord tear down with a big noise and the little ones with little noises, but they will all go. People will be terrified even to mention the name of the Lord.

"The way you Jews have acted has been as ineffective as horses trying to race on flat rock, or oxen plowing in the stone quarry. Some of you conceited ones might begin to declare how important you are and how smart, but the Lord will bring a nation against you that will grind you to pieces, from one end of the country to the other. That is what the Lord God himself has proclaimed.

Chap.
7

"God has withheld his punishment, for when in a vision I saw the destruction of crops by caterpillars and other plans of the Lord, I asked God to give Israel time to repent. The Lord agreed, and so I am preaching to you a warning which you must heed. Then in my vision I saw God planning to measure Israel with the plumbline of the Lord, to see how straight Israel might be.

"After measuring, the Lord decided to destroy a portion of Israel. There is great wickedness everywhere, especially in high places."

Even before Amos had finished preaching, word was sent to the President of the Council of Churches[1] telling him that there was a real troublemaker preaching in a way that would foul up the system. As a result, a message was relayed to Amos, who had stopped his sermon briefly for a coffee break, telling him to leave town at once. The message also suggested that if Amos had to preach, then be a foreign missionary and preach a long way away.

Amos then turned to the big cheese from the Council, for he had by this time come to the temple steps, and said, "I am not prophet, nor the son of a prophet. I am a layman. I've never been to Seminary. I am a sheepherder and I have raised some fruit, but the Lord came to me and spoke to me, and it was the Lord that ordered me to preach. Now, you big stuffed shirt, you hear what the Lord has to say. You tell me not to prophesy against Israel, but God says that you, you over-inflated churchman, shall have your wife turn bad on you, your children shall be killed, your land divided by the state, and you will be taken captive to a dirty, heathen country, and Israel will be taken into captivity."

Chap.
8

"Do you know what God said to me?" asked Amos. "God showed me a basket of summer fruit, ripe for eating, and God told me that Israel was the same way, just ripe to be eaten by an enemy. The hymns of the church shall no longer be sung, but replaced by the groans of the wounded, while the dead shall be silently cast aside.

"Now you people here today listen to this, most of you are ones that take advantage of the needy, that raise motel rates when Egyptians come to play, and all you think about is money, the market, land values, interest rates. You crummy characters, you make use of one scale to measure when you sell and another for when you buy.

"God doesn't plan to forget any of this. The land will tremble and the people mourn because of these sins. The Lord will make the occasion an awesome one for there will be an eclipse of the sun, and all your gay parties shall suddenly become full of wails and groans. It will be a bitter time and some men will turn grey overnight. The time will then come when God will send something worse than a drouth or want of food, there will be a great scarcity of the comforting word of God.

"People will wander everywhere searching for a word of encouragement. They shall travel in every direction seeking the word

[1] Amaziah

of God, but God will withhold his word as punishment. Idol worshippers shall perish, and many shall faint, even the young men and young women as they vainly seek the word of God."

Chap.
9

"The anger of the Lord is ready. There is no escape from God's justice. God will get the evil ones even if they try to hide in a church, or if they dig down thinking to be safe in hell, or if they try to dodge God and rent a skylab or a space ship, God will find the evil ones and destroy them. God will not let any escape, even if God has to let a sea monster catch those who try to hide in the deep sea.

"Do you people really know who God is? God is the one who can cause the earth to melt by a touch of his hand. God is everywhere, his home may have the ground floor on the earth, but his building rises on to the heavens. God is the one who controls. The Lord is his name.

"Don't you nuts realize that God is the Lord of everyone, not just some few? You are no better in God's sight than the Ethiopians, or the Indians, or the Eskimos. Don't you know this? God brought Israel from Egypt certainly, but God delivered the Moscow Muggers a time or two, and he helped the Assyrians, the English, the French, the Germans. God is the Lord of all.

"God's eyes are on any sinful kingdom and he will destroy it. In the case of the Jews, the Lord will not destroy all the Jews, but shall save a remnant, and shall scatter them throughout the earth. The Israelites, or anybody else that says 'it can't happen to us' — look out!

"There will come a day though when God will repair the temple of David and the Jews will return to Israel. Prosperity will then return to Israel and no sooner than the harvest is gathered than a new crop will be sown and there shall be great vineyards and plenty of wine. The Jew will return and rebuild, and plant gardens, and vineyards, and fruit orchards, and again the children of Israel will have a land of their own, and God will see that they are able to keep it."

There was a man called Reb[1] and he had a vision from God concerning the fate of a small nation named Edom.[2]

In a public place Reb stood forth and made the following pronouncement. "Look out, Edom! God has created unrest against the little nation of Edom and Edom is now despised by its neighbors. People should never deceive themselves by seeking the wrong type of security. Just hiding in a rock on a high place is not security. Success has gone to your head, you people of Edom.

"Don't you puffed-up characters know that even though you soar as high as eagles, or fortress yourself in inaccessible cliffs, the Lord can easily bring you tumbling down. Actually, you would be better off if you had a few thieves and plunderers take things, but the Lord is causing your own allies to turn against you and you are doomed for real.

"Your friends in the next county will set traps for you and your wise men will lose their confidence and appear very stupid. The soldiers that protect you will be confused by conflicting orders. Why is this going to happen? The answer is simple, because you mistreated the Israelites. You are going to be exposed and then destroyed.

"When Jerusalem was in great distress you did not lift a finger to help. In fact, you aided the heathen and told the enemies of Israel where some of the Jews were hiding. The day is fast approaching when the Lord God will balance the books. What you have done and what you have failed to do will come back to haunt you, and you will disappear from history, a vague memory of a nation is all that will remain.

"Israel will again exist. Jerusalem shall be restored and shall be a refuge to the people of the Lord. The land that is now possessed by heathen tribes shall be placed under the rule of God's own people. Gradually shall this kingdom of God grow and encompass the earth, and the Lord shall be the King.

---

[1] Obadiah
[2] God takes a look at little nations as well as big ones

JONAH

God communicated with a young man named Jonah and urged him to go to Nineveh, a well known wicked city, and to preach reform. Jonah did not want to go and decided that he would get out of town for awhile and let the idea subside. As a result, Jonah bought a ticket on a ship bound to Bermuda[1].

The Lord, however, caused an especially strong wind to blow on the sea and the ship carrying Jonah began to groan as if it were breaking. The seamen were afraid and paused briefly to pray to some god or other before casting the cargo over the side and rigging a sea anchor. Jonah was asleep in his bunk until the captain came and said, "What are you doing asleep? If you have a special god, call on him as we are in great distress."

The sailors, being a superstitious group, decided that one in the crew was bad luck, and they began throwing dice to see who was low man and therefore the culprit. Jonah threw the snake eyes.

The sailors began asking Jonah, "What business are you in? Where is your home? What is your native state? What is your racial extraction?"

Jonah replied, "I am a Hebrew. I fear the one God, Jehovah, who made the land and the sea. I am trying to flee from God."

Then the sailors were all the more afraid and they said, "What shall we do with you to make the sea calm?"

"Throw me overboard," said Jonah.

The sailors were reluctant to do this, however, and began making a desperate effort to row to the shore.

Seeing that this would not succeed, the sailors prayed saying, "Let us not perish because of Jonah, and yet we do not like to cause an innocent man to drown, but we can't last any longer." Then the sailors threw Jonah over the side and the sea began to grow calm.

The sailors immediately made a lot of promises to God and offered sacrifices and went on their way.

The Lord, however, had prepared a giant fish to swallow Jonah and Jonah remained in the belly of the fish three days and three nights.

Now Jonah began to pray saying, "O Lord, even though I am in the belly of hell, I know you hear me. You have caused me to be thrown into the sea, in the middle of great and terrible waters, and the waves and white tops came over my head. I knew then that I was cast aside, but I yearn to look again upon the holy temple. As I was sinking, the seaweeds wrapped about my head, I felt as if I'd been

[1]Tarshish

514

thrown from a mountain, and was strapped hopelessly in one place, but when my soul fainted within me, I remembered God. And so my prayer comes to you, O God, in thine own holy temple. Save me, and I will be thankful and I will do your bidding for I know salvation is of the Lord."

And the great fish became discomfited by God and spit Jonah upon the dry land.

Chap. 3

And again God encouraged Jonah to go to Nineveh and to preach as God had directed, and this time Jonah went without objection.

It took Jonah three days to reach Nineveh but he did not postpone his preaching. Immediately he began to exhort the people to repent and to tell the people that because of their wickedness God would destroy the city in forty days. Jonah poured it to them in brilliant and moving fashion.

The people believed and acknowledged God, repenting of their sins. The people began to fast, put on clothes proper for worship, and then the king of Nineveh set aside his royal robe and joined the people. The king then published a decree of worship and repentance, calling on every man to quit eating and drinking, not even should a man feed his animals, but everyone should concentrate on calling on God in the hopes that God would no longer be angry and would not therefore destroy the people of Nineveh. The king also called on everyone to desist from evil and from any form of violence.

And God saw their new works, and noted their change from their evil ways, and God did not destroy them.

Chap. 4

Jonah, however, was greatly irritated, as he didn't like the people of Nineveh and he had wanted to see them destroyed; so he prayed to God a lament saying, "You went to a lot of trouble, God, to get me here, and I went through a lot. I have always known, of course, that you are merciful and compassionate, slow to anger and of great kindness but I, Jonah, am disgusted. I wish you would take my life as I'm mad enough to want to die."

And God said, "Think about it a bit, Jonah, why are you so angry?"

Jonah then went out on the east side of the city, and built a small booth, and sat in it and sulked, watching to see if God might perhaps destroy the city.

And God pitied Jonah, and caused therefore a gourd to grow on a vine near Jonah to give him some shade and cool him down a bit. Jonah rejoiced over the gourd and felt better, now that he was getting a little attention himself.

The next day, however, God prepared a worm to eat part of the gourd so that it withered. After this God prepared a strong east wind, and the sun shone full on Jonah and he felt hot and miserable. Again Jonah began to feel that life was not worth living, and he mumbled to himself, "I'm better off dead than alive."

"Is it sensible, Jonah, to be irritated about the gourd?" asked God.

"Yes," said Jonah, "I'm sick to death of the whole thing."

Then God reasoned with Jonah saying, "You were sympathetic with the gourd, a plant which you didn't make or cause to grow, why should I not bless the city of Nineveh which has some 120,000 people in it, most of them not even having had a third grade education, not to mention all the cats, dogs, and cattle?"

MICAH

There was a man named Mickey[1] who was born in Utah[2] and he was a prophet, a man who prayed and meditated, who observed life around him, and who spoke forth for God, putting things right bluntly.

"Now hear this, everybody," spoke Mickey,[3] "The whole world should know how God deals with evil people and evil places. When the Lord takes the notion, he visits the earth, he flattens out the mountain tops,[4] and he cracks open the valleys. God is planning to do such things because of the sins of Samaria and Jerusalem.

"Samaria will become a pile of stones, the foundations of the city will be uprooted and the place will look as if it is a deserted vineyard. The precious images and keepsakes that the strayed-from-God worshipped shall be broken to pieces. There is nothing to do about it except wail and moan and run around the house naked in misery and discomfort.

"Eventually evil gets its comeuppance. Take Monte Carlo, Las Vegas, the dens of Panama, they will suffer. If a person was smart they would get the fastest car[5] available and drive away from such places at once. Some people keep thinking better times are ahead and that evil scheming will finally help them, but God says 'No'. Find a righteous place and take your children there or they will become slaves to evil or to evil people."

"Woe to you, you evil men. God knows what you do," spoke Mickey. "You lie awake at night plotting and scheming to take away another man's land or his money. Some of you lawyers cheat on handling a will, but God is planning to fix you plenty. In the long haul, you will get what is coming to you, for the cheater will get cheated. You may even wonder why God has done this to you. You asked for it!"

"You want me to hush, don't you? You don't care to hear such talk. Well, the righteous don't mind. They are comforted to know that God is tending to his business. God doesn't like to threaten people, but it is one way of trying to get you on the right road. In spite of all God's pleas you skin your neighbor, you will take the shirt off his back, you pay no attention to the plight of women and children. Because of this, the people of Judah must leave their land.

"You don't like that kind of sermon, do you? You'd rather have me encourage you to drink wine and get stoned. Well, you'll have to get another prophet for that. The time will come, however,

---

[1]Micah   [2]Morash   [3]Maybe at a Rotary meeting
[4]Sometimes God has army engineers who save him the trouble   [5]chariot

when for the sake of his own name, God will gather you again, those that are left, and under a new leader with a new covenant shall there be a new kingdom.

"Now a word to the leaders of Israel. You are supposed to know right from wrong, but you seem to love evil and care nothing for good. You are incessantly taking advantage of God's people, the poor, and the disadvantaged. You treat people as dirt under your feet and then you piously pray to God for deliverance from hard times.

"Do you think God is going to listen to you? You forked tongue leaders, God is going to completely disregard you. Your system is to bless those who pay their church pledges and punish those that don't pay as you think they should.

"One thing that will happen to you is that you will lose contact with God, and your preaching shall be practical hogwash, you will be speaking in darkness, and there will be no revelation to you. When this happens you will come apart at the seams, and go to visiting local shrinks.

"I speak, however, with confidence, for God has empowered me to declare to Judah and Israel their sins. I speak without fear. Now listen, you prosperous leaders, who deal unfairly and simply dwell on making a profit. You are murderers and money grubbers, and yet you tell the people that God is with them and that all is well. Well, because of you God will make a mess of Jerusalem and even the place of the temple will become a place of ruins.

"Toward the end of time, however, there will be a change," prophesied Mickey, "for the holy mountain of God shall be a place where tourists come from all over the world to see where God declared himself to be Lord. In those days all the world will be ruled by the Lord, and the place of his headquarters will be Jerusalem.

"The new king of this new kingdom[1] shall judge and rule, and the nations of the world shall adopt a disarmanent plan, and instead of weapons of war, the nations shall make tractors and all forms of farming instruments. There will be universal peace as God has promised.

"At this time the righteous shall be brought forth by God, and they shall be the leaders and for once goodness shall be synonymous with prosperity. God will bless his people and restore their power, and the center of this operation will be Jerusalem.

"For the present, however, you've got it tough. Your king might as well be dead and your ministers have chickened out. You have reason to groan as a woman in labor, and so groan away. You must leave this wonderful city and this delightful countryside. You

---

[1] I think this refers to Christ

are going to be captured.

"Nations continue to plot against you, but the time will come, far off as it may be, when God will not allow anyone or any nation to tamper with his people.

"The day will come when the Lord will make the righteous appear to have horns of iron and feet of brass, and there will be no people who can contend with them. The wicked nations and people shall then be subservient to the people of God.

Chap. 5

"Try getting organized. At least begin to prepare for a great new kingdom. For out of Bethlehem shall come a new king, one who was with God at the very beginning. Greatness shall come from the tiny little town of Bethlehem. There will be, however, a period of time when the people of God will seem to be fighting on their own, but God plans to correct all of this.

"The new king will feed his people with the food of the Lord and his name and his kingdom shall gradually encompass the earth. In time there shall be specially appointed leaders, seven or eight of them, and at the proper time these leaders will save the people from the Assyrians, and the spirit of God's people shall be refreshing to the world even as morning dew refreshes the grass, and God's people shall be as strong as a lion.

"Another sign of this time will be that God will do away with weapons of war and walled fortresses, and tanks and the like, and all the worship of material things shall end and man's selfishness will perish. Those who do not conform to this plan will be destroyed.

Chap. 6

"Now listen. The Lord has a complaint to file against his people and the Lord has a plea to make to Israel. God wants to know what you have against God? Where has God wronged you? Speak up! Didn't God bring you out of Egypt, furnish you with leaders such as Moses, Aaron, and Miriam, did not God confound the king of Moab?[1] What do you think God wants in return for all his goodness? Do you think God wants a bunch of sacrifices? Or a new church building? Or airconditioned temples? God has already said what he requires, it is for you to do justly, to love mercy, and to walk humbly with your God.

"God calls to all Jerusalem. If you've got a dime's worth of brains, listen to him. Armies are already heading this way. Are you going to continue cheating, using loaded dice, and measuring cloth with a short stick? Is there no end to your wickedness?

"You are so accustomed to falsehood that you don't know how to tell the truth. Because of this God will make you pyschologically ill, even your food won't taste good, and your puny savings and

[1] Omri

so-called securities will be confiscated by the enemy. You'll plant and have lousy crops, and olive oil will turn sour on you. You follow the rules of the Playboy Club and you use as your example for living ole Dean Martin.[1] Just for that I will make you a pain in the neck to the people of the world and you shall be constantly despised. People will snicker at you and make fun of your plight.

"It is a tough time for me," groaned Mickey, "for I continue searching for honest, upright men, and they are scarce as hen's teeth. It seems as if all the good men are dead, it is like looking for a fig after the pickers have finished with a tree.

"The money-mad people are scrambling for the dollar in a pitiful manner. The people bribe judges, the rulers take kick-backs, how skillfully they connive and cheat. Justice almost doesn't exist. A man cannot even trust his own kinsman, they squabble over inheritance, and tell lies about one another even though they serve the God of my salvation. I'm certain God will in time hear me.

"Don't count me out, you foolish, wicked enemies. I may get knocked down, but not out. I'll come back, for God is with me. When I sit in darkness, God brings me a light. I know I am a sinner and that I deserve punishment, but I have repented and I will be restored. Some of you may taunt me by asking where my God is, but you just wait. When God decides to act, you are going to be in big, big trouble.

"The cities of the people of God will be eventually rebuilt, bigger and better than ever, and then people will come from all over the world to visit and to recognize your success. Before that happens, however, you must suffer terrible destruction because of your sins.

"Naturally, I pray to God for all of us, asking God to come and establish his rule, to make the people live in peace, and bring prosperity again to the Holy Land. I have prayed to God for a return of the good old days.

"God has answered and has promised to do mighty miracles, like those the Lord did when he delivered his people from Egypt. Everyone will be astounded, some shall put their hands over their mouths in awe and some shall plug their ears so as not to hear, but to no avail. The wicked will be as worms crawling helplessly around, and they shall fear God.

"How could there possibly be such a great God as our God. Surely he pardons sins, he allows his anger to last for only a brief period, our God delights in mercy and is full of compassion. God will take the sins of the repentant people and cast them into the depths of the sea. At this time God will fulfill his wonderful promises to Jacob and Abraham."

Amen.

[1] Ahab

NAHUM

Matty,[1] from Pensacola,[2] was a theologian who in his study of God had some visions and insights, and as a result he made some significant pronouncements.

"God is not one to accept second place. When a person or a city places good less than first, God takes a dim view of the situation and he always punishes wickedness and disregard of God's power or his commandments.

"The Lord doesn't have a short fuse, and he angers very slowly, but once his wrath is aroused then things begin to really happen. You must realize that God is in charge of the whirlwinds, the sea, the earthquakes, and God is not subject to General Motors[3] or the Senate Foreign Relations Committee.[4] God has the control over all the earth.

"Who thinks he can stand up against God? Doesn't God control landslides? God particularly loves those who trust completely in him, and the Lord is a good, strong refuge to the faithful in time of trouble. The enemies of God, however, may be washed away in a flash flood or they may just live in mental darkness. The enemies of God don't have a chance, they will be folded up like a blanket and put away. That's the way it will be with you, you wicked city of Nineveh. Who does your mayor think he is defying God? He must be nuts for sure! Your stupid king could gather an army of tremendous numbers and they would be nothing to God.

"As for the people of God, they have been punished enough and God plans to free them. The Assyrian king that holds the people captive, however, is on the way out. God will destroy him, so thoroughly that not even one of his sons will inherit the dynasty.

"Look up! There coming down the mountain you can see the feet that bring good tidings, that tell of peace. Be happy, Judah, and keep the commandments of God and follow his statutes. Nineveh is already handled, and she will no more be a source of trouble to Judah.

"Do anything you wish, try gathering together your strongest men, but it is a waste of time. Nineveh, you've had it. You have previously desolated the land of God, but not any more. The Lord has prepared an army that flashes as scarlet, and pandemonium should reign. The chariots shall be in a traffic jam rushing uselessly back and forth and even though the king calls forth his ablest men to man the walls, it will be in vain.

"The incoming army shall descend as a flood breaking through

---

[1]Nahum   [2]Elkoshi   [3]Bashan   [4]Carmel

521

the gates of the city and the palace itself shall be over-run.

"The beautiful Queen Liz[1] shall be made captive and she will be led forth practically naked with all her handmaidens following along crying and exposing their own breasts in shame and sadness.

"The soldiers of Nineveh suddenly become yellow bellies and begin to sneak away and hide so that the city appears to be a leaky bucket. Some of the leaders call for the men to stand their ground, but they don't, and shamefully flee.

"Looting will begin immediately. There is great wealth in the city and soon it is gone, for those seeking spoils take everything. Soon all is gone, and the glory of Nineveh exists no longer. You can see the pathos on the faces of the defeated people. You can't help but wonder what happened to the fierce young warriors, the strong men of Nineveh. The answer is that God has turned against Nineveh, and God is the real reason that the chariots are broken in pieces, and there is no more respect for voices that come from Nineveh for her power is gone forever."

Chap.
3

"God repeatedly denounces Nineveh. Woe to such a city, or any city, that lives on violence, crime, and lust. The men of Nineveh have had no respect or concern for people, and they have needlessly slain others just for practice. It is almost unbelievable the number of dead that you can see in the streets, and nobody cares.

God has seen this and God doesn't like it. As a result, God will expose Nineveh as simply as pulling a skirt over a girl's head exposes her nakedness. God will cause other nations to despise Nineveh and to detest its existence. In fact, when Nineveh is destroyed no one will regret it and there will be no sad resolutions passed by the United States. Because Nineveh was a completely wicked city the Lord decided to destroy the city, and to ruin its reputation as a place to visit or a business center.

"The people of Nineveh will be captured, the leaders will become slaves, and Nineveh will reel under her hardships as a drunken man, with no direction or stability. Other wicked cities and countries have perished because they became ungodly in their conduct.

"The city of Nineveh will seemingly have an army of women, and the city will be destroyed by fire and by pillage. You can prepare all you wish, store water, assemble arms, man the walls, strengthen the barricades, but the Lord will manage the destruction of all these devices just as simply as moths handle cloth or worms gnaw away on the wood.

"There is no escape for you people of Nineveh. Your sins are

[1]Huzzab

about to catch you. Your leadership is rotten and when the trouble starts you will find that your princes and your rulers have deserted. There is no cure for your plight and your destruction and your loss will not be mourned as other nations will be glad you no longer exist. Wickedness has its day, but it has its sad end."

HABAKKUK

Chap.
1

There was a prophet of the Lord and his friends called him Hub.[1] Hub became greatly distressed by the existing conditions in the world and he prayed to the Lord saying, "How long, O Lord, must I pray? How often I have told you of the violence in the land and yet nothing happens. Everywhere I look I see evil at work. Why is this? The law is real slack. The judges let people go, they postpone trials, they give all kinds of extensions, and the courts turn free criminals regularly. Why?"

"Just keep your shirt on, Hub," replied the Lord. "You are going to be amazed at what I plan to do. My plan is to bring a bunch of heathens, worse men than you ever saw, and turn them loose on the sinners you are seeing every day. These Cossacks[2] are fierce and mean. Their horses are swifter than leopards, they make their own laws to suit themselves. These warriors will descend on your area like an eagle swoops down on its prey.

"These Cossacks are unbelievably terrible. They love violence, they disregard kings and princes, and they only leave a pile of dust behind them. These toughies claim to receive power from some strange god, but it is a god of their own making."

"Wait a minute, now, O Lord. You don't mean you are sending this awful outfit down on us, do you? You are only going to use these people to punish and correct us, certainly not to eliminate us," prayed Hub to the Lord. "For one thing, we are bad, but these Cossacks are worse. Certainly you don't plan to sponsor them. I know you dislike sin in any form; so how can you let these Cossacks crush us?

"The way you talk, we will be just like fish caught in the Cossacks' nets, or snared on their hooks. When they have captured or killed all of us, the Coassacks will bless their equipment, they will not acknowledge God. Do you plan to let them get away with their cruelty? Will the Coassacks punish us, and then go unpunished themselves?" asked Hub.

Chap.
2

After this Hub climbed to his meditation seat on top of the wall and waited for God's answer.

God then spoke to Hub and said, "You can print my words. Put them on a public bulletin board. The things that I have planned will not come suddenly, but will gradually through the years work to the fulfillment of my plan. Have a little patience, Hub.

"The man who puts his trust in man like a Cossack does, these kind eventually fail, but the man who puts his trust in God, who has

[1]Habakkuk   [2]Chaldeans

524

faith, and pursues righteousness, such a man in time really lives.

"The Cossacks fill themselves with wine, and with vainglory, and they are never satisfied, but pursue one endeavor after another, never knowing where they are going.

"The very people that the Cossacks mistreat will in time rise up and crush them. Because the Cossack type spoils many nations, so shall it work around that these nations shall eventually destroy the Cossacks. The desires of evil are very perishable. Such things only look successful, but eventually all evil is to be crushed.

"If the stones or bricks would talk, they would tell you that a wall or building built at the expense of the blood of innocent people is a construction that will definitely tumble. Godless nations can work as hard as they wish, but it is in vain. God will not always tolerate evil doings of evil people.

"Woe to you who tempt your neighbor or your friend with strong drink," says the Lord. "Particularly is this evil if you use it as a means of taking advantage of a girl. Shame on those who do such things! God's judgment will come down on all sinners. There are plenty of you in the area where Hub lives," God continued, "who have cut down trees needlessly, in fact, who have often made idols to worship from the wood. Woe to those who pray to idols of wood and stone, expecting them to do something. Idols covered even with silver and gold are worthless."

"Remember all of you, the Lord is in His holy temple and all the earth should keep silence before him," spoke Hub to the people.

Chap.
3

On another occasion Hub voiced a prayer to God which was also a song of hope as he said, "O Lord, when I hear your pronouncements I am filled with wonder. Let us again see you in action, God, mingling wrath and mercy. I can see the manifestations of God in every direction, his glory in the heavens and his handiwork on the earth. God shines as a bright light and power is in his hands.

"God has complete control of disease, God knows everything there is to know about the earth. The hills themselves stand in testimony to the Lord, people of all nations are impressed, even those nations of Russia[1] and China[2], whether they admit it or not.

"Sometimes when you see the sea in great upheaval with monstrous waves and whitecaps on the rivers, man wonders if God is angry with the waters, while actually this is just the way God made things. God made the rivers to divide the land.

"God created the sun and the moon and he started them on their regular rounds, just because God ordered it that way. God sometimes paces the earth in indignation and beats the wicked as

[1]Anshan   [2]Midian

grain on a threshing floor.

"God continues to arrange to save his chosen people, those who believe on his name. The manifestations of God in nature are truly impressive. Particularly is this true of the sea, for when the sea is terribly rough one thinks that God has his own horses thrashing in the deep, and it is a fearful sight to behold.

"I know this though, even if hard times come, if there are no figs, if the olive crop fails, if the grain fields have no yield, and the cattle perish, yet I will rejoice in the Lord, I will be delighted to know that in God is my salvation, for the Lord God is my strength, God will give me speed when I need it, and will make me capable of climbing mountains."

Hub suggests that the above song be sung accompanied by stringed instruments.[1]

[1]If he had known, he would have added with volume down.

ZEPHANIAH

There was a prophet in the land named Sim[1] and he was a great grandson of ole Hez.[2] As a prophet he spoke forth for God and he addressed the people of Judah with the following exhortation.[3]

"The Lord has decided to clean out the land of Judah. The Lord is angry and he will destroy fish and game, man and beast, and God will avenge the sins of Jerusalem, and everywhere that Baal was ever worshipped will be punished. Men who have served strange gods or simply neglected to worship the true God, these will be punished as God will vent his wrath on the area.

"The day God has appointed for His vengeance is close at hand. Those men who wear the garb of the heathen, the leaders of Judah who are selfish and phony, the criminals, and those who take advantage of the weak and innocent, on all such God is ready to pounce. Don't worry, you'll hear about it. From the front gate to the back the cry of terror and alarm shall be yelled. Death is bearing down on the money grubbers and the conniving merchants.

"There will be a period of great distress, so that men will wander around in a daze wondering what has happened to them. Some of the fellows will try to buy their safety, but they will find it is not for sale. The Lord is going to burn the whole place and the people of Judah will suddenly disappear."

On another occasion[4] Sim arose, and inspired by God, spoke to the people saying, "In God's name I urge you to gather yourselves together and turn to the Lord in prayer, for the Lord is extremely angry over your disgraceful behavior. Seek ye the Lord. Strive toward righteousness and study the ways of God so that you might follow in his path. It is still perhaps not too late to abate the anger of God and avoid his punishment.

"Look out, you wicked places! Las Vegas, the Riviera, the dark haunts of Panama, perhaps even Acapulco shall be shredded. Woe to the wicked coastal cities, the French Quarter, all the habitations of sin, for God in his own time will utterly destroy such places. All places shall finally come into the hands of the people of God.

"God knows about places like New York or parts of Mississippi or Nevada where those who served God are ridiculed. God has decreed the same treatment for all such places as that of Sodom and Gomer. God's people will in due time control all these places. The people who have made fun of those who worship God shall get it in

[1]Zephaniah   [2]Hezekiah
[3]Probably a family night supper speech that no one liked
[4]Would you believe a Rotary program?

527

the neck, but plenty! The Lord will be a terror to them, God will eliminate the effectiveness of all other gods, and men will worship the living God.

"God is not limited. God will make Ethiopia desolate and reduce Assyria to a nothing nation, and eliminate Nineveh. This is what finally happens to the wicked. The wicked city Ninevah that bragged of its greatness, that distributed tremendous brochures of self-praise, this wicked city shall be a place for ground hogs to burrow, for wild animals to use as a habitation, while owls and buzzards roost on the remains of the city. People will pass by the ruins and talk of the shame of the place and denounce it with words and chariot stickers saying 'Long gone Nineveh!'

Chap. 3

Since Sim had spoken to Rotary he was shortly thereafter asked to speak to the Kiwanis Club. On this occasion, again inspired by a revelation of God, he spoke about the city of Jerusalem.[1]

"Woe to Jerusalem! God has clearly seen that this is a wicked and corrupt city. The people have not obeyed God. Apparently the attempts of God to show the people how God works has made no impression, although God has destroyed a number of wicked places seen and known by the people of Jerusalem.

"The leadership of your city is rotten, most of your judges are crooked, and your preachers are dull, dreary reciters of stale platitudes.[2] The so-called godly church people are among those that pay no attention to the laws of God or man. The people go about in a corrupt city as if there was no God at all. Yuk!

"God is in no big hurry. Just you wait," continued Sim. "The day is coming when God is going to give a mighty whack to all the wicked nations and wicked places at once. The whole earth will feel the impact of the anger of God. At that time, God will begin to give all those that believe on him a new importance. The people of God will have one common language, and the people of God will be worshipping God all over the earth, even throughout all Africa.

"A great nucleus of these believers will be among those normally considered poor and ignorant, or disadvantaged, but the whole operation of God's people shall be honest, sincere, truthful, and their word of greeting shall be 'peace be with you all.'

"Sing, rejoice, be glad, all you believers. Your day will have arrived. Where you were accustomed to be treated shamefully, you will be honored, God will bless all his people, and the name of the people of God will be great throughout the whole earth, and the spirit of the Lord will constantly be living in the midst of his people. Amen."

---

[1] This was not well received. He was not asked back to speak again.
[2] This turned some of the preachers against him, too.

There was a prophet of the Lord known as Haggy[1] and he was inspired by the Lord during the second year of Darius the King to go to the governor of Judah[2] and to the Archbishop[3] and speak to them.

"Governor and bishop," said Haggy, "the Lord has asked me to come to you and inquire as to the reason for letting the church get so rundown and neglected."

"The people say that now is not a good time economically to do any building or add to the present church,"[4] was the reply.

"Well, God suggests that you take a look at the situation. You plant a lot of seed, but you get a poor crop. You eat all right, but you don't get enough. There is some wine, but not near enough. You all have some clothes, but not enough to stay warm on a real cold day. You all have jobs and get some income but the deductions leave you under the impression that you are bringing your pay home in a bag that is full of holes."

"Now God knows all this. God says though that now is the time to get with building the church. Go up the mountain and cut wood and build on to the house of God. Do you know why your economics are in bad shape? That's God's way of telling you that your worship of him is inadequate. Because you have been more concerned with your own house than with the house of God, the Lord has encouraged a drouth and brought on a recession."

Then the governor, the bishop, and the people repented and recognized the truth of what Haggy said to them. As a result, the Lord was pleased and he encouraged the leaders of the people, and everyone pitched in, doing each his own thing for the building program of the church, and all was well.

A few months later Haggy, again inspired by God, called on the governor and spoke to him.

"God appreciates the work which the building committee is doing. God is also aware of the fact that this building program is nothing compared to the great temple of Solomon. God, however, does not want you or the people to be discouraged because of this.

"The time of the great renewal of all the people of God is coming. You must remember that all silver and gold, and all precious things, all these are the Lord's. God doesn't need such, but in time all these things will be under the care of the believers. The wicked are doomed!

"God doesn't want you to worry about the inadequateness of

---

[1]Haggai [2]Zerubbabel [3]Joshua of Josedeck
[4]I've heard that song before

529

the present work, for the future splendor of the temple of God will be caused by the peace which God will bestow on his church."

A couple of months later Haggy again received word from God and this time he was sent to speak to the bishop.

"Bishop," said Haggy, "let me ask you a question. If a holy man is carrying a holy object, and his pants leg brushes against a table or touches a loaf of bread, does the table or the bread become holy?"

"Not on your life, Haggy. What a stupid question. Holiness is not contagious," replied the bishop.

"If, however, a person touches an infection or hangs around measles, now that will be apt to spread to the person, isn't that right?"

"Right on, Haggy, right on," said the bishop.

"In just such a manner will the Lord bless his people and his spirit in time will spread from one to the other like measles."

Haggy then visited the governor and spoke to him for the last time.[1]

"God wants me to inform you," said Haggy, "that eventually he will get with his program at full speed. The whole earth will be aware of what God is doing. God will destroy all the wicked kingdoms, and chariots, horses, and armies will be as nothing before the power of God. God says that you are a good man, Governor, and because of your faithfulness you will be rewarded, and you shall be among those who sit on the right hand of God. Amen."

---

[1] As far as we know

ZECHARIAH

There was a young man living during the reign of Darius named Izzy[1] and he was a preacher's son, and he made his first public speech at a family night supper at the church. At this time he spoke to the people telling them that he was inspired by God and that God was urging the people to repent. In fact, Izzy told the people that if they would turn to God, that God would bless them.

"Why don't you learn a lesson from your fathers?" shouted Izzy. "God warned them and pleaded with them, and they paid no attention. That's why we are all in trouble now. Your fathers finally realized this too late."

Several months later Izzy had a vision in which he saw a man riding a red horse and behind him there were black horses, white ones, and speckled ones, each with a rider.

Izzy in his dream then cried, "What is all this?"

"I'll show you," spoke forth an angel. "These men on their horses have been commissioned by God to patrol the earth in the interest of peace and good times."

Then an angel of the Lord prayed publicly to God asking, "How long will your anger against Jerusalem last, O Lord? Hasn't Jerusalem been suffering now for 70 years and isn't that enough?"

Then the Lord replied in such a way that the angel was comforted. As a consequence, the angel encouraged Izzy to speak out and to say to the people that God did care, that God felt kindly toward his people and the city like a man feels about a wife who has been taken into captivity.

The Lord revealed to the angel and thus to Izzy that the Lord was exceedingly angry at the nations who as heathens conquered Israel. The Lord decreed that his temple shall be rebuilt, that the cities of God will again prosper, that they will be restored, and God shall bless his people and their habitation with His own presence.

Then Izzy, who was still dreaming all this, dreamed of four horns and so Izzy in his dream asked the angel, "What gives with these horns?"

"These four horns," said the angel, "represent the four great powers that are reponsible for scattering my people and for destroying Judah, Israel, and Jerusalem."

Then Izzy saw four carpenters in his dream.

"What gives with these?" asked Izzy.

"These are the powers that will punish the horns and their power, and do away with them."

[1]Zechariah

Izzy continued in his dream state, and he saw in his dream a man with a measuring line.

"What are you planning to do?" asked Izzy.

"I am going to measure Jerusalem," replied the man.

"Why?" asked Izzy.

"To see if it is big enough to hold the crowd that will some day be there."

Then Izzy saw an angel in his dream go to another angel and say to him, "Go to the young man with the ruler and tell him that Jerusalem will not be large enough for all the people, but there shall be many who will live outside the walls, and they shall create suburbs and rural communities and there shall be great prosperity. There will be no need for a wall, as the Lord himself will serve as a wall for his people, and the glory of the Lord will be in the midst of the people."

The Lord then revealed to Izzy that God was pleased with the way the people who had been taken north into captivity had conducted themselves.

"The Lord says it is a time for rejoicing. Get with the program!" said Izzy. "The fulfillment of the promises of God is not too distant. Sing with joy! All the earth will be silent before the Lord, and the glory of God will again fill the earth with gladness."

As Izzy continued dreaming or dreamed again on another occasion, Izzy saw Joshua, the great leader and high priest of the early days, standing in the presence of God and standing opposite the devil.[1]

God spoke to Satan and said, "You are not to get your way. I am going to deliver Jerusalem, just as man would pull a log out of the fire."

Now Joshua was in dirty clothes[2] as he stood before one of the angels, a Mr. Clean,[3] who said, "Get some clean clothes for this man. Just as the Lord has forgiven your sins; so also will your clothes be made clean."

Then Izzy interrupted and said, "Don't forget to get him a clean hat." As a result, Joshua was suddenly spic and span.

Then one of the angels spoke to Joshua and said, "The Lord has authorized me to tell you that if you will obey his laws, and if you will encourage many other priests, ministers, and teachers to do the same thing, then you will be cleared to pass back and forth in his presence."

"You see," the angel continued, "all of you who will speak and teach in this manner, you will represent and will continue to represent the Branch that the Lord will bring forth to save his

---

[1] I continue to think of him as being red with horns
[2] No drip-dry clothes then   [3] Zerrubebel

people. There will be an event in one day which will remove the sin of the world, just as has been illustrated to you. When that day comes, the equality of man shall be pronounced, and rich or poor shall all be neighbors."

Then an angel came and awakened Izzy and asked him, "What did you see?"

"This last time I saw a candlestick of gold, with a bowl on it and seven lamps, with seven pipes, with two olive trees on each side. What in the thunderation does such a vision mean," asked Izzy.

"You don't know that?" said the angel.

"No, I don't," said Izzy.

"This vision is the word of the Lord to the Christians saying 'not by might, nor by power, but by my spirit,' saith the Lord of hosts, you will succeed this way regardless of your few in numbers or your strength.

"Even the mountains will flatten out before the Christian movement. Nothing can stop this. The Christians shall build to the glory of God and through the church, and with mighty shouts shall proclaim God's mercy, and shall credit all these things to the grace of God."

Then Izzy received another message from God saying, "It is the Christians, acting as the hands of Christ, who have laid the foundation. Do not be upset by the small number at the beginning, or the slow growth, the eyes of the Lord, represented by the seven lamps, are everywhere, seeing the worth of God's people, and watching how the will of God progresses."

"What about the two olive trees?" asked Izzy.

"Don't you know?" asked the angel.

"Absolutely no," replied Izzy.

"The two olive trees represent the annointed ones who watch over all the earth for the Lord."[1]

Izzy dreamed again a few weeks later[2] and in his dream he saw a flying blackboard.

An angel then turned to Izzy and asked, "What did you see?"

"A flying blackboard about 25 ft. long and 14 ft wide," replied Izzy.

"This blackboard represents the word of God being made known everywhere to everybody. It declares that it is wrong to steal or to lie. The Lord has ordered this to be a conscience that shall torment everyone who does wrong willfully."

The angel of the Lord then said, "Izzy, look up again."

"What is that thing I see?" asked Izzy.

---

[1]Christ and Holy Spirit   [2]Certainly not the next night

"It is a container. There is a woman sitting in the container, and the whole thing represents evil and man's abuses of God's gifts."

Then Izzy saw two women with great wings fly by and seize the container of wickedness and fly off.

"Where are they going with the wickedness?" asked Izzy.

"To the city," said the angel. "There it is easy for it to survive."

Chap
6

Izzy had another vision and in this dream Izzy saw brass mountains and there came forth from between the mountains four chariots, one chariot had red horses, another black, a third white, and the fourth was pulled by dappled greys. Izzy then turned to the angel who was present and asked, "What are these?"

"These chariots represent four spirits which come from God," replied the angel. "The black horses and the white horses represent spirits that for the most part deal in the northern areas and the dappled greys were assigned to the south. The Lord was soon pleased with the work of the spirit in the north area."

The Lord informed Izzy in a vision that he would soon be visited by representatives from the north and that he was to accept their gifts, and then take the silver and gold contained in the gifts and make a crown, and then to put the crown upon the head of the son of the high priest.

Then the Lord instructed Izzy to speak to Joshua, the son of the high priest, and to tell him that although he wore the crown, he was merely symbolizing the king and high priest who was yet to be born. The great one to come will be known as the Branch.[1] In time, the Branch shall be the real ruler, both ruler and priest, and there shall be peace and understanding between church and state.

Izzy then instructed Joshua to place the crown in the temple as a memorial and a reminder of what was to come.

The Lord further revealed to Izzy that people would come from all over the world to acknowledge God and that the Lord has promised all these things, contingent upon man's diligently obeying the word of God.

Chap
7

A committee from the Jewish community at Bethel came to Izzy with Leo the Lip[2] as chairman and spokesman.

"We have come to inquire if it might be permissable for us to drop the fasting and mourning period during the month of August. We really don't understand what it's all about anyway."

"The Lord has often questioned the sincerity of the observance of your fasting. God is certain that many of your observances were conducted for appearance's sake, and not as an act of worship. Maybe you need to brush up on the pronouncements of God when

[1]Christ   [2]Sherezer

God instructed the children of Israel during times of prosperity."

"Do you know what God has always sought?" asked Izzy. "God says for you to execute righteous judgment, to show compassion, to deal with mercy. It is not the performance in the temple that impresses God, but the way you deal with widows, the disadvantaged, the poor, and strangers. God is concerned more with your heart than your liturgy."

"Your fathers would not listen to this fine preaching," continued Izzy, "and they shrugged their shoulders and hardened their hearts. For this, the Lord became angry. As a result, you find yourselves scattered, the enemies of Israel prospered, and the good land was made desolate."

Chap
8

Izzy again received another message from God, this time pointing out that the Lord was real hot over the way the enemies of Israel had taken advantage of her. Because of this, the Lord told Izzy that Jerusalem would be some day restored, there would be a place in the city for the young as well as the senior citizens. God announced plans to gather the scattered people of Israel and restore them in fact as well as in prestige.

As surely as God punished as surely will God restore. Prosperity will return and such sayings as 'poor as a Jew in Judah' will be outmoded.

In order that these things be accomplished, God has asked everyone to begin speaking the truth, to use fairness, to promote peace, and to think of good things to do rather than evil ones.

The Lord also indicated that the more people observed the teachings and commandments of God, the less need was there for liturgy.

Because of all this, God has declared that some day Jerusalem shall be truly the holy city, a great center for tourists, many people, some church groups, some prayer groups, and many leaders of great nations shall come to Jerusalem to praise the Lord. At this time there shall be an organization of ten great nations and they shall choose a Jew to lead them, and they shall choose him because they will have heard that God is with him.

Chap
9

Further word from God came to Izzy and he passed along the information that in spite of the craftiness and cunning of such evil places as Tyre and Sidon, their doom was sealed. The Lord will not allow wickedness to be permanent. Disaster will come to the nations and the cities that defy God and that persecute God's people.

"The word from God," said Izzy, "is to rejoice. There is a great king coming, unlike any ever born, even though the king may be seen riding on a lowly donkey, the king is real. The king will carry with him salvation.

"This great new king who will come will pronounce peace and gradually his influence and his kingdom shall spread from sea to sea, and from the nearest river to the ends of the earth.

"The people of God will be leaders in this great movement and victory, though gradual, shall be a sure thing from the very beginning. This new kingdom will finally bring peace and prosperity, and the abundance of food and drink shall provide health and cheerfulness to whole generations."

Chap.
10

"God will send rain when rain is requested, and the earth shall be a blessed place. Why do people depend on weird rites, or strange charts, when all the powers of existence reside only in God?

"The Lord is angry that people go to fortune-tellers, that they seek odd ways of success through man devised programs. God plans to restore Judah and Israel and to let them be part of the great rehabilitation program of peace on earth.

"Even though the scattering of the Jews has been cruel and effective, the Lord will re-build from the remnant. In time the Lord will gather the Jews again, bringing them from England, Russia, Germany, Syria, and even some from the U.S., and the land will be crowded with them. At the proper time, the Lord will dry up the river Nile as a protection for his people.

"The believers in God will grow in strength, and their power will not be the power of men, but the power of God. It shall be known that they live as witnesses to the power of God."

Chap.
11

According to Izzy, the Lord revealed to him the fate of Lebanon. "It is a wicked country, and it will be destroyed. It will be as if a great fire comes raging and burns the whole place."

Then Izzy was urged in a vision to go out and get a job as a shepherd; so that not only would he know about what was going on, but also as a means of teaching God's message visually.

As a result, Izzy took the job as a shepherd of a flock that was being fattened for the butcher. The owners did not save any sheep, they were poor stewards, and they sold only to make the most possible money.

Izzy then spoke to the people and said, "You are not mindful of God's things, but are only interested in your own wealth; so as you have done to the sheep, the Lord will do to you. You will be completely destroyed. Even as I broke the staff marked to point out the sheep to be saved, so has God broken the staff which could save you."

After this Izzy turned to his employers and said, "Pay me for what you think I'm worth."

As a result, Izzy received 30 pieces of silver and the Lord instructed Izzy to donate it to the church, as it was obviously a means of scorn for the work of a prophet.

The Lord then told Izzy that he had illustrated the punishment part of God's plan and now he was to take a job as the shepherd for a poor man, and to give the appearance of being a poor and worthless leader.

When this was done, Izzy said to the people, "Now this recent act of mine illustrates to you that God will provide a worthless leader for you, one that cares not for individuals. It is this type of leadership that will bring Israel to trouble, but the Lord will punish such a leader who does not care for his flock and shirks his responsibility."

Chap.
12

Izzy came to the people again with another message.

"The Lord God, the one who laid the foundations of the earth, who stretched out the heavens into limitless space, who created man and breathed into him a living soul, this Lord of All," said Izzy, "has announced that he will eventually bless Jerusalem. It will again someday be God's holy city, and the city itself will be the focal point of all international relations. Anyone who attempts to destroy Jerusalem in that day shall be destroyed.

"Because of this, the people of Judah shall wonder and be impressed, and they shall seek to join again with the people of Jerusalem. The power of God will be with the people of Judah at this time and their strength shall be great. The Lord will deliver Judah first, in order that the people of Jerusalem may not become too self-impressed.

"In that distant day, a feeble person living in Jerusalem shall feel protected, for the strength of the Lord God of hosts shall be in the city.

"In that day, God will begin to destroy any nation that turns its strength against Jerusalem.

"At this time there shall be a great revival in Jerusalem, and a tremendous feeling of repentance shall fill the mind and heart of everyone, for they shall know that the one who was pierced and crucified was their saviour.

"There shall be a great period of worship, of mourning for sin, and each person will try to find a place apart and pray fervently in private to the Lord."

Chap.
13

"In that great day to come," continued Izzy, "people will understand forgiveness, and it will seem as simple as washing at a fountain. False gods will no longer exist, and those who do not follow the Lord and believe in his messenger shall be denounced. A father or mother will even denounce a son for this in that day.

"There will be no distinction between minister or priest and the laity. All will live under the spirit of God. In fact, if a man ask another where he received certain scars, he would lie and say 'in a brawl,' rather than admit that the scars came from falling down the library steps at the Seminary.

"There is a great deal of trouble ahead for the people of God, but a good nucleus will always be retained, and they shall be blessed by God and protected. God will say to such "You are my people," and they shall reply, "The Lord is our God."

"About all I can say is to tell you," Izzy said, "to watch carefully for the coming of the time of the Lord. Now here is what is going to happen. The enemies of God and of Jerusalem shall attack the city, they shall steal treasures, rape women, and take away captives by the hundreds. About half of Jerusalem in men and materials shall be left.

"Then the Lord God of hosts shall go forth in his power against the warring nations. First God will create a mammoth earthquake which shall split the land open, creating a great valley running east and west, and the believers in God will begin to gather in this valley. It will be an awesome time, for there will be neither darkness nor light, but everything will be gray and murky, and only God will know what time it is, and whether it be day or night.

"As a result, living waters shall flow in every direction, through the saints of the Lord, and there shall be one God, and only one name worshipped. Jerusalem shall again be safely inhabited.

"For all the people who fought against Jerusalem will be struck with a plague of such horror that it destroys tissue, tongues shall shrivel to nothing, and people will seem to melt. There shall be such suffering and confusion among the non-godly that they shall begin to turn against each other. The plague will also affect the animals. Judah and Jerusalem will assemble most of the confiscated wealth.

"There will be those people in enemy nations who worship God, and they shall come to Jerusalem each year on a holy pilgrimage. If there happens to be a nation that does not properly represent itself in the worship of God, the Lord will simply withhold rain from that nation.

"Should Egypt not come to be represented, another punishment will come to Egypt, as it doesn't rain there anyway.

"The whole atmosphere of life in the city will be changed in the time of the rulership of God on earth, and bumper stickers in Jerusalem will say such things as "Holy Property," and trash cans will be marked "Sacred Bowl." In fact, everything in Jerusalem will be considered a holy object, and this is for the convenience of the pilgrims coming to the holy city. In this great day, there will be no money changing or trading in connection with the Lord's temple, but the church of God shall be a holy place for the worship of the Holy God."

There was a man named Edwards[1] who was the guest speaker at a lecture series in Israel. Inspired by God, Edwards spoke to the people saying, "The Lord has loved his people always. How has he shown it? By choice. God didn't have to bless Jacob from whom you are descended. God could have just as easily blessed Esau, but instead he made a curse of all that Esau did, for he was selfish and anti-godly.

"It will always be this way with the wicked. Every time wickedness prospers God in his time comes along and wipes it clean. You will someday see the glory of God throughout all Israel.

"You yourselves teach that a son should honor his father. Why then don't you honor God? Even your preachers are not free from blame.

"What do you do wrong? I'm glad you asked! For one thing, you bring gifts to the church, leftovers to the family night supper, and stale bread for the communion table. How does that grab you?

"What's more, you pay your church pledge with blind animals, or sick doves, and you claim more deductions than you give. You wouldn't try to cheat the IRS, would you? Why then do you try to cheat God?

"Why don't you ask God for forgiveness? If God closes the door on you, it is for a reason, just as you have a reason for closing a door. God is rightly disgusted with you and God will not accept gifts reluctantly given.

"Even the gentiles are beginning to acknowledge God and the name of the Lord will grow in importance everywhere. You have made fun of the worship of God and trifled with the holy symbols. You have complained about being bored with the services and you have reflected this in your church giving. For those who are guilty there is trouble, for the Lord is the one Great God of all."

Chap.
2

On another occasion Edwards was invited to lecture at a ministers' retreat, and he spoke to them saying, "The Lord will punish you if you do not begin to emphasize more the need to glorify the name of God. You are far too much concerned with your own image and your own problems.

"God promised life and peace to the members of the ministry who follow the Lord and preach in his name. The priest or minister should be knowledgeable in the law, for he is the one chosen by the Lord to teach the law of God. You have strayed from this, and you have tried to water down the law and mislead the people.

[1]Malachi

539

"You have violated the arrangement God made with Levi and therefore you will be held in contempt by the people, some of whom will sneeringly refer to you as 'just another preacher.'

"God has explained that there is only one father and we are all brothers, how can you teach otherwise? Yet you are careless with the law of God.

"Didn't God warn everyone about marrying heathen women and then following their strange gods? A lot of you have done this, not only the general populace, but even some of the ministers. Then you wail to high heaven when there is a drouth or you do not receive all the blessings you think you should have.

"Another thing that God dislikes is the way so many of you are unfaithful to your wife, in spite of your vow in the presence of God. There is no excuse for this! Stay with your wife.

"Finally, you have bored the Lord with all your creeds and liturgy, for you have not followed your own testimonies. You even intimate that God won't punish you because God doesn't care that much. You are wrong again!"

Chap. 3

On still another occasion Edwards was invited to speak to a men's conference[1] and he spoke strongly saying, "God says that he will send a special messenger ahead to prepare the way of the Lord. Then suddenly there will appear the great one for whom you have always been looking.

"He is coming. There is no doubt about it. It will be difficult to be in his presence, for he will search your soul. He will be like a refiner of silver, one who removes all sham and all blemishes.

"This great one shall purify the ministers of God and they will once again serve him because of their love for God. Then again will the Lord be pleased with the worship services and the gifts of the people.

"The Lord will then move quickly against the wicked, the witchcraft crowd, the adulterers, the cheaters, those who take advantage of the poor, who shun the stranger, and who do not worship God.

"Repent. God is always willing to forgive. Return to the Lord, and the Lord will return to you. Then you say, 'When did we ever leave God?'

"Let me ask you, will a man rob God? Yet you have robbed God. Do you want to know how?

"In tithes and offerings. The whole nation has neglected the fulfillment of this requirement. God says, however, to test him, just try it, bring the full tithe to God's house and see if God doesn't open the windows of heaven and pour out such a blessing that there shall

[1] Apparently he was never invited back

not be room to receive it.

"If you give properly to the Lord, God will bless the land for your sake and the whole nation will prosper and be respected by other nations.

"You know, you have actually spoken against God often. You immediately say 'when?'

"Well, you've often said that it didn't pay to serve God, that the wicked seem to prosper, that they get rich and are often voted into positions of leadership.[1]

"God noticed all this and God had the names of all those put in a book who did not do this. You better believe that God has a record! The day will come and the righteous shall be rewarded and the wicked punished. God will care for the righteous as for his own son.

Chap.
4

"The day is coming for judgement, and for the wicked it will be an experience like being thrown into a furnace, while for the righteous it will be as if crippled wings were healed and a person could fly as free as a breeze. The righteous shall be separated from the wicked, who will be as ashes under their feet.

"Remember the law of Moses. Also I will send to you a prophet like Elijah[2] who will preach before the coming of judgment day, and he shall convert many and save many and be a great and helpful influence, for the people will sense that they must respond or the Lord will smite the whole country."

[1] You can say that again   [2] Maybe Billy Graham

Dear Reader:

Although I often found reading the King James
version of the Bible quite difficult in many places, it
is still the real Bible to me. I have been well aware,
however, that many, many people are not in a
position to take the time and effort to really study
the Bible. I long for the day when everyone reads the
scriptures.

It is with the intent of making the general
outline, basic truths, and character elements involved
in the scriptures easily understandable that I have
compiled this unusual version. This work is not
intended as an accurate translation or even a
paraphrase, but an instrument for leading people to
the scriptures and at the same time showing how real
the characters of the Bible are, and how modern and
relevant are the truths contained in God's word.

This version is in no way designed to be helpful
to the Biblically orientated and trained person, but it
is written with the hopes that those who have found
the Old Testament language too archaic may in this
version at least see a reasonable measure of the truth
of God.

Andrew Edington